PIMLICO

359

TECUMSEH

Author, college lecturer and recently a senior research fellow at the Newberry Library, Chicago, Dr John Sugden holds degrees from the universities of Leeds, Lancaster and Sheffield, and has pursued historical research in archives throughout Britain and North America. He has contributed to numerous journals and his previous books, *Tecumseh's Last Stand* (1985) and *Sir Francis Drake* (1990; also available in Pimlico) received overwhelming critical acclaim. *Tecumseh* won the 1999 Society for Military History Distinguished Book Award.

TECUMSEH

A Life

———

JOHN SUGDEN

PIMLICO

For the 5S Class of Ainthorpe High, 1963
and two great teachers, Joan Wright and Stanley Roger Thomas,
who encouraged me to write.

Published by Pimlico 1999

2 4 6 8 10 9 7 5 3 1

Copyright © John Sugden 1997

John Sugden has asserted his right
under the Copyright, Designs and Patents Act 1988
to be identified as the author of this work

First published in the United States of America by
Henry Holt and Company, Inc. 1998
First published in Great Britain by Pimlico 1999

Pimlico
Random House, 20 Vauxhall Bridge Road,
London SW1V 2SA

Random House Australia (Pty) Limited
20 Alfred Street, Milsons Point, Sydney,
New South Wales 2061, Australia

Random House New Zealand Limited
18 Poland Road, Glenfield,
Auckland 10, New Zealand

Random House South Africa (Pty) Limited
Endulini, 5A Jubilee Road, Parktown 2193, South Africa

Random House UK Limited Reg. No. 954009

A CIP catalogue record for this book
is available from the British Library

ISBN 0-7126-6508-0

Papers used by Random House UK Limited are natural,
recyclable products made from wood grown in sustainable forests.
The manufacturing processes conform to the environmental
regulations of the country of origin

Printed and bound in Great Britain by
Biddles Ltd, Guildford and King's Lynn

CONTENTS

ILLUSTRATIONS
AND MAPS

Hopoithle Mico
Fort Harrison
Battle of Tippecanoe

ILLUSTRATIONS *(following 334)*

The Detroit frontier
William Hull
Isaac Brock
John B. Glegg
The River Raisin massacre
Tecumseh saving the prisoners
Fort Meigs
Tecumseh rebuking Procter
Robert Heriot Barclay
Chatham
The Indian village at Moraviantown
The allied line at Moraviantown
Battle of the Thames and death of Tecumseh
Tecumseh at Moraviantown
Indian delegation visiting Sir George Prevost
Tecumseh or Paukeesaa?
Powder horn
Headcrushers
Wampum
Search for Tecumseh's grave
The Dying Tecumseh
Canadian literature on Tecumseh
German literature on Tecumseh

MAPS

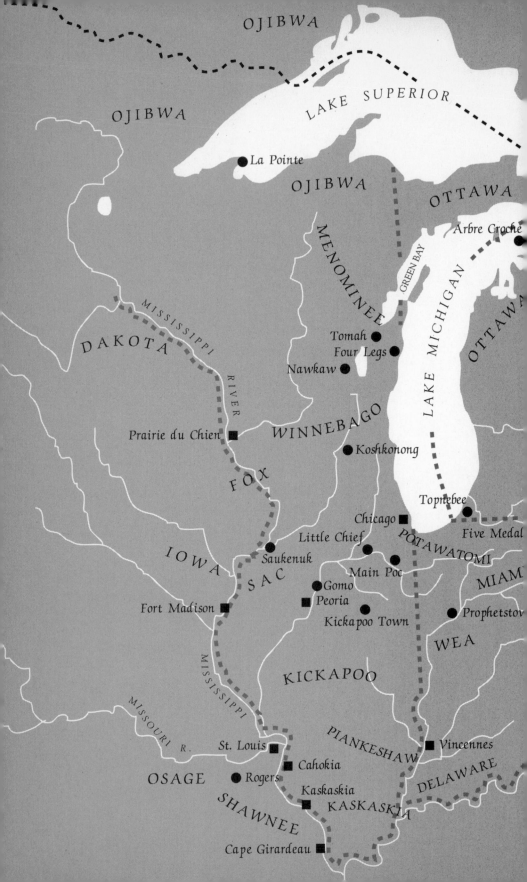

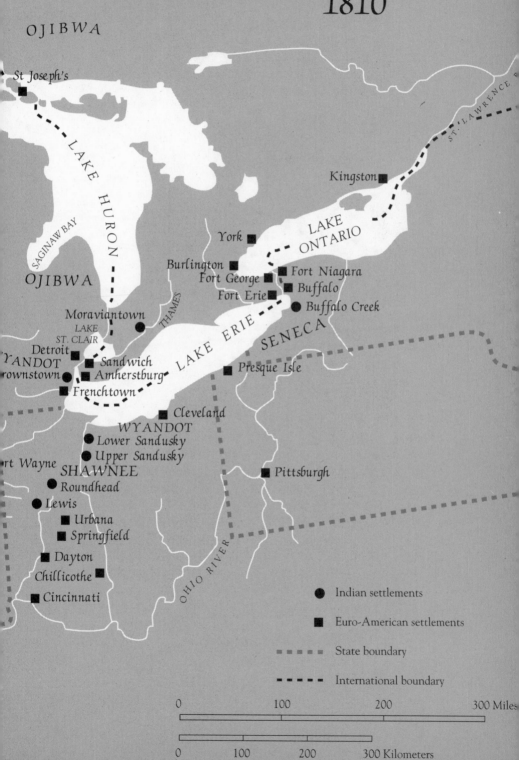

Tecumseh's Country
1810

OJIBWA

St Joseph's

LAKE HURON

SAGINAW BAY

OJIBWA

Kingston

ST. LAWRENCE R.

York

LAKE ONTARIO

Burlington

Fort Niagara

Fort George

Buffalo

Fort Erie

Buffalo Creek

Moraviantown

THAMES

LAKE ST. CLAIR

LAKE ERIE

SENECA

Detroit

WYANDOT

Sandwich

Presque Isle

rownstown

Amherstburg

Frenchtown

Cleveland

WYANDOT

Lower Sandusky

Upper Sandusky

Pittsburgh

rt Wayne

SHAWNEE

Roundhead

Lewis

Urbana

Springfield

Dayton

Chillicothe

OHIO RIVER

Cincinnati

● Indian settlements

■ Euro-American settlements

▪ ▪ ▪ ▪ State boundary

▬ ▬ ▬ International boundary

| 0 | 100 | 200 | 300 Miles |

| 0 | 100 | 200 | 300 Kilometers |

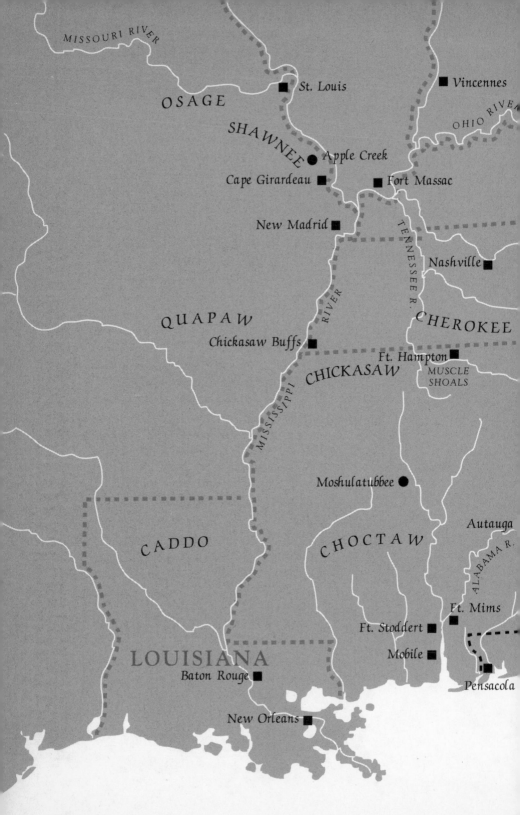

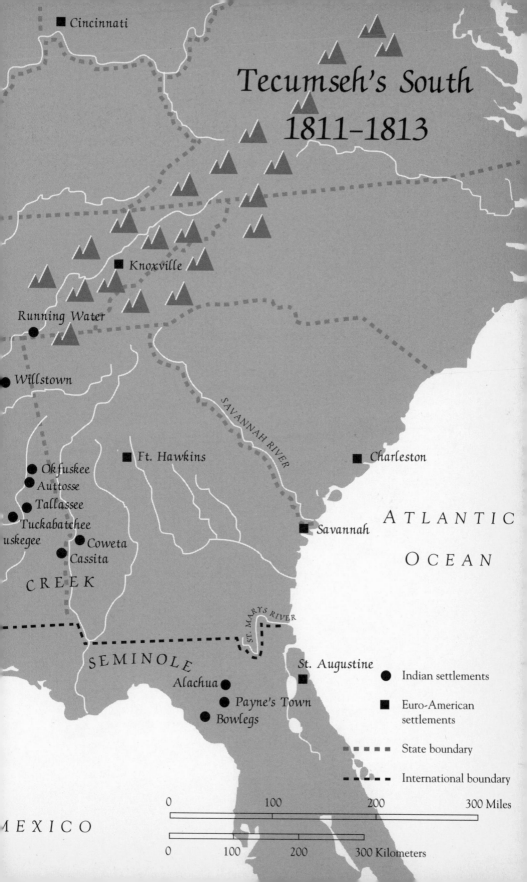

Tecumseh's South
1811–1813

■ Cincinnati

■ Knoxville

● Running Water

● Willstown

SAVANNAH RIVER

■ Ft. Hawkins

■ Charleston

● Okfuskee
● Auttosse
● Tallassee
● Tuckabatchee
uskegee
● Coweta
Cassita

■ Savannah

ATLANTIC

OCEAN

CREEK

ST. MARYS RIVER

SEMINOLE

● Alachua
● Payne's Town
● Bowlegs

St. Augustine
■

MEXICO

● Indian settlements

■ Euro-American settlements

State boundary

International boundary

0   100   200   300 Miles

0   100   200   300 Kilometers

PREFACE

Almost two centuries after his death, on a desperate smoke-filled battlefield beside the swampy reaches of the River Thames in Ontario, Tecumseh has become one of the great American heroes. Today, American Indian peoples recognize him as the most ambitious of a small number of leaders who dreamed of a brotherhood of tribes capable of resisting white expansion, and who tried to replace intertribal indifference and conflict with unity and common purpose. Canadians honor him as a savior of their country at the time of the War of 1812. In his own day the United States regarded Tecumseh and his brother Tenskwatawa, known as the Prophet, as astonishingly active and dangerous foes. Since then generations of writers have endorsed the opinion of anthropologist James Mooney that Tecumseh was "the most heroic character in Indian history." Truly, he has entered the pantheon, and new titles about him are published nearly every year.

Indeed, the literature of Tecumseh far exceeds that of any other American Indian. If fiction is included, the number of full-length treatments of his career and campaigns tops one hundred, while the list of shorter items is enormous. Despite that, relatively little of this literature has historical value, and not a single biography that is both comprehensive and reliable has hitherto been written. Many aspects of Tecumseh's life have escaped the attention of serious modern writers completely, and the best recent research has focused upon the Prophet rather than his brother. Even Tecumseh's important role in the War of 1812 has been without an authoritative and detailed appraisal. Not only that, but errors persisting in the accounts, and the appearance of numerous pretentious novels on Tecumseh, have increased public mystification. It is time to mount a rescue.

This book began thirty years ago. Given the state of the literature at that time, it became apparent that the biography would have to be based upon a fresh and thorough overhaul of all the relevant primary sources. The task, I discovered, was frustrating and sometimes grueling. Tecumseh left no written papers, and references to him were often slight and scattered, hidden in collections vast distances apart. But over the years the searches were fitted in, and an enormous body of documentation, much of it previously unknown, was brought to hand. I have tried to evaluate it without fear or favor, or regard to preconceived theories. The opinions in this book may be fashionable or unfashionable, and I certainly make no claims to infallibility, but I believe they faithfully reflect all the surviving evidence on Tecumseh known to me. My differences with other scholars, where they exist, are honest ones.

This is also the first book on Tecumseh to be grounded in thorough research into the history and historical culture of Tecumseh's people, the Shawnees. Some excellent work has been done on the Shawnees, notably by Erminie Wheeler Voegelin, whose project was never completed, but no satisfactory history of the tribe exists, and authors have been unable to fit Tecumseh into his essential context. Much of what was written about Shawnee life in the accounts of Tecumseh, for example, was drawn from studies of late nineteenth- or early twentieth-century Shawnees without sufficient regard for the profound changes that occurred in most aspects of the tribe's culture, particularly after 1830. The authors' material, therefore, was true for 1900, but not always so for the eighteenth-century society to which Tecumseh belonged. It was no substitute for a proper investigation of the historical sources.

To address these problems, I extended the scope of my investigation, and worked simultaneously upon a history of the Shawnees in Ohio. As I came to grips with that subject, much of what had hitherto been mysterious about Tecumseh fell into place. Although this research into the Shawnees is designed ultimately for independent publication, many of my findings have duly found their way into the present book.

Condensing the results of such a protracted undertaking into a book of this kind, with a text accessible to the general reader, has not been without its own problems. I can only plead for tolerance. The footnotes will be inadequate for some, daunting for others. I have identified quotations and important sources, particularly those dealing with Tecumseh as an individual. Some difficult matters of interpretation have been discussed, but while every story and theory about Tecumseh has been traced to source and tested, there is simply not the space to explain the absence of all the material I have had to discard. Similarly, the bibliography is selective, and is confined to items either cited in the notes or generally indispensable to an understanding of the man and his times.

Terminology usually threatens the lay reader. In some cases almost every alternative was clumsy and imprecise. The word "tribe," for example. As used here, it denotes people sharing a language, culture, and sense of common identity, but not always leadership. Single-village tribes might enjoy a shared polity, but most tribes were divided between villages that were sometimes geographically far apart, and in which there was little, if any, overall political organization. Readers should bear these limitations in mind over the following pages. On a similar matter, after consulting Indian friends and acquaintances, I decided against using the term "Native American."

I could not have written this book without the help of many willing, and some self-sacrificing, hands and minds, particularly in the United States and Canada. In several respects the result is theirs as well as mine, and I am proud to record their names in my acknowledgments. However, as usual it has been those who live closest to me who have carried most of the responsibility for sustaining a weary traveler on his strange quest. I owe a special debt to my partner, Terri, for suffering the seemingly endless days I spent at my desk, and to my brother, the historian Philip Sugden, whose exacting standards never ceased to spur me on.

East Yorkshire, England, September 1997

PROLOGUE

1

⊷┼ 〓◈〓 ┼⊶

THE SHOOTING STAR

Saturday morning, 19 September 1807, saw more than the usual air of excitement about the frontier town of Chillicothe, which sat beside the Scioto River and was then the capital of the infant state of Ohio. A great concourse of settlers, many from outlying districts, wound through the streets, between the neat houses of freestone, brick, and painted timber, toward the impressive two-story courthouse where the acting governor was to preside over a most singular session. Some of the men and women crowding into the building that day were mere curiosity-seekers, but others were frightened, frightened for their lives and homes, and they had come for reassurance. For these were troubled times in the backcountry.

About one hundred miles to the northwest hordes of strange tribesmen had been congregating that year at a Shawnee Indian village only recently established at Greenville, on land the tribes had long ago ceded to the United States. Some of those visitors had journeyed great distances, from as far as the Mississippi and beyond the Great Lakes, and it was said that they had gathered to listen to a prophet who had risen among the Shawnees to carry the word of Waashaa Monetoo, the Great Spirit, to the Indians and lead them back to grace. Throughout the year the influx of such large numbers of warriors, from tribes the whites of Ohio hardly knew, had spawned one fear-ridden rumor after another.

Then in the summer a clash between an American and a British frigate at sea had brought Britain and the United States to the brink of war. In the

American settlements of the Old Northwest there were many who charged the British with encouraging Indian hostility to the United States and furnishing angry warriors with arms.

Exposed homesteaders in Ohio shuddered at the prospect of British-backed Indian onslaughts upon the frontier, and the sound of tomahawks and scalping knives rattling at their doors. They posted guards and threw up blockhouses, but a hundred white families still abandoned the vulnerable Mad River country.

As the summer faded, acting governor Thomas Kirker had come under great pressure to deal with the Indians at Greenville. William Wells, a choleric Indian agent at Fort Wayne, Indiana Territory, told him to turn out the militia and order the Indians away on pain of having their village burned around their ears. Frederick Fisher, who had been trading at the Indian town for several weeks, repeated indiscreet remarks of the Prophet, including the comment that he could overturn the Americans as if they were a basin of water. And another correspondent impugned the motives of Indians who were supposed to be worshiping the Great Spirit but carried muskets supplied by British traders.[1]

Kirker was only a caretaker governor, and he had little formal education. He could easily have buckled before such an onslaught and thrown a match into a situation already tinder-dry, but he had kept cool and taken good advice. Although he had summoned nearly fifteen hundred militiamen into service, he kept them under close control until his representatives could go to Greenville and see for themselves what was happening.[2]

Now, those representatives had returned, and not alone, for with them had come four chiefs from Greenville, and the day after their arrival they attracted the anxious crowds to the Chillicothe courthouse.

The citizens stared and whispered as Governor Kirker and the emissaries he had sent to Greenville, Thomas Worthington and Duncan McArthur, ushered the four chiefs into the jury box. Two of them, a tall middle-aged Wyandot chief named Stayeghta, the Bark Carrier, but generally known as Roundhead, and a Shawnee named Blue Jacket, took seats on the left of the clerk's seat, which the Governor himself occupied. On Kirker's right sat the two other Shawnees, Panther and a remarkably striking-looking Indian whose name, it was mentioned, meant the Shooting Star. In his own language it was Tecumtha or Tecumseh.[3]

Worthington and McArthur, both well known and respected by their fellow citizens, seated themselves in front of the Indians, but eyes were inevitably drawn to two very different whites stationed close at hand. They were the Ruddell boys, and they were there to interpret. The sons of Isaac and Elizabeth Ruddell, they had been captured as children in Kentucky, when a British-Indian army had taken Ruddell's Station in 1780. Stephen was then only twelve, and his brother Abraham six years his junior. Raised by the Indians, they had fledged into fine warriors, and fought for their adopted people until the wars were ended by the treaty of Greenville in 1795.

Both boys were tall and well formed, but their careers had diverged since the peace. Stephen had taken his Indian foster mother to what is now Missouri, but had returned to Kentucky about 1798 and become a Baptist preacher. Since 1806 he had regularly visited Wapakoneta, a Shawnee village in Ohio, proselytizing for the Kentucky Baptist Church. Abe had made a poorer readjustment to white society. He spoke only broken English, and shunned company; his appearance was as wild as any Indian's, with the rims of his ears split for ornaments and trailing on his shoulders. Bizarre the Ruddells may have seemed to some that day, but they certainly enjoyed the confidence of the Shawnee chiefs.[4]

The Governor opened the proceedings, although one observer thought him "a weak and rather blundering speaker." Then heads turned toward Blue Jacket as he rose to his feet. He was an old man, but fifteen years earlier he had been the most noted war chief of the confederated tribes, and it had seemed as if almost no one could refer to him without adding "the famous Blue Jacket" or "the celebrated Blue Jacket." He had lost none of his skill as an orator since. One witness thought him "an eminently dignified" man "of calm persuasive eloquence," and another saw him as "very grand and stately."

Blue Jacket's words were those of one who remembered how Indians had not only fought their own wars in the past, but been used as military pawns by the French and British. Reviewing the conflicts of sixty years, he said with every appearance of sincerity that he had seen too much bloodshed. "We have laid down the tomahawk, never to take it up again. If it is offered to us by the French, English, Spaniards, or by you, our white brethren, we will not take it."

This seemed to clear up the worries about whether the Indians would support Britain in a war. But what about all those comings and goings to Greenville and its supposed prophet? Blue Jacket began to explain that the Indians wanted to pray, not to fight, but he grew emotional; his voice faltered and he sat down. Governor Kirker was impressed, and said so.

Then the Shooting Star, brother of the Prophet, stood. He looked first at the Governor and then turned confidently toward his wider audience.

In 1807 Tecumseh was not the legend he afterward became, but, dressed in a suit of neatly fringed deerskin, he cut a remarkable figure. No authenticated portrait of him exists, but over fifty descriptions of varying quality help us to form a comprehensive picture of him as he would have appeared to the people of Chillicothe. Over the years everyone who saw him agreed that he was exceptionally fine-looking. It is tempting to dismiss this point as the sort of hyperbole that often surrounds famous heroes, but it was made unrelentingly by many different witnesses. People spoke of Tecumseh as "one of the finest-looking men I ever saw," as "very prepossessing," "noble-looking," and "one of the most finished forms I have ever met." We are compelled to accept that Tecumseh was an unusually impressive sight.[5]

He stood about five feet ten inches—a little over medium height, though his erect carriage made him look taller—and he had an athletic, spare, and well-proportioned frame, with a full chest, broad square shoulders, and finely formed muscular limbs. He exuded energy and activity, and an old leg injury did not prevent him from walking with a graceful, brisk, elastic step. Tecumseh's complexion was light for an Indian. His head was moderately sized, his face oval, and his features were regular, large, and handsome. Beneath a full and high forehead, big dark penetrating eyes flashed dramatically under heavy arched brows. The cheeks were high, the nose slightly aquiline, and the well-formed mouth, when opened, revealed fine white teeth. Although some remembered his features as stern, they were mobile and expressive, and became animated in conversation. Tecumseh spoke fluently in the Shawnee tongue, adding weight to his emphatic and sonorous words with elegant gestures. Watching him in the courthouse, one listener was reminded of Aaron Burr, and marveled at his "impetuous and commanding" speech.

Tecumseh had been to the town before, but it took courage to confront the settlers now, when the air was thick with such dark rumors, and the bitter memory of a recent murder of a white settler had still to be exorcised. Thinking even further back, Tecumseh and Blue Jacket may have remembered one of their old leaders, Cornstalk. He had been assassinated in 1777, visiting the whites on just such an errand of peace as this.

Now words fell from Tecumseh's lips swiftly and forcefully. He was adamant that the Greenville Shawnees meant no harm to the whites. They were there to obey the will of the Great Spirit, as interpreted by the Prophet. Nothing more. It was true that allegations had been made, but these had been the malicious lies of enemies. One such was Black Hoof, head chief of the Shawnees of Wapakoneta. So many of his followers had joined the Prophet that he was left "a king without subjects" who "filled a station of but little consequence." Another was William Wells. Tecumseh's eyes had rested steadily upon the interpreter for much of the time, but when he dwelt upon the United States Indian agent at Fort Wayne they swept angrily across the room. The blood vessels in his forehead swelled, as if in passion, and his voice rose effortlessly to a higher key, startling some of the listeners.

Congress has a great many good men [he said]. Let them take away Wells and put one of them there. We hate him. If they will not remove him, *we will*! When the Indians are coming in to hear the Prophet, he sets doors to stop them. He asks them, "Why go ye to hear the Prophet? He is one possessed of a devil. I would as soon go to see a dog with the mange." When we want to talk friendly with him, he will not listen to us, and from beginning to end his talk is blackguard. He treats us like dogs.

Tecumseh was asked what he meant when he said he would remove Wells, and sensing the concern he softened his tone. The Indians would simply ignore him, he said. He explained that the Shawnees intended to leave Greenville shortly, and asked help for a new establishment he was planning. He needed a store, where the Indians could obtain necessary trade goods, and a reliable agent. Tecumseh suggested Stephen Ruddell as the perfect appointment.

Tecumseh performed with the panache of a born orator, and John McDonald, who witnessed the speech, remembered its decisive effect:

When Tecumseh rose to speak, as he cast his gaze over the vast multitude which the interesting occasion collected together, he appeared one of the most dignified men I ever beheld. While this orator of nature was speaking the vast crowd preserved the most profound silence. From the confident manner he spoke of the intention of the Indians to adhere to the treaty and live in peace and friendship with their white brethren, he dispelled as if by magic the apprehension of the whites. The settlers immediately returned to their farms, and the active hum of business was resumed in every direction.[6]

The meeting lasted for several hours, into the late afternoon, and was an unqualified success for the Indian speakers. They did not neglect to complain of American encroachments on native lands, but throughout they stressed their commitment to peace. A local newspaper enthused about their frequent appeals to the Great Spirit "for the rectitude of their intentions and the truth of what they advanced," and lauded the chiefs' "manly, firm and majestic deportment," their "familiar, unassuming and engaging" manners, and the "cool, dispassionate and rational" arguments.

Certainly Governor Kirker had no more doubts. He dismissed the militia, and on 8 October wrote to President Thomas Jefferson, passing on Tecumseh's objections to Wells and his other requests for support. The Indians, said the Governor, had given "every satisfaction I could ask . . . I sincerely believe these people are injured . . . for there does not appear on strict examination anything against them. On the contrary, their lives are peaceable and the doctrines they profess . . . are such as will do them honor."

Tecumseh and his friends did not return to Greenville immediately, but bunked for a few days at Worthington's farm, Adena, which occupied a hill in the woods, half a mile or so north of Chillicothe. It was a spanking new freestone residence, with two stories and two large receding wings that accommodated the kitchen and servants. The chiefs must have been impressed.

Worthington's family remembered Tecumseh as a plainly dressed, quiet man, but he had no English and they got little from him. Sometimes he accompanied the other Indians into the town during the day. Often, however, he seemed lost in thought.[7]

Now that the summer had almost gone, the leaves were softly turning to flame and the woods were at their best. Possibly they stirred memories in the Shawnee leader, for this was no ordinary country to him: it had been his first home. Coming from Greenville he had shown Worthington and McArthur a place on the Mad River, a little to the northwest, where he had lived as a child, but his earliest memories were of the Scioto. It was here, to the neighborhood of the original Chillicothe, a Shawnee town for which the Americans had later named their own settlement, that Tecumseh's parents had come from the south almost fifty years before.

Within the short space of Tecumseh's life the Shawnees had lost most of this land. They had been driven west from the Scioto to the Great Miami, then north into central Ohio toward the Maumee, and now their villages occupied scattered sites in Michigan and Louisiana Territories and Ohio. With their land had gone dreams of reunifying their broken tribe on the Ohio, their ancient home, along with much of their importance and independence, and part of their traditional way of life. As far as some Shawnees were concerned, the tribe's misfortunes could only mean that they had also lost the benevolence of their creator, Waashaa Monetoo. An inexhaustible tide of white settlement was forcing upon them simple but brutal options. Change, and live the American way, or retreat.

Tecumseh's visit to Chillicothe was itself but one of many protests the Shawnees had registered against the process. He was making a plea for coexistence, one of his last. He wanted the Americans to respect the right of the Indians to live and worship in peace as they wished, free from the interference of United States officials and unfriendly tongues.

A small protest this, two Shawnee voices raised in the courthouse of a growing frontier town, but it was not without significance. For Tecumseh's patience was being exhausted fast, and in just a few years he and the United States would be on a collision course. Despairing of reconciliation, the

Shawnee chief would be orchestrating the most ambitious Indian resistance movement ever mounted against English-speaking peoples in North America.

As his brother, the Prophet, acknowledged, Tecumseh planned a mighty Indian confederation, from the Great Lakes to the Gulf of Mexico. Tecumseh was "a great general," the Prophet told the artist George Catlin, "and nothing but his premature death defeated his great plan."[8] Whereas most Indian resistance in the three centuries after 1600 was relatively local, Tecumseh believed that the lands and cultures of all Indians were endangered by the advance of powerful white civilizations, and he worked on a national scale.

Tecumseh was by no means alone in his understanding that powerful external threats demanded greater unity and strength from historically disparate and diverse native peoples. Far from it, for before and since Tecumseh far-seeing leaders and groups have worked toward the same end. The Mohawk Joseph Brant labored hard to unite the Indians of the Great Lakes and the south against American land hunger at the end of the Revolutionary War, and at the same time a southern mestizo, Alexander McGillivray, was attempting to centralize power among a loose collection of Indian towns known as the Creek confederacy. In the following decade the Shawnees Blue Jacket, Red Pole, and Captain Johnny were putting together a shaky but large confederacy of northwestern tribes to defend the Ohio country, and in so doing they inherited a tribal tradition that was already old. They were the direct forerunners of Tecumseh. Almost a century later, long after Tecumseh had passed from the scene, the Hunkpapa war chief and mystic, Sitting Bull, made a belated attempt to bring members of the Lakota Sioux and other tribes together to check the American sweep toward the Rockies.

Tecumseh, nevertheless, stands out. Not for the originality of his purpose and principles, but for the sheer breadth of his vision and the energy, determination, courage, and ability he put at its service. His was a task of staggering difficulty. Divided by language, culture, and intertribal enmities and jealousies, the Indians were also politically decentralized. They had no powerful executive capable of controlling their people through police and courts, as had the Americans or the British. Even tribal authority was either weak or nonexistent, and the powers of chiefs of any description were extremely limited.

In their quest for unity, all Indians wrestled with these problems. Brant relied solely upon the power of his logic. McGillivray tried to enforce compliance by threats and coercion, and by controlling the distribution of trade goods among the Creeks so that supporters were rewarded and opponents penalized. Tecumseh strengthened his arguments with religion, building upon the foundations laid by his brother, the Prophet.

By comparison with Tecumseh, the Prophet may have looked unimpressive, with his hangdog look, reduced frame, and disfigured right eye, and his talents certainly blazed less brightly. But he was a crucial figure in Tecumseh's plans. Indeed, it was he, not Tecumseh, who had founded their reform movement. He said he was the medium of the Great Spirit, chosen to show the way to salvation, and he warned the Indians about the adverse effects of contact with the whites and taught them pride in their native identity and traditions. Increasingly, Tecumseh politicized and militarized the movement, and became its driving force, but the Prophet remained important. For long he was the principal figurehead. He threw divine sanction behind Tecumseh's plan, picturing the confederacy as the wish of the Creator. Waashaa Monetoo himself would help overthrow the Americans, and would punish those Indians who refused to listen.

The difficulties confronting the brothers were greater, far greater, than those faced by the founding fathers of the American republic, or by any European statesman, but combining strong religious and political appeals, the two made surprising headway. Their influence radiated from Indiana, in greater or smaller measure, as far northeast as the state of New York, south into the Florida peninsula, westward as far as Nebraska, and north deep into Canada. They forced the United States to mobilize thousands of soldiers, who at one point were simultaneously embattled with followers of the brothers on the shores of the Great Lakes, the banks of the Mississippi, and the margins of the Gulf coast. And Tecumseh's help was instrumental in the survival of British Canada during the War of 1812.

Ultimately, the brothers lost. They did not—could not—halt the misfortunes overwhelming their people. But they left a mark upon the times.

Those who watched Tecumseh in Chillicothe that day in 1807 recognized a spectacular orator, but few would have predicted the astonishing future of the tall Indian leader. Like the meteor for which he had been named, Tecumseh's star climbed suddenly and steeply, burned brilliantly but briefly in the darkness, and was then blotted out forever in the gunsmoke and war cries of his final battlefield. With his defeat an era in Indian history—the period during which the tribes had helped decide the fate of great international powers struggling to possess North America—came to an end. Yet such was the impression Tecumseh made, upon grateful friends, beaten allies, and victorious enemies alike, that he lived on in folklore, story, and rhyme, at home and overseas, and became one of the most legendary figures of the American past.

Tecumseh died in Canada. He had spent most of his life fighting for the broad sparkling blue reaches of the Ohio River, which he loved. But his story did not begin there. It started in the sultrier climes of what is now Alabama, in the lands of the Creeks.

THE PRELUDE

2

THE PANTHER AND
THE TURTLE

It was in the south that Tecumseh's parents met and married.
Pukeshinwau was a rising warrior of the Kispoko division of the
Shawnee tribe. His young wife, Methoataaskee, belonged to a re-
spected family of the Pekowi division.[1]

Every Shawnee belonged to one of the five divisions of the tribe:
Mekoche, Hathawekela, Pekowi, Kispoko, and Chillicothe. Originally, each
division seems to have formed more or less autonomous villages, with their
own chiefs; together, they made up the loose confederacy that was the
Shawnee tribe. Binding the divisions were a common language, culture,
and sense of identity, and the right of each division to exercise certain responsibilities on behalf of the tribe as a whole. The Mekoches, for example,
jealously guarded their privilege of handling the tribe's external relations, a
prerogative that enabled the Mekoche head civil chief to act as the tribal
head civil chief. But even in the time of Pukeshinwau and Methoataaskee
these traditional monopolies were weakening. The Shawnee divisions often
parted company; indeed, in historic times the tribe was never completely
united, either in geography or policy.[2]

Pukeshinwau was a Kispoko, and his wife a Pekowi, but among Shawnees
divisional identity descended patrilineally, and their children of both sexes
would become Kispokos. From their fathers, too, Shawnee children took
a clan.

There were about a dozen of these, every one of them symbolized by a
creature, such as a snake, raccoon, or turkey. Unlike the divisions, the clans

were exogamous: each person chose a sexual partner from a clan different
from his or her own. The clans, therefore, regulated kinship, and clan affiliation was so important that Shawnees generally advertised it in their
personal names. So it was with the parents of Tecumseh. Pukeshinwau belonged to the panther clan. The particular panther (*meshepeshe* in Shawnee)
from which members of the clan believed they derived certain powers
was believed to be a spirit, one that could only be seen leaping through the
heavens, like a shooting star. Hence Pukeshinwau's name, which meant
Something That Falls. As for Methoataaskee, her name, which meant A
Turtle Laying Her Eggs in the Sand, boldly proclaimed that she belonged to
the turtle clan.[3]

Both parents appear to have been Shawnees, but they lived in Shawnee
communities that had found havens among the Creeks. The Creeks, whom
the Shawnees named Muskogees (people of the swampy ground), made
their homes in what is now Alabama and Georgia, along the rivers of the Alabama, Coosa, Tallapoosa, Chattahoochee, and Flint.

By the time Pukeshinwau and Methoataaskee met, the Shawnees had already earned a reputation for fragmentation and remarkable wanderings.
They spoke in a soft, attractive tongue that belonged to the Algonquian family of languages, which was strong around the Great Lakes, but early references to groups who may have been Shawnees, as well as their name (which
meant "southerners"), indicate the tribe had also dwelt in the south in the
distant past, perhaps on the Savannah River of South Carolina. In the 1660s
and 1670s, when they first emerge clearly in written records, the Shawnees
were settled on the Ohio and Cumberland Rivers.

Iroquois war parties from the northeast dislodged the Shawnees from
the Ohio in the closing decades of the seventeenth century, scattering them
westward to the Illinois, south to the Savannah, and east across the Allegheny Mountains, as well as elsewhere. These migrations were further
stimulated by a desire to reach Spanish, British, and French trade outlets.
They gave the Shawnees connections among many different tribes, and
helped develop their unusual resilience, versatility, and independence.

Tecumseh's parents both found themselves among the Creeks, but they
seem to have arrived by different routes. Pukeshinwau was probably born
by the Tallapoosa, where Shawnees had lived since the beginning of the
eighteenth century. In 1811 Tecumseh once described himself as a man of
Tuckabatchee, a Creek town on the Tallapoosa, and an early name for this
town, Ispokogi, may have been a corruption of "Kispoko." We are encouraged to believe that Kispoko Shawnees may have helped to found Tuckabatchee, and that it was to this community that Pukeshinwau belonged.[4]

During their years among the Creeks, the Tallapoosa Shawnees intermarried with the neighboring Indians, and probably also with white traders who frequented the native villages. Creek towns contained large numbers of mestizos, most the offspring of relationships between British or French traders and Indian women. It is not surprising that there were persistent rumors that Tecumseh was not pure Shawnee, but that he had inherited Creek and even white blood.

In 1810, for example, a Potawatomi Indian acquainted, but not friendly with Tecumseh, claimed Tecumseh's mother had actually been a Creek, rather than a Shawnee. Much later Methoataaskee's grandson John Prophet made the same statement, and it was probably he who started a tradition that grew among both the Creeks and Shawnees that Tecumseh's mother had been a Creek.[5]

In fact, the better evidence is that it was through Pukeshinwau, not his wife, that Tecumseh and the Prophet may or may not have acquired Creek blood. The Prophet himself (John Prophet's father) said so in 1825. True, he embroidered the story to the best of his ability, as was his wont, and he even claimed that Pukeshinwau had been a mestizo, born of a Creek father and the daughter of an English colonial governor. The boy, he said, was raised by the British and returned to the Indians as a youth. But an independent, and entirely credible, version of the same story was given by the Shanes. Anthony Shane was a mixed-blood who spent most of his life in Shawnee towns, and his wife was Lameteshe, one of Tecumseh's relatives. They testified that Pukeshinwau was reputed to have had a British father (presumably a trader) and a Shawnee mother, and that he was resigned to the latter because he was unruly.

There is nothing at all improbable in the assertion that Pukeshinwau had Creek and English, as well as Shawnee, blood in his veins. The press styled his eldest son, Cheeseekau, a "half-breed" at the time of his death in 1792, while the Shanes stated that Tecumseh's complexion was "of an intermediate cast between a half white and a full-blooded Indian—rather inclining to yellow."[6]

The truth about Pukeshinwau's ancestry must remain a mystery, and no more information has survived about Methoataaskee. She may have arrived in Creek country as late as 1748, and been part of a Shawnee band which had migrated from Pennsylvania in 1745, under the leadership of a mixed-blood Frenchman named Peter Chartier. Chartier's party, which included Pekowis, built their principal southern town near Tallasseehatchee Creek, close to the Indian village of Talladega, on the Coosa River.[7]

Somehow the Kispoko warrior and the Pekowi maiden met and married. According to their son the Prophet, she was not Pukeshinwau's first wife, since Pukeshinwau had been married previously to a Creek; but if so he carried no children forward to his new household. Shawnees were generally polygynous, but thereafter Pukeshinwau took no other wife. He and Methoataaskee would remain together until death parted them.

In 1759, probably, the couple came north.

Again, the Prophet's reminiscences yield important clues. He said that about half of the Alabama Shawnees, including his mother's people, decided to join some of the tribe who were then reoccupying the Ohio. Rather than force his wife to leave her family by staying in the south, Pukeshinwau threw in with her people and went north. This story fits the events of 1758 and 1759, when Shawnees on the Ohio appealed to kinfolk in Pennsylvania and the south for support, and when, in the spring of 1759, the Chartier band quit the Coosa and journeyed north.[8]

The Ohio. The river some Shawnees knew as Mosopelea-sepe, or Big Turkey River, and others as Kiskepila-sepe, the Eagle River. A long twisting blue band, spotted with islands and weaving through lush country that offered everything Shawnees desired. The soil was rich, especially in the bottomlands, sluiced each spring by the rising waters. The hills were clothed in chestnut, yellow poplar, oak, black ash, and gum, while in the valleys snuggled beech, sugar maple, walnut, elm, and sycamore. Wild grape and honeysuckle colonized the trees, and fruits and nuts abounded. Their importance was commemorated in the names the Shawnees gave to the months: the Moon of Strawberries (May), the Moon of Raspberries (June), the Moon of Blackberries (July), and the Moon of Plums (August). Fish darted in the many clear streams—pike, bass, and redhorse sucker—and geese, pigeons, ducks, turkeys, and other birds started from the diverse cover, the thick timber and patches of prairie, marsh, and canebrake. Deer fed at the salt licks, beavers industriously engineered new pools along the streams, and bison broke clearings in the forest. The Shawnees, who hunted most animals from bears to raccoons, found the Ohio country a paradise for game.

There was no better place to reunite the tribe than here, thought the Shawnee leaders on the Ohio. Increasing numbers enhanced the tribe's strength and consequence, something that was important in view of the greedy eyes already being cast upon this country by British and French colonists. But there was another reason for the reunification plan, a spiritual one. The Shawnees wanted the blessings of Waashaa Monetoo, the Great and Good Spirit.

Like other Indians, Shawnees believed their fortunes depended upon the forbearance of the spirits. Spirits were omnipresent: in all living things; in the actions of the elements; in the sun, the moon, and the stars; and in all places, from dark glades to watery depths. It was the interplay of these spirits which controlled every event, bringing success or failure, and it was essential to invest a great amount of time and effort in securing their goodwill.

For the world of the Shawnees was uncertain and dangerous. The deities had continually to be respected, courted, and appeased, because they were the arbiters of the Indians' fate: the sun, which yielded warmth and light; the star people and the thunderbirds; the Four Winds, who controlled the seasons and night and day; Earth Mother and Corn Woman, whose blessings were so essential to a rich harvest; and many lesser forces. Indeed, the annual festivals of the Shawnees were ceremonies of thanks and supplication. Every spring several days were occupied in rituals, dances, sports, and feasting that celebrated the bounty of the winter hunt and prayed for the fertility of the new crop. And the following August the harvest would be acknowledged by a festival of green corn.[9]

In everyday life, too, all Shawnees understood that obeisance to the spirits was crucial to success. If a hunter killed an animal for food, he performed a simple thanksgiving to lay its spirit to rest, and every Shawnee occasionally sprinkled offerings of tobacco onto a fire so that the rising smoke might carry a prayer, and manipulated fetishes to summon supernatural aid. Every Shawnee respected the holy men and shamans whose unusual rapport with the spirits was turned to the public benefit, and every Shawnee had been taught to fear those who used spiritual power for evil purposes. *Weasaloageethee skee*, or witches, were men and women who commanded influence with Motshee Monetoo, the Bad Spirit, or with malignant water monsters of Shawnee mythology. According to one tradition, medicine had once been made from the remains of two of these great horned water serpents, and it was this that witches preserved and hid in sacred bags and used to cause drought, sickness, and death.

But there was one spirit more powerful than all the rest. The Great or Good Spirit, Waashaa Monetoo, he who had re-created the world after its destruction in a flood, who had listened to the entreaties of its one survivor, an old woman, and repopulated the earth. Shawnees worshiped the old woman, Waupoathee, and called her their grandmother. They believed she assisted the Great Spirit to supervise the Shawnees, and made herself visible to those on earth as the moon. But it was Waashaa Monetoo himself whose favor was the most important. From his home above the roof of the sky he saw all things, dispensing favors or punishments accordingly.

The Shawnees had been the Great Spirit's special people. They were the first humans he had introduced to the new earth, and he had located them on the Savannah River, at the center of the island Europeans would call America. He had done more. He had given the Shawnees a portion of his own heart, as well as a sacred bundle of objects which would help them summon spiritual assistance on important occasions.

Shawnees believed these things to be true. They knew the tribe's sacred medicine bundle existed, in the custody of the Ohio Chillicothes or Mekoches, and that it was accommodated in its own lodge, guarded by appointed keepers and consulted by holy men. And the Mekoches, particularly, insisted that it was they who had been the firstborn not only of all nations but of other Shawnees, too, and that this conferred upon them a unique status. Said one, "The Great Spirit . . . ordered that everything upon the earth should obey us . . . He put his heart into our tribe and made it the chief of all the tribes . . . We think we have a right to look upon ourselves as the head tribe of all nations."[10]

To be sure, this Shawnee claim to superiority was not admitted by other Indians. But the tribe was universally respected for its fighting spirit, and the language of intertribal diplomacy paid homage to that. Shawnees addressed the Delawares as "grandfathers," and the Iroquois and Wyandots as "uncles" or "elder brothers." But apart from their "first brothers," the Kickapoos, who spoke a tongue close to their own, they termed all other tribes "younger brothers."

Yet there was a problem for the Shawnees. If they had been such favorites of the Great Spirit, why were they so reduced in numbers, and broken apart, some of them in Ohio and others in Pennsylvania and Alabama? The Shawnees despondently suspected that they had offended Waashaa Monetoo, and he had withdrawn his patronage. They could only guess why. Some declared the tribe had grown corrupt, while others blamed their separation from the Kickapoos, a tribe they knew had once been part of their own.

Whichever, there were Shawnees who looked to a successful reunification of the tribe on the Ohio, one of their traditional homelands, as an important step toward redemption. Once they were unified, the Great Spirit would smile upon them again, and as long as they remained in the Ohio country he would protect them.[11]

For the Shawnees, regrouping on the great river was also a search for grace.

Pukeshinwau was one of many who heeded that call. He came to live on the Scioto, a gentle stream that descended to the north side of the Ohio. In 1758 the Shawnees had built a new town beside the Scioto, about 120 miles above its mouth, and called it Chillicothe, after one of the tribal divisions. It was this town that gave its name to the white settlement which later grew up a little to the south, and which Tecumseh would visit that September day in 1807.

The Indian town of Chillicothe occupied both sides of the Scioto at a fordable place. A few houses were situated on the east bank, opposite the mouth of Paint Creek, but most of the Shawnees lived a mile or so up Paint

Creek itself and planted their corn on the rolling Scioto plains to the south. It was not the only Shawnee town on the Scioto. Small villages were established both north and south, but Chillicothe became the focus of the tribe's activities and in 1762 was said to contain three hundred warriors, the majority of the Shawnees then living in Ohio.[12]

It was probably here that Pukeshinwau settled, and Methoataaskee gave birth to her older children. Cheeseekau (the Sting) was born about 1761, and it was undoubtedly upon this son that the family rested its greatest hopes for distinction. A daughter followed, variously named Menewaulaakoosee or Tecumapease (Flying Over the Water, or Wading Over), and another son, Sauawaseekau (Jumping Panther).[13]

Then war took a hand.

In 1763 a great conflict between Britain and France, which decided the fate of their North American colonies, finally ended. The British emerged victorious from the French and Indian War, but no sooner had they taken possession of Canada than they were faced with a sudden Indian uprising. Between the Ohio and the Great Lakes and the Genesee and the Mississippi the Indians had many and different grievances against their British "Father." Threats to land, reductions in the amount of goodwill presents and supplies given by the redcoats, nostalgia for the largesse of the overthrown French regime, and fears that the British were planning to destroy the tribes and that their contamination of native cultures was turning the spirits against the Indians all played a part. The fires of revolt crackled fiercely across the frontier, and from Michilimackinac to Fort Pitt (Pittsburgh) angry warriors threw themselves upon local British garrisons. In June 1763 the Shawnees joined in, attacking traders in the Indian villages before assaulting a line of white settlements that had just begun to break through the Allegheny Mountains from the eastern colonies. In western Pennsylvania and Virginia hundreds of homesteaders were killed, captured, or driven from their cabins, and Pitt, Carlisle, and Bedford were crowded with refugees.

Peace was restored the next year, but it left a new face in Pukeshinwau's household: Shawtunte, a white boy. Whether Pukeshinwau captured Richard Sparks himself or purchased him from another warrior is unknown. The boy was taken while playing in the vicinity of Wheeling, West Virginia. He was three or four years old, and Pukeshinwau probably thought him a good companion for his own son, Cheeseekau, who was about the same age. Certainly the boy was treated with the humanity that marked several members of Pukeshinwau's family, including Tecumseh himself.

One who later interviewed Sparks's wife testified that Richard was given the name Shawtunte and raised "with unusual kindness and indulgence." It is a tribute to the affection Pukeshinwau had for him that the family refused to give the boy up for some twelve years, despite the heavy pressure the British put upon the Shawnees to surrender prisoners. And perhaps it is an even greater tribute to the relationship that Shawtunte himself fiercely resisted repatriation. "I remember his telling me how great a calamity he considered it to be taken away from the Indians," recalled his brother-in-law, "and of his schemes for making his escape and returning to them."[14]

The decade that followed the war of 1763–1764 was a peaceful one for the Shawnees. Their settlements on the Scioto multiplied, and by 1773 no less than seven Shawnee towns clustered on the several streams that fed into the west bank of its upper reaches. Among them there was a Pekowi town, on Deer Creek, above Paint Creek, and the Kispokos erected a separate village, too, a mile up another small stream, which emptied into the Scioto some eleven miles north of Deer Creek. Between all these settlements considerable traffic passed up and down narrow but well-worn Indian paths, and other trails led farther afield, plunging into the wilderness. The most famous, the Warrior's Path, ran beside the Scioto north to Sandusky Bay on Lake Erie and south across the Ohio into the favored hunting grounds of Kentucky.

Usually the Shawnee towns occupied high ground and overlooked fertile bottomlands which the women laid out in crops. They were by no means all insubstantial creations. Every village was dominated by the council house, a large strong building in which public and ceremonial business of all kinds was transacted. The traditional family houses were raised by the women. Constructed of bark fixed around a framework of posts, they enclosed rectangular floor plans that were often fairly commodious. Even at that time, however, some houses betrayed European influences, and were made from logs or sported chimneys instead of mere holes in the roof. Interiors varied. By the standards of the time, Shawnee homes had a reputation for cleanliness, even among colonial whites. However, they were sparsely furnished. Platforms commonly served as seats, tables, and beds, but sometimes the furniture might consist of little more than skin or brush bedding.

The villages were fully occupied only during the springs and summers, and women and girls were their mainstay. While the warriors occasionally hunted, fished, and made weapons and other implements, they also whiled away long hours smoking, talking, and gambling. It was the females who grew and harvested the maize, beans, tobacco, and pumpkins in the common fields, and who gathered the maple sugar in the spring, and salt from the licks. It was they who collected wild fruits, maintained and cleaned the houses, and kept the fires. They turned corn into breadcakes, roasted meat, and made stews and hominy, and they found time to barter with traders, make clothes, and raise young children. Yet busy as life in the village was for women such as Methoataaskee, it had a lively community atmosphere, and the eagerly awaited spring and fall festivals contrasted with the starkness of the winters. The summers were social times, and hospitality marked these people. If food was there it had to be made available for guests. As one who knew the Shawnees remarked: "Nothing is too costly or too good to be set before a friend."[15]

Each autumn the Indians broke into family groups and scattered for their hunting grounds, throwing up small dome-shaped lodges made of poles and skins as temporary homes. Now, it was the men who shouldered the economic burden, for it was their job to stalk or snare the game throughout the cold season. The animals provided not only meat, and bones and pelts from which implements and clothes could be manufactured, but skins that white traders would later exchange for valuable trade goods, such as muskets, flints, knives, hatchets, kettles, combs, paint, and cloth.

Even in Pukeshinwau's time the influence of the Europeans was not difficult to discover along the Scioto. It was in the linen and cotton shirts worn by Shawnees of both sexes; in the blue and scarlet English strouding that the women made into leggings, breechcloths, and skirts; and in the beads and ribbons that were replacing traditional quillwork decoration. It could be seen in houses, in the belled horses that grazed freely about the towns, and even in occasional herds of cattle kept by the more entrepreneurial of the Indians. It manifested itself in a diversifying diet, which might include tea or chocolate, and no more clearly than in the number of white traders and smiths who dwelt in the towns. On Paint Creek Moses Henry was at Chillicothe and Alexander McKee at Crooked Nose's Town, while Richard Butler lived with the Kispokos.

The Scioto Shawnees were still a fiercely independent people. Their older technologies continued to exist alongside new trade goods that might have replaced them. Bows and arrows were to be seen along with muskets and rifles, and the basic pattern of the people's lives still followed ancient rhythms. The deerskin and fur trades had slotted easily into the aboriginal tradition of summer planting and winter hunting, and Shawnee beliefs and ceremonies, unlike those of the Delawares, were stubbornly impervious to Christian influences. Nevertheless, slow as it may have been, there was a creeping dependency upon the whites, even among the Shawnees, and its pace was increasing. The old ways were in retreat.

Pukeshinwau may not have cared. His family flourished and his standing rose. It is probable that he moved out of Chillicothe, and helped found Kispoko Town. Indeed, he may even have been its chief. Stephen Ruddell, a friend of Tecumseh, later described Pukeshinwau as "a great war chief . . . highly respected . . . both as a statesman and warrior," and John Johnston,

who would serve the Shawnees as agent, testified that he was the "chief" of
the Kispoko division.[16]

Shawnee villages had both civil and war chiefs, most elevated by merit.
During periods of sustained conflict, the war chief became the principal
leader, but normally it was the civil or peace chief who presided over the
town's business, in consultation with a council of chiefs and elders. Sometimes one person was honored with both the civil and war offices, and
Pukeshinwau may have been an example.[17]

Shawnees also recognized war and civil female chiefs, who superin-
tended the women. However, the power of all chiefs was, in fact, very limited. They had normally earned their place by their judgment, commitment,
and success—success which told everyone that they were favored by the
spirits and could command sacred power—but their role was to advise and
persuade rather than to command or instruct. Even decisions reached after
rigorous debate inside the council house might still be rejected by independently minded villagers, although considerable pressure to comply might be
levied if the public interest was at stake.

Still, Pukeshinwau had reason to be proud of his rise. Like most
Shawnee chiefs, he stood at the head of his people not because of any hereditary distinction but because he enjoyed their confidence.

Tecumseh was almost certainly born on the Scioto, at either Chillicothe
or Kispoko Town. Many early commentators erred in putting his birthplace
farther west, at towns which did not exist at the time.

The date of his birth is difficult to establish. Tecumseh's younger brother
the Prophet once said that Tecumseh was ten years older than himself,
and that he was born in 1764 or 1765, but this would seem to have been
too early. Anthony Shane and Stephen Ruddell both knew Tecumseh well.
Shane gave the date as 1771, and Ruddell was sure that Tecumseh was the
same age as himself, and had been born in 1768. This is the most authoritative estimate. Ruddell was twelve years old when he first met Tecumseh, an
age when a few years' difference between boys is all too evident. He told his
son that Tecumseh was six months older than himself, which put his birth
about March 1768.[18]

The baby was weaned after a month and then kept in a cradleboard during the day. Small objects were placed against his limbs so that they, as well
as his back, grew straight. From his father the infant took his division, the
Kispoko band, and the clan of the panther. Some six months would have
passed before an official naming ceremony was held. Pukeshinwau invited
his friends and relatives to share a feast, but it was customary for an elder

from another clan to choose the name and offer a prayer for the child's protection.

Tecumseh. The Indians pronounced it *Tecumthé*, with the final *e* short, but it has become so familiar to us in its distorted form that the use of any other form now seems pedantic. Shawnee names were highly symbolic, and some ink has been spent on the meaning of this one. The short translation was generally understood to be Shooting Star or Blazing Comet, and there were those who believed the name had been inspired by an actual astronomical event. Ruddell said that Tecumseh's mother had seen a meteor the evening the boy was born. Forty years ago an ingenious Canadian, Wallace Havelock Robb, attempted to tie Tecumseh's birth in with the transit of Venus in 1769! But in fact, like most Shawnee names, "Tecumseh" suggested the clan to which the child belonged. As mentioned earlier, in tribal mythology the spiritual patron of Tecumseh's clan was a celestial panther, a brilliant starry creature that jumped across the skies. Thus, the strict rendering of his name was I Cross the Way, but some, including John Johnston, interpreted it to signify A Panther Crouching for His Prey.[19]

The panther motif also distinguished the names of the younger children of Pukeshinwau and Methoataaskee. There were four of them, all boys. First came Nehaaseemoo, and then, during the winter of 1774–1775 the remarkable birth of triplets. One of the trio died at birth. The other two were Kumskaukau, whose name has been variously transcribed as A Cat That Flies in the Air or A Star Which Shoots in a Straight Line Over Great Waters, and Laloeshiga. Laloeshiga meant A Panther with a Handsome Tail, but this particular brother quickly disgraced himself. He was given unprepossessing nicknames. In later years he took the name Tenskwatawa, which meant the Open Door, but the one under which he grew to manhood was Lalawéthika. Perhaps it commemorated the love he had for his own voice, or that he had cried often, for it signified a noisy instrument such as a rattle.[20]

Yet there were to be no more children, and Pukeshinwau never held the last of his sons in his strong arms. The triplets were born in the winter, several months after tragedy had cruelly robbed them of their father.

3

AN OHIO CHILDHOOD

A s an adult Tecumseh was noted for his generosity and compassion, and those who knew him said these qualities had been "fully developed . . . while he was yet a youth."[1] What was even more unusual, he could extend his sympathies to enemies. Enmeshed as he became in barbaric border fighting, Tecumseh was often pragmatic and ruthless, willing to cut down anyone who opposed him in arms. But he was rarely indifferent to an appeal to humanity. As his boyhood friend Stephen Ruddell remembered, Tecumseh "was by no means savage in his nature" and "always expressed the greatest abhorrence when he heard of or saw acts of cruelty or barbarity practised."

This compassion was not the least extraordinary fact about Tecumseh, because his was a childhood savaged by the ferocities of war. Personality, we know, is laid down in those early years, years which for Tecumseh were marked by disruption, insecurity, brutality, and want. He knew hunger, fear, and grief. Five times, between 1774 and 1782, invading armies penetrated his tribe's territory, burning and killing. Tecumseh fled for his life, with his home in flames behind him. His father and many other Shawnees met violent bloody deaths defending their people, and Tecumseh saw prisoners tortured and slain. And yet he survived, sad and distrustful, but neither morose, maladjusted, nor irredeemably embittered.

The shadows that hung over Tecumseh's childhood were cast by the relationships between the Shawnees and the advancing white frontier which tried to push them aside, and by the quarrel between Britain and her rebel-lious American colonies.

During the first years of Tecumseh's life, difficulties between the Ohio Shawnees and the British colonies east of the Allegheny Mountains in-creased. The trade which brought desirable European manufactures into the Scioto villages also exacted severe, and sometimes terrible, penalties. Diseases, such as smallpox, introduced by the whites occasionally ripped holes in Indian communities. The liquor traffic went hand in hand with drunkenness, violence, and poverty when some Indians squandered their possessions and dignity to satisfy their thirst for rum. And now and again the political temperature on the frontier was driven up by thefts and mur-ders, of which no party was entirely blameless. A number of Shawnees also regarded European influences upon Indian customs and beliefs as contam-ination, offensive to the spirits whose goodwill was so essential to the tribe's well-being.[2]

However, more than anything else it was the land which sat at the heart of the conflict embroiling the infant Tecumseh. The population of the British colonies was mushrooming. It had expanded eightfold to two mil-lion since the beginning of the century, and continued to increase, fed by a high birthrate and immigration. Thousands of Scotch-Irish immigrants could be found on the frontier, from New York to Georgia. There were other reasons for expansion, too. Poor agricultural practices in the east fueled a search for new land in the west. Impecunious colonial governments used land to reward their military veterans, and speculators tried to get their hands on large tracts so that they could sell or lease them to others for profit. Some merchants wanted land as compensation for losses they had sustained during the Indian uprising of 1763.

The powerful Six Nations of the Iroquois Confederacy of New York claimed to have conquered the Ohio country in the previous century, and they were willing to sell part of it to the British, assuring them that the Shaw-nees and other Indians lived there only by their sufferance. Sir William Johnson, the British superintendent of Indian affairs in the north, endorsed that view. As a result, at Fort Stanwix in New York in 1768 the Iroquois es-tablished a new Indian boundary line with the British. They surrendered what is now western Pennsylvania and Kentucky for over £10,000. The new line ran from the head of the Mohawk River in New York, and down the Ohio from Fort Pitt as far as the mouth of the Tennessee.

At a stroke the Shawnees and other Ohio Indians were deprived of their rich hunting grounds in Kentucky, south of the Ohio. The Shawnees did not recognize the Iroquois claims to the Ohio. Shawnees, not Iroquois, had traditionally occupied this region, and apart from a small splinter group

known as the Mingoes, the Iroquois did not use it now. The Iroquois Confederacy did not even share the proceeds of the sale with the Ohio Indians.

Whatever the Shawnees thought of the treaty of Fort Stanwix, it was
manna to the speculators and settlers. The ceded land was offered for sale
on favorable terms, and when the land office in Pittsburgh opened on 3
April 1769 a total of 2,790 applications were filed before close of business.
The colony of Pennsylvania was one springboard for expansion into the new
purchase, but it was the governor of Virginia, John Murray, Earl of Dunmore, who was the most ardent advocate. To the chagrin of Pennsylvania,
he seized control of the Fort Pitt region in 1773, and planned to turn Kentucky into a new county of Virginia.

The Shawnees deeply resented the gathering invasion of lands they considered their own, lands they had never sold; but with little more than a
thousand of their people on the Ohio, a mere three hundred warriors or so,
they needed help to resist. For several years they urged Indian communities
to put aside intertribal and interband feuds and unite behind the Shawnees
to protect the land. While the boy Tecumseh blissfully played with his
friends beside the Scioto, Shawnee leaders were embarking upon exactly
the kind of pan-Indian diplomacy for which he would one day be famous.
Their messengers traveled north to the tribes of the Great Lakes, west to the
Wabash and the Illinois, and south to the villages of the Chickasaws, the
Cherokees, and the Creeks. They even approached the troublesome Iroquois
Confederacy. The Shawnees also tried to stockpile guns, powder, and lead,
and at least four times between 1770 and 1774 hosted intertribal conferences at their villages. Indians everywhere, they said, should "be all of one
mind and of one color."[3]

It was not enough. The Indians were unable to overcome their own differences, and few had stomach for a fight with the British, who supplied
them with trade and presents. The British and their Iroquois allies also tried
to isolate the Shawnees diplomatically, and only the Mingoes gave the tribe
consistent support. Unfortunately, the Mingoes could only field about one
hundred warriors.

As Shawnees noticed the ever greater number of surveyors descending
the Ohio, and the aggressive Virginian militia assembling at Fort Pitt, they
grew uncertain about what to do. Some wanted war, while others spoke for
caution, and even suggested sending a deputation to London, where it was
believed that their Great Father, the King, might look more favorably upon
their grievances than Johnson and the colonial governments. In 1773 one
party of Shawnees despaired completely, and withdrew farther down the
Ohio. Perhaps to Missouri, perhaps to Alabama.

Whatever innocence and tranquillity Tecumseh knew in his childhood
ended in the summer and fall of 1774. Shawtunte may have been one of

the first to hear the rumblings of the storm. About the end of April he had traveled north along the Warrior's Path to visit Pluggy's Town, a Mingo settlement on the Olentangy River. Suddenly the village was thrown into excitement, as a party under a respected Mingo named John Logan came in. He had always been a friend to the whites, but now he was burning with grief and anger. The Big Knives, as the Indians called the Virginians (and later Americans generally), had been to his home at the mouth of Yellow Creek during his absence. They had slaughtered his family, including his mother and sister. Now, Logan was beside himself with rage, and begged kinsmen to join in taking revenge.

Tecumseh's people were also directly involved. Two Shawnees were killed on the Ohio in separate incidents. The tribe's leading war chief, Hokoleskwa, the Cornstalk, was the son of Puckshenose, one of the few Shawnee headmen influenced by the Moravian missionaries, and he was not disposed to war, especially a war for which the Shawnees were still unprepared. Given time he might have kept the peace, if only for a little while. But when the Mingoes and a few Shawnees avenged the deaths of their relatives by attacking white settlers, Lord Dunmore saw an opportunity to crush the Indians. He went to war.[4]

In August a few Shawnee villages on the Muskingum River were destroyed, and then, as the leaves of the forest turned red and gold, two more armies of Big Knives advanced, bound for the towns on the Scioto. One consisted of eleven hundred men under Colonel Andrew Lewis, and headed down the Kanawha toward the Ohio. The other was led by Dunmore himself, and descended the Ohio from Fort Pitt. Dunmore planned to link with Lewis's column for the final march to the Scioto. Against such forces the Shawnees seemed helpless. They were outnumbered and outgunned, but they decided to try their fortune. If they could defeat one of the approaching armies, they might inspire other Indians to join them.

This was no minor foray to repay personal injuries or reap plunder, scalps, and prestige. It was a tribal effort, decided in tribal council. The head civil chief, Kishshinottisthee (Hardman), surrendered his authority to Cornstalk, the main war chief, and the red tomahawk was sent to the village and divisional war leaders, calling for their support. Pukeshinwau heard that call, and prepared the Kispokos for battle. His eldest son, Cheeseekau, although only some thirteen years old, was allowed to attend him, perhaps at the boy's insistence.[5]

For the first time Tecumseh watched the departure of a big war party. He saw the dances, in which painted warriors clad only in breechcloths brandished their weapons and raised their ardor to the throbbing of a drum. He pondered their ceremonies of purification, in which they drank a vegetable concoction to boost their energies and fasted to implore the assistance of

the spirits. He may even have understood the importance attached to the
ministrations of the holy men as they summoned supernatural aid. Almost
certainly Tecumseh was there when Pukeshinwau and the warriors made
their noisy departure. Guns were fired. The soldiers, painted, feathered, and
their heads shaven to the scalp lock on the crown, whooped and fell in behind the war chief as he led them onto the Warrior's Path singing his war
song. With the party went a sacred bundle. It contained objects which
would be used to request further spiritual help during the course of the
campaign.

On the morning of 10 October 1774 the Shawnees made a furious attack
upon Lewis's army at Point Pleasant at the mouth of the Kanawha. They
were vastly outnumbered, but they fought like lions. "From what I can
gather here," wrote one who was on the battlefield shortly afterward, "I cannot describe the bravery of the enemy [Indians] in the battle. It exceeded
every man's expectations . . . Their chiefs ran continually along the line ex-
horting the men to 'lie close' and 'shoot well,' 'fight and be strong.'"[6] The
battle raged all day, but although the Indians stove in the Virginian van during the initial assault, and later made desperate rushes upon Lewis's line, inflicting a total of 140 casualties, they were fought to a standstill. Unable to
defeat the Big Knives, Cornstalk withdrew his forces, knowing that the path
to the Scioto was now open to his people's enemies.

But several warriors did not return, some of them the bravest. Among
the dead was Pukeshinwau. We do not know whether the Shawnees brought
his body home, or whether they hid it or threw it into the Ohio with some of
the other dead, but according to a family tradition young Cheeseekau carried a thought alongside his grief as he struggled back to the Scioto. It was
the command of his dying father. Pukeshinwau had probably always looked
upon this boy, his firstborn, as his successor. Now, in his final moments, he
charged him "to preserve unsullied the dignity and honor of his family" and
"in future lead forth to battle his younger brothers."

The months following the death of her husband were difficult for
Methoataaskee. If the Prophet's account is to be believed, she was pregnant
with the last of her children, and there was the stipulated period of mourning to complete. She had to withdraw from society and abstain from merriment of all kinds. She had to wear the plainest clothes, and even refrain
from washing her hands and face. After twelve days all of Pukeshinwau's
other relatives would declare the end of their mourning with dancing, feasting, and gift-giving, but as his widow, Methoataaskee was expected to
mourn for a full year.

She had too many children to remain idle, however. Some, no doubt, de-

manded regular attention. Tecumseh, Shawtunte remembered, was an enterprising, mischievous boy who was always getting a whipping from his
mother. Her oldest boy, Cheeseekau, was at an age when he needed a father
figure to teach him the skills of hunting and to guide him through the ado-
lescent sacred vision quest. Methoataaskee never had more need of support
than in that year, and possibly she returned to her Pekowi relatives.

The family crisis mirrored a greater one that was pulling the Ohio
Shawnees apart. Cornstalk and the Mekoches stopped Dunmore's advance
by conciliation. In 1774 and 1775 they "brightened the chain of friendship"
by agreeing to surrender all "prisoners" and, apparently, by acknowledging
the loss of Kentucky. Both Cornstalk and Hardman strove to get their people
to hand over any whites or blacks originally acquired as captives, and to return stolen horses. When the Virginians built Fort Randolph at Point Pleasant, Cornstalk kept it informed of hostile intentions among the Indians.

This appeasement policy gained a temporary respite for the Shawnees,
but it also drove a wedge between the Mekoches, and a few of their supporters, and the rest of the tribe. Most of the Pekowis, Chillicothes, and
Kispokos accused Cornstalk and his Mekoches of being "wedded" to the Big
Knives. They declared that "they still loved the land and would not part with
it," and they watched with growing bitterness the construction of the first
white settlements in Kentucky.[7]

Cornstalk's attempt to return "prisoners" caused particular heartaches,
because powerful emotional bonds had been forged between many former
captives and their Indian foster families. So reluctant were some Shawnees
to part with their captives that in 1776, despite the best efforts of the chiefs,
observers from Virginia and the Continental Congress were sent into the Indian towns to consummate the process.

One victim was Shawtunte. The family's love of the boy had weathered
two attempts to repatriate prisoners, in 1764 and 1774, and he had lost his
English and become proficient in the Shawnee language. He grew into a
tall, strong, athletic youth. In later years he would remember wrestling and
racing with Tecumseh—who, he said, was not as strong as he, but was
faster. Much to Shawtunte's distress, it was probably early in 1776 that he
had to part with the only family he knew. He remained on the frontier, and
became a soldier, but seems never to have met his foster brothers again.[8]

The schism among the Shawnees was suddenly intensified by another
war, one in which they had no ostensible interest: the American Revolution.

Both the Crown and the colonies recognized the military potential of the
thousands of armed warriors living on the frontiers, and from 1775, as they
slid into war, they competed for Indian support. The Virginians, with whom

Cornstalk had been negotiating, now became part of the larger union of the thirteen colonies rebelling against Britain. For the most part colonial lead-ers initially urged the Indians to remain neutral. On the Ohio Cornstalk's Mekoches and the turtle division of the Delawares under White Eyes lis-tened. They saw no advantage in becoming entangled in a white man's war, and continued to advocate peace.

But other Shawnees were not so sure. Britain wanted the Indians to be allies of the Crown, and from posts such as Niagara, Detroit, and Michili-mackinac began building support among the tribes of the Great Lakes, the Ohio, and the upper Mississippi. The superior quality of British presents and trade goods, long-standing relationships between British officials and the Indians, and the hostility that had been developing between the tribes and the colonists encroaching upon their lands all bolstered Britain's cause. At Detroit Lieutenant-Governor Henry Hamilton handed out ammunition and advised the Indians to unite beneath the British flag. In 1777 he was au-thorized to incite them to attack the frontiers of Kentucky, Virginia, and Pennsylvania as a diversionary tactic. For the more militant Shawnees and Mingoes, who had criticized Cornstalk's temporization, this situation was a heaven-sent opportunity to use British arms, provisions, and help to clear Kentucky of the invading Big Knives.

In 1777 the peace and war factions of the Shawnees parted. Some of the Mekoches, the followers of Cornstalk and Hardman, moved with a few Pekowis to the Tuscarawas River, where they joined neutral Delawares at Coshocton. Most of the remaining Shawnees also abandoned the Scioto, but they traveled westward, to the valleys of the Little and Great Miami, where they built homes that were less exposed to American attack.[9]

Time would reveal that neither party could claim the greater wisdom. It proved to be impossible to regain Kentucky, equally so to remain neutral. In November 1777 Cornstalk died in a volley of bullets, massacred with one of his sons and two other Shawnees, not by enemies but by a crowd of Ameri-can militiamen at Fort Randolph angered by the raids of other Indians. The next year his Delaware ally, White Eyes, was also murdered by Americans. In 1782 ninety Christian Delawares were butchered by borderers at Gnaden-hutten on the Tuscarawas. The United States was not only unable to provi-sion friendly Indians satisfactorily, it was unable to protect them, against either the enemy or Indian-hating frontiersmen. Before the end of the war the neutral Shawnees and Delawares had rejoined their hostile kinsmen.

Methoataaskee was among those who founded the new towns farther west, and we can be sure which particular village it was, because Tecumseh himself identified it to Thomas Worthington and Duncan McArthur in 1807. Pekowi, as it was named, stood on the northwestern bank of the Mad River, a tributary of the Great Miami, a few miles west of present-day Springfield in Clark County, Ohio. It was an idyllic place. Sweeping gracefully over a bed of flat stones, the river skirted the town in a wide bend to the southwest, cutting through a prairie of grass and flowers set on both sides against a backdrop of high ground clothed in timber. Pekowi crowned a low hill some twenty feet above the water, which it approached toward the east. North and northeast it was overlooked by bluffs which almost struck the riverside; west and southwest stretched marsh and level wooded bottomland; while on the south, two miles of prairie, which the Indians turned into cornfields, extended to the river. The Kispokos established a smaller town at the same location, on the plain southwest of Pekowi. Here was an ideal playground for a boy of Tecumseh's spirit. He could explore swamps, scale the cliffs behind the town, or cross the cornfields to ford the river and set up ambuscades in the timbered ridges across the prairie on the other side.[10]

Not far away were the other new settlements. North, upstream, were Mackachack, a Mekoche village; Wakatomica, which contained Mekoches and Chillicothes; Blue Jacket's Town; a Mingo town; and a village of sympathetic Delawares under Buckongahelas and Wyondochella. The largest settlement was to the southeast, however. A fresh Chillicothe, often known as Old Chillicothe, was erected on the southeastern bank of the upper Little Miami, near modern-day Xenia. Its enormous council house ran the length of the village, which squatted on a hill flanked on both sides by cornfields.[11]

Tecumseh may have been as familiar with Old Chillicothe as with Pekowi, for it was the home of Blackfish, the formidable war captain of the Chillicothes. It was Blackfish who, encouraged by the British, led the first Shawnee raids into Kentucky in 1777 and 1778, harassing stations and pouncing upon straggling settlers. His greatest coup occurred in February 1778, when he captured Daniel Boone and twenty-seven companions as they gathered salt on the Licking River. The prisoners were brought to the Shawnee towns. Some were adopted, others were eventually purchased by the British for release, and a few, including Boone himself, escaped. Boone was thus back home, in Boonesborough, in September, when three hundred Indians and eleven whites under Blackfish unsuccessfully besieged the settlement for several days.

One of the Kentuckians taken at the salt licks was sixteen-year-old Benjamin Kelly. He remained with the Indians until the end of the war, five years later, but eventually became a Baptist minister. In 1821 he met a fellow preacher, Thomas Spottswood Hinde, in Ohio County, Kentucky, and gave him an interesting account of his captivity. Kelly said that he had been adopted by Blackfish himself, and lived at his house near a spring in Old Chillicothe, on a site later named Saxon's Lot. What is more, he said that Tecumseh and the Prophet were his foster brothers. Tecumseh was known as Tecumsekeh, Shooting Star, and was ten to twelve years old in 1778. Kelly

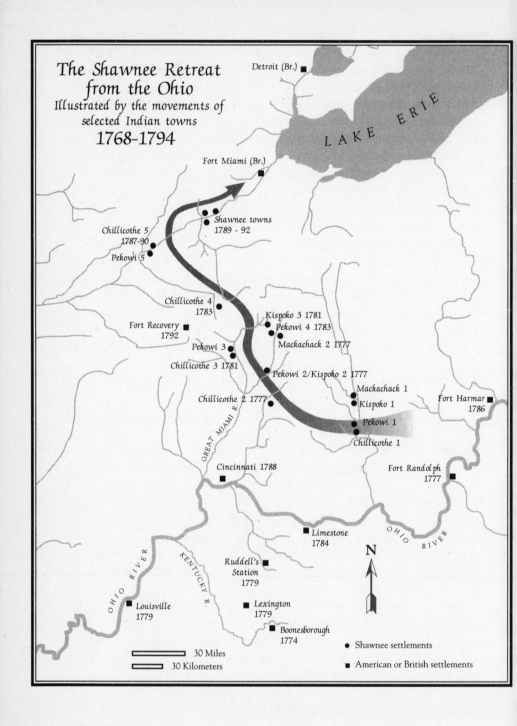

The Shawnee Retreat
from the Ohio
Illustrated by the movements of
selected Indian towns
1768-1794

Detroit (Br.)

LAKE ERIE

Fort Miami (Br.)

Shawnee towns
1789 - 92

Chillicothe 5
1787-90

Pekowi 5

Chillicothe 4
1783

Kispoko 3 1781

Pekowi 4 1783

Fort Recovery
1792

Mackachack 2 1777

Pekowi 3

Chillicothe 3 1781

Pekowi 2/Kispoko 2 1777

Mackachack 1

Chillicothe 2 1777

Kispoko 1

Fort Harmar
1786

Pekowi 1

Chillicothe 1

GREAT MIAMI R.

Cincinnati 1788

Fort Randolph
1777

OHIO RIVER

Limestone
1784

N

OHIO RIVER

KENTUCKY R.

Ruddell's
Station
1779

Louisville
1779

Lexington
1779

Boonesborough
1774

30 Miles

30 Kilometers

● Shawnee settlements

■ American or British settlements

remembered him as an exceptional boy, of good judgment, and dexterous with bow and arrows.

A question mark will always hang on Kelly's reliability, but his account could have been true. Blackfish was a middle-aged man, an orator and warrior, and he would have known Pukeshinwau well. There is nothing impossible about the Chillicothe war chief offering to adopt some of Methoataaskee's children. Among the Shawnees orphans might be taken by friends or relatives, according to their circumstances.[12]

But if Kelly's story was a true one, and Tecumseh spent time in Old Chillicothe as well as Pekowi, the patronage of Blackfish did not last long.

After dark on the evening of 29 May 1779, three hundred men stealthily enfiladed Old Chillicothe. John Bowman had marched them from Kentucky, up the Little Miami, and they were determined to repay the Shawnees for three years of warfare. A lone Indian strode out into the darkness, perhaps to investigate a noise. Bowman's men had not yet completed their cordon, but one of them eagerly shot the Indian down. Immediately, Old Chillicothe erupted into pandemonium. Some warriors disgracefully took to their heels, leaving only a few behind to defend the women and children, who ran to barricade themselves in the council house. One poor woman failed to reach the refuge. She broke her leg and lay outside the council house for the rest of the night, crying as the battle raged around her and flames leaped up from cabins the Kentuckians put to the torch.

Blackfish knew his duty. Mustering what warriors he could, he led them forward in a counterattack, but they were driven back by heavy fire, and the chief himself was struck down with a fearsome wound. A bullet entered his right knee and ripped upward, shattering the bone before emerging from the thigh. The warriors fell back to a few houses at the center of the town, Blackfish himself occupying one some thirty yards from the council house with three or four of his men. The night was long. In the council house a small group of warriors maintained a defending fire, urged on by an old man named Asstakoma, while the Kentuckians fired houses and tried to dislodge their remaining adversaries. But finally, afraid that Indian reinforcements would soon be arriving, Bowman's force gave up. Blackfish sent men to shadow the retreating army, but it did not return.

The raid severely damaged but did not cripple the Shawnees. Seven Indians had been killed or fatally wounded, including Blackfish, who lingered painfully for about six weeks while his wound mortified. However, although buildings had been damaged and property seized, much of the town and most of its people had been saved, and even the corn, which was burned, sprouted anew to yield a harvest that year. The Americans, who lost ten of their men, had struck too early in the year for maximum effect.[13]

The night Blackfish received his mortal wound, men from Pekowi rode

so hard to Old Chillicothe to help turn back the Big Knives that some of
their horses died of exhaustion. Tecumseh may have seen them setting out
in the darkness to fight, or perhaps he was even in the stricken village itself.
The boy would quickly have realized that even if he spent most of his war at
home, it was still a battle zone.

For the Shawnee towns were alive with the clamor of war in the five
years after 1777. British agents brought provisions and speeches, assembled
warriors for campaigns, advised the chiefs, and erected wooden stockades
at Old Chillicothe and Pekowi. There were French Canadians, such as Charles
Beaubien, Louis Lorimier, and Fontenay Dequindre, alongside Alexander
McKee, Matthew Elliott, the Girty brothers, and others of British ancestry.
Most of them had traded with the Indians before the war, and many had
married Shawnee women. Now they had become invaluable intermediaries
between the Indians and their British allies.

Through the Shawnee villages were also funneled British rangers and
the other tribesmen of the alliance, local Mingoes and Delawares, as well as
Wyandots, Potawatomis, Ottawas, and Ojibwas from the Great Lakes. All
used the towns as bases while they moved backward and forward in their
expeditions against the frontiers of Kentucky and Virginia.

Tecumseh grew accustomed to the excitement that attended the return
of Shawnee war parties. He heard the whoops and the crash of guns that
signaled the approach of successful warriors, and saw the scalps raised aloft
on a pole and wretched prisoners being prodded forward, singing, with rat-
tles in their hands. He learned that those captives whose faces had been
painted red were to be spared, and he watched the condemned, their faces
blackened, being driven to the council house or the war post, dogs darting
around their feet, and men, women, and children beating them with sticks
as they passed.

During the first years of the war, prisoners were usually well treated, although each captive was considered the property of the individual captor, to
be sold, given away, or dealt with as he saw fit. When the conflict grew more
bitter, with losses mounting on both sides, the prospects for prisoners deteriorated. Tecumseh saw men running between rows of shouting Indians
who thumped them with sticks or fired powder from their muskets at them.
He probably saw others, even less fortunate, stripped and surrounded, and
put to death in a fearful fashion—cut, beaten, and even burned.

Some prisoners were bought and released by the British, but most were
adopted by Shawnee families. Many, like Shawtunte, adjusted fully to the
Indian life and remembered it with affection. Indeed, it was common for
repatriation to be evaded or rejected, even by men and women who had
been assimilated into Indian society as adults.

It was thus that Tecumseh met Stephen Ruddell in 1780. That year the

British finally responded to Shawnee demands for greater support by organizing an expedition into Kentucky. Commanded by Captain Henry Bird of
the 8th Regiment of Foot, the expedition consisted of two pieces of artillery
and about 1,000 men, some of them Lakes Indians and British, but others
Ohio Indians, including Shawnees mustered at Pekowi by Alexander Mc-
Kee. They invaded Kentucky in June, frightened a couple of stations into
submission, and returned with about 350 prisoners, males and females of
all ages. Twelve-year-old Stephen Ruddell was one of them. His parents, and
most of their children, did not wait long for their release, but Stephen remained with the Indians for years. He got a new name, Sinnamatha, or Big
Fish, and almost immediately struck up a friendship with a Shawnee boy of
his own age. Tecumseh and Stephen became "inseparable" companions.

Most forcibly of all, the war came to Tecumseh in the fierce counterattacks made by the Kentuckians. Bowman's was but the first of several,
bursting suddenly and furiously into the Shawnee villages. In August 1780
George Rogers Clark brought 1,000 men and a six-pounder across the Ohio
and burned Old Chillicothe to the ground. The inhabitants had been able to
evacuate the place before the Big Knives arrived, but they lost their crops
and many of their possessions. Pekowi had more time. Indian runners and
an American deserter brought warnings, and all the refugees streaming
from the Little Miami had their own stories.

Many of the warriors of Pekowi and Kispoko Town were away at Detroit,
but riders sped for help while seventy Indians and a handful of white allies,
including James and George Girty, prepared to fight. The issue was considered so doubtful that some male prisoners among the Shawnees were killed
to prevent them from defecting to Clark's army. Women and children, one of
whom was likely Tecumseh, were sent up the bluffs behind the town, while
the warriors squatted down behind ridges, trees, and a pole fence to await
the attack.

On the evening of 8 August the Americans came along the main trail
from Old Chillicothe and reached the Mad River, below the town. Mounted
detachments fanned out, one toward the east along the south bank of the
river to prevent the Shawnees from escaping that way, and a second west,
with the hope of flushing Indians from wooded bottoms. Clark's main force
forded the stream and advanced directly upon Pekowi with his six-pounder,
through the prairie and cornfields and in front of Kispoko Town. At first the
Shawnees tried to stop the Big Knives from reaching Pekowi. They delivered a fierce musketry upon the oncoming soldiers, bringing some of them
down. But on their right the outnumbered defenders were driven from their
cover and forced back into the town. The Indians made a brief stand in a
stockade in the lower part of the village, but after the artillery opened up
their whole force fled eastward. The Kentuckians who had been detailed to

cut them off had mired down and were unable to prevent the Indians from reaching Wakatomica.

After two days Clark withdrew, leaving Pekowi and Kispoko Town in ruins. His losses were reported at 14 killed and 13 wounded, although the fatalities might have been as high as 29. The Indians said six of their men were killed and others wounded, and that a man and a woman were taken prisoner. The woman, they complained, was found murdered, her stomach slashed open. Indian graves at Pekowi had also been plundered for scalps. But the greatest damage by far was economic: the harvest destroyed and ammunition needed for the fall hunting exhausted. Starving Indians were soon traveling to Detroit to apply to the British for relief.[14]

Once again Tecumseh and his people had been uprooted, but they were nothing if not durable. The spring found the hardy Shawnee women building new villages to the northwest, the Chillicothes at Standing Stone (Piqua, Ohio) and the Pekowis a few miles north, both on the west bank of the Great Miami. The Kispokos evidently joined the cluster of towns on the upper Mad River, regrouping around McKee's trading post, located on a creek about two and a half miles southeast of the site of modern Bellefontaine.

Not even all of these settlements were safe. In the very last campaign of the war the Kentuckians struck at them, regarding the Shawnees as their most inveterate enemies. In November 1782 Clark was with another army destroying Standing Stone and neighboring settlements, including Louis Lorimier's trading post on Loramie's Creek, New Pekowi, and a village named Willstown. Seventeen Indians were killed or captured. McKee led a war party from Wakatomica to worry Clark's retreat, but the enemy was 1,000 strong, and after losing a few men the Shawnees had to withdraw. This American attack was considerably less effective than its predecessor. It occurred after the Indians had taken in their harvest and largely dispersed to hunting camps, but it forced another troublesome removal upon the Shawnees. The first year of peace found the battered but still defiant Chillicothes on the headwaters of the St. Marys, and the Pekowis with the other Shawnees at the sources of the Mad River, building a town where West Liberty now stands.[15]

The Indian onslaught upon the frontiers during the Revolutionary War was one of the most destructive in border history. It was far more severe than anything that later occurred west of the Mississippi. Although it was the Iroquois who did the most damage, scourging New York, on the Ohio the Shawnees and their allies fully justified a Cherokee prediction made in 1775 that Kentucky "was the bloody ground, and would be dark and difficult to settle." According to one estimate the Indians killed 860 "effective" men in Kentucky between 1776 and 1782. But still the tide of emigration into the new purchase continued, obstructed and endangered but not deterred, and when the war ended Kentucky contained 1,300 men capable of bearing arms. This was a far greater force than the Shawnees, Mingoes, and Delawares on the Great Miami could field. One thing was certain. The Shawnees had lost control of the lands south of the Ohio for good.[16]

The Shawnees had not been defeated, but it was they, not the Big Knives, who had retreated, from the Scioto to the Little and the Great Miami, and then farther upstream. True, they had lost little in manpower. Some Shawnees had tired of the struggle and headed south in 1780, but white prisoners adopted into the tribe had made good their few battle losses, and there had been occasional Indian reinforcements. A band of Cherokees under the Swan had joined them in 1781. Nor, despite their sufferings, did they lack spirit when the British suddenly stopped fighting. But the tribe's grip on the Ohio, and with it their dream of reuniting the nation along the waters that drained into it, had undeniably weakened.[17]

From his earliest childhood Tecumseh regarded the Big Knives as his enemies. They were responsible for the seizure of Shawnee hunting grounds, the death of his father, and the destruction of his towns. More than that, the fates of Cornstalk and the praying Delawares told him the Big Knives were fundamentally treacherous. It would have been understandable if Tecumseh had emerged from such a boyhood, punctuated by trauma and pain as it was, vengeful and brooding, but to his credit it was not so. The boy gave early evidence of generosity and humanity, as well as the ability to respond to the goodwill he found in individuals. And somehow, in all that disruption, he also learned the skills he needed to earn his livelihood.

Tribal elders sometimes taught Shawnee children hieroglyphics, oral traditions, and oratory, but Tecumseh's family were the major influences upon him. Methoataaskee was increasingly supported by her daughter, Tecumapease, who grew to be a superior and intelligent girl. Tecumapease formed a close relationship with Tecumseh. Throughout his adulthood he would regularly visit her and bring her gifts. Tecumapease had less to do with her youngest brothers, probably because marriage took her from home. At some stage, possibly before the end of the war, she married Wahsikegaboe (Stands Firm), a fine warrior who eventually became a chief and a leading supporter of Tecumseh.[18]

As Tecumseh grew older, Cheeseekau became perhaps even more important to him than Tecumapease. During the war the elder boy did what Tecumseh only dreamed of doing. He fought the Big Knives. No details of his experiences exist, but there was no shortage of engagements in which he may have honed his skills. He may have helped defeat an American military convoy on the Ohio in October 1779, and the following year was probably with Bird's expedition, which attracted a pretty full turnout of Shawnee warriors. Perhaps he defended Pekowi against Clark in 1780 or was one of the 140 men that Blacksnake decisively led into a battle with Colonel William Crawford's militia on the Sandusky two years later.

Maybe it was during these first years as a warrior that Cheeseekau earned a new name. The Shawnees were soon calling him Pepquannake or Pepquannakek, which meant Gun Shot. In 1790 an American report named him Popoquan, the Gun.[19]

In between military adventures Cheeseekau did what he could for his younger brothers, Sauawaseekau and Tecumseh. Stephen Ruddell testified that Cheeseekau taught Tecumseh "to look with contempt upon everything that was mean" and instilled in him "correct, manly and honorable principles." Cheeseekau must have taken his brother hunting, demonstrating how to track, stalk, and shoot, and describing the different habits, sounds, and signs of animals and birds. Probably he supervised some of the daily plunges that Tecumseh, like other boys, took into cold streams, so that they would develop endurance, hardihood, and self-control.[20]

Cheeseekau must have taken pleasure from his brother's progress. Tecumseh was bold and enterprising, and quickly displayed qualities of leadership during the summer games he played about the villages. Ruddell recalled that Tecumseh generally divided the boys who followed him into parties so that they might fight sham battles, forays "in which he always distinguished himself by his activity, strength and skill."

These childhood encounters were no doubt entertaining, but they were very different from the uncertain hazards of the real war trail. The peace that brought the American Revolution to an end in 1783 could have restored some tranquillity to the land of the Shawnees, but it didn't. It was no longer the territory south of the sweeping Ohio that was at issue, for now the new United States made a bid for the Indian country to the north, and once again the Shawnees were driven to war. Now, as Tecumseh exchanged adolescence for manhood, he would have to fight in earnest.

4

RITES OF PASSAGE

The Kispokos were the smallest of the Shawnee divisions, but Tecumseh was proud to be one of them.

It was true they lacked the standing of the Mekoches and Chillicothes. Mekoches regularly boasted that it was they who had been the first creations of Waashaa Monetoo, and that he had placed them at the center of the island and given them the right to govern the tribe. The Chillicothes, the Shawnees believed, had joined the Mekoches after making a journey across the sea, and enjoyed a comparable standing. But the Mekoches referred to the Pekowis, and probably also the Hathawekelas and Kispokos, as "younger brothers." There were different stories of their origins. One had the Pekowis and Kispokos being discovered by the Mekoches in the south, but most appear to have implied that they were in some way or another the creations of the senior divisions. The ancestor of the Pekowis, for example, was variously said to have risen as a child from the ashes of a Mekoche fire or to have been formed from the backbone of an elk killed by the Chillicothes.[1]

Nevertheless, unlike the Mekoches, the Kispokos had not temporized with the Big Knives, and for fighting ability they had a reputation second to none. Young Tecumseh longed to take his place among the ranks of their warriors.

As he reached puberty Tecumseh took important steps toward achieving that ambition. It was the age when young Shawnees began to look for their own guardian spirits. Spirits, as we have seen, controlled all things for the

Indians, and could receive appeals for help, but all Shawnees also had guardian spirits, peculiar to themselves as individuals, spirits which would offer personal protection during the difficult business of life. Every boy had a guardian spirit, but its identity was only discovered when he reached puberty and endured a program of fasting and prayer. The spirit would normally appear in the form of a creature, perhaps during the youth's dreams or trances, and while it would thenceforth be a source of power to him he was forbidden to identify it to anyone else.[2]

Cheeseekau probably supervised Tecumseh's vision quest, blacking the boy's face to signify his fast, and sending him alone into the woods to meditate. The experience was normally repeated several times. Each time, the length of the fast was extended, and its completion was denoted by the washing of the face. After his final quest, which might have occupied several days, Tecumseh not only would have felt stronger for the new powers his guardian spirit conferred but would also have moved closer to assuming the responsibilities of adulthood.

While Tecumseh cultivated his spirituality, he did not ignore the skills of the hunter and warrior, upon which his ability to support and protect a family would depend. He loved hunting, and many were the stories of his prowess in that field. One which seems to have been grounded in truth but confused in detail was told by John Ruddell, the son of Tecumseh's boyhood companion Stephen. John wrote that he "often heard [his] father" tell the story of a buffalo killing that "was the first notable event in the life of Tecumtha."[3]

If the details are correct, the incident must have occurred about 1786 or 1787, after warfare between the Shawnees and the Big Knives had broken out again. The Indians were maneuvering in the vicinity of an American force, when Tecumseh and a friend came upon two or three buffaloes at a stream, and they killed them and cut them up. They sent word by some hunters that they had meat ready for packing, but when the news reached the main body of Indians it did not meet with the war chief's approval. The boys had killed the animals directly in the path of the Americans, despite the chief's instructions that all should keep clear, and he was so annoyed that when the boys made their appearance he struck them across the shoulders with a ramrod to punish them for disobedience.

Chastened but undaunted, Tecumseh set out to hunt again the next day, accompanied this time by Stephen Ruddell. After ascending a long ridge the boys heard coming toward them some other hunters pursuing a herd of buffalo with dogs. They scaled some trees, and as the animals lumbered by they opened fire on them. Stephen carried a single-shot musket and was able to account for only one animal, but Tecumseh loosed arrow after arrow and killed sixteen of the buffaloes. With this feat he expunged his former dishonor, and was rewarded with the present of a gun. The story, like so many about Tecumseh, had obviously grown in the telling, but John Ruddell mentioned it so regularly that it likely had some historical foundation.

As an accomplished hunter, Tecumseh was a good provider. He developed into a finely formed young man, elegant, athletic, and handsome, and his disposition was friendly and generous. All in all a young man of exceptional promise, and one who attracted friends and admirers of both sexes.

In this he followed a path blazed by his older brothers, particularly Cheeseekau. Cheeseekau may have married during this period. He was eventually survived by a daughter, who was living beyond the Mississippi in 1825. But Tecumseh's youthful ambitions left him little time for girls. He stood ready to defend them from abuse, and according to a statement that may have originated with the Prophet, once ("while a mere boy") upbraided a warrior for beating his wife. Yet while many girls had eyes for him, Tecumseh refused to make a commitment.[4]

There were many occasions when young Shawnees might fraternize with the opposite sex, especially during the warmer months when they occupied their villages. In fact, the spring festival, which beseeched the deities for a fertile crop, traditionally included a football match between the men and the women. In attempting to drive a ball through the men's goal, the women could employ their hands and feet. The men used feet only, but they could jostle any woman carrying the ball in an attempt to dislodge it from her grasp. One such game was described by an American observer in the 1790s. "The young squaws were the most active of their party," he said, "and most frequently caught the ball, when it was amusing to see the struggle between them and the young men, which generally terminated in the prostration of the squaw upon the grass before the ball could be forced from her hand."[5]

An even more favored public opportunity was furnished by the "bringing dance." The men would begin the dance, sometimes in a ring, sometimes in a long wandering file, chanting a love song. The women looked expectantly on, but as they felt the inclination each would join the dance, selecting any man she wished as a partner. Sometimes the man and woman exchanged small presents as they danced together.

For the young, the "bringing dance" was exciting. A group of American officers who saw it in 1786 noted that "the girls were very fond of getting a few of us engaged in this dance." During Tecumseh's lifetime the character of the dance evidently changed. It became common for men, rather than women, to select their partners. This was usually signified by a pull upon the dress of the woman concerned, but it was even considered legitimate for a man to seek a favorite person who was not actually present. According to the Prophet, "If a young man chooses to go in a wigwam and give the usual sign to a young woman, she is obliged by custom to follow him, even if she have [has] retired to bed."[6]

On occasions such as these Tecumseh was a prime target, but he avoided serious connections and even treated the matter with levity. He told a friend that he was determined to disappoint the many attractive girls vying for his attentions—and if necessary he would marry a plain woman to do so! Possibly to avoid the more insistent of his admirers, or perhaps for no other reason than that he found women a distraction, Tecumseh surprised companions by his reluctance to join hunting parties that were accompanied by females.[7]

More than anything else, it seems, Tecumseh aimed to be a warrior, to achieve that final distinction that would make him an equal among men. No quality was more admired by Shawnees than bravery, and Tecumseh knew from childhood that nothing gave quicker access to prestige and influence than the warpath. Some of the civil chiefs owed their positions to heredity, especially among the Mekoches. Not so the war chiefs. Every one of them had been tested and retested in action, and had won his authority by repeated displays of courage and the ability to inflict the maximum damage upon enemies at the lowest possible cost to his own party. It was said that the brave would be the first to be rewarded in Heaven.

In his quest for military distinction, Tecumseh had to measure himself against high standards, standards set by his father and eldest brother. Even Sauawaseekau, the second son, was proving himself a good warrior. It was hard working out of such long shadows, but armed with the powers of his new guardian spirits, the boy was ready for that test.

It came suddenly, in 1786. After barely three years of a threadbare peace, all-out war returned to the Shawnee country.

In 1783 the treaty of Paris ended the Revolutionary War, but not the conflict over the Ohio. By the treaty Britain transferred the sovereignty of most land south of the Great Lakes and east of the Mississippi to the new United States without the feeblest attempt to protect the rights of its undefeated Indian allies who occupied much of the region. The American Congress moved quickly to take advantage of the situation. Before the end of the year it resolved to annex enormous territories north of the Ohio and east of the Great Miami—the very lands of the Shawnees and the Mingoes, Delawares, and Cherokees who lived with them—on the spurious grounds of conquest. Once seized, the land could be used to reward military veterans or sold to replenish the treasury of the needy federal government.

The beleaguered Shawnees found all this sickeningly familiar. Just as the Fort Stanwix treaty of 1768 robbed them of their hunting grounds in

Kentucky, so now the new republic planned to strip them of their remaining territory.

The British soon became aware of Indian discontent. They were frightened that it would rebound against them, so they postponed evacuating important posts such as Oswego, Niagara, Detroit, and Michilimackinac, even though they were on the American side of the new international boundary. Encouraged by the failure of the United States to live up to all of its obligations under the Paris treaty, Britain retained some of these posts for thirteen years, and used them to issue presents and supplies to the Indians and to prove to the tribes that, after all, their Great Father the King had not abandoned them. Britain's position was certainly difficult. On the one hand, the Indians were indispensable to the protection of the Crown's weak Canadian colonies, as well as valuable partners in the fur trade, and it was essential to maintain their vigor and goodwill; on the other, Britain did not want to be pulled into a war between the Indians and the United States, or to be accused of inciting the tribes against their American neighbors. For the time being British officials supplied the Indians, and advised them to insist upon their rights—but peacefully![8]

Those Indians who lived close to the white frontier felt particularly threatened by the new republic's land-hunger. They saw the increasing numbers of hunters building shelters in the woods, and the proliferation of crude homesteads sprinkling the valleys of western New York, Pennsylvania, Virginia, and Kentucky. In 1783 the Iroquois Confederacy presided over an intertribal conference at Lower Sandusky near Lake Erie. The Shawnees were represented, of course, and communities of Wyandots, Ottawas, Ojibwas, Potawatomis, and Delawares, even southern Cherokees and Creeks. They listened to Iroquois spokesmen advocate an Indian union to defend the land.[9]

Some who have written of Tecumseh's later efforts to create a large-scale pan-Indian resistance movement have said that there was something unusual or even original in the idea. That is nonsense. Tecumseh was distinguished by the new life he breathed into a strategy that was already tried and tired, indeed one that had already failed several times. He worked in a well-worn tradition, particularly among the Shawnees.

It is true that the Indian world was deeply divided, by language, standing intergroup hostilities, and differences in circumstance and outlook. The logistical obstacles to widespread concerted action alone were formidable. It is also true that the typical native political unit was the village, and that even there authority was decentralized and weak. Those who would tie such elements to a common purpose experienced massive frustrations. At best their success was partial and ill sustained. And yet efforts to build alliances and confederacies that crossed ethnic divisions among the Indians had long been a response to situations of exceptional danger, and such efforts had steadily grown in scale.

In the late seventeenth century broken Algonquian tribes had clustered together on the upper Great Lakes and the Illinois River to resist the onslaughts of the Iroquois. A few years later, early in the next century, it was the Iroquois themselves who dabbled in extensive pan-Indianism after they had been forced to terms by the French and French-allied tribes. Before Tecumseh was born, Shawnees, Delawares, and Mingoes, sandwiched on the Ohio between threatening French and British colonies, had formed their own united council fire. Both the Indian revolt against the British in 1763 and the Shawnee diplomacy that preceded Lord Dunmore's War involved far-reaching attempts to coordinate resistance, and the many military successes of Indian forces allied to the British during the Revolutionary War had demonstrated the potential of united action. In short, the idea of confederating Indians to meet a strong enemy may have been difficult to implement, but it was old when Tecumseh was young.[10]

There can be no doubt that the ambitious phase of pan-Indianism between 1783 and 1795 was Tecumseh's greatest inspiration. That was the movement that began at Lower Sandusky in the late summer of 1783. Its ablest advocate, the Mohawk Iroquois leader Joseph Brant, designed the confederacy to be more than a simple military alliance. It should also block American attempts to play one tribe off against another in order to buy land. The confederacy declared that land negotiations made with small groups of Indians or individual tribes were invalid; only the confederacy as a whole could ratify sales.

To strengthen the argument, the Iroquois put forward an idea that would become part of the intellectual baggage of pan-Indianism, and pass from one generation to the next. Some have attributed it to Tecumseh, but we find it stated boldly here, while Tecumseh was a mere youth. Instead of each Indian group or tribe possessing an exclusive right to a territory, with its village sites and hunting and fishing grounds, the land must be regarded as the common property of all Indian peoples, and it could be sold to the United States only with the consent of all Indian peoples.

Although Indians often abandoned territory to colonize new areas, and intertribal towns were not unusual, the notion that the land was held in common by all the tribes does not seem to have been a widely recognized principle among the natives of the trans-Appalachian country. But it made a powerful argument in the hands of a man as astute as Brant, because its acceptance meant that land deals had to be struck with the whole confederacy, rather than with smaller units, if they were to be legitimate. Over the next few years Tecumseh heard much excited talk about this idea, and it was expressed by the Indians in typically allegorical language. The land was likened to a common meal from which everyone ate. They called it "a dish with one spoon."[11]

Just how hard it was to preserve unity was soon obvious. Despite the brave front presented at Lower Sandusky, the United States was able to stage a series of treaties defeating the tribes piecemeal. At Fort Stanwix in 1784, in the absence of Brant, federal commissioners told the Iroquois that they were a conquered people and dragooned them into relinquishing their claims to what is now Ohio. Then, the next year, the Wyandots, Delawares, Ottawas, and Ojibwas were brought to heel at Fort McIntosh (Pennsylvania), where they agreed to cede a huge swath of southern and eastern Ohio, including the Shawnee homeland. These Indians did, however, secure their own villages, which were situated north of the proposed boundary.

Great was the fury of the Indians on the Great Miami. The Shawnees had been enthusiastic supporters of Brant's confederacy, and had sent their emissaries to recruit for it in the south. Now they were angry that their allies had given way with such little spirit. Kekewepelethy, a Mekoche leader known to whites as Captain Johnny, spoke for many when he angrily reminded his listeners of the vision that had moved them at Lower Sandusky. "All nations of us of one color were there," he said, "and agreed as one man not to make peace or war without the consent of the whole, and you likewise know that one or two nations going to our brothers' council fire cannot do anything without the whole were there present."[12]

But the United States isolated and intimidated them. In 1785 the Shawnees were summoned to a meeting at the mouth of the Great Miami, where the Americans erected a square stockade they named Fort Finney. The embittered Shawnees insisted that representatives of all the tribes in the confederacy must attend, but the American commissioners would have none of it. They bluntly told the tribe that it must choose between peace or war.

Under threats such as these some Shawnee chiefs believed they had no alternative but to attend, and 230 members of the tribe were at Fort Finney in January 1786, led by the head civil chief, Moluntha, an elderly Mekoche. The mood was dark, with many of the younger warriors openly hostile to the Americans, and the federal commissioners belligerent and unyielding. Discussion quickly faltered. Making a desperate stand, Kekewepelethy rejected the absurd contention that the Indians had been conquered in the war and that their lands were consequently forfeit. "We do not understand measuring out the lands," he protested. "It is all ours!" The commissioners refused to listen, and threatened force. "We plainly tell you that this country belongs to the United States," they said grimly. According to some accounts they advertised their contempt for the Shawnees by sweeping the Indian wampum from the negotiating table and trampling it underfoot.[13]

The Ohio country had been the gift of Waashaa Monetoo, and it was with anger, confusion, and fear that the chiefs finally gave way. The treaty, dated 31 January, surrendered almost the whole of their homeland: the bulk of present eastern and southern Ohio.

Fort Finney was the last of the three "conquest" treaties, but it can only be counted an American blunder. It could have transformed the fragile armistice that had existed since 1783 into a peace, but instead it struck that peace down. For whatever Moluntha and his chiefs had done was simply repudiated by the rest of the nation. Supported by the local Mingoes, Cherokees, and Delawares, the Shawnee warriors prepared for war. Their messages went urgently westward, to the as yet uncowed Indians of the Wabash, inviting them "to destroy all the men wearing hats . . . who seem to be leagued against us to drive us away from the lands which the Master of Life has given to us."[14]

Cheeseekau had by this time earned the reputation of an outstanding warrior, and he almost certainly disapproved of the weakness the Mekoches had shown at Fort Finney. By his side was Tecumseh, now ready to follow his brother into battle, as Pukeshinwau had willed. Possibly they talked of the forays they would make into Kentucky, or against the immigrant traffic that was now regularly to be seen descending the Ohio River. The pulse of many another warrior quickened at the prospect of war. But the Big Knives had anticipated them, and struck first.

Eight hundred mounted militia under Benjamin Logan, striking across the Ohio from Limestone (Maysville), reached the principal Mekoche town of Mackachack, where Moluntha lived, on the afternoon of 6 October 1786. It was not the happiest choice of targets as far as the Americans were concerned. If any of the Shawnee divisions still worked for conciliation, it was the Mekoche, and Moluntha was one of the few chiefs trying to restrain the military ardor of the young warriors. The Kentuckians did not care. Most of the Indians had left their summer villages to hunt, and little resistance was offered. Some of the townspeople tried to raise an American flag in a futile attempt to halt the attack, but the whites shot down a few warriors and rounded up some prisoners, nearly all of them women and children.

One of the captives was old Moluntha, who surrendered calmly. He was interrogated under guard by Colonel Hugh McGary. McGary had bitter memories of a disastrous defeat suffered by the Kentuckians at the Blue Licks on the Licking River in August 1782. He asked if Moluntha had been there. In fact few Shawnees had been involved in the ambush, which was largely the work of Great Lakes Indians and British rangers, but McGary took the chief's answer to have been an affirmative. He took a tomahawk and struck the defenseless old man to the ground. As Moluntha struggled to rise, McGary turned the edge of the axe and sank the blade into the side of his head, and then he scalped him. Later, he would be suspended from duty in the militia for a year as punishment for his deed. The Shawnees dismissed it less lightly. Moluntha, like Cornstalk, had tried to reason with the Big Knives. Moluntha, like Cornstalk, had paid the ultimate price.

News of the attack swept through the nucleus of Indian towns that hugged the headwaters of the Mad River, and frantic calls for help sped out to the scattered hunting camps. The villages were evacuated, but there were not enough men to make a fight of it. When the whites moved into Wakatomica a handful of warriors could not resist waiting to exchange shots with them before slipping away, but that was all. Logan's army left after two or three days, shepherding about thirty women and children as prisoners. Behind them half a dozen villages lay looted and ruined: Mackachack, Wakatomica, a Pekowi and a Mingo town, and the villages of Blue Jacket and Alexander McKee. At McKee's Town, where Tecumseh lived, the Kentuckians noted the British agent's residence, with its brick chimney and orchard. In all, Logan's men destroyed about two hundred houses in the towns, fifteen thousand bushels of corn, and some livestock. Along with the prisoners, the Kentuckians brought away ten scalps, twenty horses, and considerable booty.

Outnumbered, and afraid to hurt their people who were being marched off into captivity, the Shawnees could do little to harass Logan's retreat. Some warriors fired on the American camps or hung on the flanks and rear of the American army as it withdrew toward the Ohio, sniping at it as opportunity arose. Still, the campaign cost Logan no more than three men killed or fatally wounded.[15]

Cheeseekau and Tecumseh may have been among the outraged warriors who converged upon their threatened towns to fight the Big Knives or worry their retreat. Tecumseh was then about eighteen, and this could have been his baptism of fire as a warrior. If it was, some Shawnees remembered it as a humiliating debut. Long afterward John Johnston, who served the Shawnees as agent, was told by chiefs who had known Tecumseh that his first action had been against the Kentuckians on the Mad River. The youth was filled with fear and fled, even though other warriors, including Cheeseekau, continued the contest, and Cheeseekau was wounded and carried from the field. Tecumseh's first biographer, Benjamin Drake, who corresponded with Johnston, added that the engagement occurred near the site of Dayton and that the Kentuckians were commanded by Benjamin Logan. If true, this pretty safely places the incident in 1786.[16]

Whether Johnston's informants spoke from hearsay or were themselves eyewitnesses we are not told, but if the episode occurred Tecumseh must

have felt thoroughly ashamed. However, Logan's expedition opened another
nine years of border warfare, and there would be many more opportunities
for Tecumseh to prove that he was, after all, the son of Pukeshinwau.

The winter snows came and went, the streams filled with the thaw, and
the flowers recarpeted the valley floors, but most of the Shawnee fighting
men stayed their hand. In the spring and summer the Indians were busy
starting afresh, as they had so often done before, moving their families to
places of greater safety. Retreating yet again, closer to potential allies and
the British supply line, and farther from marauding Big Knives.

Tecumseh went with most of his tribe to where the St. Marys and St.
Joseph met to form the head of the Maumee River, near present-day Fort
Wayne, Indiana. Two important Miami towns were already established
there. Chief Pacanne lived in Kekionga on the west bank of the St. Joseph,
while across the St. Joseph and tucked into the fork that river made with the
Maumee was Miamitown, under Le Gris. Some Shawnees built their houses
in one or another of these Miami villages, while others constructed their own
towns close by. Above Miamitown, on the St. Joseph, Blacksnake raised a
Shawnee town; below it, but on the Maumee, and close to a new Delaware
village under Buckongahelas, yet another Chillicothe was erected, the home
of an aged Shawnee chief named Blackbeard.[17]

This complex of Miami, Shawnee, and Delaware towns at the head of
the Maumee became the new focus of opposition to the "conquest" treaties,
and the remaining Shawnee communities tended to live within supporting
distance, either in what is now Indiana, or farther down the Maumee, at the
mouth of the Auglaize River.

The removal was only one reason for the unusual restraint exercised by
the Shawnees in the first half of 1787. Negotiations were afoot to release the
prisoners taken by Logan, and Joseph Brant was throwing his influence behind moderation. At an intertribal council fire at the Wyandot village of
Brownstown, at the mouth of the Detroit River, Brant resuscitated his confederacy at the end of 1786. The Indians unanimously pronounced the
treaties of Forts Stanwix, McIntosh, and Finney null and void, and called
upon the United States to renegotiate with the whole confederacy. Ultimately, Brant achieved a small measure of success. The United States
wanted the land, and had no intention of yielding it, but fighting another Indian war would be expensive. The government renounced the conquest
principle, and authorized the governor of the newly created Northwest Territory to purchase the disputed lands in a new treaty.[18]

But diplomacy was slow, and in 1787 and 1788 impatient Shawnees,
Mingoes, Delawares, Cherokees, and Wabash Indians launched fresh raids

against the Big Knives. In these excursions Cheeseekau achieved the standing of a minor war chief. Sometimes he made depredations on his own, accompanied only by Tecumseh, and the bond between them strengthened in the face of common dangers and through the laughter they shared around many lonely campfires.

Among the most tempting of targets for war parties were the flatboats that carried immigrants with their livestock and possessions down the Ohio to Kentucky. They had been coming in increasing numbers since the conquest treaties, large boxlike ungainly vessels, sometimes forty feet long and fourteen feet wide, with turned-up sides and a shelter. At Fort Harmar, which had been built at the mouth of the Muskingum in 1785, officers were astonished at the flood of boats down the Ohio. Between 10 October 1786 and 15 June 1788 no less than 631 vessels with 12,205 people aboard were counted passing the garrison.[19]

The flatboats were often difficult to steer, especially when swept forward in a strong current, and the Indians found it easy to intercept them in narrows and board them from canoes. Occasionally they even used white Indians, former captives, to lure boats to the shore, where they could be suddenly attacked. It was in an attack on flatboats that Tecumseh first proved himself as a warrior. The particular incident is not precisely identified by Stephen Ruddell, who was apparently present, but from the details he gives it was almost certainly the savage raid conducted in the spring of 1788.[20]

Tecumseh was one of about a hundred Shawnees, Cherokees, and Mingoes who made the attacks. Their leaders included Blacksnake (Peteasua), Nenessica, and Kakinathucca, and among five whites said to have accompanied the expedition appear to have been Stephen Ruddell, George Ash, and Frederick Fisher, all of whom had been captured as boys in Kentucky during the Revolution. The weather was improving and the trees were in leaf, but the nights were frosty. Waiting in ambush just above the mouth of the Great Miami, Tecumseh and his friends built fires close to the river to keep themselves warm. They chose a spot where boats descending the Ohio came around a point and had little time to adjust to sudden difficulties ahead. Somehow the Indians snapped up a flatboat, which they then hid beneath the foliage inshore.

On the morning of 21 March the Indians saw another boat rounding the point, and about forty Indians crowded into the flat and pushed out to board it. The five white men and a black woman aboard offered no resistance and were brought unharmed to the bank. Two of the men were earmarked for special treatment, and were bound at the foot of a tree and had locks of their hair removed, but eventually the captors returned them to their companions.

The same afternoon another boat was attacked. As the Indians clambered aboard they found a sixty-year-old Baltimore merchant named Samuel Purviance and his manservant; a thirty-four-year-old Englishman, Thomas Ridoubt, destined to become surveyor-general of Upper Canada; and two other men. None resisted, and after stripping from them hats, coats, and waistcoats the Indians sent them ashore to join the other prisoners. Ridoubt was presented by his captor as a gift to the Shawnee Nenessica, and Nenessica and other Indians shook hands with the prisoner and offered him a pipe.

The following day the Indians divided their considerable booty. Ridoubt's property alone amounted to a wardrobe of clothes, a watch, cloth, a cane, two flutes, prints, a writing desk, trunks, a portmanteau, and fifty books. The ownership and fates of the prisoners were also decided. The Cherokees ominously slung a black wampum belt around the neck of William Richardson Watson, who had been taken on the second boat, and placing a rattle in his hand ordered him to accompany a song they began to perform. Poor Watson, a man in his forties, had already lost seven hundred guineas, and now judged that his life was in danger. He tried to pass Ridoubt his gold watch. The mood of the Indians was indeed uncertain. A stocky, fearsome fellow painted black started marching prisoners away one by one at the point of his sword, driving them into the woods to their various fates.

But most of the captives were taken out at noon in weather appropriately dark and cold. They crossed a river where a fallen tree served as a bridge, and late in the afternoon they camped in a valley. During the evening the Shawnees got drunk on liquor and provisions pillaged from the boats, but the twelve Cherokees present remained sober to protect the prisoners, who were tied beside a fire that was kindled on a small eminence. Ridoubt remembered that during the night one of the revelers came shouting from the Shawnee camp, a few hundred yards away, but two of the Cherokees overpowered and bound him, and threw him into the fresh snow for the night.

On 23 March Kakinathucca, a middle-aged Shawnee chief, took the prisoners forward with a small party while most of the other warriors returned to the mouth of the Great Miami to resume their blockade of the Ohio. Two boats under the direction of Ballard Smith and a man named Hinds were intercepted on the twenty-sixth, but the whites made a stubborn defense and got by relatively unscathed. Two Indians were said to have been hit in the firing. The warriors were definitely in an ugly mood when the final boat appeared a few hours later.

It contained three French scientists and another man. Eight or ten Indians boarded the boat from their flat, and mercilessly fell upon the unresist-

ing whites. A Monsieur Ragaut, who stood at the stern and offered his hand
to help a warrior aboard, was immediately tomahawked, and one of the
other Frenchmen was shot dead. The remaining two men jumped over-
board. One was badly wounded, but the current helped the two escape. As
they did so the triumphant warriors rifled their prize, finding several rich
suits of clothes among the plunder.

The raid shocked white communities. "The sympathy of all ranks has
been excited in an extraordinary degree by this deeply affecting catastro-
phe," thundered *The Kentucky Gazette*. For Tecumseh, too, the incident was
significant. Ruddell recalled that it was "the first engagement in which he
[Tecumseh] particularly distinguished himself" and that he behaved "with
great bravery and even left in the background some of their oldest and
bravest warriors." Tecumseh's exertions obviously met with the approval of
his seniors, but that was not the only reason that the event stuck in Ruddell's
memory. He recalled how the young warrior made a stand for common humanity.

Many of the prisoners taken that March eventually got home. Some escaped, and some were adopted, ransomed, or sold. Others were not so lucky.
Apart from the two men murdered on the French boat, as many as five prisoners may have been put to death. Ridoubt heard that Watson, who was
claimed by the Cherokees, was burned. Purviance, who had been separated
from the other prisoners on 22 March, also died, although whether he was
battered to death, as Ridoubt was told, or burned at the towns of the Wea
Indians of the Wabash, as another report suggested, is unknown. Ridoubt
also understood that a man named Simmonds was burned, and that Purviance's servant, John Black, was beaten to death.[21]

Doubtless it was one of these wretches whose fate stirred young Tecumseh. He was a ferocious opponent, but did not approve of the murder of
helpless captives. As Ruddell remarked, Tecumseh "was always averse to
taking prisoners in his warfare, but when prisoners fell into his hands he
always treated them with as much humanity as if they had been in the
hands of civilized people. No burning—no torturing. He never tolerated the
practice of killing women and children."

It was after watching a prisoner from the flatboats being burned that
Tecumseh first made that plain, Ruddell reported. He had no power to interfere with the fate of a prisoner deemed to be the property of others, disposable at their will. But even then he was deeply upset by the torment of
the miserable captive. When it was done he "expressed great abhorrence of
the deed, and finally it was concluded among them not to burn any more
prisoners that should afterwards be taken, which was ever after strictly ad-
hered to by him."

Tecumseh's aversion to the use of torture was by no means unique among the Indians, and Ruddell undoubtedly exaggerated the effect of his protest, but the incident of the flatboats represented an important milestone in Tecumseh's development, both as a warrior and as a human being.

Shortly after the raid on the river, Cheeseekau made an important decision. Perhaps, like some fellow tribesmen, he was despairing of finding a secure home on the Ohio, or maybe it was just the wanderlust that had for so long been part of his people's character. Whatever his motive, he planned to assemble a party and emigrate to what was then Spanish territory across the Mississippi, away from the Big Knives. The idea had no doubt been stimulated by invitations from a singular character named Louis Lorimier.

The son of a French colonial officer, Lorimier was then forty years old, a slim, well-formed man, but otherwise unprepossessing in appearance. The impression created by his large aquiline nose and diminutive height of barely five feet was accentuated by an eccentricity of style. His hair sometimes fell behind in a long ribboned queue, and his dress was a mixture of Indian and fashionable European clothing. But Lorimier's speech was polished and courteous; he spoke French, English, and a number of Indian languages; and he was known to be honest, enterprising, and brave.

None doubted his standing among the Indians. He had traded with the Miamis, Shawnees, and Delawares; had fought alongside them in the Revolution, when his store had been sacked by Big Knives; and by 1788 he had a son and daughter by his wife, Pemanpich, a woman of Shawnee and French ancestry related to the Shawnee chief Blackbeard.

The spring of 1787 found Lorimier in financial difficulties, and he fled to Spanish territory to escape creditors. He soon established himself as an Indian trader in the vicinity of Ste. Genevieve (Missouri), but attracted the attention of the Spanish government by offering to colonize the area with Shawnees and Delawares if land could be made available. It was a suggestion that suited all parties. The Spaniards wanted to bolster their flimsy defenses against warlike Osages to the west and the potential threat from the United States to the east. As for the Indians, some of them welcomed a haven under Spanish protection.[22]

By the summer of 1787 Lorimier's invitations were crossing the Mississippi and tantalizing the war-weary Indians of the Ohio valley. They helped Cheeseekau and Tecumseh embark upon their next adventure.

5

THE RAIDERS
OF LOOKOUT MOUNTAIN

The first of Louis Lorimier's hopeful Indian colonists arrived in Missouri in 1788. Two hundred Shawnees and Delawares had left the Maumee as early as the summer of the previous year, bound for their new life beyond the reach of the United States. Others followed. In October 1788 Major John Francis Hamtramck, commander of the American post at Vincennes on the Wabash, remarked that "the greatest part of the Shawnee nation are gone to the Mississippi." He exaggerated, but many Pekowis, Kispokos, and Hathawekelas, as well as Delawares and a few Cherokees, did make the trip. Hamtramck was estimating that six hundred of them were on the Mississippi by the spring of 1788.[1]

Cheeseekau's party was ready in the autumn of 1788. Tecumseh was there, of course, and his younger brothers Lalawéthika and Kumskaukau. The two were only about fourteen years old, and Lalawéthika at least seemed destined only for obscurity. As a young man he was nicknamed Wahneshga, the Crazy Fellow. The group may also have included Methoataaskee, who is known to have ended her life at a venerable age among the southern Cherokees.[2]

After gathering their harvest, Cheeseekau's party left their homes near the Miami villages and moved to the Mississinewa River, where they spent a few months hunting and stocking up meat before heading down the Wabash to the Ohio. They crossed the Ohio and followed it downstream toward the Mississippi. Then, just below the mouth of the Tennessee and opposite the remains of the old French fort Massac on the north bank of the Ohio, a serious accident occurred.

The Indians spotted some buffaloes, and Tecumseh and other hunters were soon galloping in pursuit. Suddenly Tecumseh was thrown from his horse, and he fell heavily to the ground. The youth was in great pain, for one of his thighbones was shattered. Further progress was now out of the question. There was nothing for it but to find a sheltered place nearby to bivouac for the winter and give Tecumseh's leg time to heal.

The spring came, but there was little comfort for the stricken warrior. His bone was so badly fractured that it could not be set properly, and Tecumseh sank into a depression as bleak as the wintry weather. He had always wanted to be a warrior and a hunter, and he had been showing promise in both activities, but now, in his darker moments, he was haunted by the specter of life as a dependent cripple. According to an important source, his despair was such that he tried to kill himself.

Throughout his life Tecumseh drew upon deep reserves of courage and determination, and a stubborn refusal to be beaten. In the spring of 1789 Cheeseekau could wait no longer. He urged his brother to stay behind with a few warriors to hunt for him until he was fit enough to follow, but the youth would not listen. Painfully, with the aid of crutches, Tecumseh carried on with Cheeseekau to Missouri. In time his injury healed, but its mark was always there. Some said there was a distinct scar. Certainly he was left with a slight limp, on account of one leg's being bowed and shortened. Close friends impishly nicknamed him Pernete, which described one buttock as being higher than the other, but others occasionally referred to him as Broken Thigh.[3]

When Cheeseekau reached Missouri he found that the Spaniards, supervised by Lorimier, were indeed carving out land for the Indian arrivals. Evidently, they originally considered Bois Brule, below Ste. Genevieve, a home for the Shawnees, but finally they plumped for establishing two villages on Apple Creek (Perry County, Missouri), about eighteen miles above Cape Girardeau. However, Cheeseekau was no doubt disappointed to find that the Indians were not the only newcomers.[4]

There was George Morgan, whom older Shawnees remembered as a trader and United States Indian agent during the Revolutionary period. Morgan was now the central figure in an attempt by the Spanish to strengthen their colonies by bringing in American settlers. He was granted favorable terms, including cheap lands, for bringing colonists into Missouri. Accordingly, seventy pioneers recruited by Morgan descended the Ohio in four armed boats and reached the Mississippi in February 1789, shortly before the arrival of Cheeseekau. They began building New Madrid on the west bank of the Mississippi, a few miles below the mouth of the Ohio.

For the Shawnees and Delawares this invasion of American colonists awoke memories of everything they had wanted to avoid. Morgan knew that. He brought a few Shawnee, Delaware, and Iroquois friends with him to reassure Lorimier's Indian colonists, and in April held a council at New Madrid, promising the local Indians that he would preserve the peace and that his grant would not interfere with their rights. His men were cautioned not to agitate the Indians by excessive hunting. But despite all that, the potential for friction was there for all to see. As early as June 1789 some Americans passing through New Madrid fired upon Cherokee and Delaware hunters and stole their furs, and the enraged natives talked about sacking the town. Trouble was averted, but the dream that had drawn many of the Indians to Missouri, a dream of a life free of American interference, had already been tarnished.[5]

In fact, Morgan's colony did not prove the obstacle some Indians feared. Morgan himself soon left for the east; he got tired of his project and never returned, and New Madrid was slow to grow. Within a year the settlers had been battered by severe floods and many went home. On the other hand, the Shawnees of Apple Creek flourished in the following decade despite the proximity of white settlements at New Madrid and Cape Girardeau.

Cheeseekau did not wait to find out, however. Likely Morgan's presence had broken the spell for him, and sometime in 1789 or perhaps at the beginning of 1790 he took his following back across the Mississippi. Yet he did not turn northeast toward the Maumee and his old haunts back in Ohio. He went southeast, to the strongholds of the Chickamaugas, the fiercest Indian opponents of the United States to be found in the broad lands of the south.

Where the state lines of Tennessee, Georgia, and Alabama now meet there is a majestic, rugged, and wild landscape. The Tennessee River slices through the narrow gorges of the Cumberland Plateau, dividing around small islands, twisting one way and then another, and crashing and rebounding against the rock to create the dangerous waters the Indians knew as Untiguhi, the Boiling Pot. Overlooking the turbulent stream are broken, sometimes impenetrable heights dominated by Lookout Mountain, which rises seventeen hundred feet from the south bank near present-day Chattanooga.

Here Cheeseekau and Tecumseh came, seeking the secluded fastnesses of the most consistent defenders of the aboriginal south, the feared warriors of the Chickamauga Cherokees. The Chickamaugas had settled here over the previous decade, retreating down the Tennessee in their long guerrilla campaign against the Americans. They had tucked four towns into a hilly area enclosed by the swirling river in the north and west and the long narrow ridges of Lookout Mountain to the east and south. By the riverside were Running Water and Nickajack, with some two hundred houses apiece, located in what is now Marion County, Tennessee. Close by was the smaller Long Island Town (Bridgeport, Alabama), while perched upon a creek running along the foot of the mountain in present-day Georgia was Lookout Mountain Town. Farther distant still other settlements had developed, two downstream, and Willstown on a tributary of the Tennessee in Alabama.

From these mountain strongholds the Chickamaugas struck in all directions, running off horses and levying a steady but growing toll of the lives and property of hardy white pioneers resolutely spilling across Tennessee. Furnished by traders operating out of Spanish Pensacola or Mobile, and occasionally reinforced by Upper Creeks, the Chickamaugas passed along Indian trails northwest to raid settlers on the Cumberland, or traced the Tennessee upstream toward the northeast to attack targets on the Holston or French Broad. Their stranglehold on the river prevented the Tennessee Company, a group of land speculators, from colonizing the lower Tennessee.

Nowhere would embattled Shawnees find closer kindred spirits than among the Chickamaugas, who owed their identity partly to a formidable leader, Dragging Canoe. When Tecumseh first saw him, Dragging Canoe was in middle age, tall and powerful with a face scarred by smallpox. One of the Overhill Cherokees of the Little Tennessee, Dragging Canoe had defied the established chiefs more than a dozen years before, and led attacks upon whites squatting on Cherokee land on the Holston and the Watauga. Defeat in 1776 and three invasions of his towns since had not broken his spirit. Dragging Canoe's defining quality was obduracy. He refused to recognize treaties, and when pressed simply withdrew farther down the Tennessee with his followers, first to Chickamauga Creek, and then to the wilds of Lookout Mountain. And from each new location, his soldiers continued to fight.

Only recently the Chickamaugas had been joined by embittered warriors from the more peaceful Upper Cherokees. Up to now these Indians had clung to the principles of conciliation and negotiation, even though the United States had failed to control local expansionists and a Cherokee boundary established in 1785 had not been honored. Unfortunately, it was they, rather than the relatively inaccessible Chickamaugas, who generally suffered when angry frontiersmen led retaliatory raids. In 1788 the principal chief of the Upper Cherokees, Old Tassel, an advocate of peace, was barbarously murdered under a flag of truce by North Carolinian borderers.

The incident brought the Chickamaugas new recruits from among the outraged Upper Cherokees. Some, such as the red-haired Bench and the ambitious Doublehead, were ready and ruthless raiders. But John Watts, the mestizo nephew of Old Tassel, was cut from different cloth. In other circumstances he would have been disposed to peace. Watts, or Green Corn Top as the Indians named him, was about forty years old and had supported the efforts of his uncle to avoid bloodshed. Brave and enterprising, "the life and spirit of the junior part of the Cherokee nation," Watts was also friendly and levelheaded. Yet he threw in his lot with the war party. Three years after the savage killing of his uncle, he could not speak of it without tears.[6]

The Chickamaugas identified with the Shawnees as an oppressed people, and several of them even reinforced the Shawnee towns north of the Ohio. From 1781 records contain several references to small bands of Cherokees living among the Shawnees and encouraging their hostility to the Americans. "The Cherokees are always in their towns," remarked one witness, "and look upon the Shawanoes and themselves in the same light." Some of these northern Cherokees may have joined the migration to Missouri, but Cherokees were to be found with the Ohio Shawnees until the end of the war, in 1795.[7]

Similarly, Shawnees visiting the southern tribes always found a welcome in the Chickamauga villages. In fact, some Shawnees seem to have settled among the Chickamaugas as early as 1780, perhaps living in Dragging Canoe's own village of Running Water. From this perspective, Cheeseekau's journey to the Chickamaugas becomes understandable. He must have already made friendships with Cherokees in Ohio, and he knew that not only were there Shawnees already at Lookout Mountain, but also that in the towns of the Chickamaugas he was among friends.

Probably it was late in 1789 that Cheeseekau brought his people to Lookout Mountain. In 1790 a hundred Shawnee houses were at Amo-ga-yun-yi, or Running Water, twelve miles below the whirlpool, where the river flowed more leisurely to the southwest, but some Shawnees settled at Ani-kusati-yi, or Nickajack, the town of Chief Breath, located on level ground a few miles downstream, where bluffs featured the distinctive Nickajack Cave.[8]

It did not take Cheeseekau long to show the Chickamaugas his usefulness. Spring 1790 found him hunting with about forty warriors—Shawnees, Cherokees, and a few Creeks. Tecumseh was probably with them, but his name does not appear in any of the accounts. They had gone a hundred miles or so down the Tennessee, and set up a camp at the mouth of Bear Creek (the Ochappo River). On 15 March one of the Shawnee warriors, with three Creeks and a woman, was searching for food down the Tennessee when the party stumbled upon a detachment of American soldiers camped on an island. There was a brief parley. The American officer, Major John Doughty, told the Indians that he came in peace and wanted to trade, and he gave them corn and tobacco. On their part, the warriors feigned friendship. They explained they were camped above, and offered to hunt for the Americans. But both sides were suspicious, and the Indians scurried back to their comrades with the news.

Indian opinion was divided at their new camp on the Tennessee, a few miles above Bear Creek. The truth was that Doughty had been sent by the United States on a mission of peace to the southern Indians, and carried a message from President George Washington. He had descended the Ohio and was rowing up the Tennessee hoping to link with some Chickasaw guides who were supposed to be meeting him. At their camp the Shawnees and their allies knew nothing of this, but some were willing to give the Americans the benefit of the doubt. According to a French trader, Chatelier, who was with them, the Cherokee leader the Swan pointed out that Doughty seemed to have been friendly. However, the Swan was very sick at the time and failed to carry his points.

The reasons for doubting the Americans were strong. If they intended to trade, as they said, why did their party consist entirely of soldiers? It seemed more likely they were looking for somewhere to build a fort. This area still belonged to the Indians by treaty, but the Georgia state legislature cared little for that. In 1789 it sold its claim to thirty thousand acres on the lower Tennessee to speculators. Even the federal government would condemn the enterprise, but in 1790 the Tennessee Company planned to settle the area about Bear Creek. The rights of Cherokees, Creeks, and Chickasaws alike were threatened by the development, and it is possible that as early as March rumors about it were making the Indians sensitive to unusual activity on that part of the river. Now here was Doughty and his soldiers. After a long discussion, the three Creeks who had met Doughty persuaded their comrades to attack. The Indians chose Cheeseekau to lead the assault.

Cheeseekau might have planned to engage Doughty in conversation, to learn more about his business before committing himself to making an attack, as a later Indian account suggested. But on the Ohio his people were already at war, and it is doubtful if Cheeseekau had any qualms about attacking the Big Knives. He used deception. The Americans would be lured ashore with a white flag and invited to join a meal. When Cheeseekau dropped his spoon the warriors would pull tomahawks from under their blankets and finish the job.

This plan was entirely consistent with the common Indian tactics of surprise and ambush. Their aim was to minimize their own losses at the expense of those of the enemy. Indian communities were small, and every warrior was needed to hunt and support his family. Manpower was a valuable resource, not one to be squandered needlessly. Consequently, Indians were unwilling to fight in the face of heavy losses. Some Europeans felt differently. Inured to battlefields on which mass armies stoically stood before appalling volleys of artillery and musket fire, they regarded Indian tactics as

cowardly and treacherous. In reality, those tactics were geared to the survival of the community. As Cheeseekau led his forty warriors, evenly spread
between four large canoes, downstream on the morning of 22 March he had
no intention of incurring the slightest unnecessary risk.

About noon, six miles below Bear Creek, the Indians rounded a bend to
see Doughty's barge laboring upstream under oars. Aboard were Doughty
and sixteen regular soldiers. Raising a white flag, the Indians came alongside, exhibiting every appearance of friendship. They smiled, and reached
up to shake hands with the Americans. Cheeseekau declared his party to be
Shawnee and Cherokee, but Doughty noticed that the Creeks he had met
and distrusted some days before were in the canoes, and he remained on
guard.

With a few attendants Cheeseekau climbed aboard the barge. Doughty's
interpreter, Francis Vigo, had been sent forward to search for the missing
Chickasaw escort and had disappeared up Bear Creek, so it was with signs
and broken English that the Indians invited the whites to camp ashore for
the night. Munificently, Cheeseekau explained that the Indians would supply them with buffalo and turkey. Doughty was wary. He declined, saying
there was no suitable landing place, but he tried to explain his mission. He
intended to meet Vigo at Bear Creek that night, he said, and the Indians
were welcome to visit his camp there, either that evening or the next day. In
the meantime, he gave the warriors presents of tobacco and corn.

Cheeseekau's plan was now in disarray. He could neither interrogate the
Americans properly, nor maneuver them into a vulnerable position, but he
kept calm, and after an hour shook hands with Doughty and left. The Indians paddled to the shore. Then, as the Americans stood aside from their
weapons to man the oars and work the barge into the stream, the warriors
saw their opportunity. They raised their muskets and delivered a furious fire
upon the Big Knives.

The sudden fusillade slashed into Doughty's detachment, sending dead
and wounded to the floor of the boat. The Major thought of beaching his
vessel, but the riverbanks were fringed with thick willows, so he ordered the
boat to be put about. That way it could run downstream with the current,
allowing some of the men to exchange oars for muskets and return the fire.

Cheeseekau's whooping soldiers pushed out their canoes again, and
tried to intercept the barge as the river swept it past. But the Big Knives
were now replying with a ragged fire, and the Indians could not close in
time. Instead, there followed a grueling and grim chase of four hours.
Doughty's barge lurched with the stream, while the yelping warriors pursued, vigorously plying their paddles or firing and reloading while American
musket balls smacked into their canoes or zipped into the water about
them. At one point the Indians seem to have tried to overtake the retreating

vessel, in order to seize some islands at a narrows ahead from which they could intercept Doughty, but he stayed in front. Exhausted, Cheeseekau's warriors finally gave up the chase.

They had done enough, for Doughty's mission was finished. Only six of his men were unhurt, and of the remainder six were dead or fatally wounded and another three seriously wounded. His boat limped down the Tennessee, but was unable to work its way up the Ohio, and had to fall back to the Mississippi and get help from a new Spanish garrison at New Madrid. Cheeseekau's party were satisfied with their work. On their way upstream the warriors met the interpreter, Vigo, but offered him no violence. Rather, they boasted of having routed the Americans, and, as they thought, of killing their commander.[9]

Those early months with the Chickamaugas must have reminded Cheeseekau and Tecumseh of their forays on the Ohio, for there was much to do on the river, watching for boats coming and going. In April the Indians fired upon a descending vessel at Muscle Shoals, killing one man and wounding another, but failed to stop it. The Shawnees may have been involved, for they were specifically mentioned in connection with a more important fracas that took place on the river early in May. This time the victims were the land speculators trying to establish an illegal colony on the lower Tennessee.

They had loaded three big bateaux with what the literate Creek chief Alexander McGillivray called "desperadoes," and armed each vessel with swivel guns. Under a man named Hawkins the bateaux tried to force their way down the river to the Muscle Shoals region above Bear Creek, where the speculators planned to erect a fort and trade with the friendly Chickasaws. A determined attack was made upon the boats by Cherokees, Creeks, and Cheeseekau's Shawnees. The Indians didn't have canoes on this occasion, but simply chose a spot from which to pour a fierce fire upon the passing boats. Casualties were heavy in one boat, which got out of control and drifted ashore. The Indians boarded it, and according to McGillivray found thirty-two dead and wounded men aboard. However, the two consorts used the width of the river to get beyond effective musket range, and the principal vessel turned its swivel upon the captured boat and drove the Indians out. The success did not give the invaders any lasting advantage, though. It was not until the following year that the Tennessee Company was able to establish a settlement on the river, and then Indian opposition quickly caused it to be abandoned.[10]

Tecumseh remained with the Chickamaugas for almost two years, sharing their triumphs and tribulations, and imbibing a wider sense of the Indian plight. The Cherokees, no less than the Shawnees, were suffering a powerful and relentless dispossession. In the summer of 1791, for example,

Glass and other headmen brought word to the Chickamaugas of yet another tribal cession, made by the Upper Cherokees at the treaty of the Holston. William Blount, the new governor of the Territory South of the Ohio, secured large portions of northeastern Tennessee. Confronted with colluding settlers, speculators, and local and federal government officials, the Chickamaugas felt they had no other recourse than armed resistance. These events probably encouraged Tecumseh to believe that a pan-Indian resistance, based upon the solidarity of all men "of one color," was both viable and necessary.

Far away from the roar of gunfire, however, there were some softer moments for Tecumseh. It appears to have been at this time that Tecumseh took up with a Cherokee girl. The relationship may not have been his first. At the time the traditional Shawnee marriage, in which the family of the prospective groom made the initial approach to the family of the girl, was in decline. In the words of Lalawéthika, Tecumseh's brother, it was increasingly common for couples "to live together without being married . . . Every couple nowadays connect themselves and separate as suits their convenience or inclination." In either case unsuccessful marriages were easily dissolved among the Shawnees, and no stigma attached itself to a separation. Children normally remained with their mothers.[11]

Tecumseh's "marriages" were of the modern kind, but unlike many, if not most Shawnees, he never had more than one wife at a time. He had difficulty in developing lasting relationships with women, but Stephen Ruddell remembered that the Cherokee girl remained with him "the longest of any." They had a daughter, and she remained with her mother's people and was living in Arkansas in 1825. Later in the nineteenth century there were Cherokees claiming descent from Tecumseh through this daughter.[12]

During the summer of 1791 Tecumseh left Cheeseekau at Lookout Mountain and went home to Ohio. No one says why. It might have had something to do with a growing crisis in the north, where Joseph Brant's confederacy induced the United States to renegotiate the conquest treaties but then promptly fell to pieces. There were new treaties, at Fort Harmar in 1789, but once again the Indians completely failed to present a united front. Most boycotted the proceedings in frustration, but a few Lakes Indians and Iroquois did attend, and for a paltry nine thousand dollars they confirmed the previous cessions of southern and eastern Ohio.

At the head of the Maumee the Shawnees quickly denounced those actions. Taking up the mantle of Brant, they struggled to fit the fractured confederacy together again. At first their only significant allies were the local Miamis, Delawares, Mingoes, and Cherokees, but then they scored a military triumph. When the United States sent its first army against the Maumee towns in the autumn of 1790, to silence the hostiles, it was thoroughly thrashed. Indian morale soared. Soon the new confederacy was growing, but no one doubted the Americans would send another army to redeem their arms. A major battle was looming, and in April 1791 the Shawnees had sent messengers in all directions, calling in warriors to fight the Big Knives.[13]

Those calls may have reached the remote strongholds of the Chickamaugas and prompted the Shawnee brothers to make their decision. Cheeseekau would remain, while Tecumseh, whose standing as a warrior was now assured, would take a small party home. Eight followers went with him, including Lalawéthika and Kumskaukau. Whatever deficiencies Lalawéthika may have had as a warrior, Kumskaukau was turning into a jovial, good-natured young man, capable of entertaining many friends, and he had the makings of a good warrior. Tecumseh led the party on a long circuitous journey through Virginia. Eventually they crossed the Ohio near the mouth of the Scioto, and were traveling through the lush country Tecumseh had known as a boy, hunting along the way, and stirring the ghosts of the past.

While moving northwest toward the Auglaize in August, the band was overtaken by a wounded Indian. He had met an army of Big Knives on the march, and been fired on. Tecumseh sent a man ahead with a warning, and then joined the main body of the Indian confederacy where it had been concentrating at the "Glaize," a name given to the confluence of the Auglaize and Maumee Rivers.

One presumes that those who fired at the Indian were from the five-hundred-strong army of militiamen which had left Fort Washington, at the mouth of the Little Miami, on 1 August. Under Lieutenant-Colonel James Wilkinson it moved north, and then turned west hoping to find the villages of hostile Indians on the Wabash. The army struck the headwaters of the Mississinewa on the fifth, and that day and the next skirmished with small parties of Indians, scattering them eastward and northward. It was probably one of these who came across Tecumseh's trail. Wilkinson himself admitted that "the whole country" was "in alarm," but he pressed on to destroy two Indian towns on the Wabash. Neither of them belonged to the enemy confederacy.[14]

The nucleus of the new confederacy, the Shawnees, Delawares, and Miamis, were shifting their towns to the Glaize, and it was there that Tecumseh apparently spent the next months. There were old friendships to be renewed, and many stories to be told of his adventures in the south. Among these Indians Tecumseh now enjoyed a different status. He was a minor war chief, with a band of faithful adherents, and it was not long before they were following him into battle in defense of Ohio.

⊷ ⊨✦⊨ ⊶

Many years afterward, Shawnees remembered Tecumseh's early military escapades with undisguised admiration.

In his youth [they said] and before the treaty of Greenville [1795], he was of the boldest warrior[s] who infested the Ohio River—seizing boats, killing emigrants, loading the horses he took with the most valuable plunder from the boats and retiring to the Wabash where, careless of wealth himself, he soon lavished the treasures of his rapine upon his followers, which when exhausted he soon replenished by fresh depredations. Tecumseh is considered as the boldest warrior of the West.[15]

Shawnees were impressed by Tecumseh's bravery and skill, and from his success they deduced that his guardian spirits, or sacred power, was strong. Moreover, Tecumseh's practice of distributing booty to others rather than keeping it himself clearly showed he had the generosity and paternalism expected of a chief. On all counts he was a man to be followed, and his influence increased.

Nevertheless, Tecumseh was unfortunate in one respect. He missed the largest battle of the war, the greatest victory ever won by Indians over English-speaking opponents. On 4 November 1791, in a cold inclement dawn, one thousand warriors under Blue Jacket, Little Turtle, and Buckongahelas intercepted the United States Army under Arthur St. Clair, as it came to attack their towns. Although inferior in strength, the Indians overran the American camp on the Wabash and inflicted almost a thousand casualties, putting the survivors into a panic-stricken flight.

Some contemporary testimony gave Tecumseh a distinguished part in this battle, one he would have loved to have played, but our better authorities are clear that he was not there. Many Indians were absent, hunting and scouting for their fellows, and Tecumseh was among them. Ruddell said he was hunting. The Shanes maintained that Tecumseh had headed a small party of scouts, shadowing St. Clair's ungainly column of troops and camp followers, with its artillery, carts, and pack animals, as it pushed northward to the upper Wabash. One morning, while waiting on Nettle Creek, a tributary of the Great Miami, he heard the thunder of distant artillery, but was too far away to reach the battle.[16]

St. Clair's defeat electrified the frontier, and some grand ambitions flickered briefly into life. The Indian confederates believed for a moment that they really could drive the Big Knives back across the Ohio, and even British diplomats began to anticipate the United States yielding ground. Fleetingly, some toyed with the notion of creating an Indian buffer state in the northwest, separating the British and American possessions. But President George Washington's administration saw it differently. Despite criticism from political enemies opposed to strengthening the military on constitutional grounds and from easterners who regarded the war as expensive and unjust, the government did not flinch in its determination to hold the Northwest Territory. In the midst of planning a new military campaign, the furthest it would go was to consider yet again what additional sums might be given the Indians to reconcile them to their loss.

The spring after St. Clair's army was annihilated on the Wabash, Tecumseh and Stephen Ruddell went hunting with seven or eight followers and some of their women. They found a wooded rise surrounded by a low swampy prairie on the southeastern bank of the east fork of the Little Miami, several miles above present-day Williamsburg, and set up a camp with a marquee taken from St. Clair, a tent, and several bark shelters. It rained on 9 April 1792, and the Indians lingered in camp, jerking venison by a fire. Their horses grazed freely, and when some strayed one of the warriors rode off to search for them. The others were in good spirits. Even the failure of their companion to return did not warn them of an approaching menace. Some of the women were said to have come from the camp to halloo loudly into the woods for their missing friend, before returning to the tents laughing, as if amused at the idea of his getting lost. In the evening the Indians danced and sang to the beat of a drum, and there was more laughter. They had no sentries out, and sensed no danger.[17]

When the Indians retired for the night, Tecumseh stayed outside and lay down to sleep beside the remains of the fire. He was a light sleeper, easily awakened, but nothing told him of the soft approach of a party of Kentuckians. Some thirty strong, they stole silently from the surrounding forest and converged on the camp.[18]

The attackers were rangers, mustered two days before to pursue Indians who had stolen horses in Mason County, Kentucky. They were led by Simon Kenton, then about thirty-seven years of age and one of the most experienced and durable of all the backcountrymen. Earlier that day an advance party had been alerted to the approach of an Indian by the bell on his horse. They ambushed and killed him. This was the man from Tecumseh's camp. Following his trail, the rangers came upon the Indians, and then waited until dark to attack. The presence of women among the Indians should have told the Kentuckians that this was not a war party. They said they thought they had found their horse thieves, but perhaps they did not care. Anyway, about midnight they moved forward in different divisions, and when they got close enough they fired a volley of bullets into the Indian tents and shelters.

Kenton had not reconnoitered the camp in a good light, and did not know how many Indians were before him. He attacked in the belief that he had enough men to do the job, and that a surprise attack would panic his opponents. His blind fire, directed at tents rather than individual targets, did little harm, and Kenton reckoned without the inexperience of many of his men, some of whom were little more than boys, and without the special quality of Tecumseh's leadership.

Tecumseh was a stubborn fighter. He hated to accept defeat, no matter how formidable the odds against him, and he relished the challenge of combat. His steadiness and enthusiasm for the fray also infected others. "He was a man of great courage and conduct, perfectly fearless of danger," remembered Stephen Ruddell. "He always inspired his companions with confidence and valour." Anthony Shane also testified that the chief seldom refused battle, and was generally surrounded by followers prepared to stand or fall at his side. "Tecumseh," he said, was "proud, courageous and high spirited, [and] would never yield, but would any time fight double his numbers, and to decide these conflicts would not unfrequently resort to his bow and arrow or war club."

There was no way the Kentuckians could have known the unusual competitiveness of their quarry. Away from the tents, Tecumseh had been overlooked when the first shots were fired. By his side, as he slept, was his war club, a weapon he favored because, he used to say, it had been used by his forefathers. Now, as that first volley of rifle balls startled him from sleep, he snatched it up and rose to face the oncoming rangers, who rushed yelling toward the camp.

"Big Fish! Where are you?" he shouted for Ruddell.

Inside one of the tents Ruddell had been jerked into action by the bullets ripping about him, and then he heard Tecumseh calling. Seizing his musket he ran outside. "Here I am!" he shouted.

Tecumseh told him to make a charge against one group of the Big Knives, while he led an attack on the others. From beside his tent Ruddell threw up his musket and fired at a big man leading the Kentuckians on his side. But the wet weather had damaged his powder, and when the ball hit Simon Kenton it was already spent.

Tecumseh rushed boldly upon the rangers at his side. According to the accounts from the Indian side, Tecumseh struck down and killed Samuel Barr, although a few of Barr's companions later asserted that he died in an exchange of gunfire. All we know for certain is that Barr was slain, and that Tecumseh's followers credited him with the deed.

In the short confused fight that developed, the Indians tumbled out to support Tecumseh, and Kenton's attack faltered. The death of Barr and the unusual confidence of the Indians unnerved the whites, who were also gripped by a fear that Tecumseh was being reinforced by warriors from across the river. Probably the impression was created by the Indian women splashing into the water for safety. Convinced that they were facing a much larger force than they had anticipated, the Kentuckians made an undignified retreat. They separated from each other in the darkness and ran for home. Over the next few days they straggled wet, cold, and hungry into Limestone or Massie's Station.[19]

Tecumseh was relieved to find that only two of his people, a man and a woman, had been wounded. But some of the horses had been run off, and there were now serious worries about the warrior who had disappeared the previous day. As soon as it was light Tecumseh took four men and followed the trail made by the fleeing rangers. After a while they came upon a short, robust, middle-aged Irishman named Alexander McIntyre cooking his breakfast in the woods. The ranger instantly bolted, with the Indians streaming in pursuit. Unable to outpace the warriors, McIntyre stopped and raised his gun. According to Ruddell, the two leading pursuers started for cover, but Tecumseh rushed upon McIntyre before he could fire and overpowered him. The prisoner was tied and triumphantly brought back with his horse to the Indian camp.

The Shawnees were packing up, ready to withdraw, but Tecumseh and Stephen made a final search in the trees, hoping to round up more horses. When they returned they found a tragic sight. McIntyre had been murdered by the angry warriors, presumably because of the death of their comrade. Tecumseh "was very angry," Ruddell recalled, "telling them that it was a cowardly act to kill a man who was tied . . . in the strongest terms." The young Shawnee had undoubtedly advanced his reputation by his defeat of the rangers, but in his opinion the killing of a helpless captive had tainted the achievement.

Time allowed white veterans to immerse the skirmish in controversy, as they exonerated their defeat by an inferior force, or claimed credit for whatever they felt had been accomplished. They disagreed about who killed the Indian on the ninth, and about who located Tecumseh's camp. There were different views as to exactly where the fight took place. Some frankly admitted the rout, but others transformed the small band of Indian hunters into an army of one hundred warriors or more, and related how the rangers steadily withdrew before potentially overwhelming numbers.

Capping all was Charley Ward's story that as he crept upon the sleeping camp and drew a bead upon an Indian figure, he was astonished to see the "open bosom" of a fair young woman, and no less so to subsequently learn that she was his own niece. Fifteen-year-old Sa-taw-nee Ward was, he maintained, the daughter of his older brother John, who had lived with the Indians since his capture as a child of three in 1758.

Tecumseh was already stepping from life into legend.

6

❖

AN HONOR

TO DIE IN BATTLE

I f Tecumseh's reputation was growing, and his loyal following of ten or so warriors entitled him to be regarded as a minor war leader, it was not he but the oldest of Pukeshinwau's sons who first won a place in frontier history. Cheeseekau was acknowledged by the Shawnees and Cherokees to be a fine hunter and a great pugnacious fighter, and that year of 1792 his name was feared throughout the Tennessee backcountry. He was now calling himself Pepquannakek, but to the Chickamaugas and their white enemies he was Shawnee Warrior, a chief renowned even among Dragging Canoe's fiery people as a rank foe of the Big Knives.[1]

Shawnee Warrior's immediate following was small, a mere 150 Indians of whom about 30 were effective soldiers, few enough in a complex that could field 700 Cherokee warriors and attract substantial Creek reinforcements. However, Cheeseekau pulled well above his weight, and his opinions were respected by the most powerful of his allies.

Partly this was because he represented the tribe that, more than any other, was marshaling Indian resistance to the Americans, a tribe that in the afterglow of the victory over St. Clair even then had its recruiters among the Choctaws, Chickasaws, and Creeks. Even Dragging Canoe himself, the leader of the Chickamaugas, was inspired by the Shawnees. His brother, White Owl's Son, led a delegation of Chickamaugas north in 1791, and some fought St. Clair. When White Owl's Son returned to the south, he brought a Shawnee pipe inviting Indians to join the war. Dragging Canoe had gone personally to argue the cause to the Creeks and Chickasaws. Worn out by his labors, he came back to Lookout Mountain in the spring of 1792 and died there. But his independent spirit remained very much alive; his forces were unbroken and unbowed, and they admired no Indians more than the Shawnees. Cheeseekau undoubtedly benefited from that standing.[2]

Mainly, though, Cheeseekau enjoyed Chickamauga respect because he earned it, seeking out enemies wherever they could be found. About February 1792 some American boats passing Running Water, where Cheeseekau lived, were hailed by the Indians. Sensibly, they declined to reply and were fired upon. Cheeseekau's warriors may have been involved in this and other attacks. Early in April Creeks from Oconee joined the Shawnees in an assault upon another American party on the river. Two white men were killed, and two women and a boy captured. It seems that the Tennessee River traffic was receiving Cheeseekau's attention early that year.[3]

Cheeseekau was an angry man, as angry as the whirlpool that agitated the waters of the Tennessee above Running Water. He remembered keenly the death of his father and the many hardships of the years that followed, and his bitterness held in its service a bold adventurous spirit that had little tolerance of temporization. In May 1792 some Chickamaugas, including John Watts, who had succeeded Dragging Canoe as principal war chief, met Governor Blount at the mouth of the Little Tennessee. They accepted annuities paid on account of the treaty of Holston (1791), and manifested every peaceful intention. Watts was playing a delicate double game, disarming his opponents with talk of peace while preparing for war, but Cheeseekau distrusted such fraternization. And his Shawnees were not slow to show it. One of those who had accompanied Watts was Fool Charles, a chief of Running Water. When Fool Charles came home some of Cheeseekau's men "fell on him and much injured him."[4]

The respect which attended Cheeseekau among the Chickamaugas was perhaps best exemplified by an incident that took place in July 1792. Blount planned a meeting with the Chickasaws and Choctaws in Nashville, on the Cumberland, and shipped presents for those Indians down the Tennessee. The boats were met at Tuskegee by Chief Breath of Nickajack and Fool Charles, both of whom were among the more peaceful leaders in the towns of Lookout Mountain. They agreed to escort the vessels downstream, but were frightened that Shawnee Warrior might attack them when they reached Running Water. Breath declared that his men would defend the boats if the Shawnees attacked, but Fool Charles had a better idea. When the convoy reached Running Water, Fool Charles put some whiskey into a canoe and took it ashore as a present to the Shawnees. It diverted their attention from the river, and the convoy passed, but the fact that the ruse was perpetrated powerfully argues the influence of Cheeseekau's small but vocal band.[5]

Among Cheeseekau's favorite targets were the white settlements on the Cumberland River in northwestern Tennessee. Perhaps somewhere there was a dim memory that this beautiful stream had once been a home for the Shawnees, back in the previous century, when they called it the Skipakysepe, or Blue River. Since 1780 the Americans had been building farms and forts on both sides of the river in increasing numbers, and by 1792 over four thousand colonists could be found on the Cumberland. In a treaty of 1785 the Upper Cherokees had accepted the Cumberland settlements, but Dragging Canoe's faction always opposed them. The Chickamaugas did their utmost to dislodge the pioneers, directly and by severing their communications with eastern Tennessee and Virginia. Their war parties tried to close the Tennessee River and haunted the overland trails.

In June 1792 Cheeseekau once again led his Shawnees against the Cumberland settlements, accompanied by a party of Cherokees under Little Owl and a few Creeks. Fording the Tennessee at Running Water, they crossed the headwaters of the Elk and Duck Rivers, and eventually passed the Cumberland to reach a picketed cluster of houses known as Jacob Zeigler's Station, thirty miles northeast of Nashville. Probably it was an eager advance party that made the first attack on 26 June, recklessly killing a man working in the fields and a black girl they also found outside the station. When three men went out to bring in the bodies, Indians hiding behind a fence some fifty yards from the murdered man opened fire. The whites threw down their guns and ran. They were all wounded, but succeeded in getting back. Disgruntled, the Indians shot two horses they found outside, and then to all appearances left. Toward evening, when the Americans retrieved their dead, the Indians seemed to have gone.[6]

However, that night Cheeseekau and Little Owl directed a furious attack upon the station, where twenty-one people had gathered together in one blockhouse for safety. The Indians set the undefended buildings on fire, and watched the flames spread to the blockhouse. Finally, a man named Joseph Wilson threw open the door. He was immediately wounded in the chest, but he ushered out his wife and six children, who were seized by the Indians; he discharged his piece at the attackers, and then raced off between the blazing buildings. He escaped, but when four other men bolted for freedom, one got only a hundred yards before being overtaken and killed. The others made it. Jacob Zeigler himself died in his burning home, but his wife slipped away and hid with her youngest child, whom she gagged with a handkerchief. Her other three children, Mary, Elizabeth, and Hannah, fell into Indian hands. Three other women, two of them black, were also captured, but for some reason one of them was apparently killed on the retreat, a few miles from the station.

Cheeseekau and Little Owl recrossed the Cumberland on 27 June, and retreated up a creek to the vicinity of modern-day Lebanon. They had too much plunder, so they stored it in twenty-one bundles, each carefully protected from the elements by peeled bark and hung from the branches of trees. Then, while some Indians went to steal more horses so the goods could be shifted, the main party pressed on with their prisoners.

The children were barefoot, despite the difficult ground. When the Indians stopped a little farther on to rest and smoke beside a fire, they fashioned tiny moccasins for the children from dressed skins. Coming behind was a posse led by James Winchester. One of the pursuers later recalled that "at the next muddy spot, we saw the little footprints of moccasins. There was that much of kindness in them."

Night found the Indians camped with their prisoners in "an open forest." Later, when they reached the Duck River, they waited for their comrades, who were following with the plunder, to catch up. Unfortunately, these Indians reported that while the Americans had given up the chase they had discovered the bundles left in the trees and recovered them. According to Mrs. Wilson the news occasioned a quarrel between the two groups of Indians, and weapons were drawn.

Cheeseekau's capture of Zeigler's Station was the severest blow yet dealt the Cumberland settlements, "the boldest stroke ever made . . . in this quarter," as a commentator in Nashville put it. Most, if not all, of the prisoners eventually returned to their people, ransomed unharmed. The Creeks were awarded three prisoners, the Cherokees others, and Cheeseekau secured the three Zeigler children. He released the girls to intermediaries within a few weeks in return for payment of fifty-eight dollars each.

The raid greatly encouraged the Indians, and soon a greater assault upon the Cumberland settlements was under way.

In 1792 Spain controlled Florida, the Gulf coast, and the west bank of the Mississippi. Her officials shared with Canadians a fear of the territorial ambitions of the United States, and understood the importance of maintaining the Indians as a buffer between the American possessions and their own. This policy was actively pursued by a new governor of the Spanish provinces, Baron Francisco Luis Hector de Carondelet. Carondelet was encouraged by, among other things, Indian military successes in the north. He hoped to construct a league of southern tribes under the direction of Spain. In May a British trader, William Panton, invited John Watts to visit Pensacola and see the Spanish commandant there, Arturo O'Neill.[7]

The northern Indian confederacy, the appeals for Indian unity being circulated by the Shawnees north of the Ohio, and the new noises being made by the Spaniards all stimulated the militant elements among the Cherokees.

On 29 June members of the tribe addressed a letter to the Spaniards at Mobile. "Now is the time if ever you mean to assist us," it said. "Do it now . . ."[8]

Watts also made the trip to Pensacola, returning in August with seven packhorse loads of goods. He summoned the excited Indians to Willstown to hear what the Spaniards had told him, and to discuss the next move.

At the beginning of September 1792 hundreds of Indians assembled at Willstown. The festivities of the green corn ceremony were disposed of, and Watts opened his council in the town square. He had a message from the Spaniards at Pensacola to interpret. O'Neill promised to help the Cherokees as far as he could, but as Spain could not be seen to be inciting the Indians against another power, O'Neill cautioned the Indians to remain on the defensive. They should avoid acts of aggression. However, the fact that Watts had brought supplies from Pensacola, powder, lead, and ammunition, spoke more loudly than the letter. Watts related how he had seen warehouses of goods, all intended for the Indians. Despite his friendly posturing to Blount earlier that year, he urged the Chickamaugas to fight. "You now must show yourselves," he cried. "All of you young men who like war, go with me tomorrow!"[9]

Cheeseekau approved, but as Watts sat down it was Bloody Fellow, another of the Willstown chiefs, who took the speaking block. Bloody Fellow had visited Philadelphia the previous winter, and he had persuaded the United States to increase the annuities the Cherokees would receive under the treaty of Holston. He had returned embracing a medal, an American flag, a uniform coat, and a much improved opinion of the Big Knives. Now he drew attention to the presents he had brought back. "Look here at these things I fetched for myself. Likewise for you warriors . . . I did not go [to Philadelphia] by myself. Others went with me. If I had gone by myself, perhaps you might have thought that I had made it [them] myself. You had better take my talk, and stay at home, and mind your women and children."

Doublehead found this too much. He interrupted Bloody Fellow in the middle of his speech, and said he preferred the words of Watts. "I think a great deal of his talk," he declared, "for it is good. I shall try to do as he directed me." He spoke for the majority of the listening warriors.

Struggling to maintain his position, Bloody Fellow said that the Americans were too powerful, and to attack them was folly. He pointed to the American flag which he had proudly displayed. "Look at that flag!" he cried. "Don't you see the stars on it? They are not towns. They are nations. There are thirteen of them. These are people who are very strong, and are the same as one man!"

This time it was the tall, impressive figure of Watts himself who rose to intervene. With scant regard for Bloody Fellow, he stated that he would send a runner to the Creeks "to fetch my friends in," and ready himself for battle. The council adjourned with the war spirit undiminished. For the remainder of that day, and into the early hours of the morning, Cherokee warriors performed war dances in the square or the council house, their bodies painted black.

On the second day of the council, about 3 September, Bloody Fellow renewed his appeal for peace. He showed his new uniform and epaulets and his American medal. "See how well they have used me. I mean no war with them," he explained. Indicating the medal he went on, "This is silver, and surely must have cost a great deal of money." As for the clothes: "When was the day that ever you went to see your old brother [Britain] and that you brought home the like of this? I have brought a good deal of good rich clothes to many of you, as well as myself. I would wish none of you to go to war, but lay at peace, as I intend to do myself."

White Owl's Son, brother of the late Dragging Canoe, strode forward while Bloody Fellow was still on the speaking block. "My father was a man," he proclaimed, "and I am as good as he was. To war I will go, and spill blood in spite of what you can say."

John Watts was moved by his support. He stepped up and shook White Owl's Son by the hand. "You are a man," he said, "and I like your talk. To war we will go together!"

Bloody Fellow's cause melted, but he continued to protest. "You had better not go," he said, "for you know nothing about what you are going to do."

At this point Cheeseekau rose and advanced to Bloody Fellow, who remained standing. The Shawnee war chief stretched out his hands. "With these hands," he is reported to have said, "I have taken the lives of three hundred men, and now the time is come when they shall take the lives of three hundred more. Then I will be satisfied, and sit down in peace. I will now drink my fill of blood." The wording, rendered from memory a few days later by a mixed-blood, Richard Finnelson, must be inexact, but no doubt Cheeseekau made a fearsome declaration in support of Watts. Bloody Fellow sat down dejected, and Watts adjourned the council, requesting the Indians to reconvene at Lookout Mountain Town the following day, when the campaign would be planned. The Indians then returned to their dancing, and some fired guns into the American flag until Bloody Fellow intervened.

The final arrangements for the campaign occupied several days of discussions at Lookout Mountain Town, punctuated by a day needed to overcome the aftereffects of some whiskey introduced by an Indian named the White Man Killer. Eventually, an initial plan to assault the Holston settlements in four divisions was thrown out in favor of a strike against Nashville on the Cumberland. Richard Finnelson and Joseph De Raque, who had brought messages to the Chickamaugas from the Spaniards, were sent on to

Nashville to gather intelligence, and Glass and Bloody Fellow went to Knoxville to speak to Governor Blount and deceive him as to the intentions of the Indians. The two chiefs did their work well, although Bloody Fellow must have been uncomfortable implementing a plan he had passionately opposed. When Watts finally got his army under way, there were no militia in arms to oppose him.[10]

Tecumseh joined his brother for that last fateful raid on the Cumberland. A contemporary statement tells how Cheeseekau established a camp "at the Creek Crossing Place of the Tennessee, a small distance above the shoals, at the mouth of a creek on the south side, there to be joined . . . by a party of Shawanese, who are expected to arrive at that place by water, by way of the Ohio and Tennessee." Anticipating the campaign, Cheeseekau probably invited his brother to reinforce him, and Tecumseh responded. Judging by accounts of Tecumseh's activities in Ohio, his personal following amounted to about ten men, so he might have increased Cheeseekau's force to around forty. Not a strong reinforcement, but the Indians from Ohio were well supplied with blankets and other goods.[11]

The Creek Crossing Place, thirty miles below Nickajack, was part of a trail used by Creeks making forays north of the Tennessee. Here Cheeseekau assembled his band, before leading it to the general rendezvous, Black Fox's camp at the junction of several Indian paths near what is now Murfreesboro, southeast of Nashville. The Shawnees were a small part of perhaps four hundred men under John Watts. Most of them were Cherokees, whose leaders included John Taylor, Otter Lifter, and Middle Striker, but there was a substantial contingent of Creeks under Talotiskee.[12]

As the Indians marched in lines three abreast toward Nashville, an unusual tension troubled the Shawnee party. A few days before, Cheeseekau had spoken to his warriors and told them that he had had a sign. Perhaps it had been a disturbing dream, for Shawnees believed the spirits communicated with people through dreams. Whatever it was, Cheeseekau regarded it as a warning. He predicted that at such a time on such a day the Indians would arrive at a fort, and that they would attack it in the morning. If they persevered they would capture it, but at noon Cheeseekau himself would be shot in the center of the forehead. The Shawnees were shocked, and Tecumseh and other friends urged Cheeseekau to turn back. He refused. Cheeseekau valued the code of the warrior. It was, he said, "an honor to die in battle," as his father had done. As for himself, he did not want to die at home like an old woman. Better that the fowls of the air should pick his bones.[13]

On the morning of 30 September the Indian advance was making its way through thick timber, some of it felled by a storm, when it ran into two enemy scouts, sent from Nashville to reconnoiter toward Black Fox's camp.

It was said that the Indians used two young mixed-bloods, George Fields
and John Walker, to draw the American "spies" within firing range. Both
were killed.

Four miles south of Nashville stood John Buchanan's Station. It occupied rocky high ground on Mill Creek, a stream that babbled into the Cumberland through pastures in which the cows lowed. Buchanan's Station was
a simple fortification. It consisted of a few buildings surrounded by a picket
stockade, with a blockhouse dominating the front gate overlooking the
creek. John Buchanan, popularly known as Major Buchanan, commanded,
and that night of 30 September and 1 October he had a few families forted
up with his own. In all there were about fifteen armed men.

The Indians surrounded Buchanan's Station about midnight. There are
stories that Cheeseekau quarreled with Watts about the propriety of the attack, but the details are hazy. The original source for the story has been lost,
and its reliability is impossible to evaluate. It seems to have stated that
Watts wanted to delay the attack until daylight, when the men of the station
dispersed to their daily chores, while Cheeseekau favored a night attack.
Such was the Shawnee's influence that he got his way. However, in the
1840s, some twenty years after the story first appeared in print, locals were
remodeling it. Some said that the issue between the two Indian leaders was
whether Buchanan's Station should be attacked at all. Watts opposed the attack, pointing out that it would alert Nashville, the real target of the expedition, whereas Cheeseekau said the Indians could not continue their advance
leaving this garrison in their rear. By the mid-nineteenth century memories
of the event were vaguer still, and Cheeseekau was being confused with
other Indian leaders, or dropped from the tale altogether.[14]

Leaving their horses about a mile from the station, the Indians reached
it on foot. Above, the moon shone clear and full. For a while all went well,
and Cheeseekau stealthily led the attackers to within ten yards of the gate.
Then some cattle gave the game away. Frightened by the shadowy figures
stealing upon the garrison, they started running, from east and southeast of
the gate toward Nashville. From his position in the blockhouse at the gate a
man named John McRory peered into the gloom. He saw the Indians,
pushed his gun through a porthole, and fired. That first shot seems to have
hit Cheeseekau in the head, and he probably died instantly.

The Indians darted to the available cover, including the open cellar of an
unfinished cabin outside of the pickets, and turned a savage fire upon the
blockhouse and stockade, aiming at the portholes. In the station the defenders fought like devils, making a defense that deservedly entered the
folklore of Tennessee. The men returned the Indian fire with rifles and muskets—except for Jimmy O'Connor, who had to use a blunderbuss. The
women, among them the Major's wife, Sarah Buchanan, went around with

ammunition and brandy, and, it was claimed, molded additional bullets from plates and spoons.

For about an hour the contest continued. Despite their numbers, the Indians failed to silence the defending fire, and their own losses mounted. Watts went down after a bullet passed through both of his thighs, and White Owl's Son was also hit. A young mestizo Cherokee from Nickajack desperately tried to break the stalemate. The offspring of a French mother and Indian father, Chiachattalley was tall and strong, and a distinguished participant in village dances and ball games. Exploiting his athletic prowess, he now grabbed a burning brand and scaled the roof of the blockhouse. The defenders saw him, and shot him down. Chiachattalley fell close to the wall, crippled, but he still struggled to set fire to the bottom logs until further bullets killed him. His body was so close to the enemy fire that the Indians could not recover it.

Two Creeks and a Cherokee from Running Water were also killed or mortally wounded, and perhaps another three Indians less seriously hurt, before the attack was given up. Litters were used to carry away the casualties, but a large amount of debris was left behind, including swords, hatchets, kettles, and pipes. The raiders had seized corn and some of the animals, and shot other livestock in the fields, but they failed to hit a single defender inside the station. Their retreat was disciplined. The warriors fell into their three-column formation, but there could be no doubt that the invasion of the Cumberland had turned into a fiasco.

A personal tragedy for Tecumseh, too, who fought on in fury and grief at the loss of his brother. He brought away the body for a Shawnee burial. Cheeseekau had watched over Tecumseh ever since the younger brother could remember, and more than anyone else had been his teacher and guide. He epitomized the ideals to which young Tecumseh aspired, and had been a touchstone by which all actions and opinions could be measured, and by which Tecumseh could set his own goals and standards. To Tecumseh, much of what he himself had done was significant only inasmuch as it had won the approval of Cheeseekau. Now their partnership was over, and a vacuum opened in Tecumseh's life that no one ever managed to fill. The first of the brothers to achieve a wide reputation, Cheeseekau was noticed in American dispatches and newspapers merely as a formidable enemy, and so whites remembered him, even attributing to him attacks in which he had no part. His greatest legacy, however, was Tecumseh. Long after Cheeseekau's death, his combination of courage, enterprise and honor lived on in his younger brother.[15]

Shawnee custom now required Tecumseh to avenge Cheeseekau's death, and lay his spirit to rest. Stephen Ruddell, who was never in the south, wrote that Tecumseh told his friends that he would revenge his brother before he returned to Ohio. With eight or ten men he attacked a cabin, perhaps killing a man, and taking the women and children prisoners. In the wake of the defeat at Buchanan's Station, discrete parties of Indians did attack white settlers or their homes, but nothing that reasonably conforms to Ruddell's account appears in the records. Possibly the facts had become confused, or Stephen had misplaced an incident that occurred at another time. Tecumseh may have had to wait almost two months to repay the loss of his brother.[16]

25 November 1792. A clear and frosty morning on Cumberland Mountain in central Tennessee. About sixty Cherokees, Creeks, and Shawnees waited in ambush near the Walton trace which connected Knoxville to the Cumberland. Their principal leader was Middle Striker, but after the death of Cheeseekau Tecumseh was likely a leader of the small Shawnee contingent, looking for his revenge.

The Indians had killed a couple of express riders on the trace a day or two before, and then they had struck the fresh trail of a party of American militia at a place named Crab Orchard. The Americans were on their way to the Cumberland from Knoxville. During the previous night the warriors had passed the militia, and just before sunup they crouched waiting for them where a path crossed a creek.

When the first of Captain Samuel Handley's forty-two militiamen began to ford the run the hidden warriors enveloped them in a sudden fire, and then dashed out with tomahawks, knives, and war clubs. The captain tried to rally his panic-stricken force, but his horse went down, trapping one of his legs beneath it. The Indians took him prisoner. Eight of his men appear to have been killed, while the rest fled back toward Knoxville.

Middle Striker's war party withdrew along the Sequatchee River Valley to the Tennessee, and Handley ultimately found himself at Willstown. During his captivity he was much abused, forced to run the gauntlet, and prepared for burning, perhaps more than once. He lost his hair through a fever, and when it regrew it was snow white. Eventually he was escorted to the Upper Cherokee towns and released at the beginning of 1793.

Several stories were told about his ordeal, variously crediting John Watts, Arthur Coody, and Middle Striker with helping to spare the captain's life. Probably several Indians stood up for him, and one may have been Tecumseh. Handley's son and a pioneer named Alexander McCoblom both insisted that at Willstown it was a Shawnee chief who had been in the battle who interceded for the prisoner's life. The first informant also implied that the chief was not resident in the south, but "was on a visit to his Cherokee mother." These circumstances more or less fit Tecumseh. He was due to return to Ohio soon, and his mother, Methoataaskee, seems to have taken up a home among the Cherokees. Without more precise evidence, this is mere speculation, but it would be pleasing to believe that even at that time, wounded by the loss of his brother, Tecumseh upheld his reputation for humanity.[17]

Tecumseh did not remain with the Chickamaugas. He had come to help Cheeseekau, and that job was finished. Although he had relatives in the south, his mother and probably also a daughter, he went home. Whether any of Cheeseekau's following chose to go with him is not known. Some Shawnees certainly remained at Lookout Mountain, and in March 1793 were believed to have killed an American mail rider. By then Tecumseh was back in Ohio.[18]

It was probably on his way home, or soon after his return, that Tecumseh fought another lively skirmish with the Big Knives. Both Stephen Ruddell and Anthony Shane describe the incident, although they disagree about where it took place. Confessing his uncertainty, Ruddell associated it with Tecumseh's southern trip, and placed the engagement "on the edge of a cane brake, perhaps on the waters of the Tennessee." This suggests that if the fracas did not occur in the south, it happened soon afterward, and was told to Ruddell by Tecumseh as part of his southern adventures. Shane is much more precise, and he dated the incident about December 1792, or about the time Tecumseh returned north. Shane put the skirmish at Big Rock, between Loramie's Creek and the site of present-day Piqua, Ohio.[19]

Tecumseh had established a hunting camp with ten men and a boy, and they were cooking one morning when a greatly superior force of whites attacked them. Their leader was said to have been Robert McClellan. McClellan had just come to Ohio, and turned to ranging after serving the army as a packer. Energetic, fiery, and brave, he was a slender but muscular adventurer who would later travel up the Missouri and reach the Pacific. Now, however, he repeated Simon Kenton's mistake of the previous spring.

The Shawnees were outnumbered, but Tecumseh stood his ground. He shouted to the Indian boy to run, and raised a war whoop to call the rest of his men to arms. None of his warriors, in fact, was much older than the boy. Shane said that every one of them, excepting only Black Turkey and Tecumseh himself, was eighteen years or less. Unfortunately, Black Turkey set a poor example. As Tecumseh turned, he saw the warrior showing a clean pair of heels. Black Turkey had got about two hundred yards before Tecumseh's shout brought him back to his duty, and he then bravely supported his companions.

The short fight started badly for the Indians, as two of them, one of them Black Turkey, were disabled in the early firing. But they steadied, and when Tecumseh led a charge the whites broke before them, retreating so quickly that they left some of their baggage behind. Tecumseh was said to have been responsible for one of the two opponents slain in the skirmish, and McClellan's casualties might have been higher had not Tecumseh broken the trigger of his gun and called off the pursuit.

The assault on the Cumberland had misfired, with tragic consequences for Tecumseh, but his reputation was further advanced by these new adventures. Listening to his stories, the Shawnees in Ohio realized that Cheeseekau had left a not unworthy successor.

7

WARRIOR OF
THE CONFEDERACY

When Tecumseh returned to Ohio at the end of 1792 the movement for Indian unity was still at high tide. The victories over American armies, particularly St. Clair's, made armed resistance to the United States seem credible. As long as the Indians kept together, and as long as the British continued to supply the Shawnees and their allies, shipping goods from Detroit to the Maumee, and then upriver by pirogue to a depot of McKee's at the foot of the Maumee rapids, the Americans could be defeated. So the Shawnees believed, particularly the younger warriors such as Tecumseh. The Big Knives would be forced to dismantle a string of military forts they were erecting north of the Ohio. They would have to annul the 1789 treaties of Fort Harmar, by which the United States claimed most of Ohio. And they would have to restore the old boundary along the Ohio, established by the British in 1768.

The Shawnees and their most ardent confederates, such as Buckongahelas's Delawares, the Mingoes, and the Ohio Cherokees, were determined to regain control of the north bank of the Ohio. But many Indians saw this as an issue that went beyond land. The Creator had given the Indians distinct identities and ways of life, but if the tribes lost their lands, their independence and the mixed hunting, gathering, and horticultural economy would become unsustainable. The Indians would be vulnerable to missionaries and government officials, who would turn warriors and hunters into farmers. Complained Red Pole, one of the most respected Shawnee civil chiefs, the President of the United States would put "hoes in their hands to plant corn for him and his people, and make them labor like their beasts, their oxen and their packhorses." At risk with the land was the very essence and mode of existence that had been given the Indians by the Great Spirit.[1]

These were inspirational times for Tecumseh, for never had the Shawnees seemed closer to achieving their ambition of creating an Indian confederacy. In 1792 and 1793 their chiefs led delegations to the Mississippi, and as far south as Alabama, carrying a pipe which they invited the Indian nations to smoke as a symbol of their support. In October 1792 the Shawnees hosted a great congress at their headquarters at the Glaize. Here, where the Auglaize flowed into the Maumee, gathered representatives from across a vast region: Shawnees, Delawares, Mingoes, Munsees, Cherokees, Miamis, Conoys and Nanticokes from the heartland of the confederacy about the Glaize; Wyandots, Ottawas, Ojibwas, and Potawatomis from the shores of the Great Lakes; Weas of the Wabash, and Sacs and Foxes whose homes were on the banks of the muddy Mississippi; Mahicans and Iroquois from New York; chiefs from the Seven Nations of Canada, on the St. Lawrence River; and Creeks and Cherokees from the south. The redcoats had once orchestrated a larger Indian confederacy than this, during the Revolutionary War, but never had Indians themselves organized a greater union to defend their territory. At the Glaize this mighty concourse promised the Shawnees that they would help them fight for the Ohio.

The Wyandots were respected as the "elder brothers" of the tribes, and they were the custodians of the great wampum belt, the symbol of the union, at their villages on the Sandusky and Detroit Rivers. But the Shawnees were the acknowledged organizers of the confederacy, as well as its opinion leaders.

The Indian villages at the Glaize were the headquarters of the confederacy. A community of French and British traders, bound to the Indians by economic and social ties, also lived at the Glaize. They included the Scot George Ironside, the French-Canadian Jacques Lasselle, and the Pennsylvanian James Girty, all of whom had, or would form, kinship links with the Shawnees. There, too, were the towns of the leading chiefs of the confederacy. On the Auglaize lived Kekewepelethy, Great Hawk, the principal civil chief of the Shawnees, and the great Delaware war captain Buckongahelas, the Giver of Presents. The Miami war leader Little Turtle had his village on the Maumee, above the Glaize, while below the Glaize were the towns of his Shawnee counterparts, Blue Jacket and Blacksnake.

Blue Jacket had a distinguished record of combat which went back to the battle of Point Pleasant. His position as the premier Shawnee war chief, and his personal sway with both key chiefs and Canadian traders, had helped give him a reputation as "the greatest warrior among all the tribes." But downriver, on the lower Maumee, there lived a figure no less significant:

Egushawa, a heavily built Ottawa war chief, the most influential leader among those tribes known as the Three Fires, the Ottawas, Ojibwas, and Potawatomis. Since the American Revolution Egushawa had been an astute broker between different Indian peoples and the servants of the British crown, and his support for the confederacy was essential for the cooperation of the Three Fires.[2]

This great confederacy, rather than vague traditions of the Indian rebellion of 1763 or the Shawnee diplomacy of his father's time, was the model for Tecumseh's own confederacy in the early years of the next century. This—pioneered by Brant and his associates in 1783, and revitalized six years later by the Shawnees—was the union he would recall to life before the War of 1812.

Back in 1793 the weaknesses of the confederacy may not have been so obvious to the twenty-five-year-old Tecumseh. In fact, the confederacy was far weaker than a mere list of the many participating tribes and groups suggests. For one thing, most of those participants put their own local interests above the welfare of the confederacy as a whole. They were not all interested in the Shawnee war for the Ohio boundary, whatever their representatives might say in intertribal conferences at the Glaize and elsewhere. The Senecas of New York, the largest tribe of the Iroquois Confederacy, for example, were too close to the white frontier, too open to retaliation, to relish any war, while for other tribes, such as those on the Mississippi, the Ohio issue was simply too remote to arouse much more than token enthusiasm. On the other hand, there were other allies, such as the Chickamaugas and Joseph Brant's Iroquois community on the Grand River (Ontario), whose sympathies were far more engaged, but who just lived too far away to be of practical help to the Shawnees.

Ultimately, the confederacy depended primarily upon the two thousand warriors in the Maumee villages, and in those of supporting Wyandots and Three Fires in what is now Ohio, Michigan, and Indiana. But even here the Indians did not always speak with one voice. The Three Fires, like Joseph Brant, were apt to criticize the Glaize chiefs for their intemperance and reluctance to compromise.

As for the British, they were truly a rope of sand. Alexander McKee and Matthew Elliott, who administered Britain's affairs with the western Indians, were both married to Shawnees, and felt deeply for the Shawnees' situation. Probably they gave their Indian friends the impression that the redcoats might eventually furnish more direct military aid. But Britain was far too cagey. Important as the tribes were to Canada's economy and security, the British had no intention of getting into a war with the United States on their account. They continued to supply the Indians from Detroit and other western posts, and looked for an opportunity to broker a peace be-

tween them and the Americans—a peace that would protect British influence—but that was all.

The tragedy for the Indians was that in 1793 armed resistance to the
United States was already too late. However Herculean the efforts of native
pan-Indianists might be, however vast their courage and perseverance, the
historical circumstances were against them. They might win victories, even
great ones, as Blue Jacket, Little Turtle, and Buckongahelas had done. But
in the end the new republic was too powerful, and the oncoming tide of
American settlement would engulf them.

At the beginning of 1793 both sides suspended military operations to
talk peace, but the prospects were bleak. Inflated by their victories, the
Shawnees and their allies wanted nothing less than the Ohio boundary of
1768. President Washington's government was no less unyielding. The
United States hoped to persuade the Indians to accept the Fort Harmar
treaties, ceding southern and eastern Ohio. If necessary, it would pay more
for that land, and the Indians were assured that in the future the Americans
would take no territory the tribes did not wish to sell. Only Brant made a serious attempt to bridge the gap, by suggesting a compromise boundary. He
proposed the Indians give up those lands north of the Ohio that were east of
the Muskingum River. But neither side was listening.

So deep-rooted was the hostility between the Shawnees and the Kentuckians that even the temporary truce brought no halt to the blows they
fiercely exchanged. At the beginning of April 1793 a group of Indians
crossed the Ohio and made a bloody raid on Morgan's Station at Slate
Creek. Two people were killed on the spot, and shortly afterward the Indians
slaughtered nineteen of their twenty prisoners for fear of being overtaken
by pursuers. Posses of incensed Big Knives were soon scouring the woods
for the culprits, who were believed to have retreated up the Scioto.

Tecumseh knew nothing of the raid. He was out with a party of seven or
so hunters, one of them the white Shawnee John Ward, who was several
years Tecumseh's senior, and a few women and children. They were passing
down the north bank of Paint Creek, a branch of the Scioto, and about 4
April camped on the riverside. The weather had been poor, with heavy rain
and strong winds, and the Indians got three fires going. Just before daylight
on 5 April some of the Indians stirred, and began rekindling the fires. Suddenly a camp dog began to bark, and a gun was fired.

It was a party of thirty-three rangers, led by Tecumseh's old adversary,
Simon Kenton, and Joshua Baker and James Ward. (By a sad irony, James
Ward was the younger brother of John Ward.) They were after the Indians
who had raided Morgan's Station, and had planned to head them off by
crossing the Ohio at Limestone and striking across Paint Creek to reach the
upper Scioto.

On 4 April Kenton's men had forded Paint Creek about two miles east of modern-day Bainbridge (Ross County, Ohio), and stumbling on Tecumseh's fresh trail north of the river, they had surmised that this was a new war party on its way to Kentucky. Following the tracks downstream for about a mile, they had come upon the Shawnee encampment.

The rangers had Tecumseh in a very difficult position. In front of him ran the stream, across which rose a steep hill. As it was late, Kenton decided to wait until daylight, and then to surround the Indians, trapping them against the river. Leaving their horses in the rear, the Kentuckians formed three equal divisions. Baker's group was sent off early, to circle around the camp and cut it off downstream. Kenton would attack from upriver, while Ward's division spread out to the left to form the link between the other two. After hearing that Baker's men were in position, Ward and Kenton advanced upon the sleeping encampment. They passed the Indian horses on their approach. At this point Tecumseh's situation seemed hopeless. His party was heavily outnumbered, separated from the horses, encircled, and unaware.

Then a gun was fired! Ward and Kenton's divisions, still stealing into position for an attack that was not due to begin until dawn, heard it, followed by a sudden burst of firing from downstream. They realized that Baker's men had started the fight prematurely, before they could be supported. As Ward's men plunged forward with a ferocious yell, they had a second surprise. They ran right into Baker's division. Despite the message Baker had sent back, to the effect that he was ready, his division was not even in its allocated place. There were some heated words. Ward accused Baker of trying to capture the glory for himself, while the other excused his precipitancy by explaining that his men had been misled by seeing the Indian fires being rekindled.

That confusion was what saved Tecumseh. His noncombatants fled downstream, away from the attack and through the gap Baker was supposed to have plugged, while the men made a stand. The Indians fell back to some trees, and clambered into the branches, from which they opened a steady fire upon the whites and treated them to a loud and constant whooping. It was still dark, and neither side knew the exact strength or position of the other. The rangers had the advantage, but they were not confident enough to charge forward against an unknown foe.

The firing had done some damage. The Indians killed one of Baker's men, Joseph Jones, and wounded some others, but they lost John Ward, who lay fatally wounded, unaware that his brother was among the attackers.

Conscious of the dangers that daylight would bring, Tecumseh displayed his usual presence of mind. Using the remaining darkness and their stealth in the forest, the Shawnees performed an adroit and decisive maneuver. While their comrades maintained the fight, some warriors dropped quietly from the trees and crept around the rangers. They recovered the Indian horses and brought them back to the rear.

As the light improved, and the militia prepared to complete their encirclement, Tecumseh and his men abandoned their position, jumped on their horses, and rode off downriver, taking the dying John Ward with them. The young war chief had lost his baggage, including valuable powder, ball, and blankets, but he had extricated his force under extremely adverse circumstances.[3]

Inactivity, Stephen Ruddell said, didn't suit Tecumseh. After returning from Paint Creek, he went hunting again. Indeed, he was generally out hunting, and reading Ruddell's narrative it is easy to conclude that Tecumseh did little else. Not much was said about the successful raider that Shawnees remembered.

Ruddell's reticence on such matters is understandable. He himself had participated in forays against the whites, probably often as one of Tecumseh's warriors. For example, in the spring and early summer of 1794 a group of Shawnees, which may have included Tecumseh, loitered on the Ohio. The Indians hunted about the mouth of the Kentucky River and raided white settlements on the Licking River, making off with fifty horses. Two of the Shawnees were captured in June, and denied that any prisoners had been taken. However, they admitted, a man was killed "by a white interpreter belonging to the party, whose name is Riddle [Ruddell]." Had Stephen later owned his involvement in such raids he would have put himself in danger of retaliation; even when speaking of Tecumseh, rather than himself, he chose to remain silent.[4]

Although we know that Tecumseh made several raids, only one conducted at this time can credibly be associated with him, but neither Ruddell nor Shane mentioned it, nor does any contemporary document refer to Tecumseh in connection with it. Nevertheless, it is worth examining, if only to illustrate the difficulties of those who would rescue Tecumseh from the twilight world between myth and history which he has so often inhabited.

On 6 May 1793, a month after the skirmish on Paint Creek, several Shawnees appeared in the Clarksburg area of western Virginia. Quietly bypassing the most exposed settlements, they reached the farm of John Waggoner, on Jesse's Run, which flowed into Hacker's Creek. Waggoner was plowing in his field when the Indians arrived. He was fired upon but was unhurt, and he ran toward his house. When he saw it surrounded by Indians, he dashed off to raise the alarm. The Indians killed and scalped Mrs. Waggoner and her three oldest children. The other children, Elizabeth, aged twelve to fourteen; Mary, who was ten; and little three-year-old Peter, were carried into captivity. Despite their lack of horses, the Indians also took away some plunder, including pewter, and made an effective retreat, throwing the pursuers off their trail.

John Waggoner never lost hope of finding his children. In 1795, at the end of the war, when the Indians agreed to surrender prisoners, he asked the American army to try to secure their release. Accordingly, Betsey and Mary were recovered, in September and October, and both returned to Virginia. The boy was not found, however—at least until nearly twenty years later. A white Indian, about the age Peter would have been, was then identified as the missing boy, partly on account of his similarity to John Waggoner. With difficulty, "Peter" was persuaded to leave his Indian family and live in Virginia, where he was accepted as Waggoner's lost son. He married a local woman in 1814, but was too much of an Indian to adjust very well to his new life. Until the end of his days he spoke in the Indian manner, and he was restless, withdrawn, and uncommunicative, giving the impression that in spirit he was still with the Shawnees. He died on Millstone Run, off Hacker's Creek, on 26 February 1879.[5]

It was not until 1831, when Alexander S. Withers published an account of the raid in his *Chronicles of Border Warfare*, that Tecumseh was publicly connected with the tragedy. Withers named Tecumseh as the leader of the war party. He claimed that while Tecumseh's warriors attacked the house, it was Tecumseh himself who fired at Waggoner, resting his gun on a fence and putting a ball through the pioneer's shirtsleeve as the latter sat on a log after the day's toil. Although Withers got some of his details wrong, including the date of the attack, he became the source of subsequent accounts. But Tecumseh's biographers never liked Withers's account, because it associated their hero with the murder of members of the Waggoner family. And in legend Tecumseh was always noble, and always in complete control of his companions-in-arms.

Yet Withers was an earnest chronicler, if not always an accurate one, and a serious biographer of Tecumseh must ask where he got his information about the chief. Withers said nothing about his sources, but there is evidence that he drew his material almost exclusively from the memories of settlers in the Hacker's Creek region. In fact, the author may have himself lived in nearby Clarksburg, where his book was first published. Certainly he made heavy use of a manuscript completed before 1830 by two local men, William Powers and William Hacker. This is important, because there is a possibility that Tecumseh was identified as the leader of the war party by the Waggoner children, who came home after leaving the Indians. Neither they nor anyone else seems to have questioned the book when it was published in 1831. The fact that Withers's account had its origins in the community in

which the Waggoner family lived enhances its credibility, but of course in itself falls short of verifying it completely.[6]

It is true, as Tecumseh's admirers have said, that the behavior of the Indians at Hacker's Creek fits ill with what we know about the chief's character. This is a flaw in the identification, but not necessarily a fatal one. The
assumption that people consistently live up to their best principles is, we all
know, a naive one. Mood, time, and circumstance force compromise upon
all of us, and no one is infallible, or immune to the feelings of remorse and
guilt. To argue that Tecumseh always acted honorably and humanely is to
turn him into a superhuman who never existed. Then, too, to defend Tecumseh on these grounds assumes that he had total control of his free-spirited
followers. Readers who have followed this book so far will know that Indians didn't operate that way. No, Tecumseh was generally humane, and his
personality gave him an uncommon authority, but he was also a human being engaged in a savage border war. Those who would whitewash Tecumseh
according to the twentieth-century American values must face the possibility that the Hacker's Creek raid was retaliation for the attack on Tecumseh's
people on Paint Creek and the killing of John Ward.

That said, the evidence is far too weak to prove that Tecumseh was
there. Only Withers says so, and when he published his book Tecumseh was
a legend, a man so famous that many who had never seen him eagerly
claimed some association with him. It is interesting to note that after Withers indicted Tecumseh for the Waggoner massacre, other locals were inspired to charge him also with an attack upon some drovers in the area,
made on 4 October 1791. In this case the attribution, first published in 1839,
can be totally refuted. But it is in such ways that legends grow.

Withers must be evaluated in this context. A comparison of the contemporary documents and his account raises suspicions that Withers, or his informants, embellished their story. The casualties suffered in the raid were
raised from four to five; the three murdered offspring were described as
younger, rather than older, than those taken away; and Withers had one of
the girls finally escaping from the Indians, whereas both were surrendered
by the Shawnees after the peace. Conceivably, the use of Tecumseh's name
was a similar improvement on the facts.

The Hacker's Creek raid occurred, and Shawnees were responsible. But
was Tecumseh there, or was the use of his name simply another tribute to
his mythical stature? The question remains one of many about the Shawnee
chief that will likely never be answered.

Peace negotiations between the Indian confederacy and the United
States collapsed that August, and another trial of strength was inevitable.

Early the next year, Tecumseh and his fellow Shawnees were encouraged by a more positive note sounded by the British.

France and Britain had gone to war in 1793, and the new governor of Canada, Sir Guy Carleton, Lord Dorchester, was convinced that the United States would become an ally of the French within a year. To protect Canada, the Indian alliance had to be strengthened. A new post, Fort Miami, garrisoned by a detachment of regulars, was established on the north bank of the Maumee, below McKee's depot near the rapids, and an island in the mouth of the river was fortified. The creation of this forward base downriver was a fillip to the Indians at the Glaize. Now, if they were driven from their homes, they could fall back to the British garrison.

No less exciting was the talk of John Graves Simcoe, the bluff lieutenant-governor of Upper Canada. He visited the rapids in April 1794 and repeated to the Indians a speech of Dorchester's, predicting that Britain would soon be at war with the Americans. The King, it said, would reassert his rights south of the Great Lakes and the treaties of Fort Harmar would be scrapped. This was inflammatory, and did not meet with the approval of the government in London, but it convinced the Indians that at last their Great Father was on his feet and about to throw his full weight behind their confederacy.

But first a new American army had to be faced, and this time it was the legion of Major-General Anthony Wayne, a larger, more disciplined and drilled force than any other the confederacy had yet encountered. By the summer of 1794 Wayne's line of forts stretched ninety miles from Fort Washington (Cincinnati), and its head, Fort Recovery (Mercer County, Ohio), was only sixty miles from the Glaize. His main force had got as far as Fort Greenville (Darke County, Ohio). The Indians hoped to stop this advance by cutting the road behind Greenville and intercepting the flow of packhorses, wagons, and cattle upon which the American army depended.

On 19 and 20 June 1794 Blue Jacket led the main Indian army from the Glaize, and picking up additional recruits on the way, marched it south-southwest toward the head of Wayne's line. This was the biggest force Tecumseh had ever accompanied, about twelve hundred strong. The Indians moved forward in a dozen or so files, while ahead and on the flanks were parties of scouts and hunters. The armed host needed two hundred deer and as many turkeys to feed on each day it marched.

Waashaa Monetoo was not smiling, however. About half of Blue Jacket's army consisted of members of the Three Fires, and they wanted to attack the weak but advanced post of Fort Recovery rather than cut Wayne's communications south of Fort Greenville. It was a thoroughly bad decision, because even a success at Fort Recovery would have had little strategical value, but the chiefs felt obliged to humor so many important allies.

First light of 30 June therefore found Tecumseh and the other Indians secreted in the woods outside Fort Recovery. A convoy of pack animals, which had gone into the fort the previous evening, was turned out to graze. When the animals trotted into the forest to forage, the Indians sprang on them, seizing more than two hundred, and killing or driving away the drovers. Then Major William McMahon, who commanded the convoy's 140-strong military escort, gallantly led his men to the rescue, but as they entered the trees they were cut to pieces and driven back to the fort in disorder.

So far the warriors had won a victory. But, excited by the sight of those terrified soldiers speeding back for shelter, the Ojibwas and Ottawas made a full attack upon the fort itself. Captain Alexander Gibson commanded few more than one hundred defenders, apart from the remains of McMahon's force, but without artillery the Indians had little chance of rooting him out. The impetuosity of the attack was punished by well-directed small-arms fire and blasts of ball and canister shot, and the Indians withdrew to a safer distance. For the rest of the day and the following morning the Indian army as a whole was reduced to wasting ammunition taking potshots at loopholes.

The campaign disintegrated. After suffering most of the seventeen Indian fatalities sustained in the battle—only a few less than the Americans—the Three Fires complained that their allies had not supported them properly, and decamped for home. Even the arrival of reinforcements under Buckongahelas did not give the remaining warriors the strength to achieve their original objectives, and the expedition broke up. It was supposed to have starved Wayne's legion of supplies. It merely created divisions that the Indians could ill afford in the approaching crisis.[7]

The initiative passed to Major-General Wayne, and at the beginning of August an American deserter brought news that the legion, Wayne's self-contained army of cavalry, infantry, and artillery, had started toward the Glaize. Once again Tecumseh and the other Shawnees abandoned their homes and belongings. Once again they had to leave their ripening crops to the enemy. Unable to organize a defense in time, the Indians evacuated all the towns around the Glaize and tumbled down the Maumee. They passed the reassuring palisades of Fort Miami, and established their families on Swan Creek, which cut the northwestern bank of the Maumee above its mouth, the site of present-day Toledo. Here, at least, the British could protect and supply the women, children, and old people, while the fighting men returned upriver to make their stand against the oncoming legion.

Maybe 1,500 warriors were mustered for the battle. There were the men from the Glaize, and Wyandots, Ottawas, Ojibwas, and Potawatomis, and a small and unofficial British contribution, consisting of a few French-Canadian sympathizers and 52 Canadian volunteers under the experienced partisan of the Revolution, William Caldwell. But they were far too few, and Little Turtle doubted that they should fight at all.

Wayne left Greenville with 3,500 men, including 1,500 mounted Kentucky volunteers. They put a camp (Defiance) at the Glaize, among the empty towns of their opponents, and began a descent of the Maumee on 15 August.

The Indians occupied a defensive position four miles above the British fort. Their left, where the Shawnees stationed themselves, rested on the northwestern bank of the river, where tall meadow grass was interspersed with thin timber. Their line formed an angle with the stream, extending three-quarters of a mile upriver, its right hidden in a dense wood. Some of the trees had been uprooted by a recent tornado, and gave the spot its name: Fallen Timbers. Thus disposed, the Indians could simultaneously engage the front and left of the legion on its march downstream, but they did not have enough warriors to man their line sufficiently.

Even worse, when Wayne moved in for the kill on the morning of 20 August many of the Indians were not in their places. Some had been late leaving their camps below, and others were calling at Fort Miami for provisions. Probably only five hundred men actually defended the Fallen Timbers, outnumbered by the Americans six to one. Tecumseh was with them, at the head of a party that included Stephen Ruddell. He waited in the tall wet grass at the left of the line, where the battle would begin.

Toward them rode the enemy advance guard, some Kentuckians under Major William Price. At the right time, Tecumseh's men, and the other warriors holding that part of the line, rose from the grass, presented their muskets, and fired. Then they ducked down to reload and fire again. Six of Price's men were killed. The rest turned tail, and pursued by whooping warriors ran headlong into the legion coming up behind, momentarily throwing two companies into disorder and forcing them to fall back a short distance.

Wayne had trained his men well, however. The army composed itself, and the Indians lacked the manpower to maintain their charge. They were also vulnerable to counterattack, and soon the legionary dragoons were galloping forward, their sabers flashing. Their leader, Captain Robert Campbell, and at least four of his men were slain or fatally wounded, but they thundered into the Indians and began to outflank them on the riverside. Behind them the legionary infantry were also advancing, engaging the Indians along the whole battlefront, and flushing the painted warriors from cover with their bayonets.

The battle was lost, but some of the defenders fought on with great tenacity. On the right Caldwell's Canadians and the Wyandots made a disciplined retreat, using firing lines. On the left Tecumseh fought with all the

stubborn courage that had helped him defeat Kenton and McClellan. His
followers were soon scattered, but he tried to hold his position with two of
his brothers. In his excitement, Tecumseh loaded a bullet in his musket before putting in the powder, and found it was useless. The three then fell back
until they came upon another line of Indians. Tecumseh told them to hold
their ground, and if any of them would give him a gun he would show them
how. A warrior handed him a weapon, but it was only a small-bore fowling
piece. Nevertheless, he used it for a while until the Indians were in danger
of being outflanked, and continued their retreat.

Wayne's men were closer now, but Tecumseh at last stumbled across
some of his own followers, and he posted them in a thicket in another effort
to contain the attack. They returned the fire of the advancing soldiers, but
eventually they, too, had to flee and rejoin the main body of the Indian army.
It was then in full retreat downriver.[8]

On that retreat an incident occurred that embittered Tecumseh and
other Indians for two decades. Streaming down the Maumee before the victorious Big Knives, the fleeing tribesmen reached the gates of Fort Miami,
the British fort. They clamored for sanctuary. Inside Major William Campbell had a tiny garrison of redcoats. It was his duty, he knew, to defend his
post if it was attacked. But dare he provoke such an attack by admitting the
defeated Indians? Was he, isolated upon the Maumee, prepared to risk
plunging his nation into war for the sake of their Indian allies? Despite the
importance of retaining the goodwill of the tribes, Campbell made his decision. He kept the gates of the fort closed. According to Blue Jacket, the principal war chief in the battle, Campbell looked over the stockade at the
painted and stripped warriors packing outside his walls and called out, "I
cannot let you in! You are painted too much, my children!"[9]

Rebuffed, the Indians ran below, to their base at Swan Creek. Wayne did
not chase them. Following an acrimonious exchange of notes with Campbell, he withdrew up the Maumee, back to Camp Defiance.

The battle of Fallen Timbers was not, in itself, an irredeemable defeat for
the Indian confederacy. The tribes had probably lost less than forty men
killed, for whom they had slain forty-four of the Americans and wounded
eighty-nine. Driven from their homes, the Glaize Indians would also be dependent upon British charity as the winter closed in on them, yet such experiences were far from new, at least to the Shawnees. What really galled the
Indians was the memory of those gates at Fort Miami, shut fast against
them at the time of their need. For all the fine words offered in the name of
their British Father the King were now proven to be worthless. The redcoats
had failed them. The Indians were alone. As Blue Jacket recalled many years
later: "It was then that we saw the British dealt treacherously with us."

The Indians Major-General Wayne had pried from the Glaize spent a squalid winter at Swan Creek. A thousand Shawnees, almost certainly including Tecumseh, were with them, subsisting on rations of pork, salt beef, flour, peas, butter, rice, and maize which the British brought into the Maumee. They were dispirited. No bold words, not even those brought to them that fall by Simcoe and Brant, nor the blockhouse which the redcoats threw up for their protection at Swan Creek, could dispel the demoralizing sense of betrayal and defeat.

Gradually, piece by piece, the confederacy crumbled. Before the end of the year the Wyandots of the Sandusky River had sent their messengers to the headquarters of the legion at Greenville. A far more serious defection followed in January 1795, when Blue Jacket himself stood at the head of a peace party. Despairing of British support, the Shawnee war chief took many key members of the confederacy with him into the American camp, including Delawares, Miamis, Ottawas, and Detroit River Wyandots, but he split his own people. Work as he would, he never brought more than a fifth of the Ohio Shawnees to the final peace negotiations at Greenville. Some of the other Shawnees decided to join Lorimier's colony across the Mississippi rather than make terms with the Big Knives, while still more, among them the head civil chief Kekewepelethy, remained for the time being at Swan Creek, dreaming that the British might still fulfill expectations and the confederacy would rise again.

Blue Jacket's first visit to Wayne in February established a fragile armistice pending the major treaty negotiations scheduled for the following summer. The one consolation for Tecumseh was that he felt safe enough to return to old haunts, hunting as usual. In the spring his following established a camp in western Ohio, although whether it was on Buck Creek (Clark County) or Deer Creek (Madison County) is uncertain. There they enjoyed a period of tranquillity.

Everyone acknowledged Tecumseh to be a fine hunter, and he won many friends by bringing home game and sharing it with the needy members of his community. Soon after his group made their new camp, a few of the younger warriors, including Lalawéthika, wagered that they could kill as many deer as he in a three-day period. The competition, the Shanes inform us, took place, but Tecumseh easily won the match. He had more than thirty deerskins to show, whereas none of his rivals produced more than twelve.

One who claimed knowledge of Tecumseh at this time was Jonathan Alder, a white Mingo who made a home on Deer Creek about the fall of 1795. He lived until 1848, and recalled Tecumseh's sense of humor:

I was well acquainted with him. I sold him a keg of rum one day for a horse. The horse got sick and died, and shortly afterward I told him he ought to give me another horse. He said he had drunk the rum up, and it was all gone, and he supposed I was about as well off as he was. He said the rum was of no use to either of us, and that he had suffered all the bad consequences of drinking it. He reasoned that the horse had done [me] as much good as the rum had done him, and perhaps more, but as it was, if I was satisfied, we would quit square, and so we did.[10]

Tecumseh did not interrupt his hunting to attend the peace treaty with Wayne at Fort Greenville in June to August 1795.[11] The treaty of Greenville was signed on 3 August. Among the leaders who put their names to it were Blue Jacket, Red Pole, and Black Hoof (Catecahassa) of the Shawnees, and former leaders of the confederacy such as Tarhe the Crane, Egushawa, Little Turtle, and Buckongahelas. The boundary established by the treaty ran from the Cuyahoga and Tuscarawas Rivers in northeastern Ohio west-southwest to Fort Recovery, close to what is now the Indiana state line, and then dropped to the Ohio River. It finally confirmed the offending treaties of Fort Harmar, and in fact slightly enlarged the amount of land the United States acquired. The Indians had lost the southern, central, and eastern sections of what is now Ohio, about two-thirds of the state, and in addition they ceded a few strategic areas on the Indian side of the line, including the sites of Forts Wayne and Defiance, both formerly centers for the Indian confederacy.

The Indians were permitted to hunt over the ceded area, but their title to it had gone. For this Wayne dispensed twenty thousand dollars in treaty goods, and perpetual annuities: one thousand dollars each to the Shawnees, Delawares, Miamis, Wyandots, Ottawas, Potawatomis, and Ojibwas, and five hundred dollars to each of several tribes of the Wabash and Illinois Rivers. Some of these peoples had made only marginal use of the ceded territory, and the treaty was particularly severe upon the Shawnees and Delawares, who had yielded not only hunting lands but also some sites of their villages.

For fifty years the Shawnees had fought and suffered to defend this ground—from the French, the British, and the United States. Many had died in that struggle, including Tecumseh's father, and both of his older brothers, Cheeseekau and Sauawaseekau. Now it was over, and Tecumseh must have been glad that Pukeshinwau and Cheeseekau were not alive to see the result of their sacrifices. Sometime in the fall, Blue Jacket visited the camp of Tecumseh, and explained the treaty. The younger man listened, but he had no intention of going to the American fort, as some others were doing, to approve of what had been done.[12]

Although he had made himself a minor chieftain, Tecumseh could not undo the work of Blue Jacket and others. But somewhere in his mind he stored a memory of the great confederacy for which he had fought. And when the specter of American land-hunger again threatened the Indian peoples, he would work for its resurrection.

8

CHIEF

By the time the treaty of Greenville was signed, Tecumseh had become a war and civil chief of his people. Shawnee war chiefs always earned their places by merit. Civil chiefs, who supervised the village councils in peacetime, sometimes inherited the position, especially among the Mekoches, but both offices could be held by the same person. Such a man was Tecumseh. In 1795 enough families were attracted to his leadership to enable him to quit the complex at Swan Creek and form a separate village.

Tecumseh's village on Buck Creek or Deer Creek may even have been the principal Kispoko village left in Ohio. His band consisted of about 45 or 50 warriors, with a total population of up to 250. These were largely Kispokos, and included some who had been with Cheeseekau in the south. A few months before Tecumseh created his independent village, 114 Kispokos— 49 men, 34 women, and 31 children—were being rationed by the British at Swan Creek. Tecumseh probably took many, if not most, of these with him, along with a few families of other Shawnee divisions.[1]

Some of his followers were relatives, such as Lalawéthika and Kumskaukau, his brothers, and probably also his sister, Tecumapease, with her husband, Wahsikegaboe. Tecumapease was the principal female chief in the band.[2] Others simply threw in their lot with a young man who embodied the qualities Shawnees most admired.

Indeed, Tecumseh was the very exemplar of Shawnee manhood. His

skill at hunting was legendary, and he had proved himself to be a great warrior, willing to defend his noncombatants to the death, courageous almost
to a fault, and intelligent and cool under fire. The Shawnees later told John
Johnston that he particularly excelled in planning large-scale engagements.
Tecumseh, like many Shawnees, believed that manhood was virtually defined by success in combat. It was the role of the man to protect his women
and children from the uncertainties of life in the forest, and to bring home
game for food, clothing, and barter. Tecumseh disapproved of effeminacy of
manner or dress because in his view it detracted from the true function of
the Shawnee man.

These qualities were those of a successful provider and war chief, but
Tecumseh also displayed something rarer—the judgment, articulateness,
integrity, and commitment to the community admired in the successful
chief and counselor.

He was spoken of as "very sensible" and serious-minded, equipped with
what Johnston described as large, liberal, and comprehensive views, and his
quick mind and retentive memory made him a powerful advocate in council. The Shanes said he "never seemed at a loss for an appropriate answer to
all questions and enquiries," while Johnston acknowledged that he spoke
confidently and fluently and was "a great public speaker." Stephen Ruddell
made the same point. Tecumseh, he said, "was naturally eloquent, very fluent, graceful in his gesticulation, but not in the habit of using many gestures. There was no violence, no vehemence in his mode of delivering his
speeches. He always made a great impression on his audience." If there was
one quality useful to politicians that Tecumseh lacked, it was duplicity. He
was noted for his frankness, and put a high premium on truth—something
that did not always work to his advantage.[3]

A virtue much revered by Shawnees was generosity. Hospitality and the
willingness to share food and other resources with the less fortunate were
part of every Indian community's ability to survive. Tecumseh was uninter-
ested in personal wealth, and freely gave what he had to those for whom he
felt compassion and a sense of responsibility. Ruddell thought the chief
"free-hearted and generous to excess, always ready to relieve the wants of
others. When he returned from a hunting expedition he would harangue his
companions and made use of all his eloquence to instil into their minds
honorable and humane sentiments."

According to the Shanes, Tecumseh's friends had only to remark upon
the fineness of one of his guns or tomahawks and the chief "would instantly
tender it as a present and compel them to receive it." He dispensed the returns of war and hunting, binding families to him through a sense of both
friendship and obligation:

Te[cumseh] was remarkable for hospitality and generosity. His house was always supplied with the best provisions, and all persons were welcome and received with attention. He was particularly attentive to the aged and infirm, attending personally to the comfort of their houses when winter approached, presenting them with skins for moccasins and clothing, and upon his return from a hunting party the old people of his neighbourhood uniformly were presented with the choicest game which his great skill as a hunter had brought into his possession. This course of conduct was not confined to the rich, or those of influence and reputation, but was extended to all classes, and he made it his particular business to search out objects of charity and extend the hand of relief.

This, then, was a man able to provide leadership, succor, and understanding, a man at once inspiring to younger warriors and safe and reassuring to the more vulnerable members of the community. Although Tecumseh's brother Lalawéthika would soon transform the religious life of the band, the village never looked upon anyone but Tecumseh as its official chief.

Like all people, Tecumseh had his faults. Arrogance, impulsiveness, and a haughty pride and capacity for ruthlessness were all part of his makeup, but it was his virtues that were remembered, even by enemies. Johnston's informants were Shawnees who were Tecumseh's political opponents, but they unanimously praised the character of the Shawnee chief.

One of the main reasons for Tecumseh's ability to attract followers was his charisma. He was friendly and inviting, and the handsome contours of his face, which some considered stern, readily expressed an infectious sense of humor. Stephen Ruddell thought him "a very jovial companion, fond of cracking his jokes." He also remembered something else, far more important, but difficult to define: a rare and mysterious quality that endeared Tecumseh to those about him. "There was a certain something in his countenance and manner," Ruddell said, "that always commanded respect, and at the same time made those about him love him." Though elusive, the quality was tangible and considerable in its effects. As the Governor of Indiana Territory, who would one day become the chief's great adversary, would testify: "The implicit obedience and respect which the followers of Tecumseh pay to him is really astonishing."[4]

For some time Tecumseh seemed uncertain where to locate his band. In 1796, after the winter hunting, he moved it to the Great Miami, where he raised a crop near the site of present-day Piqua. But he abandoned this place, too, in the autumn, and the following year was planting on the headwaters of the Whitewater River in what is now Indiana.

During these years the Ohio Shawnees were divided, politically and geographically. Blue Jacket and Red Pole led a peace faction, which they
wanted to establish near Fort Wayne, but an anti-American group under
Kekewepelethy had remained at Swan Creek, within the British orbit. The
position of Kekewepelethy's band deteriorated after Britain finally surrendered its western posts, including Detroit and Fort Miami, to the United
States in 1796, to comply with Jay's Treaty of two years before. Shawnees
from both factions then formed a new town called Wapakoneta (Man with
the Club Foot), on the upper Auglaize River (Auglaize County, Ohio). It was
a little north of the Greenville treaty line and not far from where the treaty
annuities were distributed at Fort Defiance, and it quickly became the new
focus for Shawnee politics.

Tecumseh seems to have wanted nothing to do with these disputes, nor
did he wish to jeopardize his independent status by moving to Wapakoneta
and bidding for a place on the tribal council. By the time that town was
being established in 1796 and 1797 he was moving westward toward the
Whitewater. Years later jealous chiefs interpreted this act to his disadvantage. Although Tecumseh's band accounted for more than a quarter of the
Shawnees left in the north, the chiefs said that because he had never sat on
the tribal council he had never been a chief.

When Tecumseh achieved village chieftainship he was in his late twenties and at his physical peak. He was a prepossessing man, but dressed
plainly, if neatly. His hair, like that of other Shawnees, was thick and black.
Occasionally he allowed it to grow long, so that it lay on his shoulders, but
at other times he shaved his head, leaving a scalp lock running along the
crown in the ancient tradition of the warrior. At such times he left his hair
growing at the back so that it trailed down behind as far as his rump.

Shawnee men made regular and liberal use of body decoration. Tecumseh never resorted to tattoos, but he kept a pouch of paint. Often he did no
more with it than run a red line around his hair, but important occasions
spurred him to greater artistry. Then he painted his whole face dark red, and
used a finger to wipe clear streaks through it, one from the top of his forehead to the end of his nose, and others from the nostrils to each ear. A black
line was added, beginning at the bridge of the nose and encircling the left
eye. It is possible that these designs had symbolic importance, perhaps relating to some guardian spirit upon whom he relied for protection and assistance, but our informants, the Shanes, make no reference to it.

In Tecumseh's day traditional Shawnee styles of dress remained largely
intact, but European trade materials had replaced many of the native products from which clothing had originally been fashioned. British cloth was in

general use, and for decoration trade beads and ribbons were taking the place of porcupine quillwork. There was nothing exceptional about Tecumseh's mode of dress, apart from its quality, neatness, and cleanliness. He rarely made the ostentatious display so beloved by many Indians. A pendant sometimes hung from his nose, over the upper lip, and his ears had been pierced for ornaments, but he did not split the earlobe to insert objects, as Shawnee men of his father's generation had been accustomed to do.

In hot weather Tecumseh stripped to his leather moccasins and a cloth breechcloth that was secured at the waist by a belt. More often he added close-fitting thigh-length leggings, fastened below the knee and also to the belt, and made of scarlet or blue strouding; above, an imported linen or cotton shirt might be confined at the waist. On cold days Tecumseh also wore a woolen mantle or blanket. The headgear most favored by Shawnees was the turban: a cloth wound around the head, often enhanced by a feather or two. Sidearms normally completed Tecumseh's attire. Stephen Ruddell believed that the chief's favorite weapon was the war club, but the Shanes said that he carried a silver-mounted tomahawk-pipe and an otter-skin pouch.

Gifted in so many ways, and armed with the confidence and personality to display his talents, Tecumseh was destined for prominence. Women were powerfully attracted to him, and Tecumseh's friends were not slow to point out to him the importance of having a wife, not simply as a companion, partner, and mother of children, but also for the many important duties women undertook in sustaining the life and comfort of the village. Despite this, Tecumseh's experiments in matrimony were unsuccessful. Short-lived "marriages" were common among the Shawnees—in 1773 a missionary observed that "on the smallest offence they part"—and so it was with Tecumseh.[5]

About 1796 Tecumseh took Mamate as a wife after a brief courtship. An exceptionally attractive woman of mixed Shawnee and white parentage, she seems to have been about the same age as he. Tecumseh was unlikely to have been her first partner, but experience did not help the relationship. The Shanes admitted that Tecumseh's fastidiousness, the high standards of neatness that he set in the appearance of person and home, did not make him an easy man to live with, but they had heard that the final argument had been about the trivial matter of a paint pouch. Tecumseh gave his wife materials to make a pouch. Mamate seems to have been unusually inept among the versatile Shawnee women, for she confessed the job was beyond her, and said she would find someone else to do it. Tecumseh was unimpressed. He declared he would make the pouch himself, and soon afterward he gave his wife some presents and dismissed her from his house.

The story John Johnston got from Shawnees at Wapakoneta was that Tecumseh had entered the partnership without enthusiasm in the first place, "more from necessity and the urgent entreaties of his friends than from choice." His relationship with Mamate was poor, and the two kept separate beds.

That may have been true, but Mamate did conceive their only child, a boy born about 1796. His name was Paukeesaa (Crouched, or A Cat Stalking Its Prey), and after his parents split up he remained for a time with his mother. At the age of seven or eight, however, he was transferred to the custody of Tecumseh's sister, Tecumapease. Whether this was because Mamate had died or simply because Tecumseh considered her negligent is unclear. To Tecumseh, his sister was the ideal of Shawnee womanhood. "She was intelligent," said the Shanes, "and had the command of all the women." Probably she held the female peace office in Tecumseh's own village. Tecumapease was always close to her famous brother, and she dutifully reared his son. Her husband, Wahsikegaboe, may have been a better father to the boy than Tecumseh himself. Tecumseh was said to have been "not deficient in affection for his son," but he considered him "too fair and like a white man," and he was disappointed when the boy showed little promise as a warrior.[6]

Whatever domestic difficulties troubled Tecumseh, the need to find a suitable site for a permanent summer village was the paramount concern, and in the spring of 1798 the band traveled northwest to the west fork of the White River (Indiana). Tecumseh's residence on the Whitewater the previous year had taken him closer to the Delawares, who had been settling the west fork of the White since 1796. The Miamis were acknowledged to have prior claim to those parts, but just as they had given the Delaware settlements their blessing, so now the Delawares extended an invitation to their "grandchildren," the Shawnees.

Tecumseh located his new town a little northwest of present-day Anderson, close to the line between Hamilton and Madison Counties. Five miles below, a Nanticoke village was situated by the broad stream, while above and along both sides of the river sat nine Delaware villages, the nearest of them Sarah Town. The fifth along, some twelve miles upstream of Tecumseh's, was Woapimininschi, where fifteen families lived under Kiktuchwenind. His other name, Anderson, would be commemorated by the American town that eventually rose upon the spot. Of the towns above Woapimininschi the most important were the homes of the chiefs Hackinkpomska (He Walks upon the Ground) and Tetepachsit, first chief of the Munsees, and, most easterly and significant of all, the village of Woapicamikunk. Here, on the river's southern bank, close to where Muncie would stand, lived forty Delaware families and the aging war chief Buckongahelas, the most prestigious Delaware alive.[7]

On the face of it, the west fork of the White offered much. The country was rich, and the river was stocked with paddlefish, gar, catfish, eels, pike, and other fish. In the summer its banks were alive with the sounds of birds and insects, and in bottomlands flourished chestnut, walnut, linden, cherry, poplar, and plum. Grapes and berries abounded. Farther afield the environment was varied, and included stands of oak-hickory and beech-maple forest, and prairie and marsh. Game was abundant, from turkey, white-tailed deer, and wapiti to buffalo, and traders, such as John and William Conner and Frederick Fisher, were soon establishing themselves in the west fork villages.

Tecumseh's band had occupied four sites in as many years since 1795, but here they settled. The White would be Tecumseh's home for eight years.

Those years are the least documented in Tecumseh's adult life, and we catch only occasional glimpses of him, recalled by white pioneers who saw him during his visits to Ohio.

The Galloway family moved from Kentucky to the Little Miami in 1798, building a home five miles northwest of what is now Xenia. James Galloway junior remembered mixing with a good-natured party of Shawnees who camped near the house that same year. Three of the Indians had a smattering of English, the results of having been taken prisoner in 1786 by Logan's Kentuckians: James Logan, whose Indian name was Spemica Lawba (High Horn), and Peter Cornstalk (Wynepuechsika) and his wife. They were a few years younger than Tecumseh, who was one of their companions. There was a drunken spree. Tecumseh generally neither drank nor ate to excess, but on those occasions when he was inebriated he remained good-humored, and he disapproved of the violence that accompanied so many Indian drinking bouts. And that is how Galloway seems to have remembered it.[8]

Peter Cornstalk, Logan, and Tecumseh would all enjoy celebrity among their people. Peter became a fluent orator, and Logan died an American hero of the War of 1812. A tall, strong, honorable man, Logan excelled in wrestling, and he probably tried his strength with Tecumseh. Simon Kenton, who renewed his acquaintanceship with Tecumseh about this time, recalled the chief's happy and playful disposition. He remembered how Tecumseh "used to wrestle and exercise in the snow at Jarboe's." Stephen and Elizabeth Jarboe were Kenton's parents-in-law, and from 1799 they lived four miles north of present-day Springfield, Ohio.[9]

Abner Barrett's house stood at the head of Buck Creek (Champaign County, Ohio), and he, too, counted Tecumseh among occasional visitors. He used to tell the story of the big Kentucky greenhorn who came to Ohio in 1802 or 1803 hoping to purchase land on the Mad River. One night the newcomer was at Barrett's, where he grew alarmed at the news that some

Indians were in the area. Near dark, the door was suddenly thrust open, without a preliminary knock or warning, and Tecumseh strode in "with his usual stately air." Pausing, the chief looked around silently, and noticed the transparent discomfort on the face of the burly Kentuckian. After a moment of hesitation, Tecumseh pointed to the stranger and, addressing Barrett, declared, "A big baby!" He stepped up to the Kentuckian and slapped him gently on the shoulders several times, repeating the words "big baby." The stranger's alarm rose in proportion to the enjoyment of the other settlers present.[10]

Tecumseh may have been in Ohio in 1798 and 1799 to participate in important discussions held by the Shawnees at this time. Surveyors were at last running the Greenville treaty line, reinforcing the tribe's sense of loss and reawakening its insecurities. Some of the Ohio chiefs began talking about bringing the different Shawnee communities together, from Ohio, Indiana, and Missouri, ceding their claims in Ohio, and forming a united complex far away from the worrying line of American settlement. They spoke of a new home, perhaps across the Mississippi in Spanish territory, in Canada under British protection, or on the Wabash with the Miami Indians. Shawnee spokesmen even went so far as to broach their ideas to the British, and Sir John Johnson, the superintendent-general of Indian affairs in Canada, promised the tribe an asylum on British soil rather than risk losing such valuable warriors to the Spanish colonies, with whom Britain was then at war.[11]

The arguments ultimately came to nothing, but before they were through the tribe was involved in a serious frontier alarm in the summer of 1799, one that apparently first brought Tecumseh's oratorical skills to the notice of the whites.

Its roots went back to the campaign against Fort Recovery in 1794, when Shawnees and their allies had killed some southern Chickasaws, who were scouting for the United States. Now word went around that the Chickasaws were coming north in force to take their revenge. The rumor was absolutely false, and no one knew how it started. Some said a drunken white soldier had foisted the story upon a Shawnee named Waitia in Cincinnati, and there were reports of strange Indians lurking in the woods. One notable Shawnee leader, Kakinathucca (the Bonner), even credited a fanciful story that two of his fellow tribesmen had actually been seized by the Chickasaws and had only got away through the intercession of some Americans. There was no doubt the Shawnees took the reports seriously. They posted sentries about their villages, and sent some of their noncombatants to the American post of Fort Defiance at the Glaize for protection. They also applied to neighboring Indians for support and to the British for powder and ball, and summoning their warriors, they fortified themselves for battle south of the Glaize, at a place that shared the name Fallen Timbers with the ill-fated battleground of five years before.[12]

In its turn the Shawnee mobilization threw the white settlements of Ohio into panic. There was disagreement about whether the Shawnees intended all-out war, or merely to stop the boundary survey, but homesteads across a twenty-mile front were abandoned as families either fled the region or struggled into small blockhouses that were erected on the Mad River.[13]

Finally, two settlers, William Ward and Simon Kenton, sent a letter to the Wapakoneta chiefs by a Shawnee-speaking French Canadian named Francoís Duchouquet. On 13 August seven Indian leaders put their names to a reply, assuring the settlers that they meant no harm to the Americans, and explaining their precautions against a Chickasaw attack. The result was a meeting between Ward and Kenton and some Shawnee chiefs, probably on 15 August. James Galloway junior believed the council took place at Duchouquet's, about six miles north of the site of Urbana, and said that the several Shawnee chiefs attending put Tecumseh forward as their principal speaker.

He gave a long delivery "much admired for its force and eloquence," Galloway remembered. The interpreter, Duchouquet, later told Galloway that "it was difficult for him to interpret his [Tecumseh's] lofty flights of eloquence, although he was as well acquainted with the language as with the French." The meeting was successful, Kenton was able to reassure the local settlers, and Neinimsico, a Shawnee leader, went to the Great Miami to speak to the white people there. Four other leaders accompanied William Ward to Cincinnati, which they reached on 16 August, and explained the misunderstanding to the governor of Northwest Territory, Arthur St. Clair.[14]

War scares—many of them arising from periodic increases in international tension—frequently disturbed Indian villages during these years. Even on the White River, Tecumseh's tranquillity was occasionally disturbed by distant rumblings. There is a suggestion that he once contemplated taking his band to Spanish Missouri. The move was an obvious one, for Tecumseh was familiar with the Shawnee colony there. Pierre Menard recollected seeing Tecumseh at Apple Creek, where he had relatives, about 1801. However, after Spain and Britain went to war in 1796, even the Indians of Missouri were in danger of being drawn into unwanted battles.[15]

Peace shakily prevailed, and Tecumseh was able to concentrate on his hunting. While living on the White he also made two more attempts to find a suitable wife, but there were no more children. Of these two marriages, the first, to "a very beautiful woman," ended as abruptly as his relationship with Mamate. The gossip was that Tecumseh found the woman remiss in providing a meal for his friends. He returned from a hunt one day and issued his customary invitation to friends to join him for dinner, and he gave his wife a turkey to dress. When the bird was served he noticed that a few of its feathers remained unplucked. The chief kept his peace until the guests had departed, but then he gave his wife a bundle of clothing and sent her away. She was astonished, we are told, and she promised to reform, but he would not have it. Unlike many Shawnees, Tecumseh was monogamous, but the standards he demanded of whoever was his wife were exacting indeed.

The year 1802 saw him in a happier, if ultimately no more successful, partnership, this time with Wa-be-le-gu-ne-qua, or White Wing, the daughter of an influential Shawnee chief named Half Moon. Half Moon dips in and out of our sources without betraying much of himself. If he was the Half Moon mentioned by John Slover, who was captured by Shawnees in 1782, he was already a notable warrior by that time. Thirteen years later he was certainly being described as a "chief" in commissary notes issued at Fort Greenville. During December 1795 the Americans issued thirty pounds of beef, twenty-eight pounds of bread, seventy pounds of flour, a gallon of salt, and three gallons and two quarts of whiskey to "a hunting party of Shawanoes under the Half Moon, Chief." It was probably meant that he was a peace or civil chief. Tecumseh's marriage to the daughter of such a substantial figure must have improved his standing, since it bound an important family to him in obligations of kinship. And the marriage held up uncommonly well for him. Tecumseh remained with White Wing for five years. They parted in 1807, when he was living at Greenville, reportedly because she was unable to bear him any children.[16]

To the end of his life the successful hunter, orator, friend, soldier, and chief consistently failed as a husband and father.

For several winters the peace of Greenville held. Tecumseh's band was content to remain with Buckongahelas's people, distant from Shawnee politics at Wapakoneta, distant too from the troublesome white settlements that were colonizing the beautiful valleys of Ohio. When the United States carved Indiana Territory from the former Northwest Territory in 1800, enclosing within it the land between the emerging state of Ohio and the Mississippi, it had few more than six thousand white inhabitants, most of them at Vincennes on the Wabash and Kaskaskia and Cahokia in the west. Tecumseh might have hoped for a period of stability, but it would not be so. The new century found Indians across the Old Northwest being sucked inexorably into a new crisis, one felt as acutely beside the placid waters of the White as elsewhere. Poverty, internal strife, drunkenness, insecurity, and disease were reducing the Indians to desperation.

The hunting, which provided food and the means of buying valuable trade goods, was yielding ever poorer returns. In converting the wilderness into farm and grazing land the American settlers destroyed the habitat for game and drove it away, but even far from the white frontier, in places more hospitable to wildlife, Indians themselves were overhunting. Overhunting was prompted by the falling prices commanded by skins and peltries. Europe was still at war, and the market it provided for furs was declining and uncertain. Indians found that their furs bought fewer of the trade goods upon which they had come to rely, so that more animals were needed to secure them. Gradually game became dangerously scarce. Some Indians said that the spirits had been offended by overhunting, and were withdrawing the animals to punish the tribes.

As the yields from hunting fell, treaty annuities grew in importance. In the summers Shawnees and Delawares traveled to the new distribution point at Fort Wayne to collect the one thousand dollars' worth of goods due them under the treaty of Greenville, returning with hoes, adzes, saws, knives, axes, kettles, ammunition, rope, rugs, blankets, cloth, and clothing. Yet even for those warriors who made an additional journey to Amherstburg in Upper Canada to receive British presents, the issues could not compensate for the troubles of the fur and skin trade. Their communities got poorer.

The problem was accentuated by the general misuse of liquor. Although the United States passed a law in 1802 prohibiting the sale of liquor to Indians, the law was hardly enforceable. Indians of the White River had become accustomed to taking hard-won peltries to Vincennes, Fort Wayne, Fort Greenville, or Louisville to exchange them for whiskey, which they either consumed themselves or carried back to their towns for resale. The consequences were there for all to see in every town on the river: Indians neglecting their duties, squandering possessions for drink, fighting, running howling about the buildings, and slumped naked in drunken stupor. Those who disapproved, such as Tecumseh, appeared powerless to intervene. According to nearby Moravian missionaries, the chief's own town was occasionally scourged by the violent consequences of drunken revels:

> We heard that the Schawanoses had murdered in pitiful fashion in their town an Indian of their nation while drinking whiskey. First they chopped three holes in his head with their tomahawk . . . and as he did not fall dead at once, one of them jumped on him with a knife and ran it into his body while another cut his stomach open. This happened 15 miles from here, where the Schawanoses live. Thus also lately a Delaware Indian murdered a Schawano woman. A drunken bout never takes place among the heathen without one or the other losing his life or being at least terribly maltreated . . . The

guzzling of whiskey among these heathen is so dreadful that no one can imagine it.[17]

Drunkenness not only sowed division and violence but also increased poverty. Needy circumstances drove some Indians to sell their remaining asset, the land itself, to increase their treaty annuities. They played into the hands of the United States, which had no sooner surveyed the Greenville boundary than it stood ready to tear it apart.

In 1800 enfeebled Spain transferred Louisiana, including the west bank of the Mississippi, to aggressive France, and when President Thomas Jefferson took office he thought it wise to strengthen his country's control of the Old Northwest. Indian land would not simply be sequestered, however. That risked expensive Indian wars. Rather, Jefferson's administration believed that the diminishing returns of the chase would eventually persuade the Indians to sell their lands and migrate to better hunting grounds farther west. The process could be accelerated by encouraging Indians to run up debts with traders, debts that could be paid by land cessions to the United States. Further, if the Indians could be assimilated into the dominant white society, if they could be induced to give up hunting and become small independent homesteaders, they would have no need of extensive ranges and would be willing to sell their surplus land.

Altruism of a kind distinguished the Jeffersonian approach to the Indian. It assumed that European and Indian cultures could not coexist. Only by improving the efficiency of their farming, by turning their common fields into individually owned and fenced plots, and learning to spin and weave, could the Indians be saved from extinction and brought into mainstream American life. They must abandon the hunting and warrior society, and adopt the beliefs, customs, and behavior of the whites. In short, they must cease to be Indians. The "civilization" of the Indians, as the process was called, was supported by religious groups such as the Society of Friends and always had a philanthropic dimension, but it went hand in hand with dispossession. Once the Indians were set upon being farmers, they would sell their hunting grounds for tools and stock.[18]

Indian land cessions were also demanded by white farmers, who distrusted the Indians as neighbors; by land speculators with an eye to profit; and by those interested in political advancement. They found an able advocate in the new governor of Indiana Territory, William Henry Harrison. A genial, mild-mannered, and cultivated Virginian, Harrison was only twenty-seven years old when he arrived at Vincennes as the territory's first governor, but he was strong-willed and ambitious. A military man who had fought at Fallen Timbers, he was also a professional politician close to the land speculators. In his previous position as a delegate of the Northwest Territory to

Congress he had largely concerned himself with the disposition of public lands, and his wife was the daughter of the speculator John Cleves Symmes, whose Miami Purchase had made such great inroads into the Shawnee country north of the Ohio in 1788. Unlocking the land and encouraging white settlement, Harrison understood, would not only give greater security to the citizens of Indiana Territory but also advance the march to statehood. In September 1804 Indiana already had a sufficient population to qualify for second-grade government.

Harrison satisfied the republic's land-hunger with unreasonable alacrity. Between 1802 and 1805 he concluded no less than seven treaties, by which Delawares, Miamis, Weas, Piankeshaws, Eel Rivers, Potawatomis, Kickapoos, Shawnees, Kaskaskias, Sacs, and Foxes alienated their title to the southern part of present-day Indiana, portions of Wisconsin and Missouri, and most of Illinois, all for the derisory sum of two cents an acre or less. Harrison's treaties were hardly models of fair dealing. At various times important Indian leaders were bribed, annuities guaranteed by former treaties were threatened if tribesmen refused to negotiate, deals were struck with unrepresentative tribes and individuals, liquor was employed to "mellow" Indians attending treaties, the poverty of the native communities was exploited, and agreements were reached with some groups of Indians to isolate others. Nearly all the treaties provoked Indian outrage and protest.[19]

At Greenville in 1795 the United States had negotiated with all interested tribes. This was partly to meet the Indian confederacy's insistence that the land was held in common by them all, and partly to avoid further charges that some Indians were selling property that belonged to others. In the new spate of purchases, however, American officials reduced resistance and minimized expenditure by identifying and negotiating with the specific users of the desired territory. In doing so they generated divisions within and between Indian villages—between beneficiaries and nonbeneficiaries, and between chiefs who acquiesced to the treaties and the Indians opposed to them.

Nowhere was there a better illustration of this than on the west fork of the White, where the treaties renewed insecurity and created anger among the Delawares. In 1802 and 1803 four Delaware chiefs consented at Vincennes and Fort Wayne to the cession of a large tract about Vincennes, one that included the lower White and pointed uncomfortably to the Delaware, Shawnee, and Nanticoke towns upstream. The next year Buckongahelas, Tetepachsit, Hackinkpomska, Beaver, and George White-Eyes also gave their blessing to the sale of one-and-a-half million acres extending the Vincennes block to the Ohio and extinguishing Indian ownership of the north bank of the Ohio east as far as Louisville. When the chiefs returned to their villages with the meager proceeds they were so ashamed of what they had done that they kept it a secret.

In 1805 Harrison's agent had to visit the White to explain the transaction, and old Tetepachsit was so embarrassed that he "trembled and appeared very much agitated and confused whilst speaking." The ominous storm that was brewing against the chiefs had barely subsided in August 1805, when Harrison assembled Delawares and other Indians at his home, Grouseland, in Vincennes, and bought an additional two million acres linking his recent acquisitions to the old Greenville line. He had thus cleared the entire north bank of the Ohio of Indian title. Here the Miamis denied that the Delawares had had any rights to land in Indiana, which they merely occupied by the Miamis' sufferance. Consequently, the chagrined Delawares returned home without any additional compensation for the part they had played in the new treaty, and complaining that they no longer owned the ground beneath their feet. Not surprisingly, in the light of the run of land cessions, the Delawares brooded over the possibility of their homes on the White being sold by the Miamis, and they talked earnestly about migrating across the Mississippi.[20]

Living among the Delawares, Tecumseh watched the growing insecurity among his hosts, and heard the abuse hurled at chiefs party to the treaty proceedings. He also knew the anxiety among his own people in Ohio.

The Shawnees were not deemed to have had an interest in the lands purchased by Harrison, something they may have resented after so many tribes had dipped their hands into the sale of Shawnee territory at Greenville. Nonetheless, several hundred Shawnees attended the Fort Wayne treaty of June 1803 as observers, and Tecumseh may have even been one of them. Disgusted at the release of the Vincennes block, the Shawnees walked out of the council at one point. However, they too finally made a small concession by selling their rights in an Illinois salt spring for a salt annuity. Two years later a small band of Shawnees living on the Detroit River also obtained one-fifth of a thousand-dollar annuity for consenting to the cession of land east of the Sandusky, negotiated at Swan Creek. Neither the treaty of 1803 nor that of 1805 surrendered land significant to the Shawnees, but like the Delawares they dwelt much upon these new cessions and were troubled.

In fact, wherever Tecumseh looked he saw Indians afraid for their land, particularly on the upper Mississippi, where the Sac and Fox Indians resented the loss of territory taken from them by a disgraceful "treaty" concluded by Harrison at St. Louis in 1804. There, also, the acquisition of Louisiana by the United States in 1803 told the tribes of the Old Northwest that they were gradually being encircled, hemmed in east, south, and west. French-Canadian trader Jacques Lasselle, who knew the Indians better than most, declared the land issue to be "the great subject" of "Indian discontent," while Harrison himself acknowledged that tribesmen "were grumbling about the treaties and threatening to drive the Americans back over the Ohio."[21]

An ugly cycle was developing: deprivation, land sales to alleviate distress, and further deprivation. Complained the Shawnee chief Blackbeard: "the white people . . . destroyed all that God had given us for our support. I was reduced and all my younger brothers to poverty."[22]

A solution favored by American officials and missionaries was "civilization," but this only created more division and confusion in the Indian country. Some chiefs were inclined to go so far along that road. Others thought not only that exchanging the life of the warrior and hunter for the punishing discipline of farming was irksome and unfulfilling, but that it was also blasphemous. Had not their traditional ways of life been ordained by the Creator, and would he not be angry if these were forsaken? How would it serve the Indians to adopt the practices of the whites if it merely brought upon them the wrath of the spirits that governed all things on earth?

The extent to which the Indian cultures had already been modified by Europeans varied. Some, those nearest the white frontier, were in advanced states of evolution, while others farther west had accommodated some attributes of the newcomers but remained resistant to more fundamental change.

The Shawnees exemplified the more conservative Indians. Their villages were full of evidence of their long contacts with whites—of kettles, firearms, and implements; of clothing and objects manufactured from European materials; of animals such as horses and even cattle; and of houses that echoed those of white neighbors. But for all that, in 1800 life would have been instantly recognizable to a Shawnee of sixty years before. Not until after the War of 1812 had passed did the basic social, political, economic, and belief systems of the tribe undergo radical redefinition. Then the warrior and hunter life, with its attendant rituals and offices, would decline. The economy was remodeled, and the sexual division of labor altered. Divisional chieftainship would collapse, and the clan system diminish in nature and importance. The council house, with many ceremonies and dances, would disappear, and Shawnee religious beliefs themselves would be subtly reshaped. These and other transformations lay in the future, although even in 1800 there were Shawnees who saw them coming, and looked along the white man's road with suspicion and dismay.

To Tecumseh the nearest example of resistance to the "civilization" process was afforded not by the Shawnees, however, but by the Delaware villages on the White River. In 1801 a Moravian mission had been established on the north bank of the river, fifteen miles above Tecumseh's town.

The missionaries—John Peter Kluge, his wife, and Abraham Luckenbach—
were honest and hardworking, and willing to suffer for their God. Houses, a
vegetable garden, fenced land, and livestock soon eased their discomforts.
Bringing thirteen Christian Indians with them, they hoped to nurture a non-
drinking, industrious model community that would influence the nearby
villagers.

The statutes for the Moravian church embodied codes that ran counter
to Delaware culture. For example, they insisted upon a religion that recognized one God rather than a multiplicity of spirits, and taught that a man
should have only one wife. They needed to be applied sensitively, as David
Zeisberger used them at the parent mission of Goshen, in Ohio. Unfortunately, those who ran the White River mission were young and inexperienced, and they were as ignorant of Indian ways as they were contemptuous
of the "abominations" of the "heathen." They told the Delawares that the Indians were the servants of Satan, and tried to terrify them with tales of sin
and salvation, a salvation that demanded the Indians reject their rich native
heritage.

It was not surprising that they failed. Some sick and dying Indians,
preparing for the eternal torment they had been promised, came to the mission, and there was some initial curiosity about the Moravians. Nevertheless, the White River congregation peaked at twenty-three in 1802, and
thereafter lapsed to insignificance. In its five-year life only two healthy
adults were baptized at the mission. Most Indians regarded it an irrele-
vance. As the venerable Buckongahelas bluntly told the Moravians: "we cannot drop our customs and teaching and sacrifices, for our forefathers too
received them from God and left them to us. Every Indian must remain true
to these things, and not let them go. Your teaching is only for white
people."[23]

Such were the issues unsettling the Indians close to Tecumseh at the beginning of the nineteenth century. There were fears for livelihoods, for
lands, and for traditional cultures. There were beliefs that the Indians were
losing control of their lives and becoming too dependent upon the whites,
who threatened their very identities as Indians. Yet there was a greater
threat still, one that spread the length of the White in 1802, and boded the
complete extinction of Indian communities. It was the terrifying onset of
epidemic disease.

Europeans had introduced a number of diseases against which the Indians had developed little biological protection. The diseases appeared and
reappeared, stealthily and suddenly striking down whole families, tearing
Indian villages apart; and against them there were few remedies. This time

the sickness was so bad that the Delawares thought the deities were angry with them for neglecting important ceremonies of worship. They tried to reform, reinvigorating rituals and praying for long life, but one chief who supervised such a ceremony in 1803 died himself immediately afterward.

The winter of 1804–1805 was unusually cold, and the spring brought widespread floods that damaged Indian cornfields. A new wave of deaths also occurred, defeating the best efforts of native doctors. The disease was described at the time as a "bilious fever" but may have been influenza or smallpox. It struck widely, seizing people suddenly and killing them within days.

Some Indians remained convinced that the Creator was punishing them for misdeeds, and they plumbed their own consciences for behavior which might have merited such punishment. Others put the deaths down to witchcraft, the manipulation of malignant spiritual power by evilly disposed persons. As accusations against one person or another became the gossip of the villages, terror and suspicion spread. Tensions that had grown along the White River for years began to boil over.

There was sickness in Tecumseh's village, too, and in June 1805 an investigation conducted there named some Wyandots as witches. In fact, although far away on the Sandusky River, near the shores of Lake Erie, the Wyandot settlements themselves were being savaged by the pestilence. It was said that on the Sandusky "all men and children in their nation were dying, one after the other."[24]

In May the epidemic on the White claimed its most notable victim. Buckongahelas was an old man of some eighty snows, but even his involvement in the recent land treaties had not dimmed a matchless record. He was, as a contemporary asserted, the George Washington of the Delawares. When Buckongahelas died the towns along the White were in uproar.

Tecumseh felt helpless against the deadly contagion, but in his village there was one man who thought he had an answer, who offered the direction so badly needed. No influential or respected person was he, either, but a coward and a drunkard, a thorough wastrel. Yet in this moment of crisis he stepped forward.

He was Lalawéthika, the Rattle. Tecumseh's idle young brother.

THE PROPHET

9

✦ ⊞◈⊟ ✦

A REVOLUTION
ON THE WHITE RIVER

He did not look much like Tecumseh, and even less did he act like him. Indeed, next to his handsome brother, Lalawéthika was decidedly unprepossessing—"of no great appearance," one put it. He was a rather slim man of average height. His face was lent a doleful character by the downturn of the mouth, but it was distinguished by a short mustache and a closed right eye, the latter the result of an old accident. Lalawéthika dressed plainly and conventionally, but like other Shawnees he was fond of ornamentation. Clasps encircled his arms and wrists, a large silver gorget rested at his throat, and impressive pendants were suspended from his pierced nose and ears.

Lalawéthika lacked presence, but he talked often, and was good at it, adding force to his points with appropriate gestures. Sadly, neither that nor a calculating shrewdness had won him prestige. In fact, he was regarded as a misfit. The Shanes only echoed common opinion when they described him as "a talkative, blustering, noisy fellow, full of deceit." Some Indians mocked his war record, jibing unkindly about the clean pair of heels he had shown at the battle of Fallen Timbers, and most knew him as lazy and dissolute, "a perfect vagabond" who refused to hunt and was frequently drunk. Even Lalawéthika knew his reputation to be true, and acknowledged himself "a very wicked man."[1]

In 1805 Lalawéthika was a little over thirty, and had a niche for himself as a healer in Tecumseh's village. His aptitude for the work had been revealed to him early in life by guardian spirits, and he had learned the medicinal properties of roots and herbs. Although unable to perform surgery, he could bleed patients, arrest mortification, prescribe sweat baths, and probe bullet wounds. Most crucial of all, he relied upon calling spiritual aid for the sick and driving away competing malignant forces. By services such as these, and the generosity of friends, he managed to support two wives and a number of children.[2]

Lalawéthika was more than ordinarily troubled that year. The sickness that was sweeping Indian communities was stirring the guilt deep within him. Surely this was Waashaa Monetoo's way of punishing the Indians for their inattentions and sinfulness? So, at least, said an old Delaware woman, Beata, who lived at Tetepachsit's town four miles below Woapicamikunk on the White River. Beata had been baptized at the Moravian village of Friedenshutten (Pennsylvania) in 1769, but her family had abandoned the Moravian faith when she was but a child, and the missionaries had seen little of her since. Now she was having visions and insisting the Creator was sending angels to tell her how the Indians might redeem themselves.

Since February, Beata and her followers had been informing the Indians that they had become degenerate—neglecting ancient ceremonies that propitiated the spirits, and drinking, fornicating, stealing, and abusing others. The Great Spirit was offended, and he intended sending a messiah (a child, or perhaps a resurrected Delaware warrior) who would show them correct conduct. It was important that they listened, for an apocalypse was coming, a terrible storm that would destroy the wicked. As for the witches who were using their powers to poison people, Beata herself had the ability to identify them and bring them to punishment.

To the Delawares, Beata's revelations explained their misfortunes, and the visions caused a sensation along the river. "Never," bewailed the Moravians, "have the Indians been in such a state of revolution. . . . They do not want to hear anything at all except what they learn through the extravagant visions." Beata was besieged with listeners, a new house was built at Woapicamikunk to accommodate the revitalized ceremonies, and days and nights were spent in ritual. Although Beata was unable to check the alcoholism in the Delaware towns, her fame spread as far as the Sandusky River in Ohio, where the Wyandots were dying. In September 1805 a deputation of Wyandots arrived on the White, requesting Beata to return with them to hunt out the witches that were killing their people. Yet such was the prophetess's standing that the Delawares refused to let her go.[3]

Whites as well as Indians were blamed for the decline of native ceremonials, and hostility to the Moravian mission near the Delaware towns increased. The missionaries were threatened and insulted. In July eight drunken warriors, half-naked and their faces blackened, rode "like wild beasts" into the mission and butchered a hog. Later that month a Cherokee family temporarily living there hosted a "sacrificial feast" to discomfort the Moravians. The missionaries grew so frightened that they wrote their superiors asking permission to withdraw.

No less afraid were Delaware chiefs whose involvement in land sales was said to have been another cause of the Great Spirit's anger. The most criticized chief, Tetepachsit, even fled to the mission for three days in July, in terror of his life. With Buckongahelas dead, and Tetepachsit and the drunken Hackinkpomska discredited, it was the younger Delawares who held sway on the White. Fired by Beata, they intended purging their community in the most direct if brutal way.

Lalawéthika, too, must have been alarmed by Beata's revelations only a few miles upriver of Tecumseh's town. Shawnees were also falling sick, and Lalawéthika himself epitomized the degeneration condemned by the prophetess. Indeed, there were grounds for believing the Shawnees had given greater offense than most others to Waashaa Monetoo. By their traditions they had been the firstborn of nations, and particularly favored, but their difficulties had been exceptional. They had lost homelands in Ohio and were scattered in all directions. Such severe punishment suggested that the Shawnees had particularly aroused the Creator's displeasure. The diseases ravaging the White River that spring and summer forced Shawnees, no less than Delawares, to search their own souls.

They, too, believed that the problem was being aggravated by witchcraft. Shawnees regarded witches as the agents of Motshee Monetoo, the Bad Spirit. Somehow the witches had preserved evil medicine made from the bodies of malevolent water monsters the early Shawnees encountered soon after they had been created. One of the monsters had been a sea creature, discovered by the first Chillicothes after their voyage to this land from another island. The other was a great horned serpent which inhabited a lake. The Shawnees had killed it, using the sacred medicine pack Waashaa Monetoo had given them, but the evil symbolized by both animals lived on in the medicine bags of witches. In 1805 Tecumseh's town was gripped with the fear that those bags were now being turned against the people.

In the eyes of the Indians witchcraft was an entirely plausible explanation for sudden and stubborn illness. Witches were normally thought to be old people whose longevity suggested unusual spiritual power, and the accusations and counteraccusations that accompanied witch-hunting could reduce communities to chaos. Even George Blue-Jacket, a son of the famous war chief who had been educated by the whites, did not dismiss it lightly:

This witchcraft . . . is a very wicked thing. They [the witches] can go a thousand miles in less than an hour and back again, and poison

anybody they hate and make them lame, and torment them in many
wicked and cruel ways. They can go into houses with their poison
[even] if the doors are locked ever so tight, and the people cannot get
awake till they are gone. This witchcraft has prevailed greatly and
been very common among our people, and some of the white people
have learned it and practise it, and it is a very wicked thing.[4]

By May, the Shawnees on the White River were in turmoil, as Indians
sickened and died. An old prophet named Change of Feathers (Pengahshega) seems to have acted as a witch-finder, and two Wyandots were executed, but Indians continued to be stricken. Momentarily old Change of
Feathers enjoyed great influence, but then he too perished.[5]

Lalawéthika was probably involved in the prophet's attempt to check the
contagion, but about this time a message reached him from the Shawnees
of Wapakoneta in Ohio. The people were falling sick. They needed him.
Lalawéthika went, but while he was there, working with the dying, he became deeply conscious of his own sins, and "in great distress . . . prayed to
the Good Spirit to show him how he must be saved."[6]

It was about November 1805, while he was in this frame of mind, ridden
with guilt and fear, that Lalawéthika had a frightening dream.

He was on a journey. No ordinary one, but the path taken by the souls of
the dead. At a fork the road branched left and right. Lalawéthika saw a few
Indians traveling the right-hand road, which led to Heaven, but far more
passing to the left, where three houses stood at the wayside, one after the
other. At the first two houses sidetracks led back to the right-hand road, offering travelers final opportunities to repent and redeem themselves, but
most tumbled on headlong toward the final house. It was named Eternity.
There the souls suffered so many fearful agonies that Lalawéthika could
hear them "roaring like the falls of a river." Sorcerers, drunkards, and wife-
beaters all were there, each being tormented according to his crime. Horrified, Lalawéthika watched a drunkard, a man such as himself, imbibing
molten metal.

He went no farther than the fork, but returned, determined to warn
other Indians what lay in store for them if they did not reform. Indians believed the spirits communicated with them through dreams, and convinced
that Waashaa Monetoo himself was using him as a medium, Lalawéthika
could not be restrained. To the astonishment of his friends—including
Tecumseh, who may have been at Wapakoneta for yet more discussions
about tribal reunification—he changed overnight. He began to preach to all
and sundry, his body trembling with emotion and his eyes wet with tears,
urging the Indians to repent their sins before it was too late.

For the first time in his life Lalawéthika was a celebrity. Parties gathered excitedly at his door, some from Wapakoneta, but others—Shawnees, Ottawas, Mingoes, and Wyandots—traveling in from the nearby villages to hear him. Over time he related one vision after another, gradually molding the messages of the Great Spirit into a comprehensive code that addressed most of the problems perplexing Indians throughout the Great Lakes region.

Listening to the Prophet, as he came to be called, was a deeply moving experience. During a lingering silence that was pregnant with anticipation, he would sit with his eyes closed, his features a mask of gravity and reverence. Then he would speak, eloquently and emphatically, his sonorous tones accompanied by motions of the hands. His address might last half an hour, but at every dramatic pause his followers called out "*Seguy*," to signify their agreement. Some Shakers, who watched the Prophet in 1807, found his delivery "expressive of a deep sense and solemn feeling of eternal things."

He said that whiskey had been made for whites, not Indians, and should not be touched. Sorcerers must throw away their evil medicine, and murder and warfare were wrong. "Never think of war again," he urged. The physical abuse of wives and children should also stop. It was kindness that was required, particularly care of the young, the old, and women. Attacking his own family arrangements, the Prophet declared that henceforth men should take only one wife, and stop chasing other women or driving barren wives back to their parents. He condemned dishonesty and slander.[7]

Many in the Prophet's audiences recognized themselves in his denunciations. If they refused to reform, he told them, their souls would meet eternal torment in the realm of Motshee Monetoo. The possessions their relatives had had buried with their bodies to help them travel in the afterworld would be turned to ash.[8]

But it was not enough simply to renounce the past. A new beginning had to be symbolized in the most dramatic way. They must throw away their sacred medicine bags.

Indians were protected throughout life by their individual guardian spirits, to whom they gave obeisance and appealed at difficult times. The process was facilitated by medicine bags, in which Indians kept objects that symbolized the spirits concerned. A feather, for example, might represent the spirit of a bird. The objects were fetishes, essential to a person's ability to summon any spiritual help required, and the sacred medicine bags were at the center of an Indian's religious life and sense of well-being.

The Prophet associated the bags with witchcraft and the use of sacred power to cause illness and death. He called upon followers to break with the past. They should confess all the sins they had committed since the age of

seven—when he deemed them to have lost their innocence—and discard the
medicine bags and guardian spirits under whose influence they had committed past offenses. Instead, they must be guided only by the Prophet, who
would interpret the will of the spirits for them. And to be worthy of redemption they must also bathe themselves each morning, pray for the fruit-
fulness of the earth at sunrise and sunset, and attend to certain rituals and
prohibitions. There was even a dance, introduced "simply for amusement."
On the other hand, anyone who refused to destroy a medicine bag not only
rejected the Great Spirit but laid himself or herself open to suspicions of
witchcraft.[9]

To his social ethic, the Prophet eventually added what may be called a
nativist gospel. He taught that Waashaa Monetoo intended Indians and
whites to be separate, and had accordingly bestowed upon them different
characteristics, beliefs, and modes of existence. It distressed him to see de-
moralized and indigent tribes adopting the culture of the whites. They
should be proud of their native identity, independent and self-reliant, living
"as did the Indians in olden days."

This meant revitalizing traditional ceremonies in praise of "the good
spirits of the air," and dressing in the styles and materials of their ancestors.
Men should again shave their heads to the scalp lock, wear eagle feathers on
the crown, and paint their faces. They should kindle fires with sticks instead
of using flints and steel, and prefer bows and arrows to firearms. Animals
introduced by the Europeans, whether they be cats or cattle, should be disposed of, except for horses, which had become indispensable. Alien foods,
such as pork, chicken, and wheat were taboo. As for their livelihoods, the
Indians should practice the horticultural-hunting economy of the past, and
refuse to hear voices that told them to imitate the whites. The Prophet condemned the individual landholding favored by the whites, and held that Indian communities should hold their land in common. He even espoused the
restoration of traditional pastimes and games.

In short, everything must be done to protect the distinct Indian identity,
and fraternization between the races must be avoided. Indian women who
had married whites should leave their husbands and return home, leaving
their mixed-blood children with their fathers.

To those who objected that the traditional economy could not be sustained because of the decline of game, the Prophet replied that the animals
were being plundered to meet the demands of the whites and Indians who
had acquired their materialist attitudes. As rendered by one of his disciples,
the message of the Great Spirit was:

> My children, you complain that the animals of the forest are few and
> scattered. How shall it be otherwise? You destroy them yourselves

for their skins only, and leave their bodies to rot or give the best pieces to the whites. I am displeased when I see this, and take them back to the earth that they may not come to you again. You must kill no more animals than are necessary to feed and clothe you . . .[10]

The whites had no right to the bounties of the forest, which had been created for the Indians:

I made all the trees of the forest for your use, but the maple I love the best because it yields sugar for your little ones. You must make it only for them, but sell none to the whites. They have another sugar which was made expressly for them. Besides by making too much you spoil the trees and give them pain by cutting and hacking them, for they have feeling like yourselves. If you take more than is necessary for your own use, you shall die, and the maple will yield no more water.

In one of his visions Lalawéthika claimed that the Great Spirit compared the fat deer and bears that had once existed with the emaciated animals that remained, and complained that "the red people have spoiled them by killing them too young." It was up to the Indians to restrict what they took so that the environment could regenerate.

The Prophet depicted white culture as deleterious to the Indians, and he opposed land cessions, but in those early days of his religion he did not incite his followers to acts of violence against the Americans. In fact, he showed occasional sympathy for them: "If a white man is starving, you may sell him a little corn or a very little sugar." Rather the Prophet contended that Indians and whites were different and should remain so.

Long-term coexistence was another thing, however. The Prophet foretold a coming apocalypse in which the whites would be overthrown by supernatural means alone, and buried along with those Indians who had remained sinful. Then would Waashaa Monetoo release the game animals from the earth, and the virtuous Indians would repossess the land. The Prophet equivocated about when the great event would occur, but he indicated that it was close, only a few years away.

There was nothing original in the revelations of the Prophet. They belonged to a prophetic tradition far older than he. Indians had invariably attributed unusual misfortunes, such as famines, epidemics, or natural catastrophes, to the wrath of the spirits, and in the middle of the eighteenth century Delaware prophets had promulgated views very similar to those of Lalawéthika. In fact, although at least eight such prophets, two of them women, were active between 1740 and 1775, almost all of Lalawéthika's ideas can be traced to just two of them: a Munsee Indian named Wangomend, who preached on the Susquehanna and Allegheny from 1752 to 1775, and especially Neolin, who flourished in the six years after 1760. The most significant difference between Lalawéthika and Neolin is that the former predicted the whites would finally be removed supernaturally, whereas the latter threw his influence behind a war to drive the British from Indian lands. But then, in Neolin's day the Indians were in a far stronger military position.

The Delaware tradition had passed to the Shawnees. Neolin himself lived with that tribe in 1764, and seven years later another Delaware prophet, Scattamek, had an influence among them. But then the tradition languished. At times of extreme public alarm, these prophets inspired intense fanaticism in Indians brought face-to-face with the fury of the spirits. In securer days, when the terrors had abated, the tradition survived as an undercurrent. The strictures of the prophets were also formidable disciplines to maintain, particularly nativism, the rejection of European influences, which ran counter to the common hunger for trade goods.

After 1770 the Shawnees had made little use of the language of prophetic nativism, but it was probably stronger among the Delawares, with whom they associated closely. The friendships and ties of kinship which had developed between Shawnees and Delawares had led Tecumseh to establish his village on the White, and it was there that the prophetic tradition was recalled to prominence by the epidemics of 1805. More than anyone else, the Delaware prophetess Beata prompted Lalawéthika's new career.[11]

American observers occasionally saw Christian influences in Lalawéthika's ideas, and suggested that he had based them on the principles of the Shakers. Certainly the Prophet inherited some Christian notions with the Delaware tradition. Neolin had borrowed the concept of Hell, for which his people wanted an equivalent, from Christianity, and probably also an advocacy of monogamy. However, Lalawéthika's followers admitted but two direct imports from Christianity: the use of the rosary (a string of beans) and the idea of confession, which were purloined from Wyandots who had once belonged to the Catholic community at Detroit. It is nevertheless worth remembering that the supposedly pristine aboriginal culture championed by Neolin and Lalawéthika was, in fact, a syncretism forged from Indian and white antecedents.

In the anxious winter of 1805 and 1806 many listened to the Prophet, and some declared they would quit drinking whiskey for good, and adhere to other commandments. Not everyone welcomed him, however. The members of the Shawnee tribal council at Wapakoneta were unpersuaded. Men such as the head chief, Black Hoof; the aged Blackbeard; Blacksnake, once the scourge of the Ohio flatboats; Piaseka the Wolf, a son of Cornstalk;

Big Snake; and Tail's End resented the sudden pretensions of this insignifi-
cant westerner. After all, not only had Lalawéthika no personal standing,
but he was also a Kispoko. The management of Shawnee tribal affairs cus-
tomarily belonged to the Mekoches. About the stewardship of religious
matters there was some doubt, with both the Mekoches and Chillicothes
disputing the prerogative; but most of the Ohio Shawnees belonged to
these two divisions, and they had no intention of permitting any of
their Pekowi, Kispoko, or Hathawekela brethren to usurp their privileges.
Before the end of 1805 the Wapakoneta chiefs were at odds with the
Prophet.

Talking it over with Tecumseh, who was the chief of his own band, the
Prophet decided to establish a new center for his religion, away from the
jealous chiefs at Wapakoneta. They chose a site at Greenville, where the old
treaty had been signed, one that was actually on the American side of the
treaty line. The brothers sent off their messengers, inviting local followers
and the Shawnees and Delawares on the White to join them at Greenville in
obedience to the Great Spirit.

The Prophet's plans proved to be premature, for the spring of 1806
found the new site still unprepared. Those of Tecumseh's band who had already journeyed from the White, and other supporters of the Prophet,
camped instead on Stony Creek, near present-day De Graff (Logan County,
Ohio), with a group of Shawnees and Mingoes under a Shawnee headman
named Lewis.[12]

The Prophet gave little personal attention to the new settlement, for that
March he went west, back to the White River, on a grim mission.

Learning of the Prophet's powers, the Delawares wanted him to be a
witch-finder.

They were still in a state of revolution, with the young warriors impatient of all restraint, and the old peace chiefs discredited and charged with
witchcraft. Beata was busy organizing repeated appeals to the spirits, but
she declined to put names to witches, being, as was said, "after all a
woman."[13]

Lalawéthika had no such inhibitions. His injunctions were soon reinforcing those of Beata the length of the river, and a great council was
arranged at Woapicamikunk, where the Prophet would root out the witches
en masse. The event created a climate of fear, particularly among the old
and individuals whose behavior was known to be antisocial. They felt
trapped. If they absented themselves from the council, with its ceremonies
of worship, they would be accused of insulting the spirits. If they attended,
they might be named as witches. Others, with nothing to fear, doggedly

pressed on with preparations, and as early as January crowds of Indians were filing upriver toward the meeting ground.

On 21 February a warrior called at the Moravian mission to summon the Christian Indians to the ceremony. More than anyone else he wanted Joshua, the Mahican interpreter. Fortunately Joshua was away making raccoon traps, and the Indian left without him.

Christian he may have been, but Joshua was in an extremely dangerous position. He was both lonely and haunted. Born of Christian parents in New England, Joshua had spent all his life in the missions. A valuable member of the community, he spoke several Indian languages, passed as a carpenter, and exceled at canoe building. During religious services he even played the organ and spinet. Yet for all that Joshua never met the exacting standards of the Moravians. As Luckenbach severely remarked, he had a "great many faults . . . He was never quite free from superstition."[14]

Poor Joshua's life had been filled with tragedy. His first two daughters had been massacred by backcountrymen at Gnadenhutten in 1782, and his wife died at the Goshen mission in 1801. It was perhaps to exorcise her memory that the sixty-year-old Mahican had volunteered to help open the White River mission that same year. With him went his invalid son. Sadly, life did not improve. The boy died in 1802, and two years afterward Joshua also lost a new wife he had taken while among the Delawares. Riven by disaster, torn between the pull of the neighboring towns and an uncompromising creed that made him fear for his immortal soul, he was forever drinking in the Delaware villages, chasing local women, and returning to the mission begging forgiveness.

Joshua must have swallowed hard when he learned of the summons to the ceremony upriver, where the Shawnee witch-finder would do his work, for few men were more open to accusation than he. He was part of a mission the prophets condemned, and had befriended old chief Tetepachsit, who was being touted as the foremost sorcerer. Worse, in his cups Joshua had blabbed unwisely. He had claimed power with a man-eating bird spirit that would put people "out of the way" if Joshua wished. Foolish talk perhaps, but remembered chillingly now, because Joshua had virtually admitted his command of witchcraft. Even two of his fellow Christian Indians had charged him with murdering their child by sorcery in 1803. Now, Joshua brazenly declared he would have nothing to do with the business at Woapicamikunk. But he was afraid all the same.[15]

The Prophet did not instigate the Delaware witch-hunt. It was under way when he got to Woapicamikunk, and the main suspects were already known. Tetepachsit and Hackinkpomska, who had borne the greatest blame for the land cessions, had been deposed and were under guard, and excited young men had already begun the process of extracting confessions and finding out where the evil medicine was hidden.

On 13 March, two days before the Prophet's arrival, Tetepachsit was trussed between two stakes and tortured with fire. In agony the old man finally admitted sorcery, but declared that he had secreted his medicine bag in Joshua's house during a recent stay at the mission, two months before. That afternoon "seven wild Indians with faces painted black" raced to the mission, where they found Joshua and told him that he was needed at Woapicamikunk as a witness. The Mahican remained calm, and finished his meal before leaving. On the fifteenth he was brought before Tetepachsit. The old chief was broken, but he did his best for Joshua. His statements had been false, he said, made in fear. His medicine was not in Joshua's house, but was hidden somewhere else. For the moment Joshua was safe, but he was not allowed to go home.[16]

That day the Prophet arrived. No time was wasted in parading the men and women in a circle so that he might study them for indications of sorcery. Today the futility of such a purge seems obvious, and the terror inflicted upon old people indefensible. In 1805, however, the logic of it was unassailable to many Indians. Their people were dying, and someone was responsible. The Prophet believed he could flush the witches out and find their poison. It was the theory of illness—that it came down to malevolent individuals—rather than the motive that was at fault.

Lalawéthika named Tetepachsit and Hackinkpomska as witches. Joshua had no poison, but he had influence with a homicidal spirit; he was also condemned. The first person to die, however, was an old woman named Caritas, known to the whites as Ann Charity.

Ann had been baptized by the Moravians, and had lived in their missions in earlier days. Perhaps she had acquired too many of the customs of the whites, but she was also a headwoman among the Delawares, and associated with the corrupt chiefs who were also on trial. Nonetheless, it was for witchcraft that she suffered. The poor woman endured prolonged torture, until she confessed she had given her medicine bag to her grandson, who was out hunting. The young man was found and he saved his life by making a clean breast of it: he had used Ann's medicine to fly from Kentucky to the Mississippi and back between dawn and dusk. His grandmother died.

Tetepachsit's turn came at last, on 17 March. After mentioning several places in which he claimed to have hidden his poison, none of which yielded anything, he indicated a tree near the mission. Ten warriors with blacked faces took him there. Their patience exhausted, they built a fire within the sight of the helpless missionaries, tomahawked the wretched chief, and pitched him alive into the flames, indifferent to his pitiful cries. Allegedly the chief's own son delivered the hatchet blow, blaming his father for discarding his mother and older children for a young wife.

Some of Tetepachsit's executioners then entered the mission for provisions, and the terrified Moravians inquired after Joshua, pleading that he was no witch but a Christian. The Indians left with piercing yells, while the Moravians cried and prayed. "We shall never forget how we felt in that terrible hour," they wrote. That night Luckenbach bravely decided to set out the next day to seek Joshua's release, but he was already dead.[17]

He died courageously, the same day as Tetepachsit. Before being hatcheted and burned Joshua said some words the Indians did not understand, and the Moravians assumed that he had been praying in German.

There were other executions. Tetepachsit's widow and his nephew, Billy Patterson, were condemned. Billy was put to death. But as the woman was being prepared for execution, her younger brother, a lad of only twenty years or so, pushed through the crowd, took his sister by the hand, and led her away to the astonishment of the warriors. When he came back he turned upon the Prophet. The devil had come among them, he said, and they were killing one another.

Apparently a rebellion among the friends and relatives of the accused halted the witch-hunt temporarily. The eight prisoners who were being held at the end of March included Hackinkpomska, but early the following month supporters of the chief threatened the lives of any who harmed him. Various rumors reached the Moravians—that attempts had been made to buy the lives of the accused, or that one faction of the tribe had rebelled and civil war was imminent. But there were other reasons why the witch-hunt ran out of steam. On 18 April a message from William Henry Harrison, the governor of Indiana Territory, reached the Delawares. It urged them to drive the "imposter" from their towns and "let your poor old men and women sleep in quietness," and it contained a strident challenge to the Prophet:

> But who is this pretended prophet who dares to speak in the name of the Great Creator? Examine him . . . Demand of him some proofs at least of his being the messenger of the Deity . . . If he is really a prophet, ask of him to cause the sun to stand still, the moon to alter its course, the rivers to cease to flow, or the dead to rise from their graves. If he does these things, you may then believe that he has been sent from God.[18]

The Indians appear to have disregarded Harrison's protest, though it may have strengthened those who questioned the witch-hunt. More important was the decline in the number of Delawares falling sick. This indicated that the purge had succeeded—but not for long. In August some Indians threatened to renew the proceedings, and in 1809 they did so, executing a dozen people within a year.

The Prophet is deservedly associated with the "revolution" on the White River, but we should be careful not to exaggerate his involvement. The reform movement had begun long before Lalawéthika's intervention, and he was an expression, not a cause of it, its disciple rather than its mentor. He added impetus, but made no changes to the direction of the process; nor was he able to control the energies it released. The removal of established chiefs left a vacuum of authority and gave free rein to intemperate young men, and even the prophets were unable to restabilize the situation. They could not even stop the debauchery in the villages. The Prophet left the Delawares as he found them, in chaos. One of the few lasting achievements of the revolution was the expulsion of the Moravians, who abandoned their mission the following September.

Lalawéthika's next venture was no more successful. The Wyandots and Senecas of the Sandusky River were also being scourged with disease, and their local doctors admitted themselves defeated. Failing to secure the services of Beata, they applied to the Prophet, who was at work in Lower Sandusky a month or so after quitting the Delawares. On 13 May he held forth in a crowded meeting, pronouncing "four of the best women in the nation" to be witches. The basis of the charges is unknown. It was proposed that the prisoners be executed that night or the next morning. This time the Prophet's antics aroused instant opposition, and his opponents were fortified by the providential arrival upstream of a Presbyterian missionary, Joseph Badger. The previous year he had been invited by the chiefs to serve the Wyandots, and as soon as he heard of the inquisition he fired off a protest. The accused were released, and the Prophet was frustrated.[19]

The Wyandots were dissatisfied, and turned to other witch-finders. In June Badger reported "great confusion among the Indians by reason of their dreams and prophets." He may have referred to the Seneca prophet, Handsome Lake, who was brought from New York sometime that year, or to Wyandot doctors such as Longhouse. Eventually the Wyandot witch-hunt, like the one on White River, would subside, only to be revived a few years later.[20]

Lalawéthika's ministry had begun inauspiciously. Neither the Delawares nor the Sandusky Wyandots would furnish many adherents to his cause in ensuing years. They regarded him with suspicion. If the witch-hunts had not advanced the Prophet's standing with the Indians, far less did they endear him to Americans. He passed into folklore and history alike as a malicious, dishonorable figure, a shifty charlatan exploiting the superstitious and lurking in the shadow of a noble brother.

Today we can be more charitable to Lalawéthika. The witch-hunts were not the creations of the Prophet, and however regrettable they were, to the Indians of that time—and it is only by their standards that he can fairly be judged—his purpose was commendable and his course rational. They believed that sickness was being caused by sorcery, and that its practitioners had to die to ensure the survival of the community.

The Prophet was not a likable man, but he was the voice of an oppressed people. Around him the tribes were losing almost everything—their lands, security, livelihoods, cultures, dignity and self-respect, even their very identities. Their villages were disintegrating, divided by factionalism, drunkenness, violence, and the erosion of communal values. The Prophet told them to be proud of their Indian heritages, proud and free, to unshackle themselves from the European economies by standing apart from the whites and rediscovering the self-reliance of the past and the richness of their own ways of life.

He may have been backward-looking, artless and prejudiced in his analysis, and predestined to fail, but at least he stood up for his people and tackled the problems that seemed about to accomplish their destruction.

10

SURELY GOD

IS IN THIS PLACE!

T hose who knew Tecumseh noticed the changes that came over him after his return to Ohio. Most obvious was the change in his appearance. Suddenly Tecumseh reminded older Indians of a past they had thought lost forever. He began to dress in a fashion that had been obsolete for at least half a century. The chief put aside his European shirts, the linen hunting frocks sometimes worn over them, and the cloth leggings, and commonly turned out in simple, neat and clean suits of soft deerskin—figure-hugging leggings gartered below the knee and long knee-length hunting shirts, the seams of both garments, and the hem, shoulders, and front opening of the latter, improved by tidily cut fringe. No longer were his frocks and his leather moccasins decorated with the beads and ribbons hawked by whites. Now he used the dyed quills of the porcupine.

Tecumseh was seldom entirely consistent. He saw no reason to disbelieve his brother's claim to represent the Great Spirit, and understood the argument against white manufactures. Indeed, sometimes he refused to handle European clothing, but passed it to others on a stick as if it were unclean. But he was far from a slavish adherent to the Prophet's religion, and his appearance was less that of a fanatic than that of a practical man balancing the benefits of the European trade system with the message of self-sufficiency. The blue or scarlet woolen breechcloths he fitted to a leather thong about his waist, the silk scarves he sometimes wound about his head, the silver ornaments and ear bobs, and the white shirts that now and again peeped from beneath his hunting frock: all indicated concessions to the white man's manufactures. So did the beloved silver-mounted tomahawk-pipe and the knives in their leather cases at the belt confining his waist, and the muskets that he continued to carry.

However, it was not in dress only that Tecumseh proclaimed his new religious leanings. The Shawnee chief was more discriminating about his food and drink. He was happy to eat native products, such as the potato, but demurred when served foreign dishes, and he quit drinking whiskey for good. His transformation was less dramatic than his younger brother's, but it was real nonetheless.[1]

Tecumseh also saw from the beginning that there was political capital to be made of the Prophet's crusade. Even as Lalawéthika hunted witches among the Delawares and Wyandots, and some of the band cleared the site at Greenville, an ambitious plan was forming in the minds of Tecumseh and his supporters. If Tecumseh was bringing his band back to Ohio and settling them at Greenville to worship the Great Spirit and reform themselves, why not reunite all the Shawnees there? Why not employ the powerful pulling power of the Prophet's religion to combine moral and cultural regeneration with the long-cherished dream of tribal reunification?

As they later explained to the Governor of Ohio: "The Shawnese have heretofore been scattered about in parties, which we have found has been attended with bad consequences. We are now going to collect them all together to one town [Greenville] that the chief [Tecumseh] may keep them in good order, and prevent drunkenness from coming among them, and try to raise corn and stock to live upon."[2] Omitting the reference to livestock and corn, doubtless introduced to please American officials interested in the "civilization" program, these words revealed that the ambitions of Tecumseh and the Prophet were high indeed.

Apart from the Shawnees in what is now Alabama and Missouri, in 1806 the tribe had villages on the White River in Indiana Territory (Tecumseh's), the Detroit River in Michigan Territory (Blue Jacket's), and at three sites in Ohio, Wapakoneta (Auglaize County) and Stony Creek and Captain Johnny's Town, within two miles of each other (Logan County). To bring them together would not only realize an old tribal ambition, but it would place them beneath the direction of Tecumseh, hitherto a minor chief, and his previously disregarded brother. The two were bidding for the blessings of the Great Spirit and tribal leadership at the same time.

Straightaway the brothers ran into opposition from the Shawnees of Wapakoneta. There, in a village of up to sixty houses sprawling on the upper Auglaize River, a tribal council of sorts operated under the head civil chief, Black Hoof. That council aborted the unification plan outright.

At the heart of the resistance was Black Hoof himself. He was a small, wizened old man, with a battle record that stretched back to the French and

Indian War (Seven Years' War), but his pride and ambition still flickered fiercely, and he was intelligent, articulate, and truly formidable in cut-and-thrust debate. Black Hoof, too, had longed to unite the Shawnees, but he was a Mekoche and intended to keep the traditional right of his division to handle the tribe's political affairs. The Mekoches had been created before all the other Shawnees, and none of the Kispokos, their "younger brothers," were going to deprive them of their just standing.[3]

There was more to Black Hoof's opposition than this, however. For also at issue between the Wapakoneta council and the Prophet and Tecumseh was the future direction of the Shawnee people.

Some historians have misrepresented Black Hoof as a corrupt chief, eager to cede land, take annuities, and increase his influence by controlling their distribution. There were such chiefs, but Black Hoof was not one of them. While the Shawnees received one thousand dollars in goods each year on account of the treaty of Greenville, Black Hoof was not always in control of the goods' allocation within the tribe, and in his own way he was as good a patriot as Tecumseh. A deep spiritual love of the Ohio country burned inside the little chief. He used to say the Great Spirit would not forgive the Shawnees if they ever gave up their lands, and after the treaty of Greenville he fought for those lands with great tenacity. Black Hoof did, indeed, reluctantly put his name to three additional treaties (in 1803, 1805, and 1808) but none violated Shawnee territorial rights, and the only additional annuities the tribe was entitled to receive were a salt delivery and a one-fifth—and usually unpaid—share in one thousand dollars granted under the 1805 treaty.

Black Hoof and his chiefs made trips to Washington in 1802, 1806, and 1808, but throughout they resisted attempts upon the land. "We have it with us, and shall so long as our nation will exist," they explained. Worried about the possibility of other Indians selling the territory from beneath their feet, they also pressed hard for a written statement of tribal boundaries. Shawnee limits, they said, were contained by a line running north from the head of the Mad River to the foot of the Maumee rapids, thence up the Maumee to Fort Wayne, and then south to the White River and east to the Great Miami before turning northeast to the starting point. The block of northwestern Ohio and eastern Indiana circumscribed by such a boundary carefully avoided Miami claims to the north of the Maumee and Wyandot claims east of the rapids, but it reclaimed, perhaps accidentally, the northwestern corner of the area ceded to the United States at Greenville.[4]

Black Hoof wanted to defend Shawnee land and rescue the tribe from poverty as much as Tecumseh and the Prophet, but he had a very different plan to achieve it. Although inherently conservative, he could see the hunt was failing, and believed that the Indians would have to adopt, at least in part, the "civilization" policies recommended by American officials and missionaries. He therefore lobbied for both tools and instructors so that his people could improve their farming, raise livestock, and fence fields.

In 1806, when the Prophet and Tecumseh made their bid for Shawnee support, the project of the Wapakoneta chiefs was beginning to bear fruit. The American government envisaged that once the Indians developed a prosperous farming economy they would sell surplus hunting grounds, and that most of their weapons would eventually be exchanged for plowshares and spinning wheels. The United States promised Black Hoof aid. In 1807 William Kirk of the Baltimore Quakers came west with six thousand dollars of government money to promote "civilization." The summer brought him to Wapakoneta, where he inaugurated a brief period of successful development. In 1809 John Johnston was able to report that Kirk was "much loved" by the Shawnees and "the settlement bears the marks of industry and on the whole does him much credit."[5]

Readers will now understand why Black Hoof and his supporters had so little time for the Prophet and Tecumseh. The two Kispokos, neither of them a member of the tribal council, were building a village which they openly avowed would become the new Shawnee capital in Ohio. The Prophet, despite his professed reverence for tradition, was flatly challenging the ancient leadership of the Mekoches, and, what was more, he was offering a different vision of the Shawnee future. They must live as of old, the Prophet said, not debase themselves by imitating the whites and risking the displeasure of the Great Spirit. Black Hoof said the hunt was finished and the Indians must become farmers, but the Prophet insisted the game would return if the spirits were appeased and the Indians hunted for their own subsistence and not at the behest of white traders. As for farming, it struck at one of the proudest of Shawnee traditions: the path of the warrior, which every boy had been taught to honor. Black Hoof would emasculate the Shawnee men, making them labor in the fields like the women.

The battle between the Wapakoneta chiefs and the Shawnee brothers was more than a sordid power struggle between ambitious men. It was a sincerely fought contest for the hearts and minds of the Shawnee people.

Black Hoof's opposition smashed an irreparable hole in Tecumseh's plan to unify the Shawnees around his brother's teachings. Many of the Shawnees were also extremely suspicious of the Prophet and his disciples. While Lalawéthika was with the Delawares in March 1806, an old Shawnee prophetess undertook to stand in his moccasins. She said she too had been visited by Waashaa Monetoo, and he wanted the tribe to assemble on the Great Miami and sing one of the Prophet's songs by day and eat by night. Perhaps she supposed that the apocalypse of which the Prophet had spoken was at hand. In any case, her intervention proved embarrassing. For several days some Shawnees abandoned Wapakoneta for the appointed spot, but they returned disillusioned when the predictions turned out to be false.

Returning from the Wyandots, the Prophet tried to regain lost ground. On 16 June there was an eclipse of the sun, which lasted for several minutes. Far and wide Indians pondered the meaning of such a powerful portent. Lalawéthika used it to his advantage: he maintained that Waashaa Monetoo was fulfilling the Prophet's promise to provide a sign. Unfortunately, even this impressive demonstration failed to induce the Wapakoneta Shawnees to break ranks with Black Hoof.[6]

Tecumseh and the Prophet failed to convince the most important band of northern Shawnees, but they were successful with the smaller villages. An early convert was Quatawapea (Man on the Water Who Sinks and Rises Again), widely known as Lewis. He was older than Tecumseh, a well-formed, handsome man, and elegantly dressed, and he was a good hunter. Although he was the headman of the small band of Mekoches, Chillicothes, and Mingoes who had joined Tecumseh on Stony Creek, he had not been a strong warrior, and owed his place on the tribal council to the fact that he had accompanied the Shawnee delegation to Washington in 1802. He never stopped showing everyone the medal he had received from the President on the occasion. As late as 1812 John Johnston characterized him as merely "a minor chief of little importance." Lewis belonged to the turtle clan, the clan of Tecumseh's mother, and he was a personal friend of the Kispoko brothers. He put his band behind their movement, but didn't lend much weight.[7]

The other Shawnee band that threw in with Tecumseh and his brother was led by a very different man. Up to the middle of 1806 Black Hoof's party could dismiss the Kispokos as unrecognized pretenders. The Prophet had but one voice on the tribal council—Lewis's—and it was one to which few people listened. Then, suddenly, a man of unquestioned standing came out of retirement to stand with the reformers. He was the greatest Shawnee war chief in living memory: Weyapiersenwah, the redoubtable Blue Jacket.

Blue Jacket had been the most important leader of the northwestern confederacy of the 1790s. He had personally carried the ideal of pan-Indianism to the tribes on the Mississippi, and commanded the forces that had overthrown two American armies. It was Blue Jacket who had been the principal Indian architect of the treaty of Greenville.

An unlikely recruit for the Prophet in some ways, Blue Jacket was one of the most sophisticated and entrepreneurial of all Shawnees. Related to French-Canadian traders through intermarriage, he had built up herds of cattle in his day and ran a store, selling to the Indians goods he had purchased from his friends in Detroit. He drank heavily, and was accustomed to living in the manner of the whites, with stout frame houses and such conveniences as four-poster beds and silver spoons. Some of his children were

educated in schools the whites had established for themselves, and he enjoyed fraternizing with British and American officers. No simple woodsman
was Blue Jacket, but an accomplished Indian diplomat and soldier with ex-
pansive views.

For some years now Blue Jacket had lived in semiretirement in his own
village on the Detroit River, in what the Americans had designated Michigan
Territory in 1805. He was no longer the striking figure of old, swaggering at
the peak of his influence, in a scarlet uniform coat. In 1806 Blue Jacket was
old and fat, and he seldom bothered to take his seat on the tribal council.
Why, then, did such a materially minded man as this suddenly declare for
the simple back-to-basics philosophy of the Prophet?

Probably Blue Jacket was looking for ways to regain his preeminence.
Always a vain, ambitious man, he had been trying to put himself at the head
of a new pan-Indian confederacy for some years, and had visited tribes on
the Mississippi and Illinois Rivers in 1801 and 1803. Moreover, there was little love between Blue Jacket and Black Hoof. In 1795 Black Hoof and other
Mekoches had been infuriated when Blue Jacket represented himself to
General Wayne as the head Shawnee chief, when he was, they said, merely
a "younger brother" (probably a Pekowi) and had no right to speak for the
nation in times of peace. The supremacy Blue Jacket had enjoyed as the
principal Shawnee war chief should have passed to the Mekoche civil chiefs
after the treaty of Greenville, but for some time he had blithely sustained his
wartime status. His impudence had been neither forgotten nor forgiven.[8]

Whatever his reasons, Blue Jacket's intervention was a big setback for
the Wapakoneta chiefs. The aging warrior was still a man of great prestige
and experience, and at his home on the Detroit he was in exactly the right
place to intercept the tribal treaty annuities, which were issued in Detroit
from 1805. If Blue Jacket sequestered the bulk of those annuities for the rival bands—his own, and those of Tecumseh and Lewis—he could badly un-
dermine the authority of Black Hoof and his fellow chiefs.

Blue Jacket was the most important Indian to support the Kispoko
brothers in those early days of the Prophet's ministry, and he was soon being spoken of as the head of the group. Yet even with his support, Tecumseh
could not overcome the obduracy of the Wapakoneta Shawnees. The plan to
unite the tribe was strangled at birth.

However, there were early indications that Indians of other tribes might
be more receptive to Lalawéthika's message, and the brothers gained a particularly respected ally among the local Wyandots. Stayeghta (the Bark Carrier) was generally known as Roundhead. He was then about fifty years old,
a tall, straight man with a broad chest and dark complexion. Sometimes he
wore his black hair long about his shoulders, but when he reduced it to
the scalp lock it accentuated the bullet head that gave him his nickname.

Roundhead was the ideal friend for Tecumseh. He had been a significant war chief of the great confederacy during the 1790s, and was uncommonly spirited and steadfast in battle. But he was also a sensible and competent politician. Good in company, he drank modestly. After the treaty of Greenville, which he signed, he had maintained his own village on the upper Scioto, in present-day Hardin County, Ohio, and helped arbitrate many of the difficulties that subsequently developed between Indians and whites in the area. Evidently he had originally belonged to a band of Wyandots living near the Aux Canard River in Upper Canada, but, like Tecumseh, he had the leadership and independence to form his own party, and achieved a reputation for honesty and ability on both sides of the frontier. Both Roundhead and his younger brother, Splitlog, became lifelong friends and allies of Tecumseh.[9]

One thing Black Hoof, Tecumseh, and the Prophet agreed upon: the need for peace with their white neighbors. The plans of the Wapakoneta chiefs to stay in Ohio depended upon their ability to preserve good relations with the new state.

As for the Kispoko brothers, they had put themselves within easy reach of the American settlements. Upstream the first white settlers of Stony Creek were building their homes among the plains and white oaks, while nearby the Mad River was being spotted with American homesteads. Tecumseh and his brother were planning to move closer still, to Greenville Creek, several miles across the boundary, on lands which the treaty of Greenville had ultimately reserved for the United States. A gesture of defiance, affirming the brothers' opposition to Indian land sales? Maybe, though at this time Tecumseh was still taking his share of the treaty annuities being paid for that territory. The Prophet said Waashaa Monetoo had commanded him to the spot, which implies that the idea had come to him in a dream.[10]

Certainly Tecumseh intended no hostilities against the whites. Shawnees did not put their families in the front line if they expected fighting, and the war scare of 1807 would quickly cause the brothers to abandon the Greenville site. No, the new village was to be a religious center, inducing internal Indian reform. The Prophet believed that the whites had contaminated native culture, but he did not want a war. Rather, he counseled coexistence until such time as Waashaa Monetoo chose to overthrow the Americans in some cataclysm and restore the lands to his obedient red children.

It is important for readers to recognize this, because historians have generally failed to distinguish between the Shawnee brothers and a more militant resistance movement developing farther west. On the upper Mississippi various tribes were trying to revive the military confederacy of the 1790s. Again there was talk of the dish with one spoon—the idea that the land was not owned by one group but by all Indians in common, and could not be alienated except by the consent of all. Again there was talk of a united attack on American forts.

The Indians involved were motivated by regional concerns. Foremost was the frightening growth of American power. The United States had usurped Spain's control of the west bank of the Mississippi, and it had established Fort Dearborn (Chicago) and now spoke of erecting other posts among the Dakota Sioux. William Henry Harrison's land purchases vividly demonstrated what might follow. They climaxed in the treaty of St. Louis in 1804, when several million acres in Illinois, Wisconsin, and Missouri were unjustly stripped from the Sacs. The cession even included the site of the tribe's principal village, Saukenuk, at the mouth of the Rock River. Small wonder that a Potawatomi described the United States as a hungry beast, "the white devil with his mouth wide open."[11]

There were also running difficulties between American settlers on the Illinois and the Mississippi and the Kickapoos and Sacs, and in 1806 the governor of the Territory of Upper Louisiana, James Wilkinson, had threatened to deprive the Sacs of trade goods and dispatched an unsuccessful military expedition to Saukenuk.

Encouraged by Dakota "war" pipes, the Sacs tried to form a confederacy. In 1805 they claimed it included members of ten nations, of which the Sacs, Foxes, Dakotas, Kickapoos, Potawatomis, Ojibwas, Ottawas, and probably the Winnebagos and Menominees were part. It soon hit difficulties. In the west many tribes were riven by old animosities, and farther east, where Indians were more obviously within the shadow of American power, there was less enthusiasm for a confrontation. On the Detroit River, Wyandots, Shawnees, and Delawares rejected appeals from the western confederates, and in 1805 and 1806 delegations to Fort Malden in Upper Canada failed to win British encouragement. Still, the westerners persisted into 1807, when some American officials confused their activities with those of the Prophet and Tecumseh.

In Ohio the Shawnee brothers worked independently of the Sac initiative. They had no plan to attack the United States—not yet. In 1806 they merely wanted to be left alone to build their new town and worship the Great Spirit, but inevitably misunderstandings developed. There were Indian runners plying the paths between the White River, Stony Creek, and Greenville, and warriors in paint and feathers conferring at the camp on Stony Creek. Local American settlers grew surprised and alarmed. Some homesteaders abandoned Stony Creek for the Mad River, where panic spread and the people forted up in various places. Despite heavy rain, sentinels were put out.

On 17 February an Indian council at Stony Creek was interrupted by the approach of three well-known backcountrymen. They were Thomas Moore, a militia officer, James McPherson, once a captive of the Indians but now a respected trader and interpreter, and Simon Kenton. They had been sent to find out what the Indians were doing.

Their action was entirely sensible, but they caught the Indians at an inconvenient time, and did not receive a fulsome reception. The trio were signaled away from the council fire, and were preparing to leave without further discussion when the Indians invited them into one of the houses. There, a "chief" gave the whites some wampum as a token of friendship and disavowed any hostile intentions. Indeed, the chief, who may have been Tecumseh, promised to meet and reassure the settlers in four days' time. Nonetheless, when Moore's party left "almost all [the Indians] gave us their left hand in a very cool manner." Moore was unimpressed, and soon had a report, his second, speeding to the state governor in Chillicothe.[12]

Edward Tiffin was only three years into his governorship, but when Moore's messengers kept him from his bed at the dead of night, babbling that the settlements were breaking up and that the Indians would be in Chillicothe by the end of the week, he stayed calm. He doubted the Shawnees were in a position to make war, and he seized upon the fact that Moore's party had been offered no violence. In reply, he reminded Moore of his powers to raise the militia, but warned him to act only in self-defense and to avoid provocation. Moore should meet the Indians again, as planned, and the Governor sent him a fine belt of white wampum to give them as a gesture of goodwill. He also forwarded a speech assuring the Indians of his favor and pledging that he would consider any grievances they put before him.

Tiffin had judged the situation soundly. In fact, the Shawnees were just as alarmed as the settlers. Frightened by rumors that the militia were turning out, Shawnee leaders from both Stony Creek and Wapakoneta met on 19 February to compose an address to the whites. Lewis and the Wapakoneta chiefs recalled the friendship they had pledged to President Jefferson four years before in Washington, and blamed the trouble on mischievous reports of some Delawares and Ottawas. They said the Indians had offered Moore's party the left hand, contrary to Shawnee custom, because it was nearer the heart, and in addition to sending the Governor their white peace wampum they promised to visit him at Chillicothe.

Restraint on both sides restored equanimity. Two chiefs and an interpreter met local settlers two days later to renew their reassurances, and on 20 March Tecumseh's band made a formal reply to Tiffin's speech. The Indi-

ans were not interested in war, they explained, but had "things . . . more important than that to mind, which is to believe in God." They approved of the
Governor's speech, but Moore's speedy recourse to the militia worried them,
and they recommended that "good men" be "appointed" to "live near" the
Indians to understand them.[13]

Tecumseh knew that ill-considered gossip could quickly poison relations
with the whites, and he was angry when he learned the following June that
the Black Hoof party had been denouncing the Prophet to William Wells,
the Indian agent at Fort Wayne, and urging that he be driven from
Greenville before he drew the Shawnees into conflict with the settlers. This
was a song Wells was prepared to sing, and not he only, for Tecumseh heard
that other associates of Black Hoof also were defaming his band. These included the middle-aged French-Canadian trader and interpreter François
Duchouquet, a quiet and honest if ill-educated man, and Frederick Fisher.
Fisher, a former captive of the Shawnees, had recently transferred his trading activities from Indiana Territory to Ohio, and was regularly about the
Shawnee towns.[14]

Tecumseh's anxiety increased in August when Blue Jacket came to Stony
Creek from Detroit, where he had spoken to Governor William Hull of
Michigan Territory. In those parts the settlers were alarmed lest the hostile
Indians of the west, those forming a confederacy against the United States,
should agitate the Lakes Indians. Malicious rumors—started by Black Hoof,
Wells, or anyone else—could soon tar Tecumseh's band with similar ill designs toward the settlers and threaten the new town that was being laboriously raised at Greenville. It was time for the Stony Creek Shawnees to
fulfill their promise to talk to Governor Tiffin.[15]

Three chiefs made this first journey to Chillicothe—Blue Jacket, the
principal speaker, Tecumseh, and Lewis—along with two interpreters—one
of them Blue Jacket's twenty-five-year-old son, George, who had been
schooled in Detroit, the other James Logan. Lewis wore the silver medal
and chain he had received from Jefferson in 1802. On one side the medal
bore the President's image. On the other the two hands clasped in friendship
beneath the motto "Peace and Friendship" symbolized the purpose of the
current mission.

The mission seems to have been a success, for Tiffin was a reasonable
man. The meeting took place on 11 August 1806. The Indians explained that
they were being vilified by the Wapakoneta chiefs and others, and that their
only purpose was to unite the Shawnees at Greenville and remain at peace
with the Americans. Lewis displayed his medal, and the chiefs said that they
also intended to visit Detroit to clear up any misunderstandings about them
there.[16]

And it is probable that Blue Jacket did so. He did even more, for the

Shawnee treaty annuities were being issued at Detroit and Blue Jacket went away with more of them than the Blue Jacket–Tecumseh–Lewis bands deserved, at least according to Black Hoof.[17]

By the spring of 1807 relations between the rival Shawnee factions had sunk to an all-time low. In the winter Black Hoof had led another delegation to Washington. The Prophet and Tecumseh distrusted the little Mekoche headman intensely, and quite unjustly suspected he was engaged in selling more Indian land to the United States. However, he *was* seeking instructors to improve the efficiency of Shawnee agriculture, instructors the Kispoko reformers regarded as taskmasters who would turn the warriors into women and put them to work in the fields. When the Quaker William Kirk called at Wapakoneta that spring, on his way to Fort Wayne, the Prophet saw him as a harbinger of an unhappy future.[18]

Lalawéthika struck back angrily, turning his reputation as a witch-finder to political account by denouncing his enemies as sorcerers. In April 1807 two of Black Hoof's party were murdered by supporters of the Prophet. Lalawéthika then accused four more Wapakoneta men, including three influential leaders—Black Hoof himself, the noted war chief Blacksnake, and Butler, whose father, Richard Butler, had traded at Shawnee villages before perishing as second-in-command of St. Clair's army in 1791. This was a dangerous, even a foolish, move on the part of the Prophet, for had such men been killed their kin would have retaliated, and the Shawnees might have been plunged into civil war. Fortunately for both parties, no attempt was made against the Wapakoneta chiefs.[19]

Eighteen moons after the Prophet's first visions, the dream of a nation united beneath the benedictions of the Great Spirit had shattered upon the grim reality of two armed factions with different visions of the future in open and ugly defiance.

In truth the Kispoko brothers were not interested in war, with either Indians or whites. Through 1806 a labor of love was occurring in western Ohio, a few miles south of the treaty line that marked unceded from ceded Indian country. Here Mud Creek flowed into Greenville Creek, slipping by the scarred acres of ground on which the ruins of Wayne's old fort still crumbled. At the point of land where the two creeks met, a place which Americans would one day name Tecumseh's Point, many Shawnee men and women toiled to a common purpose. They were building a town, a special town where believers could live and worship in peace. About September, their work was finished.[20]

The village rested between the point and a large prairie sprinkled with groves of oak. The women had erected fifty-seven houses, but the pride of the community was the enormous council house that rose upon a hill in their midst. From it Tecumseh could see the ruins of Fort Greenville, some three miles to the north, while to the west and east were extensive views over the rolling prairie.

The council house itself had been built by both sexes. It ran 150 feet east to west and was 34 feet wide. Three parallel rows of carefully hewn posts, the center row higher than the others, supported crossbeams that formed a pitched roof. "Even the weight poles on the roof were neatly hewed," wrote one visitor, "and everything looked new and white." Each of the four walls had an entrance in the middle, while inside, peeled logs ran along the sides as seats and the earth floor was beaten into a level and hard surface and swept clean. Between the posts in the center two trammels facilitated cooking, while the fuel for the fires was stored neatly in the northeast and southwest corners of the room.[21]

Nearer the point was further evidence of the deep spirituality and industry which pervaded the settlement. Roundhead's Wyandots had pitched a collection of tents around an open-air religious ground almost the same dimensions as the Shawnee council house. Two parallel rows of logs extended east-west, and many smaller logs were scattered about as additional seating. A large tent with open sides stood nearby, perhaps to offer shelter in bad weather.

The Shawnee women had planted maize on the margins of the prairie, enclosing some fields with pole fences—an unusual arrangement—and they harvested a crop that year.

It was to this village, emerging from the winter snows, that three strangers came on 23 March 1807. They were whites, but unlike any who had come before, for they were Richard McNemar, Benjamin Youngs, and David Darrow, brothers of the United Society of Believers, known as Shakers. Today, when few Shakers survive, the name is apt to suggest highly priced antique furniture, but in Tecumseh's day this Protestant monastic sect was expanding vigorously from its base in the state of New York. A new Shaker community had been established at Turtle Creek, Ohio, some seventy miles from Greenville.

The Shakers, so called because of the peculiar rocking motion they employed in worship, knew all about being ridiculed and persecuted for faith. Their founder, Mother Ann Lee, whom they believed to be a female Christ, had died in 1784 after being wounded by a mob. Now Brothers McNemar, Youngs, and Darrow came to Greenville to learn rather than to preach, and to encourage rather than to condemn. They did not regard the Indians as superstitious pagans. Rather they suspected that God's word appeared to them exactly as it had come to others, through chosen prophets and revelations, and the more they listened to common denunciations of this Indian named the Prophet the more they recognized the same prejudices they had often met themselves. "We began to feel a great concern for them [the Indian reformers], which continually increased on our minds with great weight," the Shakers wrote. "At length the situation and need of help became so urgent and impressive that we could feel no longer justified without going to see them and seek out the truth of the matter." Thus developed this bizarre expedition. Three white men, ignoring all ill-natured reports, came to the Prophet to offer help.

Tecumseh and Lalawéthika were with many of their people at a sugar camp four miles from their village the day the Shakers arrived, and it was on a casual trip back that Tecumseh heard about the unusual visitors. They were speaking to Peter Cornstalk, one of only two resident Indians who understood English, who was telling them that the Shawnees were "brothers" of the whites and the Prophet was merely teaching "us the way to be good."

Tecumseh was proud of the good relations he had established with Tiffin, and wanted to show the Shakers a paper he had got from the Governor, so he sent word for them to wait while he rummaged through his possessions for the testimonial. Then the chief mounted his horse and led the visitors to the sugar camp, stopping briefly on the way to converse with three Indians they encountered, all "very solemn and under the fear of God, loving and kind-spirited." At their destination the Shakers watched Tecumseh go into a large tent, where he remained about an hour talking to the Prophet and others. Lalawéthika had been sick for some time, had a bad headache and could not sit up, and he was reluctant to see the Shakers. Eventually the literate George Blue-Jacket was sent out to find what they wanted.

George wanted to know whether the whites had come to scoff. "His preaching is different from the white people," explained George. "The ministers of the white people don't believe what he says. They call it foolishness—what he believes in, and we don't like to tell them much about it because they don't understand what it means."

The Shaker brethren understood. "We are not those kind of ministers," they said. "We are a people that are separated from them by the work of the Great Spirit. They count us foolish too, and speak against us."

George asked if they believed a man could know God without reading books. Yes, replied the Shakers. In fact the best way to learn was from the heart. George told them that the Prophet was "seeing more and more wonderful things" but cautioned: "I cannot tell you the wonderful strange things which he speaks so you can understand me. I cannot interpret to you what he says." The Shakers accepted that such was the case, but required him to tell the Prophet that they, too, believed he was doing the work of the Good Spirit. They were not like other ministers.

For perhaps an hour the Shakers sat patiently around a fire in the gathering dusk. Eventually George reemerged and sat with them. The Prophet, smoking a large pipe, followed him and also took a seat. He "appeared under great sufferings and in deep labour and distress of mind, and not under any real bodily disorder," wrote Brother Youngs. After a silence the Prophet spoke for half an hour with his eyes closed and his face set solemn. "About five and twenty men were in and about the tent paying attention, five of whom George told us were Delaware chiefs who had come to hear the Prophet. At every remarkable pause of sentence a solemn assent sounded through ye tent in the word 'Seguy,' which signified their approbation of the things that were spoken."

The words could not be translated, but the Shakers were deeply impressed nonetheless. They ascertained that the Indians accepted that Waashaa Monetoo had once made himself known through Christ, and explained that Shakers believed that "the good people" he had made had now gone and men had grown cruel and unjust. Now, "wherever the Good Spirit works they will hate it and call it foolishness and nonsense, and speak against it." But, they went on, God had promised to raise up witnesses to lead people back to virtue. Such a person had been Mother Ann, but while "many believed" and "were obedient and put away all their sins and wicked ways," others derided the mission. The visitors added that they were sure the Prophet was another such witness, and "the time was come" for God to reclaim his Indian people. "We knew it was the work of the Great and Good Spirit, and we were come to encourage them and to help them," they wrote.

Lalawéthika seemed to appreciate what was said before he retired for the night, leaving George to give the Shakers the history of the Prophet's ministry. The visitors shared a communal meal—boiled turkey passed around in a large wooden bowl followed by a broth made from it—with thirty warriors and their women and children, and marveled at the "uncorrupted manners and unaffected modesty and simplicity" of the women, "not to be found among the whites."

But the most poignant moment was the evening prayer. The Indians believed that the Great Spirit was most accessible at the rising and setting of the sun, and Skelawway, the Prophet's cousin, stood in an open place at the center of the camp and spoke powerfully for fifteen minutes or so, while the people in their various tents greeted every pause with a solemn cry of approbation. A full moon above the horizon seemed to electrify the scene, and as the excited Shakers listened to Skelawway's voice carrying far into the night and that final low shout passing from tent to tent, they were reminded of the reverential words of Jacob: "How terrible is this place! Surely God is in this place and the world know it not!"

That night the whites slept on puncheons beside a fire back in the village, but they were up before daylight visiting Blue Jacket, "the principal chief" of the community. The Indians described their efforts to banish drunkenness and other vices, and answered many questions the visitors fired at them:

Q: Does he [the Prophet] say anything against fornication? You know what that is, viz. young men and women being together in the carnal works of the flesh? [Shakers are celibate.]

A: Oh yes. From seven years old he can tell it all.

Q: What do those do who have been wicked when they believe The Prophet?

A: They confess all that they have done.

Q: Who do they confess to?

A: To The Prophet and four chiefs in council.

Q: Do they confess all the bad things they have done and lay open their whole life?

A: Yes. From seven years old they confess all, and cry and tremble when they do it.

The Shakers breakfasted on turkey, broth, and wheat-flour cakes, and listened to the morning prayer. Again it was delivered by Skelawway, who stood on a log at the southeastern comer of the town at daylight and spoke for an hour, pausing only to secure the same cries of agreement from the houses the visitors had heard before. The Shakers also examined the council house, which they learned was used for communal meals as well as worship and debate.

That day five more whites arrived, sent from the settlements to search for signs of Indian hostility, but for their part the Shakers had no doubts. They left a letter for the Prophet, opining that "the same Good Spirit is working in you and in us" and inviting him to Turtle Creek, and they donated ten dollars to help the Indians buy supplies.

Although early commentators believed the Kispoko brothers were influenced by the Shakers, there is no evidence that they understood, let alone adopted, any of their principles. However, they recognized genuine goodwill when they saw it, and contacts between Greenville and Turtle Creek continued. Two Shakers were in the Indian town again in August, watching Lalawéthika lead an all-night meeting, and in May and August parties of Shawnees observed the Shaker services at Turtle Creek. The second Indian visit, when a Shawnee named Nancy (probably Blue Jacket's half-white daughter) interpreted, may have been motivated by a need for provisions. The first party had returned from Turtle Creek with twenty-seven horse-loads.[22]

Like Governor Tiffin, the Shakers had disregarded popular tittle-tattle, and seen the Shawnees for themselves. The Shakers missed much in the Prophet's doctrines, particularly his nativism, but they were profoundly moved by his simple, hardworking, self-sustaining community of some two hundred adults, peaceful, temperate, and godly, sharing what they had and enriching their souls at the expense of material wealth.

It formed a powerful contrast with the neighboring white settlements, of which the Shakers despaired. At Greenville, at least, they felt "the very air filled with His fear and a solemn sense of eternal things, and this light shines in darkness, and the darkness comprehends it not."

Among the Shakers the Prophet had found friends.

11

PROPHETS AND
PILGRIMS

Despite the orderly community at Greenville, the Prophet was disappointed by his mission to the Shawnees. The villages of Black Hoof and Captain Johnny remained hostile, and even Lewis and most of his people declined to move to the new town. That spring a few Delawares from the White River visited Greenville, but hardly any of them would eventually count themselves disciples, and only Roundhead's Wyandots provided substantial reinforcements.

Still, north and west, on the shores and rivers of the Great Lakes, were the villages of the populous peoples of the Three Fires, the Ojibwas, Ottawas, and Potawatomis, powerful tribes that had repulsed the incursions of the imperial Iroquois over a century before, and been the mainstay of the old French regime, while west toward the upper Mississippi dwelt Kickapoos, Potawatomis, Sacs, Foxes, Winnebagos, and Menominees. It was to these Indians that the Prophet sent his messengers early in 1807, inviting them to hear him preach at Greenville.

They came. During April alone four hundred men, women, and children—Potawatomis from the St. Joseph, Ottawas from the Grand River, and Ojibwas and Ottawas from Michilimackinac—passed through Fort Wayne in Indiana Territory on their way to the Prophet. Lalawéthika's heralds had done their work well, spreading curiosity the length of the Michigan peninsula, and the best efforts of William Wells at Fort Wayne could not dissuade them from continuing.[1]

The numbers flocking into Greenville seem to have taken even the

Prophet and Tecumseh by surprise. At this time of the year food was scarce. A handful of the northern people were allowed to remain, but most were sent away with the promise that the Prophet would have more to say at harvesttime, when there would be plenty to eat. Lalawéthika seems to have grasped the impracticabilities of holding open house, because he told one important Ottawa to urge each village to send two or more of its leading men as representatives so that he could instruct them and send them home to proselytize. By entertaining and preparing disciples, who would return to their towns, Lalawéthika could spread his word without being inundated by pilgrims.

Long into the nineteenth century people around the Great Lakes remembered the excitement of that time, and told many stories about it. Stories of hundreds of Ojibwas abandoning the southern shores of Lake Superior for the Indian Mecca, and of the hundreds who died of disease and starvation on their pilgrimage, and the few who returned, shrunken in body and spirit. Of the lakeside at La Pointe (Wisconsin) strewn with medicine bags rejected at the instance of the Prophet and washed up after being thrown into the deep. And of the fleet of Ojibwa canoes that left La Pointe with the body of a dead child they hoped the Prophet would restore to life. Somewhere behind these doubtlessly exaggerated stories lay a kernel of truth. Fortunately, we do not need to use these traditions; we can trace the Prophet's mission in the north from more reliable, contemporary, sources which preserve vivid pictures of its course and evolution.[2]

First, the Ottawa town of Arbre Croche (Michigan), more than four hundred miles north of Greenville. On 4 May the Trout, brother of the principal chief there, was back from the Prophet, enthusing in full council. He delivered a speech from the Prophet, accompanied by strings of white and blue wampum which Lalawéthika had said should pass "all round the earth." It appears that the Prophet was now describing himself as the reincarnation of the first man ever created, and his speech, while containing the common injunctions, betrayed a sharper anti-Americanism.

This hostility was expressed in colorful terms that Shawnees would have easily recognized. As long ago as 1752, when the tribe had been resisting French expansion into the Ohio country, a Shawnee orator had declared that the British, but not the French, had been made by the Great Spirit. The French were the progeny of evil spirits. Later, Mekoche speakers had admitted all whites to be the children of Waashaa Monetoo, but whereas the Indians had been made from his brain, the whites were manufactured from the "inferior" parts of the body such as the hands and feet. Now, the Prophet proclaimed the Indians, Spaniards, French, and British to be the work of the Great Spirit, but not the Big Knives: "the Americans I did not make [he quoted the Creator]. They are not my children, but the children of the Evil

Spirit. They grew from the scum of the great water, when it was troubled by the Evil Spirit [the malevolent sea monster of Shawnee myth], and the froth was driven into the woods by a strong east wind. They are numerous, but I hate them. They are unjust. They have taken your lands, which were not made for them."[3]

This differentiation between the Americans and other whites indicates that the Prophet's antagonism originated less in the contamination of Indian cultures, of which the British were no less guilty, than in resentment at American land policy.

Some explanation of the Prophet's outburst is offered by Letourneau, an important Ojibwa chief who left Greenville soon after the Trout, and who reported many rumors then circulating among the Ohio Shawnees. From the Mississippi had come stories of a forthcoming war that would pit Spain and Britain against the United States, a war that would inevitably embroil the Indians, and the Wapakoneta chiefs who had just returned from Washington were said to have been told, among other things, that after the present year the Americans would stop issuing treaty annuities until the Indians sold more land.[4]

Although the Prophet condemned Big Knives above all others, he continued to preach racial separatism generally. He even advised Indians to avoid shaking hands with white people and to pay traders only half the prices they asked so as not to be cheated. However, he stopped short of inciting hostilities, and advised the Indians to treat whites as brothers. The Prophet still expected his Creator to overthrow the whites for the Indians. He told the Trout that he had persuaded Waashaa Monetoo to postpone the destruction of the world for four years to give the Indians time to repent and reform, but then the Great Spirit would sweep across the land in two days of darkness, restoring the game and returning the Indians to their previous prosperity.

Nevertheless the Prophet's opinion of the United States was explosive at a time when many Indians, particularly those west of Lake Michigan, were being stirred by the war talk of the Sacs and Sioux and their confederates. The point was not lost upon Captain Josiah Dunham, who commanded the American post of Fort Michilimackinac, just north of Arbre Croche. He noted that the Prophet was urging the Indians to protect their traditional war dances, along with more innocent activities such as lacrosse, and he lost no time in sending speeches to the nearby Ottawas and Ojibwas debunking the Shawnee pretender.[5]

He achieved nothing, for the Trout left the Ottawas at Arbre Croche firmly in the grip of the new religion. They began throwing away European hats (Shawnees often referred to whites as "those who wear hats") and refusing whiskey, much to the dismay of traders. Said one of the latter that

September, "I saw upwards of sixty of them at one time together. Spirits, rum and whiskey was offered for nothing to them if they would drink, but they refused it with disdain."[6]

In May the Trout himself slipped by Dunham's fort and visited the Ojibwas on nearby St. Joseph Island, on the British side of the international boundary, and rumor had it that the chief danced among them with a war club painted red. Then, about June, he turned westward, pausing at Whitefish Point to conduct the first of a series of councils with Ojibwas along Lake Superior's long southern shoreline.[7]

Now we pass five hundred miles or more west, beyond Lake Superior into what is now central Minnesota, where a white man, John Tanner, was living with the Ojibwas in 1807. Tanner was hunting on the prairie when he saw a stranger approaching. The Indian was an Ojibwa, but "when he came up there was something very strange and peculiar in his manner," and at close quarters he would neither speak nor look Tanner in the eye. Tanner thought the stranger "crazy" but took him into his lodge, where he smoked silently for a while and then said he had brought a message from the Prophet.[8]

Astounded, Tanner listened to such commandments as killing dogs and throwing away medicine bags, flints, and steels, and to the extraordinary requirement that Tanner must always keep a fire burning in his wigwam. "If you suffer your fire to be extinguished," explained the messenger, "at that moment your life will be at its end." He stayed overnight, and the next morning Tanner pointed to the remains of their fire and scoffed at the futility of maintaining it at all times. But the stranger was undismayed. The Prophet was coming to shake hands with him, he said. Only when that happened would the injunctions come into force.

The Ojibwa stranger was in the area for some time, and made such progress that the village headman organized a day when the Indians could shake hands with the Prophet. For this the Ojibwa prophet and his assistants prepared a special lodge. The locals were led into it, and in the gloom they discerned a recumbent man-sized figure hidden under a blanket and guarded by two keepers. The effigy's guardians "made its bed at night . . . and slept near it" and suffered none but themselves to touch its blanket. The instructions of the Prophet were now solemnly repeated, and the listeners exhorted to obedience. The Ojibwa prophet then produced a string of old discolored beans and offered it to each Indian in turn, having them run it through their hands. They had now shaken hands with the Prophet and were subject to his commands.

Tanner admitted that such a climate did the Prophet's message create that even skeptics such as himself were obliged to make an outward show of compliance, and the religion spread to "the remotest Ojibbeways of whom I had any knowledge." But it soon subsided:

> For two or three years drunkenness was much less frequent than formerly; war was less thought of, and the entire aspect of affairs among them was somewhat changed by the influence of one man. But gradually the impression was obliterated, medicine bags, flints and steels were resumed; dogs were raised; women and children were beaten as before; and the Shawnee prophet was despised.

Tanner's narrative yields a good insight into the Prophet's use of Shawnee traditions. As we have seen, by throwing away their medicine bags the Indians were renouncing the spirits which had guided and governed them through life and accepting a new set of obligations from the Prophet. Since it was impossible for the Prophet to meet all of his followers personally, he circulated an effigy of himself. The Canadian Ojibwas learned that one effigy, representing half of the Prophet, had been sent north, and another, symbolizing the other half, was carried south. Contact with the figure, and shaking hands with it by means of the string of beans, indicated acceptance of his authority.

This effigy was modeled upon the most sacred Shawnee symbol of all, the tribal medicine bundle, given by the Great Spirit to the first Chillicothes. Sometimes described as an everlasting fire encased in a stone, the medicine bundle was guarded in its own lodge by two keepers, and on every important occasion it was consulted by Shawnee holy men. Even at the end of the nineteenth century the unwrapping of such a bundle involved the ceremony of running a string of beans through the hands of those present. In 1807 the tribal bundle seems to have been held by the Mekoches and Chillicothes. The Prophet would have loved to wrest this important source of spiritual power from the possession of his rivals, and he claimed the Mekoches had forfeited their right to its custody by mismanagement. He maintained that the office of keeper was a prerogative of the Kispoko and Chillicothe divisions and the turtle and panther clans, to which, of course, he was himself connected.

Failing to secure the tribal medicine bundle, the Prophet had created a new one in his own image. Like those of the original, its codes and powers derived from Waashaa Monetoo himself, rather than from inferior deities.[9]

Our last glimpse of this northern mission comes from early 1808 and takes us northwest into the lakes region of present-day Manitoba, where George Nelson traded with Ojibwas about the Dauphin River. Nelson attested to the influence of the Prophet upon the local natives, and the secrecy which shrouded the movement. Among the few details he salvaged were the Prophet's prohibitions on some uses of the drum and on the smoking of tobacco with any but a prescribed herb.[10]

As far as records tell, the religion of Lalawéthika spread farther than that of any predecessor, and not until the 1880s would a prophet of comparable influence, Wovoka of Ghost Dance fame, appear. While the Prophet's ideas passed north through the Ojibwas, other agents took them west, and there is evidence that ultimately they ascended the Missouri River to reach the Dakota and Lakota Sioux, the Poncas, Arikaras, and Mandans, and perhaps even the Blackfeet of Montana and Saskatchewan. Eventually Tecumseh took the religion south, to tribes in what is now Mississippi, Alabama, and Florida.[11]

In response many far-flung tribesmen made the journey to Greenville, including Sacs, Foxes, Kickapoos, Winnebagos, and Menominees. Some, like the Potawatomis of the River Huron (Michigan), left their corn standing in their eagerness to visit the great man, oblivious of the severe winter they would suffer in consequence.

But the weary pilgrims also brought tensions, and while the Prophet sent his religion afield, it was Tecumseh, the band chief, who dealt with the repercussions at home.

There was one man who invariably tested Tecumseh's patience to the limit: the Indian agent at Fort Wayne, William Wells. Wells was about thirty-seven years old, a handsome, bluff, energetic man who had been appointed five years before with orders to issue treaty annuities, promote "civilization" among the Indians, and further American interests generally. There are few more controversial figures than Wells. None disputed his influence with some Indians, or his knowledge of them. Captured by Miamis in 1784, he had spent several years as one of their warriors, and married a daughter of the great Miami war chief, Little Turtle. He was also busy and able, and undeniably a man of courage. Wells has had apologists, but many—rather too many—who knew him told a different story, a story of ambition, dishonesty, and corruption.

William Henry Harrison, the governor of Indiana Territory, suspected Wells of appropriating treaty money, and believed he "blended a disposition for intrigue and for the accumulation of property" inconsistent with his office. John Johnston, who ran the trading house at Fort Wayne, described Wells as "an unprincipled bad man" who defrauded both the Indians and his government, and it was Wells who the Quaker William Kirk blamed for the failure of his mission at Fort Wayne in 1807. The Delaware chief, Beaver, also complained about the agent, and in 1808 the secretary of war, Henry

Dearborn, would finally dismiss Wells after uncovering irregularities in his accounts.[12]

But during his peak Wells fired letter after letter to the War Department, partly, one suspects, to keep his name before the government. He felt bound by neither responsibility nor truth. In 1804 he even appears to have advertised his usefulness to the United States by forging a British document. It indicated that the British were tampering with the Indians, but regarded Wells as an obstacle to their designs!

In 1806, primed by Black Hoof's party, Wells turned his fire upon the Prophet. His ceaseless tirade against the reformers interwove accurate information, astute observation, outright invention, and irresponsible alarmism. Tecumseh and his brother regarded Wells as a serious problem, someone capable of undermining their relations with the whites by distortions and lies. They were not mistaken. On 31 March 1807 the agent had reopened his campaign by informing Dearborn that the Prophet's people were committing depredations upon settlers, that up to one hundred Indians at a time were drunk at Greenville, that they would not allow whites to occupy the ceded lands, and that the Prophet had invited the Lakes Indians to reside at Greenville. His solution was to urge the government to drive the Indians from their new town. He thus incited the United States to attack a peaceful but fanatical community, whose warriors, once inflamed, were capable of avenging themselves upon a sparsely settled and vulnerable frontier.[13]

April saw Wells coping with floods of Indians passing through Fort Wayne to see the Prophet. Interviewing the visitors, Wells found them entirely peaceable, and moderated his tone. Now the Prophet was not in "any ways dangerous," but he unsettled his neighborhood and his visitors would probably kill the settlers' livestock for food. On 22 April Wells invited the Prophet to incriminate himself. In a letter to Greenville, Wells charged the Indians with keeping the locals "in a continual state of uneasiness" as well as settling on land that belonged to the United States. In the name of the President, he requested the Prophet to quit Greenville. What is more, he demanded an answer in writing so that it could be put before the President. In short, the brothers should either remove or give written evidence of their refusal so that it could be held against them.

Tecumseh was having none of it. Anthony Shane brought the letter to Greenville, and found four hundred Indians there. He interpreted Wells's message in full council, but without consulting any of his followers Tecumseh replied decisively. He peremptorily sent Shane back to Fort Wayne to inform Wells that the Great Spirit himself had approved of the Indians' kindling their council fire at Greenville. If Wells had anything to say he should come himself, when Tecumseh would arrange for two respected whites of the area to attend and hear his charges. The chief asked Shane to bring Wells's answer.

By the time Wells got to replying he had a disappointing letter from Dearborn to digest. Dearborn failed to take the strong action the agent had recommended against the Prophet. He merely remarked that the Indians ought not to have been allowed to occupy Greenville, but if the agent's influence was insufficient to persuade them to remove he must apply to the governor of Indiana Territory.

Brief and restrained as Dearborn's note of 15 May was, Wells had Shane take it to Greenville as evidence of the President's disapproval of the settlement. This time Tecumseh lost his temper. After listening to Shane, the chief rose to deliver an impassioned harangue to his council. He was annoyed that the whites had seized so much Indian land. The Great Spirit did not recognize boundaries, and neither would he. Then he told Shane that if their Great Father the President had something to say he should send a man of note to deal with the Indians, for Tecumseh would have no further communications with this Wells.

Inspired by his brother, the Prophet rose with a typically reckless contribution. Why, he wished to know, did the government not send their greatest man to Greenville? The Prophet could cause darkness, or put the sun under his feet, and what white man could do this?[14]

At dusk on 25 May 1807 a man named John Boyer was burning logs in a field he had cleared by his cabin near the line between Champaign and Miami Counties in Ohio. A musket banged, and Boyer was hit. He started to run, but a second shot brought him down. With a yell a party of Indians fell upon him. They tomahawked and scalped him, and then disappeared into the forest. Boyer lay dead on his face. A few objects had been placed upon his body, a "death hammer," war feathers dyed black on one side, some hairs from what was believed to be the murdered man's scalp, pieces of birch bark, and a rattle made of deer hooves. This sinister display suggested that this was no casual atrocity but a coldly premeditated murder.

Two women and three children were in Boyer's cabin when he was cut down. They heard the shots and the Indian yell, and fled in terror two miles to their nearest neighbor. There, horrified occupants of another isolated cabin joined the flight, stumbling through the night for eight difficult miles to a second settlement. One old man fell exhausted and lay all night in the woods. The news reached Urbana the next morning and twenty men set off to recover what was left of Boyer.[15]

At first, suspicion fell upon some Indians who had wintered near Boyer's place, but it did not take long for fingers to point at the northern pilgrims tramping back and forth between Greenville and the Great Lakes, and some even accused the Black Hoof and Prophet parties of Shawnees of the murder. Tecumseh and his brother had endured a difficult winter, and they had just got rid of their northern visitors, apart from five warriors and a few women and children. But hopes of a more tranquil summer faded when a message from two militia officers, Thomas Moore and Benjamin Whiteman, arrived demanding information about the murder.

Roundhead replied on 6 June. He denied any "evil" intent on the part of the Greenville Indians, and brazenly accused Black Hoof of the killing. In his opinion the items left on Boyer's corpse had been intended to incriminate the Lakes Indians coming to Greenville. Roundhead offered to meet the officers if they brought an interpreter, and sent the news to his fellow tribesmen on the Sandusky. Roundhead's allegation showed that he believed Black Hoof capable of any trick that might injure the Prophet. It also damaged Black Hoof's campaign to maintain good relations with the Ohio settlers. The Wapakoneta head chief had already been investigating the murder, but when he was told of Roundhead's charge he moved quickly to clear the air. He urged the whites to keep calm, and through Whiteman arranged for them to meet both factions of Shawnees in a council.[16]

In fact neither group of Shawnees had been responsible for Boyer's death. Somewhere at the head of the Mad River, above Urbana, Tecumseh tried to clear his band in preliminary discussions with local settlers. It was a reasonably amicable meeting. Tecumseh and Simon Kenton exchanged yarns about their old skirmishes, and Kenton told the chief that Whiteman, the principal American spokesman, had also been in the party that Tecumseh had defeated back in 1792. The Shawnee chief strode over to Whiteman, jocularly slapped a hand on his shoulder, and remarked that he himself was the "better man" of the two "for he had whipped him when they were young men."[17]

The most important council was the one that brought the rival Shawnees together. It took place on 24 June at Springfield, then a tiny settlement of some eleven blockhouses and Griffith Foos's tavern. Each faction turned out sixty or more warriors, strong, heavily armed, and committed to defending their chiefs if words turned into blows. They agreed to stack their arms a few miles north of the town, where McBeth's cabin and Moore's gunshop sat across the road from each other, and assembled at the council ground in a maple grove just north of where the National Hotel would be built. William Ward and Whiteman, who commanded the militia, formed a substantial body of armed men into a hollow square around the council, ready for trouble.[18]

At first there was a difficult moment. Tecumseh walked into the council carrying his splendid silver-mounted tomahawk-pipe in his right hand and resting it carelessly upon his left arm. The militia officers fidgeted nervously, afraid to allow any weapons into the charged atmosphere. When they stopped Tecumseh and tried to remove the tomahawk, the chief declared he wanted to smoke. But the whites stood firm, and Tecumseh reluctantly surrendered the item, struggling to contain his anger. A Methodist preacher and schoolmaster named Nathaniel Pinckard stood close by, puffing as usual upon a stubby cob or clay pipe he was wont to carry even into his classroom. Seeing the altercation, he advanced affably and offered his pipe to Tecumseh. The Shawnee chief was dismayed at the miserable instrument, and still smarting at the loss of his own pipe, he glanced at the preacher and then took his pipe and effortlessly flicked it back over his head into the thickets to the amusement of some of the watchers.

Tecumseh resented the insult about the pipe and the bullying tactics employed by the militia throughout the council, but both he and Roundhead, who represented Greenville, knew that if their town was to survive they had to mollify the local whites and reconcile them to it. Black Hoof and Blacksnake spoke for Wapakoneta. Among their supporters were William Kirk, who had just begun work at Wapakoneta and who hoped to bring the two Shawnee factions together, and a man of a very different stamp. The younger Captain Johnny was a tall, big-boned, powerful Shawnee noted for violence and a vicious temper. James McPherson, known as Squa-la-ka-ke (the Red-Faced Man) interpreted for the Shawnees, and Isaac Zane, a man in his fifties, translated for the Wyandots.[19]

William Ward opened business. Physically he was not less impressive than Tecumseh. Tall and erect, broad of shoulder but slender and lithe, he had high cheekbones and auburn hair, which he sometimes tied into a queue. Ward was somewhat arrogant in manner, but he knew Indians well. One of his brothers had been that same John Ward mortally wounded alongside Tecumseh in the Paint Creek fight fourteen years before. Ward told the Indians that if they valued the lives and happiness of their women and children they must surrender the murderers of John Boyer or deliver as much information as they knew about the matter. This was nothing if not straight talk.

Black Hoof replied, holding a friendship medal he had received from the American President. All his warriors were at home when Boyer was killed, he said, but the items left on the body indicated the murderers were Ojibwas or other northern Indians. His remark that "from the many people that roam through the country it is hard for us to know them" clearly insinuated the guilt of Lakes Indians who had visited the Prophet.

In his letter to Whiteman and Moore, Roundhead had not only indicted Black Hoof of the murder, but had also undertaken to "show you the fellow" and to "point my finger to his breast." Ward now called upon the Wyandot chief to fulfill his boast. Roundhead refused to do so. Years later a member of the militia who was present painted a graphic picture of Roundhead rising to his feet to implicate Black Hoof, casting a look at the fuming and ferocious Captain Johnny, and then sinking back to his seat looking agitated. The contemporary record merely tells us that the Wyandot "refused" to charge Black Hoof, "but said that from *information* it was a chief of the Shawanese called Black Hoof. This was proven to be false since it is well known to two white men that on the day the murder was perpetrated he was at the town." This passage is somewhat contradictory, but taken with later reminiscent accounts, indicates that Roundhead declined to make a definitive accusation and prevaricated.

Tecumseh also spoke, rapidly and with great energy and fluency so that Dr. Richard Hunt, one of the observers, likened him to Henry Clay. The speech no longer exists, although witnesses described it as elegant and effective. The chief explained the motives of his community, and disavowed hostile intent or knowledge of the murder. According to the minutes Tecumseh stated "that he well knew that it was repugnant to the will of the Great Spirit to break friendship with the white people, and that if he knew the guilty he would give information, and desired all the Indians present to have the same resolution."

Neither Tecumseh nor Roundhead seem to have inflamed their quarrel with Black Hoof, and some kind of consensus was reached that no Shawnees were to blame. Blacksnake suspected a Potawatomi named Nannikissimo, who had wintered near Boyer's place and left the area only days after the crime. But another Indian, Thawaeasaca, piped up that he too had spent the winter about Boyer's and that relations between the Indian hunters and the settlers had been nothing but friendly and considerate. A couple of Ottawas from Greenville believed that Boyer might have been killed by a warrior who had been beaten up by a white man the previous fall. In short, no one knew who had committed the crime.

All of which left the Americans acutely dissatisfied. They warned the Indians "they must never come armed on a like occasion again." Although no one, not even Boyer's relatives, now blamed the Shawnees for the killing, Ward threatened the tribe: "If they did not give up the guilty or give sufficient information of their innocence . . . they need look for little less than that the friends of the deceased would take satisfaction, a general war would ensue, and . . . their whole people would be exterminated." The whites were disappointed that a convincing suspect had not been produced. "We looked for facts to have been this day brought to light," they said, "but still we are left in the dark." The Indians would be given more time to discover the culprits, "but if you . . . neither give them up nor use all possible diligence you need never look to us for the hand of friendship."

Neither Tecumseh nor Black Hoof had completely assuaged local outrage, and it was perhaps to relieve tension that the Kispoko chief and some friends remained in Springfield for a few days after the council, mixing with residents and participating in friendly athletic contests. It was remembered afterward that Tecumseh invariably bested the other competitors. As for Black Hoof, he continued his investigations into the murder, but it was not until 29 June that he got word from Lower Sandusky that a Potawatomi, Big Son, had accused members of his own tribe of slaying Boyer. Four years before, a Potawatomi had been murdered and another wounded, and Boyer had been killed in retaliation. The hair and feathers left on the body had belonged to the slain Potawatomi. Black Hoof rushed this information to Benjamin Whiteman in the hope that it would establish the good faith of the Shawnees.[20]

While Tecumseh was at Springfield he also made a serious attempt to bridge the rift between the rival Shawnee factions. A strong advocate of unity, he never saw much use in inter-Indian strife, and on the evening of 24 June publicly disavowed the Prophet's attempts to have the Wapakoneta chiefs assassinated as sorcerers. The tomahawk "which was given to destroy those possessed with evil spirits" would be thrown "far behind them," Tecumseh proclaimed, "never to be raised again." It was his hope, so the report said, "that an everlasting peace shall reign in the nation."

12

———— ⇥◆⇤ ————

AN ENGINE SET TO WORK
BY THE BRITISH

T he job facing Tecumseh, the diplomat of the Greenville band, was much more difficult than preaching to the travel-weary converts trundling regularly into the village. The Springfield council had not silenced criticism, and within a fortnight nearly eighty residents of the Staunton area, where Boyer had lived and died, petitioned Wells for the removal of the Indians.[1]

One difficulty was posed by the pilgrims. The more telling the Prophet's message, the more devotees he attracted, the greater the potential for alarm. That spring Lalawéthika had invited his visitors to return in August, when they could be supported by the harvests, and to remind them he sent out runners. Soon the trails were once again being worn by hundreds of travelers—Potawatomis, Ojibwas, Ottawas, Menominees, Winnebagos, Kickapoos, Sacs, and Foxes from the present-day states of Michigan, Indiana, Illinois, and Wisconsin. On 22 August 1807 Wells complained that 230 warriors were at Greenville, another 500 at Fort Wayne en route, and that others were a-coming.[2]

No one could honestly describe the pilgrims as hostile to the whites. William Kirk learned they were "all as friendly as they know how to be," while Wells himself, so apt to berate the Prophet, had to admit the travelers "all appear friendly and more desirous to find the way to Heaven than to go to war." Yet their presence unnerved settlers, and for Tecumseh there was a constant need to reassure.[3]

Another problem was the embryonic Indian confederacy in the west.

The plan to attack American posts was still being considered by militant warriors in the Illinois country, and in August there was an intertribal meeting at a Kickapoo town to debate whether to launch a war. In the end the confederates decided the time was not ripe for such an enterprise, but rumors still flitted back and forth. Not everyone troubled to disentangle the different currents that were sweeping through the Indian country, and Tecumseh and the Prophet often found themselves tarred with the military ardor of the western pan-Indianists.[4]

Then, suddenly, another and far greater shadow fell across Tecumseh's attempts to protect his band from persecution. On 22 June 1807 the British ship *Leopard* had fired upon an American frigate, the *Chesapeake*, while searching for deserters. Three men were killed, and a wave of indignation across the United States condemned Britain's abuse of sea power and called for war to extinguish national dishonor. The crisis had been looming for years. The supreme naval power, Britain, was engaged in a desperate war with Napoleonic France, but her blockade of enemy coasts in Europe had interfered with the overseas trade of such neutrals as the United States. The *Chesapeake* incident brought frayed tempers close to the breaking point, and on the frontier the possibility of a war with Britain revived memories of the Revolution, when the redcoats had loosed fierce Indian warriors against the American settlements.

With a long, ill-defended border to protect, the British in Canada had no choice but to court Indian support. British traders still visited Indian villages south of the Great Lakes, while each year presents were shipped from England so that they could be distributed to Indian visitors at Fort Malden (Amherstburg) and St. Joseph. It is unreasonable to suppose that efforts were not made to secure Indian favor, but the British did not want to be accused of inciting the tribes against the United States, and in the previous three years they had discouraged the western Indian confederacy. The war scare caught them relatively unprepared. The issue of presents had been allowed to falter, and Thomas McKee, the Indian agent at Fort Malden, the most important western post, was drunken, incompetent, and "going to ruin as fast as possible." Furthermore, for many months he had no instructions covering the new situation.[5]

Nevertheless, fraternization between the British and Indians aroused deep suspicions in the United States after the *Chesapeake* affair. Many were genuinely alarmed, but some American officials eagerly embraced a convenient paranoia. The British were to blame for Indian hostility. Instead of examining the complaints of the Indians—about relentless land-hunger, the attack upon native cultures, trade abuses, or the lopsided system of justice Indians experienced at the hands of the whites—some of the President's servants on the frontier found ready scapegoats. A mythology was nurtured:

the United States dealt justly and honorably with the Indians, and tribal dissatisfaction was simply being engineered by malignant external forces.

Especially the British and the Prophet. Thomas McKee could see it happening. "The discontent of the Indians arises principally from the unfair purchases of their lands," he wrote eleven days before the *Leopard* fired on the *Chesapeake*, "but the Americans ascribe their dissatisfaction to the machinations of our government."[6]

The Prophet was already being charged with promoting hostility to the Americans, and it was true, of course, that he had applied harsh words to them. He regarded the Americans as the ultimate authors of most of the Indians' misfortunes. But before 1809 the main thrust of Lalawéthika's mission was internal reform, such as temperance and the purging of witchcraft, rather than overt hostility to the whites. In fact, inasmuch as the Prophet emphasized regaining the Great Spirit's favor through virtuous living, and relying upon the supernatural removal of the whites, he directed Indian attention away from the war advocated by promoters of the western confederacy. Lalawéthika was increasingly resentful toward the United States, but at this time he had no intention of turning his hardworking religious community at Greenville out to fight.

In the rumor-ridden summer of 1807, when war with Britain became the talk of every frontier tavern, the Prophet began to be painted in richer colors than before: he was instigating hostility at the behest of the British!

August found William Wells declaring that "the British" were "at the bottom" of the Greenville "business" and it was to agents at Fort Malden that the concentration of visitors was due.[7] Wells was now engaged in a bitter battle with Tecumseh for the minds of United States officials. For Wells the Prophet was a dangerous agitator who deserved punishment. Tecumseh saw Wells in exactly the same terms. For the moment neither seemed to gain the advantage. After Dearborn's lukewarm response to his earlier charges, Wells attempted to goad Governor Harrison into the strong action he wanted, and to persuade some friendly Indian chiefs to visit the Prophet and urge him to move. Neither ploy succeeded, and Wells returned to imploring the intervention of the Secretary of War. He asked permission to go to Washington for a man-to-man consultation. His case was a poor one. Despite his insistence that the Prophet's removal was "absolutely necessary," he had to admit his spies had been unable to uncover evidence of hostility among Lalawéthika's followers and that those who passed through Fort Wayne were friendly. This was not an argument that even Henry Dearborn would have found convincing.[8]

William Henry Harrison wasn't ready to do anything as inflammatory as Wells was recommending—shifting hundreds of armed warriors by force— but he too propagated the fiction that the Prophet was a British agent. Even before he had heard about the *Chesapeake* he was telling Dearborn that the Indian messiah was merely "an engine set to work by the British for some bad purpose" and crediting a story that McKee himself had been at Greenville. His stories that the Delawares who had visited the Prophet had been taken there "under guard," that Shawnees were carrying war belts across the frontier, and that the tribe was "entirely devoted" to the British had no counterparts in reality, but demonstrated the climate of fear, suspicion, and slander that was gripping the Old Northwest.[9]

Only in Michigan Territory, where Governor William Hull was pressing local Indians to sell more land, was there actual evidence that the Prophet had obstructed American policy. When Hull invited the Potawatomis, Ottawas, Ojibwas, and Wyandots to meet him in June he got firm refusals. The Ottawas and Ojibwas of the Michilimackinac region, who had just been canvassed by the Trout, Lalawéthika's apostle, said they wished the whites no harm, but were dispatching a new delegation to Greenville and had no time for land negotiations. The principal chief of the Ojibwas of Saginaw Bay on Lake Huron, whose hunting grounds were threatened by the proposed treaty, frankly admitted that he had just returned from Greenville, where he had been advised to stand against land cessions. But in truth there were many other reasons for the Indians' recalcitrance, too, including the failure of the United States to pay annuities due on the last cession in 1805 and a realization that the rates being offered, less than a cent an acre, were way below market prices. These were also Indians who had been influenced by the anti-American western confederates.[10]

Sensing the depth of feeling, Hull backed off and postponed his treaty. He had to wait until November to get four to five million acres of eastern Michigan Territory, north of the Maumee. The Trout's speech, in which the Prophet declared the Americans, but not other whites, to be the progeny of an evil spirit, encouraged Hull to believe that it had been concocted in the British interest, and he added to the erroneous impression being popularized by Wells and Harrison that the Prophet was simply a creature of the British.

Hull's difficulties perturbed President Thomas Jefferson. Until then he had dismissed the Prophet as a harmless fool, but at the end of August he went so far as to order the frontier governors to make military preparations, including the raising of the militia. However, even now he was not going to be stampeded into provoking the tribes when a full-scale war with Britain loomed ominously close. He did not want the Indians disturbed, and he ordered that they be told that if they stood neutral in the quarrel with Britain they had nothing to fear. Only if they attacked the Americans would they be exterminated or driven across the Mississippi.[11]

That prudence on the part of the President gave Tecumseh another opportunity to defend his band from calumny.

While the Prophet harangued the enthusiasts thronging into Greenville, two embassies appear to have left the town. Tecumseh's absence at the end of August suggests that he was with one of them, but the evidence is just too thin to clinch it.

One delegation, consisting largely of Shawnees, reached the Iroquois in New York in July, stayed there for thirty-five days, and attended the council fire of the Iroquois Confederacy at Buffalo Creek near Niagara. The westerners were particularly interested in Handsome Lake, the Seneca prophet, and vainly endeavored to persuade him to return with them. It is this interest, along with the intertribal nature of the delegation, that suggests it originated in Greenville rather than Wapakoneta. Whatever its origin, the delegation left for home before 18 August.[12]

In the meantime Blue Jacket went north to collect treaty annuities at Detroit, and Tecumseh may have accompanied him. The $1000 worth of goods due the Shawnees for signing the treaty of Greenville in 1795 had been pared down this year to $725. One-quarter of the amount had been deducted arbitrarily to pay for five horses alleged to have been stolen by Shawnees ten or more years before. Blue Jacket claimed a half of what remained for his own and Tecumseh's bands, leaving relatively little for their Wapakoneta rivals, who had yet to arrive.[13]

Blue Jacket found Detroit buzzing with talk of war. Fortifications were being improved, and Hull seized the opportunity to interrogate Blue Jacket about the Trout's speech. The wily old chief was disarming. No, the speech had nothing to do with the Prophet, he said with less than the truth. Lalawéthika was a friend to the United States, and only wanted the Indians to unite against "the use of ardent spirits" and to "preserve themselves" as a people. Apparently Hull was satisfied.[14]

But Blue Jacket was not. The smell of war unsettled him. Both Greenville and his own village on the Detroit River would be directly in the path of any American armies marching from Kentucky or Ohio to the Canadian border.

On his return journey early in September he called at Brownstown, the Wyandot village on the Detroit River where the council fire of the great confederacy of the 1790s had been kindled. He asked the Wyandots, his "elder brothers," for advice. What should the Indians do if Britain and the United States fell to blows? The American threat to the tribes was great, as Hull's recent attempt to grab more land proved, but then the British had let the Indians down so many times. Solemnly a Wyandot chief reminded Blue Jacket how the redcoats had shut the gates of Fort Miamis to the warriors defeated at Fallen Timbers, and declared that this was a white man's war that did not concern the Indians. The tribes should unite "in a band of eternal brotherhood" but stay neutral.[15]

The aged Shawnee war chief had been the foremost leader of the old confederacy before its defeat in 1794, and he had tried to resuscitate it at least twice since. We can be sure that he agreed that whatever the Indians did, they should do it together.

When Blue Jacket and Tecumseh returned to Greenville it was to learn of more charges that had been made against the band. The trader John Conner had been in during the previous month, when three hundred warriors were in the town, and delivered an astonishing letter from Governor Harrison. It described the Prophet as "a fool who speaks not the words of the Great Spirit, but those of the Devil and of the British agents," and it accused the Indians of defiling the sacred spot where the peace had been made in 1795 by holding "dark and bloody councils." Lalawéthika had not exchanged a word with the British, but he responded with dignity. Harrison had been listening to "bad birds" and was entirely mistaken about the Prophet's motives.[16]

The threat of war and constant harassment finally pushed Tecumseh and his brother into an important decision. They would abandon Greenville for remoter parts. This was hard. Lalawéthika had always insisted the Great Spirit himself had ordered him to Greenville. He "did not remove to this place because it was a pretty place, or very valuable, for it was neither, but because it was revealed to him that the place was a proper one to establish his doctrines," he once said.[17] Seldom had more effort, hope, and faith gone into the creation of a settlement, but it was no use. It was endangered, and the brothers decided that in the spring they would move west to the Wabash.

However, they were to have one more chance to establish their credibility in Ohio. On 13 September Tecumseh was preparing for a village council when three Americans rode into the town. The Shawnees quickly recognized the athletic figure of Tecumseh's old friend Stephen Ruddell, who was the interpreter. He introduced his companions as Thomas Worthington and Duncan McArthur. They were trusted representatives of Thomas Kirker, who had been acting as the governor of Ohio now that Edward Tiffin had gone to the Senate. Kirker had heard the alarming stories about Greenville, but like his predecessor he wanted no truck with hearsay. He sent a message to the Shawnees.

Tecumseh had men from ten tribes in his village at the time, most of them Shawnees, Wyandots, Ottawas, Ojibwas, and Potawatomis, but a few

Sacs, Winnebagos, and Menominees, and even a party who lived "north" of the Ojibwas. Perhaps they were Crees. That afternoon the council house was packed with 173 Indians, while up to 30 more clustered outside the doors to hear what the Governor had to say.

After some routine business the chiefs invited the Americans to speak, and Ruddell interpreted Kirker's letter. It warned the Shawnees about the "bad men" across the Lake, the British, and asked the Indians to send a reply to Chillicothe. A Potawatomi then gave the gist of the message to the Three Fires, and members of other nations were apprised of its contents, before Worthington spoke for the emissaries themselves.[18]

In a long address, Worthington reminded the Indians of their "former misconduct," when they had supported British arms, and of how niggardly the redcoats had rewarded their services. The British had abandoned their allies in the peace of 1783, and left them to fight the United States unaided. In 1794 they had shut the warriors from Fort Miamis when they had been defeated. "These are truths, brothers. You know yourselves better than we can tell you," he said.

By contrast, Worthington went on, the United States had treated its red children with kindness after the treaty of Greenville, and the Indians had no business involving themselves in the new war "likely to take place" between their white neighbors. Even now the President was forming an army of one hundred thousand men to march north: "if they find you sitting still . . . they will take you by the hand and do you no harm." But if the Indians helped the redcoats they would be destroyed. Surely, the chiefs must recognize that if the British and Indians combined had not been able to defeat the Americans before, when "they were little and very weak like children," they could do little "now they are strong like men." As for this Indian town of Greenville, the Governor had five thousand men on hand, but he did not want a war with the Prophet. The Indians should honestly speak about why they had gathered here.

This talk was not ineffective. There were no groundless charges that the Prophet was a warmongering ally of the British. Merely a warning, a statement of the Governor's concern, and a request for an honorable declaration. Tecumseh and the other chiefs promised to reply the next day, but they felt they could deal with these men, and as the council broke up they chatted amiably to the Americans, trying to repair the damage done by the Prophet's indiscretions. Blue Jacket denied that the Trout's speech, which had been published in national and local newspapers, represented the Prophet's views, and Lalawéthika himself "seemed to resent it as a slander." The Prophet also disavowed anti-American remarks attributed to him by the trader Frederick Fisher.

The Americans camped outside the town, but the following morning they were back in the council house to hear Blue Jacket, the Indians' most practiced orator, deliver the reply. He mentioned a few sources of Indian irritation, including the building of Fort Dearborn, and remarked that many of the misunderstandings were the doing of William Wells, "a bad man" who ought to be replaced. Worthington pointed out that Fort Dearborn, which he felt would benefit both races, had been sanctioned by the tribes in the treaty of Greenville, and that only the President could remove Wells, who, after all, had been influenced partly by the Shawnees at Wapakoneta. Old Blue Jacket remained conciliatory, and reported the decision of the Indians at Brownstown to stay neutral, while the Prophet also spoke and explained why his mission had come to Greenville.

The Americans spent two more days wandering freely about the town. Like the Shakers, they had come uninvited and observed the Indians as they found them. Unlike Wells, they troubled to make personal investigations on the ground rather than to sit afar, dealing in premature assumptions and prejudices. They saw none of the "dark and bloody councils" that lurked in Harrison's imagination. Instead they concluded:

> After the most strict enquiry we could hear of nothing which left a doubt in our minds as to their sincerity. There was no hostile appearance. Their women and children, of which there was about 250, were with them, engaged generally in their ordinary labor. We were treated with great hospitality and kindness in their way from all, both strangers and foreigners, and were informed that in less than three weeks all who were able would set out on their fall hunt. Some of the Potawatomis left the town the morning we set out . . . we were unable to find one single fact on them which wore a hostile appearance.

Tecumseh and the other chiefs decided that the best way to reassure the settlers was to send a delegation to Chillicothe to address the Governor in person. Two Potawatomi leaders dropped out of the entourage at the final moment, perhaps hesitating to put themselves amid an armed and nervous militia, but Tecumseh, Blue Jacket, Roundhead, and Panther left Greenville in the company of the American party on 16 September.

Their mission, described at the beginning of this book, was a complete success, and Tecumseh and Blue Jacket not only removed the fears of the settlers but induced Kirker to take up their complaints with the President.

When he received the Governor's report, Thomas Jefferson was glad he had resisted intemperate calls for the expulsion of the Indians from Greenville. This prophet was a harmless eccentric. "I concluded," he later told John Adams, "that he was a visionary, enveloped in their antiquities, and vainly endeavoring to lead his brethren to the fancied beatitudes of their golden age. I thought there was little danger of his making many proselytes from the habits and comforts they had learned from the whites to the hardships and privations of savagism, and no great harm if he did. We let him go on, therefore, unmolested."[19]

Back at Greenville Tecumseh found the village falling strangely silent, inhabited largely by elders. Its resident population, estimated by Worthington and McArthur, had been 305 (80 of them men), but when Tecumseh had gone to Chillicothe there had still been some 200 visitors. Now the guests had departed, and the Shawnee and Wyandot residents were setting off to hunt in their family groups.

The Prophet apparently stayed at his post throughout the winter, receiving the small parties of pilgrims that continued to straggle in. From Fort Dearborn Charles Jouett wrote that multitudes of Indians were "crowding down upon us" from Green Bay. He believed that something like a thousand tribesmen from distant parts were within thirty miles of Chicago on 1 December. Some were destined for Fort Malden, others for Greenville. One group that did reach the Prophet consisted of seven Sacs and Foxes and the White River Delaware leader Beaver. Reports they made on their way home show that Lalawéthika made a significant impression upon them.[20]

It was probably late in October that a truly terrible figure rode into Greenville with twenty-six of his men. Main Poc, whose name described a congenitally deformed left hand which lacked fingers and thumb, was a boorish, bloodthirsty, drunken savage. A Potawatomi war chief from the Kankakee River (Illinois), he was also a good speaker, a man strong in spiritual power, and a fighter of tremendous ferocity and reputation. William Wells judged him "the greatest warrior in the west," with "more influence than any other Indian."[21]

Compared with sophisticated allies such as Blue Jacket and Roundhead, on the face of it this primitive barbarian was of limited use. Tecumseh must have found him repugnant. When in his cups, which was often, he sometimes rolled naked about the floor or tried to rape women. He was big, powerful, and unattractive, and was forever bullying and intimidating others. Wells, who shared a trip to Washington with him in 1808, described Main Poc's behavior as "insufferable. He exceeds every thing I ever saw. He has even attempted to eat his wife. He cannot be kept sober and it is doubtful if he ever reaches his home, as he continually threatens the lives of the other chiefs and has made frequent attempts to kill his wife." Surprisingly, the chief had numerous wives, and they gave him children. Indian agent Thomas Forsyth regarded the eldest boy as "a thick-headed fool" and the youngest as "a perfect idiot."[22]

Main Poc, in fact, epitomized most of what the Prophet and Tecumseh condemned. Not only did he drink, brawl, and treat people abominably, but far from embracing a vision of intertribal unity, he gloried in raiding the Osages across the Mississippi. Worse, he was largely ineducable, and acknowledged no teachers. He boasted that his powers were equal to the Prophet's, and that the spirits had put their mark on him by destroying his hand at birth. Often he withdrew to commune with them, and he was so loyal to them that he rejected any suggestion of yielding his medicine bag to his Shawnee rival. He drank and fought, he said, because it was the wish of the Great Spirit that he do so.

Main Poc was not a man the Shawnee brothers could easily control, but his influence among western tribes that were largely unknown to them was of great value—if it could be harnessed. The fearsome Potawatomi spent two months at Greenville. He seems to have been impressed, for when he rode home he is reported to have left six of his warriors behind.

Holding court throughout the winter, the Prophet made some useful contacts, but lodgers such as Beaver and Main Poc exacted a formidable toll upon the town's resources, depleted by previous visitors. The Shakers at Turtle Creek helped a little, but as the winter set in the brothers made their first approach to the British. Although Tecumseh's victory at Chillicothe had damaged the credibility of William Wells, the agent continued to portray the Prophet as a tool of the British. In fact, it was not until November 1807 that a party from Greenville reached Fort Malden to receive a little clothing at the King's largesse.[23]

Had the Prophet been a British agent none would have been more pleased than His Majesty's servants in Canada. They didn't hold a high opinion of Lalawéthika, and regarded him as a dangerous insurgent. In the summer, McKee, the agent at Fort Malden, had actually been advising Indians not to listen to him. But the *Chesapeake* affair alerted the British to the need to improve their relationships with the Indians in case they needed their help in a war. More presents began to be issued at the British posts, and the Indians were invited to come to Fort Malden for talks.

William Claus, the deputy superintendent-general of Indian affairs, regarded the Prophet as a "rascal" but doubtless assumed that he would have been among those responding to McKee's invitations. Yet as late as 2 November he admitted to his superior, Sir John Johnson, that none of the messages to Greenville had drawn a response. It was a surprise to the British, therefore, that later that month the party from Greenville suddenly called for supplies. But even this failed to open regular communications between the two.[24]

The policy of winning Indian favor received a fillip in December, when Sir James Craig, the governor general of Canada, issued new instructions. The agents were to avoid anything that opened Britain to charges that they were inciting the Indians against the United States, but in private meetings they could "insinuate" to the chiefs "that as a matter of course we shall look for the assistance of our brothers." Craig believed that Britain's new generosity, in increasing the issue of supplies, including arms and ammunition, and the difficulties the tribes were having with the United States, would eventually push the Indians toward the King, but special efforts should be made to win over influential chiefs.[25]

At the turn of the year, therefore, the British decided to redouble their attempts to bring the Prophet within the fold.[26]

13

THE OPEN DOOR

Amid much talk of war Tecumseh still wanted peace. He longed to establish his band in a secure home, where they could live as they pleased, unmolested, without fear of being driven from the land by purchase or sword. Freedom, security, self-respect, a sufficiency of the necessities of life, peace . . . Tecumseh shared many of the ambitions of other people. Warfare had not brought these things, but through Lalawéthika the Great Spirit was showing the Indians another way. By reforming their worship and embracing approved customs; by proscribing violence, drunkenness, and dishonesty; and by controlling the pernicious influences of the whites, they could return to grace. But they needed a place, and after being driven from Greenville the Shawnee brothers thought they had found it. On the upper Wabash, far from American settlements, they might make a home where the bounty of the earth had not been degraded.

Early in 1808 the brothers moved west to the headwaters of the Mississinewa, where hunting eked out scant provisions, and canoes were manufactured for the journey downriver to the Wabash. In April a delegation of ten chiefs found them. Distinguished visitors these, for they included the Miami war chief Little Turtle and the Earth, a leader of the Eel River Indians; but their errand was unfriendly. Spurred by the defamations of Black Hoof's Shawnees, they came to tell the Prophet that their peoples, who lived high up the Wabash, did not want him on their river.

These Indians had no doubt that the land on the northwestern bank of the Wabash which the Prophet had earmarked was theirs. Although recently

occupied by Kickapoos and Potawatomis, the territory had been acknowledged to belong to the Miami-speaking Miamis, Weas, and Eel Rivers at the
treaty of Grouseland only three years before, and it would be so again four
years hence. Nevertheless, when the delegation told the Prophet he was unwelcome it got short shrift. The Great Spirit backed his venture, boasted
Lalawéthika, and it was not in the power of mortals to obstruct it. Anyway,
he said, Main Poc and other Indians supported him, and he had invited
them to join him at his new town. Even the President of the Seventeen Fires
endorsed his plan through the agency of the Governor of Ohio. The Prophet
went considerably beyond the truth, but Little Turtle and his colleagues retired in defeat.[1]

On the White River the Delawares, too, resented the Prophet's return to
Indiana Territory, and they were disappointed at the rebuff to Little Turtle.
Lalawéthika still had a few sympathizers among his ex-neighbors, but to
most of the Delaware council he was a dangerous destabilizing influence.
After the rejection of the Miamis they sent their own party to the Prophet to
tell him his presence on the Wabash would not be tolerated. The message
was too late, because when it reached the Shawnees in mid-May they were
already erecting houses on the new site, and the Delawares were not even
admitted to the town. Tecumseh intercepted them and with a mixture of
persuasion and threats sent them scuttling home with "some indications of
apprehension and terror."[2]

In choosing their new home the Shawnees had probably taken the advice of their Potawatomi visitors, and indeed it was a beautiful place, two or
three miles below the mouth of the Tippecanoe River in what is now
Tippecanoe County, Indiana. The waters of the Wabash were rich in fish,
and turtles deposited their eggs on the islands and sandbars that abounded.
Narrow tablelands, covered in apple, maple, sycamore, and wildflowers,
and dissected by springs that coursed down the hillsides, bordered the
Wabash, and there, as well as in the gentle hills, prairies, and groves of trees
behind, lived a profusion of wildlife.

In its heyday the village, which whites would dub Prophetstown, was
impressive by Indian standards. Two hundred bark-sided houses occupied
the upper end of the site, on the high ground that overlooked the river some
fifty yards distant. On the bottomlands the Indians beached their canoes.
The houses, patterned in neat rows with lanes between, extended westward
toward the prairie, and it was there that the council house and long low
medicine lodge were constructed. On the other side, at the foot of a hill near
the river, another substantial building offered guests accommodation and
was styled the House of the Stranger. Running five hundred yards below the
town were the cultivated fields, more than one hundred acres, apparently
protected from ponies and a few foraging cattle by fences. The town was a

busy place, visited by travelers passing up and down the Wabash and along the path that traced the west bank of the Tippecanoe, but it was orderly. Liquor was kept out, and the unseemly scenes so prevalent in many Indian villages were absent from Prophetstown.[3]

It was about the time that he moved to the Wabash that the Prophet adopted a new name. He called himself Tenskwatawa, which meant the Open Door. The Prophet regarded himself as the door through which his followers might reach salvation, and even before the new settlement had been established he had taken pains to renew his mission. The Prophet's invitations had gone to the Iowas, Sacs, Foxes, Winnebagos, Menominees, and the Three Fires, summoning them to the Wabash. The brothers hoped that some would settle nearby. Certainly the ability of the countryside to support a large multitude was to be doubted, but the Prophet and Tecumseh felt that a powerful headquarters was essential to their plan.[4]

A new name for the Prophet, a new home—but neither implied an immediate change of policy toward the Americans. The brothers still wanted to coexist with the United States, albeit in a relationship which protected their interests, respected their cultural distinctiveness, and granted them some control over their lives. Tecumseh still anticipated that the requests he had made to the Americans through Governor Kirker would be met, and the government would supplant Wells and establish a new agency at Prophetstown, with a blacksmith who could mend guns and tools, and where trade goods might be had at fair prices under the supervision of Stephen Ruddell or some other honest man.[5]

Still, the brothers were drifting slowly toward certain confrontation. They still smarted at being driven from Greenville, and Hull's recent treaty powerfully reminded them of the insatiable American lust for land. Even the arrival of the Quaker William Kirk at Wapakoneta the year before signaled undesirable impositions on the part of the whites. Kirk and his workmen were building a smithy and sawmill, and encouraging Black Hoof's people to erect American-style houses and fence the open fields. Although the Indians still used little more than hoes, and very few of the men could be persuaded to assist the women in the fields, five hundred acres were put under cultivation in 1808—corn, potatoes, cabbage, turnips, and other vegetables. The increased yields lent Wapakoneta such an air of prosperity that some straggling Shawnee groups came in to form a new settlement a little upriver. Black Hoof thought his project successful, but the Prophet was inflamed by what he saw as assaults upon sacred traditional culture. He complained that the President had appointed "masters" to make the Indians toil and turn the warriors into women so they could not defend themselves.[6]

Then, too, the Shawnee brothers were being influenced by others, some more aggressive than themselves. According to Hull, Blue Jacket had been "the friend and principal adviser" of the brothers. As a leading light of the great confederacy of the 1790s, and one who had since tried to resurrect it, the old chief almost certainly encouraged the pan-tribal activities of Tecumseh and his brother. However, he was not particularly anti-American and was more concerned that whatever the Indians did they did together, united and strong. Blue Jacket was at the end of his life, and chose to spend the last of his days at his home in Michigan Territory rather than to follow his protégés to the Wabash.[7]

At their new home the brothers were mixing with less sophisticated and more militant warriors than Blue Jacket, including supporters of the immature confederacy recently proposed by members of the Sacs and Sioux. These men were smoldering with resentment against the Americans and constantly grumbling about the fraudulent treaty Harrison had pushed upon the Indians at St. Louis. Black Hawk, a Sac, remembered that cession as "the origin of all our difficulties," and Main Poc declared that those of his tribe who had supported it were "dogs . . . not fit to mend his moccasins." Here were warriors willing enough to push Tecumseh and Tenskwatawa farther toward a showdown with the United States.[8]

But for the moment the difficulties of establishing themselves in Prophetstown reinforced, rather than weakened, the hopes the brothers had of a more peaceful relationship with their white neighbors. The previous harvest, at Greenville, had been exhausted by visitors and the winter hunting disrupted by the removal. In the spring they planted a crop on the Wabash, and devoured roots and meat in the meantime—little enough to sustain the forty to eighty warriors of the band, their families, and the new pilgrims the Prophet expected to receive. The result was inevitable. Some Indians began slipping into Ohio, stealing horses from the settlers, and killing hogs and cattle.

Tenskwatawa, not Tecumseh, had to deal with the problem. Tecumseh believed in much of what his brother preached, but the Shawnee band had always looked to him, rather than the Prophet, as its founder and chief, the one who took ultimate responsibility for the community. Tecumseh did not always think his brother's approval of actions necessary, and sometimes distrusted his judgment. On occasion he even disciplined the Prophet. According to Anthony Shane, Tecumseh was once so angry when they were at Greenville that he threatened to take the Prophet's life. However, during that first summer on the Wabash, while Tecumseh went north to see the redcoats, Tenskwatawa handled diplomatic affairs, and with respectable skill.

In June he wriggled shiftily when two messengers from William Wells arrived at Prophetstown to seek the return of horses pilfered in Ohio. He was unconvincing, and the charges were transparently true, but there were then about ninety Potawatomi, Winnebago, and Ojibwa warriors visiting his village, and he needed American supplies.[9] Swallowing his pride, he sent for help to the territorial governor—William Henry Harrison, the man who had once accused him of being a British agent and a fool.

He dispatched some men to Vincennes first, down the Wabash. In an address for the Governor, stuffed with professions of peace and designed to "remove every bad impression," Tenskwatawa sneaked in the "great distress" of the band and its need for corn. He was successful. The speech, reinforced by the epostulations of its bearer, threw the Governor off guard, and he replied amiably. Religious opinions, he said, would "never be the cause of dissension and difference between us."[10]

The Prophet followed through with a personal visit in August. Face-to-face, he described his mission to Harrison and asked his help in keeping Prophetstown free of liquor. He also requested necessities, including some, such as flints, needles, hoes, powder, and ball, which he was wont to condemn as the products of European civilization. The Prophet was open about his ambition to unite the Indians around his doctrines. "The religion which I have established for the last three years has been attended to by the different tribes of Indians," he explained. "Those Indians were once different people. They are now but one. They are all determined to practice what I have communicated to them that has come immediately from the Great Spirit through me." That said, the races should live together peacefully, each respecting the differences of the other.

Harrison listened to the plainly dressed and unimpressive-looking man, and was sure the words came from his heart. He issued the Indians a few supplies, including ammunition for hunting, and in November even advanced $102 worth of provisions against the 1809 Shawnee treaty annuities. Harrison was convinced the Prophet's "sole purpose" was reform. "He is rather possessed of considerable talents, and the art and address with which he manages the Indians is really astonishing," he admitted to the Secretary of War. Moreover, far from being a British tool, he might be a force for peace. "I am inclined to think that the influence which the Prophet has acquired will prove rather advantageous," he concluded.[11]

Temporarily at least, Tenskwatawa, the Open Door, had disarmed his most powerful critic.

On his part, Tecumseh sounded out the redcoats across the Lake.

Ever since the beginning of the year they had been trying urgently to bring the Prophet to Fort Malden. In February Frederick Fisher was sent with another invitation, but the brothers didn't relish meeting Shawnees from Wapakoneta at the British post—for they too had been summoned—and they went no further than to send a friendly message by way of a reply.

Then, about the end of May, an Indian arrived at Prophetstown with a note from Deputy Superintendent-General William Claus in Upper Canada. Would the Prophet come, bringing representatives of the "several nations" who were with him along? There was an urgency in these repeated applications that could no longer be ignored, and Tecumseh finally galloped northeast with five companions. He passed Fort Wayne on 4 June and four days later gazed for the first time upon the walls of Fort Malden, Britain's bastion on the Canadian side of the Detroit, near Amherstburg.[12]

The British were glad to see Tecumseh. Their policy of winning Indian favor in case of war was having a difficult birth. Claus himself had been at Amherstburg, assembling Indians, distributing supplies, and holding innumerable councils. In public Claus was tight-lipped. He merely assured the Indians that the King was still their friend, but in private talks with selected chiefs he opened up. The best interests of the tribes would be served by an alliance with the British, for the Americans, everyone could see, were taking Indian land. Only months before, Hull had seized "upwards of five million of acres, for which the Indians will not receive three coppers an acre," said Claus. However, if there was a war and the tribes helped Britain to win, "you may . . . probably regain the country taken from you by the Americans."[13]

Unfortunately, neither enough chiefs nor ones of a sufficient caliber responded to the widespread invitations. The British desperately needed dedicated and reliable chiefs capable of mobilizing and deploying Indian forces, and their hopes were pinned upon the Shawnees, who had been the mainstay of the confederacy of the 1790s. "They are men that can be depended on," wrote Francis Gore, the energetic lieutenant-governor in Upper Canada. A spate of appointments to the British Indian Department had Shawnees in mind. Two Shawnee interpreters, Fisher and James Girty, were beneficiaries, while the inefficient Thomas McKee was replaced as Indian superintendent at Amherstburg by another Shawnee-speaker, Matthew Elliott, who was then some seventy years of age.[14]

Yet results still disappointed. In March three Shawnee veterans from Ohio called at Fort Malden, but time had wasted these once-fine warriors, and Kekewepelethy (Captain Johnny) was so ill that he could not attend sessions in the council house. By May, Claus was in despair. How could he impress the Indians when the garrison at Fort Malden consisted of no more than fifty men, "all old and some not equal to one day's march"? Ruefully he concluded that if war broke out "this country must fall."[15]

Claus was encouraged by one thing. Gore himself was on his way to Fort Malden to throw his weight behind the effort, and in June substantial numbers of Indians seemed to be coming to hear him. Then, suddenly, Tecumseh arrived at the post.

Claus was away when he arrived, so Tecumseh drew provisions and returned to the American side of the river, where his horses were grazing. He promised to be back in three days, but it was not until 13 June that his party finally sat face-to-face with Claus and Elliott in a frank three-hour discussion.

Had Tecumseh intended fighting the Americans, he would have leaped upon the British overtures, for the redcoats alone were capable of supplying the powder, lead, arms, and provisions the Indians needed to wage war. But although the Shawnee chief was courteous, he showed no desire to take the King by the hand. He admitted building a multitribal settlement on the Wabash to defend the land, and said that he would strike the Americans if necessary, but "at present" he wished to stay out of the quarrels of the whites. His experience of the last war had left him deeply distrustful of the redcoats. At that time they had refused to field a respectable force to help the Indians, and when the tribes were defeated they had closed the gates of Fort Miamis to the flying warriors. It had not been forgotten, and Tecumseh believed that several chiefs had been killed because they were shut out of the British fort in 1794.[16]

Speaking forcibly, Tecumseh impressed the British, and in the next few days they tried hard to win his favor. They gave him a "handsome" gift, and when he returned to Fort Malden on the morning of the fifteenth, after another brief trip across the river, Claus pressed him to stay for the imminent Indian council with Gore. The Shawnee chief "cheerfully" consented to wait for Gore, but in the meantime slipped back to Michigan Territory to send some of his men home and to confer with the Shawnees of Blue Jacket's Town and the Wyandots of nearby Brownstown and Maguaga.

In their hurry to humor Tecumseh the British ignored protocol. The Wyandots were the "elder brothers" or the "uncles" of the other tribes, with the right to take precedence in council, but on 1 July Claus sent a message to Tecumseh informing him of Gore's arrival without telling the Wyandots. Tecumseh also got a copy of the speech Gore planned to make to the Indians, and he seems to have been asked to deliver it. The Shawnee leader returned the speech, and when he got back to Fort Malden to speak to Claus on the evening of 9 July he had to explain that the Wyandots objected to the Shawnees' usurping their privileges. It took councils over the next two days to pave the way for the major event on 11 July.

Bold flags and a gun salute at Fort Malden proclaimed the presence of Lieutenant-Governor Gore, as he tried to breathe life back into the old British-Indian alliance before the thousand watching warriors. There were Shawnees from the Wabash and Ohio, men of the Three Fires from Michigan and Indiana Territories, the Detroit River Wyandots, and Mohawks from the Grand River in Upper Canada.

Gore delivered his speech, and then it was explained by Claus and El-liott. It warned the Indians against those who would disturb the peace of the country or Britain's historic friendship with the tribes—by inference against American officials. The Indians should adhere to "ancient customs and manners," by which Gore probably meant they should preserve their skills as warriors, and their association with the redcoats. The Lieutenant-Governor tried to please the Indians by announcing the reappointment of Matthew Elliott, a favorite among the tribesmen, and hinting that Britain did not recognize any of the northwestern land purchases made by the United States. The King, said Gore, held the Ohio boundary of 1768 "sa-cred."

Although Gore carefully avoided referring to the possibility of a war with the Americans, Indians as astute as Tecumseh detected the drift in all this verbiage. The Indians and the British should renew their friendship, and if they did go to war the warriors would have a chance of overturning all the treaties of Wayne, Harrison, and Hull. They could roll back the fron-tier and reclaim the Ohio boundary.

Gore presented a beautiful belt of wampum as a symbol of the British-Indian alliance. A broad white band ran the length of the center of the belt, sandwiched between strips of black. On it a heart stood between figures rep-resenting Gore and the Indians. The British wanted the belt circulated among the tribes to remind them of the King's friendship. Concluding his speech, Gore dined with Tecumseh and twenty-seven other chiefs, rubbing in his message. He found the Shawnee leader to be "a very shrewd intelli-gent man."

The Indians conferred and agreed on a reply, welcoming the British speech, brightening "the chain of friendship," and promising to send the belt through the nations. Reclaiming their ceremonial rights, the Wyandots delivered the speech on 13 July, and after another considerable dinner and friendly ball games and races between younger warriors, the gathering be-gan to break up.

Tecumseh probably was pleased with the result. Without committing himself, he had established a rapport with the redcoats, and, no less impor-tant, he had increased his personal standing among large numbers of Indi-ans to boot. Even the proud Wyandots bowed to the greater experience of the Shawnees as intertribal diplomats. Thus Blackbeard, one of the Ohio chiefs, was asked to take the British message to the Cherokees, while the wampum belt itself was entrusted to Tecumseh, who agreed to show it to the people visiting Prophetstown before sending it forward. Tecumseh's re-turn to the Wabash was something of a triumph. He had completely re-moved British doubts about the Prophet's utility and left them hungry to improve their relationship with Prophetstown. And not only did he bring back the regard of the Lieutenant-Governor and his officials, but he also carried their great belt of 11,550 grains of wampum to prove it.[17]

Barely four moons had shone on Prophetstown, but the brothers had won the trust of both the British and American authorities. It was a happy position, if not one they could sustain. But while Harrison and Gore had been humored, the shift to the Wabash brought no sudden transition to tranquillity. Tecumseh and his band still found themselves beneath the grim shadow of conflict.

Tenskwatawa's mission to the Ojibwas and Ottawas of Michigan Territory badly misfired. Many of these Indians had neglected their planting in 1807 to attend to the Prophet, and through much of the following year they could be seen calling at Fort Wayne, craving food to stave off starvation. Nevertheless, substantial numbers of their countrymen continued to visit the Prophet, but at Prophetstown. There they were hit by a sudden sickness in the autumn of 1808, and perhaps as many as 160 of them died, including an Ottawa chief named Little King. The mortified survivors noticed that few of their Shawnee hosts had shared their misfortune. They stormed home, complaining that the Prophet had poisoned them.

This incident mortally wounded Tenskwatawa's credibility with many Ojibwas and Ottawas, and for a while war looked to be the issue. Despite a fear that the Great Spirit might punish anyone who offended the Prophet, and warnings from Governor Hull, who insisted that even Tenskwatawa was under American protection, bristling Ojibwa and Ottawa warriors assembled on the Grand River in Michigan Territory to launch a raid on Prophetstown. One party actually made an attack. They stole into the village, murdered a woman, and abducted several prisoners.

It was fortunate that sensible heads prevailed. At Prophetstown Tecumseh forbade reprisals, while Black Hoof, who was afraid of being drawn into the vortex, appealed to the Detroit River Wyandots to broker a peace. War was averted, and the Shawnee prisoners were returned. Still, never again would the Prophet count significant numbers of the Michigan Ojibwas and Ottawas among his supporters.[18]

It was a major setback for Tenskwatawa, the Open Door. His cult soon lost momentum among the faraway Ojibwas, and of the powerful Three Fires, only part of the Potawatomis remained interested in him. The eastern Potawatomis of southeastern Michigan Territory and the St. Joseph River were much too influenced by the Americans to support the Shawnee brothers, but their western brethren on the Illinois River or in present-day Wisconsin included such formidable characters as Main Poc and his brother-in-law, Neskotnemek (Mad Sturgeon). These Indians had signed no treaties with the United States, and some had attempted to build an anti-American confederacy in recent years. At the beginning of 1808 William Wells had been dispensing presents to them on a generous scale, especially to Main Poc, in efforts to keep them friendly, but resentment remained, and Main Poc was an obdurate foe of American expansion as long as he lived. Here, among these Indians, the Prophet's criticisms of the United States were more agreeable, and he made greater headway.[19]

It was from the ranks of the western Potawatomis that Tecumseh recruited one of his closest allies. Shabeni (He Has Pawed Through) was a big burly man, but gentle, good-hearted, and loyal. He was an Ottawa by birth, but in 1808, when he first visited Prophetstown and fell under the spell of Tecumseh, he was a little over thirty years of age and a civil chief of a small Potawatomi village near the mouth of the Fox River (DeKalb County, Illinois). His wife, Pknokwe (Bear Clan Woman) was a daughter of an Illinois River headman named Spotka. Shabeni was no faintheart. He was there for the duration, and would be standing beside Tecumseh in the smoke of their final battlefield.[20]

The steadiness of the Prophet's Potawatomi supporters, increasing support from the Winnebagos, and—in 1809—from the Kickapoos, and the loyalty of Roundhead's band of Wyandots back in Ohio saved Tenskwatawa's mission from disaster. As it was, the estrangement of the Ottawas and Ojibwas left him relatively little to show for more than three years of intertribal evangelism.

Narrowly escaping a clash with the Ojibwas and Ottawas, in 1809 the brothers also saw their new, improved relationship with the Governor of Indiana Territory disintegrate in a fresh fog of rumor and suspicion. It could hardly have been avoided. Situated farther west on the Wabash, they were bound to be drawn into fresh controversy by the Indians of the Illinois and upper Mississippi.

Many of these tribesmen still wanted outright war. Time had not removed their old grievances, and fresh ones were added in 1808. Most seriously, Governor Meriwether Lewis of Louisiana Territory, from his headquarters in St. Louis, had threatened to interdict trade and use troops to coerce the Sacs and Iowas into surrendering Indians wanted for attacks on whites. The matter was an emotional one. When Iowa prisoners escaped from confinement in 1809 and the Americans applied to a principal chief for their return, he refused point-blank. In fact he threw away his American medal and threatened war. Another irritant: the erection of a trading and military post, Fort Madison, on the west bank of the Mississippi, above the mouth of the Des Moines, in September 1808. To local tribes it represented an unwelcome advance of United States power.

In March and April 1809 dire reports reached St. Louis and Fort Madison that the Sacs and Winnebagos of the Rock River were again planning to attack American posts. Once more the old rhetoric of militant pan-Indianism, echoes of the words of Joseph Brant, was repeated. The land, it insisted, belonged to all tribes in common, and all the tribes should defend it. Nicholas Boilvin, one of the most informed of American agents on the Mississippi, heard that the nations would "all join together and have but one fire and one kettle to eat out of, with the same spoon for them all; that they had but one Father [Britain] that had helped them in their misfortunes, and that they would assemble, defend their Father and keep their lands." The words had been used often in the last four years, and by the same people, but in April fifty Winnebagos brought their pleas for help to Tecumseh and the Prophet.[21]

Listening to the embittered Winnebagos, the brothers heard much that engaged their sympathies. They shared the belief that the land belonged to all Indians, and not merely its present native occupants. It was in that spirit that they had settled on the Wabash, on land claimed by the Miamis, and invited other nations to follow them. And no one needed to remind Shawnees of the American craving for land. On the other hand the Winnebago plans to surprise Forts Dearborn and Madison did not attract them at that time. Tecumseh had only eighty warriors at the most, while downstream at Vincennes Harrison had hundreds of militia at his disposal.

The brothers needed the Winnebagos to further their own plan of massing Indians on the Wabash to deter further American expansion, but they gave them no firm promises. In fact, according to Anthony Shane, who was casually employed as an interpreter at Fort Wayne, the next month Tecumseh was openly talking about the Winnebago plot against Fort Dearborn. The Prophet also acknowledged the existence of the hostile confederacy when he visited Vincennes in June, but he protested that he had declined to support it, and that it was "entirely confined" to the western Indians. On this occasion he was probably telling the truth.[22]

However, nervous American officials saw the Prophet in every hostile action. On the Mississippi Tenskwatawa's couriers had been active for more than two years, and William Clark, the Indian agent at St. Louis, among others, credited them with stirring revolt—a hostility which in reality had, as we have seen, preceded the Prophet's movement and outstripped it in its militance. Some absurd stories were circulating, including one whopper that identified the Prophet as a mixed-blood educated in England. Not everyone was so uninformed, however. Dr. Robertson, the agent at Fort Osage; Nicholas Jarrot, a trader who had passed through Saukenuk, the main Sac village; and Boilvin, who dealt with all the upper Mississippi tribes from his base at Prairie du Chien: each reported on the origins of the unrest, but made no reference to the Prophet.[23]

Scare stories were also running the length of the Wabash, wild yarns and rash assumptions, stoking genuine fears among the settlers. A trader came hurriedly to Fort Wayne to tell of the Winnebagos he had seen at Prophetstown. The Miamis, who lived near Fort Wayne and who had a reputation for cooperating with the United States, worried that the Prophet might turn upon them after scourging the whites, while the irrepressible Wells, now dismissed from his post by a dissatisfied Secretary of War, fired a parting shaft into his old enemy. He said the Three Fires were deserting the Prophet because he had ordered them to attack the Americans. All contributed to a sudden but sharp panic. Outside of Vincennes the white population of Indiana Territory was scattered and isolated, and even the town itself was poorly protected. Two miles above the settlement stood Fort Knox, but it was only an arsenal with an unpicketed barracks and blockhouse and a skeleton garrison.[24]

The scare did not last long. Harrison raised two companies of militia and threw them in a screen about Vincennes, but by 12 May he knew that the Prophet's Winnebago guests had departed, and understood that apart from some Kickapoos his influence had considerably diminished anyway. The Governor discharged his troops, but he never trusted Tenskwatawa again. From then on he sent spies to Prophetstown, disguised as honest traders.

At Fort Wayne the new agent, John Johnston, was more willing to give the Shawnees the benefit of the doubt. He invited the Prophet to visit him as a "friend," and on 25 May Tenskwatawa made his appearance, accompanied by seven Shawnees, a Kickapoo, a Potawatomi, a Winnebago, and an Ottawa. The Indians handed over a couple of horses taken in Ohio the previous year, and the Prophet spent five days speaking with Johnston and others. He even talked to the hated Wells, who still loitered about the post, and who the Shawnees blamed for many of the slanders made against them. Johnston, at least, was convinced. He was sure the alarm had been bogus, and acknowledged that "the traders all declare the Indians guiltless."[25]

The Shawnees had not been implicated, but the plan to attack the American posts was no fiction. It was real enough, but like the previous attempts of the western Indians to unite against the whites, it quickly fell prostrate. At Fort Madison Lieutenant Alpha Kingsley was so vigilant that in April the frustrated Sacs and Winnebagos gave up all hopes of surprising the post. A weak attempt was made upon Fort Dearborn, but not until August. One hundred and fourteen defiant Winnebagos rode to the post looking for an opportunity to attack it. Charles Jouett, the Indian agent at the fort, alerted the troops to the danger, persuaded the traders to shut their doors, and issued a little powder and some provisions to the Indians to calm them down. They left without committing violence, and it was not long afterward that the whole plan against the garrisons was abandoned.[26]

The alarm of 1809 drew Tecumseh and his brother farther down the road to war. Moreover, it was obvious that they would forge closer connections with the militant western Indians in the future. Hitherto, the brothers had not had an extensive relationship with them. The Sacs and Foxes had sent a small deputation to the Prophet in 1807, and another visited him in the summer of 1809, but there is no evidence that any great number of them embraced his religious ideas. However, other western tribes were awakening to the Prophet's usefulness. Large parties of Winnebagos had journeyed to see him in three successive years, and numerous western Potawatomis, too, were attracted to his teachings. In 1809 Kickapoos from the Illinois River began to pay homage. Grieving western tribesmen found much of what Tenskwatawa had to say a convenient rationale for their hostility to the Americans. If the Great Spirit wanted to protect distinct Indian cultures and lands, and if he regarded the Americans as the spawn of an evil spirit, then surely he would support a war to drive the settlers back. As the discontent of the Indians on the Illinois and Mississippi Rivers deepened, so did their interest in the Prophet.[27]

The forces impelling the Shawnee brothers to war were indeed strong, but they were perhaps not yet unstoppable. Had the United States listened to the growing protest in the west, and tried to meet the complaints, the fire that was developing might have been contained until it burned out. Restraint, fairness, and conciliation could still have denied Britain essential Indian allies.

It was not to be so. A few months after the war scare of 1809 Tecumseh and Tenskwatawa heard news that reduced them to fury.

With astonishing abandon, and a disregard for both the mood of the tribes and the need of his country for good Indian relations at a time when a war with Britain seemed imminent, the Governor of Indiana Territory pressed ahead with another land treaty.

14

A TREATY TOO FAR

About the late summer of 1809 Tecumseh led a party of determined warriors into Ohio. It was the first of his journeys in the cause of Indian unity. Hitherto the Shawnee brothers had relied upon messengers to broadcast their news, but from now on Tecumseh put himself in the vanguard of intertribal diplomacy. With fiery and expressive oratory he would excite Indian listeners across the frontier, antagonizing some, spellbinding others, unsettling most.

His message was clear. The Indians must stand together to save their lands, their cultures, and their independence, as they had done twenty years before. They must revive the great confederacy for which many of their fathers had fought. The land was the common property of all the tribes, and its defense was the responsibility of all. Tecumseh said the days of white supremacy were ending, for if the Indians united behind the principles of the Prophet, they would be blessed by the Great Spirit, and they would prevail.

There was a new firmness in Tecumseh, and perhaps it had something to do with invitations that had been sent from Fort Wayne on 4 September. They summoned various tribes to the fort for the middle of the month, and few Indians could have avoided the apprehension that more land negotiations were in the offing. Tecumseh and the Prophet's plan to mass Indians on the Wabash to protect the existing boundary suddenly became a top priority.

This first tour took Tecumseh to the tribes which had led intertribal resistance in the years of his youth and early manhood. He was not ignorant of the changes time had wrought. Those of the once-mighty Iroquois who had not fled to Canada had been engulfed by white settlements and left scratching a living on small reservations in the state of New York. The Wyandots of the Sandusky held grimly to territory wedged between two great land cessions, made in 1805 and 1807, blocks joined by a strip across Wyandot lands yielded only the preceding year. So far Black Hoof's Shawnees had defended what they conceived to be their territorial limits, but cessions to the east, north, and west were slowly encircling them. Every one of these communities lived close to American settlements, and was wide open to attack if they raised the tomahawk against the whites.

They knew this, and pursued a policy of conciliation and accommodation. Aided by the Quakers and the Seneca prophet Handsome Lake, some of the Iroquois tribes were developing their economy. Black Hoof and his friend Tarhe the Crane, the most important Wyandot chief on the Sandusky, were united in their ambition to save what was left of their lands, but they hoped to do it by proving that they could live peaceably with their white neighbors and exploit their soil as effectively as anyone else.

Tecumseh knew the established chiefs were against him, but he didn't care about them anyway. He regarded them as corrupt, selling the ground from beneath their people to gain bribes or secure their positions by controlling treaty annuities. No, Tecumseh's hopes were pinned upon the warriors, particularly the younger warriors. He reasoned that they would be finding the compromises that came with living within surrounding white settlements irksome, and they would welcome a haven on the remote Wabash. Ironically, Tecumseh was actually advising these Indians to give up ancestral lands, but it was to create a stronger barrier somewhere else.

Returning to Wapakoneta, which seems to have been his first port of call, Tecumseh saw much that worried him. The Shawnees had not been adopting white culture wholesale, and they were working hard to control the liquor trade, but most of what had been achieved under the supervision of William Kirk was nothing short of blasphemous. It rejected the Indian heritage which had been the gift of Waashaa Monetoo. Kirk himself was no longer at Wapakoneta, having surprisingly been dismissed by the American government, but one of his hired laborers was still at work, and a stock of tools supplied by the Americans had been left in the care of James Logan. A sawmill stood unfinished—and progress would not be resumed until October 1811, when the Quakers took full responsibility for the project—but there was no doubt about the path the chiefs intended to follow.[1]

Tecumseh held a meeting in the council house, but most of the chiefs absented themselves rather than confront him. Stephen Ruddell was there, though, in his new role as a Baptist missionary, and he used the occasion to interpret a letter from Governor Harrison to the chiefs—possibly one relating to the treaty proceedings then under way at Fort Wayne. Tecumseh acted boldly. He took the letter and threw it into a fire, declaring bitterly that if the Governor himself were present he would serve him the same way. He told the Shawnees that previous treaties were null and void, and that he would defend his cause to the death. Nor would it die with him if he was killed, for others would stand in his place.

John Johnston minimized the impact of Tecumseh's visit when he reported it to Harrison. Tecumseh "made no impression," he said, "and went away much dissatisfied." This was not entirely true, and in another letter, to the new secretary of war, William Eustis, Johnston admitted Tecumseh had left the Shawnees in "much uneasiness." When John Norton visited Wapakoneta the following spring he found "only a small number" of the Indians at home "with the old chiefs" and heard that most had gone to join Tecumseh. Stephen Ruddell was one of Norton's informants. Norton exaggerated Tecumseh's success, because the chief gained few long-term recruits, but Tecumseh clearly had the Indians of Wapakoneta wavering.[2]

Tecumseh looked up his old friend Lewis, who was still the headman of a mixed village of Mingoes and Shawnees in Logan County. Lewis was still interested in the Prophet's mission, and is said to have promised to travel with Tecumseh to the southern tribes. In the meantime, he went northeast with Tecumseh's party to the Sandusky River, where an important community of Wyandots and Senecas was living.

These Indians were in danger of becoming a pitiful enclave, hemmed in by American settlements. Most recently they had complained of encroachments on the Scioto River. Tecumseh tantalized them with a vision of a better life on the Wabash, where the game was richer and there was room to breathe, and he appealed to the idealism of the young warriors.[3]

An old but illustrious chief rose to reply. Most Indians in the northwest knew of Tarhe the Crane, for he had been the leading spokesman of the Sandusky Wyandots since the death of Half King in 1788. He was known to be an advocate of moderation. He had signed the treaty of Fort Harmar in 1789, and tried to stay out of the war that followed. True, when he was eventually dragged in he had fought bravely, and been wounded at the battle of Fallen Timbers, but afterward he had been the first important confederacy chief to break ranks and treat with General Wayne. Since 1805 Tarhe had been cooperating with the Presbyterian missionary Joseph Badger in implementing a policy identical to Black Hoof's. Land had been plowed and fenced, houses improved, and a school constructed. This grizzled warrior was not going to listen to Tecumseh. He replied evasively, explaining that his people would bide their time and see how Tecumseh's settlement fared for a few years before considering removal.[4]

But once again Tecumseh's visit, paradoxically a plea for unity and the protection of native territory, opened up divisions among his listeners. He stimulated suspicions about the chiefs—and the young warriors were soon insisting on monitoring their actions—and he created a debate between those under Tarhe who clung desperately to the remaining tracts on the Sandusky, and others who wanted to move to the Wabash. The most important supporter of the latter cause, it was said, was Leatherlips, who was reckoned by Governor Hull to be "a good old man and the second chief of their nation." A dozen or so Wyandot warriors did, in fact, establish a town a few miles from Prophetstown in 1810, but the sources are unclear as to whether these came from the Sandusky or from Wyandot villages on the Detroit River.[5]

Tecumseh may have got as far east as New York state, the country of the Six Nations. No contemporary document tells of such a visit, but many years later, in 1838, the historian Caleb Atwater claimed to have served Tecumseh as an interpreter to the Iroquois in 1809. His account was brief indeed, and said little more than that Tecumseh, the Prophet, and two Winnebagos, Four Legs and Caraymaunee, went to the council fire of the Iroquois Confederacy at Onondaga to enlist its support.

Now, in 1809 Atwater did live in New York, but he was preaching and practicing law, and there is not a scrap of evidence that he could ever speak either Shawnee or Iroquois. And apart from the absurdity of Tecumseh's entrusting such a position to a white man, Atwater's account contains errors that could not possibly have been made by anyone who had actually made such a trip. Most decisively, the council fire of the Iroquois was not at Onondaga in 1809, nor had it been since the American Revolution. It was on the Buffalo Creek reservation near Niagara.

That said, Atwater may not have invented the story entirely. Nine years before he published it, he served as a commissioner of Indian affairs at Prairie du Chien, and met there the very two Winnebagos he later said were with him in New York. As Atwater artlessly admitted, they told him about Tecumseh's travels. "Carrymauny the elder three times reported to me his history," Atwater wrote. "He complained to me that in all our accounts of Tecumseh we had only said of him that [he was the] 'Winnebago who always accompanied Tecumseh,' without calling the Winnebago by his name—Nawkaw Carrymauny."[6]

There is a fair possibility that in 1829 these Winnebagos told Atwater of a trip they had made to the Iroquois twenty years before, and the historian simply decided to write himself into the story, adding some fictional details and distorting factual ones. In this, as in so many episodes of Tecumseh's life, the truth has been buried beneath mythology.

While Tecumseh was recruiting, an event of greater importance was occurring at Fort Wayne. Over a thousand Indians congregated at the behest of the Governor of Indiana Territory. The reason? A determined bid on the part of Harrison to grab nearly three million acres of Indian land for less than two cents an acre.

Harrison may have wanted to encourage settlement above Vincennes to give the town greater security from Indians, but the assembly at Fort Wayne owed more to the political and economic aspirations of the Governor and his associates. In February 1809 Indiana Territory was divided, and present-day Illinois and Wisconsin became the separately administered Illinois Territory. Indiana's march to statehood, which depended upon its population, was thus retarded. One way of bringing in more settlers, as well as securing the rich lands along the Wabash, was to attack the Indian estate. So, despite native discontent, and the danger of driving the tribes toward the British at a time when war between the United States and Britain was still possible, Harrison did not hesitate.

Only four days after dismissing the militia called out to meet the Indian threat in the spring, Harrison was beseeching the federal government to authorize negotiations for two tracts on the Wabash. President James Madison had just taken office, and his administration placed too much trust in Harrison's judgment. In July it sanctioned negotiations, providing that the price paid was consistent with earlier purchases, and that every Indian nation "who have or pretend right to these lands" was present. Moreover, the treaty should go ahead only if it "will excite no disagreeable apprehensions, and produce no undesirable effects" among the Indians. Apart from the matter of cost, these were conditions Harrison did not feel obliged to fulfill.[7]

Harrison also decided to buy three, not two, tracts. One was an unauthorized strip in eastern Indiana which extended the Greenville boundary west to secure for the United States the head of the Whitewater. The authorized tracts took American land ownership up both banks of the Wabash, almost as far as the Vermilion River, more than half the distance from Vincennes to Prophetstown, and consolidated United States control of southern Indiana.

By comparison with the notorious treaty of St. Louis, the negotiations at Fort Wayne that September were well managed, but they still fell short of the standards that justice or even the federal government demanded.

Harrison packed the proceedings with members of the populous and needy Potawatomi villages—not the western Potawatomis who would have nothing to do with the treaty, but those of the St. Joseph River and southeastern Michigan. Throughout the proceedings one of their chiefs, Winamek, the headman of a small village on the Tippecanoe, "waited" upon Harrison like a pet dog. Like most Indians, the Potawatomis were suffering greatly at this time, hit by the fall in the price of peltries and the depletion of the game. Harrison knew full well that the Indians were "more miserable than they have ever been" and "half starved." Hungry Potawatomis were useful, however. They were eager to participate in land cessions because they wanted to boost their treaty annuities, and they acted accordingly at Fort Wayne, even though they had no recognized claim upon the territory being sold. In fact, the Governor's previous treaty, in 1805, had expressly stated that the Potawatomis had no rights on the Wabash.

The Potawatomis, who by Harrison's lights had no business with the treaty, were at Fort Wayne, but several groups from whom resistance might be expected, including the only people who actually occupied any of the tracts, were strangely absent. The Weas should have been there. Harrison's treaty of 1805 had vested in them, with the Miamis and Eel Rivers, the sole right to dispose of the Wabash lands, and they alone had villages in the areas Harrison wanted. A sale would drive them upriver to find unceded land. Also missing were groups who hunted across the tracts, including the Kickapoos of the Vermilion, the Piankeshaws, and Tecumseh's band of Shawnees.

Miamis and Eel Rivers from the upper Wabash were there, and rightly so, for with the Weas they were the acknowledged owners of the Wabash country. The Delawares were also there. They had been granted equal rights in the White River area by the Miamis, and used the Whitewater tract for hunting and gathering. But overall this was far from the full representation sought by the government. It was true that the final treaty was made dependent upon the subsequent approval of the Weas and Kickapoos, but the practical effects of the contrivances were obvious. At Fort Wayne the Miamis, Eel Rivers, and Delawares, for whom the tracts were of limited importance, were pressed by Harrison and the volubly insistent Potawatomis to sell. Later the more obdurate Kickapoos and Weas were confronted, each in isolation, and presented with what was almost a fait accompli.

Courtly as ever, the Governor spoke to the Indians disingenuously. He told them that no more cessions would be sought—a promise he would forget within eighteen months—and he charged the Miamis and the British with costing the Indians Ohio in the wars of the 1790s. The disappearance of the game was put down to Canadian traders and Indian "improvidence." Fictions, half-truths, appeals to sell, reasoned advice, reminders of what the increased annuities would mean . . . all fell from the Governor's lips. The Delawares stood neutral, but the Potawatomis took it all in, and "vehemently urged the sale and reproached the Miamis in the most bitter terms."[8]

Venal Miamis such as Little Turtle supported the cession, but many Miamis made a stand, particularly the Mississinewa band represented by the Owl, who lived close to the disputed area. They resented the inclusion of the Potawatomis, and told Harrison that he ought to have been talking to the Weas; but eventually they gave in. On 30 September 1809 the treaty of

Fort Wayne was signed. The Indians got $5,250 in goods, and additional annuities, and by the end of the year both the Weas and the Kickapoos had ratified the agreement. The Kickapoos were even induced to extend the purchase on the west bank of the Wabash to the Vermilion River.[9]

The treaty of Fort Wayne did not extinguish native rights to hunt and gather on the ceded areas, but inevitably those activities would wane as the settlers moved in. With other cessions, however, it left the old Greenville boundary in tatters.

The scale of Indian dispossession was alarming. Since 1800, title to part of northern Ohio, the southern third of Indiana, southeastern Michigan, most of Illinois and Missouri, and part of Wisconsin had been transferred by one treaty or another to the United States. Settlers followed in the wake of the treaties—filling up the old Greenville cession; penetrating southern Indiana; filtering up the Wabash, Mississippi, and Illinois Rivers; and skirting the shores of Lake Erie.

But the treaty of Fort Wayne was a watershed. It spread disaffection to tribes such as the Miamis, who had previously been counted friends of the Americans, and exhausted what remained of the patience of Tecumseh and Tenskwatawa. It was a stark vindication of Tecumseh's complaints, and it materially affected the course of Indian relations with the United States and Britain on the eve of the War of 1812.

And even from the viewpoint of American expansion it had not been necessary. The game was getting harder to find. As John Johnston remarked, "there is no part of this country now where 500 men can subsist ten days at a place on what the woods may furnish."[10] In time the Indians would probably have ceded their lands and moved, and no great urgency to acquire the tracts purchased in 1809 had been demonstrated.

Some people in Vincennes understood this, among them enemies of Harrison happy to embrace any pretext for his discomfort. A Canadian merchant, William McIntosh, who had served as territorial treasurer before falling out with Harrison, believed the treaty to be unjust, and openly held that if it was proved so the United States should not only refuse to enforce it but also remove Harrison from office. Harrison dismissed McIntosh as a vindictive old British Tory, but others held similar views. John Badollet and Nathaniel Ewing of the Vincennes land office held a meeting in June 1810 to consider bypassing the Governor and sending the grievances of the Indians to the President. A dangerous opponent, too, Badollet, for he had the ear of James Madison's treasurer, Albert Gallatin, and there was more than a grain of truth in what he told him. "It is my opinion that Government ought to look closer into this business," he wrote, for "the Indians want nothing but good treatment to become well disposed to the United States."[11]

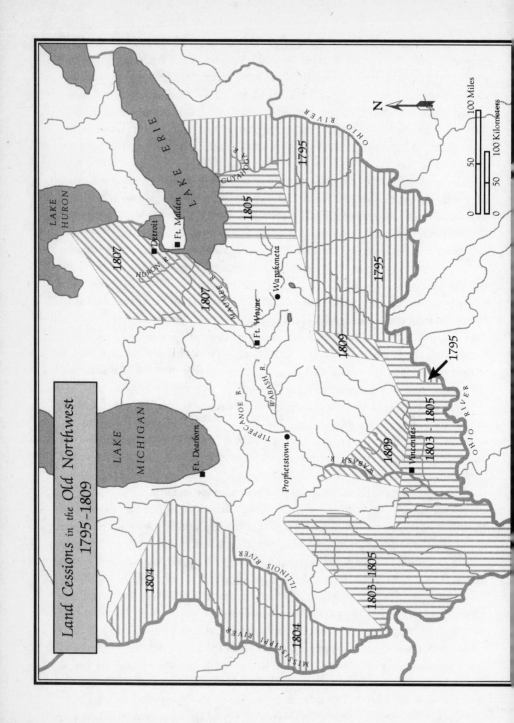

Land Cessions in the Old Northwest 1795–1809

Tecumseh was roused to fury by the news that greeted his return to the Wabash. To his mind the treaty was an act of robbery in which the United States had exploited the Indians' poverty and once again found willing coadjutors among the established civil chiefs. His anger was twofold. It was directed as much at chiefs such as Winamek, whose marks had been scratched on the treaties, as at the American dispossessors themselves.

More Indians were agreeing with him, for no ground upon which they trod seemed safe. People who had counted themselves friends of the United States—Piankeshaws, Weas, and Miamis for example—now began to appear among the ranks of the dissidents. Even the Delawares, whom Harrison considered the staunchest of his Indian allies, talked about taking a leaf from Tecumseh's book and inviting other tribes to live with them on the White River so they could defend it from the Americans. The day the treaty was signed the Wyandots of the Detroit were speaking for many when they complained to Governor Hull that "the United States should take as much upon himself as the Great Spirit above" for "he wants all the land on this island."[12]

To measure the impact of the treaty upon Tecumseh we need look no further than his visits to Fort Malden in 1808 and 1810. On the first occasion he refused to be drawn into a British alliance. He had grievances against the United States, but there was some residual optimism that they might be resolved peacefully. Two years later Tecumseh spoke altogether more gravely. He wanted the British to help him fight a war. Between those two Tecumsehs, of course, was the treaty of Fort Wayne.

The treaty, then, put Tecumseh on the road to war. But there was another change, too. Before, he had been content to stand in his brother's shadow. He was the chief of the band, handled the diplomacy, and evidently took ultimate responsibility for most of the decisions, but still, to the public eye, he was simply the most important supporter of the Prophet. Indeed, for some years yet whites would as often refer to him as "the prophet's brother" as by name. Yet although the Prophet deserved the credit for founding the Shawnee reform movement, and his religion continued to be a keystone of Indian resistance, Tenskwatawa lacked the determination, courage, energy, and leadership skills to be an effective multitribal head. As the years passed it became obvious that Tecumseh, rather than his brother, was the engine room of the confederacy. After the treaty of Fort Wayne he exercised control more openly, effectively setting the agenda. "I am alone the acknowledged head of all the Indians," he boasted in the summer of 1810.[13]

It was Tecumseh, the civil and war chief of the band, who put the brothers on the more desperate course they adopted after the treaty, but the two fully complemented each other. The opinions of the Prophet, medium of the Great Spirit, were potentially more influential than the more secular arguments of Tecumseh, and Tenskwatawa put them at the service of his brother's plans.

Tecumseh had always modified his brother's teachings in the interests of practicality. The Prophet had preached self-sufficiency and independence of the whites, but Tecumseh had once applied for a government agency to be established at Prophetstown, and he still recognized the need for gunsmiths and traders. Likewise, Tecumseh had never supposed the Great Spirit alone, by some sudden apocalypse, would protect Indian land. That was why he had tried to build a strong intertribal position on the Wabash, and why he advocated a great confederacy to dam back the "great water" of American settlement. It was not enough to live according to Waashaa Monetoo's creed. The Indians must unite, and if necessary, they must fight.[14]

Together the brothers were a fusion of two traditions of Indian resistance that had often, but not always, run in company. One was the political and military tradition of pan-tribalism, with its emphasis upon confederation. It had been a common strategy of Shawnees since the 1740s, but it peaked in the great confederacy of Tecumseh's youth, the one defeated in 1795. This was the idea most recently promoted by the Sacs, Winnebagos, Sioux, and others, but Tecumseh hijacked the movement, and extended it. He occasionally talked wildly about reaching every tribe on the continent.

To this Tenskwatawa annexed a prophetic tradition, which had often strengthened the political and military strategy, most notably in the case of Neolin, whose religion had fueled the Indian uprising of 1763. The Prophet told the Indians that they might appear powerless, even when bound together in an alliance, but they could also depend upon the support of the Great Spirit, an incalculable advantage. And his codes taught them how to deal with strife in Indian villages, and about the value of economic and cultural independence of the whites.

Together these traditions spoke to all the major problems being experienced by Indian communities, and championed by the combined talents of a charismatic, intelligent, and energetic warrior and orator and an astute and plausible holy man, they made a potent force.

The treaty of Fort Wayne provoked Tecumseh to even greater efforts. Like pan-tribalists before him, he tried hard to spread the view that the land was owned by the tribes in common. As he said the next year, the Americans "have taken upon themselves to say this tract belongs to the Miamis, this to the Delawares, and so on, but the Great Spirit intended it as the common property of all the tribes, nor can it be sold without the consent of all." By this criterion, all the treaties since Greenville were invalid. He went so far as to recommend that Indians refuse the annuities or presents the United

States distributed on account of these treaties. Any goods the Indians needed could be got by honest trade.[15]

Common land ownership, if accepted, would have prevented any one tribe or small group of tribes from selling land in which other Indians had rights, as they had done at Fort Wayne. But how was Tecumseh to enforce it? He thought he saw one way of succeeding: the removal of weak or rotten chiefs, whose responsibilities could be discharged by the warriors. "We have endeavoured to level all distinctions," he would recall, "to destroy village chiefs by whom all mischief is done. It is they who sell our land to the Americans. Our object is to let all our affairs be transacted by warriors." Some corrupt chiefs were threatened with death, others simply deposed. In August 1810 a Winnebago chief complained, with tears in his eyes, that he and the other chiefs had been divested of their authority, which had been transferred to the warriors.[16]

The odds against Tecumseh were gigantic. In 1810 the population of the white settlements in Ohio and the territories of Indiana, Illinois, and Michigan amounted to 270,000. Against this the Indian population of the Great Lakes area was little more than 70,000. Tecumseh didn't have the figures, but his travels gave him an inkling of the opposition, and stimulated his determination to bring in as many tribes as possible and to enlist the help of the redcoats. Four years earlier he had discovered an old British wampum belt in possession of the chiefs. It had been given to the King's Indian allies during the French and Indian War, and Tecumseh had retrieved it and kept it safe. Now he planned to take that belt to Fort Malden to renew the old British-Indian alliance.[17]

In the meantime messengers were dispatched to the tribes early in 1810. They went along the Wabash, and to the Great Lakes, and they reached the Kaskaskias and Iowas on the Mississippi, and perhaps also the Dakota Sioux of Minnesota. The brothers entreated the Indians to send some of their people to the Wabash and to attend an intertribal conference in the summer, when the land problem would be thrashed out. The Prophet said the Great Spirit would punish those who refused to listen, and Tecumseh seems to have circulated a belt symbolizing the confederacy.[18]

More sophisticated men, of the stamp of Brant or Blue Jacket, would have considered making an appeal to the United States government, as Indians had done with some success in 1786. But Tecumseh' s faith in the Americans had evaporated, and there can be little doubt he hoped the upcoming conference would carry a vote for war.

Despite furtive Indian councils and Tecumseh's pleas for secrecy, details of his plans inevitably leaked out. From French traders, Indians friendly to the Americans, and spies such as Michel Brouillet, there came dark fearful rumors of an armed rising. Mrs. Ash, a Potawatomi married to an interpreter at Fort Wayne, spent several days with relatives in Prophetstown about May. They warned her that war was coming. One night, as she lay trying to sleep in a cabin, she overheard some warriors talking outside. They were speculating about how the war would be fought. One bemoaned the lack of ammunition, but another supposed the chiefs would get some from the usual supplier, who Mrs. Ash took to be a British trader then in the village.

The problem of war materiel was certainly one that Tecumseh had considered. He said that the Indians' "first stroke" should "put them in possession of an ample supply of arms, ammunition and provisions." In Winamek's town it was believed that a coordinated attack upon the American posts was in the making. The Potawatomis were assigned Fort Wayne, although Main Poc's party would fall upon Fort Dearborn, which powerful pickets had made a harder conquest. Tecumseh was to surprise Vincennes with Shawnees, Kickapoos, and Piankeshaws. The Ottawas and Ojibwas were to assault Detroit, the Sacs Fort Michilimackinac, and St. Louis was also targeted. Report had it that Indians who supported the Americans would be slain with them, but that the French people in Vincennes and other places, with whom the Indians had no quarrel, would be warned in advance so they could escape.[19]

Such detailed plans, if they existed, were no more than mere proposals, awaiting the decision of the intertribal council that Tecumseh was planning, but they suggested a truth. After the treaty of Fort Wayne the pungent smell of gunpowder was never far away.

THE
FEDERALIST

—•— ≍◆≍ —•—

15

THE MOSES
OF THE FAMILY

T he winter that followed the treaty of Fort Wayne was a hard one
for the Indians of the Old Northwest.

There was a desperate shortage of trade goods. The United
States had never provided a sufficient Indian trade, and in 1809 it made
matters worse by passing the Non-Intercourse Act, which suspended commerce with Britain, France, and their dependencies. The act was aimed at
the European powers, who were damaging American trade and pride, but it
also punished the Indians by trying to shut out the British traders upon
whom they greatly depended.

Game was also scarce, and the Prophet accused the Americans of poi-
soning the land. In the spring exceptional numbers of Indians applied for
help at the British posts of Fort Malden and St. Joseph—hungry, impover-
ished, and discontented.[1]

The snows, biting winds, and icy streams came and went, but the fire inside Tecumseh was not put out. Spring brought something like a thousand
Indians to Prophetstown: Kickapoos incensed by their chiefs' cession of the
additional tract to Harrison, Winnebagos, a few of the Three Fires, and up to
thirty Creeks from the south. Others were on their way, including Foxes and
Sacs and some Indians who, it was said, came from as far as the Missouri
River. They were responding to the recent appeals of the Shawnee brothers,
and were coming to hear the words of the Great Spirit and debate the issue
of peace or war.[2]

Tecumseh left his brother to receive the visitors, and went northeast on a particularly important mission to the Detroit River. Some Ottawas, Potawatomis, Ojibwas, and Shawnees lived in the vicinity, but Tecumseh was likely interested in the Wyandot villages of Maguaga and Brownstown, south of Detroit. In addition to enjoying a special status among the tribes, the Wyandots symbolized pan-tribal unity. Between 1786 and 1795 Brownstown had been the very seat, or council fire, of the great confederacy. The Detroit River Wyandots were relatively acculturated and kept farms similar to those of white neighbors, but if Tecumseh could exploit their fear of being dispossessed by the United States and win them over, he could strengthen his claim that the new confederacy was the true successor to the memorable union of the 1790s.

Tecumseh's diplomacy with the Wyandots resulted in some little reward. In May a few of the Detroit Wyandots were at Prophetstown, while early in June Tecumseh's previous visit to the Sandusky seems at last to have borne some fruit. Evidently he had asked why the "uncles" of the tribes, the keepers of the great wampum belt of the old confederacy, sat so quietly while the tribes were being plundered. And he had requested to see that belt, and the Indian copies of any treaties the Sandusky Wyandots had in their custody. The Wyandots had said that it had been so long since anyone had inquired about the belt that they supposed it had been forgotten.

But early in June one Sandusky chief broke with his fellows and led a party down the Wabash, carrying the great wampum belt with him and declaring solidarity with the Prophet. The Wyandots flaunted it before the Mississinewa band of Miamis, urging them to attend upcoming conferences, and it was probably these Indians who shortly established a village of their own near Prophetstown.[3]

Tecumseh was back at Prophetstown about the same time. He found several barrels of salt standing by the riverside. They had come from Vincennes as part of a salt annuity granted by the treaty of 1803. In previous years the delivery had not been challenged, but the new cession had alerted Tecumseh to the danger of accepting annuities, and when the salt pirogue had reached Prophetstown to deposit the barrels due the Shawnees and Kickapoos there, Tenskwatawa had demurred about accepting them. He explained that his brother was absent, and without him no decision could be taken. However, Tecumseh was expected back daily, and the barrels could be stacked ashore for his consideration.

Tecumseh left no one in doubt about his opinion. When the young French boatmen returned to Prophetstown after making deliveries upriver they found him in a stormy mood. As the rejected barrels were being rolled back into the pirogue Tecumseh strode forward angrily, seizing the master, Gamlin, and "several others" by the hair, and shaking them "violently." He demanded to know if they were "Americans." Other warriors, standing around, grew excited. Some referred to Michel Brouillet, Harrison's spy, as "an American dog," and plundered the storehouse of tobacco and provisions he kept at the village. Badly frightened, the boatmen hurried back to Vincennes.[4]

The fracas over the salt indicated the deteriorating temper of the Indians at Prophetstown. But despite his success with the Wyandots, Tecumseh suffered a setback in the intertribal conference, which took place about the end of May at Parc-aux-Vaches, near the south bend of the St. Joseph River. This, it seems, was considered to be a more secluded venue than Prophetstown, safer from prying American officials. Tecumseh was not there, and his band may have been represented by the Prophet. The brothers had their supporters, including western Potawatomis, Kickapoos, and Winnebagos, but not enough to persuade other Indians to join strong action against the Americans. Most of the Weas, Piankeshaws, Miamis, Delawares, Ottawas, Ojibwas, and those Potawatomis from the St. Joseph and Michigan areas stood firmly against war. After the council ended and the warriors had departed, a fresh Delaware delegation arrived with a message from Harrison. It warned the Indians that if the tomahawk was raised all Indians would be endangered, because the Americans would not be able to distinguish friend from foe. The Prophet was furious at the Governor's attempt to interfere with the deliberations of the tribes.[5]

The council denied Tecumseh the support he needed to fight, but it lifted the gloom in Vincennes, which had been shuddering at ominous rumors of Indian hostility. In June, for example, a Piankeshaw had reported the tribes to be on the brink of insurrection, and said that Vincennes would be treacherously attacked by a large party of Indian visitors. At a given signal four or five warriors would assault each house. Harrison had taken precautions. He knew that his militia was being weakened by repeated fears of an Indian war. In 1809 several hundred families had fled the frontier, and others were still going. That meant fewer men available for service. On 25 June he raised two companies of Vincennes militia, but was relieved when a company of United States regulars marched in from Kentucky a fortnight later and enabled him to dismiss them.[6]

By high summer the immediate threat of war had gone. The Indian conference had declared for peace. Tecumseh's men were well armed, but they had little ammunition, and were scattering in search of game. In August only the Winnebagos remained in force at Prophetstown, and they intended going home in the fall.[7]

Tecumseh, momentarily frustrated in his plan for a general war, began to think of negotiation.

He was not entirely ignorant of what went on in Vincennes. Touissant Dubois, who had been spying for Harrison in Prophetstown, had spoken of the Governor's mobilization. He had also told the Prophet that Harrison had offered to hear the Indians' complaints in Vincennes. But Tecumseh had other sources of information, including some white man who had witnessed the treaty of Fort Wayne and subsequently visited Prophetstown. Tecumseh never named him, but learned from him that even in Vincennes there were those who opposed Harrison's treaty and favored conciliating the tribes. The chief was also informed, this time falsely, that Harrison had only two more years left in office.[8]

This made sense to Tecumseh, who doubted that the frontier was so crowded that the Americans needed more land. It occurred to him that the land purchases were merely the work of a clique of speculators, for whom Harrison was the instrument, and that the Indians might get justice elsewhere. There was another reason to start talking to the Americans. After the failure at Parc-aux-Vaches, it was necessary to temporize until the brothers could build more support.

Incidents that occurred in July brought negotiations closer. Although Tecumseh and the Prophet advised their followers to avoid premature hostilities, they had few means of controlling inflamed warriors. Four Kickapoos, returning from a visit to the small Shaker community on the east bank of the Wabash above Vincennes, stole five horses belonging to local whites. The Creeks at Prophetstown, with some other warriors, ordered settlers on the Driftwood fork of the White to get out and pilfered stock, and a couple of shots were fired at a man on the Wabash.[9]

These outrages encouraged counterattack, and Tecumseh sent two Shawnees to Vincennes in an effort to deceive Harrison into believing that while the warriors had wanted the war the chiefs had refused to go along with it. Harrison also hoped to calm the situation, and at the end of July a thin, hook-nosed Frenchman named Joseph Barron arrived at Prophetstown with a message from the Governor.

In old age Barron was happy to embroider his reminiscences, which have always to be approached with skepticism. However, he claimed that he was brought before the Prophet in the presence of Indians from different tribes. Tenskwatawa looked Barron over silently for a few minutes and then demanded to know his business. "Brouillet was here," the Prophet said fiercely. "He was a spy. Dubois was here. He was a spy. Now *you* have come. You too are a spy." He pointed to the ground near Barron's feet. "There is your grave!" he declared. "Look on it!" At that moment Tecumseh emerged from a lodge and took command. He was formal and cold, but assured the frightened messenger that he was safe, and asked him the purpose of his mission.[10]

Harrison's message was addressed to the Prophet, who the Governor still believed to be leading the movement. He said he regarded Tenskwatawa as an enemy of the United States, but the "chain of friendship" was not beyond repair. The Indians must choose whether they would travel the "large, open and pleasant" path to peace or the "narrow and crooked" way to misery and ruin. Harrison went on:

> I know your warriors are brave. Ours are not less so, but what can a few brave warriors do against the innumerable warriors of the Seventeen Fires [United States]. Our Blue Coats [regulars] are more numerous than you can count, and our hunting shirts [militia] are like the leaves of the forests or the grains of sand on the Wabash. Do not think that the Red Coats [British] can protect you. They are not able to protect themselves. They do not think of going to war with us. If they did in a few moons you would see our flags wave on all the forts of Canada.

The Governor concluded his address by offering to hear complaints about the treaty of Fort Wayne. He had the power to restore the land to its "rightful owners" if it had been wrongly sold. Or if they preferred, the Indians might take their case directly to their Great Father, the President, and Harrison would arrange the trip to ensure their safe return.

Harrison had no intention of surrendering the Fort Wayne cession, nor of admitting Tecumseh's contention that the land belonged to all Indians, but he sounded compromising. That evening Tecumseh invited Barron into his cabin, and the two talked long into the night. The chief explained that he did not want war, but he could not see how he could remain at peace with those who were robbing his people. The Indians owned the land, and it was not for the United States to decide who held what in order to purchase it from them. Nevertheless, he was glad Harrison had sent the speech, and he would go to Vincennes. He warned Barron that although he would choose thirty principal men to accompany him, he expected that one hundred Indians might visit the town, "as he knew that the young men were fond of attending on such occasions."

Barron was back in Vincennes on 2 August. Harrison rushed Brouillet back to Prophetstown with the additional message that only the chiefs and a few of their young men should make the visit. He remembered those warnings, only months old, that the Indians would attack the town under the guise of a friendly visit. In reporting to the Secretary of War, Harrison renewed an appeal he had made for authority to establish posts on the up-

per Wabash at the boundary of the new purchase, and belatedly discovered
the identity of the real power at Prophetstown: Tecumseh. "This brother," he
wrote, "is really the efficient man—the Moses of the family . . . He is . . . described by all as a bold, active, sensible man, daring in the extreme, and capable of any undertaking."[11]

On 14 August 1810 Captain George Rogers Clark Floyd, the newly arrived commandant at Fort Knox, wrote a letter to his wife:

> Nothing new has transpired since my last letter to you except that
> the Shawanoe Indians have come. They passed this garrison, which
> is three miles above Vincennes, on Sunday last [12 August], in eighty
> canoes. They were all painted in the most terrific manner. They were
> stopped at the garrison by me for a short time. I examined their ca-
> noes and found them well prepared for war, in case of an attack.
> They were headed by the brother of The Prophet, who, perhaps,
> is one of the finest looking men I ever saw—about six feet high,
> straight, with large, fine features, and altogether a daring bold-
> looking fellow. The Governor's council with them will commence to-
> morrow morning. He has directed me to attend.[12]

Perhaps seventy-five warriors camped with Tecumseh a mile or so above
the town, while word of their arrival went ahead. Then on the fifteenth
Tecumseh led his party into Vincennes, toward a clearing in a small grove of
trees close to Grouseland, Governor William Henry Harrison's two-story
house with its tall chimneys. Here, fenced from the crowds, Harrison had
prepared the council ground.

This was a legendary meeting, the first confrontation between Tecumseh
and the man he regarded as his principal opponent in the fight for the
northwest. One popular story about it was vouched for by eyewitnesses, albeit after uncredited versions had appeared in print, and may have been
true. When the Indians reached the ground, it went, they found Harrison
and his entourage seated on a dais, on which the Governor affably offered
Tecumseh a seat. In reply Tecumseh declared "the earth was the most
proper place for the Indians, as they liked to repose upon the bosom of their
mother," and he seated himself with his fellows upon the grass. One who
knew some of the participants recorded that the effect was "electrical, and
for some moments there was a perfect silence."[13]

Of the two men who now faced each other, Tecumseh was the more
striking and impassioned. The handsome chief saw before him a long-faced
man with brown hair, a wandering nose, and a mild but alert expression.

Not a man to be persuaded, however. Tecumseh spent several days explaining his point of view to Harrison, but his speeches were reported to be "sufficiently insolent and his pretensions arrogant." When the conference resumed on 20 August the sides were deadlocked and tense.·

Tecumseh was frustrated by his inability to make the Governor understand. Harrison sat with several officials, including judges of the territorial supreme court, the secretary of the territory, and several army officers and unarmed citizens. Close by, a guard of thirteen soldiers from Fort Knox stood ready. In addition to Tecumseh's following, several other Indians were in attendance, including some Piankeshaws and Weas. One was the principal chief of the Weas, who had consented to the treaty of Fort Wayne. He had been boasting that he would tell Tecumseh that he had no business interfering in Wea affairs, but now he sat silently, unwilling to fulfill his promise. Another supporter of the treaty was present: the much-despised Potawatomi chief Winamek, who had been living under the threat of assassination for his part in the business. He lay on the grass to Harrison's left, silent but nursing a brace of pistols.

Patiently, Tecumseh put his case again. He began by explaining that the Indians regarded neither the Americans nor the British as satisfactory successors to their old French father. Indian oratory normally included an appeal to history, or at least to history as the Indians now chose to represent it. The French, Tecumseh said, had treated the Indians as their children, bestowing gifts on them but asking little in return. By comparison, the British Father had been wanting. Forgetting how the British colonies had taken Kentucky from the Shawnees when he had been a mere child, Tecumseh claimed the British had not threatened Indian land, though they were niggardly with their presents, and had used the Indians to fight their wars for them.

However, Tecumseh reserved his severest criticism for the Americans. They had never been trustworthy, complained the chief. He instanced the murder of the Christian Delawares at Gnadenhutten in 1782 and the slaying of Moluntha by Big Knives four years later. "My brother," Tecumseh asked Harrison, "after this conduct can you blame me for placing little confidence in the promises of our Fathers, the Americans?"

Dealing with more recent grievances, Tecumseh accused the Seventeen Fires of deliberately goading the Indians into a war. Occasionally Indians had been killed by whites, and many Kickapoos had contracted smallpox, which some attributed to infected annuities delivered them by the United States the previous year. More important, the Americans were taking the land. "I do not see how we can remain at peace with you," the Shawnee said openly, "if you continue to do so . . . You try to force the red people to do some injury. It is you that is pushing them on to do mischief."

Tecumseh repeated his opinion that the Indians held their lands in common, and he attacked the Americans for identifying individual tribes or groups of tribes as owners of tracts for the purpose of facilitating purchases. He fully admitted that he was deposing the village chiefs who had put their names to land deals and substituting the authority of the warriors, and he even threatened the lives of those chiefs involved. As for the treaties themselves, Tecumseh did not know whether they had been approved by the President or not, but they were invalid, and had been unfairly negotiated. The deficiencies of the recent treaty were not lost on the Shawnee chief. The Weas, he complained, had been isolated "because of their small numbers," while the Potawatomis had been employed to bully other Indians into signing. Tecumseh poured abuse upon Winamek. The Potawatomi suffered the tongue-lashing without protest, but he checked his pistol, ready for trouble.

Tecumseh explained that the tribes would meet soon at Brownstown to find out which chiefs had abused their trust by selling land, so that they could be punished. Their deaths would be the responsibility of the United States. He also announced that he was uniting the tribes against further cessions, and would resist any attempt to settle the recent purchase. Yet he did not want war, and he offered Harrison an escape from it. He asked the Governor to return the land and to permit more traders to serve the Indians. The Indians wanted no annuities or presents, and would buy what they required; beyond this, they needed no more than the occasional services of a gunsmith.

Harrison had spent years speaking to Indian leaders, but he had never met one like Tecumseh before. Here was no humble supplicant or surly dissembler. The man standing before him boldly claimed to represent every tribe on the continent, candidly denounced the land cessions, and fiercely declared his determination to resist them. Although he disavowed hostile intentions, he predicted that war would be the result of American policies, and showed no fear of it. Tecumseh confirmed that he would accept powder from the British, and proudly proclaimed himself "the head" of a defensive confederacy. He wanted no charity from the white man, only an honest trade. Yet although the speech was defiant it was not aggressive. Rather Tecumseh pleaded for justice. He was trying to tell Harrison that his people were being oppressed, and if nothing was done about it, they would fight.

Some whites would have understood, but the Governor could or would not listen. As far as he was concerned, the land had been bought from its rightful owners, and the idea that the Indians held land in common was not only manifestly preposterous but dangerous. It would undo every treaty he had made, and block the further purchases he had in mind. His reply was translated into Shawnee, Potawatomi, and Miami by Joseph Barron. The

Governor denied that his government had treated the Indians dishonestly and unjustly. The Indians were not one nation, nor owned the land in common, for had not the Great Spirit given them different tongues?

Then it happened. Tecumseh lost his temper. While Harrison was still speaking the chief rose to his feet in anger, gesticulating violently. The warriors at his back also stood. They had left their firearms behind, as the parties had agreed, but their hands fell to war clubs, knives, and tomahawks. Tecumseh "spoke for some time with great vehemence and anger," and the surprised Barron turned to Harrison to tell him he was being called a liar.

For a few terrible moments it looked as if the council would disintegrate into bloodshed. John Gibson, secretary of the territory, flashed an anxious glance at the Governor. "Those fellows intend mischief!" he said. "You had better bring up the guard!" He signaled the small band of regulars, who started forward from where they had been standing in some shade. Harrison drew a dress sword, and Captain Floyd a dirk, while Winamek cocked a pistol. A civilian, the Reverend William Winans, scurried to the governor's house to find a gun to defend Harrison's family, and other citizens pulled rails from a fence to defend themselves.

Governor Harrison was never cooler. He told Barron to tell Tecumseh the council was finished. He would reply to the Indians' complaints in writing, and if the chief wanted to speak to him again he must act through another person. Heated, but restraining themselves, the Indians returned to their camp.

That night was charged, and Harrison put together three companies of militia in case Tecumseh attacked the town. In fact the Shawnee chief was already regretting his show of temper, which had done his cause no good whatsoever. Early the next morning Barron appeared at his camp, accompanied by Sheriff John McCandless and a man named Whitaker, with a message from Harrison. Tecumseh readily apologized for his conduct. He excused himself by saying that some people in Vincennes blamed Harrison personally for the treaty of Fort Wayne, which had not been authorized by the President. Barron left Tecumseh smoking his pipe beside his tent pole with McCandless and Whitaker, and amity seemed to have been restored. Later in the day the council resumed, but the militia were ready, and a nervousness hung in the air.

Tecumseh rose to speak, a model of courtesy. He repeated, more by way of apology, the information he had been given that Harrison did not represent the views of all the people of Vincennes. But when the Governor asked if the surveyors running the new purchase would be safe, and whether Tecumseh's Kickapoo followers would receive their annuities, Tecumseh stood firm. The Indians wanted their land, not annuities.

Brothers [he said] they want to save that piece of land. We do not wish you to take it. It is small enough for our purposes. If you do take it you must blame yourself as the cause of trouble between us and the tribes who sold it to you. I want the present boundary line to continue. Should you cross it, I assure you it will be productive of bad consequences.

When Tecumseh sat down, Wyandot, Kickapoo, Potawatomi, and Winnebago orators spoke to the same intent, approving Tecumseh's principles and confirming that he was their leader.

Neither Harrison nor Tecumseh would yield ground. Harrison insisted that the lands had been fairly bought and would be defended by force if necessary. Tecumseh's speech would be sent to the President, but the Governor warned the Shawnee that he should not expect a favorable answer, for the United States would never acknowledge the Wabash lands to have belonged to any Indians but those who had been occupying them.

Both men sensed the inevitability of conflict, and would return to prepare for it. Tecumseh would canvass the western Indians, while Harrison would temporarily suspend the survey of the new purchase but recommend to the government a show of force and the establishment of one or more military posts on the upper Wabash, where trouble was likely to begin.

According to Moses Dawson, later Harrison's associate and biographer, Harrison and Barron visited Tecumseh's camp on the evening of 22 August, for a final but private meeting. The Shawnee chief tried to reach Harrison. If the treaty of Fort Wayne was rescinded, and the Americans agreed to hold future negotiations with all, rather than a few, of the tribes, Tecumseh would prove himself a good friend to the United States. He would even join them against the British. He was not deceived by the redcoats, he explained. They only wanted the Indians to fight their wars. He clapped his hands and imitated a person shouting for a dog to illustrate the way the redcoats summoned the tribes to fight. However, Tecumseh spoke frankly. In the end, he believed, he would be forced into a war with the Americans. But he promised that if that happened, he would do his utmost to protect women and children.

The Governor said that he would send Tecumseh's complaints to the President, but he very much doubted that the chief's terms would be acceptable.

"Well," replied Tecumseh with an air of resignation, "as the Great Chief [the President] is to determine the matter, I hope the Great Spirit will put some sense into his head to induce him to direct you to give up this land. It is true, he is so far off. He will not be injured by the war. He may still sit in his town, and drink his wine, whilst you and I will have to fight it out."[14]

16

TECUMSEH'S DIPLOMACY

The task of building an Indian confederacy was enormous.

Many had trod the path to Indian unity before, men of stature such as Guyasuta and Pontiac, Brant and Blue Jacket. They had tried to persuade diverse and independent-minded Indian villagers to lay aside their differences in the common interest, but they had all failed. Even their greatest successes had been partial and transitory.

The problems were daunting. The forbidding geographical distances between remote native communities, and their sense of powerlessness in the face of the awesome and seductive power of the Seventeen Fires. The ease with which intertribal ventures fell apart, sometimes because of competition between varied local priorities, or the jealousies of proud chiefs. There were simmering intertribal rivalries, such as those that set the Ojibwas against the Dakota Sioux or the Potawatomis against the Osages, and ferocious storms could suddenly break from nowhere to fracture relationships between even generally amicable peoples. In the summer of 1810, for example, the Illinois Kickapoos were planning to attack the Rock River Winnebagos, who had massacred a Kickapoo party near the mouth of the Missouri. Yet these were the greatest supporters of Tecumseh and the Prophet.[1]

Not the least difficulty was the problem of communication among peoples speaking different languages. The Indians Tecumseh was trying to mold to his purpose were spread in a huge arc across the white frontier, stretching from New York in the northeast, sprawling across the Great Lakes country and the midwest, and through the southern states to reach its

southeastern terminus in Florida. The Wyandots, Cherokees, and the six nations of the Iroquois Confederacy spoke different Iroquoian languages. The
Winnebagos and Dakotas used Siouan languages, but ones that were mutually unintelligible. Among the Choctaws and Creeks of the south, Muskogee-
speakers predominated. Even those tribes which belonged to the great
Algonquian family of languages needed interpreters to speak to each other.
Shawnees could understand Kickapoos, but not Sacs and Foxes, whose languages were next-closest to their own. And among the other Algonquian
tongues Tecumseh encountered were Ojibwa (the Three Fires), Miami (Miamis, Weas, Piankeshaws, and Eel Rivers), Delaware, Munsee, and Menom-
inee.

Working within such diversity—of language, predicament, and purpose—Tecumseh faced greater difficulties than those of any American or
European statesman. Yet he would not be deterred. When William Wells
had the temerity to tell him that his task was impossible, Tecumseh merely
replied that Wells would live to see otherwise. Little wonder that one observer referred to the Shawnee as "a man of enterprise and energy."[2]

A few circumstances did play to Tecumseh's advantage. Centuries of
trade between Indian villages, as well as more than a century of political
pan-Indian activity among the Lakes Indians, had eased the communication problem between different and potentially hostile groups. From the
Pawnees these Indians had borrowed the symbol of the calumet and tobacco. When an emissary from one group presented the ceremonial pipe to
members of another it signified that he wished to speak, and that he should
not be attacked. Some trade jargons had also developed, eroding if not erad-
icating linguistic barriers, and belts of wampum bearing easily recognizable
symbols were important tools of intertribal diplomacy. Describing the
British belt he took to Fort Malden at the end of 1810, Tecumseh said: "On
one end is your [British] hand. On the other, that of the red people (both
hands in black wampum, but the Indian end of the belt darker than the
other) and in the middle the hearts of both."[3] Such designs clearly indicated
peace and solidarity.

Likewise, ideas promulgated by Tecumseh, such as the common ownership of land, had been widely circulated by pan-Indian diplomats since the
1780s, and were well known to most of Tecumseh's audiences.

Most obviously, Tecumseh's strategy was supported by the times themselves. Such widespread intertribal movements as had occurred in the past
had been responses to powerful external threats. The defeat of the French
and the stresses of adjusting to the triumphant British had fueled a general
Indian revolt in 1763, while the attempt of the new United States to seize the
northwest after the Revolutionary War had produced the more sophisticated confederacies of the 1780s and 1790s. Tecumseh, too, was rallying the

Indians around a crisis, the deep inroads being made into the territory and cultures of the tribes since the beginning of the nineteenth century.

Another, and superficially unlikely, advantage was the decentralized political structure of Indian communities. Everywhere, tribal organization was weak, and the village chiefs had limited ways of enforcing discipline and compliance. They relied upon persuasion, example, and consensus. Individual Indians might be persuaded to follow this or that course of action, but ultimately they were very much free agents. This helped Tecumseh. Although many of the village chiefs were cautious, the Shawnee leader could pull the power from beneath their feet by inducing the warriors to follow him. For the most part he was not harnessing tribes to his standard, so much as some villages or individuals within tribes.

Tecumseh recruited discreetly, avoiding whites who could report his activities and urging secrecy upon Indian audiences. Consequently, we have little information about his tours, and must reconstruct them from scrappy contemporary references and unreliable and murky traditions passed down by eyewitnesses. No better example of this is a strenuous journey conducted by Tecumseh in the summer of 1810, after his clash with Harrison. He had gone east in 1809, north early in 1810, and had originally planned a southern trip for the summer, but decided to postpone that arduous venture. Instead, he evidently went west, rallying his most enthusiastic allies about the upper Mississippi. Reports to that effect must have reached Harrison, who wrote the following summer that "you hear of him [Tecumseh] on the shores of Lake Erie or Michigan or on the banks of the Mississippi," but none of them have survived. Unsatisfactory memories, recounted long afterward, have to form the backbone of our account of Tecumseh's next adventure.[4]

Unlike the tribes in New York, Ohio, and Michigan Territory, the western Indians included the most inveterate enemies of the United States. Several of their chiefs, such as Gomo and Sequenebee of the Illinois River Potawatomis, wanted nothing to do with war, but the martial spirit was already manifesting itself in attacks upon American citizens in these regions. In July a Vincennes post rider bound for St. Louis was killed, and on the twenty-first of that month a party of Potawatomis under Mad Sturgeon, the brother-in-law of Main Poc, attacked the camp of a posse of six whites on a branch of the Salt River. The Americans, led by William Cole, had left the district of St. Charles (St. Louis) to pursue Indian raiders. Cole and three of his men were killed, a fifth wounded and left for dead, while the sixth man survived by hiding in a sinkhole. The culprits were certainly followers of the Shawnee brothers, and one would spend the coming winter at Prophetstown. But Tecumseh disapproved of such premature hostilities. He knew they could disrupt his plans before he was ready.[5]

Details of Tecumseh's western tour were given to Nehemiah Matson by Shabeni during long conversations in 1836. Shabeni was a headman of the Potawatomi village on the Fox River (Illinois), and became a devoted disciple of Tecumseh—although strict accuracy in his reminiscences, rendered long afterward by Matson, cannot be expected. He remembered that he was playing ball with his warriors during the early part of an Indian summer when Tecumseh arrived at his village with three of his chiefs, all mounted on spirited black ponies. The next day a dog was killed, and a feast honored the visitors, with songs and dances performed into the night. If true, this account suggests that Tecumseh had ascended the Tippecanoe, crossed the divide to the Kankakee, and then come downstream, visiting such Potawatomi villages as those of Main Poc, Moquongo, and Little Chief before turning up the Fox to find Shabeni. Inspired as usual by the charismatic Shawnee, Shabeni agreed to join Tecumseh's party.

Tecumseh descended the Illinois River to Peoria. The western Potawatomis he visited on the river had not signed Harrison's treaties, but chiefs such as Gomo, Comas, and Sequenebee declined to support Tecumseh. Matson picked up a tradition, apparently from Illinois pioneers, that the Shawnee also visited a French trader, François Racine, at Peoria, but left the town without even speaking to some of the Indians camped about.[6]

The Shabeni account then describes how Tecumseh led his party to the Rock River, which they ascended northward into present Wisconsin, calling at several Winnebago towns along the way. Tecumseh would have had a stronger welcome here, but after negotiating Lake Winnebago and following the Fox River to Green Bay he was among the Menominees, who had never been much interested in the Prophet's religion. At Green Bay, for the first time, independent traditions support the Shabeni story.

James Biddle, who was in the area six years afterward and knew the Menominees and one of their chiefs, Tomah, wrote an account of Tecumseh's visit in 1854. He said Tecumseh held a council with the Menominees, but Tomah resisted his call for war. The warriors were free to join Tecumseh if they wished, explained the chief, but as for himself, his hands were unstained by human blood. "The effect," wrote Biddle, was "described as tremendous . . . and the gravity of the council was disturbed for an instant by a murmur of approbation." Despite Tecumseh's efforts, Tomah's "prudent counsels prevailed."

A trader with the Menominees, Augustus Grignon, also heard that Shawnee emissaries visited the tribe in 1810, when he himself was at Michilimackinac. He doubted that either Tecumseh or the Prophet came in person, but he may easily have been mistaken. In 1810 Tecumseh was not the legendary figure he afterward became, and his presence in the delegation was not a detail a fur trader would have deemed worth remembering,

Tecumseh. Benson J. Lossing's engraving, adapted from a drawing said to have been made from life by Pierre Le Dru. Because Tecumseh was erroneously believed to have been a brigadier-general in the British army and certainly possessed a uniform coat, Lossing replaced the Indian costume with regimentals. No fully authenticated portrait of Tecumseh exists.

Thomas Worthington, who visited Tecumseh at Greenville in 1807 and escorted him to Chillicothe to address a public meeting.
(COURTESY OF THE OHIO HISTORICAL SOCIETY.)

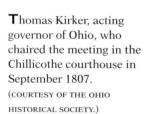

Thomas Kirker, acting governor of Ohio, who chaired the meeting in the Chillicothe courthouse in September 1807.
(COURTESY OF THE OHIO HISTORICAL SOCIETY.)

The Chillicothe courthouse, where Tecumseh reassured American settlers of Indian goodwill. The engraving, from *The American Pioneer* (1842), somewhat inaccurately reconstructs the view of 1801. The mound to the right was larger than represented here, while the barracks and Governor Edward Tiffin's house in the distance should have been farther right and out of the picture.

Simon Kenton, who attacked two of Tecumseh's camps, but after the peace of Greenville fraternized with the chief in Ohio. (COURTESY OF THE WISE INN, VIRGINIA.)

"Peter Waggoner," photographed in his final years. A white Indian, he was persuaded to abandon his Indian family around 1812 and to repatriate to the Virginian community around Hacker's Creek. There he was accepted as Peter Waggoner, a three-year-old carried off by Shawnees in May 1793. Locals credited Tecumseh with leading the raid. "Waggoner" died in 1879.

The Prophet, around 1808, from a drawing by Pierre Le Dru. Previously known as Lalawéthika (the Rattle) and later as Tenskwatawa (the Open Door), this younger brother of Tecumseh started the Shawnee reform movement in 1805.

The Prophet, 1824. A lithograph published in *The Aboriginal Port Folio* (1835–36), made from a painting done from life by James Otto Lewis around 1824. The original has disappeared.

The Prophet, painted by Charles Bird King and engraved for Thomas L.
McKenney and James Hall, *The Indian Tribes of North America* (1836–44).

Rival Shawnee headmen. (top) An elderly Black Hoof, head civil chief of the Shawnees of Wapakoneta, Ohio, who saw Tecumseh and the Prophet, as challengers to his leadership. (bottom) Quatawapea, known as Colonel Lewis, head of a band of Ohio Shawnees and Mingoes. Although proud of the medal he had received from President Jefferson, he sympathized with Tecumseh and the Prophet, but he lacked the courage to give outright support. Both portraits engraved for McKenney and Hall.

William Wells, Indian agent at Fort Wayne, Indiana Territory, from 1802 to 1809. He was both ambitious and apparently dishonest, and his intemperate reports fueled American difficulties with the Prophet and exasperated Tecumseh. Nevertheless, he died a hero's death at Dearborn in 1812. (COURTESY OF THE CHICAGO HISTORICAL SOCIETY, ICHi-14160.)

William Henry Harrison, painted around 1800, shortly before he became governor of the Indiana Territory. The major-general's uniform was added during the War of 1812. Harrison's mishandling of Indian affairs, particularly his relentless demand for Indian lands, created unnecessary hostility to the United States before the war. He was a significant cause of Tecumseh's revolt. (COURTESY OF THE FRANCIS VIGO CHAPTER DAR, VINCENNES, INDIANA.)

Amherstburg, painted by Margaret Reynolds from Elliott's Point in 1813. Bois Blanc Island is on the left. On the right the town, dock yard, and Fort Malden are visible. The *Queen Charlotte* is shown under sail and the *Detroit* being built on the stocks. The figures have not been identified, but some have supposed the British officer to have been Henry Procter and the Indian standing profile in the right-hand corner to be Tecumseh. (COURTESY OF THE DEPARTMENT OF CANADIAN HERITAGE: FORT MALDEN NATIONAL HISTORIC SITE.)

Thomas McKee, British Indian agent, shown in the 1790s, while he was a member of the 60th Regiment. Dissolute and belligerent, McKee was replaced by Matthew Elliott as Superintendent at Amherstburg in 1808 but continued to help administer Britain's Indian affairs. During the War of 1812 he fought alongside Tecumseh dressed as an Indian. The portrait was conclusively identified by R. Alan Douglas of the Windsor Community Museum, where it now hangs. (COURTESY OF THE WILLIAM L. CLEMENTS LIBRARY, ANN ARBOR, MICHIGAN.)

Francis Gore, lieutenant-governor in Upper Canada in 1808, at which time Tecumseh met him at Fort Malden. Capable, if sometimes impetuous, Gore spearheaded Britain's attempts to cultivate relations with the Indians after the *Chesapeake* incident of 1807 threatened war with the United States. The portrait was painted in England in 1814. (COURTESY OF THE METROPOLITAN TORONTO REFERENCE LIBRARY.)

Indian allies: (top) Shabeni, an Ottawa by birth but headman of a Potawatomi village when he first met Tecumseh in 1808. A devoted follower of the Shawnee chief, he retired to Illinois after the War of 1812 and died near Morris in July 1859, dependent upon the charity of local white friends. This photograph was taken around 1857. (bottom) Nawkaw (Wood), also known as Caraymaunee (Walking Turtle), leader of the Green Lake Winnebagos, Wisconsin. Some six feet in height, erect and powerful, he was fond of dress. He was fiercely proud of his friendship with Tecumseh until he died in the 1830s. An engraving made for McKenney and Hall from a painting by Charles Bird King.

Tecumseh confronting Harrison at Vincennes in 1810. One of several interpretations of the famous event, this nineteenth-century reconstruction by W. Ridgway is extremely inaccurate. The costumes of the Indians are fanciful, and the artist located the incident in front of the Vincennes legislative building rather than Harrison's home, Grouseland.

Choctaw opponents. (top) Moshulatubbee, last hereditary district chief of the Choctaws. His name, which meant "One Who Perseveres and Kills," suggests he had been a ferocious warrior, but when Tecumseh visited him in 1811 Moshulatubbee was tall but corpulent, a heavy drinker, and pleasant-natured. Though he was sympathetic to Tecumseh's cause, Moshulatubbee ultimately threw his influence against him. Years later the United States forced him from his traditional homelands and he died in Oklahoma in 1838. His portrait was painted by George Catlin. (bottom) Pushmataha, another of the three district chiefs of the Choctaws at the time Tecumseh canvassed the tribe. Pushmataha is believed to have opposed Tecumseh throughout, and he later helped the Americans to defeat the Shawnee's Creek allies during the War of 1813–14.

Creek allies. (top) Josiah Francis, a mestizo Creek, variously described as a silversmith or blacksmith. Also known as Hillis Haya (Medicine Maker) he became the leading Red Stick prophet, developing a fiery brand of Tenskwatawa's religion. Retreating to Spanish Florida after the defeat of the Red Sticks, he took his son to Britain in 1815–16, lobbying for military intervention on behalf of the Creeks. There he made this crude self-portrait. He was captured and hanged in Florida in 1818. (bottom) Hopoithle Mico, head civil chief of the Upper Creek town of Tallassee, as he appeared to John Trumbull in 1790. An opponent of land sales and American attempts to "civilize" the Creeks, his support for the Red Stick revolt fomented by Tecumseh was partly motivated by his desire to overthrow a rival, Big Warrior, who supervised the tribal council. Then a man of great age, Hopoithle Mico was surrendered to the Americans by defeated Red Sticks in April 1814.

Fort Harrison, built by Harrison's army on the march to Prophetstown in 1811.

The battle of Tippecanoe, 7 November 1811. In this nineteenth-century print Alonzo Chappel celebrated the daybreak charge by which the Americans eventually dispersed the Indians.

even if he had been told it. Grignon, like Matson and Biddle, wrote many years later of an event he had not witnessed personally.[7]

Shabeni said that Tecumseh's next move took him to the Mississippi. He visited the trading mart at Prairie du Chien, which attracted Indians of many tribes, and then went downstream, appealing to the Sacs and Foxes, particularly in Saukenuk, at the mouth of the Rock River, and in nearby Wapello. This is the first evidence of Tecumseh reaching the Sacs, but it was far from an opportune time to visit. Once the most anti-American warriors of the region, the Sacs had quieted down since Fort Madison was strengthened in 1809, and they had begun to improve their economy by exploiting local lead mines. In 1811 Benjamin Howard, the governor of Louisiana, even reported that the tribe was "now very friendly to us."[8]

Even the most militant Sac, Black Hawk, remembered how indifferently his tribe had treated the Shawnee reformers. A Sac delegation was sent to Tenskwatawa in 1809, and it returned with one of his "prophets," about the winter of 1809–1810. This individual told the Sacs at Saukenuk that "if you do not join your friends on the Wabash, the Americans will take this very village from you!" Ruefully Black Hawk admitted that the "prophet" proved to be right, but he did not think so at the time.[9]

Only one Sac account actually mentions Tecumseh visiting their towns, but it is a confused statement, made in 1823. The narrator, Wennebea (Spinning Top), said that both Tecumseh and the Prophet convened a council at the Sac villages. Now, Tenskwatawa never visited the Sacs. To be frank, he showed little disposition to go anywhere in pursuit of his mission, and we must conclude either that Wennebea confused a Sac visit to Prophetstown with one of Tecumseh's calls upon the Sacs, in 1810 and 1812, or that he erroneously thought one of the party Tecumseh brought with him was the Prophet. It is likely that Tecumseh's entourage did contain someone instructed in his brother's principles, because Tecumseh was still representing his views to be those prescribed by the Great Spirit.

Wennebea recalled that the Prophet told the Sacs to discard their medicine bags, and some obeyed. Others challenged him, demanding he raise the dead to prove his supposed powers. The Prophet shifted nervously, avoiding the challenge, and Wennebea refused to put aside his medicine bag and openly protested that it had served him well. The Prophet "was very angry at me," he said, "and his brother, Tecumseh, who was near to us, laid his hand upon me and offered to strike me, which he would have done had he not been prevented."[10]

Whatever happened when Tecumseh visited the Sacs, no one remembered that he had much success.

Shabeni parted with Tecumseh at Saukenuk and went home, leaving the Shawnee's party to visit the Indians of Missouri. Although Shabeni had nothing to say about the rest of Tecumseh's tour, his allusion to the trip to Missouri is supported by other evidence. Undoubtedly, Tecumseh was heading for the villages of the Missouri Shawnees, where he had relatives. He had once considered making his home among them, but apparently had not been there for several years. In the summer of 1810 he found the place in ferment.

The Shawnees had settled Missouri from 1787, establishing two villages on Apple Creek, about fifteen miles apart, on land later officially awarded them by the Spanish government. The towns accommodated some 150 warriors, and prospered, boasting log houses, some two-storied, granaries, barns, and a variety of livestock. About eighteen miles below where Apple Creek flowed into the wide Mississippi was Cape Girardeau. There, Louis Lorimier, who had led the Shawnees to Missouri and successively kept two Shawnee wives, had established a community of Anglo-Americans with their black slaves. Relations between them and the Indians were friendly.

However, in 1810 Tecumseh would have had no difficulty in appreciating that the fortunes of the Missouri Shawnees had slumped. Their hunters were having to ride farther than ever before to find the bigger game, such as deer and buffalo, and their trade had been hit by the fall in the value of skins. The Shawnees were also complaining about whites trespassing on their lands, pilfering horses and hawking liquor. In truth, an American officer wrote that the Shawnees were "said to be the most wealthy of any [Indians] in the country, but they are greatly debauched and debilitated by the use of ardent spirits."[11]

Forty Shawnee families under a mixed-blood chief named Onothe (James Rogers) were so dissatisfied they built a new town on the Maramec River, sixty miles above its mouth. The future of both the Apple Creek and Maramec villages was threatened when sovereignty of the area passed to the United States in 1805. The Americans seemed in no hurry to confirm the grants the Spaniards had made the Indians.

When Tecumseh arrived he found the Shawnees, and their neighbors, the Delawares of the St. Francis, more troubled than usual, for they were being riven by an outbreak of witchcraft hysteria and threatened by a war with the Osages. Both problems seem to have embroiled Tecumseh.

The witchcraft killings in Missouri were part of a wider problem that echoed the events of 1805, when Beata and Tenskwatawa had begun their ministries. Epidemic diseases had returned to the Indian country, ravaging communities and provoking widespread charges of sorcery. In 1809 some Kickapoos died of smallpox, and an old Kickapoo was put to death for refusing to surrender his medicine bag, which it was presumed he had used to bewitch the sick. Tecumseh and his brother had turned the tragedy to account. Tecumseh said the disease had come from infected annuities the

Kickapoos had got from the United States. The Prophet invited the Kickapoos to Prophetstown, which he claimed was protected by the Great Spirit and impregnable to disease.[12]

In the spring of 1810, Death called upon the Delawares on White River and the Sandusky Wyandots. A dozen Delaware witches were said to have been executed, while a Wyandot witch-finder began charging venerable members of his tribe, both men and women, with causing deaths by magic. At least five Wyandots were killed as witches during the year, the most famous the senior and aged civil chief Leatherlips. He was believed to be a malicious sorcerer who had brought sickness and death, but his execution was also supported by political enemies who feared he would turn his powers upon them. Leatherlips was said to have connived with Roundhead to get the Wyandots to accept Tecumseh's invitation to move to the Wabash. Opponents of that plan, particularly the principal chief, Tarhe the Crane, got the council to order his death, and an execution squad found him on the Scioto River about June and split his head open with a tomahawk. As late as 1811 Tarhe's political opponents were still complaining that the chief's party were "murdering us day by day."[13]

In Missouri the witch-hunt may have been even more ferocious, and when Tecumseh reached Apple Creek it was already a year old. It appears to have originated in the summer of 1809, in a council attended by Chief Waabeletheh of the Delawares and Chiefs Thathaway and Rogers of the Shawnees. Some kind of court to try offenders was established. A woman was acquitted, but three men were marched into the thick woods by about a hundred warriors, axed, and thrown onto a pyre.

No one can tell how many died afterward. One report of 1810 put it at seventeen Delawares and Shawnees, and another at twenty among the Delawares alone. Godfrey Lesieur, a boy who belonged to a local family of Indian traders, later said that some fifty were executed in a year. Most of the unfortunates were accused of transforming themselves into beasts— by which Lesieur meant witchcraft—and were condemned by a court with three judges.

Tecumseh, recalled Lesieur, disapproved of the whole business, and threw his influence against it. Indeed, the boy credited Tecumseh with bringing the Missouri witch-hunt to an end.[14]

If so, he was less successful in dissuading the Missouri Shawnees from attacking the Osages. Intertribal warfare always distressed Tecumseh, strong as he was on Indian unity. The year before, he had prevented his warriors from retaliating against the Ottawas for murdering a woman in Prophetstown, and he took the same stance now. He could see no sense in the Indians, greatly outnumbered by the Americans, fighting each other.

Ever since their arrival in the west, the Shawnees and Delawares had been squabbling with the Osages. During Tecumseh's first summer on the Wabash their messengers had reached him asking for warriors to help them scourge the Osages. Trouble flared up again in the spring of 1810, when some of the Great Osages then living near Fort Osage on the Missouri River butchered two Shawnees of James Rogers's town and a Delaware on the Gasconade River. One of the Shawnees who died was related to Tecumseh. Ever since he was a boy, Tecumseh had been taught that the responsibilities of kinship included revenging injuries done his relations. When the Shawnees and Delawares called upon neighboring tribes, including Cherokees, to join a large war party to avenge the deaths, Tecumseh must have been torn between his familial duty and his principles of Indian unity.

The expedition was being prepared at the time of Tecumseh's visit, but again he counseled forbearance. According to his own report, he had "even taken the tomahawks out of the hands of those who were ready to march against the Osages."[15] Ironically, on this occasion his most effective supporters were the American authorities in St. Louis. William Clark, the Indian agent, had already sent the trader Pierre Chouteau to turn the aggrieved Shawnees and Delawares from their course. It was Chouteau, not Tecumseh, who eventually got the Osages to promise compensation and brokered a short-lived peace in the ensuing fall.

According to Godfrey Lesieur, family matters of a different kind troubled Tecumseh in Missouri, although in this case we cannot be sure whether the interesting story he tells occurred in 1810 or during the chief's next visit to Apple Creek more than a year later. Lesieur was an honest chronicler, but he did not give his account until just before his death in 1872, and his details are hazy.

He tells us that a sister of Tecumseh's lived at Chillicothe, one of the Shawnee towns on Apple Creek. She had recently married a young French Creole, François Maisonville, whom she had met when visiting the area of New Madrid. The marriage had taken place Indian fashion, but when Tecumseh heard of it he was angry. Perhaps influenced by the Prophet's teachings that mixed-race marriages offended Waashaa Monetoo and would not prosper, he insisted the couple part. However, the lovers would not be so easily thwarted. A few months after Tecumseh's departure the girl returned to her husband and they raised a family.

The Maisonvilles certainly existed. François was probably the same listed in the 1797 census of New Madrid as an unmarried man, without children or property. Mrs. Maisonville, whom Lesieur took to be Tecumseh's sister, died in New Madrid County about the age of thirty-one, if we may believe Edward Meatt, who married one of her granddaughters. A grandson of the Maisonvilles, Joseph Maisonville, was still living in 1886. But, as so often in our search for the historical Tecumseh, the facts are clouded.

Just who was Mrs. Maisonville? Lesieur thought she was a sister, but our best authorities are clear that Tecumseh had only one full sister, Tecumapease, and the little we know about Mrs. Maisonville indicates that she was too young to have been even a half sister of the famous chief. Still, he exercised some kind of stewardship over the girl. It is tempting to believe that she was, instead, Tecumseh's niece, the daughter of Cheeseekau. In 1825 the Prophet admitted that a daughter of Cheeseekau was living west of the Mississippi, and Tecumseh might reasonably be expected to have been interested in her welfare.[16]

The main purpose of Tecumseh's visit, to enlist the western Shawnees in his confederacy, failed. In fact these Indians had only recently embarked upon a program of economic development similar to Black Hoof's at Wapakoneta, and they showed no interest in Tecumseh's conservatism. He made his way home, probably passing through the Kickapoo villages in present-day Illinois, and there he would have found a better welcome. Although the Kickapoo band on the Vermilion, a tributary of the Wabash, had endorsed the treaty of Fort Wayne, these Illinois River Kickapoos and their leading chief, Pamawatam (the Mink), had been at loggerheads with the Americans for years. They had been involved in attempts to forge an Indian confederacy to defend Indian land before Prophetstown had ever been built, and in 1809 they had became some of the first adherents of the Prophet. In all his travels Tecumseh found no greater kindred spirits.

As usual Tecumseh found that grueling advances were accompanied by smart steps backward. While he was looking for new allies in the west, the Indians he had left behind wavered on the issue of land cessions. Opposition to such sales was increasing, especially among younger people who saw their birthright being frittered away, but many of the established village chiefs both depended upon and feared the United States.

Tecumseh returned to find that in September two thousand Indians from the tribes that had made the old confederacies—Iroquois of New York and Upper Canada; Ohio Shawnees, Wyandots, Delawares, and Munsees; and people from the Three Fires—had met at Brownstown. They were provisioned by the Governor of Michigan Territory, and far from grappling with the land problem, as Tecumseh had anticipated, they bound themselves to a policy of neutrality in any war between white powers and condemned Tecumseh's confederacy. Indeed, they said the Shawnee brothers had no right establishing an intertribal council fire on the Wabash, when everyone knew that honor belonged to Brownstown.[17]

One problem was that anger did not fill Indian bellies or clothe Indian bodies. Treaty annuities did. Tecumseh's view that they ought to be rejected called for unusual resolution when the first chills of autumn whipped up. Even on the Wabash, where there was so much discontent about the recent treaty, Indians packed into Fort Wayne for their annuities that October.

Some held out, though. For the first time Tecumseh's band refused to share the Shawnee annuities, and the western Potawatomis also ignored the distribution. The Miamis came into Fort Wayne shamefacedly after many other Indians had dispersed. Although they complained "the tomahawk was hung over their necks" at the treaty and grumbled about petitioning the President for Harrison's removal, all but the Mississinewa band of about thirty warriors and an Eel River chief backed down and took their annuities. Threats and poverty ate the Indians' resolve. Before the end of the year even the Weas and about half of the Kickapoos, who had initially turned down their annuities, had called for them at Vincennes.[18]

Tecumseh would not be discouraged. Chiefs such as Tarhe, Black Hoof, Little Turtle, and Five Medals might sit silently while the Indians lost everything, but he still held the moral high ground. Scarcely bothering to rest from the fatigues of his western tour, Tecumseh set out at the end of October. He was going to the most powerful of all his potential allies, the redcoats at Fort Malden.

He arrived there about 12 November with 134 men, 28 women, and 8 children—Shawnees, Potawatomis, Ottawas, Winnebagos, and Sacs. The British had been strenuous in winning Indian friendship. Their agents were supposed to achieve this feat without inciting the Indians against the Americans, but they were finding that United States policies were doing their job for them. By the autumn of 1810 Matthew Elliott, the Indian superintendent at Amherstburg, was struggling to keep the lid on a boiling pot. He warned his superiors that Indian resentment against the Americans was growing, and on 25 November the Canadian governor, Sir James Craig, went so far as to notify the British chargé d'affaires in Washington that the tribes were planning war and that the American government should be alerted.

Tecumseh saw the British walking their tightrope again, here blowing hot to nurture Indian favor, there trying to restrain them lest Canada be pulled into an unwanted war. On 15 November Tecumseh's party received presents from Elliott, in the presence of George Ironside, the keeper of Indian stores, James Girty the interpreter, and officers of the garrison of Fort Malden.

The Shawnee chief began talks by delivering some strings of white wampum to mark the death of Frederick Fisher, an interpreter who had died of "a violent cold" some days before. Then he rose for his main speech. He displayed an old British wampum belt depicting their former alliance

with the Indians. He had taken it "from under our kings" [chiefs], Tecumseh
said. The warriors, not the chiefs, now controlled tribal affairs, and they intended to renew that ancient friendship with their British Father.

On his previous visit to Fort Malden in 1808, Tecumseh had withheld
firm promises to back British arms, but now he wanted to involve the redcoats in a war he felt the Indians would have to fight:

> You, Father, have nourished us, and raised us up from childhood.
> We are now men, and think ourselves capable of defending our
> country, in which cause you have given us active assistance and al-
> ways advice. We now are determined to defend it ourselves, and af-
> ter rising you on your feet, leave you behind, but expecting you will
> push forwards towards us what may be necessary to supply our
> wants.[19]

Tecumseh expected a war. "We sit [live] at or near the borders where the
contest will begin," he said, and he wanted supplies, if nothing else, from
the British. He asked that the alliance belt he had brought be handled by all
present, and he outlined his plans to extend his confederacy to the southern
tribes:

> Father, I intend proceeding toward the Mid Day [the south] and ex-
> pect before next autumn and before I visit you again that the busi-
> ness will be done. I request, Father, that you will be charitable to our
> king[s] [old men], women and children. The young men can more
> easily provide for themselves than they.

Elliott was deeply disturbed by this further evidence of coming conflict.
He promised to send Tecumseh's request for aid to the King, and did so the
following day, asking at the same time for new instructions on how he
should proceed. Particularly troubling to Elliott was Tecumseh's reference
to "the business" being "done" before next autumn. At a subsequent private
conference Elliott asked the chief what he had meant. Tecumseh replied
that his confederacy would then be complete. He had hoped to keep his
plans secret, but the Americans had learned of them, and he now thought it
time to inform the redcoats of what he intended.

Tecumseh's visit sent a shudder through Craig. Dreading that an Indian
war would be blamed on Canada, he wrote Lieutenant-Governor Gore on 2
February that British officials should dissuade the Indians from fighting.
While the redcoats would remain their friends, the Indians should not expect assistance if they attacked the United States. In other words, as soon as

the alliance with the Indians became inconvenient to Canada, the tribes could be abandoned.

Tecumseh would have been disappointed, but hardly surprised. He had never trusted the British. This time it did not matter. While Tecumseh was indulging in his frontier diplomacy, the United States and Britain were sliding steadily toward their own war.

17

AN UNCOMMON GENIUS

William Henry Harrison was beginning to recognize the driving force behind the Indian confederacy. On a warm August day in 1811 he scratched a remarkable tribute to the Shawnee leader:

> The implicit obedience and respect which the followers of Tecumseh pay to him is really astonishing, and more than any other circumstance bespeaks him one of those uncommon geniuses which spring up occasionally to produce revolutions and overturn the established order of things. If it were not for the vicinity of the United States, he would, perhaps, be the founder of an empire that would rival in glory that of Mexico or Peru. No difficulties deter him. His activity and industry supply the want of letters. For four years he has been in constant motion. You see him today on the Wabash and in a short time you hear of him on the shores of Lake Erie or Michigan, or on the banks of the Mississippi, and wherever he goes he makes an impression favorable to his purposes.[1]

Tecumseh worried Harrison. The Governor desperately wanted Indian land. He was "heartily tired of living in a Territory" and blanched at the thought of "one of the fairest portions of the globe" condemned to be "a state of nature, the haunt of a few wretched savages." This Tecumseh was a blot upon Harrison's vision of expansion, statehood, and civilization. If anyone could settle large numbers of warriors on the Wabash, infuse them with his theories of landholding, and block further purchases, surely it was this talented Shawnee orator and his mystical brother.[2]

Prudence suggested the best course might be to halt land purchases temporarily. The white settlers had no immediate need of them, and in time the declining game and growing Indian poverty would induce the tribes to sell and move on. At least John Johnston at Fort Wayne thought so. But not Harrison. He was almost impervious to the consequences of his policies. Despite Tecumseh, despite the fact that the Indians were "more uneasy and dissatisfied than I ever before saw them," despite even the promises Harrison had made at Fort Wayne that no more land would be required, the end of 1810 saw him advocating further purchases. Fortunately, the United States government disagreed. The Governor was told to postpone surveying the 1809 purchase and was denied permission to erect a new army post up the Wabash. His plans for further land negotiations were negatived.[3]

Tecumseh was no less obdurate. Relentlessly traveling, camping in lonely woods and prairies, living off the land, and pleading unity before untold council fires, he was systematically canvassing every tribe on the frontier.

The one area that had so far eluded his personal attention was the south, and Tecumseh's plan to visit the land of his father had probably been stimulated by conversations with the Creeks who visited Prophetstown in 1810. Tradition says that one of them was Tuskenau, the eldest son of Big Warrior, the most important chief in the Creek Nation. In these conversations, Tecumseh would have learned that the southern Indians were also taking alarm at American land-hunger, and that Big Warrior was making his town, Tuckabatchee, the council fire of a southern confederacy. Jealous rivals, such as the chiefs of Tallassee and Coweta, were frightened of Big Warrior's ambition, but it suited Tecumseh. If representatives of all the southern tribes congregated at Tuckabatchee when Tecumseh was there he could address the lot at one stroke. Nevertheless, the journey to the Mid-Day was a formidable enterprise, and Tecumseh's project was postponed, first in the summer of 1810 and then again the following spring.[4]

Tecumseh's hesitation to commit himself to the southern marathon probably had something to do with the fluid nature of Indian opinion in the north and west. The Shawnee chief had to counteract discouraging speeches sent from the Brownstown council and revitalize flagging supporters. He was constantly having to recultivate old ground.

Not single-handed. That spring of 1811, a belt was being passed through Indian villages on the Mississippi and Missouri summoning the warriors to join the stand, and the redoubtable Main Poc was abroad, whipping the Sacs, Foxes, Dakotas, Kickapoos, and Potawatomis into a fighting mood. He made up a party of 230 of their warriors and led them to Fort Malden in July, where the British were told that "all the nations as far as the sea coast have entered into a close alliance." The warriors had put the village chiefs "behind their backs" and were ready for war.[5]

But Tecumseh was by far the ablest advocate of a united Indian resistance, and he decided that his priority was to beat back east, retracing the steps he had made in 1809. He spoke confidently of bringing hundreds of soldiers from the Sandusky Wyandots and Senecas, the Ohio Shawnees, and the Iroquois Confederacy of New York back to the Wabash.

Before leaving, Tecumseh had the dubious pleasure of entertaining William Wells, newly reinstalled on the payroll of the American government as an interpreter, and John Conner at Prophetstown in April or early May. They had been sent to find out about the attack on the Cole party the previous summer, and they also complained about the theft of a dozen horses from Busseron. Tecumseh and Tenskwatawa disclaimed responsibility for the latter, but they admitted the thieves had been Potawatomis from among their supporters, and restored four of the animals. About the Cole affair they could do nothing, however, for the murderers were under the protection of Main Poc. Tecumseh was much more positive when the subject of white encroachments came up. He told his visitors that he would certainly resist them.[6]

In May, the Strawberry Moon, Tecumseh rode into Ohio with a few trusted warriors. He made a final but unsuccessful appeal to the Shawnees at Wapakoneta, and called again upon the Wyandots and Senecas on the Sandusky. Once more Tecumseh targeted the younger warriors. He probably reminded the Wyandots that some of their people were already building a town on the Wabash, and certainly suggested the rest should follow. The Shawnee also spoke of his confederacy, and mentioned his plan to enlist the Creeks. The Wyandots accepted some wampum from Tecumseh, signaling that they had not rejected his speech. They were divided, but even a few chiefs saw merit in moving west and selling the beleaguered lands on the Sandusky, trapped as they were against Lake Erie by American possessions. Some Indians committed themselves to joining Tecumseh on the Wabash within two years. It was a modest success, but far less than he had predicted.[7]

Nor did Tecumseh reach the Iroquois in New York. Deciding to send a deputation to them when he got home, he turned back for Prophetstown, and was home at the end of June.

During his absence little had occurred. Brouillet, who had been spying at Prophetstown while heavily disguised as a trader, had been withdrawn by Harrison and replaced by one Jean Baptiste Laplante. The salt annuity had also been delivered. This time the Prophet had seized more than his fair share—with the flippant remark that it was needed to provide for the two thousand Indians Tecumseh was bringing back with him! Tecumseh may have disapproved of his brother's action, but if so there is no record.[8]

He had more than enough to do, preparing an embassy to the Iroquois Confederacy and his own journey to the south. The New York party was large, and it was led by some of Tecumseh's Mingo supporters. Mingoes were Iroquoians, former members of their confederacy, who had long since lived among the western Indians, particularly with the Shawnees. Early in August Tecumseh's deputation reached Buffalo Creek, at Niagara, where the Six Nations of the Iroquois Confederacy had their united council fire. Representatives of them all gathered to hear Tecumseh's message—Senecas, Cayugas, Oneidas, Mohawks, Onondagas, and Tuscaroras. A United States agent, Erastus Granger, was also on hand, although the significance of the proceedings largely escaped him.

The prowess of the Iroquois as warriors and statesmen was legendary, but since the American Revolution they had been a shadow of their former selves. Many had removed to Canada, and those who remained, maintaining a forum at Buffalo Creek, were living on pockets of land in New York encircled by white settlements. To people in such circumstances Tecumseh's invitation to come to the Wabash was seductive.

When Tecumseh's ambassadors left for home on 10 August, amply provisioned by their Iroquois hosts, an argument raged behind them. Many Iroquois families were determined to go to the Wabash, while others, including "the chiefs who receive annuities," bewailed the loss of ancestral lands as well as the terrors of a long journey to "a strange land." The matter festered, but some Iroquois warriors went to Prophetstown that very year and fought in the battle of Tippecanoe. Others were then said to have been on their way, and some Senecas were reported to have accompanied Tecumseh when he went to Canada in 1812. Obviously the appeal to the Iroquois Confederacy, the most northeasterly of Tecumseh's many campaigns, was not entirely without fruit.[9]

After dispatching his party to New York, Tecumseh had attended to the details of his southern trip. But he was interrupted. Violent and hot-blooded warriors again threatened his plans.

"The time is drawing near when the murder is to begin, and all the Indians that will not join are to die with the whites." These bloodcurdling words, spoken by an Iowa Indian in St. Louis in May 1811, marked the beginning of a new war scare in the west.

In June several killings occurred. One or two men were slain by Menominees on the Mississippi, and Potawatomis raided a house on Shoal Creek in

Illinois Territory, killing a man and abducting his sister. For two months the territory was in turmoil. Indians evacuated their villages, and whites fled from farms to towns and blockhouses. Governing the new territory from Kaskaskia, Ninian Edwards had militia patroling for hostiles.[10]

In August Edwards demanded the Potawatomis surrender the murderers of 1810 and 1811, warning them that the whites were losing patience and the Indians must choose peace or war. It was strong language, but even moderate chiefs such as Gomo and Little Chief called the Governor's bluff. They were caught between two fires, they explained. The Americans accused them of listening to the Prophet, their own warriors of partiality to the United States and selling land. The chiefs denied they had the power to hand over the murderers, but said that "if the whites had kept on the other side of the waters the accident of today would not have happened." Edwards should not threaten war, or he might force the Indians to fight. These were flinty words from leaders who had been known for their friendship to the Americans.[11]

The western crisis helped prompt William Henry Harrison to make a final effort to bring Tecumseh to heel. When fifteen warriors from Prophetstown arrived in Vincennes in June to have weapons repaired, the Governor sent them packing. He wrote a letter to Tecumseh, whose "great talents" alone, he believed, were holding "together the heterogeneous mass" on the Wabash.

Harrison upbraided the chief for plotting war, and told him that despite his protestations of innocence the evidence was clear: on the Mississippi some Indians had said that Tecumseh meant to murder Harrison and fall upon the settlements, while the Prophet had unlawfully seized the salt annuity. Their course was futile, however. At a word from Harrison the Kentuckians would come "pouring forth" like "swarms" of "mosquitos on the shores of the Wabash," and these were but a fraction of the numbers that would be mobilized against Tecumseh.

Tecumseh must satisfy the people of Vincennes that he meant them no harm "or they will not lay aside their arms," and an explanation of the taking of the salt was required. The Governor had heard that Tecumseh hoped to visit the town with his young men. He would be welcome, providing he brought only a small entourage, but Harrison could say no more about the treaty of Fort Wayne, since the matter now lay with the President. If Tecumseh and the Prophet wished, they could be sent to Washington to speak directly with the President, and Harrison would guarantee their safe return.

The letter was entrusted to a tall militia officer named Walter Wilson, and Harrison added a personal postscript: "My friend Tecumseh, the bearer is a good man and a brave warrior. I hope you will treat him well. You are yourself a warrior, and all such should have an esteem for each other."[12] The appeal was not made in vain. Although Wilson's interpreter, Joseph Barron, and his son would later tell some tall stories about the mission, at the time Harrison was able to report that his messengers had been well received "and treated with particular friendship by Tecumseh."[13]

Wilson apparently delivered Harrison's letter on 3 July, stayed overnight at Prophetstown, and received Tecumseh's reply the next day. Tecumseh might have been advised to take up Harrison's offer to send him to Washington, but he probably distrusted the Americans too much to put himself in their power, and had little faith in negotiations. He decided to stick with his plan of recruiting the southern Indians. But it was important to mollify Harrison, particularly as Tecumseh would be away from Prophetstown all winter. He sent Wilson back with word that he would visit Vincennes in about eighteen days and "wash away all these bad stories."

Tecumseh made the trip to Vincennes the first leg of his southern tour. Rather than return after seeing Harrison, he would head for the lands of the Chickasaws, Choctaws, and Creeks, and he intended to return by way of the Mississippi, chancing his life with the fierce Osages, with whom his fellow tribesmen in Missouri were still having a simmering dispute.

Harrison, too, was making plans. Spurred by the disturbed state of Illinois Territory, he spent part of July seeking authority to take the offensive. This time he got it. The Secretary of War ordered reinforcements to Vincennes. He stressed the President's "earnest desire" for peace, and warned the Governor that force should be avoided unless "absolutely necessary," but he ordered Harrison to punish Indian raiders and protect the settlements. Although it was hoped that Harrison would not need to march up the Wabash, he had permission to use his troops if the Prophet commenced or seriously threatened hostilities.[14]

It was enough. Harrison had the authority to attack if he judged it necessary. Even before his last council with Tecumseh he was planning to strike.

Several hundred warriors followed Tecumseh downriver. Someone counted fifty-three canoes, and another part moved separately by land. They moved slowly. Tecumseh was within eighty miles of Vincennes on 21 July, but four days later his canoes were at Busseron, twenty miles above the town.

Here he was intercepted by Walter Wilson, who wanted to know the reason for the delay. He also told Tecumseh that Harrison was concerned that the chief had brought so many adherents, when he had been expressly forbidden to do so. Tecumseh replied that he had been waiting at a rendezvous for his land contingent to catch up. As for the other point, only twenty-four men had been chosen to attend him. The other travelers had made the journey of their own accord.

This was mere prevarication, of course, but it is not difficult to see why Tecumseh ignored Harrison's attempts to reduce his following. First, Tecumseh wanted to meet the Governor on something like equal terms, not as the head of a pitiable delegation. Second, and much more important, was the question of safety. Tecumseh was not massing men to surprise Vincennes. In fact he intended leaving for the south immediately after the council. But he knew he was placing himself at Harrison's mercy. It took courage for Tecumseh and his supporters, grossly outnumbered and outgunned, to confront the Governor. We know that Harrison was not the man to dishonor a truce; Tecumseh did not. He *did* know that friendlier chiefs than he had perished in the hands of whites. If the positions had been reversed, and Harrison had agreed to negotiate in Prophetstown rather than Vincennes, he would quickly have understood the need for a strong guard.

Tecumseh dropped in on the Shakers who lived above Vincennes. Their friendship had been proof against every malicious tongue, and they had enjoyed an immunity from the occasional thefts that worried nearby settlements. Then the chief continued his journey, arriving in Vincennes late on 27 July. He put off meeting Harrison until the thirtieth, by which time he had about 270 warriors and 20 to 30 women and children in his riverside camp. These included a party of Weas under Lepousser, who had followed him down.

The town was on full alert. Gunpowder was concentrated under a guard, and the regulars from Fort Knox, about 80 dragoons, and the militia were on duty. The day of Tecumseh's arrival, Harrison, wearing a fringed hunting shirt, reviewed his militia, near 800 strong. According to John Badollet, he whipped them into such a mood that "it was with difficulty that they could be restrained from running to Tecumseh's camp."[15]

Tecumseh's nervousness was obvious the day the council opened. An hour before talks were to begin he sent to Harrison, asking him if he intended bringing armed men to the ground. The Governor replied that if Tecumseh's warriors left their guns behind, Harrison would have only 30 or so dismounted armed dragoons by him. Eventually Tecumseh marched from his camp with 180 men packing tomahawks, clubs, knives, and bows and arrows, but no firearms. It was a mile into the town, where an arbor had been prepared for the talks. The road ran between crowds of militia, dressed in hunting shirts and bristling with arms. Badollet claimed they had "bayonets fixed and glistening in every direction." When Tecumseh reached the arbor he saw Harrison at one side. Behind him, seated on benches, were 80 dragoons, without rifles or muskets but with pistols stuffed into their belts and swords.

The Indians squatted at the other side of the arbor, and Harrison began to speak. Tecumseh interrupted to tell him he could not be heard, and he moved closer to his audience. Getting into his stride, Harrison went straight into the attack. The previous year Tecumseh, on behalf of "all the tribes of the continent, " had alleged malpractice at the treaty of Fort Wayne. Harrison had not yet heard from the President on that issue, so he would say nothing about it. Tecumseh might go to Washington if he wished. What Harrison now wished to know was why the salt had been confiscated some months back.

Tecumseh rose to speak. He explained he had not been at home when the salt was seized, and suspected that without him his people had been at a loss as to how to act. They had finally taken and distributed it. Then, verging on the flippant, Tecumseh said it was impossible to please Harrison. One year he complained that no salt was taken, the next because extra salt was accepted. This was a trite response, unworthy of Tecumseh, and it was well that a fierce summer shower broke and enabled him to get an adjournment.

The following day the Indians did not arrive until nearly two in the afternoon, and talks went on well after dark. The Wea leader Lepousser, whose people were being driven from their homes by the treaty of Fort Wayne, opened for the Indians. They called him Ashenonqua, the Speech Maker. He roved over Harrison's treaties, and remarked that while he himself had not been consulted at Fort Wayne over the fate of his lands, the Potawatomis had held tomahawks over the heads of the Miamis to force their consent. He wanted an inquiry to discover who was responsible for this misconduct. Listening uncomfortably, Harrison gathered that it was Winamek, and not himself, who was the object of the Wea chief's scorn. Nevertheless, dutifully supported by some Miamis present, he contradicted Lepousser's interpretation and pressed on to other subjects.

Looking for firmer ground, Harrison said that Tecumseh could banish all suspicions instantly by delivering two Potawatomis in his camp who had participated in the Cole incident. Of course, Tecumseh could not have surrendered Potawatomi murderers without damaging his relationships with that tribe and its war chief, Main Poc, and perhaps Harrison knew it. The demand was unreasonable, and Tecumseh easily sidestepped it by stating that the wanted men were not at Prophetstown. However, he offered wampum in atonement for the deaths—an Indian method of expressing remorse and sympathy—and asked the Americans to forgive the offenders. He had done no less himself when Ottawas had killed one of his band and Osages had slain a relative.

Harrison suffered what he described as a "long and somewhat artful" speech, but pricked up his ears when Tecumseh spoke about his plans. The

Shawnee enjoyed a reputation for straight talking, and now perhaps he spoke too freely. Tecumseh volunteered the information that he had united the northern tribes "after much trouble and difficulty" and that as soon as this council ended he was going south.

This was a considerable exaggeration. Tecumseh had considerable support among the western Potawatomis, Kickapoos, and Winnebagos, but only scattered followers elsewhere, among them his own Kispoko Shawnees; the Mississinewa band of Miamis; a number of Wyandots; substantial portions of the Wea and Piankeshaw tribes; and a few Sacs, Foxes, Iowas, Menominees, Dakota Sioux, Ottawas, and Iroquois. This amounted to a formidable achievement, though it fell short of matching the great confederacy of the 1790s. Tecumseh may have been unwise to exaggerate his success, for it only amplified Harrison's alarm. Perhaps the chief sensed this, for he tried to reassure the Governor by an apt comparison: "The U. States had set him the example of forming a strict union amongst all the fires [states] that compose their confederacy. That the Indians did not complain of it, nor should his white brothers complain of him for doing the same thing with regard to the Indian tribes."

In answer to a question as to whether he would stop the settlement of the new purchase, Tecumseh made a clumsy attempt to dissuade Harrison from acting against him during the months he would be away. He tried to preserve the status quo:

> . . . he replied that he hoped no attempts would be made to settle it [the new purchase] until his return next spring. That a great number of Indians [Wyandots and Iroquois] were coming to settle at his town this fall, and that [they] must occupy that tract as a hunting ground, and [even] if they did no further injury, they might kill the cattle and hogs of the white people, which would produce disturbance. That he wished everything to remain in its present situation until his return, our settlements not to progress further, and no revenge sought for any injury that had been or should be received by the white people until his return. That he would then go and see the President and settle everything with him. That the affairs of all the tribes in this quarter were in his [Tecumseh's] hands and that nothing could be done without him. That he would dispatch messengers in every direction to prevent them from doing any more mischief . . .

John Badollet, a critic of Harrison, wrote that Tecumseh spoke "in a most able and spirited manner." But in fact he had committed a tactical blunder. By informing Harrison that large numbers of Indians were coming to settle the disputed lands he incited him to act quickly, and by advising the

Governor that he himself would be absent until the spring he advertised an
opportunity to strike. This was a serious mistake to make before a man as
shrewd as Harrison.

It was now late, and Harrison wound up the proceedings. In the flicker-
ing torchlight he soberly informed Tecumseh that "the moon which they
beheld . . . would sooner fall to the earth than the President would suffer his
people to be murdered with impunity, and that he would put his warriors in
petticoats sooner than he would give up a country which he had fairly acquired from the rightful owners."

The chasm between them was as wide as ever, each protesting injustices
the other refused to recognize.

In three more days most of the Indians had broken camp, but Tecumseh
lingered awhile. In town at the time was an irascible Potawatomi. He was
hard of hearing, and people generally knew him as the Deaf Chief. Like
Winamek, the Deaf Chief belonged to the part of his tribe least influenced by
Tecumseh, and greatly valued—and voiced—his independence. Word had it
that he was not a man to be meddled with, and he was reputed to have once
marched into a Kickapoo camp, confronted one of the warriors, whom he
blamed for the death of his brother, and shot him dead on the spot.

The Deaf Chief had once been in Prophetstown when a message from
the British had arrived, and he was wont to broadcast the opinion that the
Shawnee brothers were simple slaves of the redcoats. Now, after observing
the talks between Harrison and Tecumseh, he began shooting his mouth off
again, to the effect that Tecumseh was fully bent upon war and had lied in
the council when he described himself as a friend of peace. Soon afterward
someone told the Deaf Chief that Tecumseh had reacted angrily to these allegations, and that he had ordered his followers to assassinate the Deaf
Chief when he went back upriver.

One day Tecumseh was in his camp, speaking to Barron, when a canoe
sped from across the river. In it sat the Deaf Chief, paddling furiously. He
wore his war regalia and had painted his face, and he was armed to the
teeth. The Deaf Chief stormed ashore, and finding Tecumseh at his tent
challenged him to combat.

"Come and kill me!" shouted the infuriated Potawatomi. "You and your
men can kill the white people's hogs and call them bears, but you dare not
face a warrior!"

Tecumseh did not reply. He merely treated the spectacle with complete
indifference, and calmly continued his conversation with Barron.

Exhausting his epithets, the Deaf Chief even employed "a term of re-
proach which can never be forgotten by an Indian," but still Tecumseh ignored him. Finally, the frustrated Potawatomi gave a whoop, strode back to
his canoe, and paddled away.

It is extremely unlikely that Tecumseh had ever considered the Deaf Chief important enough to be assassinated. Winamek, who had earned much greater resentment, was suffered to remain at large, and so was the Deaf Chief. Later in the year he was carrying messages between the tribes and Vincennes.[16]

On 4 August, the day before he left town, Tecumseh made a courtesy call upon Governor Harrison. He "labored hard to convince me that he had no other intention by his journey [to the south] than to prevail on all the tribes to unite in the bonds of peace," the Governor reported. Unfortunately, it was too late to forestall Harrison's offensive.

With some insight Harrison informed the Secretary of War that the Prophet was "imprudent and audacious, but . . . deficient in judgement, talents and firmness." Tecumseh was another matter. But although the "greater part of his followers are attached to him from principle and affection," many supported him through fear. The application of a strong counterforce was necessary, and he intended to provide it.

Tecumseh, he wrote, "is now upon the last round to put a finishing stroke to his work. I hope, however, before his return that that part of the fabric which he considered complete will be demolished, and even its foundations rooted up."[17]

18

STORM ON THE WABASH

Tecumseh had gone to the Mid-Day, but Tenskwatawa remained at Prophetstown, where several hundred Kickapoos and Winnebagos camped to listen to him preach. Nerves were steadying in Illinois Territory, where Edwards had disbanded his militia, and briefly there seemed little reason for the Indians to expect a fall that held anything livelier than the customary hunting. Tecumseh wished it so, and at council fires in the south he spoke, rather misleadingly, of the strength of the confederacy in the north and the reformed and orderly community his brother had planted at Prophetstown. He was too far from home to hear the rumble of the approaching storm.

The Indians at Prophetstown heard it, though, in the messages sent to the tribes from Vincennes. Harrison told them to withdraw their people from Prophetstown, or at least to declare those who refused to leave beyond their protection. He reminded them of the pledges they had given at Greenville to report and obstruct the movements of men hostile to the United States. Touissant Dubois brought the Governor's words to the Miamis, Eel Rivers, and Weas at Fort Wayne on 4 September, stating baldly that Harrison intended to disperse the Prophet's congregation. Even according to the Americans, the upper Wabash belonged to the Miamis, but that did not deter the Governor from requiring the Indians to disavow the Prophet and order him to dismantle his establishment. Speaking grimly of "an army . . . more numerous than the leaves of the trees" being at hand, Harrison cautioned: "My warriors are in motion . . . I must have satisfaction for the murder of my people, and the war-pole that has been raised on the Wabash must be taken down."[1]

Some Miamis shivered, but others were angry at such a blatant threat to invade and bloody their unceded ground. Speaking for Miami chiefs such as Pacanne, Stone Eater, and Big Man, and his fellow Wea, Negro Legs, Lepousser warned: "We have our eyes on our lands . . . with a strong determination to defend our rights, let them be invaded from what quarter they may."[2]

At Prophetstown Tenskwatawa and his councilors met in consternation. Tecumseh had warned them to avoid trouble, and they needed what powder and ball they had to survive the cold season. They sent a group of Kickapoos to conciliate Harrison. The deputation included an old headman of the Vermilion, who had been deposed for signing the 1809 treaties, but with whom Harrison was familiar. The key figure, however, was a Kickapoo described by the Governor as a "war chief of talents entirely devoted to the Prophet." He might possibly have been Pamawatam, the principal chief of the Illinois River Kickapoos.[3]

Whoever the Kickapoos were, they arrived in Vincennes to find that their position had been undermined by more raids perpetrated by hotheaded warriors. Tecumseh had always tried to restrain such men, believing that they could precipitate a premature conflict, and now his fears were being realized. Three Indians, perhaps Potawatomis, had stolen horses on the White and Wabash Rivers, and dispersed a three-man pursuit party. The attacks annoyed Harrison, and strengthened him during his talks with the Kickapoo deputation on 23 and 24 September.[4]

The news the Kickapoos brought back to Prophetstown was not good. A great army had assembled in Vincennes, and was about to march up the Wabash toward them, and Governor Harrison had complained of repeated acts of hostility and delivered an ultimatum: the Indians must restore stolen horses and surrender those guilty of murders. Harrison would not be put off by promises that the matter would be sorted out in the spring. He was marching now, and the Indians could stop him only by meeting him along the way and complying with his requirements. How the Indians needed Tecumseh's leadership at that moment! Whether they intended to negotiate or fight, they had no one with his talents and authority.

The chiefs at Prophetstown could not satisfy Harrison's demands, but he did not believe this. The Kickapoo deputation had left Vincennes promising to return the stolen horses and search for the murderers. Harrison planned to advance up the eastern bank of the Wabash and erect a post near the far boundary of the late disputed purchase. Then, by a formidable display of American military might, he hoped to force the Prophet to meet his terms. The Governor thought the sheer size of his army would deter attack, but he reckoned without the reckless courage the Indians could bring to the defense of their country, especially when filled with enthusiasm by the Prophet.

More than a thousand men began the march from Vincennes to Prophetstown, a distance of 180 miles along the riverside. About a third of Harrison's army were regulars, men of the 4th Regiment of United States Infantry, dressed in blue long-tailed coats, close-fitting breeches, and shakoes crowned with colorful cockades. Their commander was Colonel John Parker Boyd. There were over 400 Indiana militia under Lieutenant-Colonel Joseph Bartholomew, many in deerskin hunting smocks with tomahawks and knives in their belts, and appearing, in the opinion of one regular, "nearly as destitute of discipline as the savages themselves." About 120 mounted Kentucky volunteers, attired in blue coatees, pantaloons, and hats or caps covered in bearskin, rode under the command of Joseph Hamilton Daviess. The military personnel of Harrison's expedition was completed by 80 Indiana mounted riflemen under Captain Spier Spencer and Touissant Dubois's detachment of "spies," while wagoners, cooks, and drovers handled baggage and drove the meat on the hoof.[5]

In mild autumn weather the American army lumbered upriver until 1 October, when it halted near the site of present-day Terre Haute to throw Fort Harrison up on the high banks of the stream. The progress of the invaders was monitored by scouts from Prophetstown, where the Indians were determined to fight. They were short of ammunition, and needed men desperately, but they were not cowed, and calmly began moving noncombatants from the town and dispatched riders and runners to find their wandering hunters and appeal to neighboring tribes for help.

One party was sent to the White River Delawares early in October. It ran into a group of Delaware chiefs on their way to Fort Harrison, and brought some into Prophetstown instead. The embarrassed Delawares protested that they intended remaining neutral, but that Governor Harrison had invited them to meet him on his march for a talk. The Prophet's warriors were unimpressed and insulted the Delawares, but finally allowed them to complete their journey to the American camp.

The failure of the Delawares to help Prophetstown would have surprised no one, and although some Miami and Wea hotheads wanted to stand with Tenskwatawa, their chiefs—more sensible of the dangers of bringing hot lead, cold steel, and burning brands into their villages—held them back. However, other Indians did respond to the cries for help, and several hundred warriors gathered in Prophetstown. The Delawares who visited the town put the number of fighting men at 450 or less—mainly Winnebagos, Kickapoos, and Shawnees—but additional reinforcements arrived in time for the battle. These seem to have included Wyandots from the nearby town, the men from two Potawatomi towns a few miles up the Wabash (one of them Winamek's), Piankeshaws, and a few Kickapoo and Potawatomi war parties from the Illinois River region.

Tenskwatawa was no warrior, but he had a crucial function to perform on the eve of battle. He pleaded with the spirits for their assistance. This was of great importance, because Indians convinced that the Creator or other deities were giving them strength were capable of unusual bravery and determination. In military terms, the Prophet's incantations increased the morale factor, enabling the Indians to confront what might otherwise have been deemed an insuperable task. The encouragement of Tenskwatawa, the anger at Harrison's invasion, the purification rituals and war dances, which went on day and night, brought the warriors to the necessary psychological condition. Man for man they were probably far more determined than most of the American soldiers marching toward them.

An indication of that occurred on the night of 10 October, when Shawnees from Prophetstown crept up on the American camp at Fort Harrison and shot a sentry through both thighs. After a little confusion among Harrison's inexperienced soldiery, a number of Kentucky dragoons galloped into the dark woods to search for the snipers. The Indians had gone, but when the dragoons returned they were fired at by jittery marksmen in their own camp.

The attack taught Harrison that the Indians had not been intimidated by his advance, and when the Delaware chiefs came in from Prophetstown he was in no doubt that his plan to overawe the Indians had failed. According to the Delawares, the Prophet was boasting of burning the first American prisoner he took. While at Fort Harrison the Governor also received a fresh letter from the Secretary of War, enlarging his powers. He was now authorized to disperse the Prophet's band, by persuasion if possible, by force if he must. Harrison decided to prolong his expedition and threaten Prophetstown itself, but like the Indians, he must have realized that a battle probably lay ahead.

On 29 October the American army marched from the fort. The Governor had sent back for reinforcements, and two companies arrived in time for action. When he reached Prophetstown his strike force may have amounted to 950, but nonmilitary personnel would have brought the number of men capable of bearing arms to something like 1,000. The Indians ignored the oncoming soldiers. Some Kickapoos later admitted that the warriors considered attacking Harrison at the fort or if he marched on at such places as Raccoon or Pine Creek, suitable spots for an ambush. Yet except for an attack on a provision boat working its way upriver from Fort Harrison, an attack which cost a boatman his life, the Indians were strangely inactive.

Not only was Harrison's final advance undisturbed, but the Indians appeared surprised on the afternoon of 6 November when the American army picked its way across the thickly timbered ravine and swampy bed of Burnett's Creek below Prophetstown to form up on a plateau overlooking the village. The Indians had not even removed all their women, children, and old people from the town. One reason for this might have been the unusual course of Harrison's march. The Americans had crossed to the west side of the Wabash, stationed a depot (Fort Boyd) at the mouth of the Vermilion, and then swung away from the wooded margins of the river into the open prairie, where the army was less vulnerable to surprise attack. Harrison returned to the river only on the final approach to Prophetstown.

Another explanation for the failure of the Indians to challenge Harrison's march might have been the arrival at Prophetstown, a few days before the army, of Miami and Delaware messengers from Fort Harrison. They had been sent to present the Governor's latest terms for peace: the return of the stolen animals and either the surrender of Potawatomi murderers or proof that they had not lately been under the Prophet's control. There is some evidence that the Indians took this to mean that Harrison would do nothing further until he had received a reply to these demands. About 4 November a conciliatory answer was indeed sent back by the same intermediaries, one of whom was a Miami chief named Little Eyes. Most probably the reply was designed merely to buy time for the Indians to complete their preparations for battle, but it missed Harrison anyway. Little Eyes and his companions descended the river toward Fort Harrison on the east bank, and thus passed by the army, which had crossed to the west bank above Raccoon Creek.

Although the speed of the last leg of Harrison's march had surprised the Indians, they had not been idle. They had hewed and hauled logs to form a breastwork about the village, starting at the riverside below the town. It was said to have been "laid in a zigzag form so as to present salient angles," with trenches behind it to accommodate defenders who could fire through holes cut in the logs.[6] The people must have been thankful for those fortifications when they saw the American army penetrating the open oak wood on the plain above the village. Even so, there was a brief panic. Horses shied in excitement, as warriors ran hither and thither, grabbing weapons and speeding to the point of danger, and women gathered startled children to bring them to safety.

No attack came. Mindful, perhaps, of Eustis's caution to exhaust persuasion before applying force, Harrison planned to camp for the night and, if he could not impose his demands, attack the next day with his men refreshed. The Indians quickly overcame their confusion. The men kept their distance, making occasional defiant gestures but wary of conversation. Then they saw Dubois advancing with an interpreter and a white flag to arrange a talk. Three Indian leaders, one a trusted counselor of the

Prophet's, met with the Governor. They disclaimed any hostile intentions, and told Harrison that they had said as much in the message sent him by the Miamis and Delawares. It was agreed that a major conference would be held the next day, and Harrison said he would pitch a camp nearby. In a second talk the Indians even suggested the Americans might find suitable camping places northwest of the town, and the Governor made his way to a narrow oak-wooded knoll that rose above the swampy prairie.

The American camp was about a mile northwest of Prophetstown, at present-day Battleground, situated on a sliver of high ground running a few hundred yards in a roughly north-south direction alongside Burnett's Creek. The bank of the creek, sprouting brush and willows, lay west of the site and along its full length. There the small plateau was a little higher, perhaps by ten feet, than at its eastern and southeastern side, where it shelved to the prairie that extended to Prophetstown. At the northern end of the campsite the plateau was broader, for it tapered toward a point as it ran south. Confined as it was, the site allowed Harrison to establish his force over some ten acres of ground.

From the air his camp would have resembled an irregular trapezoid. The front and rear lines, composed of regulars and militia, were about three hundred yards long, the former facing the prairie, the latter overlooking the creek. Harrison's northern or left flank stretched 150 yards and was defended by Kentucky riflemen under Samuel Wells, while his southern or right flank, near the point of the plateau, extended a mere 80 yards or so and was manned by Spencer's riflemen. The dragoons were posted in the corner formed by the left flank and the front line, while the command tents as well as the baggage and horses and cattle occupied the securer center. The ensuing night was cold, dark, and cloudy. Few expected the brittle truce to last, and the men slept in their clothes, fully accoutered, their weapons ready— the regulars in their tents, pitched a few paces behind their lines, and the rest relying for warmth upon the large fires that Harrison ordered to be kindled.

The few scholars who have seriously considered the "battle of Tippecanoe" have examined it from the viewpoint of Governor Harrison and his troops. Rarely have the difficulties that faced the Indians been appreciated. Yet the Prophet's warriors were confronted with one of the most hazardous of military assignments: the prospect of a force, vastly inferior in numbers and firepower, assaulting a defensive position.

Even with those final reinforcements the Indians may have been outnumbered two to one. Their exact strength is unknown. Claims made by Harrison and Captain Josiah Snelling that 600 or 700 warriors attacked the camp are not supported by most of the statements made by Indians themselves. Agents at Fort Wayne learned that some 300 to 400 Indians were in the fight. Matthew Elliott was told at Fort Malden that while up to 300 men were with the Prophet, most quickly fell to plundering horses and stock, leaving about 100 to do the firing. These assertions may have been less than candid, but a consideration of the different statements and what the Indians achieved leads to the conclusion that the Prophet's assault force amounted to up to 500 men—Kickapoos, Winnebagos, and Potawatomis sprinkled with Shawnees and Piankeshaws, with a few Wyandots, Iroquois, Ottawas, and Ojibwas. Weak numerically, the Indians were also disadvantaged in weaponry. The Americans were armed with bayonets and muskets, some of them using cartridges containing twelve buckshot each, and a few of the men had rifles. Most of the Indians carried firearms, too, but their supply of powder and shot was meager.[7]

Some Indians took encouragement from a previous occasion when the tribes had thrown their full weight against a superior entrenched force: Blue Jacket's victory over Arthur St. Clair's army in 1791. But that great battle had been won by a consistent withering musket fire. Here the lack of ammunition forbade such tactics. The Indians would have to rush the American lines and use the war club and tomahawk in vicious infighting.

The night Harrison established his camp the warriors sent their non-combatants to safety across the Wabash and laid their plans. A key figure seems to have been a black cook named Ben. Ben had been with Harrison's army, but fell into Indian hands, whether by capture or desertion is uncertain. There are several versions of what Ben blabbed, but he may have told the Indians that Harrison intended to attack the next day, and that he had no artillery. The Prophet and his chiefs are said to have considered assassinating Harrison at the scheduled conference; Ben's information was probably important in prompting a night attack. If there was to be a fight, it was better to have it on Indian terms, rather than to wait for the Americans to advance in battle array.

Tenskwatawa was needed to secure the blessing of the spirits. Early statements based on Indian information had it that he promised his followers that the Americans would be stupefied during the attack. Their gunpowder would be turned into sand, and the Indians themselves would become bulletproof. Winamek, whose warriors took part in the battle, reported that the Prophet said the night would be too dark for the whites to see, while the Indians would find it light as day. There is little reason to doubt Tenskwatawa said something of the sort. He had survived rash pronouncements before. The failure of his bold claim to have rendered Prophetstown impregnable to disease had not escaped criticism. It was normally possible for a prophet to explain the failure of predictions by saying the spirits had become offended and withdrawn the assistance they had promised. Perhaps the necessary obeisance had been inadequate, or some impurity had invalidated the ritual upon which the supernatural support depended.[8]

On this occasion, if the Prophet's remarks were given correctly, his predictions would quickly have been vindicated, for as the Indian sentries reconnoitered Harrison's camp on the black and cloudy night of 6–7 November 1811, they could see the Americans had no breastworks. The fires kindled within Harrison's lines threw a glare over his camp. Had not the Prophet said that the whites would look into darkness but the Indians would see as bright as the day?

In the early hours of the morning the Indian army filed silently from the rear of Prophetstown and circled north and then southward to steal along the creek bed to the northwestern corner of Harrison's camp. The war chiefs who led are unknown. Shortly afterward American commentators threw out names carelessly. The most convincing statement came many years later from Lewis Cass, whose connections with Indians gave him means of securing accurate information. He was seldom free from prejudice and cannot be believed implicitly, but he named a Kickapoo, Mengoatowa, who was killed in the battle, and a Winnebago, Waweapakoosa, as the Indian leaders. This is entirely credible, because in the absence of a war chief with the prestige of Tecumseh or Main Poc, the Indians presumably used their own recognized fighting leaders, and the Winnebagos and Kickapoos formed most of the assault force. According to British information the Winnebagos agreed to fire from one side and the Kickapoos from the other. Finally, Cass's account has some slight support in the remark of a Kickapoo chief, made in December, that his brother, likely also a leader, had been slain in the battle.[9]

Whoever they were, the chiefs got their warriors into position unheard and unseen. To the discomforts of the cold had been added a constant drizzle, but the American fires were still burning. It was about four-thirty in the morning, not yet dawn. The soldiers had not been turned out, but some men were up, chatting to the sentries, sitting by the fires or throwing more wood on them. The Governor himself was dressing in his tent.

Stealthily the Indians crept forward, realizing that their best, perhaps their only, chance of success lay in a sudden surprise assault. Perhaps it was an incautious warrior. Perhaps the sharpening glare of some replenished fire. But an American sentry saw something. He whipped up his musket, fired into the darkness, and the battle of Tippecanoe began.

That shot forced the Indians to act straightaway. Raising a terrifying yell they fired upon the guards and scrambled forward, emerging from the dark with blackened faces and feathered heads as if they were fiends from Hell. The sentries fled before them, some dropping their guns, and the Indians crashed into the northwestern corner of the American camp, where

Captain Robert Barton's regulars held the rear line and Captain Frederick Geiger's Kentucky riflemen protected the left flank.

The American line buckled under the impact. Captain William C. Baen was tomahawked, and another officer cut down as he stepped from his tent, while a few of Barton's men were killed and wounded as they struggled to form battle order. For a moment it was touch and go. Thirteen new recruits broke and fled to the center, and two Indians broke through and were shot within the lines. Still, the troops held their ground. They formed an uneven line and began firing back into the night. Harrison and his aide, Colonel Abraham Owen, rode to the point of attack. Almost immediately Owen was pitched, mortally wounded, from his horse by Indian snipers, but Harrison, always steady in a crisis, reinforced the section. Unable to break through, the Indians resorted to exchanging ferocious volleys of musketry with the American lines, advancing from the gloom to the rattle of deer hooves and whistles, discharging their guns into the soldiers, and melting back into the darkness.

While some Indians were thus engaged, others scurried clockwise around the American camp, passing along Harrison's left flank and empty-ing a hail of bullets upon the northeastern corner. Some of the whites la-bored feverishly to extinguish the bonfires that were now illuminating them to Indian marksmen, and glowing coals and logs danced eerily in the air as they were struck by balls from the fusillade. Harrison's men were realizing a disadvantage, as they strained to see into an inky night deepened by the smoke of gunpowder or fired hopefully at the flashes of the Indian muskets.

It was too much for Captain David Robb's mounted riflemen, stationed at the extremity of the left flank. They gave way, scattering to the center. Colonel Boyd, the commander of the regulars, was a fierce critic of irregu-lars and did not lose the opportunity to note this "dastardly" behavior, later describing how some of the men cowered behind trees and wagons inside the lines. The collapse of Robb's company exposed James Bigger's Indiana riflemen, who defended the adjacent part of the front line, to fire from both front and flank. They, too, weakened, and they fell back in some disorder until they rallied behind another company. Unfortunately for the Indians, the American regulars behaved magnificently, forming along the front line in less than a minute, spreading to atone for gaps, and returning fire for fire.

A terrible scene unfolded, defined by the constant crash of gunfire; the cries of the wounded, of Americans hobbling or being carried to the hospi-tal tent in the center and of fallen Indians being borne across the prairie; the bellowing of the terrified cattle herd as it stampeded from the camp with some of the American horses into the clutches of surrounding Indians; and the "infernal yell" of the Prophet's warriors with the answering cheers of Harrison's soldiers. Firing upward from their low ground, many Indians trained their muskets on the mounted dragoons until Colonel Daviess dismounted his men. He had little time to live. A particularly severe fire was being administered by Indians sheltering in an oak grove some twenty paces from the American lines, and with twenty or so gallant followers Daviess tried to flush them out by charging on foot. As his party floundered forward in the dark, exultant warriors fell upon their flanks scourging them with gunfire. The whites retreated, but Daviess's white coat stood stark in the darkness and he was killed. Finally, Captain Josiah Snelling led his company against the same oak grove and expelled the Indians from it with the loss of only one man tomahawked.

When the Indians reached the right flank of Harrison's tormented army they concentrated a punishing fire upon the southwestern corner of the camp. Officer after officer dropped among Spencer's riflemen on the flank and Jacob Warwick's militia company at the end of the rear line. Captain Spencer himself, struck in the head, continued to animate his men until he fell, shot through both thighs. As the poor man was raised another bullet tore into his body and killed him. Not only Spencer but also his first and second lieutenants were mortally injured. On his part, Captain Warwick received a shot through the body during the first fire and was taken inside the lines for treatment. He was dying, but insisted on returning to his company. His example was not to be in vain. Reinforced by Robb's men, dislodged from the other flank, the right also maintained its position.

Now the Indian attack was in serious trouble. The failure of the surprise attack, the inability to drive in the tenacious enemy lines, the swiftly dwindling supplies of ammunition, and the approaching daylight all told against them. Masked by night, they had been able to scamper around the American lines, probing for weaknesses without revealing their own numerical inferiority. As the dawn began to sear the sky they made a last desperate attempt to break the American front line, and then the fury of their assault diminished.

When visibility improved, Harrison was ready to counterattack, launching dragoons, regulars, and militia from both flanks. They stormed onto the prairie, driving the remaining Indians before them. The warriors streamed back toward Prophetstown, carrying those dead and wounded comrades within their reach, and leaving the small plateau beside Burnett's Creek still in the hands of Harrison's bloodstained and tired soldiers. Firing had lasted for two and one-quarter hours, and left the field strewn with dead and wounded men.

Harrison's casualties amounted to 188 men, 68 of them killed outright or fatally wounded. The Indian losses were slighter, because for the most part the Americans had fired blind. They defy exact enumeration. Statements of one party about the damage it inflicted on another are hardly ever reliable, and usually have at least one eye open to the advantages of propaganda and self-promotion. Harrison said that 36 to 40 Indian bodies were found on the field, and believed, entirely plausibly, that others had been taken off for burial. A total of 50 Indians killed would be a reasonable estimate to make from the Governor's evidence. This roughly equates with the statement of a Kickapoo made in December. It claimed 51 Winnebago and Kickapoo dead, a figure that would have to be increased by a fatally wounded Potawatomi found by the Americans on the prairie after the battle.

However, although guesses made by Indians varied greatly, most gave significantly lower figures for their losses: 25 killed according to a Kickapoo informant of the British; between 24 and 39 killed if we believe information acquired by the Illinois Indian agents, Thomas Forsyth and John Lalime; and 28 dead according to John Johnston. Tecumseh's own band did not, it seems, escape unscathed. Lewis Cass, who interviewed the Prophet years later, said that the Shawnees lost one man, Paaksgee, dead, and three, Kathooskaka, Mamatseka, and Maipokseka, wounded.[10]

The Prophet is represented to have continued his incantations throughout the battle, and to have urged the warriors to fight until the end. One thing is certain. The Indians of Prophetstown had far from disgraced themselves. By assailing a superior army on its chosen ground, and inflicting greater damage than they had themselves suffered, they had made one of the most creditable military defenses in the long history of the American Indian wars.

Nevertheless, without the ammunition to destroy or dislodge the enemy, or indeed to defend their town, the Indians had no further option than to withdraw. Harrison's force had been badly shaken, and for some time it failed to press its advantage. It spent the whole of 7 November and most of the next day in camp, waiting for the Indians to renew the attack, building a breastwork, and tending the wounded. Some of the scalps of dead Indians were fixed to the muzzles of guns to be taken back to Vincennes as trophies. Only after dark on the eighth did the Americans venture into Prophetstown.

They found it deserted, but for a wounded Indian and an old woman who had been accidentally left behind when the warriors hurriedly departed. Both were treated humanely. However, Harrison then dealt his adversaries his cruelest blow. The whites plundered the towns of utensils, such as kettles, seized some of the corn for their own use, and put the village to the torch. The wise Kickapoos had hidden their winter corn reserves, but the Shawnee granary went up in flames. Without those supplies and ammunition for hunting, the Prophet and his band faced a hard winter.

On 9 November the battered American army, its wounded loaded painfully onto wagons, turned back for Vincennes, leaving behind them the black and smoking ruins of Tecumseh's town.

19

RED STICKS
AND EARTHQUAKES

Tecumseh had not seen Prophetstown since July. When he had paddled down the Wabash to confront Harrison at Vincennes he had merely begun a remarkable six-month odyssey that would take him some three thousand miles and into ten or more of the present-day states of the Union. It was arguably the most impressive journey ever made on behalf of Indian unity. With him went a handpicked party, six Shawnees, six Kickapoos, six Winnebagos, and two Creek guides. Sadly, the names of few who shared the rigors of that marathon with him have come down to us. One of the Shawnees may have been Tewaskoota, or Jim Blue-Jacket junior, the grandson of the famous war chief. Jim would then have been in his twenties. Of the guides the most important was certainly Seekaboo. A contemporary American report described him as a Creek from Tuckabatchee who had been living with the northern Shawnees for twenty years, but Choctaw and Creek tradition remembered him as a mixed-blood Creek related to Tecumseh and fluent in the Muskogee and Choctaw languages. He probably also commanded southern trade jargons such as Mobilian, and he was as important an interpreter as he was a guide. Yet more, he remained in the south after Tecumseh's departure, nurturing the seeds the chief had broadcast, and serving against the United States in the ensuing Creek and first Seminole wars.[1]

As Tecumseh and his friends descended the Wabash to the Ohio early in August, and then traveled overland through Kentucky and Tennessee, they must often have debated the prizes and prospects that lay before them. They were moving into the south, an area the Spaniards and Americans affected to have carved up for themselves, Spain clinging tenuously to most of the Gulf coast south of the thirty-first parallel, and the United States recognizing the states of Tennessee and Georgia and the territory of Mississippi, which occupied what would become Alabama and Mississippi. To Tecumseh it was Indian land. Some seventy thousand Indians, equal to those scattered across the Great Lakes region, inhabited this richly varied landscape. The mountainous area of the southern Alleghenies could still field about two thousand Cherokee warriors, while about half as many Chickasaw men lived with their families about the Tombigbee watershed of northern Mississippi. More formidable still were the Choctaws, whose six thousand warriors commanded most of what is now Mississippi, and the Creek (or Muskogee) Confederacy, an affiliation of Muskogees, Alabamas, Yuchis, Hitchitis, Shawnees, and others, which probably had five thousand men.

The Creeks occupied present-day Alabama and Georgia, the warm lush country in which Tecumseh's parents had met and married half a century before, its hills under forests of oak and hickory and its reedy streams intersecting cane meadows and broad savannas. Over forty villages of the more numerous Upper Creeks were sprinkled along the Alabama, Tallapoosa, and Coosa Rivers; the Lower Creeks were settled upon the Chattahoochee and Flint; and parts of the confederacy which had moved south to colonize the subtropical swampy wilderness of Florida were acquiring a separate identity as Seminoles.

Shawnees had tried to integrate these tribes into pan-Indian confederations before, but never entirely successfully. In 1793 a delegation under Red Pole had toured the south, but the Chickasaws had even enlisted with Anthony Wayne and raised the hatchet against the northern confederates. The bad blood then brewed between them and the Shawnees had yet to be forgotten.

Tecumseh had a much more difficult job than Red Pole. The southern Indians may have shared many burdens with their northern fellows, but their prospects for armed resistance to the United States were distinctly dimmer. They had no powerful counterpower to the Seventeen Fires, no Britain to offer assistance or at least an alternative source of supplies. Spain was patently enfeebled, barely capable of maintaining its precarious foothold in the Gulf. In addition, the American grip on the tribes was tighter in the south, not merely by means of its forts but also because of the greater success of the "civilization" program in that quarter.

In each of the tribes American agents were encouraging the Indians to improve their farming, and to manufacture cloth, rather than to hunt; to produce for the market instead of for mere subsistence; to replace the old values of cooperation and sharing with thrift and acquisitiveness; and to emphasize individual rather than communal ownership of the land. Among the Cherokees and Creeks, where effective agents Return Jonathan Meigs and Benjamin Hawkins were respectively at work, many Indians were in rapid retreat from the basically traditional culture that Tecumseh and the Prophet espoused.

And among all the southern tribes this process was promoted not only by agents but also through the development of mixed white and Indian bloodlines. Far more than in the north, the offspring of white traders and Indian mothers were rising to prominence through their familiarity with European culture. Everywhere mestizos were gaining control of tribal affairs. The most famous Creek of the period, Alexander McGillivray, had been only one-quarter Indian. John Ross, who would soon become the most prominent Cherokee, had one-eighth Indian blood, and however much he identified with his Cherokee nationality and defended tribal homelands, he had culturally more in common with the whites than with the traditionalists among his fellow tribesmen. By 1800 mixed-bloods were managing Chickasaw affairs, largely through the five sons of a Scots trader, James Logan Colbert. Among the Choctaws the full-bloods held out longer, and in 1811 all three district chiefs—Apukshunnubbee, Pushmataha, and Moshulatubbee—were such, but their days were numbered, too, and the future belonged to mestizos such as the Folsom brothers, the Leflores, and John Pitchlynn.

Many mixed-bloods, like the Colbert brothers, preferred the acquisitive entrepreneurial lifestyles of their merchant forebears to the simple egalitarianism of the Indians. They were seldom indifferent to the threat to native land, but their extensive connections with whites as well as their inclinations tempted them to turn deaf ears to Tecumseh's plea for a self-sustaining and revitalized traditional Indian culture. As Tecumseh led his men to the Mid-Day he knew a powerful phalanx of influential opponents—American agents and military commanders, government chiefs whose positions and wealth depended upon the United States, and many of the upcoming prosperous mestizo leaders whose vision of the future was so different from his own—would stand with the fainthearts against him.

Tecumseh was ever an optimist, finding words to cheer weary followers, to inspire hope and laughter in the face of uncertainties and awesome difficulties. Even here, in the south, he was not without some advantages, and we may be sure he had learned about most of them.

The "civilization" program, for example. It had bitten deep, but it had its critics, even within the most "advanced" (Tecumseh would have said "corrupted") of nations, the Cherokees, where a nativist backlash was in the making. Furthermore, throughout the south Indians were sensing a looming crisis. Like their northern brothers and sisters, the southern tribes were being punished by European diseases, alcohol abuse, ongoing problems with intruders upon Indian lands, and the declining yields of the hunt. Like the northerners, they were deeply troubled by the inexorable erosion of their territory.

Encouraged by the United States to accumulate trade debts that could be extinguished by land cessions, all the tribes had suffered. In 1805 the Choctaws had ceded four million acres for less than two cents an acre, nearly all of it to offset debts. The Chickasaws lost land northeast of the Tennessee, also for a derisory pittance. Between 1801 and 1823 the Cherokees relinquished ten million acres in nine cessions. By another treaty, concluded in Washington in 1805, the Creeks had been bullied into allowing the rapacious Georgians to drive the eastern limits of the Creek Nation from the Oconee to the Ocmulgee at a cost of a scant ten cents an acre. Gradually the Indian domain was being squeezed from all sides, between swelling American settlements on the Mississippi in the west, in Tennessee to the north, and in Georgia to the east. In that same treaty of 1805 the Creeks were also compelled to accept a federal horse path across their territory, linking the Georgian settlements to Fort Stoddert, near Mobile. Tired of waiting for the Indians to unlock their land by "civilizing" and turning themselves into small homesteaders, many American expansionists clamored for the removal of the tribes west of the Mississippi.

Even before Tecumseh arrived in the south, these problems were feeding a rising anti-Americanism, as well as tensions within Indian villages— tensions between the proponents of "civilization" and nativists, and between pro-American chiefs and defenders of the land. Resistance movements similar to those led by Tecumseh and the Prophet were already surfacing. In February 1811 three Cherokees said that they had spoken to envoys of the Great Spirit and learned that he disapproved both of the land cessions and of the decline of traditional customs and beliefs. And from 1798 the Upper Creeks had been hosting intertribal conferences in which Choctaws, Creeks, Cherokees, and Chickasaws had discussed the common defense of Indian land. The most recent revival of the idea had occurred in 1810, and Tecumseh knew about it. Indeed, he was coming to attend just such a pan-Indian council, to be held at Tuckabatchee on the Tallapoosa.

Tecumseh had other reasons to keep his spirits high. Ahead, on the Tallapoosa, were several villages of Shawnees, most of them Hathawekelas, who would surely give him a welcome. It was from these communities that his father had moved north. Tecumseh hoped to exploit these connections, but his thoughts must also have been nostalgic. He had kinfolk here, men and women he had never met but about whom he had heard. As Tecumseh traveled on, he knew he was going home.

‣—‣ ▆◆▆ ▬—‣

Tecumseh wanted to mask his activities from American officials, so he decided against descending the Mississippi, where regular traffic would have been encountered, and which would have taken him beneath the nose of the United States trade factory at Chickasaw Bluffs (Memphis, Tennessee). Occasional glimpses of him were gained as he rode through the Chickasaw Nation.

About 27 August he passed Levi Colbert's home, probably the one at Buzzard Roost Creek a little south of the Tennessee River. The Colbert brothers, born of a Scots father and Chickasaw mother, had easily been accepted as clan and tribal members of the matrilineal Chickasaws, but they would never have enjoyed the Shawnee leader's confidence. Tecumseh was an old-fashioned chief, who cared little for material wealth but distributed what he had to the neediest of his followers. The Colberts were of a new breed, eager for personal profits. To them roads hacked through Indian lands meant less an unwelcome intrusion than an opportunity to make money through running inns and ferries. In 1805 George Colbert had received one thousand dollars for services in securing the cession of Chickasaw land north of the Tennessee to the United States. When George called upon Tecumseh to discover his purposes, the Shawnee chief was tight-lipped. He told Colbert that his business must await the intertribal meeting at Tuckabatchee. Tecumseh did not delay among the Chickasaws. Probably remembering how they had helped the Americans in 1794, he sent messages ahead to the Choctaws and pressed on into Mississippi Territory.[2]

Contemporary reports are even sketchier about the weeks Tecumseh spent among the Choctaws. They tell nothing beyond the fact that the tour took place, and for details it is necessary to consult traditions Henry Sale Halbert collected among the Choctaws later in the century. Although Halbert was a dedicated enthusiast, scrupulous and precise, even his material has to be approached with extreme caution. He had four substantial accounts, but only one from an eyewitness, Himonubbee, who had been a boy of twelve years when Tecumseh went through his nation. The other narratives came from people who had no personal knowledge of Tecumseh, but who had received eyewitness accounts from others many years before. Charley Hoentubbee was one such informant. His father, Chief Hoentubbee, had been Tecumseh's host in 1811. He often spoke to Charley about Tecumseh's visit until his death in 1859, when Charley was thirty-nine years old. The point to remember is this: Chief Hoentubbee had valuable information, but the years misted and distorted his recollections, and even after the vestiges had been passed to his son, Charley suffered some two dozen more years to elapse before giving them to Halbert in 1882. Halbert cross-checked his accounts carefully, but his reconstruction of Tecumseh's tour of the Choctaw nation is inevitably tentative.[3]

Despite this proviso, the broad outlines can be salvaged. According to statements alleged to have been made by a Choctaw named Red Pepper, Tecumseh's party, on horseback and accompanied by Chickasaw guides, reached Choctaw country near present-day West Point, Mississippi. They crossed Oktibbeha Creek and were escorted by a number of Choctaws southward, along the Six Towns trail. Fording the Noxubee River about eight miles above the site of Macon, they eventually reached the village of Chief Moshulatubbee (Mashulaville). There were three district principal chiefs among the Choctaws, and Moshulatubbee was one of them. The hereditary head of the northeast, he was then some fifty years of age, a tall but gross, good-humored man. With Seekaboo interpreting, Tecumseh explained his purpose. The large Choctaw listened patiently, and did not seem unsympathetic. He sent runners to convene a council, and while preparations for the meeting went forward, Tecumseh took his message to neighboring towns.

One such village, in the northwestern part of today's Kemper County, was the home of Chief Hoentubbee, who became enough of a friend to Tecumseh to receive the gift of a silver crescent-shaped gorget. Traditional accounts of the appearance of the northerners at this town, like Shabeni's narrative of Tecumseh's 1810 tour, suggest the care the Shawnee took to standardize the dress of his emissaries. His men appeared in uniform. Here they wore buckskin shirts and fringed leggings, breechcloths, and moccasins. Their heads were shaven, except for long scalp locks that fell in three plaits, adorned with hawk feathers, behind them, and they wore red flannel headbands beneath silver bands. About his arms each man sported three silver bracelets, above and below the elbows and at the wrists, and as weapons he carried a rifle, pipe-tomahawk, and knife. The Indians had painted themselves alike, too. Semicircular red lines were traced beneath each eye and terminated on the cheekbones; there were small red spots on each temple, and a large spot at the center of the breast. Tecumseh himself, said Himonubbee, whose father attended the council, had inserted a single large plume into the front of his headband; part of it was stained white, the other red.

After several days at Hoentubbee's town Tecumseh held a heavily attended council. The Shawnees performed a dance, and when it was over Tecumseh spoke, naked in the sultry air but for a breechcloth, moccasins, and his red headband. Beside him Seekaboo, a man of forty or so years, translated, inviting the Choctaws to join the northern confederates. Moshulatubbee was said to have been there, as well as the principal chief of the southern district, the warrior and orator Pushmataha. All three of the

Choctaw district chiefs were pensioners of the United States, and Push-mataha had also received five hundred dollars for facilitating the sale of tribal lands in 1805. On the second day of the council, it is claimed, he spoke against Tecumseh, urging the Choctaws to remain peaceful, and he is represented to have shadowed the northerners from town to town thereafter, opposing them on every appropriate occasion.[4]

Tecumseh repeated his appeal at other villages, including Yazoo and the important Mokalusha, both in what is now Neshoba County, and at Chunky Town in Newton County. There Halbert's information diverged. Charley Hoentubbee, whose father acted as Tecumseh's guide, insisted the Shawnee went no farther than Chunky Town, but Himonubbee said the northerners journeyed south into Pushmataha's district, visiting the Six Towns in modern Jasper County, and the towns of Coosha (Lauderdale County) and Yahnubbee (Kemper County). Whichever version is correct, there is agreement that Tecumseh finally spoke at the great council Moshulatubbee had convened. Whether it occurred at the Mashulaville site or northeast of it, at present-day Brooksville, is immaterial. It was a considerable gathering—one of the largest ever seen, if we may believe an account obtained from John Pitchlynn, who was present as an interpreter for the United States. Tecumseh asked the Indians to join him in his war, reminding them of the probability of British assistance, but once again Pushmataha counseled against him, and the meeting turned him down.

Tecumseh had suffered a severe defeat. One contemporary account of no great authority speaks of him as persuading three hundred Choctaw warriors to support his cause, and tribesmen later remembered forty-five members of their families helping the Creeks in their eventual rebellion against the United States, but the prevailing impression of Tecumseh's tour of the Choctaw Nation is one of failure. He was not disheartened. Redoubling his efforts, he took his entourage eastward, across the Tombigbee into the lands of the Creeks.[5]

Here, if anywhere in the south, Tecumseh would find allies.

Here were fellow Shawnees, most in a town named Sauvonnogee on the Tallapoosa, some of them Tecumseh's kinfolk.

Here, too, were Creeks who had already been curious enough to visit the Prophet on the Wabash, and Creeks concerned enough for their lands to revive southern pan-tribalism. Big Warrior (Tastanagi Tako), the head civil chief at Tuckabatchee, speaker for the Upper Creeks, and the most important leader on the tribe's national council, was no friend to the United States agent, Benjamin Hawkins, and was keen to place himself at the head of the four southern tribes.

When Tecumseh arrived at Tuckabatchee on the evening of 19 September he found the town alive with the excitement and bustle of an important intertribal convention. Creeks from across the nation were there, including some Seminoles. There were nineteen Choctaws, forty-six Cherokees, and a number of Chickasaw representatives. Hawkins had come from his base on the Flint, among the Lower Creeks, to force the Indians to consent to another road the Americans intended blazing across Creek territory, from Tennessee to Mobile. With him were a number of his colleagues: John Halsted, the Indian trade factor at Fort Hawkins on the Ocmulgee; Christian Limbaugh and Nimrod Doyle, the agent's assistants; and Alex Cornells, a mestizo who served Hawkins as an interpreter.

Even in that colorful throng the handsome Shawnee chief and his followers stood out. In all quarters tongues were wagging about the intentions of the strange northerners, but the objects of the speculation held their peace. The council was already a few days old when Tecumseh arrived. After waiting for Hawkins to finish speaking on 20 September, the chief led his party into the public square, where the council house stood, to greet his hosts.

The northerners were dressed in a fantastic manner. Stripped to breechcloths, moccasins, and ornaments, they had placed eagle feathers on their heads and painted their faces black, while buffalo tails hung behind from their belts. Other tails were attached to their arms, ingeniously "made to stand out, by means of bands." Tecumseh led his people on several rounds of the square, and then approached the Creek chiefs, cheerfully shaking them with the full length of the arm, and presenting them with tobacco to proclaim his goodwill.[6]

In the days that followed Tecumseh also introduced the Creeks to what seems to have been the war dance Shawnees used to prepare themselves for battle. The Creeks found it a novelty, since their war dances followed rather than preceded their military forays, and they were soon trying to imitate the songs and movements of the visitors. The dance was a striking three-part affair, performed by nearly nude warriors painted in a fearsome manner, all armed with tomahawks and other weapons. Initially they danced in a circle to a solemn tune, but then a war whoop sent them to their seats, where they observed a brief silence. In the second phase, the dancers rose one after the other, capering to a drumbeat, recalling their feats of war, and inciting their fellows by reminding them of the injuries they had received. During the finale all the warriors were on their feet, commencing "the most tremendous yelling, jumping and figuring about" in imitation of the impending fray. The "dance of the Lakes" soon became a rage "in all the towns on the Tallapoosy."[7]

For the time being Tecumseh allowed Hawkins the stage and remained content to observe and gather information. Disappointed to see the American officials, he steadfastly refused to declare his business, and after each day's proceedings would insist that the sun had gone too far down for him to speak. He evasively parried probing questions. On 21 September Hawkins reported that a war pipe had been forwarded from the Indians of the upper Mississippi. It had come through the Chickasaws, urging the tribes to unite against the whites. Of course Tecumseh knew the purpose of that pipe, but in the agent's presence he stood aloof from it.

> The chiefs here unanimously refused to smoke the pipe on its presentation and of course refused to join in the war [reported Hawkins]. The Shawanese leader stated last evening that he had followed this pipe from the north and recommended its rejection to all the Indians he had seen, and that the Indians should unite in peace and friendship among themselves and cultivate the same with their white neighbours . . .

When a Cherokee chief told Tecumseh that if he had come to rouse the southern Indians to war he should go home now, Tecumseh still refused to be drawn. He made them wait.[8]

In the meantime, if Tecumseh needed an illustration of American arrogance to the Creeks, Hawkins readily supplied one during that first week. Still smarting from having had a federal road imposed upon them six years before, the Creeks were now being told that nothing they said would prevent the second horse path from slicing across their domain. A protest sent by Hopoithle Mico, the chief of the Upper Creek town of Tallassee, to President Madison in May was dismissed as "unreasonable." According to one witness, Hawkins and the chiefs tossed the subject to and fro for three days without agreement, until "Col. Hawkins, at length, told them he did not come there to ask their permission to open a road, but merely to inform them that it was now cutting." Hawkins sugared the pill by granting the Creeks the profits from ferries, toll bridges, and inns along the way, and promised that one thousand spinning wheels, one thousand cotton cards, and "waggonage" would be given the tribe. Still, it took the agent until 28 September to force the agreement upon the reluctant Big Warrior and his chiefs.[9]

Hawkins had what he wanted. He was increasingly suspicious of Tecumseh, but he left for his agency, giving the Shawnee the opportunities for which he had been waiting.

United States officials were not admitted to Tecumseh's principal presentation, which was delivered over the best part of a day in the public square before hundreds of eager listeners. No record of his speech was made, and he seems to have cautioned his audience against unwelcome questions, charging supporters to hide their plans until the right moment. Publicly the Indians should remain friendly, and steal not so much as a bell from the whites.

However, from disparate remarks made about the speech, it is clear that Tecumseh emphasized his family connections with Tuckabatchee and invited the southern tribes to join his confederacy. They must stand against land cessions, and remove venal chiefs, and if necessary they must fight. Tecumseh predicted that guns would soon be fired in the north, but the British would help them, and a greater power still—the one the Creeks called the Maker of Breath, the Great Spirit himself, who spoke through Tecumseh's brother, the Prophet.

One of Tecumseh's party, perhaps Seekaboo, had imbibed the Prophet's principles, and it was probably from him (as well as through later communications with Tenskwatawa himself) that Tecumseh's Creek followers eventually drew their extreme nativist ideology. In fact, these disciples, soon to be dubbed "Red Sticks" because of the red clubs used to raise war parties, returned to fundamentals of Tenskwatawa's religion that had been waning in the north. They spoke not only of resisting the "civilization" program—with its transformation of warrior-hunters into women-farmers—by destroying looms, plows, and spinning wheels, but also of killing animals associated with the whites, such as hogs, poultry, and cattle. And wars could be won as easily as mouths were filled. The Red Sticks had only to shake their clubs at enemies and the Maker of Breath would mire the enemies in boggy ground and render them helpless. Much of this sounds far more like Tenskwatawa than his more secular and practical brother.[10]

Yet Tecumseh, too, believed in the benevolence of the Great Spirit, and promised the Creeks supernatural aid. He proved it by giving a sign.

It was already there for all to see. The sign had first been noticed in March, in France. From the end of August it was visible in America, but lay so close to the horizon that few would have observed it. But throughout September, as Tecumseh came into the Creek Nation, it grew in brilliance, and during October it appeared at its brightest, glowing eerily over the forests during the night. It was a great comet, its head a million miles across, and its tail one hundred million miles in length. In November the visibility of the comet declined, and the next month it had all but vanished.

Tecumseh seized upon the appearance of the comet, alluding to it as an omen that boded ill to his enemies. To the Creeks it was a powerful argument. Consider, here was this celebrated Shawnee, brother of the Prophet, his very name—Tecumtha—signifying the Shooting Star. His appearance coincided with that of the comet, and while Tecumseh remained, visiting Creek towns, the splendor of the heavenly visitor intensified. No sooner had he moved on than it faded, disappearing as mysteriously as it had come. No Creek could be blamed for believing that this man had truly been favored by the spirits.[11]

Under the patronage of the great comet, Tecumseh spent a month or more among the Creeks, touring their towns, speaking to their leaders, and soliciting support. It was a nation full of overlapping conflicts, he discovered, many of them useful. Nativists opposed the "civilization" process, while others, largely from the non-Muskogee section of the Creek Confederacy, resented both the Muskogee-dominated National Council and Hawkins's efforts to centralize power in it so that he could turn it to his account. The Upper Creeks of the Coosa and Alabama were particularly incensed by the forthcoming road, which threatened their homes, while Seminoles' fears for their land had been revived by American filibustering in Spanish Florida. A complicated network of grievances played into Tecumseh's hands, allowing him to find several important allies.

Big Warrior, a huge man, "spotted as a leopard" it was said, proved a disappointment. He wanted to protect Indian land, and to head a southern confederacy, but he lacked the stomach for a serious confrontation with the United States. However, others came forward.

A Creek tradition named as one of Tecumseh's supporters Menawa of Okfuskee, on the Tallapoosa, but more important were the chiefs of the Upper Creek town of Tallassee, and Josiah Francis, an Alabama *hillis haya*, or medicine man.

The civil chief of Tallassee was Hopoithle Mico, known also as Tame King, a man of extreme age who had once been a friend to the United States, until he considered himself slighted by its agents. He condemned the "civilization" plan and land cessions. He was also deeply jealous of the National Council, partly because it was controlled by Hawkins and the Muskogees (the Tallassees were not Muskogees) but more so on account of its elevation of his personal rival, Big Warrior, to the supreme office. The Tallassees hated Big Warrior. For about three years Hopoithle Mico and his skillful head warrior, Peter McQueen, a wealthy slave-owning mestizo, had even ousted him from his position in the council, but Big Warrior regained his place and the Tallassees lost power. Nonetheless, Hopoithle Mico still claimed that he, not Big Warrior, was the rightful head, not only of the Upper Creeks but also of the southern confederacy they were forming. His opposition was so bitter that on one occasion his town had been raided, the buildings burned, and some of its residents abused.

The Tallassees were tailor-made for Tecumseh, who offered external aid for the defense of Creek land. After the dismissal of his protest about the road to President Madison earlier in the year, Hopoithle Mico had been casting about for new allies. He believed the Spaniards would soon surrender their forts to the Americans, so on the first day of September he had been at Apalachicola in Florida, sending an appeal for help to the British in the Bahamas.[12]

Josiah Francis was another non-Muskogee, a mixed-blood Alabama warrior, whose hometown was Autauga. He was a trader, but one heavily in debt to the John Forbes Company, which he blamed for encouraging land cessions. (The Indians were expected to apply the proceeds of their land sales to debts.) But Francis was also deeply spiritual, a *hillis haya*, and he was impressed by Tecumseh's claim to have spoken for the Creator. Just as Creek creation stories told how the spirits had rescued the world from chaos and flood, so in Francis's view might the Maker of Breath now intervene during this time of crisis to save the Creek Nation. One report indicated that Francis was interested enough in Tecumseh to accompany his entourage north.[13]

In the Upper Creek country many others listened to Tecumseh. Some joined his delegation, taking the place of Seekaboo, who remained in the south to develop the connections Tecumseh had made. More made straight for Prophetstown to speak to Tenskwatawa and learn whether all Tecumseh had said about the northern confederacy was true. In January 1812 two hundred Creeks were reported to be on the Wabash. Although many Creeks remained uncommitted or hostile to Tecumseh, he seems to have left the Creek Nation with some firm promises of support.[14]

Contemporary reports are silent about Tecumseh for the next two months. That he was not idle, we can be assured, and that he spent much of that period among the Creeks, as was later alleged, seems certain. During the last half of the nineteenth century misty traditions of visits to the Cherokees were mentioned. One said that Tecumseh penetrated the mountainous regions of North Carolina and called upon the Cherokee chief, Junaluska, "at his home, and at the town house on Soco Creek, in Swain County." Others, that he was in Tennessee. Searches have failed to confirm these traditions, but if Tecumseh did visit Cherokee settlements he clearly intended no extended canvass of the tribe. Perhaps he considered it to be too influenced by the Americans. A clearer sight of him occurred in November, heading westward toward the Mississippi through Chickasaw territory. He called upon the principal chief, Chinubbee, and asked him to join the confederacy. Chinubbee had an annuity from the United States, and showed no interest in Tecumseh's plans. Some of his younger warriors, aggravated over intrusions upon their lands and damage to tribal property, might have responded to a general appeal from Tecumseh, but the Shawnee did not make one, and he continued his journey.[15]

Tecumseh's tour of the south was over, and as he passed from the scene so the comet that had illuminated his travels disappeared from the sky. Yet he had one more surprise for the southern Indians. He had another sign for them, one far more terrifying than the mysterious comet. In the early hours of 16 December 1811, shortly after Tecumseh's departure, it came, rousing white, red, and black alike from their sleep. The very ground began to shake.

Today scientists refer to them as the New Madrid earthquakes, and estimate that the severest tremors were greater than any others known in North America in modern times.

The epicenter was in what is now northeastern Arkansas, about sixty-five miles southwest of New Madrid, Missouri. The first shocks, beginning about two o'clock in the morning, destroyed Little Prairie, a small settlement close to the epicenter. They were not felt in New Orleans, but steeple bells rang in Charleston, South Carolina, buildings trembled, furniture shifted, and clocks stopped.

The Cherokees were horrified. The next day the Moravian missionaries at Springplace, Georgia, were visited by many Indians pleading for an explanation of the tremors. Some cried that the earth was collapsing. A Christian Indian who visited neighboring Indians said she "could not describe vividly enough the perplexity in which she found the people everywhere. Some of them attribute the occurrence to the sorcerers; some to a large snake [evil spirit] which must have crawled under their house; some to the weakness of old age of the earth, which will now soon cave in."[16]

Those shocks were simply the first of many. Altogether there were three series of them, beginning 16 December, 23 January, and 7 February. A Louisville survey counted a total of 1,874 up to 15 March, over 50 of alarming proportions. At times the convulsions were felt from Canada to the Gulf of Mexico. Fissures opened in the earth, spewing out sand and water. The Mississippi temporarily reversed its flow, and the small town of New Madrid was rubbed out. Many reported strange sights: birds settling on people's heads and animal prey and predators milling together, as if the need for company of any kind overruled natural caution. Someone near the epicenter during the fierce tremor of 7 February recalled that

the surface of the earth on this side of the River St. Francis [Missouri] appeared to be compressed in such a manner as to force the water mixed with fine sand through small apertures as high as the tops of the trees. That although he was at that time on a ridge the water covered the surface several inches deep but soon disappeared. That himself and another Indian were so astonished that they sat down and looked each other in the face without either attempting to speak for a considerable time.[17]

None were more astonished than Indian peoples. Unusual phenomena like this told them that the spirits were angry, and often sparked incredibly intense if not always long-lived spiritual resurgences. The epidemics of 1805 had spawned the religions of Beata and the Prophet, both attempting to restore the equanimity of the spirits by revitalizing worship, restoring old practices, and reforming behavior. The New Madrid earthquakes likewise unleashed waves of fear and guilt.

At the Moravian mission at Goshen, Ohio, where the shocks caused headaches and sickness, an Indian remarked that the Great Spirit was displeased with the Americans for stealing land and killing Indians in the battle of Tippecanoe. The Cherokees, said another missionary, were in "real tumult," living beneath "a dark heavy feeling" that some fearful apocalypse was approaching. "Ugly and terrifying appearances of God" were reported, and the talk was that "a new earth would come into being in the spring." Cherokee prophets bubbled with predictions. During the final series of tremors the miserable inhabitants of one town fled, terrified that it was about to be obliterated by a monstrous hailstorm. "As the stated terrible day passed without hail, they came back to their dwelling places, ready and willing to believe every new deceiver," wrote the missionaries.

Engulfed in consternation, the Cherokees were unable to rally around any definitive explanation of the phenomena. Those touched by Christianity thought the Day of Judgment had arrived. Some claimed that the earth was dying, and others that the Great Spirit was annihilating the whites for their theft of the land. It was as heatedly argued that the Indians themselves had provoked the events because they had neglected the spirits and allowed old traditions to die. There was no consensus, no single prophet who could interpret the earthquakes to everyone's satisfaction and prescribe a course of action. When the tremors ended, the agitation among the Cherokees, nativist and otherwise, receded with them.

Not so among the Creeks, who were also thrown into ferment, for Tecumseh had already armed them with an explanation. The Great Spirit wanted the unnecessary trappings of white civilization to be discarded, land sales to end, and the tribes to stand together. The Red Stick prophets who emerged among the Creeks in the wake of the earthquakes endorsed that plan relatively single-mindedly. They had no reason to doubt Tecumseh. He had promised them signs of his power, and he had delivered.

Within months of the final quakes it was being reported that Tecumseh had actually predicted the event to the Creeks, and over time the story became an accepted part of tribal oral history. Thomas L. McKenney got a version during a visit to Tuckabatchee in 1827. Tecumseh, he was informed, had told Big Warrior that when he reached Detroit he would stamp his foot upon the ground and shake down every house in Tuckabatchee. Tecumseh's boast was fulfilled, and his powers confirmed. George Stiggins, brother-in-law to a Red Stick leader, gave another account. He related that Tecumseh left the Creeks with the promise that in about four moons he would climb a mountain, whoop, clap his hands, and stamp the earth three times until it trembled. The pledge was redeemed, and with the comet—"two such uncommon occurrences in succession"—convinced the Creeks of Tecumseh's veracity. As late as 1883 an aged Creek who had been fifteen at the time of the earthquakes declared that they had been predicted by Tecumseh.[18]

What is to be made of this? The significant fact is not whether Tecumseh did or did not predict the earthquakes, but that the Creeks believed that he had done so. That belief was crucial, for it established Tecumseh's credibility. Even among the Chickasaws there were now warriors who believed it "the duty of every Indian implicitly to adhere to The Prophet."[19]

Many Creeks had no doubts. There were extensive standing grievances against the United States; Tecumseh had sharpened that hostility, outlined a strategy, and claimed supernatural support; and the earthquakes proved that he was right. These were the three linked factors that took the Red Sticks into one of the most desperate Indian revolts in American history.

20

REBUILDING THE UNION

Tecumseh was near the epicenter when the first shocks of the earthquake raised the people of the midwest from their sleep. His itinerary was running true to the one he had given Harrison the previous August: "After having visited the Creeks and Choctaws he is to visit the Osages and return by the Missouri." Accordingly, Tecumseh had crossed the Mississippi, and in December, when the tremors began, he was in Missouri. He made "great exertions" to bring the Shawnees and Delawares there into his confederacy, but could not break their traditional indifference to his movement.[1]

Even the earthquakes didn't help him here, although some of the local Indians were willing to attribute them to the powers of the Prophet. An Indian from the New Madrid area, who, it was said, had been swallowed and then disgorged in the spasms, opined that "the Shawanoe Prophet has caused the earthquake to destroy the whites." On the Maramec River the Shawnees had been badly frightened, too, but despite Tecumseh's visit before or during the tremors, they refused to develop a serious anti-American interpretation of the phenomenon. They put everything down to their neglect of Waashaa Monetoo, and organized a three-day ceremony in which the people purified themselves, fasted to communicate with the spirit world, and offered prayers, thanks, and venison to appease angry deities. It was instinctive nativism, but in this instance it failed to work to Tecumseh's advantage.[2]

The Osages were also pondering the meaning of the shocks. According to John Dunn Hunter, a white man who said he had been raised among these proud predatory riders of the Midwest, the earthquakes filled the Indians "with great terror . . . the trees and wigwams shook exceedingly; the ice which skirted the margin of the Arkansas River was broken in pieces; and the most of the Indians thought that the Great Spirit, angry with the human race, was about to destroy the world."[3]

Many Osages had little love for the United States. The tribe had relinquished its claims to the west bank of the Mississippi to the Americans in 1808 and 1809 and had lived to regret it. A large Osage delegation had been in St. Louis that September to plead for the treaty to be rescinded. The payment of the first annuities due under the agreement may have mollified some of the Indians, but dissatisfaction survived, and Tecumseh might have used the fear engendered by the earthquakes to turn it to account.[4]

It took courage and vision on the part of Tecumseh to approach the fierce Osages, courage because a two-year dispute between them and the Missouri Shawnees was still unsettled, and vision because Tecumseh had to subordinate the obligation to take personal revenge for injured kinfolk to his plan of Indian unity. As mentioned earlier, one of the two Shawnees slaughtered by Osages in 1810 had been a relative of Tecumseh's. He must have felt the urge to repay the murder in the usual manner, but instead he had urged the Shawnees to forgive the Osages, and now proposed to invite them to join his confederacy. The mission was certainly dangerous. The Shawnee-Osage quarrel would persist until May 1812, when the Americans sponsored a peace in St. Louis, and some of the tribes allied to Tecumseh, such as the Potawatomis and Kickapoos, had been feuding with the Osages for years. Tecumseh was bargaining that all this bad blood could be laid aside, and these formidable warriors would stand with him against a greater enemy.[5]

John Dunn Hunter's *Memoirs of a Captivity Among the Indians of North America*, published in 1823, gives the only account of Tecumseh's visit to the Osages. For a while the book made Hunter a celebrity, but after an English periodical used it to fuel an attack upon United States Indian policies, overzealous American patriots made venomous attempts to discredit the author. He was described as "one of the boldest of imposters" and his book as "a worthless fabrication." A few rallied to Hunter's defense, including George Catlin, who had met Indians who remembered the author's captivity, but the *Memoirs* fell under a cloud. Only recently has Hunter been rehabilitated, the prejudices of his detractors understood, and the pendulum begun to swing in his favor.[6]

Hunter's information about Tecumseh was part of the original criticism of the book. Governor Lewis Cass of Michigan Territory, who orchestrated the assault, insisted Tecumseh had never been near the Osages. In 1826 four

Osages and a white man who had lived with the tribe were produced to state that they had never seen Tecumseh, although they had heard of him "as we have heard of the Devil."[7] Whether witnesses assembled in such circumstances are entitled to belief may be doubted. They could have been trying to disassociate themselves from Tecumseh to establish their own loyalty to the United States, or they may simply have been members of one band of Osages ignorant of what had happened in another.

Contemporary records support, rather than refute, Hunter's description of Tecumseh's visit to the Osages. The author does not date the event, but he clearly related it to the earthquakes, which reliably puts it at the turn of 1811–1812. Records of the United States War Department prove that the chief—far from being elsewhere, as Cass and other detractors claimed—was in Missouri that December, and, moreover, that he had gone there for the express purpose of visiting the Osages. If Hunter invented his story he was singularly fortunate that it fit so snugly with the official documentation.

A fair judgment of the context and content of Hunter's account suggests that it is probably authentic. Most likely the Shawnee chief traveled westward after visiting the Missouri Shawnees to call upon the Osage band on the Osage River, to which it had retired during recent intertribal difficulties. Hunter recalled visiting those towns at the time, and evidently he had joined the considerable numbers the Shawnee attracted to his council. He was struck by the quality of Tecumseh's address:

> I wish it was in my power to do justice to the eloquence of this distinguished man, but it is utterly impossible. The richest colors, shaded with a master's pencil, would fall infinitely short of the glowing finish of the original. The occasion and subject were peculiarly adapted to call into action all the powers of genuine patriotism; and such language, such gestures, and such feelings and fulness of soul contending for utterance, were exhibited by this untutored native of the forest in the central wilds of America, as no audience, I am persuaded, either in ancient or modern times ever before witnessed.
>
> My readers may think some qualification due to this opinion, but none is necessary. The unlettered Te-cum-seh gave extemporaneous utterance only to what he felt. It was a simple but vehement narration of the wrongs imposed by the white people on the Indians, and an exhortation for the latter to resist them . . . This discourse made an impression on my mind which, I think, will last as long as I live. I cannot repeat it verbatim, though if I could, it would be a mere skeleton, without the rounding finish of its integuments: it would only be the shadow of the substance, because the gestures, and the

interest and feelings excited by the occasion, and which constitute the essentials of its character, would be altogether wanting.[8]

The speech, as outlined by Hunter, was along the lines of those Tecumseh had already given in the south. The Indians had aided the whites when they were weak, but were now suffering because they had grown strong. The Americans wanted aboriginal land "from the rising to the setting sun" and even "to kill us, or drive us back, as they would wolves and panthers." The tribes were all members of one family, but they would be destroyed separately if there was no unity. Again there was emphasis upon the help available. "Our Great Father over the great waters"—the British king who was angry with the Americans—would help them fight, and he would supply his "red children."

The Great Spirit was also important. He was annoyed that the whites, who had been given "a home beyond the great waters," should seize the lands of the Indians. "Brothers," said Tecumseh, referring to the earthquakes, "the Great Spirit is angry with our enemies. He speaks in thunder, and the earth swallows up villages, and drinks up the Mississippi. The great waters will cover their lowlands. Their corn cannot grow, and the Great Spirit will sweep those who escape to the hills from the earth with his terrible breath."

By this account Tecumseh told the Osages that the confederacy needed help, for it was too weak to fight alone. "Brothers, we must be united; we must smoke the same pipe; we must fight each other's battles; and more than all, we must love the Great Spirit. He is for us. He will destroy our enemies and make all his red children happy."

Allowing for imprecision in this report, which Hunter himself admitted, this mixture of the expedient and the spiritual is exactly what would have been expected of Tecumseh, and the exploitation of the earthquakes is entirely consistent with the way he had drawn attention to the comet. Hunter said that the following day another of the visitors, the Creek prophet Francis, also addressed the Osages, enlarging "considerably more on the power and disposition of the Great Spirit," but that his speech lacked the effect of Tecumseh's more protracted discourse. Nevertheless, though the Osages gave serious consideration to the proposals over several days, they eventually declined entering into Tecumseh's plans.

The visit to the Osages completed the itinerary Tecumseh had given to Harrison in Vincennes. The Governor understood that Tecumseh would "return by the Missouri," by which it must be assumed that he intended descending the Osage River to the Missouri and striking for home across Illinois Territory after crossing the Mississippi. However, that did not happen, for once Tecumseh reached the Mississippi he followed it northward.

The reasons for this are unknown, but one possibility suggests itself: that in Missouri Territory Tecumseh learned for the first time of the battle of Tippecanoe and the destruction of Prophetstown, and that he extended his tour to revive morale.

To one who had gone so far, and striven so hard, to carry the confederacy forward, the news must have been crushing. It raised many questions— about what had actually happened, the damage done, and the safety of friends and family. In times such as these Tecumseh was generally at his best. He never considered defeat. If the confederacy had been broken, it would simply have to be rebuilt. Urgent as the need to go home must have been, he turned north, probably as much to steady former allies as to find new ones.

The northwestern leg of Tecumseh's tour bore a very different character from its preceding phases. Here Tecumseh moved among tribes long exposed to the seductions of the Shawnee brothers and their allies, and far readier to take up arms against Americans. Only a few months before, an old Potawatomi, White Pigeon, had traversed the Illinois and upper Mississippi calling upon the villages to prepare for a war in the spring and to collect arms from the British. Winnebago veterans of Tippecanoe had reinforced the call. Boiling over their losses, they had come home full of vengeful talk about attacking Fort Madison, Fort Dearborn, and other places as soon as the hunting season ended. Tecumseh shared the anger. But in the final days of his tour he played a double role, recruiting warriors to the cause but also inviting others to stay calm and wait until all was ready before disclosing their hands. It was not easy. On 1 January a Winnebago war party visited some lead mines on the Mississippi (in Dubuque, Iowa), plundered the place, and murdered two of the workers.[9]

As far as recruits were concerned, Tecumseh was successful. Governor Ninian Edwards remarked tersely that Tecumseh had "visited the tribes on our Northwestern frontier with considerable success." From St. Louis William Clark also kept "a watchful eye" on the Shawnee chief. He reported that after moving through Missouri "he proceeded to the Sacs and Sioux country, where his councils have been more attended to."[10]

Tecumseh probably dropped in on the Iowas beyond the Des Moines before crossing the Mississippi to reach the Sacs, who occupied the east bank as far as the Rock. The Sacs had been divided on the issue of war, but they held a "very general council" on 8 January. At first American officials believed that it decided to keep the peace, but some Sacs were soon inciting Foxes and Winnebagos to attack Fort Madison. Whether Tecumseh was involved in the council is not known, but he possibly had some connection with it.[11]

Following the Mississippi north, Tecumseh must have traveled through Fox country, and above Prairie du Chien and on the lower reaches of the Minnesota River to find villages of the Mdewakanton division of the Santee Dakota Sioux. Again, his influence may be suggested by the increasingly hostile mood of these Indians. The Dakotas were shortly sending the Sacs and Winnebagos red wampum, indicating their support for a war, and Governor Edwards admitted that if they joined the hostile confederacy, "it will be the most formidable one with which the western country has had to contend."[12]

Throughout the region Tecumseh found the spirit of resistance unimpaired. He retraced his steps beside the Mississippi and made for home, riding over Illinois Territory and speaking to Kickapoos, Potawatomis, Ojibwas, and Ottawas along the way. Some Kickapoos, including chiefs Pamawatam and Little Deer, had gone to Vincennes to paper over the breach with Harrison, but others were in council at Peoria, weighing the consequences of Tippecanoe. There is no record of Tecumseh's presence at the Peoria council, but it occurred about the time he passed through the area.[13]

In the final weeks of his trip, Tecumseh lost many of his traveling companions. His Winnebago and Kickapoo adherents were tempted home, and others, including two Creeks, went on ahead to Prophetstown. It was not until late in January, apparently, that Tecumseh brought the remainder of his party back to the Wabash. There he confronted the grim reality of what Harrison's army had left behind—as he later told the British, the "great destruction and havoc, the fruits of our labor destroyed, the bodies of my friends laying in the dust, and our village burnt to the ground, and all our kettles carried off."[14]

Tecumseh was furious. With the destroyers, and also with his brother, the Prophet, who had been trusted to keep the peace. One account says that Tecumseh seized Tenskwatawa by the hair and shook him, threatening to take his life.[15]

The wretched fellow was already chastened. Tenskwatawa's prestige had suffered greatly as a result of the battle. Indians who had lost friends or relatives blamed the Prophet for failing to protect them. Tenskwatawa tried to excuse himself. He explained that the spirits had refused his prayers because his menstruating wife had, unbeknown to him, contaminated the ceremony. (Shawnees regarded menstruating women as unclean and required them to withdraw from public life.) On this occasion the excuses had not been believed, and the Prophet was bound with ropes and threatened with death. Eventually, the Indians calmed down and let him go. He was still a holy man, and there was a lingering fear that if violence was done him a price would have to be paid.[16]

Piecing together the story, Tecumseh learned that the Indians had reoccupied Prophetstown immediately after Harrison's army had gone. They found that the Americans, in addition to burning the town, had opened Indian graves and in macabre revenge had unearthed the bodies of their slain opponents and thrown them aside to rot above ground. The Indians then split up for their traditional hunting grounds. The Shawnees had little ammunition to hunt, and they had also declined their treaty annuities that year and lost their granary at Prophetstown. Their winter was a harsh one. They crossed the Wabash and spent some time with the local Wyandots, and finally wintered on the headwaters of the White River before returning to Prophetstown in January.[17]

By the time Tecumseh returned the tension of the military campaign had eased. Those tribes amenable to American discipline had gathered at Fort Wayne a few weeks after the battle to collect their annuities and disassociate themselves from the Shawnee brothers, whom they offered to seize or assassinate. Indians who had supported Tecumseh were also quiet, for a while. They had not been cowed by the battle, but the winter that followed was peculiarly severe. There were exceptionally heavy falls of snow, and many game animals died or retreated before the cold. In the spring, droves of Indians huddled into Fort Wayne for relief. Given such conditions, Tecumseh's followers needed peace to search for food without fear of further attack. So, in December and January they temporized with the Americans, using the Weas and Miamis, who had not been in the battle, as intermediaries.

When Tecumseh returned he found Kickapoos, Winnebagos, and Piankeshaws camped near Prophetstown. Their deputations to Vincennes and Fort Harrison had ascertained that no further American military operations were under way. Harrison had said that if the Indians expelled Tecumseh and the Prophet from the Wabash and returned peacefully to their own homes they would be pardoned. In short, the Governor was determined to disperse the concentration at Prophetstown, but he was not exercising the military option to achieve it. Not yet. Tecumseh's arrival occurred just as Pamawatam and other chiefs were composing a reply.[18]

He approved of their actions, which at least defused tension. More than anything else he needed a period of tranquillity in which to rebuild the union.

Hopes for a quiet spring were drowned beneath the worst wave of violence that had engulfed the frontier in fifteen years.

William Henry Harrison had confidently proclaimed the battle of Tippecanoe to be a complete and decisive victory, one that would put an end to sporadic Indian attacks on American settlements. The Governor was lionized in many newspapers, particularly in the west, and his view of the battle was endorsed by President Madison in his message to Congress on 18 December. It was a new Congress, bristling with "War Hawks," and unlikely to spare much sympathy for Indian revolutionaries who were generally regarded as tools of the British.

Not every politician exulted, however. John Randolph of Roanoke openly attributed the Indian war to the United States's own lack of moderation, and the Ohio congressman Thomas Worthington, who had negotiated with Tecumseh in 1807 and been impressed by him, regarded the battle as a "melancholy" event. With others he proposed the government appoint commissioners to investigate Indian grievances.

New instructions which the secretary of war, William Eustis, addressed to Harrison on 17 January 1812 also contained the germs of reconciliation. Peace talks that were already under way between Harrison and the disaffected Indians should continue. The Indians should be told that although their American Father was angry and was prepared to send another army against the tribes, he preferred peace. If the Indians buried the hatchet forthwith they would be pardoned. Tecumseh, the Prophet, and other chiefs were invited to Washington for talks.

Two years earlier such actions might have achieved something, but in 1812 those hesitant exploratory steps toward meeting Indian grievances were taken too late.

In Canada British officials also wanted to contain frontier conflict in the wake of the battle of Tippecanoe. Their Indian policy had been remodeled after Tecumseh's visit to Fort Malden in 1810 had revealed how close some Indians were to rebellion. Caution was now the name of the game, lest Britain be drawn into a war. The Indians were to be informed that the British would not help them fight the United States; if the tribes were attacked, they should withdraw rather than retaliate. During 1811 the faces at the head of Canadian administration changed. Sir James Craig was replaced as governor-general by a talented diplomat, Sir George Prevost, and Gore was succeeded by a tall, dashing soldier named Isaac Brock. But the new men continued the prudent policies of their predecessors. Agents were ordered to maintain friendly relations with the Indians and to furnish them with essential supplies, but dissuade them from a war with the Americans. The battle of Tippecanoe convinced the King's servants that they had judged the mood of the Indians correctly, that their moderation had been vindicated, and that it was necessary to maintain it to avoid fanning the flames.[19]

Unfortunately, neither Tecumseh's influence on the Indians, leniency on the part of the United States, nor British restraint could prevent the eruption of Indian raiding early in 1812.

It proved the complete futility of Harrison's expedition. Harrison had raised a fort to guard the 1809 purchase and damaged the Prophet's standing, but in every other respect his expedition had failed. He had not secured the surrender of Indian murderers, nor dispersed Tecumseh's followers, who reoccupied Prophetstown as soon as the Americans left. The Indians had not been overawed by American power, for the battle had left them with their pride intact and their fighting spirit unquenched. And he had not, as he boasted, brought an end to Indian hostilities. He had increased rather than satisfied native grievances, for now there were spirits of the dead to be avenged. Even before the winter had ended, war parties were moving through deep snows in search of scalps.

The Winnebago attack upon the Mississippi lead mines at the beginning of January was merely a curtain-raiser. In February and March the Winnebagos turned upon Fort Madison (Iowa), killing a few people around the fort and bottling up the small garrison and the agents at the trade factory, and on 6 April they murdered two settlers working in the fields above Fort Dearborn (Chicago). As terror spread throughout the countryside, American traders fled from the northwest, and the trade factory at Fort Dearborn suspended all issues of ammunition to Indians.

Kickapoos joined in on 10 February, butchering the O'Neil family in the district of St. Charles (Missouri), and throwing the territory of Louisiana into alarm. In neighboring Illinois Territory western Potawatomis added to the panic. On 11 April a party led by Kichekemit and Mad Sturgeon, both of whom had been involved in the attack on the Cole party back in 1810, burned a house a few miles above Vincennes and killed six members of the Hutson family and a hired hand. It was perhaps the same group that committed another shocking atrocity eleven days later by slaughtering the Harryman family, including five small children, on the Embarras River, west of Vincennes.

Throughout the American settlements fear and fury followed the Indian raids. "Every effort to check the prevalence of such terror seems to be ineffectual," complained Governor Edwards. In June he estimated that the number of males over twenty-one available to serve in his militia had fallen from 2,000 to 1,700 in a few months because of the flight of settlers from the frontiers. Both he and Governor Benjamin Howard of Louisiana raised volunteer companies to patrol, strengthened fortifications—including the erection of Fort Mason above the mouth of the Salt River (Hannibal, Missouri)—and called upon the Secretary of War for a new campaign against the Indians.[20]

Edwards was also sensible of the threat to friendly Indians from outraged whites, and in April set up meetings with more pacific leaders such as Gomo of the Potawatomis and Little Deer of the Kickapoos. He wanted the murderers surrendered, or at least punished by the Indians themselves. They had to remind Edwards that they did not possess the powers the Americans supposed. "You probably think I am a great chief," said Gomo. "I am not. I cannot control my young men as I please."[21]

The chiefs could not execute members of their communities without incurring the risk of retaliation, and ultimately of civil war between Indians supporting the chiefs and those acting on behalf of warriors punished by the chiefs. As for surrendering malefactors to the United States, that had been done before, when chiefs had been better able to muster public support for the action. No such consensus was possible in 1812. American justice was patently one-sided. As Pamawatam once explained, Indian murderers had been executed, but no white man had paid for Indians killed in the recent past at St. Charles and Cahokia and on the Kaskaskia and Missouri Rivers. Edwards's appeals for the surrender of the killers went unsatisfied.

During April, Ohio and Indiana Territory were also scourged by war parties, most of them Potawatomis, who axed three traders to death in their beds near Fort Defiance and struck at the White River and its Driftwood fork. Local whites were whipped into a frenzy. "Armed parties of our people are out in all directions, breathing destructions against the Indians indiscriminately," complained John Johnston from his new Indian agency at Piqua, Ohio.[22] They found an innocent group of Potawatomis near Greenville and killed two of them.

These raids made nonsense of Harrison's claim that his battle would end Indian hostilities. It had stimulated rather than stifled atrocities. In 1810 and 1811, prior to the battle, Indians loosely connected with Tecumseh's confederacy had killed 8 or 9 whites, and during the Tippecanoe campaign itself Harrison lost another 69 killed or fatally wounded. In the first six months of 1812, some 46 additional American lives were lost in Louisiana, Illinois, and Indiana Territories and in Ohio. With the possible exception of two men murdered near Sandusky Bay by an Ojibwa bad hat named Semo, all were killed by warriors from groups which had fought at Tippecanoe. These were not the first blows of a full-scale onslaught on the frontiers, as some believed at the time. They were revenge slayings. They began on 1 January, peaked in April when the winter hunting and trapping had been finished, and ended in May, when the Indians judged themselves satisfied. The attacks must be reckoned the final accounting of the battle of Tippecanoe.

By the middle of April Harrison was acknowledging his complacency. Vincennes was bursting with fugitives from the outlying homesteads, houses (including the Governor's) were being picketed, and with the regulars he had used in 1811 being withdrawn by the government for a projected campaign against Canada, Harrison was deploying militia to cover the approaches to the town. He joined Edwards and Howard in clamoring for "a war of extirpation" to be waged against Tecumseh and his allies.[23]

For Tecumseh the raids were another embarrassment. Once again, headstrong warriors were destroying carefully laid plans, putting the Americans on their guard, and encouraging massive retaliation before the confederacy was ready.

Even in the south Tecumseh's schemes were being blighted by violence after an early blossom. Into March the earthquakes had continued to remind the Creeks of the disapproval of the Great Spirit, and of Tecumseh's explanation for it. A religious revival had grown in the Creek Nation, particularly among the Alabamas. Red Stick shamans tried to resuscitate old obeisance, and they demanded the destruction of symbols of white colonialism, which they said were offensive to the Maker of Breath. Fervored prophets such as Francis, and perhaps Seekaboo, claimed to command the powers of nature. They could make the earth shake, turn the ground into swamp, make their followers bulletproof, and protect their towns within magic lines. To intimidate opponents the prophets leveled accusations of witchcraft and threatened them with destruction.

This revival owed its initial inspiration to the Shawnee brothers and looked to them for leadership, but it became a more extreme movement than its northern counterpart, in its proliferation of prophets, the ferocity of its attack on Indian enemies, and its bizarre ritual. Samuel Manac recalled how he met a Red Stick prophet named High-Headed Jim in 1813:

> An Indian came to me who goes by the name of High-Headed Jim, and whom I found had been appointed to head a party sent from the Auttasee Town on the Tallapoosa on a trip to Pensacola. He shook hands with me, and immediately began to tremble and jerk in every part of his frame, and the very calves of his legs would be convulsed, and he would get entirely out of breath with the agitation. This practice was introduced in May or June last by the Prophet Francis, who says he was instructed by the Spirit.[24]

Whether, given time, this kind of fanaticism was capable of uniting the Creeks behind the Red Sticks is doubtful, but divisions were introduced early by attacks on whites. A dozen whites were killed in the first half of 1812, most of them travelers on the post roads which the United States had arrogantly blazed across Creek territory and on which surly warriors, their faces painted black and red, sometimes congregated to obstruct fords and bridges or demand tolls. On 26 March a drunken Indian killed a white man with a stick as he tried to cross Catoma Creek. Arthur Lott was shot dead from ambush on the post road by four Creeks, two of whom were believed to have been relatives of the Tallassee chief Peter McQueen.

The most serious incident took place in May on Duck River, in Tennessee. A party of Creeks led by Ellipohorchem, returning from a visit to Prophetstown, broke into a house; massacred a man, a woman, and five children; and carried another woman, Martha Crawley, back to the Creek Nation in captivity. There is evidence that the attack was prompted by a false report that whites had killed some Creeks. That aside, Crawley luckily escaped, but the incident raised a storm among southern whites, who thirsted to drive out the Creeks. As Andrew Jackson informed the Governor of Tennessee, "the fire of the militia is up. They burn for revenge, and now is the time to give the Creeks the fatal blow."[25]

Northern chiefs refused demands for the surrender of Indians wanted by the United States. Not so the Creeks. Benjamin Hawkins convinced Big Warrior that to avoid punishment the Creeks must prove their friendship for the United States by apprehending the murderers. In June three Indian posses went in search of the fugitives. In all, eight were killed, including the leader of the Duck River massacre, whose body was tossed into the Coosa. One of Lott's killers hid in the house of Hopoithle Mico, the civil chief of Tallassee, but his pursuers stormed into the sanctuary and shot him through the head and body. Other offenders were whipped for theft.

But the price paid by Big Warrior and his National Council was high. Family and clan members of the "executed" warriors called for revenge, and the rift between the Muskogee chiefs on the council and their non-Muskogee rivals deepened. All the executed men came from Tuskegee, Tallassee, or Tushatchee, Upper Creek villages of the non-Muskogees. In Tallassee, Hopoithle Mico and Peter McQueen sulked over these new insults, while Red Stick prophets reviled Big Warrior and his coadjutors as the minions of the Big Knives. There was every appearance that in the south Tecumseh's vision of an Indian brotherhood was far less likely than a Creek civil war.

Tecumseh had barely begun to recover from the setback at Tippecanoe when from one end of the frontier to the other premature bloodletting once again threw his plans into turmoil.

21

❖

LAST DAYS OF PEACE

Three main problems faced Tecumseh after his return to the
Wabash: the deprivation of his Shawnee band, the danger of another American campaign, and the need to reestablish his support. He moved quickly on each front.

His Shawnees needed food, supplies, and ammunition. Tecumseh intended planting a large crop in the spring, but in the short term his band
was dependent upon the generosity of allies whose reserves had escaped destruction the previous November. Ammunition particularly was lacking.
Tecumseh set his men to fashioning bows and arrows, and in February dispatched a deputation to Fort Malden for help. The party was finely balanced
as usual, and consisted of eight Shawnees, eight Winnebagos, and eight
Kickapoos under a Kickapoo "orator" described by William Wells as "the
third man in this hostile band." On 13 March the delegation delivered
Tecumseh's message to the British, along with gifts of tobacco and
wampum.

Tecumseh notified the redcoats of his return, and of the destruction of
Prophetstown. He recalled his former visit to Fort Malden, and requested
supplies. His messengers asked for ammunition, arms, knives, razors, brass
wire (for use as tweezers), red paint, firesticks, tobacco, kettles, clothes, and
food. They wanted a keg of powder for each of the three visiting nations,
and another thirteen put aside for the chiefs when they came later in the
spring.

Matthew Elliott must have shaken his aging head in perplexity. He sympathized with the Indians but was under orders not to incite them against the Americans, and he had little food and powder and no shot to give. In fact, although Americans continued to accuse the British of supplying the Indians with large quantities of ammunition, during the first half of 1812 no shot was issued from Fort Malden and only twelve hundred pounds of powder, far less than previously. Tecumseh's party received some provisions, but they were so low on food that on their way home they risked going into Fort Wayne for bread and meat.[1]

At the same time as he sent the deputation to Fort Malden, Tecumseh addressed the need to appease Governor Harrison, a process already begun by the Kickapoos, Winnebagos, and Piankeshaws. Harrison had encouraged the Miamis and others to drive Tecumseh from the Wabash, and some pro-American chiefs had offered to assassinate the Shawnee brothers if it would restore peace. Tecumseh scoffed at such threats. He was said to have remarked that he and his brother would readily submit to execution if the Americans promised not to take any more Indian land.

The threat of another American campaign was a different matter, because his people were in no condition to meet a second invasion. Inside, Tecumseh seethed with anger at the attack on Prophetstown. He wanted to hit back hard, but forbearance was never more necessary. Tecumseh tried to disarm Harrison with reassuring if duplicitous professions of goodwill. Late in February he sent a message to the Governor by eighty Kickapoos, Winnebagos, and Piankeshaws who were being chaperoned to Vincennes by Wea intermediaries. It announced his return and, reminding Harrison of a promise he had made the previous summer, stated that he was now ready to visit the President.

Tecumseh's messengers were a colorful lot. One had half of his face painted green, and the other half red. Another wore cow horns upon his head, while the women shocked their American counterparts by riding astride instead of sidesaddle. They sported themselves entirely amiably, and the message they carried expressed Tecumseh's desire for peace, but in other respects the chief's words fell far short of Harrison's terms, which required the breakup of Prophetstown. However, the Governor was having to temper his tone after opening new instructions from the Secretary of War. They made no demands of the Indians beyond their observing peace. Eustis was interested in conciliation, and also ordered Harrison to invite Tecumseh, the Prophet, and other chiefs to Washington. Ironically, therefore, while Tecumseh's speech to Harrison did not meet the Governor's stipulations, it fitted Eustis's like a glove, and Harrison had no alternative but to accept it. He broached the matter of the Washington delegation to Tecumseh's messengers, but added that while Tecumseh could go he would not be allowed to be the party's leader.

Tecumseh had forestalled further operations against him, but his attempts at rapprochement went no further, and he refused to have any more truck with the idea of visiting Washington. Harrison told him to contact John Shaw, at Fort Wayne, who was organizing the trip, but Shaw heard nothing. On Harrison's advice, Shaw eventually sent wampum to the Shawnee brothers, inviting them to discuss the matter. Shaw got his wampum back, but no answer. Tecumseh was simply not going.

Perhaps he suspected the delegation would be packed with American minions such as Little Turtle and Five Medals, or maybe he resented being treated as just any old chief, without the authority of an intertribal leader. Also, Tecumseh was unwilling to put himself in American hands, and indeed Harrison was happy to consider using the chief as a hostage until the idea was squashed by Eustis. Finally, Tecumseh saw the mission as futile. Despite early successes in negotiating with decent Ohio politicians, Tecumseh had shown no interest in discussing the treaty of Fort Wayne, and he visited Vincennes only at Harrison's invitation. Rather he put faith in war and the threat of war. Yet Tecumseh was not inherently a man of violence or a warmonger. He wanted peace to hunt and travel and to allow his people security. His attitude to negotiation, therefore, betokened a deep and total despair. He simply could not believe that the United States would give him justice.

This was unfortunate, because by boycotting the delegation (which eventually collapsed through lack of interest) he rejected an opportunity to take his case around the local officials who had engineered the treaties, the Harrisons and Hulls, to a national administration that was then more interested in appeasing the Indians, especially as a war with Britain was looming. Thomas Worthington and others were even then pressing the government to appoint a committee to investigate Indian complaints. In June the government acted, naming Worthington, Return Jonathan Meigs (Governor of Ohio), and Jeremiah Morrow as federal commissioners with orders to meet the Indians at Piqua. Whether the United States would have made sacrifices to gain Indian opinion—have offered a more comprehensive trade, paid treaty annuities in full, or put a brake, even a temporary one, on land purchases—is questionable, but it was this type of initiative which offered the best path forward. Alas, it came too late.[2]

Tecumseh's third task was to revitalize the confederacy. The earthquakes, which rumbled on into the spring, helped him. In the west and north Indians were venturing diverse interpretations of the tremors, but even a chief as pacific as Gomo of the Illinois River Potawatomis was capable of believing that they supported what the Shawnee brothers said. Gomo acknowledged that the "Great Spirit is angry and wants us to return to ourselves [traditional cultures] and live in peace . . . You see many children [Indians] have sold their lands. The Great Spirit did not give them the land to sell. Perhaps that is the cause [why] the Great Spirit is angry."[3]

Tecumseh's messengers ran from Prophetstown in February with messages for the Indians of the Illinois and the Mississippi, rallying them in case the Americans attacked him again. Tecumseh decided that he would go on the offensive if Harrison came. His exact plans, if he had any, are unknown, but various rumors were reported. Fort Dearborn, which the Indians considered an easy conquest, would be sacked for arms and ammunition; supplies would be seized from traders; the Ottawas and Ojibwas would be told to attack Forts Wayne and Detroit; American troops trying to reinforce the posts would be intercepted; and Tecumseh would descend the Wabash in canoes, wasting Vincennes, and seizing guns, ammunition, and provisions.[4]

As soon as he felt safe from attack, Tecumseh may have gone recruiting personally before the end of February. Wells was told that he had "gone . . . to hurry on the aid he was promised by the Cherokees and Creeks," and Indians in the Illinois country soon afterward reported the chief to be on the Tennessee with three hundred men. The Governor of Tennessee also heard of a party of northern Indians, Creeks, and Choctaws encamped near Bear Creek, a tributary of the Tennessee in what is now northeastern Alabama. Whether Tecumseh went south again remains uncertain, but the Ohio, Mississippi, and Tennessee waterways were undoubtedly being used as important routes of communication between Prophetstown and the south.[5]

Tecumseh's peculiar difficulty was to invigorate resistance on the one hand and to counsel restraint and patience on the other. As the winter drew to a close, the Shawnee chief had reasons for believing that he had stabilized the situation, steadied the confederacy, and stayed the hand of the Big Knives. But then came that spate of frontier violence committed by Winnebagos, Kickapoos, Potawatomis, and Creeks, and in May Tecumseh headed for the Mississinewa, a tributary of the Wabash, to address an intertribal council on the new crisis.

It was not an ideal occasion from Tecumseh's point of view. American officials were observing, and most of the Indians at the Mississinewa meeting came from tribes opposed to him rather than from allies. The representatives spoke for the Delawares, Ojibwas, Ottawas, Potawatomis, Eel Rivers, Miamis, Weas, Piankeshaws, Shawnees, Wyandots, Kickapoos, and Winnebagos.

Isidore Chaine, a mixed-blood Wyandot from the Detroit, was there on an errand for the British. Afraid their prudent Indian policy had not been stated strongly enough, the redcoats had sent him to remind Tecumseh that the King disapproved of hostile acts against the United States. Opening the proceedings, Chaine offered the usual condolences for the tribulations of his listeners. He was sorry to see "your path filled with thorns and briers, and your land covered with blood," but it was the wish of the Wyandots and the British that the Indians should not go to war.

When Chaine finished all eyes turned upon the Shawnee chief as he rose to speak. Venerable chiefs such as Five Medals and Little Turtle, who sat watching, may have regarded him as an upstart, but none doubted that this man, standing elegantly before them in the traditional deerskin garb of their ancestors, carried more power for peace or war than anyone else.

Speaking for the Shawnees, Kickapoos, and Winnebagos, Tecumseh thanked his "elder brothers" the Wyandots for their concern. "We thank the Great Spirit for inclining your hearts to pity us," he said. "We now pity ourselves. Our hearts are good. They never were bad." This was the keynote for his address. Neither the attack on Harrison's army nor the recent Indian raids had been part of his plan, and by expressing his genuine outrage at them he was able to mask his own plans for a general war. He could present himself as a peacemaker:

> Governor Harrison made war on my people in my absence. It was the will of God that he should do so. We hope it will please God that the white people may let us live in peace. We will not disturb them, neither have we done it, except when they come to our village with the intention of destroying us. We are happy to state to our brothers present that the unfortunate transaction that took place between the white people and a few of our younger men at our village has been settled between us and Governor Harrison. And I will further state that had I been at home there would have been no blood shed at that time.

He went on to blame the Potawatomis for the recent attacks—a charge that as far as Indiana Territory, Ohio, and much of Illinois Territory were concerned was largely the truth. "We are not accountable for the conduct of those over whom we have no control," he protested. "Let the chiefs of that nation exert themselves and cause their warriors to behave themselves, as we have . . ."

Chiefs from the peaceful bands of Potawatomis were present, and one of their spokesmen rose to answer. The Prophet had been to blame. Yes, Potawatomis had participated in raids, but

> they were encouraged in this mischief by this pretended prophet, who, we know, has taken great pains to detach them from their own

chiefs and attach them to himself. We have no control over these few vagabonds, and consider them not belonging to our nation, and will be thankful to any people that will put them to death wherever they are found.

Tecumseh did not enjoy being lectured by chiefs he considered to have betrayed their people by selling tribal lands for personal gain. He regarded them as creatures of the Americans, and he knew that one reason why they were losing control over their warriors was that they had lost the confidence of many of their own followers.

It is true we have endeavored to give all our brothers good advice, and if they have not listened to it we are sorry for it [he replied]. We defy a living creature to say we ever advised anyone, directly or indirectly, to make war on our white brothers. It has constantly been our misfortune to have our views misrepresented to our white brethren.

Here we can imagine Tecumseh looking sternly at the venal chiefs sitting before him.

This has been done by pretended chiefs of the Potawatomies and others that have been in the habit of selling land to the white people that did not belong to them.

Also indicted on that charge were a number of Delaware chiefs, whose spokesman quickly retorted:

We have not met at this place to listen to such words. The red people have been killing the whites. The just resentment of the latter is raised against the former. Our white brethren are on their feet, their guns in their hands. There is no time for us to tell each other you have done this and you have done that. If there was, we would tell The Prophet that both the red and white people have felt the bad effect of his counsels. Let us all join our hearts and hands together and proclaim peace throughout the land of the red people.

There were other speeches, but nothing new was added. The Miamis chided the Shawnees, Kickapoos, Winnebagos, and Potawatomis for failing to "keep their warriors in good order" and neglecting the women and children who would be the victims of conflict. The Kickapoos replied by insisting that they had made peace with Harrison, and it was the intemperate Potawatomis who had created the new predicament.

About 15 May the council broke up. No one had spoken for war. None had been indifferent to the desirability of peace, and all agreed to control the liquor trade, which was universally deemed to be an evil. However, the real issues had been skirted, although they lurked in the mind of everyone present. As Chaine told the British, "all the nations are aware of the desire the Americans have of destroying the red people and taking their country from them."[6]

During the proceedings on the Mississinewa, Chaine took Tecumseh aside to pass on the messages from the redcoats and the Wyandots. The Shawnee told him that he was on his way to plant corn, but that he intended sending another party to Fort Malden for powder and lead, despite the danger of such groups' being intercepted at Fort Wayne or by Miami and Potawatomi supporters of the United States.

Tecumseh spoke bluntly about his frustration with his impetuous and incompetent followers, who were dragging him into premature hostilities. Pointing to the Potawatomis present, he told Chaine that "our younger brothers, the Putewatemies, in spite of our repeated counsel to them to remain quiet and live in peace with the Big Knives, would not listen to us." Their raids of 1810 and 1811 had brought an army up the Wabash, and their new outrages were wrecking the fragile peace which he, the Winnebagos, and the Kickapoos had patched up with Harrison.

The Prophet had also botched the business by not avoiding hostilities the previous November. "Had I been at home and heard of the advance of the American troops towards our village," Tecumseh informed the Wyandots and British, "I should have gone to meet them, and shaking them by the hand, have asked them the reason of their appearance in such hostile guise." Bitterly he reflected that "those I left at home were . . . I cannot call them *men* . . . a poor set of people, and their scuffle with the Big Knives I compare to a struggle between little children who only scratch each other's faces."

But in closing his speech, Tecumseh said that if the Wyandots and the redcoats expected him to retire if attacked, rather than to defend himself, they had misjudged their man. He concluded flintily:

Father and Brothers! We will now in a few words declare to you our whole hearts. If we hear of the Big Knives coming towards our villages to speak peace, we will receive them. But if we hear of any of our people being hurt by them, or if they unprovokedly advance against us in a hostile manner, be assured we will defend ourselves like men. And if we hear of any of our people having been killed we will immediately send to all the nations on or towards the Mississippi, and all this island will rise like one man.

Then, Father and Brothers, it will be impossible for you or either of you to restore peace between us.[7]

War, indeed, was on everyone's lips that spring of 1812. For Europeans the war between Britain and France, and their respective allies, seemed endless, and in Washington a new Congress was being stirred by the passion of its War Hawks, who railed against abuses of British naval power. Although maritime grievances dominated the debate in Washington, War Hawks had begun to add the alleged British instigation of the Indians as grounds for war—an argument which may have influenced representatives of such frontier states as Kentucky, Tennessee, and Georgia.

President Madison also was looking for a military solution. He was not convinced that Tecumseh's confederacy owed its existence to British interference. The government's attempt to bring Tecumseh and the Prophet to Washington, and its appointment of commissioners to examine Indian complaints, indicated the President's awareness that he was not being well served by western officials. It was not Tecumseh's confederacy that pushed James Madison toward war. Rather, he was troubled by his inability to deal with the maritime issues between the United States and Britain, and by the rifts that were opening in his Republican Party. War might bring his party together, and the seizure of Canada, which everyone knew to be weakly defended, might compel the haughty Britons to make concessions at sea. But Madison, like others, was willing to use Indian resistance to justify actions taken for other reasons. Thus it came to be that on 1 June 1812 Congress heard a message from the President itemizing the nation's grievances against Britain and hinting at a declaration of war. The story that Britons had connived with Tecumseh found its place on the list. Indeed, it was the only nonmaritime issue so distinguished.

The talk was of war, in Europe, the United States, and in Canada, where the American mood was quickly sensed. On the frontier Tecumseh was preparing his own challenge to the United States. Here was no pawn of British imperialism, but a man with his own war aims, taking his battalions into conflict whether the redcoats fought or not.

Fortunately, even in those final days he was gaining, rather than losing, support. The pro-American chiefs of the Potawatomis admitted they were losing their warriors, about 150 of whom had joined Tecumseh from the Elkhart and St. Joseph. More than 200 Miamis did the same.[8]

In June Tecumseh made his final canvass of the western tribes. In the name of the Prophet, who still spoke for the Great Spirit, he sent parties of men, carefully chosen to represent the different tribes which supported him. They went as far as the Oto Indians on the Platte River (Nebraska). At

Lake Peoria the messengers were described as carrying black wampum with carrots of tobacco painted red, a recognized invitation to war. A Sac reported how twenty-five of the envoys, including Shawnees, Winnebagos, Kickapoos, Potawatomis, and Miamis, arrived at Saukenuk, the Sac capital on the Rock River, on 26 June. Each of the soliciting tribes handed over wampum tied with red ribbons, and the envoys invited the tribes meeting there to smoke a pipe in solidarity. If the report can be taken at face value, the Sacs, Foxes, Iowas, and Menominees present demurred, but Sioux and Oto warriors promised to take the appeals to their villages.[9]

Tecumseh, no less than Mr. Madison, was launching a war. But whereas the President's war message is part of public record, little is known about the plans of the Shawnee chief. One report said that Tecumseh's speeches asked Indians to congregate at Prophetstown when the corn was high to co-ordinate an attack upon the Big Knives, but from what Thomas Forsyth heard in July a plan for a great assault had already been concerted. Over 1,500 Dakotas and Foxes were to attack Louisiana. Main Poc would lead Sacs, Winnebagos, Potawatomis, Menominees, Kickapoos, and the Ottawas and Ojibwas of Green Bay and Milwaukee against Illinois Territory. Tecumseh would attack Indiana Territory with up to 800 warriors, including Potawatomis from the Wabash, Kankakee, St. Joseph, and elsewhere. And the Indians of the Maumee and Michigan Territory would rendezvous at Fort Malden. The first three of these groups were supposed to field over 4,000 fighting men.

That this plan was not entirely whole cloth is suggested by the simultaneous report of Antoine Leclair. It told how Dakotas called upon the Winnebagos of the Upper Rock with the news that they were eager to attack Louisiana but unsure about when they were required to do so. On the Fox River Leclair also picked up the information that "the chain of friendship was so well brightened among all the redskins" that "from north to south it would be a war of extermination."[10]

The plan Forsyth discovered may well have been mooted, but it magnified the support for the confederacy. Many Indians mentioned in the report were willing to play the part they had been assigned, but others displayed no such inclination. So just what was the real state of Tecumseh's union on the eve of conflict? As the fear of war spread, Indians across the northwest abandoned outlying villages to coalesce in areas, seeking safety in numbers. Tecumseh counted individual supporters in many Indian communities, but the hard core of his following were to be found in the discrete concentrations that were appearing west and northwest of the Wabash.

First there was Prophetstown itself, where 40 Shawnee cabins had been raised on the original site destroyed by the Americans. Below, but adjoining them, some 160 Kickapoo houses sheltered over 100 soldiers, while about five miles distant the Winnebagos built 40 longhouses as well as numerous temporary huts on Ponce Passu Creek. Extensive cornfields attended all of these settlements. When local Potawatomis, Wyandots, and Piankeshaws, and the 250 or so new Miami and Potawatomi reinforcements, are taken into the reckoning, the Prophetstown concentration may have contained 800 warriors.[11]

Westward, at the northern end of Lake Peoria on the Illinois River, another 650 warriors grouped, living principally on corn and fish. These were Potawatomis of the Illinois and its tributaries, some Kickapoos and Miamis, and a few Ottawas and Ojibwas. Some of them wanted to keep out of trouble, but attitudes to the United States had hardened. They posted sentries to watch for enemy rangers, and were in constant communication with Prophetstown.

North, in present-day Wisconsin, two other important centers of anti-American activity had formed. Those Winnebagos who had not moved to the Wabash were concentrated at Lake Koshkonong on the upper Rock, and had spent the winter performing war dances. At the Great Rapids of the Fox River the followers of Main Poc were assembling, although "that vile fellow" himself was still in the Detroit area, from which his messages crisscrossed Indiana and Illinois Territories.[12]

Across the Mississippi some of the Dakota Sioux appear to have regarded themselves as part of the military combination, and they had up to 1,200 warriors on the Minnesota River. The ferocious winter, with its shortage of game, powder, and ball, had grievously injured them, and many grumbled at the insufficiency of American trade goods and the attempts of the United States to restrict the access of British traders through nonimportation laws. A key figure among the Sioux was the red-haired Scottish trader Robert Dickson, who was married to a Yanktonais Sioux. The Indians liked him, and his standing increased when he distributed the whole of his stock to native villages to help them ward off starvation. Dickson's influence was undoubtedly important in prejudicing the Sioux against the United States. Not only were these powerful people reputed to have joined the Indian confederacy, but they also apparently had a prophet of their own, who may have taken views from Tenskwatawa.[13]

Tecumseh's northern allies may have numbered as many as 3,500 warriors, but they were not all reliable, they were spread thinly over a massive area, and there were notable gaps in their ranks. Tecumseh probably supposed that once a war began it would suck in men who were now faltering. As it stood, along with its southern supporters and a few warriors, mainly Wyandots and Potawatomis, at Fort Malden, the confederacy was considerably wider than the pan-Indian action of 1763 and 1764, and comparable with the confederacies of the 1780s and 1790s, the most extensive Indian efforts before Tecumseh's own. The strength of the previous confederacies had been the Shawnees, Delawares, Mingoes, Wyandots, Miamis, and Three Fires of what is now Ohio, Michigan, and Indiana. But since then Indian resistance had been pushed west. Tecumseh drew upon such peoples as the Winnebagos and Dakotas who had hitherto been marginal actors in pantribal movements.

In June Tecumseh made his final preparations. Until the harvest, Prophetstown was still short of food, and Tecumseh even sent thirty Kickapoos, Shawnees, and Winnebagos to Fort Harrison to make an unsuccessful application for corn. Then he took ten young warriors and set out himself for Fort Malden. He wanted to make another effort to win over the Wyandots, Ottawas, and Ojibwas of the Detroit River, and to call upon the redcoats for those essential supplies of food, arms, and ammunition.[14]

On 17 June Tecumseh brought his party into Fort Wayne for his last talks with American officials. He was relaxed, content to spend several days at the fort, conversing with the new agent, Benjamin Stickney, a man approaching forty.

Years later Ann Forsyth, who had been raised by Indians and was then a tender fifteen, remembered attending a dinner held by Captain James Rhea, the commandant of Fort Wayne. She took a place next to the famous Shawnee. He wanted to know why she wasn't married, and when she told him that she planned to marry an Indian, he idly went through the different tribes with her to discover which one had earned her favor. Another story came from John Johnston, the former agent at Fort Wayne. He was no longer at the post, but his brother served there as clerk, and presumably told John that Tecumseh refused all food at the table but for potatoes, which he considered to be aboriginal and therefore acceptable to the Great Spirit.[15]

Tecumseh gained valuable information during his visit to Fort Wayne. Expresses arrived carrying proclamations for the Indians from Governor William Hull of Michigan Territory. The Governor was now at the head of a big army cutting its way north from Urbana in Ohio to reinforce Detroit, and he wanted to make sure the Indians stayed neutral in the coming war between the redcoats and the Americans. If they did not, he warned, they would be defeated and dispossessed.

Tecumseh showed no alarm. On 19 June he spoke for three hours, reviewing Indian relations with the United States over the past year, and again indicting the Potawatomis for the spring raids. He told the agent that a fresh white man's scalp had been hung on a pole near his village, and he was sure the Potawatomis had done it. As for the messengers Tecumseh had just sent to the tribes, they were merely on errands of peace, he said.

Stickney was new to his post, but he was not deceived. Although Tecumseh had put as innocent a gloss as he could upon his intention to visit Fort Malden, when Stickney replied the following day he told the chief that it could only be deemed a hostile act when the two countries were about to go to war. Tecumseh then tried to represent his main motive for a trip north to be a desire to bring the Wyandots, Ottawas, and Ojibwas of Michigan Territory into a general peace, but this was no more convincing. Probably trying to intimidate Tecumseh, Stickney said that the chief would probably encounter Hull's army on his way north, and that the General would be able to give him more details about the likelihood of a war with Britain.

Tecumseh had failed to reassure Stickney, but neither the agent's threats nor the advance of Hull were going to deter him from continuing to Fort Malden. When he left on the morning of 21 June, as he had said he would, he did not even shake hands with Stickney. He did, however, leave one of his entourage, who had fallen sick, behind.

As he hurried northeast Tecumseh's pulse may have quickened. This time the spirits seemed to be smiling upon him. For just as he prepared to launch his war, a bigger conflict between the Big Knives and the British appeared about to burst. Now at last the old dream that had tantalized Blue Jacket, Little Turtle, and Buckongahelas so long ago—the dream of a joint pan-Indian and British defense of the northwest—was becoming a reality.

The cloud had already broken. On 18 June, while Tecumseh was at Fort Wayne, the United States formally declared war upon Great Britain.

ALLY OF THE REDCOATS

22

WAR ACROSS THE

DETROIT

Deep forebodings greeted Tecumseh when he reached Fort Malden about the end of June. News of the declaration of war, which reached the little community on the last of the month, filled officials there, as elsewhere in Canada, with unease, and with good reason. With the mother country embroiled in a European war, unable to send help, how could underdeveloped Canada, its white population outnumbered twelve to one, defend itself against the United States? Small wonder that some of the War Hawks in the American Congress drooled over what they believed to be an easy conquest.[1]

None of the four Canadian provinces was more exposed than Upper Canada. The British held a significant naval supremacy on Lakes Erie and Ontario, it was true, but the province was vulnerable to overwhelming attacks on two fronts, across the Niagara in the east and the Detroit farther west. Its isolated settlements yielded a mere 77,000 white inhabitants—a small enough number when compared to the 677,311 then living in the states of Kentucky and Ohio and the territories of Illinois, Indiana, and Michigan—and a goodly proportion of those Canadian colonists were recent American immigrants of doubtful loyalty. Major-General Isaac Brock, who commanded in Upper Canada, could disperse only 1,600 regulars and 11,000 militia to defend his enormous charge.

It was not simply manpower that bedeviled Brock's attempts to save Upper Canada. Economically the province was primitive, and supplies were few. To make matters worse, it was at the end of a tortuous communication

line that ran twelve hundred miles from Quebec to the most westerly post,
St. Joseph's, at the head of Lake Huron. For several months of the year the
water route along the St. Lawrence and the Great Lakes iced up. When it
opened in April, goods had to be shipped in bateaux and hauled painfully
over portages. Such overland trails as existed were flimsy indeed, mere
paths marked by "nothing but cuts made on the barks of trees by tomahawks," and they were buried beneath snow for most of the winter. Everything was in short supply at Forts Malden and St. Joseph's—provisions,
specie, weapons, medicines, and clothes—and after the outbreak of war
their fragile communications were exposed to enemy attack at numerous
points along their great length.[2]

Seventeen miles below Detroit, but on the Canadian side of the narrow
strip of blue water, barely half a mile wide, that marked the international
frontier, stood the small town of Amherstburg, hiding behind the leafy island of Bois Blanc. It had a dockyard, where the three tiny ships upon
which Britain's command of Lake Erie depended had been built—the brig
Queen Charlotte, the schooner *Lady Prevost*, and the diminutive *General
Hunter*. At the northern end of the town Tecumseh found the redcoats fran-
tically putting Ford Malden, until recently a dilapidated work, into a state of
defense. Its red-roofed buildings and corner bastions were being strengthened, and the palisades, cut with loopholes for muskets, repaired. Soldiers
sweated to deepen the surrounding ditch, while twenty pieces of artillery
were being mounted on powerful platforms. There was a great deal of wood
in Fort Malden, wood that could quickly be turned into lethal flying splin-
ters by enemy artillery, and Tecumseh saw the men setting up a magazine
and a splinterproof shelter inside the fort.[3]

He would have noticed, too, how few were those who guarded this remote part of the empire. Lieutenant-Colonel Thomas Bligh St. George had
overall command, but although the two months before 25 July saw his regular force tripled in size it still amounted to only 300 men of the 41st Regiment of Foot, under an experienced, gallant, and middle-aged Scot, Captain
Adam Muir; and a subaltern's detachment of Royal Artillery headed by Lieutenant Felix Troughton. About 600 Canadian militia were mustered, most
without uniforms. A few of the regulars and about 460 militiamen had to be
stationed upriver, to protect the village of Sandwich, across the river from
Detroit. Considering that Fort Malden was the King's most important post
west of Lake Ontario it was not impressive. Even after the Indian storehouse inside the fort had been stripped, and some private property im-
pounded, the militia had insufficient arms and wanted to go home. St.
George, who shuttled back and forth between Sandwich and Amherstburg,
seemed complacent.

Camped on Bois Blanc, a thickly wooded island about a mile in length, or between the fort and the skirt of the forest that closed in on the northern end of the settlement, were the assembled Indians. Three hundred and fifty warriors strong, they sat smoking and talking in their hastily erected huts or gathered in the council house that occupied the riverbank close to the garrison. At any time it was difficult to find more than two hundred of them, for they and their families came and went as they pleased.

Apart from the few who had accompanied Tecumseh from the Wabash, this small band of British allies consisted of Canadian Wyandots under Tecumseh's old comrade Roundhead, his brother Splitlog, and Warrow; Potawatomis led by Main Poc; thirty Menominees sent by Robert Dickson from Green Bay; a few Winnebagos and Sioux; some Munsees, such as the Goshen mission Indian Philip Ignatius, who had come from the Sandusky; and probably several Ottawas, Kickapoos, and Ojibwas. On 4 July a substantial party of Sacs appeared, and four days later they performed a war dance on the wharf at Amherstburg. The crew of the *Queen Charlotte* replied with fifes, drums, a gun salute, and three cheers delivered from the ship's rigging.

Nevertheless, the Indian force was not a large one, considering the many invitations sent from Fort Malden. Across the river were two villages of Wyandots, Maguaga and Brownstown, with a combined population of less than three hundred souls, as well as a small Shawnee settlement, the remains of Blue Jacket's old following. Elliott had sent them a red tomahawk, but they preferred to sit quietly. Like most of the Lakes Indians they did not relish entering a war on what they deemed to be the losing side.[4]

Servicing their "Indian arm" was the British Indian Department, a small staff of agents, interpreters, and storekeepers, but it was manifestly incompetent. The superintendent at Amherstburg, Matthew Elliott, was brave, but too old for active service, and ridden with lumbago, while Thomas McKee, who he had replaced, was choleric, imprudent, and frequently drunk. Their control of supplies and their official status gave them some sway, but just as the department had once influenced the intertribal confederacy of the 1790s through Shawnee chiefs such as Captain Johnny and Blue Jacket, so now it relied heavily upon Tecumseh to direct the Indian allies. Elliott, McKee, and the storekeeper, George Ironside, were related by blood or marriage to the Shawnees, and Elliott considered the Wyandots, Winnebagos, and Shawnees to be his best warriors.[5]

A handful of regulars, a dispirited and meager militia, and a few Indians whose loyalty depended upon Britain's ability to serve them . . . a chronic shortage of supplies and a long and threatened communication line . . . an adversary superior in both men and materiel . . . It was hardly a recipe for success. Plodding ominously toward Fort Malden was the army of Brigadier-General William Hull. His Tippecanoe veterans, the 4th Regiment of United States Infantry under Lieutenant-Colonel James Miller, and twelve hundred Ohio militia commanded by Duncan McArthur, Lewis Cass, and James Findlay, struggled through the standing water and timber of the Maumee swampland, assailed by blackflies, mosquitos, and heavy rain, and then skirted the head of Lake Erie to pick up the path that led north to Detroit. Tecumseh, of course, expected them. He had heard about Hull's army when he was at Fort Wayne, and as the Americans hacked their way up the Detroit, clearing a path through the woods for their wagons, he would have been alerted by the gun which Hull fired each day at sunset. Excited friends and scouts also kept him informed. The Shawnee chief instantly proposed making an attack on the enemy column, but St. George was unable to support him, and persuaded him to hold back. Unchallenged, the American troops reached Detroit on 6 July, where the small resident garrison and Michigan militia raised Hull's force to around two thousand.[6]

The situation in which Upper Canada found itself was bleak. Expecting a massive attack from another American army in the east at Niagara, Major-General Brock was now confronted with a large force in the west, one that was already neutralizing most of the Indians and sealing off Tecumseh and Main Poc from their main supporters west of the Wabash. Hull had it in his power to invade Canada over the Detroit, sweep away Fort Malden, and advance eastward to threaten Brock's rear. Throughout Upper Canada there was despondency. When Brock convened the provincial legislature at York (Toronto) on 27 July he found its members convinced that Canada would fall. Fearful for their own property and livelihoods, they were afraid to resist the American invaders lest they antagonize them. Brock suspended the legislature in disgust and declared martial law, but privately he was close to despair. As he wrote on 29 July,

A full belief possesses them all that this province must inevitably succumb. This prepossession is fatal to every exertion. Legislators, magistrates, militia officers, all have imbibed the idea, and are so sluggish and indifferent in their respective offices . . . Most of the people have lost all confidence. I, however, speak loud and look big.[7]

Isaac Brock was no milksop, but Canada was fortunate in having more than one strong man that eventful summer. Tecumseh was soon at work among the Indians at Amherstburg. Their chiefs determined policy in councils that were to a considerable extent dominated by the Shawnee leader. This was allowed by witnesses of every description—by British officials, Americans who fell into enemy hands, and by the Indians themselves, in statement after statement. Thus officers of Hull's army, captured by the allied forces, told John Lovett that the Indians were "the finest fellows they ever saw . . . commanded by . . . Tecumseh," who, they said, was "a warrior of almost unbounded influence." Thus, too, did the Procter family, who knew Tecumseh well, describe him as "the recognised head of the Hurons [Wyandots]," the "chief among chiefs" who "in some way possessed the secret of swaying them all to his purpose, though without any formal authority . . . the engine by which they [the Indians] could be moved." And thus did John Richardson, a volunteer with the 41st, mark the Shawnee as "far above" his fellow chiefs "in nobleness of person, as well as in brilliancy of intellect."

In reality, Tecumseh's authority rested upon little more than the power of personality, example and argument, and he was far from always able to control the Indians; but that his influence was both great and surprising was universally admitted, and it was to him, rather than any other individual, that the British looked for the management of their "Indian arm." In his mid-forties, Tecumseh was then in the prime of life. William K. Beall, who saw him at Amherstburg that July, found him typically unostentatious ("very plain") and "stout-built" (perhaps meaning strongly built), with a "noble set of features and an admirable eye," and noted that he was always accompanied by six important chiefs "who never go before him."[8]

The first demonstration of Tecumseh's influence occurred when two hundred Indians met St. George and a few officers in a council at Fort Malden on 7 July. The British commander reported that "the usual ceremonies of the wampum" were enacted, but little else. Probably the meeting had been occasioned by the arrival of Indian messengers from across the river, one of whom was the Shawnee James Logan, who had put himself at the head of a small party from Wapakoneta and helped guide Hull's army to Detroit. The messengers invited Tecumseh and others to join an intertribal council just opening at Brownstown, the seat of the old confederacy. Tecumseh wanted none of it. The Brownstown affair had been got up by Hull to secure Indian pledges of neutrality and agreement to talk to the American commissioners at Piqua. Evidently Logan and his fellows made no converts at the council at Fort Malden. It was satisfactory to the British, who reported that "Tecumtha . . . acted a conspicuous part on the occasion."[9]

Tecumseh and James Logan were friends, both destined to end their lives in this war, fighting for different "Fathers" in whose causes they took no intrinsic interest. The two men spoke long into the night, arguing about where the best course for the Indians lay, but they could not agree. Logan felt that Tecumseh would be crushed with the British; Tecumseh that the confederacy and British alliance were the red men's only hope of saving their lands, culture, and independence. He told Logan that the Creeks were pledged to join him, and spoke of many other Indians who stood ready to fight. Still, sadly they parted for the last time, committed to different but unsuccessful paths.[10]

Deep inside, Tecumseh expected Fort Malden to fall. Hull's force seemed to be overwhelming. But the old warrior spirit still burned brightly within the Shawnee leader, and he was ready for battle. A large belt of wampum, stained red, was carried from Amherstburg urging the tribes to stand with the redcoats and warning them not to leave their families undefended by visiting the United States commissioners at Piqua. Again, Tecumseh's messengers circulated in Ohio and Indiana Territory. On 19 July two of them found the Prophet, with some Shawnee, Kickapoo, and Winnebago followers, at Fort Wayne. Tecumseh told his brother to raise as many men as possible, send his women and children toward the Mississippi, and strike at Vincennes. "If he lived" Tecumseh would meet him in the Winnebago country. According to William Wells, who was at Fort Wayne, Tecumseh's emissaries were also charged to go to the south, pledging the Indians and any enslaved blacks who could be induced to join them by promises of freedom that the British would supply them with arms from Florida.[11]

The fears of those who gloomily predicted the capture of Fort Malden seemed about to be realized on 12 July, when American troops were ferried across the river and occupied Sandwich. The invaders were not resisted. Most of the inhabitants of the small Canadian town fled their homes; the troops garrisoned there had pulled out the previous day, at the first sign of enemy activity. The chagrined redcoats and militia retired southward to Fort Malden, hauling their guns and baggage and driving their cattle before them. Hull set up headquarters in a brick house on the riverside, the home of the Baby family, and hoisted the American flag on Canadian soil, while his men dug in, or foraged the countryside for provisions. On 13 July the American general addressed a frightening proclamation to the "Inhabitants of Canada." It represented his troops as liberators, expelling the "tyranny and oppression" of the British, and advised Canadians to stay at home, where their lives and property would be inviolate. If, however, they resisted and fought alongside the Indians, they would be killed. Hull's entrenched fear of the Indians was never more obvious than in this bloodthirsty no-quarter declaration: "No white man found fighting by the side of an Indian will be taken prisoner. Instant destruction will be his lot."[12]

At this point the defeatist mentality in Upper Canada appeared vindicated. Hull seemed vigorous and adroit. He had invaded and threatened opponents with apparent confidence and determination, and the effect upon Canadian morale was devastating. Hundreds of civilians, including whole settlements such as Delaware and Westminster, applied for Hull's protection. Some even offered their services. The Canadian militia began to desert in droves. At Fort Malden they fell to below four hundred, and the survivors were said to be "in such a state as to be totally inefficient in the field." Amherstburg verged on panic, expecting the Americans to sweep down upon the town daily. Bemoaned Elliott: "The people here are much dejected and have removed all their effects out of the place."[13]

Many Indians upon whom the British had placed their hopes refused to assist them, unimpressed by the redcoats' efforts to defend their border. Under Hull's supervision the intertribal council took place at Brownstown, attracting Black Hoof and Lewis of the Ohio Shawnees and Tarhe the Crane from the Sandusky. Walk-in-the-Water (Myeerah) represented the Detroit Wyandots, and a few Indians of other tribes attended. It was a predictably compliant gathering, and agreed to stand clear of the fighting. Other Indian communities also considered it wise to appease rather than to defy the Big Knives. The Ojibwas of Lake St. Clair and the Iroquois on the Grand River, both residents of Upper Canada, sent deputations to Hull seeking his protection in return for neutrality.

Never had the British needed Tecumseh more. With the help of Roundhead and Main Poc, the Shawnee chief held his little band together at Fort Malden. Elliott wrote gratefully that "the Indians with us are between three and four hundred, who have resisted every allurement which Genl. Hull laid before them. Tech-kum-thai has kept them faithful. He has shown himself to be a determined character and a great friend to our government."[14]

More than that, Tecumseh's ardor for battle was undiminished. St. George admitted the eagerness of his Indian allies but knew he lacked the resources to support them afield, and he declined to allow them to be exposed unnecessarily. But the situation was desperate and about the middle of the month he relented. Deciding that his redcoats would have to help where they could, St. George finally loosed Tecumseh upon the oncoming invaders.[15]

About five miles north of Amherstburg, perhaps two-thirds of the distance to Sandwich, a deep stream flowed sluggishly westward into the Detroit, its environs a flat grassy prairie largely devoid of trees or thickets, its channel unfordable near the mouth, where the main road passed over the only wooden bridge. Not a famous stream, the Aux Canard, but for a few weeks the frontier between the forces contending for Upper Canada.

The Aux Canard was not a difficult obstacle to an army with the strength and resources of Hull's, but it was the only place in the open prairie north of Fort Malden where a stand could be made against the American advance. Unfortunately, St. George had too few men to mount much of a guard. Far-

ther east Brock stood ready to meet an attack at Niagara, and without reinforcements from his superior, Sir George Prevost, in Quebec, he could
afford little help for Fort Malden.

On 16 July the Americans suddenly appeared at the Aux Canard. Two
hundred and eighty men, a few of them regulars, under Colonel Lewis Cass
arrived in the clear afternoon. The redcoats were caught napping. Only a
handful of soldiers were on guard with a couple of small fieldpieces, and
they had not even destroyed the bridge. Cass left some riflemen north of the
river to entertain the British—a job they accomplished by wounding two
sentries, one fatally—and led the rest of his detachment upstream to find a
ford. He crossed, formed his men for battle with riflemen on his flanks, and
descended the south bank of the river through bushes and prickly ash. By
the time Cass was able to menace the bridge, a few militiamen and about
fifty Indians—the last led, so the Americans believed, by Tecumseh and
Thomas McKee—had hurried forward to support the British regulars.
There were not enough defenders to make a difference. An ineffective exchange of shots left Cass in control of the bridge and the allies glowering re-
sentfully out of range. With a yell the Indians retired, and the British
wheeled away their field guns. At no cost the Americans had gained the only
defensible position above Fort Malden, and the garrison's fate seemed certain.

That night the Indians were expecting a major battle, and performed a
noisy war dance in Amherstburg. The next day, stripped and painted black,
the warriors scampered like terriers toward the front. To their surprise they
found the Big Knives had gone. Instead of advancing, Cass had relinquished
the bridge and trooped back north toward Sandwich. Almost disbelieving
their luck, the British reclaimed the bridge, which, apart from a few sleepers, they ripped up. They built a small breastwork on the south bank to protect a new battery, and summoned the *Queen Charlotte* up the Detroit to
cover the mouth of the Aux Canard with its guns. As for the Indians, they
were triumphant. McKee, naked and painted like his fellows, led fifty exultant warriors into Amherstburg, brandishing a fresh scalp aloft on a pole.
Alas, it did not come from the enemy, but from the body of the British sentry, which some irreverent tribesmen had grimly exhumed and desecrated.[16]

Mystification was not confined to the British and their Indian allies. The
day after the skirmish at the bridge, Major James Denny of the Ohio Volunteers informed his wife: "Our general is losing all the confidence he had in
the army. He holds a council of war every day, and nothing can be done—
and councils again. The result is still the same."[17]

The truth was that William Hull was tortured by doubts. Yes, he had
fought with distinction in the Revolution, but that had been years before.
Intelligent, and still commanding in appearance, his portly frame and fresh
complexion crowned with a shock of white hair, he had become a cautious,

plodding leader, too willing to magnify difficulties into insurmountable obstacles. He was fretting about his communication line, which ran south
from Detroit along the riverside, open to naval attack, and, always a humane man, he was deeply apprehensive of the atrocities of Indian warfare.
Even before occupying Sandwich the General was exaggerating the "large
number" of Indians with Tecumseh, and doubting whether he could subdue
Fort Malden. And now, having put his foot on Canadian soil, he hesitated to
advance.[18] Rather, he waited, hoping that more of the Canadian militia
would desert, and that he could put his artillery in a better shape to knock a
breach in Fort Malden. The price paid for his vacillation was the demoralization of his own men, hitherto so sure of victory, and the recovery of allied
confidence.

Hull's appetite for the war wilted with every setback. The first important
blow occurred on 17 July, a day after the scrap at the Aux Canard. Far to the
north Captain Charles Roberts, the British commandant at St. Joseph's,
brought 400 Indians, a party of volunteers, and less than 50 regulars to the
little American post of Michilimackinac and persuaded it to surrender. The
Indian detachment consisted of 280 reluctant Ojibwas and Ottawas and 113
more enthusiastic Sioux, Winnebagos, and Menominees, recruited by the
trader Robert Dickson from groups that had long and successfully been canvassed by Tecumseh and Main Poc. The fall of Michilimackinac unnerved
Hull, who envisaged that hundreds of Indians who had previously been neutral would now mass against him on the Detroit.

In the meantime, whenever his forces advanced toward the Aux Canard
they seemed to run into Tecumseh and his pesky companions, gathering intelligence or probing the American positions. When the American colonel
Duncan McArthur tried to reconnoiter the allies from a low hill overlooking
the Aux Canard on the nineteenth he twice incited warriors to cross the
bridge by the remaining sleepers and attempt to cut him off. On the first occasion Main Poc was felled by a shot in the neck and had to be helped from
the field; the second time some 45 Indians retreated when the Americans
brought up 150 men from their camp at Petite Cote, near Sandwich. Both
sides then directed shots at each other across the stream, and McArthur had
two men wounded before withdrawing his force. An impudent group of
warriors, led (according to James Foster, an American memoirist) by
Tecumseh, shadowed the Americans back to camp, snapping at their heels,
firing occasional shots, and searching for opportunities to create mischief.
At one point McArthur ordered a halt, about-faced his men, and sent a volley toward their tormentors. The Indians jumped flat on their faces—except,
claimed Foster, for Tecumseh, who stood contemptuously unmoved. After
haunting the enemy militia for some distance, however, the Indians returned to their own lines.[19]

Six days later the Americans suffered their first battle fatalities of the War of 1812. Early on the wet morning of 25 July, Major James Denny marched and countermarched 120 Ohio volunteers within sight of the allied positions on the Aux Canard. Tecumseh got up a following of Shawnees, Ottawas, and Potawatomis and called in at an Amherstburg store to invite a twenty-three-year-old French Canadian, Thomas Vercheres de Boucherville, to join them in an expedition against the Americans. He agreed, and in later life gave the only inside account of the ambush of Denny's troops.

Sources disagree about how this interesting skirmish opened. Elliott, who was not a participant, reported that 13 Indians were attacked by the Americans near the ford on the Aux Canard, but drove their opponents away. Boucherville described how 150 Indians set up an ambush at Petite Cote, a mile or so of short grassy prairie beyond the bridge, and showered Denny's detachment with musket balls and arrows as it innocently passed between the hidden lines.

American accounts, including one Denny sent his wife two days afterward, give a more probable sequence of events. One of Denny's rangers, returning alone to the main camp, was killed at Turkey Creek by an Indian war party that had penetrated deep behind enemy lines. In the early afternoon the Indian party was itself intercepted by Denny's detachment, and 20 militiamen fervently chased the warriors toward the allied lines. Suddenly Denny had a disaster on his hands. Before he could regroup his scattered command, or secure a defensive position, Indian reinforcements galloped up. Some of the painted warriors dismounted and took off across some fields to gain a wood on Denny's right flank.

Indians and Americans scrambled to occupy the wood, but the militia reached it first. Tecumseh's warriors, seeing they had been outrun, poured a hot volley upon their adversaries, which the Americans returned as they got into cover. Denny had secured his right, but his left now collapsed completely, and with it all order and discipline. Momentarily the American right held its ground from the wood, but then they saw the Indians outflanking their force on the left and running to secure the road in the rear by which the militiamen must retreat. Quickly every man in Denny's force realized that they were in danger of being encircled and cut to ribbons. They stampeded like crazy steers toward the road, every soldier for himself, crashing through cornfields and thickets with the Indians on their flank all the way. Occasionally the warriors would stop and fire on the flying Big Knives from a distance as close as sixty yards.

Denny's volunteers gained the road, a straight and level path, and ran along it pell-mell. An amazing scene unfolded. As the soldiers fled, the Indians ran alongside, jamming guns through fences or from beside farmhouses and fruit trees to fire, while bemused Canadian inhabitants gazed from their windows with apparent indifference to the drama outside. Some Americans plunged into the Detroit River or Turkey Creek to escape, but not always successfully. One British report recounted how two such soldiers, realizing the futility of further flight, waded toward the oncoming Indians, holding out their hands in surrender, and saying "How do?" They were tomahawked on the spot. Boucherville remembered a similar incident. "One poor horseman, who had received only a slight wound," he recalled, "threw himself from a bridge into the river . . . It was in vain . . . A young Shawnee brave leaped upon him and killed him with a single blow of his tomahawk."[20]

It was near Turkey Creek that Denny's fractured force shook off their pursuers after a retreat of several miles. Only the speed of their flight had saved them from severe casualties. Denny's losses apparently amounted to five killed, one man taken prisoner, and two wounded. The captive was treated roughly by the Indians, who were infuriated by their own casualties: a man killed and three wounded, one so badly that his survival was considered unlikely. To make matters worse, an American volunteer, William Mc-Culloch, had found time to scalp the slain warrior. The Indians spared the prisoner's life but bound him and whipped him with ramrods, and the sister of the dead Indian struck the wretched man with her fist. Even after Elliott had ransomed the captive and the Indian dead had been buried with military honors, feelings ran high and a group of warriors attempted to rush the guardhouse. According to their lights, Indians had the right to demand satisfaction for slain relatives, and neither Tecumseh nor the redcoats could transgress that custom without difficulty.

The skirmishes over the Aux Canard, small as they were, increased the confidence of Tecumseh's warriors and indicated how quickly some of those untrained Ohio soldiers could be reduced to chaos. Conversely, they did nothing to alleviate the discontent festering within Hull's army. Denny absolved himself of misconduct in an inquiry, but the stagnation of the campaign and the miserable performance under fire damaged morale. Hull's own thoughts were growing blacker than the stormy skies and cold nights that were unseasonably enveloping the contest, and Indians populated his nightmares. Hull even spoke to some of his men about a harebrained scheme to send a party to infiltrate Amherstburg and kidnap Tecumseh. Everywhere Hull turned there were Indians, or so he thought. He pictured them descending upon him from the north in hordes. They were certainly ahead of him, between Sandwich and Fort Malden. And shortly he learned they were behind, for a few days after his fight with Denny Tecumseh transferred his operations to the American side of the Detroit and attacked what Hull regarded as his greatest weakness, his vulnerable supply line to Ohio.

Tecumseh's ability to move audiences with the passion and fluency of his oratory had not escaped the British. They had seen it at the council of 7 July, when he rebutted the overtures from Hull and kept the Indians at Amherstburg "faithful." Now a second diplomatic triumph changed the nature of the military campaign.

Guarding General Hull's communications south of Detroit were the Wyandot towns of Maguaga and Brownstown. Their inhabitants lived in comfortable houses, and most longed only for peace in which to tend their extensive crops, apple and peach orchards, and herds of cattle. But they were in a war zone. At first they had believed that the large American army offered them the greater protection, but time was not vindicating that opinion. Michilimackinac had fallen, and the Big Knives were faltering in Canada, where Tecumseh and Roundhead were proving that they could be beaten. Even the cautious, grave-faced Walk-in-the-Water, the leading man among the Detroit River Wyandots, began to reconsider their position.

On 2 and 3 August, Tecumseh, Roundhead, and Captain Muir brought a large force of Indians and a hundred redcoats across the Detroit. Embarking from Amherstburg, they passed south of Grosse Isle and landed near Brownstown, where the Wyandots had assembled with their property and animals. Probably about three hundred Wyandots and Shawnees—the populations of Maguaga, Blue Jacket's Town, and Brownstown—were escorted to the British side of the river. Altogether, they furnished Tecumseh and Roundhead with about seventy additional warriors.

Then and later these Wyandots protested that they had been captured, and years afterward still spoke of a council at Fort Malden in which Walk-in-the-Water tried to honor his policy of neutrality. Elliott, the story went, denounced the chief's protests as "American talk," and Tecumseh and Roundhead also condemned him. Finally, Tecumseh and the British simply crossed the river, surrounded the American Wyandots, and impressed the lot!

At the time American officers were not taken in by this improbable explanation for the sudden change of loyalties, and with good reason. The allies could not have so completely rounded up the unwilling populations of three villages. In fact, their force was designed to cover the Wyandot removal and to provide Walk-in-the-Water's people with a pretext for their defection if the Americans ever called them to account. Not a single British source spoke of the impressment of reluctant Indians. Instead, the sources alluded to a council in which Tecumseh convinced the Wyandots to throw in with the allies. An officer of the Canadian militia, who arrived at Sandwich a fortnight later, recalled that "by his singular tact and address"

Tecumseh "soon gained over the Wyandotts," while Colonel Henry Procter, who had succeeded St. George in command at Fort Malden, saw the Shawnee chief's intervention as decisive: "He convinced the Indians that our cause was theirs, and his influence and example determined and fixed the Wy[a]ndots, whose selection determined every tribe. The defection of the Wy[a]ndots or Hurons had the greatest effect on the enemy, whose supplies they enabled us to cut off."[21]

Unquestionably the event was significant, because Maguaga, Blue Jacket's Town, and Brownstown all sat squarely on the main path that ran twenty-odd miles from Detroit to Lake Erie, and thence into Ohio. With British ships commanding the waterways, Hull's mail and supplies had to use that road. The General had applied to the Governor of Ohio for provisions, and in response Captain Henry Brush was driving three hundred cattle and seventy packhorses laden with flour north. It was vital to Hull to secure the road in order to maintain contact with his government and bring Brush's convoy to Detroit. Yet the defection of the Wyandots enabled Tecumseh to attack the road and shut off the one artery feeding the American army.

During the operation to remove the Wyandots, Tecumseh's warriors killed a couple of men on the road below Brownstown and captured another,[22] but two days later the blockade was resumed in earnest. On the morning of 5 August Tecumseh left Amherstburg with twenty-five men, one of them Alexander Elliott, the agent's son, who was accoutered so as to be indistinguishable from his companions. Not a large force to cut the road, but Tecumseh had never troubled overmuch about numbers. That day, however, enemy forces five times the size of his own were converging from both directions upon the Shawnee's chief's position at Brownstown.

Coming from the River Raisin escorting the northbound mail were twenty-five French volunteers. A little south of Brownstown Tecumseh's men fell upon them from ambush, capturing the mail and strewing the path with enemy dead. Only seven survivors returned to the River Raisin, two of them wounded.[23]

The threat from the north was far greater, for in an effort to clear Hull's communications two hundred militiamen under Major Thomas Van Horne approached Brownstown carrying the southbound mail and hoping to link with Brush's convoy at the River Raisin. Tecumseh knew about them. His scouts had stumbled across an isolated militiaman in a cornfield, shot and killed both him and his black servant, and exchanged shots with others of Van Horne's detachment before hurrying back with the news. Curiously, the slain American soldier was William McCulloch, who had scalped the Indian killed in Denny's defeat; as the father of quarter-blood Wyandot children, McCulloch may also have been regarded by the Indians as a renegade. Despite the deaths of McCulloch and his servant, Van Horne pressed on. His men marched in two columns, the mail from Hull in the center; and both advance and rear guards containing mounted men.

Tecumseh was outnumbered almost four to one, but had the advantage of surprise, and with his eye for good ground he discovered a suitable place to stage another ambush, at the northern end of Brownstown, where the path forded a small creek that cut through a narrow prairie toward the Detroit River. Skillfully the chief dispersed his warriors. Some occupied corn-fields on the right near the river, and others squatted in the wood and brush that fringed the creek on the southern side of the ford. Their inferiority in numbers was masked because the Indians were entirely invisible to the advancing troops.

As Van Horne's men tramped forward, his two columns converged to use the ford, presenting at their head a concentrated target for the hidden muskets being leveled at them among the thickets across the creek. At fifty yards or less the warriors raised a terrific yell and fired, trying to pick off mounted men and officers first. The Americans were soon in disorder, as horses buckled, screamed, and plunged, and soldiers fell or scattered. Van Horne's men made a brief attempt to withdraw a little way to form a firing line, but they were soon flying ignominiously in all directions after making only a token resistance.

For several days the command was straggling back into Detroit, in ones, twos, and small parties. Including the servant, Van Horne's final loss appears to have been twenty killed or fatally wounded, seven of them officers, and twelve wounded, as well as the mail. By comparison Tecumseh's casualties were astonishingly low. A young Shawnee interpreter, John Logan, was slain as he attracted enemy fire during too eager a pursuit, and two men, Laury Cadotte and an Ojibwa, were wounded. Poor John Logan (no relation to the famous Mekoche James Logan) had extensive kin on the Detroit River, where he lived and where he had married a Wyandot. The Indians laid his spirit to rest by killing two Americans they had captured. Both prisoners were brought, with the body of Logan, to the Indian encampment near Fort Malden. There one of the unfortunates was conducted into the council house, and when his attention was diverted he was executed by the stroke of a hatchet. His companion received even less charity. Logan's aunt hit him with an axe, and he was finished off, stripped, scalped, and mutilated by an angry crowd. Some Britons saw it but dared not interfere. Tecumseh, who was not present, might have done better, but Shawnees accepted that prisoners belonged to their individual captors, to be treated according to their whim, and that the aggrieved were entitled to satisfaction; and not even Tecumseh might have been able to spare the captives their miserable fate.[24]

The double ambush at Brownstown, with its capture of the mail in both directions, was one of the most remarkable victories in Indian history: seldom had so inferior a force administered so severe a defeat at such little loss to themselves. A vital prize came from the southbound mailbag. A letter William Hull had addressed to the Secretary of War under the date 4 August expressed the general's fear of being cut off and overwhelmed by thousands of Indians, and admitted that the situation of the American army had become critical.[25] This insight into Hull's mind would shortly prompt the decisive act of the campaign.

The fight also sent significant ripples elsewhere: to Indians abroad, who were now exhorted by the messengers of Main Poc and Tecumseh to rise against their oppressors or rally to Amherstburg; and upon Hull himself, now referred to as the "Old Lady" by his officers. The general saw himself surrounded by Indians, and his communications had been broken. The Ohio supply convoy under Brush reached the River Raisin, thirty-five miles south of Detroit, on 9 August, but the road ahead was closed by Tecumseh's warriors. Brush had 165 men, and another 50 of the Michigan militia were at the River Raisin, but there was no question of the convoy's proceeding unescorted. It had to sit waiting for Hull to cut a way through from Detroit.[26]

William Hull was no longer interested in an offensive. It was "indispensably necessary" to devote all his attention to that supply line. He was further disturbed by news that the American attack upon Niagara had been delayed, and that Brock was shifting some of his strength to Fort Malden. Although Hull's siege train was now ready for service against the British fort, he decided not to use it. Instead, on 8 August he withdrew all but 250 of his men from Sandwich and forted them up in Detroit. There were those in his army who cried out against the retreat from Canada. "We are in as near a state of mutiny . . . as is possible," complained one.[27] But General Hull was determined to clear Tecumseh and his men from his rear before proceeding. The invasion of Canada had ended.

23

+—+ ⊠◆⊠ +—+

THE MOON OF PLUMS

T he afternoon of 9 August 1812. Several hundred men marched
grim-faced up a narrow, wet, and muddy path that stood for the
main road north to Detroit. On each side was the forest, its trees
overarching the path, their leaves shedding raindrops upon the travelers as
they passed below. More than a hundred redcoats were on that march, led
by Captain Muir, and they were accompanied by a small number of volunteers, one of them a wide-eyed boy of fifteen who would become Canada's
first novelist, John Richardson, then attached to the 41st Regiment of Foot.

This was John's first taste of frontier warfare, and he would remember
vividly that miserable tramp through the wilderness, and passing the battlefield at Brownstown where the bloated disfigured corpses of Van Horne's
soldiers lay scattered about, some with stakes driven through them by exultant warriors. Beside the redcoats, as they marched, the Indian allies
slipped noiselessly along the trail, their bodies painted and naked but for
moccasins and breechcloths, and their hair dressed so that it bristled like
the quills of the porcupine. "They might have passed for the spectres of
those wilds," wrote Richardson, "the ruthless demons which War had un-
chained for the punishment and oppression of Man."[1]

The leader of those Indians held John Richardson spellbound, haunting
the impressionable Canadian to the end of his days. For John, Tecumseh
was "all that was noble and generous in savage life," and the real hero of the
war. Testifying to the qualities that inspired both white and red, Richardson
noticed that "there was . . . that ardor of expression in his [Tecumseh's]

eye . . . that could not fail to endear him to the soldier hearts of those who stood around him."[2] Unaware of the young volunteer's admiration—an idolatry that would one day implant Tecumseh in the literature of the great land to the north—Tecumseh was once more leading his men into battle.

After the Brownstown skirmish Tecumseh had delivered the captured mail to Fort Malden, but by 7 August he was back on Hull's communication line, keeping it tight shut. Eventually Muir shipped his force across the river to join him, constructing crude shelters to shield his men from the foul weather. On the ninth some of Tecumseh's scouts who had been watching the road toward Detroit ran shouting into the camp. Many Big Knives were coming!

Tecumseh and Muir marched their men up the trail to meet them. To maximize their chances of surprising the Americans they chose a new ground for a stand, near Maguaga, fourteen miles south of Detroit. American accounts of the ensuing battle claim that the British threw a log breastwork across the path at an angle, but Richardson would hotly insist that no such work existed: the allies arrived on the ground only a few hours before the fight took place, and reinforcements, including another detachment of the 41st under Lieutenant Richard Bullock, were dribbling in until the last moment.

Muir's men occupied the center of the allied line, flattening themselves on the ground behind cover in imitation of the Indians. About 150 soldiers were there, most of them regulars. The Indian contingent numbered perhaps 300. A few, whom the Americans later believed to be led by Main Poc and Walk-in-the-Water, bounded across a small prairie to the right to occupy some trees by the riverside, but Tecumseh used most of the Indians to form a left flank in thick oak woods.

About four in the afternoon the Americans appeared, in considerably greater force than their opponents. Desperate to clear his supply line, Hull had detached nearly a third of his effectives, "the best troops of the army," as he said.[3] Lieutenant-Colonel James Miller had a little over 600 men, half of them blue-coated regulars, the rest handpicked militiamen from Ohio and Michigan, dressed in gray or blue woolen hunting shirts. With them were a six-pounder and a howitzer.

Behind a few mounted "spies" Captain Josiah Snelling of the 4th Regiment of United States Infantry led a 40-man advance guard. They were nervous because earlier in the day one of their men had been shot dead by a hiding Indian, and other near-naked observers had occasionally been glimpsed through the foliage. However, Tecumseh had chosen his ground well, and the Americans marched innocently on—first the spies and advance guard, then two columns of soldiers, one on either side of the road, with a file of cavalry between them, Miller riding at its head. In the center, too, following the horsemen, were the artillery pieces and the ammunition and baggage wagons, while small detachments of riflemen had been thrown out on the flanks. Tecumseh waited, and when he judged the time to be right, signaled the attack.

There was a single shot, a frightening cry from the Indians, and a heavy crash of musketry as Tecumseh's men sent a volley into the advance guard and the columns of approaching soldiers. Again the Americans were taken completely by surprise. Again they reeled from the impetus of that first fierce onslaught, as fire ran along the whole allied line. But this time they were stiffened by regulars, and showed their mettle. Snelling's men held firm, and Miller soon had the rest (except his rear guard, which defended the wagons) into lines of battle. They marched menacingly into the fray, firing particularly upon the British, whose bright scarlet coats could be seen bobbing up and down among the trees. The Indians were harder targets, their presence being denoted largely by the constant yelling and the flashing of guns in the timber.

Some thirty minutes of slaughter elapsed, in which both sides lashed each other with gunfire, the Americans occasionally spicing their attack with murderous discharges of grapeshot from the six-pounder. Their howitzer was less useful. The horses of its gun team panicked, and the piece was not dragged up until the main action was over, but Miller's men did not need it. They were already pushing upon the enemy lines behind their bayonets.

Something had gone amiss with the allied defense. In his official report Colonel Procter admitted that "some mistake" had occurred, but neglected to explain its nature. Richardson believed that the Indians on the right, near the river, had been driven back by the Americans, and in the fog of war the British took the retreating warriors to be enemy militiamen. Afraid of being outflanked, the redcoats fired on the Indians, and for a moment the allies had shot at each other. Boucherville, another of the British volunteers, blamed the regulars under Bullock for mistaking an order to attack for one to retreat. Whichever was the case, Miller's men forged on, expelling the allied center and right wing from their positions.

Tecumseh did not give ground easily, and he had known since his early days in warfare that steadiness under fire could sometimes overturn superior numbers. When his allies fell away, exposing his Indians to the danger of being outflanked and encircled, he elected to fight on in the thick timber, stubbornly contesting every step. "The Indians on the left, under the command of Tecumseh, fought with great obstinacy," Hull would acknowledge. For some time the chief kept his men in the field, deserted, outnumbered, and outgunned, but trying everything he knew to turn the tide of battle, forming and reforming his warriors, and twisting one way and then the other. A quarter of a mile or more behind him, Muir, although wounded in the leg, regathered his broken command on the brow of a hill, from which they could still hear the distant firing that marked where Tecumseh and his followers were making their lonely stand.

At least the redcoats drew some benefit from it. Miller declined to pursue the British too closely, concerned that Tecumseh might still get behind him, and perhaps wearied by the sharp fight and the short and rapid advance; and even when the Indians abandoned the unequal contest and melted westward into the forest the Americans failed to press their advantage. Muir got his men back to the boats near Brownstown and retreated to Fort Malden, and the Indians eventually followed in their canoes. It seemed that their blockade of Detroit had been shattered.

Tecumseh had been slightly wounded in the neck during the two-and-a-half-hour battle, and George Blue-Jacket, son of the famous war chief, nursed a wounded shoulder. He had accompanied the party as an interpreter, replacing the unfortunate Logan. According to Elliott, seven Wyandots, two Ojibwas, and two Shawnees were killed, although Henry Procter reduced the tally to two Indians killed and six wounded. The colonel had to account more accurately for the British casualties. After Lieutenant Charles Sutherland, who had been shot through the cheeks, died and some prisoners were recaptured, they amounted to five regulars and militia killed, fourteen wounded, and two missing. Among the wounded was Boucherville, who often fought with the Indians. Years afterward he gratefully recalled how "the good Tecumseh" visited him while he was convalescing, once with officers of the 41st, and once to bring him a Shawnee healer.

Miller suffered more grievously, and reported eighty-two casualties on the ground, eighteen of whom were dead. The next day the Americans searched the woods for a missing man, whose body they eventually discovered. They also came upon a wounded Indian, who lay with a broken leg and arm. The warrior was still full of fight, and slew one of his opponents before being killed himself. But there was no further action. The stiffness of the opposition, heavy casualties, a violent thunderstorm that followed the battle, and shortages in provisions seem to have discouraged the American commander. Even when McArthur risked bringing reinforcements and supplies from Detroit by boats and picked up the sick and wounded, Miller would move no farther. On the twelfth he went back the way he had come after receiving an order of recall from Hull. Ultimately, then, Tecumseh and Muir had suffered a tactical defeat only to win a far more important strategic triumph. The blockade of Detroit remained intact, and two days after the battle of Maguaga the remaining American soldiers in Canada were withdrawn.

By their refusal to be intimidated and their example in the field, Tecumseh's followers had changed the complexion of the campaign. Only weeks before, an overpowering American army had been set to march through Upper Canada in the face of dispirited defenses. Or so it had seemed. The run of victories, small though they were, had since swollen allied confidence, and it was Hull's force that was now isolated in Detroit with demoralization spreading like a pestilence through its ranks. The army was in "a critical and alarming situation," complained Cass. "For Heaven's sake send all the relief you can!" pleaded McArthur and Findlay. "Oh! If we had had a general!" cried James Denny to his wife. A round-robin was soon circulating, proposing that Hull be divested of his command. The general himself was busy turning his problems into dragons. He was convinced that the fall of Michilimackinac would bring the "northern hive of Indians . . . swarming down in every direction," but he exaggerated. Aside from thirty Menominees Dickson had sent to Fort Malden early in the campaign, only two hundred Ottawas and Ojibwas could be persuaded to leave Michilimackinac for the Detroit, and they did not arrive until the fighting was over.[4]

On the other hand, Indian opinion was certainly changing, and warriors who had once dragged their feet were now coming into Amherstburg. By the middle of August Tecumseh's force had risen to six hundred men.[5]

On Lake Michigan the shifting temper of the Indians as well as the pessimism in Detroit culminated in a tragedy. Hull sent orders to Captain Nathan Heald, the commander of Fort Dearborn (Chicago) to evacuate his post and retire to Detroit. As soon as word of the garrison's imminent departure spread, the local Indians gathered, and on 14 August Heald tried to appease them by distributing the stock of the trade factory, withholding only the ammunition and liquor. The same day, the Indians received a red belt of wampum from Main Poc at Amherstburg and news of the victories over Hull's army, one of several such messages the Potawatomi war chief was sending across Illinois Territory, presumably with the full approval of Tecumseh. Already incensed by the withholding of supplies, militant Potawatomis advocated an attack upon the retiring garrison.[6]

On 15 August several hundred Potawatomis, with some Ojibwas, Winnebagos, and Kickapoos, massed behind a sandbank some one-and-a-half miles from the fort to attack the cavalcade of soldiers, women, children, wagons, and animals that wound its way along the lakeside. There was a bloodbath, and the survivors of the massacre gave themselves up. Only a third or less of the sixty-six soldiers and twenty-seven noncombatants escaped being slain in the engagement or in subsequent captivity. Among the dead that day was William Wells, sent from Fort Wayne to escort the garrison. He died bravely, but the Indians cut off his head, lodged it on a pole, and cut out and divided his heart.

Brutal and tragic, the destruction of the garrison of Chicago starkly

voiced the changes of fortune in the frontier war. Back at Fort Malden,
Tecumseh believed that the British should waste no time in exploiting their
advantages by attacking Detroit itself. He had maintained his Indian force,
and led it into battle, reinforcing General Hull's fears that he was beset with
overwhelming numbers of warriors; he had sealed the Big Knives in Detroit;
and he had captured intelligence that laid bare the state of Hull's mind.
What he needed was a British officer with the imagination to build upon the
foundations the Indians had put into place.

Sometime before midnight on 13 August a splutter of musketry briefly
punctuated the night air in the channel between Bois Blanc and Amherstburg. The shots were fired by Indians, interrupting their war ceremonies,
but not in anger. They were a salute, welcoming boats that at last brought
much-needed substantial reinforcements to Fort Malden. Satisfying himself
that no attack at Niagara was impending, General Brock had embarked
three hundred men, fifty of them regulars of the 41st, at Long Point and set
off with them to personally direct operations in the west.

It was not long afterward that Matthew Elliott found Tecumseh. Almost
immediately upon landing, the General had spoken to the garrison officers,
and he had asked the old agent if the Indians could be prevailed upon to
conserve their ammunition rather than to waste it in salutes. Elliott went
straight to the Shawnee chief and asked him to see Brock.

When Tecumseh walked lightly into the room, a big man, considerably
taller and stouter than the Shawnee, with good firm features and a florid
complexion, stepped forward to shake his hand. A Guernsey islander of
about Tecumseh's age, Isaac Brock was a man of action head to toe. He had
known little other than army life, had served under Abercromby, Nelson,
and Moore—some of the finest warriors in Europe—and had fretted at his
subsequent exile in Canada, far from the great battles in which he longed
for a share. Not surprisingly, such a man had been less than pleased that
Sandwich had been occupied by the enemy unopposed, and he blamed the
collapse in Canadian confidence upon the sluggishness of the British response to invasion. The Indians were a different matter. A letter Brock wrote
some months later, when Tecumseh had left Fort Malden, establishes
Brock's appreciation of what they had done. "If the Indians act as they did
under Tecumseh, who probably might be induced to return to Amherstburg," he advised Procter, "that [the American] army will very soon dwindle
to nothing." They would help keep the Americans in "a state of continual
ferment."[7]

Captain John B. Glegg, one of Brock's aides, preserved a picture of
Tecumseh the night he met Brock:

Tecumseh's appearance was very prepossessing; his figure light and finely proportioned; his age I imagined to be about five and thirty; in height, five feet nine or ten inches; his complexion, light copper; countenance, oval, with bright hazel eyes beaming cheerfulness, energy and decision. Three small silver crowns, or coronets, were suspended from the lower cartilage of his aquiline nose; and a large silver medallion of George the Third . . . was attached to a mixed coloured wampum string, and hung round his neck. His dress consisted of a plain, neat uniform, tanned deerskin jacket, with long trousers of the same material, the seams of both being covered with neatly cut fringe; and he had on his feet leather moccasins, much ornamented with work made from the dyed quills of the porcupine.[8]

The hour was late and the meeting short. Brock explained the need to conserve ammunition, Tecumseh agreed, and the group dispersed with a promise to meet in council during daylight.

Brock made a bold decision. Against the advice of Procter—indeed, it was later said, against the counsel of all his officers save his aide, John MacDonnell, and the quartermaster-general of militia, Robert Nichol—he planned to attack Detroit. Weighing what he knew of Hull, Brock hoped to bluff the American general into surrendering by playing upon his fear of the Indians, and if that failed, to draw his force out of Detroit for a set-piece battle.[9]

There was no difficulty in selling this proposal to the Indians, for it was entirely in accordance with their sentiments, and the council on the fourteenth was a brief one. Brock said that he had come to help the Indians drive Hull out. There is a story, one much loved by Canadian historians, that after a pause Tecumseh turned to his people, held out his hand, and exclaimed, "Ho-yo-o-e! This is a man!" It was told by James FitzGibbon. He was not at Fort Malden, but he was an officer in Brock's regiment, the 49th, and claimed to have heard it from an eyewitness; so perhaps it happened. However, Glegg, who was definitely on the spot, remarked only that the Shawnee chief replied to the effect that he was glad their great Father the King had awakened at last and allowed his men to fight beside their Indian brethren. Other chiefs spoke in agreement and the council closed. Tecumseh and some of his companions went through the finer details of the plan with Brock at a subsequent meeting at Elliott's quarters, perhaps at his farm. Tecumseh was himself abstemious, and promised that his followers would take his example, at least until the Big Knives had been defeated. "If this resolution be persevered in," said Brock, "you must conquer!"[10]

The Indians prepared for what all presumed would be the decisive engagement. There was a war dance at Fort Malden, and on the fifteenth the warriors, some on horseback, others on foot, made their way north to Sandwich, where Brock's offensive was to be launched. Brock began by sending Hull a summons to surrender, pointedly stating that "the numerous body of Indians who have attached themselves to my troops will be beyond control the moment the contest commences." Within living memory the inability or unwillingness of European soldiers to curb the ferocity of Indian allies had been notorious. The British column, butchered near Fort William Henry after surrendering to the French in 1757, and the murder of civilians during a British-Indian attack on Cherry Valley in New York in 1778, had firmly rooted Indian outrages in the American mind. Brock evoked that legend, but his summons was rejected, and early the same evening a five-piece battery the British had established at Sandwich opened up on the American garrison. Hull's twenty-four-pounders roared back, but firing ceased at dark with little damage having been inflicted on either side.[11]

That night hundreds of canoes, carrying 530 Indian warriors, glided stealthily across the river to land near the River Rouge below Detroit. Led by Tecumseh, Roundhead, Matthew Elliott, Thomas McKee, Walk-in-the-Water, Main Poc, and Splitlog, the red men filed into the woods a mile and a half back from the waterfront, ready to assault the flank and rear of any force that contested Brock's landing. The British came over at daylight, their boats covered by the *Queen Charlotte* and the *General Hunter*, and put ashore three miles south of the town, at Spring Wells. With the ships protecting his right and the Indians advancing through the trees on the left, General Brock intended to march openly to Detroit by the main road, hoping Hull might be persuaded to come out and do battle.

It was certainly a gamble. Brock had some support from his ships, and the batteries at Sandwich were manned by gunners of the provincial marine to release artillerymen to march with the general, but his principal reliance had to be placed with the men on the American side of the river. Tecumseh had 530. Brock's column consisted of 800: 300 regulars from the 41st and Royal Newfoundland regiments; 30 members of the Royal Artillery with five six- and three-pounders; 400 militia, some of them garbed in red uniforms to give them the appearance of regulars; and 70 Grand River Iroquois and Munsees from the Thames separately recruited and brought in by John Norton. Brock had no reason to believe that Hull's strength was less than his own, but in fact the American general seems to have had 1,060 men fit for duty, along with three or four hundred Michigan militia. However, half of the latter defected as soon as the attack took place.[12]

The sixteenth of August was a pleasant day. The sun was out and the breeze slight. Soon the stillness was shattered by the renewal of the cannonade from Sandwich, and Brock's men marched calmly up the road that wound gently past the occasional farmhouse toward the town. The tall figure of the general could be seen riding at the front with his advance guard; the artillery, regulars, and uniformed militia followed; and the rest of the militia brought up the rear, some with handkerchiefs bound about their heads and paint on their faces in the fashion of the Indians. Tecumseh's men themselves swept north through the forest. Some broke away to run after horses or sheep, or to loot empty houses, but most moved determinedly onward, scooping up prisoners as they went.

Tension mounted as Brock's column reached its goal. Before them rose the fort, commanding a hill overlooking the river, and guarding the approaches to the town, which was situated at the upper end of the settlement. The 160 houses were also defended by a picket, but the inhabitants had packed into the fort with Hull's regulars. A strong quadrangular structure confining two or three acres, the post had blockhouses at each corner, four palisades a hundred yards in length, and a gate and gatehouse. Additional protection was afforded by a double row of pickets, one in a ditch six feet deep, and the other behind, struck obliquely into the large bank of earth pitched up against the fort walls. Hull's militia were widely dispersed. Many were with their tents behind pickets below the fort and town, but others were stationed in the rear of the fort or the upper part of the town, ready to fight the Indians.

As Tecumseh and Brock brought their forces closer they could hear the awful scream of the British shells and shot arching over the river. Some missiles burst prematurely overhead, like fireworks, but others found their range with fearsome accuracy. One shot fell in the fort's messroom, mutilating two officers and a doctor, while another crashed through a gate, slaying two soldiers. Lydia Bacon, who was in the fort, heard that another man was killed on the parapet. For their part the guns the Americans aimed at Sandwich performed badly, but when Brock's men got within a mile of the garrison they saw something that made them shudder. Sitting on a small rise before the fort was an advanced battery of two twenty-four-pounders and a six-pounder, loaded with grape and canister shot. It was trained upon the head of the British column.

To make matters worse, on his march Brock had received information from Indian scouts that made what had always been a risky venture seem positively desperate. A large party of Americans had been seen to the south, behind the allied troops. This proved to be a detachment of 350 militia under McArthur and Cass which had been sent two days before to reach Brush's supply convoy at the River Raisin by a circuitous route through the forest, one that avoided the main road Tecumseh had blocked. The detachment failed to reach Brush, and on the fifteenth, after the British summons to surrender had been made, Hull had sent them an urgent recall. On learning of the approach of this unexpected force, Brock abandoned his plan to draw Hull into a battle outside the fort. But he did not retreat. He decided to storm Detroit immediately, before the additional American soldiers could enter the fray.

The critical moment had arrived. Brock's column was within range of the advanced battery, and young Richardson, trying to march as stiffly as his more experienced elders, fancied he could see the American gunners with their matches burning. Then Brock filed the command aside, into a ravine near a farmhouse, and prepared to assault the enemy positions. Tecumseh circled through the trees on the left, surrounding the fort and threatening the upper town. A Canadian militia captain maintained that "Tecumseh extended his men, and marched them three times through an opening [in the woods at the rear of the fort] in full view of the garrison, which induced them to believe there were at least two or three thousand Indians."[13] Maybe so, but the officer was not himself an eyewitness, arriving only after the action was over, and no American account mentions the Indian maneuver. At a subsequent American court-martial, however, Hull was said to have been influenced by news that the Indians were breaching the outskirts of the town.

It was about ten A.M. The American batteries fell silent. A white flag was hung over the walls of the fort, and the American troops outside, including those at the forward battery, suddenly withdrew without firing a shot. There was a delay, one brimming with suspense for men on both sides, and then Brock's aides, Glegg and MacDonnell, rode to the American lines. They dismounted and were conducted to Hull's marquee, pitched about a hundred yards from the fort and garishly emblazoned in blue and red stripes. Less than an hour later they were back, reporting to Brock. Almost unbelievable news passed through the British ranks. Hull was ready to surrender the fort, the town, and the whole of his army.

Still finding the news difficult to comprehend, the British column moved into the town. The American soldiers, looking somewhat disheveled, marched out of the fort and stacked their arms on the esplanade between the garrison and the town, and a little after noon Lieutenant Bullock was given the honor of leading a detachment of the 41st into the captured stronghold. They marched to the sound of fife, drum, and a round of "The British Grenadiers." Finally the American colors were lowered, and the Union Jack fluttered bravely over the fort, symbolizing the return of British rule to Detroit after an absence of seventeen years. The captured artillery were used to fire a salute—each report greeted by a triumphant yell and discharge of muskets from the 150 Indians who had gathered around—and the whole victorious army erupted in cheering. Nearby, among the sullen vanquished troops, were many brave men who felt they had been denied an opportunity to defend their country's honor. Some, it was said, had tears in their eyes.

The extent of the allied victory gradually became apparent. Hull surrendered 2,188 men (582 regulars and 1,606 militia), including those with Cass and McArthur, with Brush, and a small party left at the Maumee rapids. Three to four hundred Michigan militia also passed into British hands, but half of these had defected to Brock during the engagement, and all of them were excluded from the surrender because they were not held to have been part of the federal army. Hull yielded thirty-nine guns, including nine twenty-four-pounders; three thousand rifles and muskets; and a large quantity of shot, flints, powder, and cartridges. The *Adams*, a new warship, not yet fully equipped, as well as the fort and all the government property in Detroit, fell as prize. Provisions, which a civil official in Detroit perhaps optimistically estimated would have sustained Hull's garrison for twenty-five days, were also secured. At a stroke the threat to western Upper Canada was obliterated, and the whole of Michigan Territory was restored to British jurisdiction. Never before had the Indians signally contributed to so great a military triumph, nor would they again. To Tecumseh it must have proved that Waashaa Monetoo had indeed begun to smile upon his people once more.

The news hit a complacent American public like a sudden crash of thunder. There was disbelief, and then fury. William Hull waited two years before a court-martial condemned him for neglect of duty and misconduct, and delivered a death sentence. The sentence was commuted on account of the general's former services, but his remaining years, and strenuous efforts to justify himself, never expunged public obloquy.

There has always been debate about what led Hull—the commander of a considerable force in a strong fort with sufficient provisions—to surrender, particularly when he had known for several days that his appeals to the Secretary of War and the governors of Kentucky and Ohio for reinforcements were being answered. Much was said after the event, in the court-martial and elsewhere, to accuse or extenuate the general, but it seems to have carried little weight at the time. Reading the earliest evidence yields the conclusion that Hull simply convinced himself that he was being attacked by an overwhelming force, and worse, a force that consisted of many Indians. If he resisted, he courted a massacre.

Some who saw him before the surrender said that fear was stamped all over Hull. He was dispirited and pale and his voice trembled, and he crammed his mouth with so much tobacco that the juice ran down his beard onto his cravat and vest. But it was probably humanity, rather than cowardice, that moved the old soldier. He was genuinely concerned for the lives of his men, for the seven hundred civilians sheltering in the fort (among whom were his own daughter and grandchildren), and for the safety of the outlying detachments under McArthur and Brush, which he protected by including them in his surrender.

To some extent Hull was a scapegoat for an overconfident and ill-prepared administration. Before the war, for example, he had drawn attention to the necessity of the United States' gaining naval command of the Great Lakes, but the plea went largely unheeded. And Hull was unfortunate that the delays in the American attack at Niagara enabled Brock to concentrate scarce resources on the Detroit.

But as the historian Harry L. Coles said more than thirty years ago, this argument does not absolve Hull of responsibility. The British and Indians, no less than the Americans, wrestled with formidable problems of supply, communication, and inadequate and unreliable manpower. The campaign of 1812 was determined primarily by leadership. We have only to compare the corresponding commanders: on the one side, Captain Charles Roberts of St. Joseph's, promptly striking out to surprise the American post of Michilimackinac; the tireless Tecumseh, molding a credible Indian force and leading it into battle on both sides of the river, often adroitly pitting paltry detachments against superior numbers; and Brock, carefully husbanding his resources to meet an invasion on two fronts, and astutely weighing and boldly exploiting the weaknesses of his opponent. On the other there was the defensive Hull, paralyzed by the blackest constructions he could put upon his own problems; James Miller, who turned victory into defeat by returning to Detroit after Maguaga; and McArthur and Cass, who, ordered to reach Brush by an inland trail, simply blundered unsuccessfully about the woods, and who, after receiving a message to return, not only failed to notify their general of their approach but also retired to kill and roast an ox while the fort was under attack.

Tecumseh, a principal architect of Hull's humiliation, felt the surrender of Detroit was the vindication of his course. The afternoon of the surrender many Indians celebrated. While the prisoners were being loaded into boats—the regulars for shipment to Quebec, the militia to be paroled shortly—some warriors joined the volunteers in the town, capering about the streets in carriages or getting drunk. There were no offenses against the person, but the need to maintain order was paramount, and Procter was installed as acting governor of the territory.

Brock and Tecumseh made their headquarters in a vacant house on the main street, presumably either St. Ann or St. Honore Street. A junior aide to Hull, Robert Wallace, remembered the British general introducing him to the Shawnee chief. Tecumseh was wearing a morocco sword belt over his deerskin hunting shirt. "As soon as Brock presented me to Tecumseh, the interpreter stood at once by his side, and with great promptness conveyed what I said into Indian. For though he could speak some English, yet he was unwilling to be exposed, in the formalities of intercourse, from using bad English. Besides the interpreter, another man as waiter was in attendance! He occupied two rooms, a front and a back one. He was tall and commanding, and straight as an arrow." Wallace reckoned Tecumseh the best general in the country, and a courteous one, too. "Well," the chief said to him, "you are a prisoner, but it is the fortune of war, and you are in very good hands."[14]

A young assistant quartermaster-general of Hull's army, William Hatch, also saw Tecumseh, in Detroit on the 17th, "mutually exchanging tokens of recognition" as a "former acquaintance" and clearing the last of the Indians from the streets. Most of the warriors had ridden back to Amherstburg the day Detroit fell. Tecumseh "was then in the prime of life," said Hatch, "and presented in his appearance and noble bearing one of the finest looking men I have ever seen."[15]

There were mopping-up operations to be completed. A militia captain, William Elliott, had been sent to take the surrender of Brush's men at the River Raisin, but Captain Peter Chambers, a regular officer, was detached to follow him up and take charge of American public property both there and at the Maumee rapids. Tecumseh and Roundhead were asked to accompany Chambers, who had a small entourage but no military escort.

On 19 August Tecumseh and a few other Indians met the British party at Brownstown. The British then left for the River Raisin by bateaux, while the Indians proceeded overland. Tecumseh rode after them with Matthew Elliott and his son, Alexander. The following morning the chief came upon Chambers again. The officer had landed at the Rocky River, just above the Raisin, and was sheltering from the rain in a deserted house, sharing breakfast with a trader, Charles Askin. Chambers and Tecumseh rode together the remainder of the way.

In their attempts to present Tecumseh as the exemplification of the noble savage—always true, wise, and powerful—storytellers frequently enter-tained listeners with accounts of the Shawnee chief's ability to arrest the excesses of his wilder companions. Some who had seen him, such as John Ruland, one of the Michigan volunteers, later claimed that they knew for certain that Tecumseh had saved this or that person from unruly warriors bent on plunder or mayhem. Now, while Tecumseh was undoubtedly a humane man, and at times a masterful one, he was not invariably able to impose an alien discipline upon the forces he led and inspired. The expedition to the River Raisin, reconstructed from the contemporary documents rather than the embroidered reminiscences of old pioneers, was evidence of that.

Captain Chambers's party reached the River Raisin on 20 August to learn that Brush's troops had absconded three days before without surrendering their arms to Brock's messenger, William Elliott. It served the fugitives little, since their names had been entered on the list of paroled prisoners and they were able to serve again only after being exchanged. More cooperative, the Michigan militia had handed in their arms, and Captain Elliott had already shipped them to Amherstburg. Other public property regarded as prize had been stored at the house of one of the Lasselles, the family of French-Canadian merchants. It was there that the British completed their breakfast.

While they were seated in Lasselle's house, the wife of John Anderson, one of the inhabitants, came hurrying up. She said that Indians were plundering her house, and begged the British to put a stop to it. Free spirits as they were, the Indians were generally impatient of restraint. Plunder belonged to the captor, and was no business of the chiefs or anyone else. The Indians also took a fundamentally different view of the Americans than did their British allies. They made fewer distinctions between men-at-arms and civilians. To the Indians, civilians and soldiers both represented an invading and often oppressive force, part of the tide of settlement that was eating tribal lands. They had been willing to fight according to some of the ground rules laid down by the redcoats, and no prisoners had been killed at Detroit or the River Raisin, but warriors who had suffered material deprivation in recent years, when trade goods had been expensive and scarce, were not slow to claim that as conquerors they had a right to the spoils of war.

The Indian allies had already become troublesome, roaming the Michigan countryside stealing horses, ransacking a few houses, and killing cattle and hogs. Even some British or Canadian subjects had been similarly served. When Mrs. Anderson appealed to the British, Chambers and Askin set off to her house and found several truculent Wyandots looting it. They brushed aside the British protests and continued with their work. When Matthew Elliott at last appeared on the scene, entreated to turn out by Askin, he was no more successful. "For all the good he did he might as well have stayed where he was," grumbled Askin.[16]

The old agent was sick at the time, but had he been well he would have achieved little more, for no one, neither Elliott nor McKee, nor even Tecumseh or Roundhead, could halt the pillaging. Tecumseh was more effective than Elliott had been, but also failed. Chambers reported: "It affords me great pleasure to say that the conduct of Tecumthe . . . and Round Head . . . was such as reflect on them the highest honor." Askin entered in his journal that "Técompsé, the Indian General, as he is called, behaved, I must say, remarkably well. He assisted us very much in trying to prevent the Indians from pillaging."

A few Sacs desisted from the plunder. Admonished by Chambers, they even returned some of the goods they had taken. But the Wyandot rampage continued unabated. A number of Wyandots remained at the Anderson house for most of the day, hauling out some goods, smashing others, and spilling flour in the yard. Others went from house to house, repeating the performance each time. It was, as Chambers admitted, "one universal scene of desolation."

The Americans had raised two blockhouses at the River Raisin, surrounded by a strong stockade; all of these structures were burned. The next day the party continued toward the Maumee rapids. At first Chambers planned to dismiss the Indians, frightened that their behavior at the River Raisin would be resumed, but rumors that 180 Americans were at the rapids demanded a strong escort. Tecumseh went ahead with some of his men. Twenty-five sick soldiers from Hull's army were all that remained at the rapids. The Shawnee chief gave them protection, and fired the blockhouse. When Chambers arrived about one or two o'clock he could find few arms to collect, but the enemy's provisions were embarked on boats and canoes for passage to Amherstburg. Once again, some Indian warriors robbed local inhabitants, although not, it seems, on the scale of the pillage at the River Raisin.[17]

Shawnees called August "Poakarmauwee Keesthwau," the Moon of Plums. Traditionally it was a time of plenty, when the summer and the crops had matured, and the harvest was taken. There was feasting, as the ears of corn roasted, and dancing and merriment. Thanks were given the deities who had provided the bounty. Yet despite difficulties with pillaging Indians, never in Tecumseh's life had he enjoyed a moon so full of benedictions as the August of 1812.

The British enthused loudly about what the Indians had achieved. Isaac Brock's general orders, written the day Hull surrendered, characterized the Indian performances throughout the war as "marked with acts of true heroism." Particularly he admired Tecumseh, whom he openly referred to as "the Wellington of the Indians." There is a story, which may be true, that the general gave his Shawnee ally a sash in recognition of his services. The following day he observed that Tecumseh was no longer wearing it, and fearing some offense had been taken, inquired as to why it had been discarded. Tecumseh showed, not for the first time, the tact that was needed in handling proud Indian supporters. He had given the sash to Roundhead, he replied, who was both an older and an abler warrior than himself.[18]

Brock would receive a knighthood for his capture of Detroit, but Tecumseh's reward was arguably greater. He had seen the Big Knives humbled. Michilimackinac, Chicago, Detroit, and the fortifications at the River Raisin and the Maumee rapids had been taken, while the Indians found a small fort at Sandusky abandoned and burned it to the ground.[19] In a brief six weeks every American post on the upper Great Lakes west of Cleveland had been eliminated. Not since 1791, when the army of Arthur St. Clair had been smashed on the banks of the Wabash, had the cause of pan-Indianism been so triumphant.

24

━┥━ ⊰◈⊱ ┝━

ATTACK AND
COUNTERATTACK

Tecumseh had helped save Canada, but one thing is certain. The Shawnee chief didn't really care a spent pistol ball for the King and his colonies. It was the plight of the Indian peoples, and his own ambition, that drove him forward, and the British, those shifty, untrustworthy beings who so often failed their native allies, were tools to be used. Their military might could be harnessed to the Indian confederacy. Alone, neither could defeat the Big Knives; together . . . His spirits soaring after recent successes, Tecumseh was even talking about clearing the Americans from all the lands north of the Ohio.

In General Brock Tecumseh had at last found a man worthy of his trust, and during the few days they had together the Shawnee made sure the English officer learned why the Indians were fighting. Brock knew the folly of promising more than he could deliver, but he was under a deep obligation to the Indians; he sympathized with their predicament; and more than anything else, he had further need of their services. He had to keep Tecumseh's hopes alive. He pledged that this time the Indians would not be deserted.[1]

Still threatened by an invasion at Niagara, Brock spent only a day or so at Fort Malden before returning east, but on 29 August he addressed a letter to the new British Prime Minister, Lord Liverpool.

Among the Indians whom I met at Amherstburg, and who had arrived from distant parts of the country, I found some extraordinary characters [he wrote]. He who attracted most of my attention was a

Shawnee chief, Tecumset, brother to the Prophet, who for the last two years has carried on, contrary to our remonstrances, an active warfare against the United States. A more sagacious or more a gallant warrior does not, I believe, exist. He was the admiration of every one who conversed with him. From a life of dissipation he has not only become, in every respect, abstemious, but has likewise prevailed on all his nation and many of the other tribes to follow his example. They appear determined to continue the contest until they obtain the Ohio for a boundary. The United States government is accused, and I believe justly, of having corrupted a few dissolute characters whom they pretended to consider as chiefs, and with whom they contracted engagements and concluded treaties, which they have attempted to impose on the whole Indian race.[2]

The Indians were vital to Canadian security, and Brock suggested that Liverpool could ensure their loyalty by including them "in any future negotiations for peace." To Sir George Prevost, governor-general of Canada, he was more pointed still. The Indians would not fight for Britain unless their interests, or war aims, became part of peace negotiations; a treaty, he said, should admit their claims "to an extensive tract of country, fraudulently usurped from them."[3]

Exactly what passed between Tecumseh and Brock is unknown. An alleged statement of the chief's grievances was wide-ranging, and included abuses at the American trade factories, the use of trading posts for military purposes, the obstructions placed in the way of British traders, and the disregard of Indian interests; but this document smacks of having been concocted by British merchants for their own purposes. On 17 September Brock instructed Procter to have Thomas McKee raise the matter with the Indians, although in a casual fashion, and learn what the tribes would want in a peace, both in the event of British success and of British failure in the war. There can be little doubt that Brock assured Tecumseh that Indian land claims would be supported, but equally that he had not entered into the detail of the subject.[4]

Prevost endorsed Brock's view. He advised the secretary of war and colonies, Earl Bathurst, of the "great assistance" the Indians had rendered Brock, and he repeated the opinion that their conciliation was essential to British interests. The British stipulations for peace should include a suitable Indian boundary. The British government agreed, and Viscount Castlereagh, the foreign secretary, was so instructed. At the same time the Canadian merchants weighed in, frightened that if the Indians were driven from the country south and west of the Great Lakes the fur trade would be ruined. The committees of trade at Quebec and Montreal jointly addressed

Prevost in October 1812, declaring that the Indians had saved Upper Canada and richly deserved a new boundary. The return of territory north of the Ohio and west of the Sandusky—in short the reversal of every treaty the United States had signed with the northern Indians since 1784—should be "a *sine qua non* of any treaty whatsoever negotiated." On 14 December the letter was transmitted to Castlereagh by Nathaniel Atcheson, secretary to a committee of North American merchants in London, and it was probably also forwarded by Prevost.

Although committed to assisting the Indians, the British had different ideas about what precisely ought to be done. The merchants most closely approximated the extreme Indian ambition to reclaim the Indian boundary as it stood at the end of the Revolutionary War. Sir George himself apparently preferred the Greenville line of 1795. At least, when he appointed Robert Dickson to recruit an Indian army on the upper Great Lakes the following January, he went so far as to suggest the Indians tell Americans to withdraw behind the Greenville boundary on pain of death. On his part, Bathurst was hoping in June 1814 that a successful war would "restore the whole of the Michigan country to the Indians."[5] That some territorial claims should be made for the Indians seemed, however, to be acknowledged.

Tecumseh's plan had looked like such a flimsy vision, so futile a gesture to challenge, at this late stage, American control of the Old Northwest, that even the most abused of Indian warriors had hesitated to give it credence. But difficulty, argument, and intimidation had not bowed Tecumseh, and suddenly his dream seemed to be coming to life. In the heat of conflict Indians and British began catching his wild spirit. The Indians began to wonder whether, after all, the Great Spirit had not reserved the lands north of the Ohio for his red children; the British resurrected the idea of an Indian buffer state that would keep the northwest out of the American hands.

Still, the priorities of the allies remained wide apart. Canada lacked the resources for more than a *defensive* war. It was essential that naval command of Lake Erie be maintained—for which purpose Procter had a ship and some gunboats being built at Fort Malden; no less important was the retention of Michigan Territory, because to relinquish it would have sacrificed the confidence of Britain's Indian allies.

Tecumseh saw it differently. He wanted the redcoats to help him reconquer the Old Northwest. The late victories would kindle the revolt and wean faltering Indians from the American flag, but to capture the remaining enemy garrisons he needed the help of the Great Father. In August the Potawatomis of the Tippecanoe and St. Joseph, who had once consorted with Governor Harrison, gathered to attack Fort Wayne, galvanized by the sudden reversal of fortunes. They sent to Amherstburg for help. Despite misgivings about campaigning far afield, the British felt obliged to respond, and a confident Tecumseh sent word to the Miamis, who lived near Fort Wayne, that they must stand aside lest they be crushed beneath his feet by the allied army he was bringing to capture the fort.[6]

The chief's confidence was, in fact, misplaced. It was true that much had changed. Most of the western tribes that had hitherto regarded Tecumseh suspiciously had been brought into line, and even among the more divided Eel River and Miami Indians the war party was rumored to be gaining the upper hand.[7] Only the staunchest friends of the United States—the White River Delawares and the Ohio Shawnees, Mingoes, and Wyandots—turned up to speak to the federal commissioners at Piqua in the middle of August, and their position was singularly uncomfortable. Afraid that Tecumseh and his allies would punish them, they withdrew deeper into Ohio, behind the American lines, to establish new settlements at Upper Sandusky, Zanestown, and Piqua; but they were never entirely trusted by white neighbors. Even after the Shawnee James Logan died gallantly in American service in November, many settlers had no time for the friendly Indians. Old Black Hoof learned that in the most direct way when he visited a militia camp on 23 January 1813, benignly offering his assistance. A soldier fired through the hut where the chief sat talking to American officers and inflicted an agonizing wound to his face.[8]

With larger numbers of warriors than ever before at their disposal, Tecumseh and his supporters were still confronted by an enormous military task. In addition to facing the distractions of normal economic activities, disrupted by the coming and going of armed parties and the danger of attack, the tribesmen were crippled by a shortage of powder; and the defenses of the American population were formidable. The Indians were brilliant bush-fighters, but they always found the problems of capturing fortified positions largely insurmountable. They had no artillery to knock breaches in stubborn wooden walls, nor the manpower and discipline to storm resolutely defended entrenchments, and native food supplies were rarely up to sustaining a long siege. Sometimes the Indians surprised careless or unwary garrisons, but if that failed their attacks on forts were almost always unsuccessful.[9]

In 1812 the Indians contended not only with substantial garrisons, such as those at Fort Wayne and Vincennes, but also with a fortified civilian population. Many white families fled in terror, piling their pitiful belongings on carts and wagons, but those who remained took asylum at military posts or forted themselves up in blockhouses, from which they seldom ventured without escorts.

Moreover, Tecumseh and his allies were squaring up to far greater forces than their own. Apart from an extensive frontier militia, available for short-term service, and the deployment of six mounted volunteer ranger companies, there was the fact that Kentucky, a state forged in Indian conflict and the home of congressional War Hawks, was equipping large armies for the field. At the beginning of September, when the Indian offensive gathered momentum, a sixty-one-year-old southern planter, Brigadier-General James Winchester, was in Kentucky raising a new army of regulars and militia, originally intended to have reinforced Hull in Detroit. William Henry Harrison, who had discarded his governorship of Indiana Territory and been honored with the brevet rank of major-general of the Kentucky militia, was in Ohio, superintending those of Winchester's troops who had already been sent forward. Besides these battalions, two thousand eager Kentucky volunteers under Major-General Samuel Hopkins were being sent to Vincennes for action on the Wabash and Illinois Rivers.

In this context, Tecumseh can only be judged to have been overconfident, but his optimism was grounded in the willingness of the British to provide supples, artillery, and necessary know-how. But at that moment the redcoats stalled. Prevost had arranged an armistice in the futile hope that Britain's repeal of admiralty orders in council, important sources of American discontent, would be sufficient to bring the war to an end. It was in vain that Tecumseh and Roundhead argued that the Indians attacking Fort Wayne needed help *now*. Until the expiration of the armistice on 8 September, Procter would not budge.

Finally the expedition moved. On 12 September Tecumseh, Roundhead, and Elliott led 600 warriors from Amherstburg; Muir was soon following with 150 regulars, 100 militia, a six-pounder, and a howitzer, embarked at Amherstburg for a voyage to the Maumee; and Thomas McKee set out on the fifteenth with 200 Ottawas and Ojibwas who had just arrived from Michilimackinac. The morale of the Indians was tip-top, and they boasted of carrying all before them, as far as Vincennes and Fort Massac.[10]

Impatient to alert the Indians ahead, Tecumseh soon put the ponderous allied army behind him as he hurried ahead with his exciting news. Somewhere along the way, that jubilation was dashed. He was too late. The siege of Fort Wayne had already been broken.

It was worse than that. When Tecumseh reached the Wabash he discovered that spirited assaults on other outlying frontier garrisons had also failed. On 5 September Winnebagos and Sacs had fiercely attacked Fort Madison on the Mississippi (Iowa), destroying the trade factory and other property outside but failing to set the post itself on fire. Three days later the Indians quit after running low on ammunition.

Fort Wayne, which was attacked in force the same day as Fort Madison, was a stronger position, with eighty men and four pieces of artillery, but its commandant, James Rhea, was grossly incompetent. "He was as drunk as a fool all night," wrote one of his soldiers that day, "and had not yet come to his perfect senses, if he ever had any." Throughout the siege he verged upon hysteria. The leaders of the Potawatomi assailants included a prophet from the Elkhart, Five Medals, and the very same Winamek who had once curried favor with Harrison, but who was now bragging about his part in the Chicago massacre and claiming that, barring Tecumseh, he was the confederacy's leading war chief. Although they spattered the defenses with bullets and destroyed everything they could find outside the walls, the Indians had little success. When Harrison appeared on the twelfth with two thousand men from Piqua, the attackers dispersed. Only four Americans were killed in the operations against Fort Madison and Fort Wayne combined.[11]

A more persistent attack was made on Fort Harrison by Tecumseh's own band on the Wabash. Tenskwatawa had held his position at Prophetstown after his brother left for Canada. Provisions had been thin during the summer, and many followers had gone to Lake Peoria to fish, but the harvest at the end of August was beginning to draw them back.[12] While the Potawatomis tormented Fort Wayne, the men of Prophetstown—Shawnees, Winnebagos, Kickapoos, and Miamis—stole down the Wabash toward the hated post guarding the limits of the infamous treaty of 1809.

Fort Harrison was weakly defended. Inside, some of the fifty-five regulars from the 7th Regiment of United States Infantry were down with fever, and nine women and children were among the civilians who had abandoned their farms for the security of the post. On the evening of 3 September the Indians made the mistake of advertising their presence by shooting to death two hay-makers some four hundred yards from the garrison. The next day they tried to allay suspicions by sending an old Kickapoo headman, Joe Renard, to parley, carrying a white flag. Joe had about thirty-five Indians with him, ten of them women, and explained that a proper delegation would be sent shortly. They only wanted provisions, he said. But the officer in charge of Fort Harrison, Captain Zachary Taylor (destined to earn greater fame as the twelfth president of the United States), did not relax his guard.

The night of the fourth was dark, and some Indians reached the apertures in the lower story of one of the fort's corner blockhouses to thrust burning materials inside. A shot from a sentry opened a savage exchange of fire, the Indians using bows and arrows as well as muskets, and Taylor's men replying as best they could from the other blockhouse and two bastions. The Indians were encouraged when they saw flames licking out of the afflicted blockhouse, enveloping its upper story and roof and threatening the adjoining barracks. That lower story had contained the fort's provisions: flour, pork, salt, soap, hides, tallow, and—most important of all—nearly 150 barrels and 25,316 rations of whiskey, which now blazed furiously, throwing upon the scene a lurid glare.

Throughout the night there was a desperate struggle, in which jubilant Indians sniped at the heads peering over the pickets or the brave illuminated figures struggling for footholds on the tops of buildings as they tried to douse them with water and tear off combustible roofing. Daylight found a smoking twenty-foot breach in the fort, the provisions gone, and three defenders dead and three wounded. But the fort had survived, and the Indians fell back upon starving the whites out. They ran off or killed the stock kept outside, infested the supply line to Vincennes, and lit a large fire on the banks of the Wabash below the fort, keeping a canoe ready to intercept any boats seen working their way upriver.

These tactics, too, failed. On the fifth and sixth the Indians turned back mounted detachments from Vincennes—the first of which was driven off with a loss of two rangers killed—but ten days later 1,350 men under Colonel William Russell got through with badly needed supplies. No sooner had the relief force arrived than the Indians returned to the siege, ambushing a provision wagon and its escort of thirteen regulars halfway between Vincennes and the fort. They killed seven soldiers, wounded one, and took the wagon, but abandoned their attempts to reduce Fort Harrison.[13]

Efforts to drive back the settlers met with no greater success. Even three hundred warriors under Gomo and Sequenebee who made a foray down the Illinois in September achieved nothing. The one devastating attack was the destruction of Pigeon Roost (Scott County, Indiana), when a Shawnee named Masalemeta, a relative of Peter Cornstalk and James Logan, led a sudden descent on 3 September, killing twenty-four people, all but three of them women and children. On their retreat they mortally wounded a soldier during a skirmish with pursuers. John Gibson, acting as governor of Indiana Territory, aptly if coldly described the victims of the raid as "foolhardy" because they had not provided themselves with a blockhouse.[14]

In truth the Indian campaign had already bogged down before Tecumseh returned to the Wabash. Many homesteaders had been frightened away, and Indians roamed at large, burning empty houses and destroying stock and stores, but those important forts and blockhouses had withstood the fury of their attack. To cap all, the allied sortie under Muir and Roundhead collapsed. The men marched up the Maumee to reach a point some forty miles from Fort Wayne on 25 September, but then learned not only that the fort had been relieved, but also that a superior American army was descending the river toward them. Roundhead wanted to fight, but some of the Indian holy men augured defeat and more than half the warriors decamped. Judging discretion to be better than valor, Muir ordered a retreat.[15]

For the Shawnee chief who had dreamed of liberating the Ohio country from his enemies it was a terrible disappointment. His movements during the rest of the year are obscure. He remained about the Wabash, although the Indian army at Prophetstown was breaking up for the fall hunting. Many Winnebagos and Kickapoos went home, and Tecumseh seems to have spent part of October at the head of the Tippecanoe before moving back to the Wabash. In December he was reported to have had six hundred men there, somewhere between the Tippecanoe and Eel Rivers. If the report was accurate, Tecumseh was already regathering his forces.[16]

His one consolation was that the American counterattacks, when they came, were generally ineffective. Before the year was out nine major expeditions were launched against the northern Indians. Riders burned twenty-one towns, seized property, destroyed crops and stores, and turned part of the Indian country into a wasteland, devoid of food and shelter. Groups of soldiers, whatever their principal business, found empty Indian villages tempting. In October militiamen marching through Ohio pillaged several, one of them Roundhead's old settlement, even breaking open graves to strip corpses of silver trinkets.[17]

In all but two cases the towns destroyed had already been evacuated, and there were few Indian casualties. Many of the towns, perhaps half, belonged to Indians who had only recently turned upon the Americans: the Miamis on the Wabash, Eel River, and Mississinewa; a Potawatomi village on the Elkhart; and an Ottawa town in northern Ohio. In one of those expeditions, which torched four villages on the Mississinewa in December, fifty Indian men, women, and children were killed or captured, but the soldiers were dislodged by a determined Miami counterstroke and retreated frostbitten through the snow after suffering fifty-eight casualties.

The hard core of Tecumseh's support was less vulnerable, but in October a force under Colonel William Russell and Governor Edwards broke up the hostile concentration near Lake Peoria. Pamawatam's village, sheltering Miamis and Kickapoos, was surprised and some Indians were killed, but all the other villages destroyed on the Illinois were found deserted.

The main effect of the American counterattacks was to throw needy Indian communities upon British supplies, thus increasing the alliance with the redcoats, and to redistribute Indian populations. Miamis grouped on the Mississinewa, and many Potawatomis coalesced around White Pigeon's town on the headwaters of the St. Joseph. The Indians uprooted from the Illinois retired to the mouth of the Rock, where they stimulated anti-Americanism among the local Sacs.

One expedition struck straight at Prophetstown. The local Indian settlements had been more or less abandoned several weeks before, and the remaining inhabitants were evacuated before 19 November, when 1,250 men under Hopkins arrived from Fort Harrison. For several days the soldiers pillaged and burned the empty villages—Prophetstown and the adjoining Kickapoo village, and the Winnebago town on Wild Cat Creek, a stream that emptied into the Wabash below Prophetstown. Parties of men ranged afar, scouring the countryside for caches of corn and for lurking Indians.

Whether Tecumseh was this far down the Wabash no one can say, but some of his followers were, waiting for a chance to punish the raiders. They had their camp on the north fork of Wild Cat Creek, about seven miles above the Winnebago town. It nestled securely between the stream, which curved rapidly around the camp in a semicircle, and a high and precipitous bluff which could be scaled by way of three steep ravines. Among the warriors was Tecumseh's younger brother Kumskaukau. Since the battle of Tippecanoe Tecumseh had grown impatient with the Prophet, and openly critical of his conduct, but Kumskaukau was much more to his liking. In fact, everyone liked Kumskaukau. His infectious good humor was not unlike Tecumseh's own, and a reservoir of stories usually put him at the center of a large circle of friends. He was a good fighter, too. On 21 November Kumskaukau and some friends were on top of the bluff when they spotted one of Hopkins's scouting parties coming upriver. The Indians fired from ambush, toppling a rider from his horse and sending the rest scurrying home.

The next day a larger detachment appeared, sixty horsemen under Lieutenant-Colonels John Miller and Philip Wilcox, coming to bury their fallen companion. Quickly the warriors crouched down in the ravines while one Indian rode in full view of the soldiers as a decoy. The Americans were riding in three columns, and when they saw the lone warrior the column on the right raised a triumphant shout and galloped after him at full speed. The other columns followed. A little over a mile farther and the Americans suddenly saw Indian heads popping up on three sides—ahead from the edge of the bluff, and from the crests of ravines to the right and left. Too late! There was a barrage of musket balls and the soldiers made a chaotic retreat, three of them wounded. Sixteen men had been killed.

Probably the Indians suffered no losses, but they expected that Hopkins would send an even bigger party against them, so they quit their camp the same day, just as a heavy snowfall, a sudden icing of the rivers, and a biting cold marked the onset of the worst of the winter.[18]

The wider war was also in a stalemate. In October an American thrust across the Niagara was bungled, and twelve hundred men were killed, captured, or wounded. The battle of Queenston Heights also cost the British dearly, despite the victory. They lost their finest leader, Isaac Brock, slain at the front of his men as he tried to capture an enemy position. Tecumseh lost a powerful and able friend.

Public opinion in the United States demanded the recapture of Detroit, the end of the Indian threat, and the redemption of the nation's honor, stained, as it was thought, by Hull's surrender. On 17 September Harrison was appointed to command a new northwestern army. He planned to unite three divisions at the rapids of the Maumee for a push against Fort Malden and Detroit. James Winchester would descend the Maumee with two thousand Kentuckians. Twelve hundred Ohio militia under Brigadier-General Edward Tupper were to follow Hull's ill-fated original route from Urbana. The third contingent, consisting of Pennsylvanian and Virginian volunteers, would mobilize at Upper Sandusky with the principal artillery. The armies advanced, protecting their lines of communication with blockhouses.

Tecumseh would have relished disrupting the vast movements the American preparations entailed. All those groaning wagons and plodding packhorses, heavily laden flatboats, and herds of cattle and hogs. The weary detachments of men going here and there. Harrison expected the Indians to attack his supply lines, but nothing happened. One reason, perhaps, was that Tecumseh's iron constitution, which had hitherto supported extreme and continued exertion, long arduous travels, and the stresses of battle, had failed. Toward the end of the year he was sick—halted on the Wabash, and attended no doubt by his new and last wife and probably also by sister Tecumapease. John Johnston heard that the Shawnee chief had lost the use of one of his legs, which had so "entirely withered" that it was believed he would "never recover the use of it." Further active service, it was said, was out of the question. At Fort Malden Colonel Procter also learned of the illness, but with greater concern. As late as 13 January he reported that "Tecumshee, I fear, has scarcely recovered his health."[19]

We can imagine the Shawnee leader chafing at his incapacity, for there was so much to do. His greatest fear was that this time the Big Knives would overwhelm the British, who were the only source of arms and ammunition for the Indians now that they had failed to capture the American forts. If the redcoats were conquered, the Indian cause would die. In the face of Harrison's mobilization, Tecumseh's priority was to recruit as many warriors as possible for the defense of Canada.

Tecumseh occupied a position near the remains of Prophetstown, possibly to make it easier for old allies to find him, and called in his supporters. It was midwinter, but by about the end of the year he had assembled some seven hundred warriors. No one challenged the operation. At one point an American force approached and the Prophet was set to run. Tecumseh threatened his brother with a tomahawk, but neither that nor an engagement with the enemy proved to be necessary.

To encourage those already at Fort Malden he sent a delegation, drawn from the different Indian communities at Prophetstown—Kickapoos, Winnebagos, Shawnees, Miamis, Delawares, and Creeks. It urged the Indians to "fight manfully . . . for their country" and to expect Tecumseh to join them at the River Raisin with his full force in about one moon. Indians who defected, the Shawnee warned, would provoke his "severest frown." He also fired a shot across British bows, entreating them not to make a secret peace with the Americans that ignored the Indians, as they had done in 1783: "should they [the United States] stretch out the hand once, twice, thence even to four times to sue for peace it must be pushed back," and only on the fifth suit "perhaps they might be listened to."[20]

While convalescing amid his anxieties, Tecumseh regularly received news of distant events. Two such reports, one from the south and the other from the north, were of immense interest. About November, fifteen Creeks arrived at his camp, perhaps those who added their names to the message for Fort Malden. Their leader, Little Warrior (Tastanagi Ooche), was a chief of twenty years' standing at the Upper Creek town of Wiwohka, and spoke with considerable authority about the progress of Tecumseh's revolt in the south. His information was not entirely encouraging, for it certainly included the unfortunate divisions opening in the Creek Nation as the National Council, pressed by agent Hawkins, executed Indians guilty of murdering white settlers. On the other hand, Little Warrior apparently also told Tecumseh that a Creek war party would come north to fight beside him when the grass was a foot high, about May.[21]

Tecumseh probably learned something else from Little Warrior. The Shawnee chief's influence had at last extended into the Florida peninsula, among the Seminoles, who had taken up arms against the Americans. Florida was a hotbed of intrigue and rebellion. It was held by Spain, but American filibusters, supported by a detachment of American troops under Colonel Thomas Smith, were attempting to annex part of it and had the Spanish governor, Sebastian Kindelan, besieged in St. Augustine. Both sides approached the Indians, but in July 1812 the Alachuan and Alligator bands of Seminoles, with a party of fugitive blacks associated with them, threw in their lot with the Spaniards.

Their principal chief, old Payne, had wanted to stay neutral, as the Americans had advised, but his younger brother, Bowlegs, listened to other counselors. Some were blacks, frightened that the relative freedom they enjoyed with the Seminoles would end if the United States seized Florida. But a key figure, the man the Creeks designated the "author" of the trouble, was none other than Seekaboo, the talented agent Tecumseh had left behind to promote his confederacy among the southern Indians. Hawkins was probably referring to Seekaboo when he wrote in September that a prophet was working among the Seminoles, who had "all . . . taken his talks." The Creeks themselves credited him with convincing Bowlegs and others that they had to fight. They must help the Spaniards now, or one day they would have to defend themselves against the Americans alone. Once attacked, assured Seekaboo, their enemies would scatter like jackdaws.

Seekaboo and Bowlegs won the argument, and 250 Seminoles and blacks, with a few sympathetic Creek Red Sticks, began attacking American houses and soldiers, and liberating slaves. When Colonel Daniel Newnan led 117 Georgian volunteers against them in September 1812 a running fight developed, and the next month the Georgians were driven out with losses of 16 killed and missing. Equally important, black and Seminole operations in the rear of the American forces besieging St. Augustine broke the siege. Many of the filibusters abandoned the army, and in September Smith's men had to withdraw behind the St. Johns. The respite would be brief, but for the moment the Spaniards breathed more easily.

In the end, of course, the Seminoles would pay for their temerity, and Payne realized it. In December he asked Hawkins to help him restore peace. The Creeks claimed that "Tusseki Abbee" (Seekaboo) was "crazy" and said that he had fled from the Seminole country to save his life. However, the Seminole uprising dragged into 1813, survived poor Payne, who died awaiting the outcome of his appeal to Hawkins, and led to the invasion of Florida by Tennessean and federal troops in February 1813. Two Seminole towns were destroyed, and the rebels withdrew to the southwest, but the embers of revolt remained unextinguished.[22]

This Seminole-black uprising in north central Florida represented the southern limit of the influence of Tecumseh and the Prophet, but it gave little practical help to their struggle around the Great Lakes. About the end of January, however, word came breathlessly into Tecumseh's camp that must have sent his spirits soaring to the sky. There had been another major battle, and the allies had completely crushed one of the American armies.

In January 1813 William Henry Harrison hoped to gather 4,000 men at the Maumee rapids and attack Fort Malden by crossing the Detroit River on the thick ice. One wing of his force, Winchester's column of 1,300, had established itself at the rendezvous by the middle of the month.

At two o'clock in the morning of 19 January Colonel Procter was roused from his sleep in Sandwich by urgent tidings: the Americans were at the River Raisin, only thirty miles south of Detroit. Gradually, the picture cleared. Without waiting for Harrison, Winchester had advanced part of his force to Frenchtown, the small settlement on the north bank of the River Raisin, and expelled an inferior party of British militia and Indians, and he was bringing up reinforcements. Winchester's impatience offered Procter an opportunity to strike at a portion of the enemy's force before it could be supported, but he would have to be quick. For all the British commander knew, Harrison might already have been massing overwhelming strength at the River Raisin.

Procter was no Brock, but he made the right decision. Summoning all the disposable forces at his command, he crossed the ice and assembled his army at Brownstown. With commendable alacrity it was soon wading through the thick snow toward the Raisin: 597 British regulars and militia, six pieces of artillery, and 700 Indians under Roundhead. They were lucky. At daybreak of 22 January Procter and Roundhead found Winchester's troops on the north bank of the River Raisin, unprepared and vulnerable. The American general had brought up the bulk of his army, a little over 900 men, but they were dreadfully positioned. The river, coated in ice and snow, was behind them, while in front open ground furnished no shelter. Part of the army was camped behind pickets, which promised some protection from small-arms fire. But its right, which included the 300 regulars, was largely exposed. The men carried inadequate supplies of ammunition. The reserve ammunition was across the river with Winchester himself, who was sleeping nearly a mile behind his lines. No one had bothered to post sentinels on the only road along which the British and Indians could come.

Nevertheless, when the firing began the American marksmen took a fierce toll of the British in the enemy center. But the redcoat artillery blasted holes in the exposed American right while the Indians and militia operated on the flanks with none of the indecision that had been so damaging on the Fort Wayne expedition. Roundhead threw his warriors upon the weakened right flank, and it fell back across the frozen river. It was at this point that Winchester himself arrived, his uniform hurriedly pulled over a nightshirt. He ordered his battered right to re-form on the south bank of the river, and a few tried to do so, but nothing could prevent the wing from collapse.

Soon the men of Winchester's right were running for their lives, some throwing aside their guns as they floundered in the deep snow with the mounted Indians outflanking and closing in on them, shooting them down like deer or butchering exhausted survivors with tomahawks. Few more than 30 got back to the rapids; the rest of the right wing were either rounded up or left to lie stiff and dead in the bloodstained snow. Winchester himself was overtaken and, stripped to his nightshirt, brought to Roundhead. Procter persuaded him to surrender the remainder of his troops, who still defiantly held their ground behind the bruised pickets.

Procter had lost 24 British killed and 161 wounded, and with hundreds of American prisoners on his hands, he pulled out as fast as he could, fearful of being overwhelmed by American reinforcements. He had promised to protect his captives, but he left about 80 sick and wounded Americans behind in houses at Frenchtown, unguarded and waiting for sleds that were supposed to be coming to collect them the next day. Instead of the transport, 50 inebriated Indians ranged Frenchtown on 23 January, hauling injured men from houses and beating, shooting, and axing them, and burning buildings over the heads of disabled men cowering inside. Some of the broken bodies of the victims were tossed into the street to be torn by foraging hogs.

For the United States the battle was another disaster. A Kentucky historian estimated the total loss at 290 killed and 592 captured, casualties all the harder to bear as details of the massacre of the wounded became known. Fear and indignation washed over the frontier, and in Kentucky, whose sons had been sacrificed, the cry "Remember the Raisin!" became a clarion call for battle.

Yet to the Indians and British it was a striking victory over invaders, if a tarnished one. The battle, along with the deepening thaw and the imminent expiration of many of Harrison's enlistments, put an end to the plan for a winter attack on Fort Malden. A new secretary of war, John Armstrong, did not in any case favor it. Equally important, the battle invigorated the Indian allies, who were soon "flocking" into Amherstburg, reassured that with the help of the redcoats they could still defeat the Big Knives.[23]

When the winter snow receded, and Tecumseh returned to the Detroit, hope had returned to his heart.

25

✦══✦══✦

FIGHTING GROUNDHOGS

Henry Procter may have been promoted to the rank of brigadier-general for the battle of the River Raisin, but on 17 April 1813 he was feeling in great need of Tecumseh. A spell of warm weather had just banished the ice from the lake, and his small flotilla of six ships and two gunboats, chafing restlessly at their moorings at Amherstburg, and the bateaux drawn up on the nearby beach, were free to transport his little army to the mouth of the Maumee, the first stage of a journey to attack Fort Meigs, the enemy's new stronghold in Ohio. Procter had a force of 983 men ready for embarkation: 485 regulars, most of them from the 41st Regiment and the Canadian Royal Newfoundland Regiment; 30 Royal Artillerymen and a captain of Royal Engineers with a field train; 462 militia; and a small commissariat. Six hundred warriors under Round-head, serviced by the Indian Department, had been preparing themselves for weeks, exciting their martial ardor in dances and purifying themselves in sweat baths and ceremonies to win spiritual favor. Now they were ready to make their way to the Maumee overland, or by using canoes. They were all waiting, as Procter wrote that day, for "the cooperation of Tecumthe."[1]

It was Procter's misfortune to be compared with Isaac Brock, and to be found wanting. Little is known about him. No one troubled to paint his portrait, either in words or on canvas, and his command at Fort Malden has always seemed rather lackluster after Brock's brilliant campaign of the previous summer. An Anglo-Irishman of fifty years, Procter lacked important qualities. An army man for most of his life, he was nevertheless inexpe-

rienced on the battlefield, and although a respectable disciplinarian and ad-
ministrator, he needed leadership skills and the ability to create teamwork
and esprit de corps. He relied upon a cabal of followers, but failed to communicate with the army at large. He was on poor terms with the Indian Department, which he castigated as incompetent; the militia, whom he found
unreliable; the civil authorities at Detroit, whom he regarded as treason-
able; and even with some of his principal regular officers, including his new
second-in-command, Lieutenant-Colonel Augustus Warburton. Since his
failure to protect prisoners at the River Raisin, American newspapers had
raised him as an ogre.

Procter's difficulties were not always eased by his superiors, Sir George
Prevost, and Major-General Roger Sheaffe, who succeeded Brock to the
overall command of Upper Canada. Understandably, their priority was the
defense of the Canadas farther east. Procter was kept short of almost every
item of supply—not the least, men. It was in vain he appealed for an additional regiment to help him garrison the Detroit frontier and encourage his
Indian "arm." Sir George was happy to authorize the raising of a ranger
force—volunteers to support Tecumseh—but he continued to regard the Indians, not regulars, as the guardsmen of the west. In the winter he appointed Robert Dickson, the trader, to recruit a thousand Indians west of
Lake Michigan, and to place them at the disposal of Procter. Dickson's
progress was slow but sure, but in April his task was far from complete.[2]

Beset with problems and inadequacies he may have been, but Procter
had a grasp of the strategical situation in the west that was keener than
Prevost's. The Commander-in-Chief was talking about a strictly defensive
campaign on the Detroit, with attacks against American positions and
communications best left to Tecumseh and his people, but Procter understood that widespread Indian support required far more from the British
than that. The Indians expected the redcoats to demonstrate a real commitment to defeating the enemy. They wanted to see soldiers in the field.

The need to present himself as a credible ally was one reason why Procter, like Brock, favored taking the offensive. But he also knew that sitting
listlessly at home, allowing the United States to mass overpowering strength
against him, gave him no chance of survival. No, he had to strike, to disrupt
American mobilization before it rapped on his door. As he wrote on 17
April: "If I tamely permit the enemy to await his reinforcements and mature
his plans, he will become too formidable." Just as a judicious blow had
crushed Winchester and crippled Harrison's winter offensive, so Procter
now planned another reprieve, by attacking the enemy's new advanced base,
Fort Meigs, near the Maumee rapids. Once it was eliminated, the small
blockhouses to its rear, on the Maumee, Auglaize, and St. Marys, might also
be attacked.

The success of the stroke depended upon Indians, as none knew better than Procter. That was why he sat waiting for the six hundred men Tecumseh was bringing with him. But he also desperately needed the chief himself, not only for his skill in the field but also for his ability to manage what had always been a volatile and unpredictable force. In fact, in some ways Procter was a prisoner of his native allies. He was expected to discipline and control them, but because their support was so essential, he could not afford to antagonize them. At times he seemed almost afraid of the fearsome-looking fighting men who outnumbered his own troops. Tecumseh, though, was dependable. No one could doubt his dedication to overthrowing the Big Knives, and his influence over the Indians outmatched anyone else's. He spoke to the British for the Indians, but no less did he listen to them, and carry their views and plans to his fellows. He was an indispensable broker between the two sets of allies, and Procter needed him for the expedition.

Recent events had driven home the problems of managing the Indians. In September the Fort Wayne expedition had ended in fiasco when many tribesmen refused to fight. In October they were reluctant to scout toward the River Raisin until Roundhead turned out a small party. Two months later some Indians had broken away and massacred the American wounded at Frenchtown.

These problems were rooted in cultural differences, as the issue of prisoners illustrated. Indians were not invariably savage, as some whites supposed; indeed, captives often testified to chivalry and gentility. Unfortunately, unlike British officers the Indian leaders had few powers to curb the excesses of wilder warriors, and the rights of individual captors to dispose of prisoners as they wished were strongly established. Moreover, when engaged in protracted warfare Indians were inclined to view the sparing of prisoners as mere foolishness. They had no cages for military prisoners, nor the means to support them, and if they released captive soldiers it was only at the risk of meeting them in battle again. It made no sense, the Indians explained, to fight the enemy twice.

Perhaps the main reason for the killing of prisoners was the right of relatives of slain or wounded warriors to take their revenge. Many Indians considered that only by doing so could the spirits of the departed be pacified. As Procter informed Sheaffe, "it is almost impossible to save any prisoner . . . where the Indians have lost lives."[3] This system of retribution served an important function in societies which possessed little in the way of police or courts, for it deterred would-be offenders from injuring others. It acted as a primitive agency of social control. However, it also fed the potential for conflict between the British and their Indian allies, each interpreting the issue according to their own cultural inheritance.

Procter needed help to handle the Indians, but Elliott was old and Mc-

Kee broken in health. "The great defect in the Indian Department," he complained, "is the want of a leader of influence in the field." The agents did a respectable job of recruiting, supplying, and interpreting for the Indians, but they were not leaders. As preparations for his expedition matured, Procter found himself thinking even more about Tecumseh.[4]

The Shawnee chief's return to Amherstburg was delayed. Leaving his Kickapoos and Winnebagos on the Wabash to follow later, he eventually brought his Shawnee band—men, women, and children—forward in March, sending word ahead so that Elliott could deposit provisions at the River Raisin where Tecumseh had arranged to rendezvous with Potawatomis, Ojibwas, and Ottawas from across Michigan Territory. He was at the Raisin on 16 April, with eighty warriors, warning the local Frenchmen that they ought to enlist in Procter's forces, and then he took twelve followers across the Detroit the same day to talk to the British after an absence of seven months. Tecumseh asked for five more days to settle his noncombatants in the protective custody of the Great Father, and Procter consented to delay his campaign. As usual, the chief glowed with optimism. Before returning to the Raisin he gave out that he expected Fort Meigs to fall, but if it proved too hard a nut to crack he would lead the Indians against Fort Wayne. Always, he had a big heart.[5]

Procter was content. His reinforcements were assembling, and he had Tecumseh. Within hours of renewing his acquaintance with the Shawnee he wrote, "I shall risk an attack on him [Harrison] in a few days, especially as Tecumseth is at hand."[6] On 23 April he finally embarked his troops.

Tecumseh spent no more time than was necessary to attend to his old people, his women and children, and unite his fighting men with Roundhead's, and then he took the twelve hundred warriors around the lake to the mouth of the Maumee River, toward Fort Meigs. His brother the Prophet marched with him, but Tenskwatawa's influence was visibly diminishing and he played little part in the expedition.

On 26 April they arrived to find the redcoats already at work, shipping artillery and supplies up the Maumee on gunboats and bateaux, and disembarking the cramped soldiers on the northwestern bank. Four miles upstream, at Swan Creek, Procter outlined his plans to the Indians in a council the next morning. Captain Chambers had examined Fort Meigs, thirteen miles above. It was situated on a plateau on the southeastern side of the river (near present-day Perrysburg, Ohio) and stood about sixty feet above the water, but batteries could be erected on the opposite bank, which was slightly higher. All Tecumseh, the Indians, and the militia had to do was to watch the flanks and rear of the fort and let the redcoat artillery do the rest.

On the following day the allies established their main camp two and a half miles below Fort Meigs, but across the river, just behind the ruins of old Fort Miami. An unfortunate symbol of British perfidy, this dilapidated bastion, and Tecumseh's mind must have gone back to the summer day when as a young warrior he, with others of the defeated Indian confederacy, had fled here a step ahead of Wayne's legionaries, and been denied refuge by the British garrison. However, this was no time for useless reflection. Day and night the weather was incessantly wet and cold, and the allies set to work erecting bark shelters and leather tents and lit fires to dry damp clothes and shivering bodies.

That day a few Indians and British surveyed Fort Meigs from across the river, until a couple of the garrison's big eighteen-pounders cleared them away. Later, in the evening, the warriors arrived in force, slipped over the Maumee in boats, and filed around the fort, effectively opening the siege. They killed some hogs and bullocks, and brought a few horses from within range of the American guns. Some of these Indians had been seasoned in action, at Tippecanoe, Detroit, and the River Raisin, but for others this was the first opportunity to attack the Big Knives. Emotions ran particularly high because they knew that behind those powerful walls their enemies were led by a man widely regarded as a major author of their misfortunes: William Henry Harrison. There was an immense feeling of anticipation and grim satisfaction that their greatest adversary was about to be delivered up to them.

On the twenty-ninth, two hundred Britons and several oxen slipped and stumbled along a dirt road that the rain had converted into thick mud, dragging heavy guns up from their encampment. Tecumseh's men resumed their work. Clambering dexterously into every promising position from which they could yelp and fire into the garrison, they shot down the few stock that still foraged outside the walls. Harrison's soldiers had made a pretty thorough job of denuding the immediate vicinity of the fort of trees and brush, so the warriors had to fire over extreme ranges. Sometimes their musket balls splashed about the walls, wounding a few men, but most were spent before they reached their targets.

The allies soon learned that the Americans occupied a position of great strength. Had they assembled faster, and the lake been navigable earlier, they might have caught Fort Meigs seriously undermanned, because the enlistments of the Pennsylvanian and Virginian troops had expired and they had gone home. Since then Harrison had moved quickly to repair the damage. Ordered to remain on the defensive until the United States could build a naval squadron to take command of the lake, he had constructed Fort Meigs as an advanced base and was determined to hold it. Its garrison had been increased to twelve hundred men, half of them regulars and volunteers, and the rest militia from Ohio and Kentucky. Furthermore, additional forces under Brigadier-General Green Clay were coming from Kentucky to Harrison's relief.

The fortress itself was truly formidable. Harrison had been blessed in possessing the services of Captain Eleazor D. Wood, one of the earliest graduates of West Point, and arguably the greatest American hero of the siege. Wood was an engineer of skill and energy, and in Fort Meigs he had created a work of uncommon resilience. Scrutinizing it, Tecumseh would have seen a tall and robust timber picket, with seven two-story blockhouses, five raised batteries, and towers at each of several gateways, enclosing nine acres of ground. Its plan resembled a misshapen ellipse, four hundred yards long and half as wide, and to repel anyone who dared attempt the pickets it was skirted by ditches and in parts an abatis, or breastwork of stakes. The fort's powerful armament consisted of four eighteen-pounders, five twelve-pounders, four six-pounders, and five howitzers, the ammunition for which was securely lodged in two subterranean magazines.

Tecumseh put his faith in the British batteries, but Wood's resources were equal even to that threat. As soon as he ascertained the position of the enemy guns over the river, Wood had the garrison working in shifts. Masked from the eyes of the allies by a line of tents, they threw up an enormous mound of earth that ran like a gigantic worm the length of the interior. This traverse, as it was called, twenty feet wide and twelve feet high, was unveiled on 1 May. Wrote its creator:

> . . . orders were directly given for all the tents in front [of the mound] to be instantly struck and carried into the rear of the traverse. This was done in almost a moment, and that beautiful prospect of beating up our quarters, which but an instant before presented itself to the view of the eager and skilful [British] artillerists, had now entirely fled, and in its place suddenly appeared an immense shield of earth, obscuring from his sight every tent, every horse . . . and every creature belonging to the camp . . . Those canvas houses [tents], which in a great measure had covered the growth of the traverse, by keeping from the view of the enemy the operations about it, were now with their inhabitants in them entirely protected in their turn.[7]

Once the traverse had been completed the men dug recesses into the reverse side of it, away from the British batteries, and sheltered there during bombardments. The accommodation was muddy, inclement, and squalid, but at least it was proof against the cannonballs and shrapnel propelled from the enemy artillery. Tecumseh was both astonished and disgusted.

Why did these men not come out and fight man-to-man? To the Shawnee chief the sight of the Big Knives popping up from their boltholes and scattering back into them at the sound of gunfire resembled nothing so much as groundhogs flitting in and out of their burrows.

During the night of 30 April a gunboat stole up the river to open the British bombardment, but it was not until the day the traverse was revealed that the redcoats started firing from their principal batteries on the north bank—two twenty-four-pounders captured at Detroit, a mortar, a howitzer, and three twelve-pounders. This was what the Indians had been waiting for, and as the balls and shells screeched overhead they raised an exultant clamor, and redoubled their own small-arms fire upon the fort. For several days a brisk duel took place. Somewhat short of ammunition, the Americans stinted their fire, but directed a largely ineffective fusillade against the British and occasionally turned grape and canister shot toward the Indians and militia. Procter's artillery was busier. One American diarist counted 1,649 discharges from the morning of the first to the fifth of May.

Tecumseh and Roundhead were soon wondering whether the redcoats knew their business. Their only artillery officer, indeed, fell ill early during the siege, but it was Wood's traverse and earth-covered magazines and buildings that were the main obstacles to progress. The British cannon fire, some of it hot shot projected by the nine-pounders, sank ignominiously into the sodden earth and clay, hissing and smoking, or scattering dirt over nearby workmen, while a few of the shells detonated in midair and most of the others extinguished themselves as they plowed angrily but futilely into the soft mud. The roof of the main magazine was damaged, the blockhouses and storerooms were stoved and opened to the rain, and a few soldiers were killed, but it was obvious to everyone that the British bombardment was failing.

By 3 May Tecumseh and other chiefs were being openly critical of the performance of their allies, and the British opened fire from additional guns on the south bank of the river, only three hundred yards east of the fort, on the brink of a small ravine formed by a creek. Three guns were thus deployed, hurling shot and shell at Fort Meigs from a different direction, but the ubiquitous Wood was as quickly in action, shielding the defenders with new traverses and littering the interior of the post with a network of mounds like some great subterranean mole. As one American boasted to his family, "There is not a stronger place of defense in the states than this is at this time."[8]

Then, in the small hours of 5 May, there came a sudden and dramatic change of emphasis. Some miles above the besieged fort, the rapids of the Maumee flashed like silver over a rocky bed and around picturesque islands just then ripening into a fresh green. The turbulent stretch of water was negotiable by shallow-draft vessels, and that morning eighteen flat-bottomed boats were swept down the rapids by a current sharpened by the spring thaw and the heavy rain. Those boats carried fourteen hundred Kentucky troops under Brigadier-General Green Clay, the relief force Harrison had been waiting for.[9]

Their arrival upset the numerical superiority Tecumseh and Procter had been enjoying at Fort Meigs. There were now more soldiers defending the fort than besieging it. Furthermore, Harrison planned to exploit his advantage. Communicating with his reinforcements by intrepid couriers prepared to pierce Indian lines, he had coordinated a plan to destroy the British batteries on the north side of the river. It was a risky maneuver, involving the temporary isolation of one of Clay's two regiments, but entirely feasible. The first twelve boats, containing over eight hundred men under Colonel William Dudley, were to land opposite Fort Meigs and spike the British guns before joining their companions in the fort.

Tecumseh seems to have been on the south bank of the river that morning, with most of the Indians and militia, preparing to renew their attacks upon the fort. Neither he, nor anyone else, was ready for Clay's sudden dash down the Maumee, and it took them by surprise. Dudley disembarked his men on the north bank according to the plan, and without opposition. The landing of Clay and the rest of the reinforcements on the south bank proved to be trickier, but after a struggle with wind and current the Kentuckians eventually got ashore above the fort in two parties. Apparently Tecumseh was on the opposite side of Fort Meigs, below it, but even in that case he would have been alerted by the firing to the south and west as Clay's men cut their way to the garrison, would have heard the crash of the covering fire spat out by Harrison's artillery, the yell of the soldiers who sallied from the fort to drive the Indians back, and the furious cries of his own warriors as they tried to fall upon the Americans as they withdrew back into the fort.

Barely had the fighting ended above the fort than Harrison launched another sortie, but against the smaller British batteries a few hundred yards below. Taking advantage of the distractions above and across the river, Colonel John Miller and 350 regulars, volunteers, and militia gamely slipped from the fort and passed along a small ravine to surprise the British guns. They captured 41 redcoats, drove others away with their attendant Indians and militia, and spiked the artillery. As soon as he realized what was happening, Tecumseh vigorously counterattacked with a party of Indians, recovering the guns and almost outflanking and encircling one of the American militia companies. Miller's regulars made a spirited charge to extricate the endangered wing, and the force regained the fort, but 30 men were dead and 90 wounded.[10]

Harrison had wanted to synchronize the attacks on the batteries on both sides of the river, but Tecumseh's action with Miller closed about ten forty-five, while the forces across the Maumee, on the north bank, were still engaged.[11]

After quitting their boats Dudley's men had formed into three columns and marched two miles downstream, over an open plain and up a hill toward the main British artillery. Dudley had thirty scouts spread out into the woods on the left as flankers, seven of them friendly Shawnees from Black Hoof's band. The going on the miry ground was hard, but the Kentuckians reached their destination and raising a ferocious whoop rushed forward to scatter the weak opposition. They brought down the British colors and tried to spike the guns, although they used ramrods instead of handspikes, and the weapons were only temporarily disabled.

Having accomplished this much, Dudley should have retreated as he had been ordered, but some of the troops came under fire from Indians to the left and stormed enthusiastically into the forest after them. Their jubilation was not long-lived, for there were no better bush-fighters than the warriors of Tecumseh, and they cunningly led the Kentuckians on, fleeing before charges, only to halt and renew their fire every time the whites hesitated. Gradually Dudley's men were drawn deeper and deeper into the rain-soaked timber, closer to the main allied camp downriver. Then, as the Indians' numbers increased, they turned upon their pursuers, closing in, firing, and rushing upon the fallen with tomahawks and scalping knives. They were indeed an intimidating sight, as one American recalled, "painted with most every color, their heads tipped off with bird wings, huge bunches of feathers, and skins of animals . . . their faces being blacked as black as coal and grease could make them, the upper and lower lips . . . marked with white stripes." Some of the Kentuckians were paralyzed with fear. According to their Shawnee scouts, "The men stood as if they could not help themselves, and got shot down very fast."[12]

Finding themselves being cut down one by one, Dudley's men broke and fled in total disorder, back toward the batteries they had just so effortlessly captured. As the terrified soldiers tried to save themselves it was almost every man for himself, but even in such extremities there were some who bravely struggled to assist fallen comrades. George Carter Dale hid a man with a broken leg under some wood, but as he fled he saw pursuing Indians pulling the wretched fellow from his hiding place and tomahawking him. Unencumbered by his musket, which he had mislaid, Dale fled past a mangled, stripped, and scalped Kentuckian, and then came upon another wounded soldier, who handed him his own gun and told him to run for his life as he knew that he himself was finished. With their blood up, some of the pursuing Indians were pitiless. One soldier, disabled and scalped, lay still alive "in a miserable plight . . . begging for water" until other warriors came along and finished him off.[13]

While Dudley's men took a beating in the woods, they also faced a determined British counterattack to recapture the batteries. News of the fall of the batteries had gone downstream to the British headquarters, and a band of solemn redcoats was soon tramping toward the guns, the mud sometimes sloshing up to their knees, and the rain incessantly sluicing down their faces. Among them were some brave officers: Muir, Captain Chambers, Lieutenant Bullock (who had left his tent despite the wound he had received over the left eye a day or so before), and Lieutenant John Le Breton of the Royal Newfoundland Regiment. As they approached the batteries, Chambers threw away his sword and took a musket from a dead soldier. Calling upon his men to follow he charged the Americans with his bayonet, and after a brief struggle the British regained possession.

The battle raging on the north bank soon attracted the notice of Tecumseh across the river. In fact according to a story later given by a British officer present,

> when Col. Dudley landed his troops, Tecumsey . . . was on the south side of the river, annoying the American garrison with his Indians . . . During this time Harrison had sent out a detachment to engage Tecumsey and did continue with him a considerable length of time, when Tecumsey was informed of what was doing on the opposite side and he immediately retreated, swam the river, and fell in the rear of Dudley and attacked him with great fury. Being thus surrounded and their commander [Dudley] killed the troops marched up to the British line [and] surrendered.[14]

This account did less than justice to the allies north of the river who had originally defeated Dudley, but there was probably some truth in it. Leslie Combs, one of Dudley's flankers, described the same movement in his first full account of the battle, written in 1815: "The enemy was during this time receiving large reinforcements from the other side of the river, which enabled him now nearly to surround us." In one of many subsequent statements Combs was called upon to make he declared that Tecumseh "had fallen upon our rear and we were compelled to surrender." A sixteen-year-old volunteer with Dudley, Thomas Christian, also recalled that the difficulties on the north bank "gave that portion of the enemy upon the opposite side of the river ample time to cross over in our rear, completely hemming us in upon every side. Our case was then hopeless."[15]

One of the military advantages possessed by Indians was their flexibility in battle. They were opportunistic, willing to attack or retreat according to

circumstance, with none of the restrictions rigid command structures imposed upon spontaneity. British regulars on the south bank also crossed to
attack Dudley, but unlike their red brothers they had to await orders and
they moved ponderously. Shadrach Byfield, a member of the 41st who had
helped the Indians repulse Miller, remembered his corps being marched to
the boats and crossing in time to see the closing phases of Dudley's defeat.[16]

Only a few of the unfortunate Kentuckians escaped. About twenty fled
back upriver, and rather more fought their way to the boats and made it to
the fort. From Fort Meigs their countrymen watched helplessly as the others were surrounded. As an old man John Plummer used to tell how he saw
an Indian on a gray horse chasing Americans into the river. Two of the soldiers, carrying a wounded man between them, got under the bank near the
boats, and the Indian wheeled his horse and was followed by his warriors
into the woods. Of course, as John told it, the Indian was Tecumseh![17]

Dudley was killed, and most of his men struggled to survive. Some
tossed down their guns, finding that they obstructed flight or that the wet
weather had made them useless. Most searched for British soldiers to
whom they hoped they could surrender in safety. Three Americans gave
themselves up to one redcoat. Parties of Kentuckians, many without officers
and the different military companies inextricably mixed together, floundered to the batteries to surrender.

The action ended about noon, after nearly three hours. It had been fruit-
ful for the Indians, more to their taste than the weary siege work of the past
days. South of the river they had inflicted large casualties, and north of it
they had been instrumental in annihilating Dudley's regiment. The hundreds of prisoners, many wounded, testified to their triumph.

Collecting as many prisoners as they could, the British sent them downriver with a fifty-man guard, to the old fort which was to become a temporary enclosure. Many of the Indians fell to pillaging captured boats, making
off with boxes and trunks and gleefully pulling from the baggage shirts, uniforms, and boots, which they busied themselves sampling. Others painted
and dried fresh scalps and stretched them over small hoops or suspended
them from poles.

Tecumseh and Elliott delayed about the battlefield, perhaps trying to
persuade more jubilant warriors to part with captives, but suddenly an urgent message was brought from the British officers at old Fort Miami below.
They needed help, and quickly. A large number of Indians had gathered
about the old fort and they had begun to massacre the prisoners.

Perhaps more than any other incident in Tecumseh's life this one lingered in the memory. "Never did Tecumseh shine more truly than on this oc-

casion," recalled John Richardson. "Ever merciful and magnanimous as he was ardent and courageous, the voice of the supplicant seldom reached him in vain."[18]

It is fair to suggest, however, that more than humanity impelled Tecumseh toward Fort Miami after he received the urgent summons for help. The Indians depended upon the British to win back their lands, if not in war then through negotiations. They had to be useful to the redcoats, and to engender a sense of obligation. They must win British respect. As Tecumseh and Elliott rode down the muddy track to the crumbling fort where the prisoners were being lodged, the Shawnee chief was probably aware that it was his cause and the Indians themselves who were on trial.

The trouble had started early. On their march to the fort the prisoners had been pestered by impudent warriors and divested of possessions such as money and watches and much of their clothing. An Indian with red and black circles painted around his eyes rode by young Leslie Combs and snatched his hat, shortly before another warrior, on foot, roughly peeled the coat from his back despite the prisoner's bandaged shoulder. Hunting shirts, waistcoats, cravats—almost any attractive item was taken, and to insult some Indians added blows, whipping stumbling Americans with sticks or ramrods.

Ahead lay the entrance to the derelict British fort, passing over a ditch to an interior enclosed by fallen walls only three or four feet high. A mere shell, this bastion that had once halted Wayne's army now looked more like a large pen. As the prisoners were shepherded toward the remains of the gateway they saw two ominous lines of Indians waiting for them, war clubs, tomahawks, ramrods, and pistols and muskets in their hands. The Indians lined both sides of the path leading into the fort for a distance of perhaps fifty feet. The running of the gauntlet was a traditional Indian way of receiving prisoners, not in itself always intended to be a means of killing them, but certainly a serious threat to weak or injured men.

Combs claimed that the dead bodies of ten or twelve naked and scalped captives were scattered nearby. As he approached the gauntlet, "a man who was walking behind stepped before me. Just as he entered the defile an Indian put a pistol to his back and fired. He fell. I ran through without being touched." Another prisoner, Joseph Underwood, darted between the flailing lines of jeering warriors and received nothing more than occasional blows from ramrods across his shoulders, but the captive before him was shot dead, and Underwood and others behind fell sprawling across his body. In making his run, George Dale saw one of his companions struck to his knees by a war club.[19]

Inside the fort, the British hoped to protect the prisoners. They posted guards on the gateway while the weary Kentuckians slumped down, some with the heads of wounded men resting upon their laps. Precious but uneasy moments of peace followed, punctuated by occasional shots outside and the cries of the warriors insulting new arrivals, but once all the prisoners had been brought in some Indians pushed the guards aside and rushed into the enclosure while others clambered over the fallen walls. Sensing what was going to happen some of the redcoats cried, "Oh! *Nichee wah!*" (Oh! Brother, desist!). But the Indians were in an ugly mood. When one aged British regular tried to protect the Americans, an Indian callously shot him dead.

A worthless Ojibwa warrior, variously identified as Split Nose or Normee, was said to have been the principal instigator of the murders. It was believed he had missed the battle, and wanted an easy way to secure scalps. Perhaps it was he who was the fearsome figure, painted black, who mounted the wall, pointed his musket at a prisoner, and killed him. The warrior then calmly reloaded his piece and shot two more before laying the gun aside and jumping down with an axe in his hand. As the blade fell upon a fourth victim, and the Indian ripped off the scalps, horrified prisoners crawled over each other to escape. The numerous assemblage of warriors raised a chilling war whoop and readied their weapons. "What were our feelings at this moment?" Combs later wrote to General Clay. "He who has never realised cannot imagine. A description is impossible. Without any means of defense or possibility of escape, death in all the horror of savage cruelty seemed to stare us in the face."[20]

Two men rode into the garrison, one an Indian in fringed deerskin and with an elegant sword, the other an aging white man whose severe features were set beneath gray hair. Tecumseh dismounted quickly, appalled by the scene before him. Combs, who stood nearby expecting the worst, saw the "noble looking chief" stride "hastily into the midst of the savages." He sprang lightly upon "the high point of the wall," where he could be seen by the whole throng, and "made a brief and emphatic address," Combs wrote. "I could not understand his language, but his gestures and manner satisfied me that he was on the side of mercy." Matthew Elliott added his authority to the proceedings, and waved his sword. Many, perhaps most, of the angry Indians were Ojibwas and Potawatomis, who had little comprehension of Tecumseh's words, but they knew that graceful figure before them, and they could not mistake his anger. Gradually they dispersed.

Another witness, the prisoner Dale, also wrote of Tecumseh's intercession. An Indian rode up, he said, with "a very mast[erful] appearance." During his harangue he pointed to the flags that were beginning to pass between Captain Chambers and Fort Meigs as the British attempted an exchange of prisoners, and some of the Indians made off, thinking the fort was about to surrender. "Some s[aid] it was Tecumseh . . . ," recollected Dale, "but who he was I knew not, but he was the only man that acted like a gentleman, as an officer."[21]

Tecumseh's saving of the prisoners, when British efforts had failed, went unrecorded in the official dispatches which the commanders wrote about the battle, but when the prisoners were eventually paroled and returned to their homes they spoke gratefully about what he had done. In time the story grew and changed, as legends do, and the boundaries between fact and fiction became almost undistinguishable. Captain William Sebree, who was in Fort Meigs, heard at the time that Tecumseh had drawn his sword and declared that it was a disgrace to kill a defenseless prisoner. Another in the fort, Anthony Shane, offered a similar tradition, but some converted the sword into a tomahawk and said that Tecumseh had used it to dare anyone to touch another prisoner.[22] Not a few lapsed into romance. They told how the Shawnee chief had buried his hatchet in the head of one or two Indians—an act which would, had it occurred, have opened Tecumseh to legitimate retaliation.[23]

The most lovingly repeated story was that after halting the massacre the infuriated chief turned on Procter, condemning him for allowing it to occur. One of Procter's soldiers, captured the following fall, is supposed to have said that the general actually watched one of the prisoners being killed, and that Tecumseh angrily rebuked him with the words, "I conquer to save, and you to murder!" The unnamed British officer who narrated Tecumseh's entrapment of Dudley also included an account. According to this version the Shawnee chief was almost in tears when he halted the slaughter. Pushing two Indians from their intended victims, and daring any of the "hundreds that surrounded him" to interfere again, he exclaimed in anguish, "Oh! What will become of my Indians?" Then he turned on the British commander, who protested that the Indians were uncontrollable. "Begone!" retorted Tecumseh. "You are unfit to command. Go and put on petticoats!"[24]

Whether there is any truth to these stories no one can say. Certainly the murders were embarrassing to Procter, whose name was already infamy in the United States because of the River Raisin massacre. A substantial number of captives perished at the fort. One prisoner saw twelve to fourteen men shot down, and Combs offered a similar figure. Harrison believed about forty prisoners died. In light of the number of captives afterward counted by the British and the bodies recovered by the Americans after the siege, forty would seem to have been a considerable exaggeration. Nevertheless, a tragedy occurred, and Procter ducked it entirely in his dispatch. It took Chambers to admit more frankly that a "dreadful slaughter" had taken place. Even after Tecumseh's intercession, when the prisoners were being counted and packed into boats for removal downriver, some Indians pulled out likely-looking youths for adoption in the native villages.[25]

Tecumseh's defense of the American prisoners became a cornerstone of his legend, the ultimate proof of his inherent nobility; but his clemency to another group of captives, one that appeared on no one's roster of battle losses, has been forgotten.

When Elliott drew his attention to them, about the evening of 7 May, Tecumseh recognized the four men immediately. Big Jim, the Soldier, and the two Perry brothers were Ohio Shawnees, caught in the service of the enemy. They had suffered accordingly. The Wyandots, no less than the Shawnees, had some of their people in Ohio, within the American lines, but they regarded them as prisoners and were even then prompting Procter to offer captured American militiamen in exchange for their release. These four Shawnees were different. They had marched with the Big Knives.

When Tecumseh saw the Shawnee prisoners, the Wyandots had stripped and beaten them, and torn hair from every part of their bodies. Walk-in-the-Water, normally a mild-mannered man, had belabored them about their heads with a ramrod. "We made a great whooping every time to show him we were not afraid of death," the Shawnees boasted later. In fact, Big Jim was miserably contrite, and complained that he was no warrior and should have remained home with the women, but William Perry mocked his captors defiantly and singled himself out for particularly hard treatment. The limbs of all four were blue and cramped through being bound for several days, and the men were still tied against posts in a camp near the old fort and suffering regular abuse when Tecumseh appeared.

"Tecumsey came to us," the prisoners reported, "and shook hands with us, and told the Wyandotts, Pottowotomies, and others to let us alone." Upon receiving their word that they would not escape, he had them untied, and promised that as soon as he could get up a council to frame a message to Black Hoof's people he would send them home with it. In the meantime Tecumseh's two friends, the Blue-Jacket brothers, took the prisoners under their protection to ensure their safety.[26]

The battle of 5 May ended action at Fort Meigs. Most of the Indians rushed home to celebrate their victory in the customary fashion, and a day or so after the battle less than twenty Indians remained with Tecumseh to prosecute the siege. The militia also disappeared. The expedition had prevented them from sowing their spring wheat, and they insisted on returning to their farms so that their corn, at least, would be planted. Procter and Tecumseh had no choice but to abandon the siege, and on 9 May the redcoats loaded their guns on boats while Tecumseh led his entourage on its two-day journey back to his base at the River Raisin.

The siege had cost the British 14 killed, 41 taken prisoner, and 47 wounded, but the Indian loss, which was probably higher, went unrecorded. Harrison sustained nearly 1,000 casualties in all: some 135 killed, over 630 taken prisoner, and 188 others wounded. In Kentucky another army was mourned, but on the frontier, as Daniel Cushing wrote from Fort Meigs, "The sight of dead men has become no more terrifying than the sight of dead flies on a summer day."[27]

Fort Meigs, with its network of earthen mounds, still stood defiant— overcrowded, disease-ridden, and ill-provisioned, but utterly beyond imme- diate conquest. It seemed that neither side was able to stage a successful offensive.

The Indians were not displeased, however. The redcoat artillery had failed, but they had been primarily responsible for the destruction of Dud- ley's command and the heavy casualties Harrison had suffered on the south bank. Procter praised their "courage and activity," and couriers from the army took their own accounts of the battle eastward. The British high com- mand rejoiced in "Tecumseth's success" and ventured that it would counter- act the effect on morale produced by the raid upon York in April.[28]

Tecumseh had lost none of his own confidence. He talked about how the British had promised to return to Fort Meigs, and how if it was captured he would demand that Harrison be discharged into his hands. He regretted fighting Indians, though, and at the River Raisin released the Shawnee pris- oners with a conciliatory message praying that the chiefs of Wapakoneta would not think hard of him or his followers for meeting their warriors in battle. Two men, one of them Jim Blue-Jacket, escorted the captives home about 14 May.

By the account of the humbled scouts, Tecumseh's hopes for spreading the revolt rode as high as ever. "It was eight years since he was working to fix this war," Tecumseh had told them, "and that he had every thing accom- plished, and that all the nations from the north were standing at his word."

26

AN ADEQUATE SACRIFICE

TO INDIAN OPINION

T he months that followed the siege of Fort Meigs saw Tecumseh
at the peak of his reputation. Indians would not always abide by
his counsel, but they believed him truly blessed by the spirits—
they believed that he had exceptional supernatural power. Knowing less
about the process of negotiation that went on between Tecumseh and his
fellows, the British tended to make him a superman. Among the soldiers
fighting grimly to hold the Niagara frontier that summer Charles Askin
wrote, "I wish we had Tecumseh here to help us out of our difficulties."[1]

On the other hand, the Prophet's influence had receded, and Tecumseh
publicly dismissed Tenskwatawa as his "foolish brother." Since the outbreak
of the war he had made less use of him. Before, the Prophet's professed
sway with the Creator had been the greatest encouragement Tecumseh
could offer Indians to join him; but once the redcoats went to war, with
promises that rode on the backs of significant military victories, it was they
who increasingly became the most effective inducement, at least in the
north. The Prophet figured little in the records of the war, and the British
found him of limited utility. He hovered in the background, behind his
brother, helping where he could.

In the summer of 1813 the armies on both sides paused to draw breath
while the naval forces contended for control of Lake Erie, and British officers had greater opportunities to observe their legendary ally.

Some were surprised. Yes, Tecumseh fought painted like his fellows, and
there were times when he was formidably forceful, as for example when he

upbraided a member of the Indian Department who had abused his wife. More often his features wore a pleasant expression, though his eyes, it was said, were "full of fire and intelligence." Far from being uncouth or ferocious, as some expected, he "readily and cheerfully accommodated himself to all the novelties of his situation, and seemed amused, without being at all embarrassed by them."[2]

He was generally accompanied by one member or another of the Indian Department, who interpreted for him, because he had few words of English. Once when he encountered General Procter on an Amherstburg sidewalk they had to exchange greetings and leave together to find an interpreter.[3]

Often Tecumseh joined Colonel Elliott for dinner at Procter's table, mixing easily with both male and female company, including the general's wife, daughters, and son. His behavior on such occasions was impeccable, although it was noticed that he invariably declined spirits, observing that he had suffered by them in earlier days and now confined himself to water. Boucherville remembered one of these banquets, which he said was hosted by Jacques Baby. "Tecumseh was seated at my left with his pistols on either side of his plate and his big hunting knife in front of him," said Boucherville. "He wore a red cloak, trousers [leggings] of deerskin, and a printed calico shirt, the whole outfit a present from the English. His bearing was irreproachable for a man of the woods as he was, much better than that of some so-called gentlemen."[4]

General Procter, at least in public, never spoke of Tecumseh other than with respect. This is worth emphasizing, because legend always portrayed the two as enemies—Tecumseh noble and brave, scarcely disguising the contempt he felt for the cowardly and vicious Procter. Several nineteenth-century stories, for example, related how Tecumseh stood up to Procter on behalf of the civilian population of Michigan Territory. Undoubtedly there were constant apprehensions, among both Indians and British, that some inhabitants were acting as fifth columnists, supplying the American forces with information. Procter's solution had been to declare martial law, administer oaths of allegiance or neutrality, order some suspects out of the territory, and ship others east for investigation. Whether justified or not, these policies hardly endeared the General to many civilians, and some, it was said, turned to Tecumseh for assistance.

The Shawnee chief was noted for magnanimity, and it is not unlikely that he would have been moved by stories of hardship brought to him on behalf of those imprisoned or banished. It is known, for instance, that he protected one of the residents of the River Raisin from being driven out, perhaps Jacques ("Coco") Lasselle, a French son-in-law of the celebrated Blue Jacket. Another who remembered his charity, it is said, was Father Gabriel Richard of Ste. Anne's Church, Detroit, a Frenchman locally re-

spected for his efforts to educate Indians and poor whites. In 1823 Richard
was elected territorial delegate to Congress, and received a letter of introduction from his friend William Woodbridge to Henry Clay. Woodbridge
testified that Procter had imprisoned Richard for urging the people of Detroit to remain loyal to the United States, and that he owed his liberty to the
chivalrous intervention of Tecumseh.

Versions of these and other stories were embellished to accentuate the
conflict between Procter and Tecumseh, but there is no real evidence that
they generated tension between the two. Indians understood the dangers
posed by the flow of intelligence to their foes, and were themselves quick to
suppress it. In January 1813 Procter had two men suspected of helping the
enemy arrested on Roundhead's entreaty, and Tecumseh himself was said to
have persuaded the general to ship a man named John Kinzie to Quebec in
irons for the same reason.[5]

As far as the record shows, the relationship between Tecumseh and
Procter did deteriorate, but not until the summer of 1813, when they disagreed about strategical priorities. The roots of their dispute are easily understood. Returning from the Maumee, Tecumseh began establishing his
people in a new home. The British had suggested the Indians quarter themselves in Michigan Territory, between the Raisin and Detroit. Such settlements would block an American advance upon Detroit or Fort Malden, and
ease the rationing problem that was straining the British commissariat to
breaking point. To a large extent, the Indians would live off the country west
of the Detroit River and Lake Erie. Perhaps it was also hinted that if Britain
forced the United States to yield territory in the war some of the Indians
might make a permanent home in the area.

The proposal was no sooner put than Tecumseh had new villages in the
making. His own followers settled on the lower Huron River, convenient for
his trips to Amherstburg; a force of Potawatomis, including, no doubt, some
driven from their homes on the Elkhart and St. Joseph, established themselves upon the same river, but twenty miles farther upstream; and a little
north an Ottawa town was built upon the River Rouge. To serve the new
communities the Indian Department was ordered to base some staff in Detroit.[6]

These new locations were important because they conditioned Indian
thinking about the conduct of the war. Although they were useful forward
bases from which to strike at American forces in Ohio, the new towns were
by the same token vulnerable to enemy attack. Fort Meigs was only forty
miles away, and mounted American detachments were penetrating as far as
the River Raisin. Further concerned that the French inhabitants on the
Raisin were broadcasting details of Indian movements, Tecumseh and other
chiefs worried that if they left to campaign afield, enemies from Fort Meigs

or elsewhere could attack their undefended villages. As far as they were concerned, large-scale Indian attacks on American positions as far east as Sandusky were out of the question unless Fort Meigs was eliminated first.[7]

So much for the Indians—but what about Procter? He had achieved little against Fort Meigs, and saw no point in a second expedition to that post. In his view the threats to his naval command of Lake Erie and his supply system were far more important. Two lines of communication supplied Amherstburg, a relatively impracticable route by way of the River Thames, and the passage along the Great Lakes and the St. Lawrence. Everything, Procter believed, depended upon keeping those lines open. His command, which the British had begun to call the Right Division, contained over ten thousand Indian dependents—men, women, and children—and imposed a burden that far outmatched local resources. Shortages in food, clothes, arms, ammunition, and equipment were already serious. "We have scarcely the means of constructing even a blockhouse," grumbled Procter.[8] If his communications were cut, his position would become untenable.

In the spring and summer the United States almost severed Procter's main supply line by furious attacks upon the British Center Division, which held on to Lake Ontario and the Niagara frontier by its fingertips. An American naval squadron gained temporary control of the lake, and York was taken, while an assault across the Niagara River gave the American army a foothold in Upper Canada. The British fought back, pinning the invading forces against the Niagara and striking across the lake at the American naval base at Sackett's Harbor, but the campaign played havoc with Procter's communications. Stores intended for Fort Malden were destroyed in American attacks, and under severe pressure the Center Division itself was constantly sequestering men and materials that were supposed to be moving forward to Procter. The General fretted and fumed. Always an irritable man, he became increasingly embittered by the tardy support given his enterprises.

Most dangerous of all, in Procter's eyes, was the threat to his naval superiority on Lake Erie. At Presque Isle (Erie, Pennsylvania) an American squadron was in the making, driven to completion by a young man of determination, energy, and daring, Commodore Oliver Hazard Perry. At his service were the superior resources of Ohio, Pennsylvania, and New York, and greater manpower. The position was desperate, for if Perry was allowed to command the lake, more than Procter's supplies would be at risk. By landing troops in Procter's rear, the Americans could surround the Right Division and its Indian allies.

For the moment the weak British squadron on Lake Erie remained in control, but it was in a deplorable condition: its prime warship, the *Detroit*, was just being completed, but the deficiency in naval ordnance had to be remedied by stripping the army of important field pieces, and there was a dearth of professional seamen. When acting commodore Robert Heriot Barclay arrived at Amherstburg to command Britain's naval squadron in June he brought only twenty-three seamen and a surgeon with him. He pestered for more, but got only an additional forty-one before he was finally forced to do battle.

Officially Barclay was a mere lieutenant, but he was brave and competent. The most obvious mark of his battle experience was the empty left sleeve of his uniform, the result of a fight with the French five years before, and Tecumseh called him "Our Father With One Arm." Certainly he grasped the essentials, and after reconnoitering Presque Isle on 16 June he urged his superiors, and Procter, to destroy the American squadron while it was still in its shell. To do this Barclay needed men. Procter had already been promised another battalion of the 41st Regiment of Foot, which he hoped would enable him to dispense with his militia, and he agreed to use his reinforced regulars to attack Presque Isle. The plan was sound, even necessary. The trouble was that Tecumseh and his Indians had a poor grasp of naval warfare, and they clamored for an attack on Fort Meigs instead. They wanted to eliminate the threat to their families. Both Indians and redcoats had their own ideas about how the war should progress. Both were right, given their preoccupations, but they clashed with each other.

Henry Procter's papers portray a different man from most published histories of the War of 1812. At this stage he understood what he ought to have been doing, better than some superiors: he knew that a strong offensive was needed to maintain Indian confidence, something Prevost barely appreciated; he had campaigned for resources in letter after letter, and since the previous winter had advertised the danger to his command of Lake Erie; he stubbornly refused to admit the possibility of retreating from Fort Malden, and resented a new commander of the Center Division telling him that it might become necessary; and he championed the inclusion of the Indians in the peace. In some respects he should have been a good partner to Tecumseh, yet after the expedition to Fort Meigs the two drifted apart.

A more effective leader than Procter might have reconciled the Indian and British views, but he was a poor communicator. In fact, his officers were divided, irrespective of rank, between those who did and those who did not enjoy the General's confidence. Inferior officers friendly with Procter found themselves better informed than superiors. Procter's bad relationships with the Indian Department, which had not been improved during the operation at Fort Meigs, also hindered communication with the Indians. Tecumseh was often in Elliott's company, and probably imbibed some of his

friend's negative feelings toward Procter, and because Elliott sympathized
with the Indians rather than the general he was inclined to take their side
rather than to search for a middle way.

About the middle of June a council at Fort Malden brought the argument into the open. Robert Reynolds, a resident of Amherstburg, gave what
may have been an account of this council in his old age. He remembered
Tecumseh making a cool, carefully worded speech, in support of a renewal
of the attack on Fort Meigs. If necessary, the chief said, the British should
give the Indians spades and they would dig their way into the fort. When he
had finished speaking, Tecumseh sat on the ground, as was his custom, and
began filling his tomahawk-pipe.

When Procter spoke he rounded on the Indian Department. According
to Reynolds, Elliott rose in fury and both he and the General put their hands
on their swords. Tecumseh rose slowly, shaking the tobacco from his pipe.
"What does he say?" he inquired of Elliott.

"Sit down," replied the old Irishman, placing a hand on Tecumseh's arm,
but still bristling. "Never mind what he says."[9]

Although no official record of the council survives, terse references al-
lude to it. Procter agreed to return to Fort Meigs, but his militia had gone
home and he explained that it was necessary to await the arrival of the second battalion of the 41st. Tecumseh would muster his warriors about
Brownstown and leave in a few days, and the troops would follow as soon
as they had been reinforced.[10]

Procter was disgruntled. He considered Fort Stephenson, a smaller post
on the Sandusky, to be a better target because its fall would have interrupted enemy communications between the Maumee and Cleveland, and it
was much less formidable than Fort Meigs. About this time, too, Barclay
began impressing upon him that the real priority was Presque Isle and the
maturing squadron of ships Perry was assembling there. Procter procras-
tinated. His reinforcements were not coming through, he explained with
justification, and blamed the difficulties in the Center Division.

The Indians had to content themselves with sending small groups to
watch and annoy Fort Meigs. On 2 July one such war party killed or captured all but two of a sixteen- or eighteen-man detail a few miles above the
fort, and evidently it also destroyed some supplies left at the head of the
rapids for the garrison.[11]

In July thunderous gun salutes in both Detroit and Sandwich signaled
the arrival of fifty bark canoes, sliding into the river from Lake St. Clair, carrying flags and hundreds of decorated warriors. The newcomers raised their
muskets, discharged them in acknowledgment, and then passed down to
Fort Malden. A tall, burly Scot with flaming red hair and a beard was with
them. Robert Dickson, the Red Head, sent to mobilize the Indians of the

northwest, had been true to his word. In all he had now forwarded about fourteen hundred warriors to Amherstburg. Some of Dickson's recruits, such as the Ojibwas, had been distant toward Tecumseh in the past, but most of the Sioux, and the Menominees, Potawatomis, and Winnebagos, had been interested in his confederacy before the war. The Sioux included Mdewakantons under Little Crow and Itasappa (nephew of Wapahasha, the principal chief) and a few Yanktonais and Sissetons under chiefs such as Red Thunder. On the other hand, Dickson won no adherents from those groups that had rejected Tecumseh—the Missouri Shawnees and Delawares and the Osages—nor did he, any more than the Shawnee chief, succeed in rallying all the Sacs. In short, Dickson had brought many warriors to the Detroit, but partly by reaping where Tecumseh and Main Poc had sowed.

The Indians Tecumseh had left on the Wabash in March also found their way to Fort Malden, and Main Poc himself returned. The previous fall he had gone to Illinois Territory to recruit from his base on the Fox River, or from the Bureau River on the upper Illinois, where Indians driven from the Peoria region eventually fortified themselves behind five blockhouses. Helped by other Potawatomi leaders such as White Hair and White Pigeon, he tried to swell the allied ranks, cajoling, boasting, and threatening. Finally, in the summer he was back on the Detroit, ready to fight the Big Knives again.[12]

Between two and three thousand warriors, with many families, rallied to Tecumseh, Procter, and Dickson that summer. It was a nightmare for the commissariat. Many Indians had little more than bread, while others, particularly Dickson's wild recruits, scoured the countryside, killing livestock and robbing some of the inhabitants.[13]

Without all the promised reinforcements, Procter was not ready to move against Presque Isle, but food stocks in Amherstburg were running out. One solution was to loose the Indians upon the enemy, letting them live off the American countryside. With many misgivings, the General postponed his plan to attack Presque Isle and in the middle of July once more set his forces in motion toward Fort Meigs.

Tecumseh had got his way, but with skimpy hopes of success. Last time, Procter's artillery, of which so much had been expected, had failed, and this time the redcoats were not even trying. Several of their guns were now equipping Barclay's squadron, and they took nothing more powerful than a few six-pounders when they left Amherstburg for Fort Meigs on 19 July. Obviously, no one expected those to succeed where twenty-four-pounders had failed.

The allies were playing a wild card. Tecumseh had come up with an idea. Harrison, it was known, had turned over the command of Fort Meigs to Green Clay, and was himself farther east on the Sandusky. If Fort Meigs was invested, might not Harrison march to its relief? More than anything else Tecumseh relished the prospect of drawing Harrison into a battle, and that was one way of doing it. Even if Harrison did not stir, Tecumseh proposed the allies stage a sham battle, with plenty of firing, on the Sandusky road, near enough for it to be heard but not seen from Fort Meigs. Tecumseh reasoned that Clay might suppose that Harrison was coming to relieve him and sally out to help the mythical reinforcements. If he did . . .

In itself Fort Meigs was actually stronger than ever. It contained ample provisions and ammunition, and nearly two thousand men, most of them fit for duty. Particularly unfortunate in respect to Tecumseh's plan, General Clay knew that Tecumseh and Procter were coming, for he had been warned by a Frenchman and some American prisoners of the allies who had escaped. Neither at Fort Meigs nor at Harrison's camp on the Sandusky were there serious fears for the post's safety.[14]

Few more than 450 regulars crossed the lake with Procter and reclaimed their old encampment below Fort Meigs on 20 July, but the Indian force, well mounted, was the largest Tecumseh had ever fielded, maybe amounting to 2,500 men. Dawn of the twenty-first saw the Indians surrounding the garrison, scooping up oxen and horses outside the walls, and killing a surprised picket guard, estimated in the different accounts as from 6 to 10 men strong. About nine o'clock, on one of a run of fine days, the familiar roar of Indian muskets and American artillery once more shattered the peace of the beautiful Maumee River.

No one had any faith in the siege itself. The British scarcely bothered to erect batteries, and the allied small-arms fire, although sometimes heavy, was desultory and ineffective. No more than two or three defenders were wounded during the entire operation. The cordon around the fort was also loose. A handful of American regulars from a nearby encampment sneaked through with a loss of only a couple of horses and some baggage, and when Clay sent out a strong detachment to recover the bodies of the picket guard on the twenty-third only three or four Indians were attentive enough to fire on them. A few hundred allies hurried from the camp across the river to intercept the Big Knives before they could withdraw into the garrison, but they were too late.

Every hope was placed on luring Harrison to Fort Meigs or Clay out of it. The allies were greatly encouraged by a report that Harrison was on his way with eight hundred men, and Tecumseh and Elliott took a large party of Indians and militia to meet him. The noisy war dance which rent the night air of the twenty-second with cries the besieged garrison regarded as "diabolical" and "infernal" may have commemorated their departure. But

Tecumseh was disappointed. The report, he discovered, was untrue. No relief force was marching to Fort Meigs.[15]

The attempt to entice Clay from the fort also misfired. On the afternoon of 26 July the Indians, who had moved their skin tents from the British encampment to the south side of the river, below and out of sight of the fort, filed unseen through the trees to the Sandusky road, about half a mile east of the rear of the garrison. About four o'clock they opened a brisk fire, while the British lay hidden, ready to rush for the fort gates to cut off the Americans as soon as they sallied forth. The display was convincing. Many of Clay's soldiers lined the ramparts at the back of the fort, straining to see through the trees and brush. The firing suggested that a large force was pushing the Indians back toward the fort, but Clay would not let his men out. That very morning two couriers had come in from Harrison, stating that the general was confident that Clay would repulse any attack. Clay knew that no relief force was on its way from the Sandusky.

After an hour or so the sham battle ended, and the frustrated Indians returned to their camp, battered by the hail and rain of one of the fiercest thunderstorms anyone had experienced. It seemed that the expedition was dogged by ill luck, and two days later the siege was raised.

Next Procter planned to go to the Sandusky, not so much to attack the small post of Fort Stephenson at Lower Sandusky as to enable the Indians to round up livestock so that the victualing problem on the Detroit could be alleviated. Once again the Indians objected, explaining that they could not leave their villages open to attack from Clay. A compromise was reached. Procter, with the regulars and a few hundred Indians under Elliott and Dickson, would try Fort Stephenson, while Tecumseh, with about two thousand warriors, would occupy the swampy ground between the Maumee and Sandusky Rivers, where he could intercept Clay if he tried to march east or hurry home toward the Raisin if the Americans went that way.[16]

The British sailed along the lake, and Tecumseh took up his position and watched Elliott lead his warriors into the woods, heading for Fort Stephenson. They were soon back. On 2 August Procter had attacked, but his artillery had been too light, and in a brave but disastrous attempt to storm the palisades he had lost twenty-nine men killed, twenty-eight missing, and forty-four wounded. An advance party of the long-awaited second battalion of the 41st Regiment, which had at last reached Amherstburg, rowed hard all night to join Procter at Sandusky Bay. They were there the day after the attack, but Procter had had enough. His battered command went home.

The severe casualties shook Procter; indeed, according to one witness, he was close to tears. But the dispatch he wrote some days later is more interesting for the light it sheds upon the general's relationships with his officers, and his standing in the allied army. Not a single officer was deemed worthy of praise. Rather Procter claimed that he alone had seen the folly of assaulting the fort, and excused his decision to attack on the grounds that he would otherwise have lost face, with both the regiment and the Indians. The Indian Department, he wrote testily, had "declared formally their decided opinion that unless the fort was stormed we should never be able to bring an Indian warrior into the field with us." Yet not a red man had joined the assault. In Procter's opinion his losses were "a more than adequate sacrifice . . . to Indian opinion."[17]

The expedition had pleased no one. Tecumseh and Roundhead still thirsted for an open battle with the Big Knives, one that did not involve wooden walls and siegework. Most of Dickson's recruits were disappointed. They had got no plunder, and they were soon on their way home, back to the upper Great Lakes and the Mississippi. Procter, consoled perhaps by the belated arrival of his second battalion of regulars and another promotion, this time to the rank of major-general, was sinking in the estimation of his forces and becoming dangerously isolated.

Away from the shimmering Great Lakes little was occurring that would have eased Tecumseh's frustration. Indian raiders continued to dodge rangers and militia, attacking where they could, but the mustering of the great army Tecumseh had led into Ohio had drained his supporters of their strength in other places. In July Winnebagos and others were active around Forts Mason and Madison; they killed a dozen men-at-arms and overran a blockhouse, but there were no important successes.

Tecumseh suffered a major setback in the south. He had hoped the fall of Fort Meigs would have released him to travel in the autumn to the Creek country, where he planned to launch a southern campaign against the United States in person, thus opening a new theater of the war. Unfortunately, the war in the north stagnated, and the southern uprising slipped from his control.

It had seemed to be on course. Among the Upper Creeks enthusiasm for war was growing, fanned by anti-American "prophets" among the Alabamas and the resentment felt by the Tallassees and other non-Muskogees toward the Creek National Council, dominated as it was by Big Warrior, Muskogee chiefs, and the United States agent Benjamin Hawkins. Eight Indians the council had put to death in 1812 for murdering whites had come from the towns of non-Muskogees.

The man Tecumseh relied upon to implement his plans for a southern revolt was Little Warrior, the leader of the Creeks who had visited Prophetstown in the autumn of 1812. After speaking to Tecumseh, the Creek delegates had proceeded to the Detroit, where they participated in the battle of

the River Raisin, some later boasting of the American flesh they claimed to
have eaten upon that occasion. In February 1813 Little Warrior and nine of
his men were back on the Wabash, finalizing plans with Tecumseh and the
Prophet before making their long journey home by way of the Ohio and
Tennessee Rivers. Tecumseh emphasized the need to wait until he and the
British were ready, and for intertribal solidarity. Little Warrior should unite
the Creek Nation (whether by eliminating pro-American chiefs or not is uncertain), bring the other southern tribes into the brotherhood—for which
purpose Tecumseh supplied wampum and speeches—and wait until the fall.
Once Fort Meigs had been captured, and the British could supply them,
Tecumseh would bring his Shawnees south and personally lead the Indians
into their war.[18]

Tecumseh's plan stressed restraint and unity, but neither meant much in
the lands of the Creeks, where the political temperature was at the boiling
point. Before completing their return journey, Little Warrior and his fellows
had themselves pulled Tecumseh's scheme to pieces. At the mouth of the
Ohio they brutally murdered seven white families. Little Warrior's principal
confederate, a Tuskegee chief named Estanngle Weeahtustkey, happily
slaughtered a pregnant woman and her unborn child. One report had it that
the Indians merely acted upon the instructions of Tecumseh, who told the
Creeks to kill some whites on their way home and report the number slain
to their nation, but this hardly seems likely. It had long been the Shawnee's
complaint that his slow-maturing plans were being scotched by premature
hostilities, and in the spring of 1813 such attacks were entirely inappropri-
ate to the plan for a war in the fall.[19]

Whatever motive underpinned Little Warrior's raid, it wreaked havoc
with Tecumseh's program. Once home, Little Warrior sent messages to the
other Creeks and to the Cherokees, Chickasaws, and Choctaws, as Tecumseh had suggested; but the atrocities visited upon the helpless settlers on the
Ohio spoke with louder voices. Throughout the south they aroused Americans to fury. To disarm aggressive anti-Indian expansionists who lusted for
just such a pretext to dispossess the Creeks, Hawkins called upon the National Council to put its loyalty to the United States beyond doubt: it must
apprehend and kill Little Warrior and his friends.

Big Warrior and his chiefs complied. A posse of Upper and Lower
Creeks left Tuckabatchee. Before dawn on 18 April it swooped around a
house in Hickory Ground Town and cornered four of the fugitives. The
house was set on fire, the Tuskegee chief burned alive inside, two of his
brothers were hauled out and tomahawked, and a Tuckabatchee man was
also slain by the posse. Little Warrior, who had been sleeping in another
house in the town, escaped, but a week later he was surrounded in a swamp

and died fighting. By 5 July eight men and a woman had perished at the hands of Big Warrior's Creeks.[20]

This time the anti-American Red Sticks did not suppress their anger. Relatives and friends of Little Warrior and his companions demanded the lives of those responsible for the executions, including Big Warrior, the principal chief on the National Council, and Hawkins himself. June and July saw a spate of a tit-for-tat killings, as the clamor for retribution was extended against all pro-American chiefs.

A particularly bloody episode involved an eighteen-year-old prophet named Letecau, a native of Aubocooche who had been raised among the Alabamas. He invited established leaders of his hometown to witness his magical powers upon the banks of the Coosa River. As the audience watched intently, Letecau and some followers performed "the dance of the Lakes," introduced by Tecumseh, inside a magic circle which they had drawn and which they supposed made them invulnerable. Suddenly, the Red Sticks gave a whoop and attacked the astonished onlookers, killing three. In their opinion they were merely cleansing the nation of its corrupt chiefs and preparing it for spiritual renewal, but the survivors of the attack, who fled, quickly rallied and mustered their own supporters. They found the prophet and his dancers still at work and slew the lot. Then they angrily descended upon Okfuskee, a town in which Letecau had built a following. The Red Sticks of Okfuskee had already killed five pro-American chiefs. Now it was their turn, and all who had taken the prophet's talks were murdered.[21]

In a much more serious incident hundreds of Red Sticks besieged Big Warrior in Tuckabatchee. After a week of fighting the defenders abandoned their town, cutting their way out with an escort of 230 Lower Creeks. The triumphant Red Sticks burned Tuckabatchee and two allied towns, Kialijee and Hatchecubbau, and seized control of the upper part of the nation.

The murders had led to executions, the executions to retaliation, and retaliation to civil war, with most of the Upper Creek towns, Muskogee and non-Muskogee, forming the Red Stick party, and most of the Lower Creeks—more influenced by Hawkins and closer to Georgia—aligning against them. This was not the Indian brotherhood Tecumseh had wanted. Not the unification of the Creeks he had planned. He and Hawkins had wrestled for the soul of the Creek Nation only to tear it apart.[22]

Tecumseh's hopes of recruiting warriors from the other southern tribes also collapsed. To give them credit, the Red Sticks tried, sending messengers as far as the Arkansas Osages, but to little avail. On the Red River of Louisiana some tribes smoked the Creek tobacco and accepted the war talk, but the leading chief of the Caddoes threw his influence upon the side of peace. Two small Choctaw towns, one on the Tombigbee and another on

Yahnubbee Creek, with a combined strength of sixty-five warriors, began performing war dances under leaders such as Ta-aboly, and some remained with the Red Sticks for at least three years, but most Indians were simply too overawed by American power to help. Many Cherokees and Choctaws fought against the rebellious Creeks.[23]

Isolated and ill-equipped, the Red Sticks had no chance of winning. Maybe if he had lived Tecumseh would have told them. To make matters worse they ignored the Shawnee's instructions to wait until he could come to lead them and until the British were able to give assistance. They rushed recklessly into a conflict with the United States. As one of them admitted, "the prophets of [the] Alabama had begun prematurely. They were to go on with their magic until Tecumseh arrived, who was to put the plan in motion, and he would come when his friends the British were ready for him."[24]

The war with the Big Knives started suddenly. After capturing Tucka-batchee the Tallassee war chief, Peter McQueen, led three hundred Red Sticks to Pensacola, seeking arms and ammunition from the Spaniards. He carried a letter of introduction Little Warrior had brought from the British in Canada. The Spanish governor had no wish to provoke the United States, but McQueen's force was a formidable one to disappoint, and Spain had need of the Creeks. Once again the Americans were trying to purloin Spanish territory, and only two months before McQueen's arrival they had annexed nearby Mobile in the most blatant fashion. Consequently, the Creeks got some powder. However, on 27 July at Burnt Corn Creek in southern Alabama they were intercepted on their way home by a party of mestizos and whites from the Mississippi territorial militia. The Red Sticks routed the attackers, but lost six men along with many of their valuable supplies.[25]

The skirmish at Burnt Corn was small but important. McQueen had intended rubbing out the remaining pro-American Creeks and uniting the nation before challenging the United States, but the relatives of the warriors killed at Burnt Corn called for vengeance upon the whites and mixed-bloods instead. In August the Tallassees, too, had reason for speedy retribution, because some Lower Creeks, encouraged by Hawkins, raided Tallassee and burned it, seizing McQueen's blacks and a boy of his family. Furious, the Tallassees withdrew to Auttosse, began performing Tecumseh's war dance, and called out the Red Sticks for an attack.[26]

Fort Mims on the Alabama River, less than forty miles above Mobile, 30 August 1813. It was a new fortification, and its only blockhouse was unfinished. Although it also contained a strong house, the residence of the settler for whom it was named, the fort had few defensible structures. The territorial forces forming the garrison, less than two hundred strong, as well as most of the civilians who had come in for protection, were quartered in rude cabins or tents. The fortress was most ineptly designed. It occupied a hill, but there was no ditch, and portholes had been cut in the pickets only four feet above the ground, where they were easily accessible to attackers. An even greater disability was the fort's commander, Major Daniel Beasley, a man of shocking complacency. He allowed the gates to remain open, and rubbished warnings that hostiles were abroad. The day before, two young blacks, out herding cattle, had rushed in to report seeing Indians. Beasley ordered a detachment to investigate, but when it was unable to confirm the report he ordered the boys flogged.

At noon several hundred Red Sticks, their naked bodies daubed black and red and their heads shaven to scalp locks, poured out of a ravine toward the open east gate of the fort. In front ran four prophets who believed themselves bulletproof. Some of the Red Sticks surged through the gate, chopping down the wretched Beasley as he belatedly tried to close it, and others ran shrieking around the post, commandeering the portholes and firing through them, turning the pickets to their own advantage. Inside, a terrible massacre of men, women, and children took place. The Creeks set fire to both the Mims house and a bastion where the last resisters fought desperately for their lives.

Later an American burial party found a horrifying spectacle. Bloody, mangled, and scalped corpses littered the area, twisted into grotesque positions, and pulled at by scavenging birds and animals: "Indians, Negroes, white men, women and children lay in one promiscuous ruin. All were scalped, and the females of every age were butchered in a manner which neither decency nor language will permit me to describe. The main building was burned to ashes, which were filled with bones. The plains and the woods around were covered with dead bodies."[27] Two hundred and forty-seven whites were buried, but if the blacks, mestizos, and friendly Indians who had been in the fort are included in the count nearly four hundred inhabitants were possibly slain or taken prisoner. Only a handful escaped.

The destruction of Fort Mims, the only time in United States history when Indians successfully stormed a large fortification, was more than a tragedy for the luckless inhabitants. Apart from suffering their own casualties, the Red Sticks committed themselves to a war in which they were vastly outnumbered. They tried to involve the Spaniards in a joint Creek-Spanish attack upon Mobile, and appealed to the British in the Bahamas to send help by the Apalachicola River, but in the end they fought their war alone, ringed by enemies.[28]

How much of this reached Tecumseh, who was in the last days of his life, is unknown. After Little Warrior left the Wabash for home Tecumseh had sent a deputation of his own after him, presumably with his latest speeches. Led by an aged but trusted chief, the Shawnees had accompanied McQueen to Pensacola to strengthen his appeal to the Spaniards in July. In the town Tecumseh's messengers refused to touch alcohol, but openly bragged that all the nations between the Missouri and the Great Lakes were "now like one fire" and "determined to make the land clean of the Americans or to lose their lives."[29]

These Shawnees were due to return to Tecumseh, and perhaps reached him before he made his own final stand against their age-old enemy. If so, Tecumseh would have been disappointed—by the murders on the Ohio, which had set the Red Sticks upon a slippery slope; by the civil war and the hostility of the other southern tribes; and by the overeager assault upon the whites. It was as well that he did not see the events that followed, for Tecumseh's intervention in Creek affairs would be truly disastrous. He had wanted to protect them, to save their lands and their independence, but he merely prompted the destruction of the once-mighty Creek Nation.

27

FATHER, WE SEE YOU
ARE DRAWING BACK!

But in the north the war had not yet been lost.

Many of Dickson's westerners had gone home, but the camps in Michigan Territory and on Grosse Isle (where Tecumseh had recently relocated his eighty Shawnee warriors and their families, the remains of his own and Blue Jacket's band) could still furnish up to two thousand fighting men. And as far as Tecumseh knew, Procter was confident of holding his ground. Not even the failure of the last foray into Ohio had seriously damaged Indian morale. Yes, the enemy forts had withstood attack, but the Americans could not keep fighting like groundhogs. They would have to come out, and in a contest without wooden walls, big guns, and earthen burrows, the Indians were sure they would prevail. Some of these men had been at Prophetstown, when an inferior Indian army had savaged Harrison's camp before running out of ammunition, and they had thrown the forces of Hull, Winchester, and Clay upon their backs.

Tecumseh's soldiers knew about the new army that Harrison was assembling, but they were sure they could beat it. If it suddenly advanced, they planned to stop it at the Huron River, near the mouth of the Detroit. Their one concern was that most of Procter's troops were stationed at Sandwich, rather than at Fort Malden, and "the business must be over before he [Procter] would arrive to render any assistance."[1]

That confidence shone fiercely when some pro-American Wyandots from Tarhe arrived to speak to their fellow tribesmen. General Harrison was coming in great force, the emissaries warned. Stand aside now, before you are destroyed! Walk-in-the-Water, whose heart had never been in the war, held his peace in public, but privately told the visitors that he and his warriors would desert the British when Harrison advanced. He wanted a foot in both camps. But Roundhead was made of sterner stuff. Far from being dismayed by the news of Harrison's preparations, he addressed the messengers bluntly in a council at Brownstown on 23 August. "We are happy to learn your Father [Harrison] is coming out of his hole," he said, "as he has been like a ground hog under the ground, and [his coming] will save us much trouble in walking to meet him!" Captain Chambers, who was present, reported proudly that "nothing could be more noble than the behaviour of our Indians."[2]

The Indians had been kept ignorant of the perilous condition of the Right Division. Probably Procter thought that if they knew the alarming deficiencies at Amherstburg, where food was scarce and Barclay's ships badly wanted men, guns, and stores, the Indians would lose heart and desert. Tecumseh got his first inkling that something was amiss about 24 August, when Perry, who had put his squadron onto the lake the previous month, demonstrated off Hartley's Point near Amherstburg, threatening Procter's naval communications. Tecumseh grew excited, for surely Our Father With One Arm would lead his squadron out to fight. When no British ships stirred, Tecumseh went over to find out what was wrong, and was told the big canoes were not ready. According to one account, some Indians were not convinced and in their council spoke of the British as cowards.[3]

Lack of courage, in fact, was not one of Commodore Barclay's shortcomings. His squadron was weak, and his crews had had to be brought to strength with 250 of Procter's redcoats; but he intended to do his utmost to clear that supply line, and on 9 September his ships weighed anchor for a decisive showdown. Tecumseh probably watched the six little vessels put out, their proud sails billowing white against the blue water as they worked their way downriver toward Lake Erie—the flagship *Detroit* of nineteen guns; the eighteen-gun *Queen Charlotte*; the *Lady Prevost* of twelve guns; the six-gun *General Hunter*; and the puny *Chippawa* and *Little Belt*. Somewhere on board, two adventurous Indians sampled the novelties of naval warfare under sail.

At noon the following day a tremendous cannonading filled the air with great clouds of powder smoke near the Bass Islands, thirty or more miles from Amherstburg. The squadrons were in action, but though the thunder rolled for three hours neither the Indians nor their allies could make out the course of what was plainly a desperate conflict. Lieutenant-Colonel Warburton, Procter's second-in-command, trained a glass on the battle from a viewpoint several miles below Amherstburg. He thought Barclay had won, but the ships were so distant and the gunsmoke so dense that none could say that he was right or wrong.

The battle ended, but no word came from Barclay, nor did the Indians who had sailed beneath his flag return to their families. The tenth turned into the eleventh, and the eleventh into the twelfth . . . Still nothing, though the wind was fair for a voyage from the Bass Islands to Amherstburg.

Those were anxious days for Tecumseh, and sad ones also. For some-time during the last week in August and the first two in September—the exact date has escaped record—Roundhead, the great Wyandot war chief, was gathered to his forefathers. He did not die in battle, as perhaps he would have wished, but of natural causes. His loss must have touched Tecumseh deeply, for the Shawnee had possessed no stauncher or abler Indian ally. Abstemious, willing to discipline his warriors, and sure and steady in battle, the Wyandot's tall figure carried great authority, and his death had a perceptible effect upon morale, particularly among the allied Wyandot and Miami warriors. Well might Procter acknowledge that "the Indian cause and ours experienced a serious loss in the death of Roundhead."[4]

Amid the melancholy ceremonies that laid the great warrior to rest, Tecumseh perhaps reflected that he had never needed Roundhead more than he did now. Roundhead had understood the compromises that went with holding the British-Indian alliance together, and had worked to deliver them if no one else did. Neither Walk-in-the-Water, Splitlog (Roundhead's younger brother), the unpredictable Main Poc, nor Naiwash of the Ottawas was capable of easing that burden, which now fell squarely upon the shoulders of the Shawnee chief.

But time was racing now. On 14 September some Indians came to Tecumseh in great agitation. They were hotfoot from Fort Malden, where they had seen a British party throwing part of the wall into the ditch. The fort, which the Indians had defended against difficult odds for fourteen months, was being dismantled. To Tecumseh there was but one interpretation: contrary to all his promises, Procter was going to retreat!

Tecumseh was not the only one to be astonished. Lieutenant-Colonel Warburton was no less flabbergasted when his staff adjutant brought him the same news. Although second in rank to Procter, he knew no more about the general's plans to retreat than Tecumseh. Warburton wrote to Procter, who had stationed himself at Sandwich, and received a curt reply that the General had the right to issue whatever secret orders he liked. Unfortunately for Procter, there was no treating Tecumseh that way.

He, more than any other Indian, had argued the necessity for a British-

Indian alliance. He had staked much of his personal credibility upon that course, despite the tribes' embittered memories of those earlier British betrayals, when the redcoats ditched their Indian allies in the treaty that ended the Revolutionary War, and when the gates had been shut against the defeated warriors in 1794. It was partly upon the strength of Tecumseh's arguments that some Indians had abandoned their old homes, and built new ones on the Detroit, on land they trusted the King would one day secure for them. Tecumseh was not going to stand by and watch the British march off leaving those families to the mercy of their enemies.

The Indian camps were soon filled with loud denunciations of the treacherous British. Some warriors threatened violence, and Tecumseh stormily demanded that Elliott bring Procter to a council. The Indians had a large belt of wampum that symbolized their alliance with the redcoats. At its center was the shape of a heart, and at each end a hand, one for the British and the other the Indians. Tecumseh was prepared to cut that belt in two and throw the pieces at Procter's feet in a dramatic renunciation of the alliance. Unable to delay further, the General finally faced the Indians in the council house at Fort Malden on 18 September, more than a week after the battle on Lake Erie.

The atmosphere was charged, as if the striking array of warriors seated in the center and the British officers and agents dispersed around the walls were sitting on a powder keg attached to a sizzling fuse. All eyes focused on the familiar but magnificent figure of the Shawnee chief, as he rose to his feet, a wampum belt in his hands. It was not the great belt, not yet, but another bearing symbols that reminded the chief of the points he had to make. Young John Richardson was enthralled as he watched his hero:

Habited in a close leather dress, his athletic proportions were admirably delineated, while a large plume of white ostrich feathers, by which he was generally distinguished, overshadowing his brow, and contrasting with the darkness of his complexion and the brilliancy of his black and piercing eye, gave a singularly wild and terrific expression to his features. It was evident that he could be terrible.[5]

With Samuel Saunders interpreting, Tecumseh made an emotional and fearsome attack upon the British:

Listen! When war was declared, our Father [Procter] stood up and gave us the tomahawk, and told us he was now ready to strike the Americans; that he wanted our assistance; and that he certainly would get us our lands back which the Americans had taken from us. Listen! You told us at that time to bring forward our families to this place. We did so, and you promised to take care of them, and that they should want for nothing while the men would go to fight the enemy. That we were not to trouble ourselves with the enemy's garrisons [forts], that we knew nothing about them, and that our Father would attend to that part of the business . . . When we last went to the rapids [Fort Meigs] it is true we gave you little assistance. It is hard to fight people who live like groundhogs.

Then he came to the kernel of the matter:

Father, listen! Our fleet has gone out. We know they have fought. We have heard the great guns, but know nothing of what has happened to Our Father With One Arm. Our ships have gone one way, and we are much astonished to see our Father tying up everything and preparing to run the other, without letting his red children know what his intentions are. You always told us to remain here and take care of our lands. It made our hearts glad to hear that was your wish.

Procter was an unpopular man in the army, and the general's juniors, Warburton and Lieutenant-Colonel William Evans, who had both, like Tecumseh, been kept in the dark by Procter, were among those beginning to enjoy the general's discomfort. The amusement became audible as Tecumseh accused Procter of cowardice:

You always told us you would never draw your foot off British ground. But now, Father, we see you are drawing back, and we are sorry to see our Father doing so without seeing the enemy. We must compare our Father's conduct to a fat animal that carries its tail upon its back, but when affrighted, it drops it between its legs and runs off.

Tecumseh had a serious point. With some twenty-five hundred redcoats and Indians at his disposal, let alone militia, a substantial fort, and a powerful battery, Procter was retreating without a battle, without (as far as the Indians knew) even seeing an enemy. Tecumseh wanted to fight the Americans. If he succeeded it would transform the campaign; if he failed, why, that was the time to retreat. Tecumseh went on:

Listen, Father! The Americans have not yet defeated us by land; neither are we sure they have done so by water. We, therefore, wish to remain here, and fight our enemy should they make their appearance. If they defeat us, we will then retreat with our Father . . .

Finally, the chief told Procter that if necessary his Indians would fight alone:

Father! You have got the arms and ammunition which our Great Father [the King] sent for his red children. If you have an idea of going away, give them to us, and you may go and welcome for us. Our lives are in the hands of the Great Spirit. We are determined to defend our lands, and if it is his will, we wish to leave our bones upon them.[6]

This affirmation ran through the excited Indians like an electric shock, and they rose to their feet with a roar of approval, their tomahawks flashing in the air. The experience was humiliating for Procter, who had been forced into the open and insulted in front of his soldiers. He now admitted what he had known for a week. Barclay's squadron had been entirely vanquished and the Americans reigned supreme on the lake.

The battle of Lake Erie, like the capture of Detroit, was a defining engagement of the war. It destroyed Britain's naval force on the lake, and gave the American commodore the power to slice the main allied supply route, which used the lake between the Center Division at the head of Lake Ontario and Procter's Right Division at Amherstburg. Perry could also sever Procter's second communication line along the River Thames, most obviously by sending ships up the Detroit strait into Lake St. Clair, where they could attack the road running along the shoreline or enter the mouth of the Thames itself. In short, Perry could starve the allies of supplies.

The British and Indians were short of essentials, and were consuming fourteen head of cattle and seven thousand pounds of flour a day, more than the locality was capable of supplying. Nor was it solely a matter of provisions. As Procter realized, the American navy could land troops above or below Fort Malden and patrol the Detroit River to separate the British from most of their Indian allies in Michigan Territory. The redcoats could be surrounded and overwhelmed.

Bitter as the taste of retreat was on Procter's tongue, he saw no alternative. He was not an officer of the dashing kind, willing to hazard battle in circumstances as risky as these. On the other hand, nor was Procter a mean strategist, and from those dark days of reflection had emerged a plan that was perfectly sound. Procter felt impelled to retreat—but how far? To withdraw to the Center Division, abandoning his district completely, would have been fatal to the Indian alliance, in Procter's view. Tecumseh would have denounced it as an act of desertion, and the warriors might conceivably even turn upon the civilians left behind. No, Procter would retreat as far as the lower Thames, at least initially. By doing so he would overcome the immediate threat to his communications at the mouth of the Thames, and upriver he could make his stand. From there he would be in a position to fall back to the Center Division if he was defeated.

Procter's plan had its merits, but he implemented it with breathtaking incompetence, producing from the first an impressive catalogue of costly errors in judgment. Instead of drawing Tecumseh, the other chiefs, and his senior officers into his plans, he remained silent, confiding in cronies and issuing secret instructions to begin dismantling the fort. It was sheer folly. How could the work party avoid attracting attention? How could such clandestine proceedings fail to rekindle deep Indian suspicions? It seemed that the British general was afraid of dealing with Tecumseh.

Procter survived the council at Fort Malden by promising to reply in two days. Then he scuttled back to Sandwich, leaving orders for the hapless Warburton to shoulder the redoubtable responsibility of squaring matters with Tecumseh. It was a charge the Lieutenant-Colonel declined to accept—understandably, since he had no knowledge of the promises made to the Indians, and little more of Procter's plan of campaign. The result was that nothing was done, and for two days the suspicions of Tecumseh and his followers simmered dangerously. As they saw ordnance and stores being transported from Fort Malden toward the Thames, they could only be certain that whatever else their council with Procter had achieved, it had not dissuaded the redcoats from abandoning Amherstburg.

The discontent still hung heavily over the fort like a black cloud when the day of the second council, the twentieth, dawned. Procter arrived at Fort Malden to meet an agitated Colonel Elliott, urgently complaining that the Indians were on the point of cutting with the British and that he himself had been threatened with the tomahawk. If nothing was done he could not answer for the consequences. Realizing that Warburton had not seen Tecumseh, Procter resolved to appeal directly to the Shawnee chief, whose "example and talents [he believed] governed the councils of his brethren."[7] Shortly a message reached Tecumseh, requesting his attendance at the quarters of Procter's staff-adjutant. Procter was there, with his aide, Captain John Hall, Warburton, Elliott, and other officers. They stood around a table "on the outer court towards the garden" with a large map of the Detroit area open before them.[8]

Using Elliott to interpret, Procter explained to Tecumseh the implications of Perry's victory. According to Hall, "Tecumseh asked many questions and made several shrewd remarks in reference to the map." He readily understood the problem, and when the General promised that he was fortifying the forks of the Thames, a place called Chatham, to make his stand there, seemed reassured. Tecumseh wanted time to confer with the other chiefs, but Procter testified that such was Tecumseh's influence with the Indians that "in the course of two hours" Tecumseh "had brought the greater

portion of the chiefs and nations into my proposal, and effectively prevented any opposition of moment."[9] The council that followed ran
smoothly, with the Indians consenting to accompany the retreat to the forks
of the Thames. The incident suggested that had Procter acted with greater
candor in the first place he might have spared himself much personal embarrassment.

Tecumseh believed that he had forced Procter into making a stand, but
the retreat itself had still to be faced. Tecumapease, the chief's sister, who
headed the Shawnee women, must have shaken her head at this further removal. The Indian women and girls are scarcely mentioned in the primary
sources, but they bore the brunt of the everyday toil in the villages and on
the trail. They packed the belongings and food and organized the trans-
portation, and it was they who would endure the principal labor of making
new homes. Tecumapease was over fifty years old now, and the rigors of the
hard work performed by Shawnee women had taken a toll. She must have
wondered what lay ahead, as she began stripping her house on Grosse Isle.
The important men in her life, her husband Wahsikegaboe, her brother
Tecumseh, and her nephew, seventeen-year-old Paukeesaa, whom she had
raised, would all be standing in that battle Tecumseh was talking about. As
Tecumapease helped bring the band, its horses, and its possessions across
the river, she knew she had much more to lose than her home.

The day after the second council, Indians began crossing to the Canadian side of the Detroit and taking the trail north toward Sandwich. Others
went by water, moving upstream to Lake St. Clair in laden canoes. In all
about twelve hundred warriors and their families joined the retreat, a cross-
section of Tecumseh's confederacy that included Kickapoos, Winnebagos,
Sacs, Shawnees, Wyandots, Miamis, Munsee Delawares, Potawatomis,
Ojibwas, Ottawas, Senecas, and even twenty-five Creek warriors. However,
not all the Indians followed Tecumseh. Several hundred, most of them
Potawatomis under Main Poc, remained in their villages on the Huron and
the Rouge, sullenly disillusioned.

As with the Indians, so with the British and Canadian inhabitants. Some
stayed, but many were moving out. Most of the artillery pieces were dismounted and shipped up toward the forks of the Thames with a quantity of
stores. Snorting cattle were rounded up and driven north, and creaking
wagons were loaded with equipment and personal baggage. Not all the
evacuees belonged to the army, for among the civilians in Amherstburg
were old Tories with good reason to fear American occupation. One abandoning his home was an elderly, white-haired frontiersman. He was almost
blind, but in Kentucky he was still detested as "the white savage" who had
led Indian raids during the Revolution. His name was Simon Girty.

On the morning of 27 September Ensign Benjamin Holmes of the Canadian Light Dragoons, on duty below Amherstburg, saw them coming across the lake. American ships, carrying Harrison and his army, on their way to invade Canada at last.

By then the British had burned Fort Malden and the public buildings in Amherstburg, and their families had gone forward, while the last of the Indians were making their way across the Detroit. The redcoats themselves were at Sandwich, poised to march for the Thames as soon as the invasion began. Now, with Holmes's urgent messages, that time had come. Holmes and his rear guard withdrew toward Sandwich, pulling down behind them the bridge over the Aux Canard, which had been repaired since the first skirmishes of the war. Muir brought over the detachment from Detroit, and in the afternoon the Right Division tramped out of Sandwich, along the path beside Lake St. Clair toward the mouth of the Thames.

Tecumseh and Colonel Matthew Elliott felt the loss of Amherstburg more keenly than most. For the chief Fort Malden symbolized the British-Indian alliance, the rock upon which his dream was founded. To the old British agent Amherstburg was his home. They tarried together, as if reluctant to admit defeat, even after the British rear guard had fallen back, and they watched from a distance as five thousand American soldiers spilled triumphantly into Amherstburg about four o'clock in the afternoon.

Then, sadly, the two old friends turned their horses and rode north.

Rain began to fall heavily the next day, soaking the deep green conifers and flaming autumnal hardwoods, brightly clad in leaves of red, yellow, gold, and orange. Water flooded the narrow paths north, already lacerated by wagon wheels and the horses and feet of the retreating army. For days the rain made the going miserable and slow. The redcoats took three days to travel the thirty or so miles to the mouth of the Thames. Procter himself was rarely with his men. First he was in the rear, then ahead up the Thames, commanding by instructions sent forward or back as the situation demanded. The Indians, both warriors and their families, were generally well behind their allies. Some passed the British army on the thirtieth, as it waited at Louis Trudelle's farm on the south bank of the Thames, three miles above its mouth, but many did not straggle in until the next day.

Tecumseh and Elliott were at the very back, sometimes dangerously close to the enemy advance, moving the Indian stragglers forward. On 28 September the two reached Sandwich, which they found empty of soldiers. They called at the riverside house of the militia officer, Colonel Francis Baby. He was at home, preparing to follow Procter's army, but Tecumseh suggested he stay with them until the enemy came into sight. They remained overnight, and early in the morning dispatched a scout back toward

the Aux Canard. He returned in one and a half hours with news that the
Americans were very close, at Turkey Creek, just south of Sandwich. Tecumseh, Elliott, and Baby then mounted and continued their journey, camping
overnight on the Belle River.

Between the Belle and the Thames the trio passed several Indians, moving leisurely along the swampy and broken plain around Lake St. Clair, and
urged them on. Tecumseh reached Trudelle's on the evening of the thirtieth.
He discovered that Lieutenant-Colonel Warburton commanded—because
Procter had gone ahead in his carriage! The more the Indians saw of Procter's behavior the less they liked it. What if the Americans came up and attacked? When the general's attendance did not improve in the days that
followed, Tecumseh asked Elliott for an explanation, but the agent, with
some honesty, was unable to supply one. The Prophet, hardly a model of
courage himself, declared that he felt like ripping the epaulets from Procter's shoulders.

On 1 October Warburton and Tecumseh continued the retreat, toward
the forks where the chief had been promised his battle. About nine miles
were covered before the allies split, Warburton crossing to the northeast
bank of the Thames and camping at John Dolsen's farm, and Tecumseh's
people remaining south of the river, where they could frustrate any American attempt to pass and outflank the redcoats by means of a path that
twisted through the dense woods on that side.

Procter also appeared at Dolsen's that day. When he learned that word
was going around the Indians that he had deserted his army and was afraid
of the enemy, he took pains to disabuse them, and spent much of the second
on the backtrail. But early the next morning he returned to form, and
rushed upriver again. He was thus once more absent when news reached
Dolsen's a few hours later that the Americans had suddenly advanced and
captured a small British detachment only seven or eight miles below. Elliott
hastened across the river in a scow to bring the news to Tecumseh.

The Shawnee chief was mystified by what the agent had to tell him. Warburton intended to stand and fight, there and then, and asked Tecumseh if
he would protect the south bank. As far as Tecumseh was concerned, it was
madness. Why fight at Dolsen's when less than five miles upstream lay the
forks of the Thames, where Procter had prepared a defensive position? No,
Tecumseh sent Elliott back to tell the redcoats that his warriors would fall
back to the forks, as they had agreed with Procter. That was the ground for
a battle. Warburton had the Right Division formed for action, but upon receiving Tecumseh's message he too marched his men up to the forks.

The forks of the Thames were formed by a small but deep run, McGregor's Creek, that cut into the south bank of the river at a place named
Chatham. When Tecumseh reached them he exploded in fury. There was no

sign of Procter! There was not even a fortified position, no works whatsoever! Only three or four dismounted guns lying helpless in the grass and a hut containing small arms betrayed any intention on the part of the General to defend the place. Twenty days had passed since Procter had made a decision to defend the lower Thames. Twenty days to mount his formidable battery of carronades, howitzers, and long guns. Twenty days to ready 880-odd regulars and over 1,500 Indians. Twenty days to rally militia. Yet nothing was in place. The General himself? Even then he was changing his plans. He was several miles up the Thames, inspecting a position on the north bank near a Delaware mission known as Moraviantown.

Testified Warburton:

> On the arrival of the troops there [the forks], Tecumseth was haranguing the Indians on the opposite bank of the river in a loud and violent manner. Colonel Elliott shortly after came over to me crying, and stated that from what he had heard, if something could not be done, he would not stay to be sacrificed. I understood that the passion of Tecumseth was caused by not finding the forks of the Thames fortified.[10]

The chief's anger was understandable. He had put his life, his cause, and his loved ones in the care of the British, and his reputation too, for it had been he, on the strength of Procter's empty promises, who had persuaded so many Indians to retreat to the Thames. He had risked everything for the alliance. Now, with those expectations dashed at the forks, even his iron fortitude must have quaked. The Shawnee had faced innumerable disasters before. Rebuff after rebuff in his visits to far-off Indian villages. The ashes of Prophetstown upon his return from the south. The failure of the Indian offensive the previous fall. The fiasco at Fort Meigs and the Creek civil war. The retreat from Fort Malden. But possibly at no time had he come closer to despair. Even Tecumseh, the eternal optimist, the man who had so often striven to turn defeat into victory, must have stood at Chatham and sensed that time was truly trickling away for the vision of a British-backed Indian resurgence in the Old Northwest.

About him the Indians were raging. They threatened Procter's life, and even Elliott's. "I will not, by God, sacrifice myself!" the agent told Warburton. Yet there were jobs that had to be done, for the Americans were close now. Tecumseh's spies told him that Harrison had passed Dolsen's, a few miles below, and that he was coming along the south bank after Tecumseh rather than crossing to follow the redcoats. Tecumseh sent Elliott to the British, asking them to come over and support him, but they protested they could not. They had no boats, they said.

That night Tecumseh conferred with chiefs and warriors at their camp near John McGregor's mill on the creek and came to a decision. Tomorrow they would retreat to Moraviantown, where Tecumseh would try again to make Procter fight. Tecumseh sent the resolution to Warburton the next morning, and his force also decamped for Moraviantown. In the meantime Tecumseh, as willing as ever to try his strength, conducted a rearguard action to delay Harrison's pursuit.

His warriors crossed McGregor's Creek and dispersed themselves in the cover on its northeastern bank. They tried to destroy the bridges that spanned the stream, but were only partly successful. An upper bridge a mile above was burned, but the larger construction at the mouth of the creek was too wet to burn, and the Indians had to satisfy themselves with merely pulling up the planking. There was a two-hour skirmish. Harrison had brought more than three thousand men up the Thames, and he turned Richard Mentor Johnson's regiment of one thousand mounted Kentucky volunteers and two six-pounders upon the Indians. Three Americans were killed or fatally wounded, and a few Indians, and a ball struck Tecumseh in the arm. The chief could do no more, and withdrew with his men after setting fire to the small arsenal the British had established at the forks.

Tecumseh's confederates were wavering now. Walk-in-the-Water quietly dropped out of the retreat with his warriors, and a few Shawnees—probably members of the Detroit River band associated with the Wyandots—and Delawares also left. Other Indians were badly scattered, and when Tecumseh formed his battle lines the following day only five hundred men got into position.

Procter had turned his retreat into a rout. He had not, as Tecumseh supposed, given up the idea of making a stand, but he dithered about where to do it. Belatedly dissatisfied with the ground at Chatham, he had toyed with defending Dolsen's instead, but at the time Tecumseh reached the forks was preparing yet another site on a plateau behind Moraviantown. His precious resources were strewn along the several miles between Dolsen's and Moraviantown, and they fell one by one to the invading Americans. The British detachment taken below Dolsen's on the third; the arms depot lost at Chatham; the Indians who defected; two small vessels with ammunition and stores sunk above Chatham to prevent them from being overtaken; and almost one hundred men, entrenching tools for building fortifications, and more boats and ammunition caught up by the Americans early on the fifth. They were all unnecessarily squandered by the British general.

A fatalistic despondency was enveloping the retreating forces, and as he looked at the large British medal suspended from his neck Tecumseh must have wondered where it was leading him. After the engagement at Chatham he chivied his people upriver, and spent the night at Christopher Arnold's mill, partly to protect it from straggling Indian warriors who might have set it on fire. Even at this stage, he could spare thoughts for the small Canadian farmers whose lands had become a battleground.

The next morning, 5 October, he rose early. Tecumseh was still at Arnold's, chatting with Joe Johnston, a neighbor who possessed several Indian languages, when sixteen-year-old Abraham Holmes saw him after scampering two miles upriver for just such a privilege. To the boy, whose parents were also small homesteaders, the chief appeared grave in countenance and earnest in conversation, but of an altogether superior presence. The Americans were not far away, for when young Abraham got home he found their horses grazing outside his house. Tecumseh was following his practice of waiting until he actually saw the enemy before riding on. That way he knew that all the Indians who could pass him had done so, and that he had fulfilled his role as a chief, chaperoning his people out of danger to the best of his ability.[11]

When the American riders approached Arnold's, Tecumseh climbed on his pony and sped upriver. There was a ford two miles beyond, but more likely he followed most of the Indians to Moraviantown, where another ford gave them access to the north bank and the new defensive position Procter was preparing. The American army forded the river above Arnold's, only a few miles behind. Both sides intended to fight. A battle was now inevitable.

28

OUR LIVES
ARE IN THE HANDS OF
THE GREAT SPIRIT!

Later that day, in the afternoon, a thousand men stood waiting on the north bank of the Thames, little more than a mile below Moraviantown. The area, later known as the Zone of Gore in Kent County, Ontario, gently undulated beneath a wet wood of white ash, oak, maple, and beech, occasionally broken by willow marsh. The men faced southwest, looking down the river which serenely slipped between high brushy banks on their left flank. On the road, which traced the bank of the stream, was stationed a solitary six-pounder, loaded with spherical and common case shot and served by five regular gunners. It was the only piece of artillery employed by the British in the battle, and there was no spare ammunition. The rest of the once-powerful redcoat batteries had been either captured or sent forward with the leading artillery officer to the Indian mission village of Moraviantown, where Procter was supposed to be making his stand.

A distance of 250 yards between the river and a small swamp, an area of open woodland, was occupied by the remains of the Right Division: those who had not deserted, fallen ill, been posted to other duties, or already been captured. Probably no more than 450 men were there. Most stood in the now faded and grimy scarlet uniforms of the 41st Regiment of Foot, the Royal Newfoundland Regiment, and the Tenth Royal Veteran Battalion, but there were a few Canadian Light Dragoons here and there, in blue jackets, gray trousers, and felt helmets with bearskin crowns.

Some of the men looked determined enough, but they were in poor shape. Confused, they had been formed for battle at Dolsen's two days before, then marched to fight at Chatham, and from there been directed to Moraviantown. They had not reached it. For on that morning of 5 October Procter had rejoined his troops as they marched. Evidently he believed that the Americans were upon him, because he had suddenly abandoned the march and formed them here, within two miles of their destination. They stood waiting on the ground for three hours, but even here Procter shuffled and reshuffled the men's position. Lieutenant Richard Bullock heard them complaining that "they were ready and willing to fight for their knapsacks, wished to meet the enemy, but did not like to be knocked about in that manner, doing neither one thing nor the other."[1]

The soldiers were also hungry and ill-equipped. They had not eaten a substantial meal for one and a half days. The previous day the retreat from the forks had been so sudden that meat could not be cooked, and only a little bread had been distributed. On the fifth, oxen were killed but could not be eaten, because the cooking utensils, it was discovered, had been sent to Moraviantown. Food was indeed waiting for them at the village, but standing now in expectation of battle the men were hungry and weak.

Much of their ammunition had also been lost. The men carried single-shot smoothbore muskets, but they had no cartridges for them other than those in their pouches.

After crossing the ford near Moraviantown the Indian warriors had deposited their families in a sanctuary some two miles distant, and then made their way downstream to find the army. Many Indians were still missing, but five hundred men got to the field in time. They occupied the thicker wood to the right of the British line, between the small swamp and a much larger one that ran along the foot of a low ridge about 650 yards from the river.

Tecumseh had spoken with Procter and agreed to turn the enemy left while the British contained their right. The chief's dispositions were admirably designed for that purpose. Squatting behind the trees and brush between the two swamps, and along the greater one which ran roughly parallel to the river and secured the right flank, the Indians were able to rake an attacker's front and left simultaneously with gunfire. Equally important, the ground was marshy and thickly forested. It would bog down the American horsemen, provide cover for the Indians, and furnish a means of escape if the day went against them.

Looking at his line of painted warriors, Shawnees and Delawares, Creeks, Foxes, Sacs, Winnebagos, Wyandots, Kickapoos, Potawatomis, Ottawas and Ojibwas, with a few members of the British Indian Department posted among them, Tecumseh may have realized that it was dangerously extended. It was too long for the number of men present. With the fifteen hundred men he had had a moon ago, Tecumseh could have made a formidable defense here, but he had only a third of that number.

He was down to his diehards now. There were seasoned warriors among them. Chiefs such as his brother-in-law Wahsikegaboe, true as his name, Stands Firm; and the Ottawa Naiwash, the second-in-command. Shawnees such as Waxiniwa, Pasheto, and Gunniwaubi, and the Potawatomis Shabeni and Mad Sturgeon. There were even a few whites who had been raised among the Indians, such as Andrew Clark, one of Tecumseh's most loyal warriors. But there were also boys of sixteen and seventeen in the line, young lads such as the Wyandot Adam Brown, nervous but proud to be standing with the man they had come to believe was the greatest warrior in the world. All of them, old and young, were thinking of their individual guardian spirits as they waited that day, praying for courage and fortune, but beyond that they trusted to Tecumseh, for they knew his power to be strong.

The prospect of battle, after so much doubt, had invigorated Tecumseh, and he breathed confidence, as any good commander would. But he was not blind to the attrition that had wasted the allied army, or to the desperate nature of the coming encounter. Some sources, ones that do not all qualify as eyewitness accounts but which come from persons close to Tecumseh, testify that the chief had a presentiment of death before the battle. There are probably few who prepare for action who do not contemplate the possibility of death or mutilation. But Indians believed in omens, in signs from the spirit world, and it is entirely possible that the Shawnee leader went into the fight convinced that he would fall. As he arranged his men that afternoon, and took leave of these most loyal of his followers, he may have recalled his own words at Fort Malden: "Our lives are in the hands of the Great Spirit. We are determined to defend our lands, and if it is his will, we wish to leave our bones upon them."

Captain William Caldwell, who was stationed between the British and Indian sections of the line, gave an interview in his last years. He remembered that before the firing began he had been seated on a log with Tecumseh, Thomas McKee, and a young Shawnee, and that the chief suddenly started as if shot. Caldwell asked him what was wrong. Tecumseh said that he "could not exactly tell, but it is an evil spirit which betokens no good." The incident was disturbing, and Caldwell suggested that Tecumseh should not fight that day, but the chief would not hear of it and shook the foreboding off. In his old age Caldwell was apt to fantasize, but he might have been preserving a genuine memory.[2]

More reliable sources indicate that Tecumseh's thoughts turned to his son in those final hours, although scarcely with charity. The boy had disappointed his father, probably through no fault of his own, and although Paukeesaa was seventeen, Tecumseh did not rate him a warrior. The Procters heard that to the end Tecumseh told his friends not to raise Paukeesaa to chieftainship, for he was too fair and like a white man. Anthony Shane understood that as he prepared for the battle Tecumseh took off his sword and handed it to his followers. They should give it to his son, he said, if he ever grew to be a warrior.[3]

Tecumseh must have had misgivings about the battle, but he knew the men needed confidence and he stood tall. After arranging the Indians, he went to review the British troops. What he saw cannot have been encouraging. Not only were the redcoats few in number, but Procter had given them no protection. There were no breastworks, despite the fallen trees and timber about, and the soldiers stood close together, their tunics standing out discordantly in the open wood. They made perfect targets! There were times when Tecumseh must have found the British way of war baffling. No Indian would have fought like that!

He moved twice along the British line, encouraging the soldiers, perhaps saying farewells. John Richardson stood in the line:

Only a few minutes before the clang of the American bugles was heard ringing through the forest . . . [Tecumseh] passed along our line, pleased with the manner in which his left was supported, and seemingly sanguine of success. He was dressed in his usual deer skin dress, which admirably displayed his light yet sinewy figure, and in his handkerchief, rolled as a turban over his brow, was placed a handsome white ostrich feather . . . He pressed the hand of each officer as he passed, made some remark in Shawnee appropriate to the occasion which was sufficiently understood by the expressive signs accompanying them, and then passed away forever from our view.[4]

Tecumseh then spoke to Procter, using Elliott as his interpreter. The men were too close together, he said, too exposed to enemy riflemen, and those soldiers near the six-pounder, they needed to be stouthearted, for the Americans would certainly make a push for the gun. "Father," said Tecumseh, "tell your young men to be firm, and all will be well." They were not good friends, the Shawnee chief and the British general, but Tecumseh now saw standing before him a brother warrior, ready to fight with the odds against him. "Father," he said, "have a big heart!"[5]

Destiny, unfortunately, was bearing heavily upon the hapless general. When Tecumseh had gone, Procter withdrew eighty men from his line to create a reserve line under the command of Muir and Bullock. He improved the chances of his men surviving enemy sniping, but those open and largely unprotected files were an irresistible target for the American cavalry. They

stood in ragged formation, some shielding themselves behind what little
cover there was, most squinting nervously ahead for a sight of the enemy
through the trees.

The force which William Henry Harrison brought up between three and
four o'clock amounted to at least 3,500 men. True, he had few regulars, only
120, but the spearhead of his army, Richard Mentor Johnson's regiment of
1,000 Kentucky mounted volunteers, was a sharp one. Armed with long rifles, tomahawks, and knives, garbed in leather hunting smocks, and drilled
in maneuvers of every description, these riders were mobile, skillful, and
afraid of nothing the allies could throw at them. Many thirsted to revenge
the losses of the River Raisin and Fort Meigs.

Behind Johnson's regiment marched five brigades of Kentucky militia,
personally commanded by the state governor, a plucky sixty-three-year-old
named Isaac Shelby. Three of the brigades advanced in lines, one behind the
other, the first under George Trotter. The two remaining brigades, led by
General Joseph Desha, formed a line along Harrison's left flank, its right
joining the left of Trotter's brigade at an obtuse angle. In addition, Harrison
fielded 260 Shawnees, Delawares, Wyandots, and Senecas, recruited in
Ohio, and two six-pounders. Standing defiantly before such a force, Tecumseh and Procter were outnumbered more than three to one.

Waiting with his own Shawnee and Delaware followers at the extreme
left of the Indian line, Tecumseh was close to his British allies but could not
see them through the profusion of thickets and timber. It was they, rather
than the Indians, who received the first assault—delivered by the first
battalion of Johnson's regiment, led by the colonel's brother, Lieutenant-
Colonel James Johnson.

The Shawnee chief heard the American bugles, the rattle of rifle fire as
American sharpshooters got to work, and then two volleys of musketry, as
the first and second lines of redcoats tried to check the four columns of
mounted Kentuckians thundering down upon them. There seems little
doubt that as Tecumseh tensed himself to meet the attack upon his position
he received shattering news: the redcoats had been broken, almost immediately. At a stroke the troops covering the Indian left had been smashed.

It had taken only a few scant minutes for the Americans to crash
through and flank the British lines. With the Kentuckians sweeping wildly
around them, and forty-three men down, eighteen of them dead or fatally
wounded, most of the redcoats surrendered. Their six-pounder, deserted by
its guard, was taken by Harrison's regulars before it could fire a shot.

After a meager attempt to rally his men, Procter left them to their fate,
and galloped away with his aide, Captain Hall. Shortly afterward and still

shaken, the general galloped through the short main street that ran straight between the cabins of the mission Indians at Moraviantown. He had some men at the settlement, preparing a plateau behind the village for battle, but Procter gave them little time. Without dismounting he gulped down a drink and then rode on, leaving a bewildered artillery officer with no more orders than to rearrange his guns. Procter had abandoned any semblance of leadership, and his force had offered negligible resistance. The most generous estimate of the casualties they had inflicted was one man killed and three wounded. For the 41st, whose battle honors included Detroit, the Raisin, and Fort Meigs, it was, as Elliott said candidly, "shameful in the highest degree."[6]

While the first battalion of Johnson's regiment annihilated the British force, the second battalion picked its way across the small swamp on the Indian left to charge Tecumseh's stand. Tecumseh had no intention of retreating without a fight, whatever might have happened to his allies. He may have remembered the field of Maguaga, when he had also been left to face a superior foe unaided. He had fought on then, and he would do so today. All along the Indian line, the warriors sat eerily quiet, pulling back the hammers on their muskets, peering from behind trees, fallen logs, and brush, and waiting. On the right many of the Indians knew nothing of the British defeat.

Johnson's men swept boldly forward, oblivious of the uncounted numbers of painted foes ahead. At the front Jacob Stucker's company formed a line of skirmishers on foot. Then, eventually passing them, there were twenty riders—volunteers all, led by Richard Mentor Johnson himself—a "forlorn hope" designed to empty the Indian guns. And finally the rest of the battalion, in two mounted columns about four hundred yards apart. Farther back still there came the long lines of Isaac Shelby's Kentucky militia, striding earnestly forward.

Tecumseh ignored the skirmishers, but as the forlorn hope sped forward the Indians rose from their cover and delivered a crashing volley into the oncoming riders. Instantly the air was filled with thick acrid black powder smoke, and the ground strewn with dead and wounded men and thrashing animals. Johnson himself was hit four times, but kept the saddle of his white or gray mare. When the charging columns also struck the Indian line at its left and center, they too met a fusillade from the screaming warriors. Colonel James Davidson, who rode at the head of the left column, was struck in the chest, stomach, and thigh.

To their chagrin the Kentuckians found their horses floundering in impenetrable and swampy ground. Many of the riders dismounted to fight on foot, closing face-to-face with their opponents over logs and shrubs.

Farther to the right the Indians appeared to gain the advantage when they fired upon the infantry where Trotter's line met Desha's flank division, and then surged forward with their tomahawks. The infantry faltered, then fell back, but reinforcements came up from behind, and Harrison and Desha themselves were soon on hand to check disorder. Rallying, the militia resumed their advance, and intermingled with Johnson's regiment to force the Indians back to their original positions. Shouting, the roar of muskets, the squeals of terrified horses, and the stench of gunsmoke were now the context of a desperate struggle.

In the thick of the battle the Indian warriors occasionally saw amid the trees and smoke the reassuring figure of their leader, firing his musket and yelling encouragement. Dressed in his deerskin leggings and hunting shirt, a sash evidently drawn about his waist, and his face painted black and red, he had little beyond his impressive presence that particularly marked him from his fellows, although a bandage around one arm indicated the wound he had received at Chatham, and the British medal was still about his neck.

Both parties charged, only to be repulsed. Desha described one such movement, when over a hundred soldiers he took to belong to Johnson's regiment fled into his line. The pursuing Indians recoiled to the left when they encountered the superior numbers of militia behind, and the offensive came to nothing.

Upon another such occasion Tecumseh sprinted forward to inspire his followers. One of the Big Knives raised a gun, loaded with a ball and several buckshot. He trained it upon the left side of the oncoming chief's chest and fired . . .

Spreading feverishly among the warriors, the news took the heart out of them. One American recalled that "they gave the loudest yells I ever heard from human beings and that ended the fight."[7] Farther right, firing went on somewhat longer, but the Indians had been let down by the British, had lost the inspiration of Tecumseh, and were fighting crippling odds. Gradually they withdrew into the swamp and the battle ended.

It could not have been more decisive. Harrison had lost only 15 men slain or mortally wounded and a similar number injured. The Indian casualties were comparable, but the British had suffered severely, losing 634 men killed or captured before, during, or immediately after the battle of Moraviantown.

As some British had the grace to admit, that was not their greatest loss, for the man who more than any other represented the British-Indian alliance lay dead on the field. Nearby were some of his greatest friends, including young Andrew Clark, fatally injured, and the chief's brother-in-law, Wahsikegaboe, the top of his head blown off at point-blank range.

Curious soldiers, gathering around the body of Tecumseh, were surprised to see a man who seemed less than ferocious. "He was a fine looking man," Peter Trisler told his father. His features seemed "majestic, even in death," thought Samuel Brown, one of Johnson's regiment. But it was Major Thomas Rowland who four days later penned to a friend the most sympathetic portrait:

> Tecumseh is certainly killed. I saw him with my own eyes. It was the first time I had seen this celebrated chief. There was something so majestic, so dignified, and yet so mild in his countenance, as he lay stretched on his back on the ground where a few minutes before he had rallied his men to the fight, that while gazing on him with admiration and pity, I forgot he was a savage. He had received a wound in the arm and had it bound up before he received the mortal wound. He had such a countenance as I shall never forget. He did not appear to me so large a man as he was represented—I did not suppose his height exceeded five feet ten or eleven inches, but exceedingly well proportioned. The British say he compelled them to fight.[8]

Captain William Caldwell recalled fleeing through the wet woods, and coming upon Matthew Elliott and Tecumseh's son. He told Paukeesaa of his father's death. There was no reply, but as the boy loaded his musket his hands were trembling.

No one can tell for sure how Tecumseh died. Not because of a lack of testimony, for perhaps there is too much of it, but because the subject became a red-hot political issue. By 1830 Richard Mentor Johnson, then a senator for Kentucky, was being presented as a possible presidential candidate, and he did reach the vice presidency in 1837. Nothing about Johnson was lauded more than a claim that he had slain Tecumseh, and columns of vehement newsprint were devoted to proving that he was or was not entitled to the credit of having vanquished the country's greatest Indian foe. Johnson's supporters eagerly searched out witnesses who saw their hero shoot Tecumseh that day on the Thames, while his detractors were no less active, and here and there other witnesses popped up, telling how someone else had killed the chief. Around Tecumseh's death there gathered an unfathomable humbug. Many many statements were made about the subject, but barely one can be taken at face value.[9]

To be fair, the claim made for Johnson, as well as the version of Tecumseh's death it offered, has to be taken seriously. There is no doubt Johnson killed an Indian in the battle. The colonel was hit four times by musket balls. His horse had also been grievously wounded, and became entangled in the branches of a fallen tree. Johnson eventually extricated the struggling animal and turned its head toward the roots of the tree. He saw an Indian before him with a musket, and received from him his fifth wound, in the bridle hand, which remained "withered and emaciated" ever after. Then the warrior pulled a tomahawk and rushed forward "with a gentle leaping trot." Johnson thrust his reins over his left arm, and with his right drew a pistol which he fired at close range, just as the Indian raised his hatchet for a throw. The Indian was hurled backward, but Johnson was weak through loss of blood, and became so faint that he had to be assisted from the field.[10]

Now Johnson had never seen Tecumseh, and neither he nor his brother James claimed that the Indian he had killed was the Shawnee leader when they wrote their contemporary dispatches. Be that as it may, others were less reticent. As soon as Tecumseh's body was discovered at the end of the battle, there were members of the mounted regiment who credited Johnson with the slaying. Throughout the 1830s, when the subject became a public controversy, Johnson prudently admitted that while he had killed an Indian, he had no idea whether the slain warrior was Tecumseh or not. For several years he allowed others to present his claim, and only in 1843, it seems, did he feel confident enough to openly pronounce himself to be the man who shot Tecumseh.[11]

Several Indian witnesses were found to shore up the story, perhaps the best-known being Tecumseh's old friend Shabeni, who lived in retirement in Illinois, dependent upon the charity of white friends. Shabeni treasured the memory of his leader, and had certainly been close by him during the battle of Moraviantown. Among several accounts the aging Potawatomi gave, none was more quoted than an interview conducted in the United States Hotel, Chicago, in 1839.

> Tecumseh was a very brave but cautious man [said Shabeni]. He had, however, been wounded in the neck and became desperate. He thought his wound was mortal, and told his warriors that, as he must die, there could be no risk in rushing forward to kill Col. Johnson. He did so, and Shaw-ben-eh saw him when he fell. His object was to strike the colonel with his tomahawk before he saw him, and a moment more of inattention and the colonel's head would have been sundered. He was shot just as his arm reached the full height to strike the fatal blow.
>
> He [Shabeni] described the colonel's horse very minutely. He was very large and white, with occasionally a jet black spot. Another Indian in company, whom Shaw-ben-eh said was but a boy at the time of the battle, interrupted him to say that his mane and tail were black. The next day he was with many others and this boy, went upon the field of battle, and saw Tecumseh's body there, and by the

side of it another Indian whose skin had been taken off. He said he had heard of this skin having been exhibited as that of Tecumseh. They might think so. But it was not. Tecumseh's body had not been touched.

Here someone asked where and how they buried him? This aroused the chief from his seat, and he was eloquent in the extreme. None but brave warriors die on the battlefield. Such, afraid of nothing when alive, don't care for dogs, wolves or eagles and crows, when dead. They want the prairie, the whole prairie, to lie upon. So Tecumseh, the bravest man that ever was, whom the Great Spirit would not let be killed by the common soldier, but sent to Col. Johnson to be killed, wanted no grave nor honors. He let every animal come and eat of his flesh, as he made every red man love, and every white man fear him.[12]

Statements such as this, made by witnesses whose qualifications seemed impeccable, convinced many that Johnson had truly been responsible for the great chief's death; but more astute historians are entitled to question that identification. How did Shabeni know that the rider was Johnson, for example? He had never seen the Colonel before the battle, and if he saw him then it can only have been fleetingly and in the excitement and haze of conflict. Nor was Shabeni in Johnson's presence again until 1836, when he saw him in Washington.

Gordon Hubbard, an acquaintance of the Potawatomi chief, was one who doubted Shabeni's identification. He repeatedly interrogated the old man about those few seconds in 1813, and found him much confused, influenced by what he had later heard said about Tecumseh's death. "You Americans say Johnson killed him," said Shabeni, "and he, Johnson, should be believed. Somebody killed him, and I saw a man on a white horse fire and Tecumseh fell. Some one else may have shot him."[13]

In fact, although Shabeni held firm on some points—he used to say the rider uttered an oath, "God damn!" as he shot Tecumseh—there are grounds for thinking he occasionally remodeled his memory of the event according to what he had afterward been told. At one time he was propagating an entirely different version of Tecumseh's death. And his story of the finding of the Shawnee's body, given in 1839, was almost certainly untrue. However, it resembles what is apparently an entirely invented narrative of the battle, ascribed to Black Hawk, published the year before Shabeni gave his interview. It is conceivable that Shabeni had adopted this story, which spared him the pain of admitting that the Indians had not been able to carry off Tecumseh's body and save it from mutilation.

Shabeni was not the only Indian to support the Johnson claim, but the possibility that these statements were tampered with, or invented, for political or partisan purposes cannot be ruled out. They may not even be independent of each other. At least one of the other Indian witnesses telling a like story, a Potawatomi leader named Ap-ta-ke-sic (Half Day), was an associate of Shabeni and might have influenced, or been influenced by, him.[14]

Richard Mentor Johnson could have shot Tecumseh, or he may have shot Wahsikegaboe, or indeed some other warrior. The evidence is simply too inconclusive. Moreover, while Johnson's claim was the first to be set down, and is still the strongest, it was by no means uncontested. Some veterans thought that a member of the "forlorn hope," William Whitley, whose body lay fairly close to Tecumseh's, might have shot the chief before being cut down himself. Others championed the claims of Jacob Harrod Hollman or David King.

Hollman was a private in Stucker's company, and used to tell how he and a companion were advancing on foot when two Indians rushed forward and threw up their guns to fire. The Americans were faster, and each killed his man. The warrior Hollman shot had "a pistol of curious workmanship" in his right hand, which in death was extended as if in the act of firing. Hollman took the pistol, and he maintained that British prisoners told him that Isaac Brock had given it to Tecumseh. His account convinced some, including the head of the United States Bureau of Indian Affairs in 1851; but it was largely uncorroborated and somewhat contradictory. For instance, Hollman seems also to have stated that Tecumseh was firing an "English fowling piece" rather than a pistol.[15]

David King, a young private in James Davidson's company, had more support. According to the fullest statement of his claim, made by James Davidson and his brother, Michael, both of whom were in the battle, King was one of several soldiers skirmishing on foot toward the right, attempting to frustrate Indian flankers. An Indian leveled a musket at King, but one of the boy's friends, named Clark, shouted a warning. The cry distracted the Indian, who turned his gun upon Clark; but before he could squeeze the trigger King shot him in the breast, close to the left nipple. "Whoop!" King screamed in excitement. "By God! I have killed one damned yellow bugger!" The warrior's body, which King later stripped for souvenirs, was, according to the Davidsons, the same identified as Tecumseh's.[16]

King's claim was published as early as 1816, and may have been a respectable one, but unfortunately a close analysis of the different statements of it made by James Davidson only invite suspicion. His was far from a dispassionate narrative of events, and he falsified details in order to square them with what was known, or presumed to be known, about Tecumseh's death. In that Davidson resembled so many others who professed to know the secrets surrounding the end of Tecumseh but who merely deepened the mystery.

The Indians, of course, were best placed to provide a solution to the problem, yet not one substantial account alleged to have come from them can confidently be accepted as authentic. They vary considerably, even when allowance has been made for the discrepancies that inevitably distort the memory of events long past.

Some Winnebagos were reported to have said Tecumseh fell at the first fire. Shabeni and Ap-ta-ke-sic recounted the classic debacle with Johnson. But perhaps the most interesting narrative, if only because it was the closest in time to the battle and predated the ballyhoo of Johnson's campaign, was given to Thomas Forsyth at Fort Clark in 1816. The witness was described variously as an Ottawa and a Potawatomi. He told how he and two Potawatomis, Kichekemit and Mad Sturgeon, defended the Indian line close to Tecumseh, who carried a saber and two pistols. They planned to run up on the oncoming horsemen, seize the animals' bridles, and unseat the riders, but Johnson's volunteers were too many and they charged too fast. Kichekemit was killed, Mad Sturgeon fled, and the narrator himself hid behind a bush. But Tecumseh tackled a foot soldier, who thrust at him with a bayonet, piercing his deerskin hunting shirt about the hips. The chief tried to disentangle himself and use his saber, when a horseman rode up and shot him through the head. Three days later some Indians returned to the ground, where they found the body of their leader, scalped and partly mutilated.[17]

One supreme fact burns brightly through the mass of conflicting testimony. Tecumseh had promised to die fighting rather than surrender his lands to the enemy, and deserted by his redcoat allies and confronting terrific odds, he had done it. More than anything else it was that martyrdom which propelled the so-called "battle" of Moraviantown—in reality a sharp fight that lasted little more than half an hour—into history and legend.

Not long after the engagement ended, Tecumseh's body was discovered on the field. It was identified by Anthony Shane, who was with Harrison's Indians, and eventually by some of the captured British officers. Observers deduced that the chief had been hit several times because his body bore numerous injuries: a bullet hole, too small to admit a man's little finger, near the heart; one or two wounds caused by buckshot; and a cut on the head.[18]

Ignorant soldiery scalped and stripped the corpse, and the next day disappointed latecomers tore pieces of skin from the back and thigh to convert into razor strops. Henry Clay was said to have exhibited one in Washington the following winter, and as late as 1862 a man named Tarrance Kirby pleaded with President Abraham Lincoln for the release of his incarcerated Confederate grandsons, protesting that he had once served his country by helping to slay and "skin" Tecumseh. Kirby proudly recalled that he "brought two pieces" of the chief's "yellow hide home with me to my mother and sweethearts."

Not everyone thought that way. Shane condemned the outrage, and when Harrison visited the body with Commodore Perry on the sixth he confessed himself "greatly vexed and mortified" by the sight. At that time the face was so swollen that Harrison could not identify it. So many false reports of Tecumseh's death had appeared in newspapers that by an understandable prudence Harrison omitted in his official report what was arguably the most significant result of his victory.[19]

No one knows where the Shawnee chief was laid to his final rest. Peter Trisler wrote on 8 October that the body was given the Canadians, who took it back to Sandwich for burial. But over the years many stories have been told, tales of secrets passed furtively from generation to generation, of burials and reburials in hidden places, and of graves privately nurtured and cherished by dedicated Indian followers and their descendants. Now and again crumbling human skeletons have been unearthed, stirring temporary excitement and speculation, but two hundred years have not yielded the spot where the troubled remains of the Indian leader finally found peace.

In 1830, when much of the passion of the border war had been spent, two Americans traveled leisurely up the Thames, thinking of Tecumseh's last retreat. Both would be involved in removing the remaining Shawnees from Ohio, across the Mississippi, James B. Gardner as a commissioner and Daniel R. Dunihue as a conductor of emigration; but they had learned to respect the memory of the chief who had defended the Old Northwest and lost.

A local guided them over the neglected and silent battlefield, pointing out the patches of sunken ground on a small ridge where the British and American dead lay buried. A short distance above the field, and close to where the wide Thames stole placidly by, the visitors were shown another grave, which they were told contained the bones of Tecumseh. There, among the marsh willows, wild rose, and witch hazel, a modest mound about a foot in height was colonized by a young gooseberry bush, some briers, and a few shrubs of white ash. Beside it lay a hewn post, five feet long. It had fallen from its place, but it still bore the remains of flaking red paint and weathered Indian characters.

Sitting solemnly alongside, one of the Americans took out some paper and wrote "lines written at the grave of Tecumseh . . . July 22, 1830, by a citizen of Ohio." They began:

> *Sleep on brave chief! Sleep on in Glory's arms!*
> *Freed from men's malice, and from War's alarms;*
> *Distinguished savage, great in mind and soul,*
> *Rest here in peace, while ceaseless ages roll.*[20]

EPILOGUE

29

SINCE OUR GREAT CHIEF TECUMTHA HAS BEEN KILLED

The fight at Moraviantown and Tecumseh's death ended serious conflict in the Old Northwest. Content to control the Detroit frontier, using its military and naval power to daunt Tecumseh's old supporters, the United States curbed the Indian war but saw no need to occupy that part of Upper Canada. Farther west, Britain was more successful, and the Indians still rallied to the redcoats. The British gained naval command of Lake Huron, and extended their influence on the upper Mississippi, where the Americans lost Fort Madison and Prairie du Chien. Even here, though, the fighting was on a small scale.

After their defeat at Moraviantown the remains of the British-Indian army retired to the Center Division at the head of Lake Ontario. Procter was court-martialed in the winter of 1814–1815. Found deficient in judgment, he was sentenced to be reprimanded in public and suspended from rank and pay for six months. The suspension, but not the reprimand, was rescinded, but Procter was never employed again. He died in Bath, England, in 1822.

What was left of Tecumseh's following shivered and starved at the head of Lake Ontario for the rest of the war, poorly fed and clothed. Although six hundred warriors eventually gathered there, with their families, they did little fighting. Attempts to find a successor with even a thread of Tecumseh's intelligence, determination, eloquence, and influence failed. Sir George Prevost invited Tecumapease, Paukeesaa, and a few other chiefs to Quebec, where they were received in March 1814. Tecumapease should have been in

seclusion, mourning the death of a husband and brother, and she was presented with some condolence presents by Lady Prevost. During his speech
Sir George remarked upon the sorrow he had felt upon hearing of Tecumseh's death, and Tecumapease burst into tears.

The Prophet had not been invited, so poor was the opinion the British
held of him, but in April the Shawnees at Lake Ontario made Paukeesaa
their civil chief and the Prophet their war chief—offices that had previously
been united in Tecumseh. Neither incumbent was fit for the duty. Paukeesaa
was turning into a handsome young man ("by his looks [he] may some day
make good the place of his father," someone wrote two years later), but he
was still a youth. While the war continued, authority in the band rested with
the war chief, Tenskwatawa, but when it ended and the civil chief was elevated to the premier position, Paukeesaa surrendered the office to an Indian
named Yealabaheah.[1]

As for the Prophet, he tried to extend his influence to all the western Indians at the lake. He retained some adherents, particularly among the
Shawnees and Kickapoos, but simply lacked the talent for the job. He bad-
gered the British for supplies, including rum—an act his brother would not
have condoned, and which the Prophet himself would have condemned in
better days. Instead of pulling the scattered tribal groups together, he exac-
erbated their differences, and he could not be brought into military service.
He decamped from the front at the first opportunity. Regarding him as a
pompous nuisance, the British ignored him. Poor Tenskwatawa tried to recall the glory of his dead brother, "the great dependence of your children,"
as he told his white allies. In frustration he complained: "The [Shawnee]
women look to me as their chief . . . I am now put in the place of my brother,
Techkumthai, who is gone from us, and it is expected *I* will be listened to as
he was!"[2]

But the Prophet was not Tecumseh and everyone knew it. The Ottawa
chief Naiwash, who had been the second chief in the battle of Moraviantown, put it succinctly in October 1814:

> We Indians . . . from the westward, perhaps the Master of Life would
> give us more luck if we would stick together as we formerly did . . .
> and we probably might go back and tread again upon our own lands.
> Chiefs and warriors, since our great chief Tecumtha has been killed
> we do not listen to one another. We do not rise together. We hurt our-
> selves by it. It is our own fault . . . We do not, when we go to war, rise
> together, but we go one or two, and the rest say they will go tomorrow.[3]

The war officially ended on 24 December 1814, just over two months after Naiwash's lament. Britain had entered negotiations at Ghent, Belgium,

with high hopes, because the defeat of France had released British reinforcements, including Wellington's Peninsular War veterans, for North
America. As a sine qua non for peace, a confident Britain demanded the creation of an Indian buffer state in the northwest, based on the Greenville line
of 1795 and inalienable by the tribes to either Britain or the United States.
It was an attempt to honor those pledges made to Tecumseh.

Inevitably, the American peace commissioners rejected the sine qua non
outright. Although the British captured Washington, the following campaigns misfired, and wearied by twenty years of war in Europe, Britain
wanted peace. When the treaty of Ghent was signed on Christmas Eve it did
nothing more for the Indians than restore the rights, privileges, and territories they had possessed in 1811. In other words, they were to suffer no
reprisals for having fought for the King. If Tecumseh's spirit lingered about
the marshy reaches of the Thames, he would not have been surprised that
the redcoats had failed the Indians in the end. They always had.

Even what protection the treaty gave the Indians did nothing for the
Creeks. After Tecumseh's death they became embroiled in the most intense
spell of conflict that ever took place between the United States and American Indians. In a short five months, between November 1813 and March
1814, the Red Sticks inflicted seven hundred casualties in killed and
wounded in pitched battles with invading armies. The names of battles such
as Calabee Creek, Tallushatchee, Talladega, and Horseshoe Bend are almost
forgotten now, but they were desperate encounters. In the north the Indians
had suffered lightly in battle. But the Red Sticks were wretchedly supplied,
often ill led (sometimes by "prophets" rather than experienced war chiefs),
and vastly outnumbered by armies from Mississippi Territory, Georgia, and
Tennessee, and contingents of pro-American Choctaws, Cherokees, Chickasaws, and Lower Creeks. They suffered appalling losses. Eight hundred Red
Stick warriors escaped to Florida, but Britons who knew them estimated
they had lost eighteen hundred men in the fighting, while several hundred
of their noncombatants also had been killed or captured. According to a
British officer, the Red Stick refugees were "such objects I never saw the like
of, absolute skin and bone."[4]

The Creeks lost even more than that. For on 9 August 1814 Andrew Jackson, who had risen to prominence suppressing the Red Sticks, imposed the
treaty of Fort Jackson upon friendly and hostile Creeks alike. It took away
half the nation's lands, some twenty-three million acres.

For a while the remaining Red Sticks, who had been no party to the
treaty, tried to overturn it. When the British invaded the south in 1814 they
joined the King's standard, with some Seminoles and blacks. Even after the
British invasion had been repelled, and peace concluded, the Red Sticks argued that the treaty of Ghent, by restoring Indians to their possessions of

1811, nullified the treaty of Fort Jackson. Helped by a sympathetic British officer, one Creek leader, Josiah Francis, even visited London to plead with the government to intervene to protect Creek land. True to form, the British refused to do so. They washed their hands of their Indian allies, and the last vestige of credibility for Tecumseh's policy fell to the ground.[5]

To salve their consciences the British paid compensation to Indian women whose husbands had been killed in service, although much less than a board of officers had initially recommended. On 25 April 1815 Tecumapease and Tecumseh's last wife duly exchanged their crosses on a receipt at Burlington, Lake Ontario, for a mere fifty dollars each.

Tecumapease was then in her fifties, and near the end of her life. Anthony Shane tells us that after the war she returned to Detroit, where she died. One suspects this statement referred to the Indian council hosted by the Americans at Spring Wells, Detroit, in August and September 1815. The purpose of the meeting was to arrange a cease-fire with Indians formerly allied to the British, and to allow those exiled in Canada to come home. Maybe it was here that Tecumapease died. One by one the members of this remarkable aboriginal family passed from the scene.

The Prophet and Paukeesaa did not sign the treaty of Spring Wells. They wanted to return to the Wabash, where they might continue as chiefs of their own band, but the Americans insisted they settle at Wapakoneta with the Ohio Shawnees. Tenskwatawa simply could not swallow living under the supervision of his old rival, Black Hoof, or abide aping the ways of the whites as the Mekoches at Wapakoneta were doing. Although a few of the Prophet's followers did sneak through to the Wabash in 1816 and 1817, Tenskwatawa and Paukeesaa remained in Canada, living on British gratuities. They and six of their Shawnee dependents were awarded a total of £388 under a British statute of 1823, which allowed for the indemnification of war losses. But they feuded with successive superintendents of the Amherstburg Indian Department, and the British were glad to see the Prophet and his nephew finally return to American territory in 1824.[6]

Aging now, and beginning to drink again, the Prophet was falling far short of the ideals he had once propagated, but he still claimed the Great Spirit spoke to him in his dreams, still insisted that he wanted to live by hunting as of old, and had not lost his skills as a demagogue.[7] Few were listening anymore, and it was to regain some of his former influence that he came out of exile.

He returned at the invitation of Lewis Cass, governor of Michigan Territory. Tenskwatawa gave Cass an account of Shawnee life and an unreliable fragment of autobiography ("he, as is usual with him, never delivers anything as he receives it," George Ironside once said of the Prophet), and he promised the Governor that he would help persuade the Ohio Shawnees to move across the Mississippi, releasing their lands to settlers. The Prophet saw an opportunity to put himself at the head of a Shawnee party in Kansas, and he grasped at it. He had become everything he had once detested: a supporter of land cessions, and a dependent and instrument of the United States.[8]

The Prophet's emigration party of Shawnees and Mingoes, including Paukeesaa, left Ohio in 1826. Two years later it arrived in Kansas, where the United States wanted to consolidate the Ohio and Missouri Shawnees. Tenskwatawa supposed the tribe might reunify there under his leadership, but his influence swiftly declined. Once more he became lonely, "silent and melancholy," dwelling in the past, and regaling occasional visitors with stories about Tecumseh. His brother, he said, had been a great general, and were it not for his death he would have built a mighty confederacy from the Great Lakes to Mexico.[9]

Even Paukeesaa left his uncle's village. Little more is known about Tecumseh's son. An old Shawnee remembered that he attended the intertribal council organized by the Cherokees at Tahlequah (Oklahoma) in June 1843, and that he died soon after. He had two sons, it was said. One, John, reached maturity, served in the American 14th Kansas Regiment, and died without issue during the Civil War.[10]

By then the storm Tecumseh had helped foment had long since blown itself out. The old rebels had been gathered to their fathers. Main Poc, incorrigible to the last, died in the spring of 1816. Pamawatam was trying to revive the Indian confederacy as late as 1816, but three years later he and other Kickapoos agreed to exchange tribal lands in Indiana and Illinois for territory across the Mississippi. The Sac Black Hawk also flirted with pantribalism, but with no more success. He made his lone stand against the United States in 1832 and was overwhelmingly crushed.

The embers of the revolt smoldered for years in the south. Red Stick survivors under McQueen and Francis sheltered among the Seminoles and blacks in Florida, where their continued hostility to the Americans eventually brought on the so-called "First Seminole War" and Jackson's expulsion of the Spanish in 1818. Francis was captured in Jackson's invasion and hanged, and McQueen died a few years later, but their bitterness passed to a new generation. Francis's son, Earle, was a leader of the Creek "war" of 1836, and McQueen's grandnephew, Osceola, achieved national fame as a prime agitator of the "Second Seminole War" of 1835.

Earle and Osceola died resisting the removal of the tribes. But if those who had inherited the mantle of armed resistance from Tecumseh failed, so too did Indians who hoped to protect their lands by cooperating with the Americans. Such a man was old Black Hoof. In a way he was even more tragic than Tecumseh, for, in the end, the years his people had peacefully co-existed with white neighbors, the faltering steps they had taken on the road to "civilization," and the military aid they had given the United States—all counted for nothing. The Ohio Shawnees were moved west with the others. Black Hoof fought against it while there was breath in his feeble body. The chief himself was mercifully spared emigration, for he died at Wapakoneta in 1831, but it was in the full knowledge that a removal treaty was imminent and that his policies had foundered as signally as those of Tecumseh. He died disillusioned, convinced that the whites had ruined his people. Among the Indians there had been no winners.

On a cold day in November 1836 Dr. J. A. Chute and a companion made their way along a winding woodland path in Wyandotte County, Kansas, somewhere in the modern district of Argentine, Kansas City. The path led down a hill to a few rude dwellings, none more distinguished than the others. The two entered one of the houses by a low bark-covered portico, negotiating a half-famished dog as they entered a dimly lit interior in which "two or three platforms built against the wall served the purpose of bedsteads, covered with blankets and skins." A few pumpkins and ears of corn were stored, but the floor was littered with spoons, pipes, trays, and other utensils, and in a corner of the squalid room, near an "apology for a fireplace," a man lay on one of the beds, a blanket thrown over him.

> Here was fallen, savage greatness [wrote Chute]. I involuntarily stop[ped] for a moment to view in silence the spectacle of a man whose wo[rd] was once law to numerous tribes, now lying on a miserable pallet, dying in poverty, neglected by all but his own family. He that exalteth himself shall be abased.
>
> I approached him. He drew aside his blanket and discovered a form emaciated in the extreme, but the broad proportions of which indicated that it had once been the seat of great strength. His countenance was sunken and haggard, but appeared—it might have been fancy—to exhibit something of the soul within. I thought I could discover . . . something of the marks which pride, ambition and the workings of a dark, designing mind had stamped there.[11]

The old Indian was sick, very sick, and had summoned help, but he was still suspicious of the white man's medicine. In that final illness he swooned several times, but each recovery convinced him that the spirits would not let him die. He still hesitated to commit himself to an alien science, and desired his visitors to return in three days. Then he would receive treatment.

True to their word, the two Americans returned at the appointed time to ask whether the old man would accept their services. But the Prophet, the last of the children of Pukeshinwau and Methoataaskee, was dying and speechless, and never did reply.

It was Tecumseh they remembered, whites and Indians both.

His own tribe exalted him. Even the chiefs of Wapakoneta, who had contested his every move, referred to him as "the great Taycomseh" in 1815, and the Prophet lived to see his brother's memory "revered as the pride of the nation" and ranked far above his own.[12] The historical facts about Tecumseh were soon forgotten, but the Shawnees turned him into a mythic figure. One tribal elder, interviewed in the 1930s, said that Tecumseh had been born of a virgin with knowledge granted him by the Creator. He was impregnable to witchcraft, except when practiced by members of his own people, and it was by such means that he was eventually overthrown.

In the twentieth century Shawnees were crediting both brothers with molding tribal ceremonial and religious life. Some ascribed the fall bread dance to the Prophet. Tecumseh, it was said, had introduced the green corn dance, which celebrated the ripening of the harvest; the buffalo head dance, said to have been communicated to Tecumseh by a buffalo that was his guardian spirit; and a warrior's dance. He was believed to have contributed objects to the Kispoko sacred bundle. In fact, the green corn festival was being held by some Shawnees when Tecumseh was only a young warrior, but the point is not whether such attributions are, or are not, true. It is that Shawnees take an immense pride in Tecumseh, and wish to commemorate him in some of their ancient traditions.

One early twentieth-century Shawnee legend even predicted a second coming. Tecumseh's reappearance would be marked, as was his birth, by the flight of a star across the heavens. When that day came all the Indian tribes would unite.[13]

Admiration for Tecumseh is by no means confined to Shawnees. A Potawatomi band once treasured a sacred bundle associated with the great chief, and alleged family connections are eagerly embraced in many tribes. Creeks and Cherokees have claimed that Tecumseh was descended from them. One Delaware tradition held that Tecumseh's father had been adopted by the tribe, and that Tecumseh was raised by Delawares; according to another, found among the Delawares of the Moraviantown reservation in Ontario, Tecumseh's mother took a Delaware as her second husband. She and her family were at Moraviantown in 1813, and it was they who gave Tecumseh a secret burial. However shallow-rooted in history some of these traditions are, they can be fiercely defended by communities that hold Tecumseh dear. Some present-day Ojibwas, for example, are convinced that they have descendants of Tecumseh among them, although the idea appears to be no

older than Iola Fuller's novel, *The Loon Feather* (1940). The invented hero-
ine, Oneta of Mackinac Island, is represented to have been an Ojibwa
daughter of Tecumseh.[14]

All peoples need heroes and heroines, their Lincolns, Nelsons, and Joan
of Arcs, people who embody ideals and aspirations and about whom a national identity can be hung. Indians need such figures, too, perhaps more
than most, for their cultures have been debased, their territories taken from
them, and through much history their communities have been broken.
Tecumseh may have been unsuccessful, but he bequeathed to Indian
peoples something of great importance: from his memory they have drawn
pride and self-respect.

Unlike most Indian heroes, Tecumseh does not stand for one tribe or
another, but for all Indian peoples. He had opposed intertribal hostilities,
and tried to bind the nations in peace and mutual solidarity. Historically, his
confederacy had been an imperfect union, unable to control its elements,
and capable of sowing divisions, such as those among the Creeks. But
Tecumseh's ambition to be a national Indian leader, rather than merely a local one, and his vision of a pan-Indian brotherhood have powerful appeal
for Indians of today.

Tecumseh was not the only important pan-Indian leader. He lived at a
time when powerful threats from Britain and the United States had stimulated a tradition of ambitious federalism, particularly among the Shawnees.
The most sophisticated apostle of the movement, however, was the Mohawk
Joseph Brant. Brant was the equal of Tecumseh in vision, ambition, energy,
and ability, and he was more pragmatic. In 1793 he discounted as illusory a
boundary Tecumseh advocated twenty years later. Yet it was Tecumseh who
became the supreme pan-Indian hero. Brant lacked Tecumseh's passion,
and had the misfortune to survive into old age; Tecumseh fell a martyr to
the cause on the battlefield.

After Tecumseh's death no one challenged his position. The death of pan-
tribalism in the east, and the sheer speed with which the United States swept
toward the west coast, denied the Indians of the far west the time that would
have been necessary to recognize the need for solidarity, to overcome intertribal differences, and to organize resistance on more than a local front. A
few leaders flirted with the idea of building confederacies—men such as the
Yaqui Juan Banderas; Coacoochee, a brilliant Seminole; the Yakima headman Kamiakin; and the Sioux leaders Little Crow, Red Cloud, and Sitting
Bull—but no one with the extent of Tecumseh's vision or activity appeared.
Tenskwatawa found a comparable successor: Wovoka, the Ghost Dance
prophet. Tecumseh never did. For Indians today he remains the ultimate
symbol not only of courage and endeavor, but also of unity and fraternity.[15]

Indians who revered Tecumseh as a patriot about whom a national identity could be constructed were not alone, for Canadians remembered his intervention in their history as decisive. The capture of Detroit had changed the complexion of the war. In Upper Canada the defenders had found a belief in themselves; in the United States the humiliation of Hull's defeat and the Indian threat compelled Americans to devote valuable resources to the war in the west, away from the strategically more significant fronts at Niagara and the St. Lawrence. Until Perry's victory in September 1813, Tecumseh and his Indians were an important feature of the defense of Canada, at a time when the country was at its weakest.

Historians are apt to portray the Indians as pawns of the British, and some undoubtedly were, but Tecumseh was hardly of that number. Arguably it was the other way around. His war with the United States had effectively begun before the British joined him, incorporating his war aims into their own. In that sense the Tecumseh so beloved in Canadian history, the patriot, never existed. His loyalty to the British, to Canada, was purely dependent upon their value to his own cause.

Without probing too deeply into Tecumseh's motivation, Canadians saw only a warrior who had given much, including his life, to their country in its hour of peril. They never raised a national monument to him, as they did to Brock, although the idea was mooted several times between 1841 and 1931, and many local efforts to commemorate the chief were made. In the mid-nineteenth century, for example, officers of the Amherstburg garrison collected money for a memorial. Nevertheless, the chief's name has always abounded: a town in Ontario; *H.M.S. Tecumseth*, a schooner, built in 1815 and raised from Georgian Bay in 1953; and the Calgary naval reserve, HMCS Tecumseh, which enlisted forty-five hundred personnel in World War II and retains as its badge the image of the crouching panther, Tecumseh's totem—to name just a few.[16]

It was through literature that Canadians paid their greatest tributes to Tecumseh, weaving in the process a literary tradition for the young nation. Two of the first book-length poems written by Canadians eulogized Tecumseh. For George Longmore (1793?–1867), whose "Tecumthe, a Poetical Tale in Three Cantos," was written in Montreal and first published in 1824, the chief was a tragic hero

> *who wanted but the polish'd mind*
> *Civilization's wand supplies*
> *To make him mighty midst Mankind.*[17]

So, too, thought John Richardson (1796–1852), Tecumseh's old companion in arms, who interwove literary and military careers. Richardson returned time and again to those haunting scenes of his youth, and the Indian who had captured his imagination so firmly. Although Richardson is now regarded as the greatest of Canada's early novelists, his first treatment of Tecumseh, *Tecumseh; or, The Warrior of the West*, was an epic poem of four cantos, published in 1828 but composed five years earlier. In it Richardson admitted a "generous anxiety to preserve the memory of one of the noblest and most gallant spirits that ever tenanted the breast of man" but steadfastly insisted that his portrait was without "the slightest exaggeration."

To Richardson Tecumseh was the soul of the allied forces, but one of many, including Brock, Barclay, and the men of the 41st Regiment, who deserved to be enrolled among the country's heroes. His history of the war, first published in a London journal, *The New Monthly Magazine and Literary Journal*, in 1826 and 1827, was intended to educate young Canadians in the "gallant deeds" of their fathers, instilling in them the patriotism and sense of community essential to a new nation. Richardson pursued his interest in Tecumseh through two papers and a novel in the Scott-Cooper tradition, *The Canadian Brothers* (1840).[18]

The nationalist poet Charles Mair (1838–1927) regarded the War of 1812 as "the turning point of Canada's destiny," the event which had brought diverse peoples together in defense of the realm and forged a conscious national identity. His five-act tragedy *Tecumseh: A Drama* (1886) was regarded in its day as the country's greatest literary achievement. Mair acknowledged that Tecumseh had fought for the freedom of his own people, but wrote that in doing so he became one to whose "genius and self sacrifice at the most critical period in her [Canada's] history is due the preservation of Canada to the empire." The chief was, thus, significant primarily as a maker of Canada, that "bright youth among the graybeards of the earth."[19]

Tecumseh the patriot was soon an essential part of the education of young Canadians, and every self-respecting series of biographies was expected to devote a volume to him: the Canadian Heroes series (Norman Gurd's *Tecumseh*, 1912); the Chronicles of Canada series (Ethel T. Raymond's *Tecumseh: A Chronicle of the Last Great Leader of His People*, 1915); the Canadian History Readers (Lloyd Roberts's *Tecumseh*, 1930); and the Great Stories of Canada series (Luella Bruce Creighton's *Tecumseh: The Story of the Shawnee Chief*, 1965). Titles such as these are still published today, but the words of Lloyd Roberts speak for all of them:

When you think of the Indians, think of Tecumseh—think of his valour, his steadfastness of purpose, his great heart; think of his loyal service to Canada, and be grateful. Tecumseh is dead? No, Tecumseh lives![20]

Although Canadian writers are still inspired by the role Tecumseh played in the birth of the nation (the poet Don Gutteridge speaks of "birth-ground" and "battleground" in his 1976 *Tecumseh*), some have seen even larger events reflected in his career. In "Tecumseh and the Eagles" the romantic poet Bliss Carman likened the chief's struggle to those of nations fighting for freedom in the First World War. Wallace Havelock Robb's *Tecumtha, Shawnee Chieftain—Astral Avatar* (1958), a blend of poetry and prose, read into Tecumseh's quest for intertribal peace and his early attempts to coexist with the whites a primitive United Nations. Glossing over, or ignorant of, the plans Tecumseh made for war after 1809, Robb turned him into one of the world's peacemakers, a model for generations raised under the threat of nuclear war.[21]

Patriotism of an altogether more sinister kind acclaimed Tecumseh across the Atlantic, of all places in the Germany of the Third Reich. German interest in the frontier was then already old. Travel literature and the great popularity of the novels of James Fenimore Cooper and Karl May had prepared German readers for yet another exemplification of the noble savage.

A few Germans had even tackled Tecumseh before. Some original books were published about him in the nineteenth century, including a biography aimed at the young, Franz Kottenkamp's *Die Ersten Amerikaner im Westen*, issued in 1855. The next year a Dresden sculptor working in Brazil, Friedrich Pettrich, produced the most impressive statue of the chief, hewn out of marble. Pettrich had lived in the United States, where President John Tyler set him to work on George Washington's statue, and he subsequently found other patrons, including the Emperor of Brazil and the Pope. His reclining full figure, *The Dying Tecumseh*, is now in the National Museum of American Art in Washington, but the original plaster model, made in the United States, has a place in the Vatican's Missionary Ethnological Museum in Rome.

However, it was not until the 1930s that Tecumseh achieved breathtaking popularity in Germany, and his elevation was entirely the work of one man: Fritz Steuben (1898–1981), a gifted writer who published under the pseudonym Erhard Wittek. Beginning with *Der Fliergende Pfiel* (The Flying Arrow) in 1930, when Steuben was thirty-two years old, he bombarded the public with a series of Tecumseh novels, building sequel upon sequel, until the final titles—*Ruf der Wälder* and *Tecumsehs Tod*—in 1939. There were eight volumes in all, taking Tecumseh from youth to death, all published by Franckh of Stuttgart.

Essentially, Steuben's books were exciting adventure stories for boys. They boasted that they were "retold from old sources" and they included illustrations of ethnographic items such as boats and houses, but they had little real historical information in them. Far from accepting the confines of anything as vulgar as fact, Steuben rewrote history to promote the ideology of the Nazis, who achieved power in 1933. Tecumseh's swastika was a bundle of black arrows, bound with a tomahawk; his SS an elite bodyguard of "dog" soldiers, something inspired by the Plains Indian warrior societies, but for which the Shawnees had no counterparts. And Tecumseh himself became Nietzsche's superman, a strong leader (führer) who overruled the weak, corrupt, and inefficient to change history. The real Tecumseh led by example and argument, because his people were tribal, with few centralized authority structures; but Steuben's hero enjoyed dictatorial powers. "Here," the author wrote in *Der Sohn des Manitu: Eine Erzahlung vom Kampfe Tecumsehs* (1938), "only a man could help who would . . . by orders of steel force down the shaking in everyone, and not only in himself."

The Tecumseh books were allowed to flourish during the Nazi regime because they had been twisted into a crude allegory of Germany's unification under its own powerful führer. The Shawnee was commonly regarded as the hero of a just cause which had failed, partly because the Indians had not united under his leadership. Now, suggested Steuben, Germany, ringed by enemies, must rally around Hitler if it was to escape a like fate. These ideas were reinforced throughout the books in various ways. Despite the appalling slaughter of the First World War, in which Steuben served, he used the Tecumseh series to glorify conflict, and he invariably portrayed the German settlers of North America as morally superior to other whites. Readers were left in no doubt that had Germany, rather than France or Britain, controlled America, the Indians would have received juster treatment. Daniel Boone was allowed to have been a hero—but only because he was equipped with a fictitious German grandfather and given a facility with the German tongue![22]

Sad as these perversions of Tecumseh's story were, they possessed enormous narrative power and bewitched a generation of young Germans. In the thirties alone 790,000 copies of Steuben's Tecumseh books were sold, and they continue to be reprinted, singly or in omnibus editions, albeit shorn of their Nazi elements. They also had imitators, such as Franz Schauwecker's *Thecumseh: Erhebung des Prarie* (1942), and as late as 1972 prompted a major motion picture, the East German *Tecumseh*, which starred a fêted Yugoslav actor, Gojko Mitic, as the great chief. The film was as bad as its only widescreen American counterpart, *Brave Warrior* (1952), in which Jay Silverheels, better known as television's Tonto, strove to bring Tecumseh to life from a lame script.

For all Steuben's storytelling skill, and the efforts of modern editors to cleanse his work of offensive elements, he remains a controversial figure. But the interest he aroused in Tecumseh has not entirely disappeared. Tecumseh novels and biographies continue to leave German presses, the last in 1996.

Tecumseh's American conquerors had fuller memories of the man. Before the peace of Ghent, while both patriotism and indignation at frontier brutalities were still running high, writers praised their archfoe. *The Republican* of Dayton, Ohio, echoed a general sentiment on 25 October 1813 when it judged him "perhaps the greatest Indian general that ever lifted a tomahawk."

This conviction only deepened as the emotions of war faded. Histories and the increasingly fashionable collections of Indian biography unreservedly lauded the chief, while rhymsters began to celebrate him as eagerly as they had once eulogized the heroes of Tippecanoe. In "Tecumthe, the Last King of Ohio," Charles A. Jones confidently predicted:

> *While heave you high hills to the sky*
> *While roll you dark and turbid river,*
> *Thy name and fame can never die—*
> *Whom Freedom loves will live forever!*[23]

Americans saw qualities to admire in Tecumseh: courage, fortitude, ambition, generosity, humanity, eloquence, military skill, leadership . . . Above all, patriotism and a love of liberty. Addressing "the Shade of Tecumseh" a contributor to the *Advocate and Register* opined:

> *War hath hush'd his stormy breath*
> *Truth and justice claim his station,*
> *While thou sleepest calm in death,*
> *We look back with admiration.*

> *Brave as he who Europe sway'd* [*Bonaparte*]
> *Conquering with an arm of thunder,*
> *Had Science lent thy genius aid,*
> *Thou hadst been an equal wonder.*[24]

To some Tecumseh was the epitome of the "noble savage" then beloved by European and American philosophers, his virtues and innocence untrammeled by the trappings of civilization. Cyrus Dunham, an Indiana politician, caught this mood in 1852 when he proclaimed Tecumseh "one of Nature's great men, made in God's own image. He spoke God's own language—the voice of Nature."[25]

Toward the midcentury Tecumseh's stature was increased by two quite different and unconnected developments. One was the evident plight of the Indian and his removal from most areas east of the Mississippi. After the War of 1812 Indians were no longer a serious military threat to the United States, and appeared to be in terminal decline. Contact with whites seemed merely to corrupt them, spreading diseases, drunkenness, and disintegration. Even those Indians who attempted to acculturate failed to win acceptance, and were sent out of the way, beyond the frontier with the rest. Gradually there grew a feeling that the Indians were a doomed race. Efforts were made to record and classify what were believed to be disappearing cultures, and it became easier to romanticize Indians. This was the age of Catlin and Alfred Jacob Miller, of Schoolcraft and Longfellow.

In his own time Tecumseh had been assured by American officials that the United States had treated the Indians with justice and humanity, and the tribes had no business in rebellion. But from the perspective of the 1830s and after, Tecumseh seemed to have been vindicated. His people had been driven out, and appeared to be on the brink of extinction. Now Tecumseh had not only been noble, determined, and brave. He had also been *right*, and deserved the admiration of every American who understood patriotism. In 1829 *The Ohio Republican* marveled at a "matchless career" in which Tecumseh had led "a broken and injured people to repeated victory, taking vengeance for the wrongs of centuries, exerting the whole energies of his soul and body to the destruction of invaders, who were likely to blot him and his people from the face of the earth . . . It is questionable if Washington lived with more patriotism, or Epaminondas died with greater brilliancy."[26]

The other development which enhanced Tecumseh's status was political. For several decades men involved in the defeat of Tecumseh and his warriors competed for public office, buttressing their candidacies with stories of their service against one of the country's most determined opponents. It was worth thousands of votes to have been at Tippecanoe or Moraviantown, or to have routed the Red Sticks in the south. The action on the Thames alone, it has been estimated, helped create one president, one vice president, three state governors of Kentucky, three lieutenant-governors, four United States senators, and a score of congressmen.[27] No less than four men who rose to prominence fighting Tecumseh and his allies ran for the presidency—Andrew Jackson, William Henry Harrison, Zachary Taylor, and Lewis Cass—and three of them did so successfully. The heady political debates between partisans of such contenders further exalted the reputation of Tecumseh, keeping it before the public.

The campaign of 1836, in which Richard Mentor Johnson gained the vice presidency on Martin Van Buren's Democratic ticket, and Harrison was an unsuccessful Whig candidate for the White House, focused tremendous attention on Tecumseh. William Emmons's five-act play *Tecumseh, or, The Battle of the Thames* (1836) which presented Johnson as Tecumseh's slayer, had already been performed on the stage before publication. In Baltimore an Indian outfit, said to have been worn by Tecumseh in the battle; a British standard captured on the occasion; and a pistol alleged to have belonged to Johnson were exhibited to accompany the drama. The weapon was presumably the smoothbore .48 caliber pistol with a walnut stock that was sometimes displayed in the Capitol House, Frankfort, Kentucky, as the gun that killed Tecumseh.

Harrison, or "Old Tippecanoe" as his admirers styled him, was elected to the Senate in 1825 and made a second bid for the presidency in 1840. His campaign reminded voters of his battles with Tecumseh and the British through ballads, biographies, almanacs, and numbers of *The Log Cabin*. It was launched at a Whig rally which reputedly drew thirty thousand people to the battlefield of Tippecanoe, which had been donated to the state of Indiana in 1836. Harrison won the election, but died a month after taking office. Superstitious hacks of a later century would note that until Ronald Reagan no subsequent president elected in a year ending in a naught would survive his term, and concluded that the Prophet had placed a curse on the presidency in revenge for his brother's death.

By-products of the political campaigns were the first full-length treatments of Tecumseh in American fiction. Some, such as George Hooker Colton's poem *Tecumseh; or, The West Thirty Years' Since* (1836) and George Jones's five-act play *Tecumseh; or, The Prophet of the West* (1844), put the Shawnee center stage. Others, including novels such as James Strange French's *Elskwatawa; or, The Prophet of the West* (1836) and Anna L. Snelling's *Kabaosa* (1846), focused on individuals who became embroiled in his activities. But all paid unequivocal tribute to the chief. In one fictional treatment, Mrs. Seba (Elizabeth Oakes) Smith's "The Western Captive; or, The Times of Tecumseh," published in *The New World* for 1842, Tecumseh was permitted to romance a white woman. Given Tecumseh's views on mixed-race marriages, at least after 1805, the story may have lacked credibility, but it possibly inspired a well-known legend that Tecumseh had once had an affair with a pioneer girl in Ohio.

By the time the centenary of his death came around, Tecumseh's reputation was secure. The frontier had closed, and the armed resistance of the American Indians ended. Dime novelists, showmen, and moviemakers pounced hungrily upon the more topical Indian wars of the far west for copy, but historically Tecumseh had been a clear watershed. Between 1740 and 1815 the Indians had occasionally been a significant force in the balance between white powers—between the French and British colonies, Spain and the United States in the south, and the British and the Americans in the north. That role ended with the collapse of Tecumseh's movement in 1814, for never again would the North American Indians play an important role in international relations.

Militarily, too, the scale of Indian-white conflict was markedly smaller in the seventy-five years after 1815 than during the corresponding period before. Custer's defeat in 1876 created such a great sensation partly because, in the desultory warfare of the far west, it was unique. Had it been part of the wars east of the Mississippi, it would have been merely one, and by no means the most remarkable, of many severe defeats inflicted wholly or instrumentally by Indians upon white armies—the defeats of Braddock, Grant, Herkimer, Harmar, and St. Clair, and the engagements at Sabbath Day Point (Lake George), Fort William Henry, and Wyoming, among others. The United States army lost only 948 men killed by Indians in all the country's wars between 1866 and 1890, but newspapers and military dispatches between 1810 and 1815 reveal that Tecumseh and his allies were substantially responsible for killing or capturing 5,500 people in the south and the Old Northwest, of which number only about 500 were unarmed civilians. The battles of the River Raisin and Fort Meigs alone accounted for over 1,600 American soldiers.

By the end of the nineteenth century, therefore, despite a succession of recent gallant stands made by different groups of Indians against the United States, it was clear that there was not going to be another Tecumseh. Writer after writer, respectably acquainted with the sad saga of Indian-white conflict—Benjamin B. Thatcher, Henry Trumbull, Edward S. Ellis, Norman B. Wood, James Mooney, Cyrus Thomas, Clark Wissler, Alvin M. Josephy, and Olive Dickason—proclaimed Tecumseh the greatest of all Indians. Whether justified or not, the view is still generally accepted today.

For all that, compared to their Canadian counterparts American writers were reluctant to see Tecumseh as a subject of serious literature. In the third quarter of the nineteenth century he became part of the dime novel tradition, inspiring such sensational titles as *Tecumseh and the Prisoners, The Skeleton Scout, The Mad Ranger*, and *The Wolf Queen; or, The Great Hermit of the Scioto*. More substantial novels also featured Tecumseh, and with relentless respect. Reviewing numerous titles relating to the War of 1812, G. Harrison Orians justly wrote: "The one consistent theme . . . was the greatness and nobility of Tecumseh . . . In some this praise became a major theme, in others it was a digressive judgment, but it was the one note invariably found."[28]

Yet it was supposed that readers would be unable to identify with an Indian whose life was spent opposing the United States, and Tecumseh was generally introduced as a supporting or contextual player, with the action built around more acceptable figures: two Kentucky boys befriended by the chief (E. S. Ellis's *Scouts and Comrades; or, Tecumseh, Chief of the Shawanoes*, 1895); an American soldier who falls in love with a white girl raised by the Prophet (John Ball Naylor's *The Sign of the Prophet: A Tale of Tecumseh and Tippecanoe*, 1901); a Scottish girl rescued from her captor by Tecumseh (Mary C. Crowley's *Love Thrives in War*, 1903); or the protagonist in Crittenden Marriott's novel of 1914, *The Ward of Tecumseh*.

Tecumseh had been assimilated into the American pantheon as much as any Indian could have been at that time. Towns in Missouri, Michigan, Nebraska, and Oklahoma bore his name, as did not a few individuals, the most famous being William Tecumseh Sherman. There was a brisk trade in supposed relics of the chief—sashes, flags, pistols, tomahawks, shot pouches, and belts—while the folklore that encrusted him was so thick historians were unable to chisel it away. Bil Gilbert has informed us that as late as the 1930s children in Michigan still enjoyed games of Pioneers and Indians, in which the most prestigious role was that of Tecumseh.[29]

However, it was only in the last forty years that Tecumseh became the American icon he is today. Those years witnessed a considerable shift in attitudes toward the Indian. Civil rights movements drew greater attention to the divisions within American society and the predicaments of ethnic minorities, and the growth of social sciences in universities heightened respect for systems of belief and practice different from our own. In the 1960s and 1970s the American Indian became a potent symbol for the increasingly fashionable radical left. A generation of young Americans was encouraged to accept a romantic picture of historic Indian societies as ecologically aware, self -sufficient, and communally responsible—worthy alternatives, it seemed, to a materialist, exploitative modern world that appeared about to destroy itself. One result of these and other currents of thought was a greater interest in, and ultimately appreciation of, Indians and their importance to the American past and character.

Given such preoccupations, it was inevitable that Tecumseh would be reappraised as an authentic American hero. He crashed his way into mainstream American literature as the subject of not only several plays, but also sprawling biographical novels of a type not seen before. Between them Allan W. Eckert's *The Frontiersmen* (1967) and *A Sorrow in Our Heart, The Life of Tecumseh* (1992), both of which had the effrontery to present themselves as historically accurate; Ruben D. Salaz's two volumes of a projected trilogy entitled *I Am Tecumseh* (1980, 1985); James A. Huston's *Counterpoint* (1987); and James Alexander Thom's *Panther in the Sky* (1989) offered 3,500 pages relating to the Shawnee chief. Of these, and the other fictitious treatments of Tecumseh, Thom's is, in my view, significantly the best. It intelligently interpreted Tecumseh's life against a background of Shawnee culture and did so within the compass of a well-paced and at times moving narrative.[30]

No less illustrative was the stampede to provide Tecumseh materials for the education of the young. Beginning with William Edward Wilson's *Shooting Star* (1942), Augusta Stevenson's *Tecumseh, Shawnee Boy* (1955), and David C. Cooke's *Tecumseh, Destiny's Warrior* (1959), the thin stream of publications turned into a flood after 1970. Between James McCague's *Tecumseh, Shawnee Warrior-Statesman* (1970) and Robert Cwiklik's *Tecumseh, Shawnee Rebel* (1993), no less than eleven children's biographies have been published in the United States, most of them slim volumes designed for elementary school grades. They testify that after nearly two hundred years Tecumseh has come to belong to all Americans.

By comparison the Prophet has fared badly. His religious principles were incomprehensible to the whites, who dismissed him as a superstitious charlatan. Some even deprived him of the credit he justly deserved for starting the Shawnee reform movement in 1805, and claimed that from the first he was a mere tool of Tecumseh. Writers also happily charged him with massive purges of political enemies, but often ignored his laudable attempts to address social and environmental problems. Unquestionably, Tenskwatawa's religion was an important rationale for the resistance movement, but when all is said it is easy to see why he was remembered as a disagreeable figure. Influential, and in some ways altruistic and talented, he was, the records nevertheless suggest, an unlikable man, indolent, boastful, cowardly, and dishonest. He was not the stuff of legend.

Much that has been written about both brothers was misleading, or downright wrong. There was nothing new or unique about their ideas, or the goals for which they strove; nor did they conjure up Indian resistance to the United States at the period of the War of 1812 single-handedly. However difficult to achieve, their ideas were all old ones, while the flagrant seizure of Indian lands was creating opposition to the Americans before the brothers ever put themselves at the head of the movement. Tecumseh and the Prophet were indeed important, but they were never the whole story. Even the Creek war, which most loudly proclaimed the influence of Tenskwatawa's religion, brought to the south by his brother, drew also upon other and varied tensions, as I have tried to show.

On the other hand, sometimes the brothers have been underrated, rather than exaggerated. They were not simple pawns of the British. Tecumseh planned his war independently, received the redcoats as his allies, and induced them to put his war aims with theirs. We speak of the War of 1812, but in truth there were two wars. The war between the Americans and the British ended with the treaty of Ghent. The war between the Big Knives and the Indians began at Tippecanoe, and arguably did not run its course until the last Red Sticks were defeated in the Florida swamps in 1818.

Among all the leaders in that brave but futile Indian revolt, Tecumseh stands out because of his astounding versatility and energy. Not only was his ambition boundless, but his eloquence made him the voice of the oppressed, his magnetism bound people to him, and he was an inspirational field commander. More than anything else he was a man of tremendous vitality and sense of purpose. In a word, of *passion*. Even today, reading garbled accounts of what he said, and the words of those who saw him, one can still feel that passionate belief that spurred Tecumseh on, that powerful spirit that again and again urged him to confront every obstacle and meet every danger. Roundhead had leadership, Main Poc raw courage, and the Prophet was for many the voice of the Great Spirit. But it was that astonishing commitment in Tecumseh, served by a formidable battery of personal qualities, that made him at once the principal organizer and driving force of the Indian confederacy.

Tecumseh has been idealized, and his faults forgotten. That he planned to unleash a ferocious war upon the frontiers was sometimes denied or passed over, and the appalling consequences of his actions for Indians such as the Creeks were often omitted. In an attempt to redress the balance Lewis Cass pointed out that Tecumseh was "a man of more enlarged views than are often found among the Indian chiefs, a brave warrior and a skillful leader, politic in his measures and firm in his purposes. But he was jealous and ambitious, and prepared to sacrifice the happiness of his people to his own impracticable objects."[31]

It is a fair point, and yet, ironically, it may also help explain his enduring fascination. For when we consider Tecumseh, and his forlorn and desperate attempt to rescue his people against what we would regard as impossible odds, we are reminded of qualities without which men and women would be infinitely the poorer: the essential nobility of self-sacrifice, and the occasional triumph, in moments of great adversity, of the human spirit.

APPENDIX:

FAMILY PORTRAITS

Writing in 1838, Richard Mentor Johnson, the reputed slayer of Tecumseh, opined that no portrait of the great chief existed.[1] Thirty years were suffered to pass before anyone challenged his statement. Then engravings of both Tecumseh and the Prophet were published by Benson J. Lossing in his richly illustrated *Pictorial Field-Book of the War of 1812* with the explanation that they were founded upon original pencil sketches made in Vincennes in 1808 by a French trader named Pierre Le Dru. Lossing had discovered them in 1848 in Quebec, where they were owned by Le Dru's son. Sadly, although Lossing had a reputation for accuracy he chose to modify the alleged portrait of Tecumseh in his book:

> I have given only the head by Le Dru. The cap was red, the band ornamented with coloured porcupines' quills, and in front was a single eagle's feather, black with a white tip. The sketch of his dress (and the medal above described), in which he appears as a brigadier general of the British army, is from a rough drawing which I saw in Montreal in the summer of 1858, made at Malden soon after the surrender of Detroit, where the Indians celebrated that event by a grand feast. It was only on gala occasions that Tecumtha was seen in full dress. The sketch did not pretend to give a true likeness of the chief, and was valuable only as a delineation of his costume. From the two

we are enabled to give a pretty faithful picture of the great Shawanoese warrior and statesman as he appeared in his best mood. When in full dress he wore a cocked hat and plume, but would not give up his blue breechcloth, red leggins fringed with buckskin, and buckskin moccasins.[2]

The portrait of the Prophet was published unbowdlerized. Tecumseh and his brother were never together in Vincennes. In 1808 and 1809 the Prophet, but not Tecumseh, visited the town; in 1810 and 1811 Tecumseh took his place. We must conclude either that Le Dru made his sketches somewhere else, for example at Prophetstown, which was frequented by traders, or that the portraits showed Tenskwatawa and one of his principal supporters, whom Le Dru later took to have been Tecumseh.

Whether Le Dru had the artistic talent to preserve respectable likenesses of his subjects is uncertain, but Lossing's portrait is the nearest we have to an authentic representation. It had no competitor until 1954, when George I. Quimby examined a collection of oil paintings acquired long before by the Chicago Natural History Museum. Among them was an unsigned portrait, twenty-three by twenty-eight inches, showing an impressive-looking Indian in a black scarf and a dark gray or black coat. Soon the museum was publishing the surprising claim that it possessed what appeared to be a lost portrait of Tecumseh.[3]

The "Tecumseh" portrait was one of a collection made by the Indian agent Benjamin O'Fallon, a nephew of Governor William Clark of Missouri, and kept at his home, Indian Retreat, in St. Louis. O'Fallon died in 1842, and in 1861 the paintings went into storage, where some were regrettably lost or destroyed. Thirty-seven survivors, all but two of them George Catlin originals, were sold by Emily O'Fallon, Benjamin's daughter, to the Chicago museum in 1894. She told both Mrs. Ulysses S. Grant, who facilitated the sale, and a trustee of the museum that "we always understood" one of the portraits to show Tecumseh. Quimby correctly identified the likeness to which she referred, although she had erroneously credited the painting to artist Chester Harding.

Have we, then, a genuine portrait of Tecumseh? It would be pleasing to think so, but probably we do not. To begin with, the pedigree of the portrait is flawed. No concrete information about it, the circumstances in which it was painted, and the artist exist. This has to weaken the attribution. Miss O'Fallon had undoubtedly been told about the portraits when she was a child in Indian Retreat, but she may have become confused in the many years that followed, and she admitted that much of what she had then heard she no longer remembered. Finally, there are those worrying clothes, white

men's clothes. It is hard to imagine Tecumseh, the fiery all-Indian, submit-
ting to being painted in a garb which, by his lights, ran counter to the
wishes of his god.

Mind you, there is a respectable if unproven case for believing that the
portrait may actually depict Paukeesaa, Tecumseh's son. Now, he met Clark,
and possibly O'Fallon also, when he passed through St. Louis in 1827 on his
way to the west. It is entirely possible that the two agents seized the opportunity to persuade the son of the most celebrated of Indians to sit for his
portrait. We know the son was striking, like his father, and the painting de-
picts a man of about Paukeesaa's age at the time, thirty-one. What is more,
a portrait of Paukeesaa definitely was made, evidently by an artist named
Joshua Shaw. The Shaw painting was listed in an inventory of the famous
collection of Indian portraits held by the War Department, catalogued in
1858. Unfortunately, it was destroyed by the fire which swept the Smithson-
ian building, where the collection was later housed, on 15 January 1865.
However, Shaw may have executed two copies, one to be forwarded to the
War Department, and one for Clark and O'Fallon's own collection. This is
pure hypothesis, but it neatly fits the circumstances, and could account for
the Tecumseh connection in Miss O'Fallon's mind. Unless some further evidence is turned up, perhaps in O'Fallon's reports and correspondence, it
must nevertheless be accepted that the identity of the Indian gazing imperi-
ously from the canvas in the Chicago Natural History Museum remains for
the time being a mystery.[4]

The only other contender as a likeness of Tecumseh is the small Indian
figure in military trousers to be seen in Margaret Reynolds's watercolor of
Fort Malden, painted in 1813. There is a tradition that the figure is Tecumseh, but it is no more than that.

The Prophet survived into a period when the painting of Indians was
gaining popularity, and was treated by several notable artists: James Otto
Lewis in Detroit in 1824[5]; Charles Bird King on another canvas that perished in the 1865 fire[6]; and George Catlin in Fort Leavenworth, Kansas, in
1832.[7]

In 1989 a joint portrait of seven Indians, four men and three women,
painted in 1814 by Rudolph von Steiger, an army officer, was purchased by
the National Archives of Canada in Ottawa. The picture shows the deputation of western Indians who visited Sir George Prevost in Quebec. Inasmuch as Tecumapease, Tecumseh's sister, was the most significant woman
with that delegation—indeed, she is the only woman known to have accompanied it—it is probable that one of the female figures shows her. Similarly,
Tecumseh's son, along with such influential leaders as Naiwash and Mitass,
headed the delegation, and may be included in the portrait.

Sadly, even here some disappointment awaits those who would learn more about this unusual Indian family. The value of the painting is compromised, because the artist caricatured his subjects rather than attempted a serious portraiture. Tecumapease, like her famous brother, remains elusive, and what seems to have been her only appearance on canvas was the work of an artist whose prejudices outstripped his interest in leaving a responsible image for posterity.[8]

ACKNOWLEDGMENTS

The biographer of Tecumseh works in a long, if not always distinguished, tradition. The pioneering work, *The Life of Tecumseh, and of His Brother the Prophet*, was written by Benjamin Drake and published in 1841. Drake, brother of Daniel Drake, the celebrated physician and writer, was a Kentuckian who spent most of his life in Cincinnati as an editor, lawyer, and author. He was an assiduous and honest scholar. Beginning his project in 1821, only eight years after Tecumseh's death, he secured statements from several friends and acquaintances of the chief while they were still in middle age. He approached, among others, Governor Lewis Cass of Michigan Territory, one of Tecumseh's military opponents. Cass admitted that he had contemplated a sketch of Tecumseh himself but abandoned the idea because of a lack of material; he promised to try to interview the Prophet, who was still alive in Canada. A few years later Cass did have the Prophet questioned, but Drake never saw the result. His project had lapsed. It was not until the 1830s that he revived it, gathering fresh information, and laboriously copying the official dispatches of William Henry Harrison.

Drake's premature death in 1841 robbed him of the praise due his *Life of Tecumseh*, which was written in a modest but concise and clear style. Because of his limited access to archival material, his account was substantially fashioned from eyewitness statements made after Tecumseh's death, and it was sketchy, imprecise, and sometimes inaccurate. Even the best of his informants sometimes confused events or got them out of sequence, and

Drake himself missed important clues and accepted some dubious stories at face value. Nevertheless, his effort was a very commendable one, and without the materials he collected it would be impossible to write a respectable biography today.

Drake's work was the basis for several simple biographies that appeared over the next century, and the only major attempt to improve upon it was unfinished and unpublished. It was made by an indefatigable collector of frontier Americana, Lyman Copeland Draper, a New Yorker who worked obsessively on numerous biographies but never completed any of them. In 1864 he purchased Drake's Tecumseh papers, which had gone to auction in St. Louis, and over the years amassed further information, including original documents, cuttings, and statements from anyone he could find who claimed to have had a connection with the famous chief.

On the whole, Draper's witnesses were far inferior to Drake's. Many were so old they could barely remember events more than fifty years before, while most had been only slightly acquainted with Tecumseh. Some merely dispensed hearsay. Tecumseh had become a folk hero, and many legends crept into Draper's files. Although he strove hard to complete his biography in the 1880s, nothing Draper wrote suggests he had the ability to evaluate such treacherous materials, and his failure to produce a book was not, perhaps, in itself, a great loss. Yet we must salute him, and heartily, for his contribution was invaluable. In all, he collected nearly five hundred volumes of papers relating to the old frontier, thirteen of them in the Tecumseh series. By preserving Drake's materials, and adding many important items to them, he left at the State Historical Society of Wisconsin, of which he was secretary, the essential foundation for further study.

Glenn Tucker, whose *Tecumseh: Vision of Glory* was published in 1956, stands by general consent lowest in esteem of Tecumseh's major biographers. Although colorfully written, in a style that held youths from play and old men from the chimney corner, the book was tediously idolatrous. Tucker's Tecumseh was forever noble and just, invariably the master of every situation, and always right. No such person ever existed. To his credit, during his research Tucker threw a wider net than any of his predecessors, scouring a broad range of printed sources and deploying Draper's manuscripts among a few other archival gleanings. He also benefited from the publication of relevant official documents by William Wood, Ernest A. Cruikshank, and Logan Esarey.

With fifty pages of documentation and bibliography, Tucker's book had a superficial authority, and for several years was widely accepted by a docile public. However, Tecumseh was far too legendary a subject for a writer as gullible as Tucker. Not only was Tucker an eager victim of bogus source materials, but he also appropriated material from avowedly fictitious works and indiscriminately packed his book with apocryphal folk tales. Justly did the historian Reginald Horsman refer to the biography as a mixture of fact and historical legend.

It was Horsman who marked the beginning of serious modern scholarship on Tecumseh. On the one hand, his solidly researched studies of the War of 1812 period were the first to systematically exploit the official archives of Canada and Britain; on the other, along with the Canadian writer Carl F. Klinck, he drew attention to the unusually difficult primary sources relating to Tecumseh and called for a critical review.

Stimulated by Horsman, Herbert C. W. Goltz devoted two dissertations, *Tecumseh: The Man and the Myth* (1966) and *Tecumseh, The Prophet, and the Rise of the Northwest Indian Confederacy* (1973) to the subject; they were based heavily upon the Draper manuscripts and material in the National Archives of Canada. Because his work was not regularly published, and was directed to a narrow academic audience, it did not receive the recognition it deserved. Goltz made two particularly important contributions. He rigorously expunged the legendary material from the record and emphasized the need for a close adherence to the canons of historical scholarship. And he removed the Prophet from Tecumseh's shadow. Undeniably the less attractive of the two brothers, the Prophet had generally been depicted as the mere tool of Tecumseh. Yet if Tecumseh ultimately controlled the Shawnee reform movement, it was the Prophet who started it, and who was initially the means by which the brothers gained extensive influence.

The most recent scholar to investigate the brothers is R. David Edmunds. His emphasis, too, was upon the Prophet, whom he rehabilitated in his most important book, *The Shawnee Prophet*, published in 1983. In addition to reasserting the Prophet's importance before the War of 1812, Edmunds made the first appraisal of his later years, showing how he struggled to regain influence after Tecumseh's death. Edmunds also dived into an excellent range of manuscript sources, utilizing many hitherto neglected documents in the National Archives of the United States and in the rich holdings of local historical societies.

After years of scholarly neglect, Tecumseh and the Prophet regained currency during the last twenty-five years, and several important histories tackled aspects of their careers. In another doctorate, George C. Chalou waded through files in the American National Archives and elsewhere to produce *The Red Pawns Go To War* (1971), which put Tecumseh at the center of Indian participation in the War of 1812. I tried to establish the facts about the chief's controversial final campaign in *Tecumseh's Last Stand*, published in 1985, and more recently Gregory Evans Dowd and Richard White set both Shawnee brothers into the context of earlier religious and pan-Indian movements.

Attempting a full-dress study of Tecumseh and his times, based in a European country in which few have heard of the chief and most found my academic interest in Indians esoteric, if not downright eccentric, has sometimes resembled scaling K2 without oxygen. Reflecting now upon a long journey, including a dozen overseas research trips, it is pleasing for me to record the names of those who furnished timely assistance along the way.

I am grateful to the Twenty-Seven Foundation and the British Academy, both of London, and the Ford Foundation for sponsoring parts of the project. The latter funded an invaluable year at the D'Arcy McNickle Center for the History of the American Indian, at the Newberry Library, Chicago, then under the direction of Fred Hoxie. Among many who then generously extended hospitality to an exiled Briton I am particularly indebted to Assistant Director Jay Miller, research fellows Tom Biolsi and Sharon O'Brien, and library staff Ruth Hamilton, John Aubrey, Harvey Markowitz, and the late Michael Kaplan. Professor Cecil King of Queen's University, Kingston, Canada, and Dr. Catherine Littlejohn were forever willing to help and to contribute information, and have become most treasured friends and traveling companions. Helen Hornbeck Tanner, senior research fellow at the Newberry, freely shared her unrivaled knowledge and enthusiasm for Great Lakes Indian history, and has followed my adventures since, never failing to encourage and help when the going got hard. The debt I owe her is immense.

Many fellow students of the period have also supplied information, ideas, advice, and support. They include Colin G. Calloway, Dartmouth College; Doug E. Clanin, whose monumental edition of the papers of William Henry Harrison will, when completed, become a standard reference; R. Alan Douglas and Geoff Raymond of Windsor's Community Museum, Ontario; R. David Edmunds, who invaluably supported my first book on Tecumseh; John Mark Faragher, Yale University; Michael Friedrichs, Augsburg, Germany; Bob Garcia of the Fort Malden National Historic Site, Amherstburg; Herbert C. W. Goltz, St. Thomas University, Fredericton, New Brunswick; George Gurney, curator of the National Museum of American Art, Washington, D.C.; Reginald Horsman, University of Wisconsin–Milwaukee; Francis Jennings, then in Chicago; Uwe Johannsen of Nortorf, Germany; Louise F. Johnson, Round Rock, Texas; Norma Luallen, Louisiana; Don B. Smith, University of Calgary; the late Dan L. Thrapp of Tucson, Arizona; Dr. Melburn D. Thurman, Missouri; and Marylen M. Williams of Tulsa, Oklahoma. To all of them I readily give my thanks.

Among other individuals and institutions providing assistance I must mention the Alabama Department of Archives and History, Montgomery; the Archives of Ontario, Toronto; the Archivo General de Indias, Seville, Spain; Carolyn Autry of the Indiana Historical Society, Indianapolis; Jane

R. Baugh of the Virginia State Library, Richmond; Graham Boxer, Mersey-side County Museum, Liverpool, England; the British Library, London, and the British Newspaper Library, Colindale; W. S. Byrne, Rhodes House Library, Oxford, England; Elizabeth Carroll-Horrocks and Martin L. Levitt, American Philosophical Society, Philadelphia; the University of Chicago Library; the Chicago Historical Society; the Cincinnati Historical Society; the Library of Congress, Washington, D.C.; Steve Cotham, Lawson McGhee Library, Knoxville, Tennessee; Charlotte Erikson of the University of Cambridge, England; Roberta Ferrari, University of Pisa, Italy; the Filson Club, Louisville, Kentucky; John J. Grabowski, Western Reserve Historical Society, Cleveland, Ohio; the Historical Society of Pennsylvania, Philadelphia; the Indiana Historical Bureau, Indianapolis; Mary Karshner of the Burton Historical Collection, Detroit Public Library, who epitomizes for me the ideal archivist; the Kingston Public Library, Ontario; the Kingston-Upon-Hull Library, England; Jane Levin of the Anthropology Department and Christine Gross, Collections Manager, both of the Field Museum, Chicago; the Eli Lilly Library, Bloomington, Indiana; the Missouri Historical Society, St. Louis; Nelson Morgan, University of Georgia Library, Athens; the National Archives of Canada, Ottawa; the National Archives of the United States, Washington, D.C.; the National Library of Ireland, Dublin, Eire; the National Library of Scotland, Edinburgh; the Ohio Historical Society, Columbus; Lieutenant Bryn Owen and Colonel W. R. Davies of the Welch Regiment Museum, Cardiff, Wales; Christopher Peebles of the Glenn A. Black Laboratory of Archaeology, Indiana University, Bloomington; Samuel Proctor of the *Florida Historical Quarterly*; the Public Record Office, Kew, England; Charles A. Shaughnessy of the National Archives, Washington, D.C.; the Metropolitan Library of Toronto; Pamela A. Wasmer and John Selch, Indiana State Library, Indianapolis; Galen R. Wilson and Arlene P. Shy of the William L. Clements Library, Ann Arbor, Michigan; the State Historical Society of Wisconsin, Madison; The Winterthur Museum, Delaware; and Chris Wright of the Royal Anthropological Institute, London. Attempts have been made to locate the owners of copyright material, but notifications of any oversights will be addressed. The sources of illustrations, other than those from the author's collection, are given with the reproductions.

Finally, during these last stages, I have been fortunate in finding an enlightened editor and publisher in Jack Macrae, whose advice and encouragement urged me into that last push to the summit.

KEY TO ABBREVIATIONS

IN NOTES

AND BIBLIOGRAPHY

Sources mentioned in the notes are keyed to the alphabetical lists of manuscript and printed materials. The first page of each document is normally cited. In addition, the following abbreviations have been used:

ANB	*American National Biography*
ASPIA	*American State Papers, Indian Affairs* (1832)
BHC	Burton Historical Collection, Detroit Public Library
CVSP	W. P. Palmer, *Calendar of Virginia State Papers . . .* (1875–93)
DCB	*Dictionary of Canadian Biography*
IHS	Indiana Historical Society, Indianapolis
MPHC	*Michigan Pioneer and Historical Society Historical Collections* (1877–1929)
OHS	Ohio Historical Society, Columbus
SHSW/D	State Historical Society of Wisconsin, Madison: Lyman Draper Manuscripts. Cited by volume, series [denoted by a letter or letters], and page. Thus, 3YY109 is volume 3, series YY, page 109
TPUS	C. E. Carter and J. P. Bloom, *Territorial Papers of the United States* (1934–75)

NOTES

1. The Shooting Star

1. Wells to Kirker, 4 August 1807, Simon Kenton papers, 7BB39; Elias Langham to Kirker, 5 September 1807, ibid., 7BB45, and his note on Wells to John Gerard, 22 August 1807, ibid., 7BB44.

2. Joseph Foos to Kirker, 10 August 1807, Thomas Kirker papers; William Creighton to Kirker, 23 August 1807, Samuel Williams papers (2); *The Scioto Gazette*, 10 September 1807.

3. Principal sources for the Indian visit to Chillicothe are *The Fredonian* (Chillicothe), 25 September 1807; Kirker to Thomas Jefferson, 8 October 1807, Daniel Parker papers; and two late eyewitness accounts, one by Thomas S. Hinde, Hinde papers, 16Y45–51, and the other in Charles A. Stuart to Lyman Draper, 17 February 1846, Kentucky papers, 8CC59. Quotations are from these.

4. Key references to Stephen Ruddell (1768–1845) include John M. Ruddell to Lyman Draper, 15 May 1867, Tecumseh papers, 8YY52; John Ruddell, interviewed by Draper, 1868, Draper notes, 22S41; W. A. Galloway, *Old Chillicothe*, 263–66; and G. E. Lankford, "Losing the Past."

5. Quotations respectively from George Floyd to his wife, 14 August 1810, Tecumseh papers, 2YY118; J. B. Glegg in F. B. Tupper, *Sir Isaac Brock*, 243; Robert Wallace in J. F. Clarke, *Campaign of 1812*, 443; and George Wallace in H. R. Schoolcraft, *Travels*, 140. The most useful of other sources are Anthony Shane interviewed by Benjamin Drake, 1821, Tecumseh papers, 2YY55–62; the Stephen Ruddell narrative, 1822, ibid., 2YY120; the statement of John Johnston, ibid., 11YY17; and the account of Tecumseh in the Return Jonathan Meigs papers (2).

6. John McDonald, writing in 1836 ("Tragical Death of Wawillowa"), conflated his memories of separate events occurring in 1803 and 1807, but they can be disentangled.

7. James Worthington to Benjamin Drake, 13 February 1840, Frontier Wars papers, 5U174.

8. Catlin, *Letters and Notes*, 2: 115–19.

2. The Panther and the Turtle

1. The main sources for Tecumseh's earlier career are the accounts of Stephen Ruddell and Anthony Shane, both collected by Benjamin Drake. Ruddell was a close associate of Tecumseh's from 1780, and was remembered as an honest witness (George Boord to Lyman Draper, 31 October 1883, Tecumseh papers, 5YY56). When Drake approached him on the recommendation of Duncan McArthur, Ruddell agreed that "the name of so great and good a man ought not to be suffered to sink into oblivion," and supplied a brief narrative of the chief's life up to 1795: Ruddell to Drake, 17 January 1822, ibid., 2YY189, and Ruddell narrative, January 1822, ibid., 2YY120.

   The interviews given by Shane and his Shawnee wife, Lameteshe (herself a relative of Tecumseh), in November 1821 are fuller (ibid., 2YY55 and 12YY passim). Shane was a mixed-blood of French and Ottawa Indian parentage, and spoke five Indian languages in addition to French and English. He was most closely associated with the Shawnees, and in 1795 he was hired as an interpreter at Fort Defiance and set about compiling a Shawnee vocabulary. He was regularly employed as an interpreter thereafter, and in 1813 commanded a party of Indians that accompanied the American invasion of Canada, when Tecumseh was killed. A treaty of 1817 assigned Shane a tract of land on the St. Marys, in Ohio, but he died among the Shawnees in Kansas. Drake was referred to Shane by Richard Mentor Johnson. See R. C. Knopf, "Surgeon's Mate," 78; C. J. Kappler, *Indian Affairs*, 2: 145; and J. Sugden, *Tecumseh's Last Stand*, 261. Shane was an older man than Tecumseh (M. D. Hardin to Mark Hardin, 20 November 1812, Frontier Wars papers, 7U4) and not as close to the chief as Ruddell, but his account, which consistently cross-checks with other records, has been much undervalued.

   In 1825 Charles C. Trowbridge, secretary to Governor Lewis Cass of Michigan Territory, interviewed Tecumseh's brother, the Prophet, in Detroit. Regrettably, the manuscript disappeared, but it was used by Cass's associate, Thomas L. McKenney, and James Hall in *Indian Tribes of North America* (1: 75) and a quotation from it is preserved. Unfortunately, although the Prophet lived until 1836, no further autobiographical fragments survive. See Cass to Benjamin Drake, 24 December 1821, Lewis Cass letter; Cass, "Indians of North America," 95–98; Trowbridge to Lyman Draper, 29 May 1868, and 12, 18, and 29 July, 1882, Tecumseh papers 5YY1–3, 5YY5; R. D. Edmunds, *Shawnee Prophet*, 167–73.

   The final significant witness for Tecumseh's early life is John Johnston (1775–1861), who served as an Indian factor and agent from 1802. His personal acquaintanceship with Tecumseh was very slight, but he was good friends with many Shawnees who had known the chief since childhood, and offered useful information. Johnston's principal account of Tecumseh was given to Daniel Drake in the 1820s, and first used by H. R. Schoolcraft, *Travels*, 138–46. The original is filed in Tecumseh papers, 11YY17–18.

2. Shawnee divisions still established separate towns in Tecumseh's day, but villages composed of Shawnees from several divisions, or indeed of Shawnees and Indians of other tribes, were also common.

   The most important source of ethnographic data about the Shawnees in this period is the account the Prophet gave Trowbridge in 1824, published as *Shawnese Traditions* by W. V. Kinietz and E. W. Voegelin. It must be used carefully, however, because the Prophet interpreted Shawnee beliefs to his own advantage. Contemporary references to Shawnee culture were trawled for my *Shawnees in Tecumseh's Time*, although sections of this now need revision. Referring to the anthropological researches of M. R. Harrington, Carl and Erminie W. Voegelin, Noel W. Schutz, and

James Howard, it contains fuller documentation for the statements made about Shawnee culture here.

    For the Mekoche right to handle tribal business, see E. G. Williams, "Richard Butler," 145; and George Ironside to Alexander McKee, 6 February 1795, E. A. Cruikshank, *Simcoe*, 3: 288. The Shanes told Drake that Methoataaskee, mother of Tecumseh and the Prophet, was a Mekoche, but I prefer Ruddell's testimony that she was a Pekowi. After her husband's death, she lived among the Pekowis, and had she been a Mekoche, the Prophet would surely have made political capital out of it. He was quick to claim privileges for the clans and divisions of which he was a member (Kinietz and Voegelin, 17, 55–57) but consistently denigrated the Mekoches.

3. For clans see Kinietz and Voegelin, 16–17, 26–27; and (when their nature had somewhat changed) L. A. White, *Morgan*, 46–47.

4. Benjamin Hawkins to William Eustis, 13 January 1812, U.S. SoW/LR/R 44: 0015; Hawkins to Wade Hampton, 21 September 1811, ibid., 37: 4252; J. R. Swanton, *Indians of the Southeastern United States*, 184–86; N. W. Schutz, *Shawnee Myth*, 426–35.

5. William Henry Harrison to Eustis, 26 June 1810, 7 August 1811, L. Esarey, *Harrison*, 1: 433, 548; Charles Tucker to Draper, 29 August 1884, Daniel Boone papers, 29C35; Tucker to Draper, 15 July and 16 August, 1887, Tecumseh papers, 1YY95–96; I. G. Vore to Draper, 12 May 1886, ibid., 1YY92. I have discounted a view that Methoataaskee was a Cherokee. The only credible authority for it is a third-hand statement alleged to have passed from Tecumseh to Henry Rowe Schoolcraft via the Vincennes merchant George Wallace and writer Samuel Conant (Schoolcraft, *Travels*, 138). A late-nineteenth-century tradition that Tecumseh's mother was a Cherokee (for example, A. N. Chamberlin to Draper, 4 February 1882, Tecumseh papers, 4YY28) may have arisen because Methoataaskee is believed to have died among the Cherokees.

6. *The Knoxville Gazette*, 20 October 1792.

7. Material on Chartier is indexed in works by Charles Hanna, Chester Sipe (1927), Randolph C. Downes, Robert S. Cotterill, David H. Corkran, N. W. Schutz, Francis Jennings, and Richard White.

8. E. W. Voegelin and H. H. Tanner, *Indians of Ohio and Indiana*, 1: 381–82; N. B. Wainwright, "George Croghan's Journal," 356.

9. For the annual festivals, O. M. Spencer, *Indian Captivity*, 102–13; B. H. Coates, "Narrative," 104; F. M. Perrin du Lac, *Travels*, 46; C. F. Klinck and J. T. Talman, *John Norton*, 174; and J. Johnston, "Account," 274. There are no references to the fall bread dance, now a part of Shawnee ceremonialism, until 1859. The Prophet treats Shawnee religion extensively in Kinietz and Voegelin, but for other accounts see the detailed study by Schutz, and Sugden, *Shawnees in Tecumseh's Time*, ch. 8.

10. Mekoche chiefs, March 1795, William Claus papers, 7: 124. Early references to the sacred bundle are Kinietz and Voegelin, 3, 55–57; H. Howe, *Historical Collections*, 32; and T. Flint, *First White Man of the West*, 140. It is uncertain whether divisional sacred bundles, in addition to a tribal one, existed at this time.

11. B. Drake, *Life of Tecumseh*, 21–22; H. R. Schoolcraft, *Information Respecting the . . . Indian Tribes*, 4: 254; John Johnston to Draper, 13 September 1847, Tecumseh papers, 11YY31.

12. Shawnee towns in Ohio during Tecumseh's period are described by Voegelin and Tanner, *Indians of Ohio and Indiana*, and Voegelin, *Indians of Northwest Ohio*, and mapped by Helen Hornbeck Tanner (1986). The Shawnee retreat down the Ohio from western Pennsylvania is also treated by Hanna, Downes, and Michael N. McConnell (1992).

13. I have followed Stephen Ruddell's dating, which puts Cheeseekau's birth in 1760 or 1761 and Tecumseh's in 1768. Given that Shawnee mothers usually spaced their children about two years apart (Kinietz and Voegelin, 33) this seems about right. How-

ever, in his account the Prophet had the three older children born in the south, and Cheeseekau six years older than his sister. He would also seem to have placed Tecumseh's birth too early.

14. The sources are imprecise on the dating of Sparks's captivity, but the interpretation here is the only one consistent with the evidence. There are four independent accounts. Sparks made a statement about his captivity, without mentioning Tecumseh, to James Magoffin in 1812 (Schoolcraft, *Information Respecting the . . . Indian Tribes*, 4: 624), and two accounts came through his family, one from his wife, Ruth Sevier (E. F. Ellet, *Pioneer Women of the West*, vii, 153–61) and the other from his brother-in-law (George Wilson Sevier interviewed by Draper, 1844, Draper Notes, 30S297). Finally, Sparks recounted his adventures to Thomas Washington during the War of 1812: Washington, "Attack on Buchanan's Station," 371–72. I am satisfied that Sparks was adopted by Pukeshinwau, but less so that he remembered details accurately.

15. H. Harvey, *History of the Shawnee Indians*, 146.

16. Johnston to *Liberty Hall*, Cincinnati, 30 November 1811, in *The Western Sun*, 11 January 1812.

17. References to the temporary wartime precedence of war chiefs include Henry Bouquet to Thomas Gage, 15 November 1764, *MPHC* 19: 280, and speech of Blue Jacket, 2 August 1795, *ASPIA* 1: 579.

18. John M. Ruddell to Draper, 5 November 1883, Tecumseh papers, 8YY38. John Johnston estimated birth dates between 1761 and 1768 on different occasions. The statement on Tecumseh obtained from Shawnees, filed in the Return Jonathan Meigs papers (2), says that Tecumseh was "about 48 years" in 1812, and implies a birth date around 1764.

19. The name was commonly written "Tecumseh" or "Tecumseth," but Shawnees usually pronounced the *s* as *th*. Hence Ruddell's insistence that the correct pronunciation was *Tecumthe* or *Tecumtheth*. See also Trowbridge to Draper, 18 July 1882, and R. J. Conner to Draper, 17 June 1891, Tecumseh papers, 5YY3, 8YY20. There may have been variations. A Shawnee friend of Tecumseh's, James Logan, gave his full name as We-the-cumpt-te. Shawnees often dropped the first syllable of a name. Conversely, "Tecumseh" may also have discarded a suffix. Benjamin Kelly, who lived with the Shawnees, gave the name as "Tecumsekeh," which sounds as if the suffix *skaka* (denoting the masculine gender) was sometimes employed (James Galloway to Drake, 12–23 January, 1839, George Rogers Clark papers, 8J245; Kelly statement, Thomas S. Hinde papers, 39Y225). "Shooting Star" was the usual translation, but see A. S. Gatschet, "Tecumseh's Name," for a discussion of the symbolism.

20. The ease with which errors have crept into the record is illustrated by the case of Nehaaseemoo, Tecumseh's brother. To accommodate apocryphal statements that Tecumseh had two sisters, rather than one, Glenn Tucker arbitrarily changed the gender of Nehaaseemoo to female (Tucker to David Botsford, 7 and 18 June, 1955, and Botsford to Tucker, 11 and 22 June, 1955, Tecumseh File; and Tucker, *Tecumseh*, 331–332). This reconstruction was not only flatly contradicted by the only genuine authorities, but also by the name itself. Shawnees often indicated gender in the suffix of personal names, and *hsimo* as in "Nehaaseemoo" was firmly masculine (C. F. and E. W. Voegelin, "Shawnee Name Groups," 618).

3. An Ohio Childhood

1. Shane interview: see ch. 2, n. 1. This, with the statements of Stephen Ruddell and John Johnston described in that note, are foundations for the early life of Tecumseh.

2. I am following my own reconstruction of Shawnee history, which is being prepared

for publication, but valuable commentaries on this period have been given by Randolph C. Downes, Helen Hornbeck Tanner (1986), Gregory E. Dowd (1992), Richard White, and Michael N. McConnell (1992).

3. John Stuart to Lord Hillsborough, 6 February 1772, K. G. Davies, *American Revolution*, 5: 33. Shawnee diplomacy runs as a thread through the documents. For examples see A. C. Flick, *Papers of Sir William Johnson*, 8: 6, 57, 417, and 12: 1055.

4. For Cornstalk's relationship to Puckshenose and the Moravians see Timothy Horsfield to William Parsons, 7 and 10 July, 1756, Timothy Horsfield letters; C. J. Fliegel, *Records of the Moravian Missions*, 93, 324, 381, 1044–45. I have written on Cornstalk for *ANB*, indicating further sources, but R. G. Thwaites and L. P. Kellogg (1905) print an excellent selection covering Lord Dunmore's War. Useful secondary accounts are given by Jack M. Sosin (1966) and Paul Lawrence Stevens.

5. Ruddell said Cheeseekau accompanied his father, but he was probably too young to have been a warrior. Timothy Flint, *First White Man of the West*, evidently got Shawnee material from Daniel Boone (pp. 139, 141, 147–48), and mentioned that war chiefs sometimes had attendants whose duties included distributing rations to warriors (pp. 140–41, 152–53). Although Flint used information from other sources, including an account by William Wells which had nothing to do with the Shawnees, this seems to be original, and may have come from Boone, who was once a captive in Shawnee towns. The Flint volume is extremely suspect, but it could explain Cheeseekau's presence in the army.

6. William Christian to William Preston, 15 October 1774, Thwaites and Kellogg (1905), 261.

7. E. G. Williams, "Richard Butler," 394–95. The experiences of the Ohio Indians during the revolutionary period are discussed by Paul L. Stevens, Gregory Schaaf, and Colin G. Calloway (1995).

8. The issue of the release of prisoners is well illustrated by the speech of Cornstalk, 11 October 1775, R. G. Thwaites and L. P. Kellogg, *Revolution on the Upper Ohio*, 100. A birthmark identified Shawtunte to his mother as Richard Sparks. He was a lifelong illiterate, but had a successful army career, partly on account of his marriage to a daughter of John Sevier, a noted southern partisan. After living in Pennsylvania, Sparks served in the U.S. Army under Anthony Wayne, and in 1796 moved to the south, where he served in Tennessee, Louisiana, Mississippi, and Alabama. He died 1 July 1815, in Claiborne County, Mississippi, a colonel of the 2nd Regiment of U.S. Infantry. See R. C. Knopf, *Anthony Wayne*, 18, 539; J. F. H. Claiborne, *Mississippi*, 221–222.

9. For the Mekoches joining the Delawares, see David Zeisberger to Edward Hand, 16 November 1777, R. G. Thwaites and L. P. Kellogg, *Frontier Defense*, 164; speech of White Eyes, 13 September 1778, L. P. Kellogg, *Frontier Advance*, 142.

10. Duncan McArthur to Benjamin Drake, 19 November 1821, Tecumseh papers, 2YY187. Matthew Arbuckle to Hand, 1777 (Thwaites and Kellogg, *Frontier Defense*, 25 n.) and the report of Matthew Elliott, 31 August 1776 (Jasper Yeates papers) indicate the removals occurred in 1777. For the Pekowi and Kispoko towns see Alexander McKee to Arent Schuyler De Peyster, 22 August 1780, Frederick Haldimand papers, 21783: 381; James Galloway to Drake, 22 January 1839, George Rogers Clark papers, 8J263; and Drake, *Life of Tecumseh*, 66–67.

11. J. Filson, *Kentucke*, 102; Simon Kenton interviewed by John H. James, 1832, Simon Kenton papers, 5BB106; and Galloway to Drake, 13 December 1839, George Rogers Clark papers, 8J260, describe Old Chillicothe.

12. Hinde prepared his account in 1825 (diary, Thomas S. Hinde papers, 39Y225) and it was published in newspapers the following year. Kelly was then dead, but Hinde re-

peated the story, without embellishment, several times (ibid., 16Y45; Hinde to Drake 17 July 1840, Tecumseh papers, 3YY130; Hinde to J. S. Williams, 6 and 30 May, 1842, *The American Pioneer*, 1: 327, 373; Draper notes, 21S252). I believe Hinde rendered Kelly accurately, but whether the latter was falsely claiming association with Tecumseh on account of the chief's celebrity is open to question. Kelly's captivity is historical (Boonesborough petition, 16 October 1779, Draper notes, 14S20), but Draper was unable to confirm his Tecumseh story with a son and grandson (Carter J. Kelly to Draper, 15 April 1852, 18 June 1867, and Benjamin H. Kelly to Draper, 15 August 1869, Daniel Boone papers, 24C124–26).

On the face of it, Kelly is supported by an account of the 1781–1782 captivity of Philemon Waters, first published in 1851. Waters (1751–1829) was well known to pioneers (Kenton, interviewed by James, 1832, Simon Kenton papers, 5BB106). His son and grandson, Thomas H. Waters and Frank Waters, claimed that he was captured in Ohio by Indians who had a camp at the Blue Licks on the Licking River. Tecumseh was at the camp. Waters was taken to the Shawnee towns and named Tu-ca-pi-ce. Tecumseh was kind to him, and used to give him jerked venison in return for help in learning English (1851 clipping, Daniel Boone papers, 13C129; inquiries in ibid., 13C133 and 13C149, and in Draper notes, 18S200). This account was produced long after Waters's death, and although it also contains the information Hinde got from Kelly, I judge that the latter, already published, was being plagiarized.

On Blackfish see the narrative of Joseph Jackson, 1844, Daniel Boone papers, 11C62, and my paper in *ANB*.

13. J. A. James, *Clark Papers*, 1: cviii, 331, 2: 30; narratives of Joseph Jackson and Henry Hall, both 1844, Daniel Boone papers, 11C62, 12C1; Josiah Collins interviewed by John D. Shane, 1840s, Kentucky papers, 12CC64; Kenton interviewed by James, 1832, Simon Kenton papers, 5BB106; John H. James statement, 1851, Draper notes, 5S181; Henry Bird to Richard Lernoult, 9 June 1779, Frederick Haldimand papers, 21782: 231; C. G. Talbert, *Logan*, 74–81.

14. Account of John Clairy, 5 August 1780, Frederick Haldimand papers, 21760: 340; Indians to De Peyster, 22 August 1780, ibid., 21782: 383; British dispatches by De Peyster, ibid., 21760: 342, and 21782: 387, and by William Honan and Alexander McKee, ibid., 21782: 377, 381; Haldimand to Lord George Germain, 25 October 1780, Davies, 18: 208; American accounts in J. R. James, 1: 451, 476; R. R. Juday, *Battle of Piqua*.

15. The invasion of the Shawnee towns in 1782 is described in McKee to De Peyster, 15 November 1782, Frederick Haldimand papers, 21783: 272; De Peyster's dispatches, 21 November 1782, 7 January 1783, ibid., 21763: 1, 21783: 272, 282, and William Claus papers, 3: 189; council minutes, 13 January 1783, Frederick Haldimand papers, 21783: 286; accounts by Clark in J. R. James, 2: 152, and *CVSP*, 3: 382.

16. Deposition of Samuel Wilson, 15 April 1777, *CVSP*, 1: 282; and Andrew Steele to Benjamin Harrison, 12 September 1782, J. R. James, 2: 115, supply the quotations.

17. The Shawnee emigrants, led by Yellow Hawk and Black Stump, were settling in the Cherokee country by 1780 (Jackson narrative, 1844, Daniel Boone papers, 11C62; Alexander Cameron to Germain, 18 July 1780, Davies 18: 120). The Swan was with the Shawnees at least from the spring of 1781: council minutes, 5 April 1781, Frederick Haldimand papers, 21783: 18.

18. Lewis Mesquerier to Draper, 8 September 1869, Tecumseh papers, 1YY98. The Shanes give information about Tecumapease, but for her husband see also return of Indians killed, 23 January 1815, Canada/IA 12: 10524.

19. Ruddell, and John Doughty to Henry Knox, 17 April 1790, Josiah Harmar papers (1). The root of the name is *popiquani* (gun).

20. Several accounts mention the bathing, for example J. H. Moore, "Captive of the Shawnees," 293. The custom survived until the late nineteenth century, at which time Shawnees explained that if a boy retrieved an object from the bed of the stream it might help him identify the spirits which would protect him through life. This function may also have existed in Tecumseh's day: T. W. Alford, *Civilization*, 24–25; M. R. Harrington, "Shawnee Indian Notes" (ms.), 101–102.

4. Rites of Passage

1. W. V. Kinietz and E. W. Voegelin, *Shawnese Traditions*, 1–8, 61–63; Mekoche chiefs, 1795, William Claus papers, 7: 124; and J. Johnston, "Account," 275. The earliest traditions of the origins of the Kispokos were collected by Erminie W. Voegelin in 1933–1934 (Voegelin papers), but they do not strike me as being of great antiquity.
2. Kinietz and Voegelin, 21, 36, establishes the existence of guardian spirits among the Shawnees, but no details of the vision quest have been found in contemporary records. Accounts of it from the end of the nineteenth century (T. W. Alford, *Civilization*, 24 and M. R. Harrington, "Shawnee Indian Notes," [ms.], 101–102) suggest it was similar to that of the Miamis (H. W. Beckwith, "The Fort Wayne Manuscript," 87–88).
3. John M. Ruddell to Lyman Draper, 5 September and 1 November, 1884, Tecumseh papers, 8YY40, 8YY42; Ruddell, interviewed by Draper, 1868, Draper notes 22S41. John was in his mid-thirties when his father, who gave him the story, died.
4. T. L. McKenney and J. Hall, *Indian Tribes of North America*, 1: 78, 97.
5. J. Burnet, *Notes on the Early Settlement*, 68–70. Modern Shawnees associate the game with the spring festival—a connection that existed at least as early as 1859 (L. A. White, *Morgan*, 47).
6. The evolution of the dance between 1751 and 1859 can be traced in C. A. Hanna, *Wilderness Trail*, 2: 152; E. Denny, *Military Journal*, 71 (first quotation); Kinietz and Voegelin, 50 (second quotation); and White, 47. See J. Sugden, *Shawnees in Tecumseh's Time*, 84–85.
7. The Shanes, Stephen Ruddell, and John Johnston treat Tecumseh's relationships with women. See ch. 2, n. 1.
8. A good survey of United States Indian policy in post-Revolutionary times is given by Reginald Horsman (1967). For British relations see the studies by A. L. Burt, G. G. Hatheway, Reginald Horsman (1964), J. Leitch Wright (1975), Colin G. Calloway (1987), and Robert S. Allen.
9. The Sandusky council: minutes, 26 August to 8 September, 1783, Britain/CO 42/45: 13; Alexander McKee to John Johnson, 9 September 1783, ibid., 42/45: 33; Shawnee statement, 5 September 1783, Frederick Haldimand papers, 21763: 248; speech of Captain Johnny, 9 August 1793, Joseph Brant journal, Canada/IA 8: 8466.
10. On these movements see accounts by A. F. C. Wallace (1957), Richard White, Francis Jennings, Michael N. McConnell (1992), Gregory E. Dowd (1992), Howard H. Peckham (1947), Paul L. Stevens, and Isabel T. Kelsay.
11. Journal of Brant, 26 July 1793, Canada/IA 8: 8461.
12. Indian speeches enclosed with Daniel Elliott and James Ranken to the U.S. Commissioners, 1785, Draper notes, 14S195.
13. For the Fort Finney treaty: E. Denny, *Military Journal*, 59–80; ms. journal of Richard Butler, 1785–86; C. J. Kappler, *Indian Affairs*, 2: 16; McKee to Johnson, 25 February 1786, Britain/CO 42/49: 258.
14. Jean Marie Phillipe Le Gras to George Rogers Clark, 22 July 1786, L. Kinnaird, *Spain in the Mississippi Valley*, 2: 175.

15. American accounts include Logan to Edmund Randolph, 17 December 1786, *CVSP*, 4: 204; Logan to Shawnees, October 1786, Frontier Wars papers, 23U38; Josiah Harmar to Henry Knox, 15 November 1786, W. H. Smith, *St. Clair*, 2: 18; Walter Finney to Harmar, 31 October 1786, Josiah Harmar papers (2), 1W241; E. Denny, *Military Journal*, 93–94; *The Carlisle Gazette*, 13 December 1786; notes from Virginian archives, Draper notes, 12S133; and interview material in Simon Kenton papers, 5BB106, Kentucky papers, 12CC79, and Frontier Wars papers, 14U114. For British/Indian accounts, Simon Girty to McKee, 11 October 1786, *MPHC*, 24: 34; statement of W. Ancrum, 13–20 October 1786, ibid., 24: 35; Patrick Langan to Daniel Claus, 14 December 1786, William Claus papers, 4: 131; Abraham Kuhn and Marrayet Haire to Richard Butler, 28 October 1786, and statement of Lewis Wetzel, 14 November 1786, both in Shawnee File; B. H. Coates, "Narrative," 126.

16. The John Johnston manuscript gives the statement of the chiefs, but see also Drake, *Life of Tecumseh*, 68.

17. M. M. Quaife, "Henry Hay's Journal," has the most valuable references to these new settlements.

18. The Brownstown council: minutes, 28 November to 18 December, 1786, Frontier Wars papers, 23U39; Indians to U.S. Congress, 18 December 1786, Britain/CO 42/50: 70.

19. Harmar to Knox, 14 May and 9 December, 1787, 15 June 1788, W. H. Smith, 2: 19, 37, 44 n.

20. Ruddell cannot be expected to have remembered the details entirely accurately, as he admitted ("in the action one prisoner, as well as I recollect, was taken"), but the important clues for an identification of the incident are that it occurred the spring before Tecumseh went south; that several boats, not one, were taken as they descended the Ohio; that they were owned by traders; and that the people on them were killed, except, Ruddell thought, a prisoner who was later burned. A conscientious search of the relevant military dispatches, and the files of *The Carlisle Gazette* and *The Kentucky Gazette* for the years 1786 to 1789 inclusive, failed to document any attack that completely conformed to Ruddell's recollections.

    Only two incidents could have inspired the account: the raid of March 1788, and another that occurred in late May 1788. About forty Indians camped on the Ohio at the mouth of the Kentucky River in May. They fired upon a military detachment under Ensign Cornelius Ryker Sedam, wounding two men, and later captured two boats, killing several persons. One boat belonged to the Ashe family. Mr. Ashe escaped, but his son was killed and his wife and six children were captured. The raiders withdrew up the Great Miami (John Wyllys to Harmar, 26 to 31 May and 11 June, 1788, Josiah Harmar papers [2], 1W409, 1W423; list of prisoners, 3 September 1794, Anthony Wayne papers [1]). Tecumseh may have been in both raids, but the events of March, involving the capture of several boats and considerable baggage, and the killing and burning of prisoners, were probably those to which Ruddell alluded.

21. John F. Hamtramck to Harmar, 16 May 1788, G. Thornbrough, *Outpost on the Wabash*, 80; deposition of James Gray and William Garland, 18 May 1788, enclosed in Hamtramck to Harmar, 21 May 1788, Josiah Harmar papers (2), 1W394; correspondence of Harmar and John Purviance, 1788–1789, ibid., 1W400, 2W7, 2W54; Wyllys to Harmar, 12, 26 to 31 May, 1788, ibid., 1W405, 1W409; *The Kentucky Gazette*, 5 April 1788, 19 May 1792; statement in George Rogers Clark papers, 33J11; J. May, *Journal and Letters*, 42–43; M. Edgar, *Ten Years of Upper Canada*, 339–56, 371.

22. I contributed a sketch of Lorimier to *ANB*.

5. The Raiders of Lookout Mountain

1. E. Denny, *Military Journal*, 105–106; Hamtramck to Josiah Harmar, 13 October 1788, 11 April 1789, G. Thornbrough, *Outpost on the Wabash*, 120, 166. Anthony Shane says Cheeseekau's party contained Pekowis and Hathewekelas. The small number of Pekowi, Kispoko, and Hathewekela Shawnees left in Ohio also identifies them as the main emigrants (return of the Indians, 4 December 1794, William Claus papers, 6: 291).

2. John Johnston's Tecumseh manuscript (see ch. 2, n. 1) states that Methoataaskee died at an advanced age among the Cherokees. She may have gone with the Shawnees who joined the Cherokees in 1780, but more probably went with Cheeseekau, who eventually settled with the Cherokees. For Lalawéthika, see Shane.

3. The chronology of Cheeseekau's trip is confused, but I have related the details given by Ruddell and Shane to the historical context. Tecumseh's injury was also mentioned to Charles A. Wickliffe in 1812 by Christopher Miller, who lived with the Shawnees between 1782 and 1794 (Wickliffe, "Tecumseh and the Battle of the Thames," 45–49; deposition of Miller, 1794, Draper notes, 16S163). William Walker and Adam Brown, both interviewed by Lyman Draper, 1868, Frontier Wars papers, 11U26, 11U74, mention that their people, the Wyandots, referred to Tecumseh as "Broken Thigh."

4. Francisco Cruzat to Lorimier, 9 July 1787, L. Houck, *Spanish Regime in Missouri*, 2: 42; James Rogers and Noma to James Madison, 29 March 1811, U.S. SoW/LR/IA M271: 0550.

5. Hamtramck to Harmar, 11 April 1789, Thornbrough, *Outpost on the Wabash*, 166; documents in L. Kinnaird, *Spain in the Mississippi Valley*, 2: 274, 275, and in Houck 1: 275, 279, 286, 310, 316, 2: 43; and Morgan to the Indians, April 1789, Anthony Wayne papers (1). Morgan had negotiated with the Spanish ambassador to the United States, but did not consult the provincial governor, Esteban Miró, who eventually "crushed" the American colony "in the cradle" (J. Wilkinson, *Memoirs*, 2: 112).

6. *The Knoxville Gazette*, 20 October 1792. Comprehensive accounts of the Chickamaugas are given by John P. Brown and James P. Pate.

7. *The Virginia Gazette or The American Advertiser*, 17 May 1786; information of Joseph Saunders, 24 July 1786, Josiah Harmar papers (2), 1W185; E. Denny, *Military Journal*, 99; *The Kentucky Gazette*, 2 May 1789; H. H. Tanner, "Cherokees in the Ohio Country."

8. Enclosure with William Blount to Henry Knox, 20 March 1792, *ASPIA* 1: 264.

9. John Doughty to Knox, 17 April 1790, Josiah Harmar papers (1); Doughty to Harmar, 17 April 1790, Josiah Harmar papers (2), 2W201; Doughty to John Wyllys, 25 March 1790, W. H. Smith, *St. Clair*, 2: 134; D. C. and R. Corbitt, "Spanish Archives," 22: 145, 23: 77; *Minutes of Debates in Council on the Banks of the Ottawa River*, 11–12.

10. Doughty to Knox, 17 April 1790, Josiah Harmar papers (1); McGillivray to Miró, 8 May and 2 June, 1790, Corbitt and Corbitt 23: 83, 88; McGillivray to William Panton, 8 May 1790, J. W. Caughey, *McGillivray*, 259; McGillivray to Miró, 8 June 1791, ibid., 291.

11. For Shawnee marriages see W. V. Kinietz and E. W. Voegelin, *Shawnese Traditions*, 30–35; D. Jones, *Journal of Two Visits*, 75–76; and T. W. Alford, *Civilization*, 67.

12. Ruddell and Johnston knew about Tecumseh's Cherokee liaison but were so vague about it that it probably occurred in the south, rather than the north: Johnston to the *Piqua Gazette*, 30 September 1826, Tecumseh papers, 1YY89; T. L. McKenney and J. Hall, *Indian Tribes of North America*, 1: 78. It appears that mother and daughter were among the Cherokees who migrated to Arkansas beginning in the 1790s. In the next century Tecumseh was said to have been the grandfather of four or five brave and intelligent Cherokees known as the "fair-skinned" Procters. John G. Harnage remem-

bered one of them as "the finest looking Indian I ever saw" (J. T. Adair to Draper, May 1882, Tecumseh papers, 4YY31; Harnage to A. N. Chamberlin, 7 February 1881, ibid., 4YY36).

13. Journal of March–May 1791, Britain/CO 42/73: 197.

14. Wilkinson to Arthur St. Clair, 24 August 1791, W. H. Smith 2: 233. Shane is the sole authority for Tecumseh's journey. General accounts of the northern war have been given by James R. Jacobs, Jack J. Gifford, and Wiley Sword, but none is satisfactory from the Indian viewpoint. Narrower, but excellent, contributions were made by Reginald Horsman (1964), Richard H. Kohn, and Isabel T. Kelsay. On the Glaize, see H. H. Tanner, "The Glaize in 1792."

15. Statement about Tecumseh, Return Jonathan Meigs papers (2).

16. The story that Tecumseh and two other Shawnees, Berry and Blackfish, armed with knives and hatchets, were among the first to break St. Clair's line was first published by Joseph Charless in *The Missouri Gazette*, 1 January 1814, but it probably came from Indian agent Thomas Forsyth (Forsyth's sketch of Tecumseh, Tecumseh papers, 8YY54). See also Benjamin Logan interviewed by Draper, 1863, Draper notes, 18S168.

17. Apart from notices in *The Kentucky Gazette* (14 and 21 April, 1792) the earliest accounts of this incident are those of Shane and Ruddell. Although congruent, Ruddell's takes precedence because he was a participant. His account is substantially the same as that given later by his son (John M. Ruddell interviewed by Draper, 1868, Draper notes, 22S41). By comparison the later reminiscences of the rangers are contradictory, defensive, and occasionally absurd. Four rangers left accounts of some length: Charley Ward, a youth in 1792 (J. A. McClung [M'Clung], *Sketches*, 188–93; "Extract From Reminiscences of a Western Traveller"; James Ward and Moses Fowler, interviewed by Draper, 1845, Simon Kenton papers, 9BB54, 9BB63); Simon Kenton himself (J. McDonald, *Biographical Sketches*, iii, 254–57, 267; Kenton interviewed by John H. James, 1832, Simon Kenton papers, 5BB106); Benjamin Whiteman (narrative, 18 October 1839, Simon Kenton papers, 9BB7; interviews by Draper, 1846 and 1851, ibid., 9BB1, and Draper notes, 5S185); and Christopher Wood, interviewed by Draper, 1852 (Simon Kenton papers, 8BB2). Another participant, Samuel Frazee, referred to the episode incidentally when interviewed by Draper, 1845, ibid., 9BB66. Whiteman's second interview shows a serious deterioration in recall and exaggerates his own prominence in contravention of his own earlier and other accounts, while Wood, who was eighty when interviewed just before his death, was influenced by his association with Whiteman. Some two dozen other documents relating to the event are scattered throughout the Kenton papers and Draper notes, but most are secondhand materials of doubtful utility.

18. A muster roll made out after Kenton's return provides twenty-eight names (muster, April 1792, Simon Kenton papers, 6BB98), but unpaid volunteers, one of whom was Cornelius Washburn, seem to have joined the expedition also.

19. Ward (in McClung), Whiteman in 1846 and 1851, and Wood say that Barr was shot, a version accepted by Barr's daughter (Ann Ellison interviewed by Draper, 1863, Draper notes, 19S143). Ruddell has Tecumseh downing Barr with a war club, and the Shanes with a tomahawk. Whatever the truth, their accounts, which were independent of each other, establish that Tecumseh was credited by the Indians with killing Barr.

6. An Honor to Die in Battle

1. The southern career of Cheeseekau has been obscured by confusion. Historians of the Cherokees give incomplete accounts of Shawnee Warrior, who was killed at

Buchanan's Station in 1792, without identifying him with Cheeseekau (A. V. Good-pasture, "Indian Wars and Warriors," 177–84, and J. P. Brown, *Old Frontiers*, 205, 342–44, 347, 359). Tecumseh's biographer, Drake, also failed to make the connection. His source, Stephen Ruddell, had not participated in the southern campaigns and was vague and contradictory. Drake was misled into believing that Cheeseekau was killed about 1788, four years too early, and neither he nor Brown was able to successfully fit Ruddell's narrative to documented events (Drake, *Life of Tecumseh*, 69–70; Brown, *Old Frontiers*, 270–71). Lyman Draper was the first historian to speculate that the Indian known in the south as Shawnee Warrior was Cheeseekau, but he neither clinched nor published his identification. Glenn Tucker (*Tecumseh*, 338–39) accepted Draper's theory, but muddied the picture by confounding Shawnee Warrior with a Cherokee named Chiachattalley.

My confirmation of Draper's hypothesis rests upon three arguments. First, the life of Shawnee Warrior provides the only known parallel to Ruddell's account of Cheeseekau. Ruddell represents Cheeseekau as having commanded a Shawnee party among the Cherokees for about three years, and as having perished in an unsuccessful Cherokee attack upon a fort. Shawnee Warrior led the Shawnees at Running Water from about 1789 to 1792, and was killed at Buchanan's Station in exactly such circumstances. Second, white pioneers of the area actually remembered that Cheeseekau and Tecumseh had been at Buchanan's Station, and the tradition was independently recorded at least three times between 1829 and 1849 (S. L. Knapp, *Lectures*, 211; speech of Baillie Peyton of Tennessee in *The Commercial Daily Advertiser*, 29 January 1834; and T. Washington, "Attack on Buchanan's Station").

Finally, Shawnee Warrior and Cheeseekau are directly linked in contemporary documents. Relying upon the information of Indian trader Francis Vigo, the American secretary of war reported on Shawnee Warrior's taking of Zeigler's Station in 1792, noting that the captors were "the very men who attacked Major Doughty in 1790" (Henry Knox to William Blount, 15 August 1792, *ASPIA* 1: 258). This led me to Doughty's report of his action (John Doughty to Knox, 17 April 1790, Josiah Harmar papers [1]), which specifically identifies the Shawnee leader on that occasion as "Popoquan, or the Gun." We know from Ruddell that this was another name used by Cheeseekau. The only conclusion from the foregoing, that Cheeseekau and Shawnee Warrior were the same person, enables me to present the first full and accurate account of this phase of his and Tecumseh's lives.

2. Report of Richard Finnelson, September 1792, *ASPIA* 1: 288; statements of David Craig, 15 March 1792, and James Carey, 3 November 1792, ibid., 1: 264, 328.

3. Report of David Craig, 15 March 1792, *ASPIA* 1: 264; Pedro Olivier to Francis Hector, Baron de Carondelet, 10 April 1792, Spain/Papeles Procedentes de Cuba, 25A.

4. Enclosure with Blount to Knox, 26 September 1792, *ASPIA* 1: 291.

5. Enclosure with Blount to Knox, 26 September 1792, and Blount to Knox, 4 July 1792, *ASPIA* 1: 291, 270.

6. The best account of the attack on Zeigler's Station is John Rogers to Henry Lee, 5 August 1792, *The General Advertiser*, 4 October 1792. The quotations are from John Carr's "Narrative," and from the letter from Nashville, 16 July 1792, in *The Knoxville Gazette*, 25 August 1792. See also the return of persons killed, captured, and wounded, *ASPIA* 1: 329; and correspondence of Blount and Knox in ibid., 1: 258, 275.

7. Spanish policy is described in books by Arthur P. Whitaker and J. Leitch Wright (1971).

8. Cherokees to Spanish governor in Mobile, 29 June 1792, McClung Historical Collection.

9. On Watts at Pensacola: Bloody Fellow to O'Neill, enclosed in O'Neill to Carondelet, 5 August 1792, Spain/Papeles Procedentes de Cuba, 39; and report of Red Bird, 15 September 1792, *ASPIA* 1: 282. Sources for the Willstown council are the statements of

Finnelson (September 1792), Joseph De Raque (15 September 1792), and James Carey (3 November 1792) in ibid., 1: 288, 291, 328.

10. *ASPIA* 1: 276, 277, 279, 280, 281, 293, 331; *TPUS* 4: 177, 181; A. B. Keith, *John Gray Blount Papers*, 2: 640; J. Robertson, "Correspondence," 2: 71, 76; J. Haywood, *Civil and Political History of the State of Tennessee*, 350–57.

11. Information enclosed in Blount to Knox, 7 October 1792, *ASPIA* 1: 293; Kenoteta to Blount, 1 October 1792, ibid., 1: 293.

12. Basic sources for the attack on Buchanan's Station are the statements collected by Blount: 10 September and 5 November 1792, and Blount to Knox, 8 November 1792, *ASPIA* 1: 294, 331, 325. Other contemporary references are James Robertson to Blount, 7 October 1792, Tennessee papers, 4XX14; Blount to Robertson, 17 October 1792, Robertson, "Correspondence," 2: 80; *TPUS* 2: 414; D. C. and R. Corbitt, "Spanish Archives," 28: 131; and P. M. Hamer, "British in Canada," 115. Not all the sources of Haywood, 356–59, have been found, but he is generally dependable.

    Accounts given by participants much later, and secondhand testimony, while abundant, have to be used with caution: *Cist's Advertiser* (Cincinnati), 2 September 1846; Washington, "Attack on Buchanan's Station"; J. Shelby, "Letter"; J. Rains, "Narrative"; J. Brown, "Captivity of Colonel Joseph Brown"; "Scalping of Thomas Everett," 265; E. F. Ellet, *Women of the American Revolution*, 3: 310, 318–25; John Buchanan Todd interviewed by Draper, 1854, Tennessee papers, 6XX64; H. R. Buchanan to Draper, 2 September 1845, Kentucky papers, 8CC51; and several statements in vol. 30S of the Draper notes.

13. This follows Ruddell.

14. The convolutions of the story can be followed in Haywood, 356; Robert Weakley interviewed by Draper, 1844, Draper notes, 32S358; Washington, 426–28; and the narratives of Joseph Brown and John Carr.

15. For erroneous stories of Cheeseekau see J. B. M'Ferrin, *Methodism in Tennessee*, 431–36, and Jeannie Cegar's account of 1934, Erminie Wheeler Voegelin papers.

16. In the days following the defeat, several parties of Indians raided the Nashville area, killing three soldiers at a blockhouse on a branch of the Little River, burning a distillery, stealing and destroying stock, and attacking isolated settlers. One party burned three houses on Sycamore Creek, eighteen miles from Nashville, on 9 October and then proceeded to the Bushy Creek on the Red River, where another house was destroyed and horses ran off. Pursuers killed an Indian and recovered the horses. Tecumseh may have been in some of these raids, for which see *The Knoxville Gazette*, 10 and 20 October, 1792; *ASPIA* 1: 331; Haywood, 332–33; Thomas Hickman interviewed by Draper, 1844, Draper notes, 30S448.

17. *The Knoxville Gazette*, 1, 15 December 1792, 26 January 1793; Blount to Knox, 24 January 1793, and information of Handley, *ASPIA* 1: 434; William Panton to Carondelet, 16 February 1793, J. W. Caughey, *McGillivray*, 353; Handley to James Scott, 10 December 1792, J. G. M. Ramsey, *Annals of Tennessee*, 573; Handley, "Narrative"; Samuel Garland, interviewed by Draper, 1841, Draper notes, 31S304; G. W. Sevier, interviewed by Draper, 1844, ibid., 30S351; Alexander McCoblom and Samuel Handley, interviewed by Draper, 1841–1842, ibid., 31S298; Brown, "Captivity of Colonel Joseph Brown," 76. *The Knoxville Gazette* of 26 January 1793 reported that only four Shawnees were in the ambush.

18. Haywood, 280; *ASPIA* 1: 446, 448, 455. Early in 1793 some Indians moved north to join the Indian confederacy in Ohio, and Shawnees from Lookout Mountain Town may have been among them (report of John McKee, 28 March 1793, ibid., 1: 444).

19. "Big Rock" is believed to have referred to a round granite boulder, some twelve feet in diameter and four feet high, that existed on the west side of Loramie's Creek until it

was blown up by a settler clearing land in 1882 (Stephen Johnston to Draper, 20 July 1882, Tecumseh papers, 11YY6–7).

7. Warrior of the Confederacy

1. Minutes of Indian congress, 30 September to 9 October, 1792, E. A. Cruikshank, *Simcoe*, 1: 218. The background sources for this chapter are many, but particularly useful are Britain/CO 42/vols. 316–20; Canada/IA vols. 8–9; Canada/C series, vols. 247–48; William Claus papers, vols. 4–7; Anthony Wayne papers (1); *ASPIA*, vol. 1; and the Alexander McKee papers.
2. J. H. Buell, "Fragment from the Diary," 268 (quotation).
3. *The Kentucky Gazette*, 6 and 20 April, 1793. A leader of the rangers, James Ward, left three accounts. At the age of seventy-six he supplied a narrative to Benjamin Drake dated 18 September 1839 (Simon Kenton papers, 9BB57). A second statement was made to John D. Shane about 1842 (ibid., 9BB58) and a third to Lyman Draper in 1845 (ibid., 9BB54). Moses Fowler, who served in Kenton's division, spoke of the fight (petition to congress, 29 January 1846, ibid., 6BB113, 115; Charles A. Marshall to Draper, 14 May 1885, ibid., 10BB50) but gave only one full account, to Draper in 1845, when he was seventy-five years old (ibid., 9BB63). Kenton's own version, offered at the same age, comes largely through J. McDonald, *Biographical Sketches*, 258–59, but this account may be partly founded upon J. A. McClung [M'Clung], *Sketches*, 194–95, whose sources are unclear. Ruddell and Shane refer to the incident.
4. Examination of Shawnee prisoners, 26 June 1794, *ASPIA* 1: 489.
5. The contemporary sources are James Wood to the governor of Virginia, 10 May 1793, *CVSP* 6: 365; George Jackson to Anthony Wayne, 19 May 1795, Anthony Wayne papers (1); and the list of surrendered prisoners, 1795, ibid., and in Draper notes, 16S178.
6. Withers, *Chronicles of Border Warfare*, 408–11. See also statements in Simon Kenton papers, 11BB10–11, and Draper notes, 25S261, and L. V. McWhorter, *Border Settlers*, especially 362–63, 372–73.
7. Among several accounts of the attack on Fort Recovery the narrative of a British observer with the Indian army (Cruikshank, *Simcoe*, 5: 90) and Alexander Gibson to Anthony Wayne, 30 June and 10 July, 1794, Anthony Wayne papers (1), are particularly useful.
8. Ruddell's account of Fallen Timbers has Tecumseh and two or three comrades rushing upon a field gun and its crew about the time the Indians began to retreat. They drove the gunners away, cut loose the team horses, and used them to ride to safety. The legion did deploy artillery during the action, but although one artilleryman was wounded it seems that the guns were left behind in the American charge (J. J. Gifford, *Northwest Indian War*, 424–25; D. L. Smith, "Greene Ville to Fallen Timbers," 293). I have searched every letter and journal bearing upon the battle and can find no confirmation of Ruddell's story, and have used Shane's account in preference. See also John M. Ruddell interviewed by Draper, 1868, Draper notes, 22S41, and his letter to Draper, 15 November 1884, Tecumseh papers, 8YY43.

    Shane does not identify which of Tecumseh's brothers stood with him, although elsewhere he remarks that Sauawaseekau was killed during this war. He may have died at Fallen Timbers, although no authority specifically says so. Lalawéthika was certainly in the battle. Years later Shawnees derided his performance by saying that he fled ignominiously from the field (John Johnston to *Liberty Hall*, 30 November 1811, *The Western Sun* [Vincennes], 11 January 1812).
9. Thomas Worthington and Duncan McArthur to Thomas Kirker, 22 September 1807, Simon Kenton papers, 7BB49. The numerous sources for the battle cannot be cited

here, but they can be sampled in R. C. McCrane, M. M. Quaife (1929), and R. C. Knopf (1954, 1960).

10. *History of Madison County, Ohio*, 284, 287 (Alder's account); R. M. Sparks, *Tecumseh's Deer Creek Village*.

11. So says Shane, and the absence of Tecumseh's name on the treaty supports him. In 1810 Tecumseh is reported to have told an interpreter, Joseph Barron, that he had been at Greenville and remembered seeing young William Henry Harrison sitting beside Wayne (Harrison to William Eustis, 6 August 1810, L. Esarey, *Harrison*, 1: 456).

12. Shane is the authority for Blue Jacket's visit, but that he toured the Shawnee camps carrying an American belt of wampum inviting them to participate in the peace is established in *ASPIA* 1: 583. Proceedings of the treaty of Greenville are given in ibid., 1: 562.

8. Chief

1. Josiah Snelling to William Henry Harrison, 20 November 1811, L. Esarey, *Harrison*, 1: 643; Thomas Fish and Enos Terry to Return Jonathan Meigs, 14 January 1812, U.S. SoW/LR/R 46: 1681; return, 4 December 1794, William Claus papers, 6: 291.

2. Shawnee villages still conferred female war and civil chief offices. The incumbents were generally related to the male chiefs. The Shanes (see ch. 2 n. 1) mention Tecumapease's position, which I presume was held in Tecumseh's town. Joseph Barron, who visited Tecumseh's band in 1811, was evidently the source for a story, preposterous in itself, which implies that Lalawéthika's wife held the female war office (J. Law, *Vincennes*, 98–105).

3. In addition to the Shane, Ruddell, and Johnston accounts see C. F. Klinck and J. T. Talman, *John Norton*, 174, and Thomas Forsyth's account, Tecumseh papers, 8YY54.

4. Harrison to William Eustis, 7 August 1811, Esarey, 1: 548. Typical remarks about Tecumseh's pride occur in Stephen Johnston to Lyman Draper, 23 August 1880, Tecumseh papers, 11YY3, and an account, apparently by James Conner, 1832, ibid., 8YY23.

5. D. Jones, *Journal of Two Visits*, 75.

6. The name of Tecumseh's son has been given as "Pugeshashenwa" and "Pah-gue-sah-ah," but the most authoritative version is "Paukeesaa" (W. V. Kinietz and E. W. Voegelin, *Shawnese Traditions*, 27). It was generally pronounced *Pauketha* (John Johnston to the *Piqua Gazette*, 30 September 1826, Tecumseh papers, 1YY89). Estimates of the boy's age are given by Shane, the Procters (whose testimony in *Tales of Chivalry and Romance*, 80, forms the final quotation), and James Witherell, 27 April 1816, B. F. H. Witherell papers.

7. Benjamin Howe to John F. Hamtramck, 8 and 9 August, 1796, Anthony Wayne papers (1), and material in L. H. Gipson, *Moravian Indian Mission*, supply evidence on the White River villages. Shane is the main source of information about Tecumseh between 1795 and 1805.

8. James Galloway junior to Benjamin Drake, 12 to 23 January, 1839, George Rogers Clark papers, 8J245; narrative of James Galloway senior, October 1832, ibid., 8J268.

9. Simon Kenton interviewed by John H. James, 1832, Simon Kenton papers, 5BB100. There is a sketch of Logan in *ANB*.

10. Galloway to Drake, 29 January 1841, Frontier Wars papers, 7U84. John Arrowsmith, interviewed by Draper, 1868, Draper notes, 24S78, remembered hearing Barrett tell the story exactly as Galloway gave it to Drake.

11. *The Western Spy*, 27 August 1799; James McHenry, to Arthur St. Clair, 30 April 1799, Edward E. Ayer manuscripts; St. Clair to McHenry, 21 October 1799, 19 May 1800,

Arthur St. Clair papers; John Johnson to Thomas McKee, 21–22 April 1799, Ironside letterbooks, George Ironside papers; E. A. Cruikshank and A. F. Hunter, *Peter Russell*, 2: 285.

12. Documents filed in Canada/C252: 213, 248, and C253: 132, 135; St. Clair to McHenry, 22 July and 19 August, 1799, Arthur St. Clair papers; *The Western Spy* 6, 13, and 20 August, 1799; *TPUS* 3: 59, 68.

13. St. Clair to McHenry, 19 August 1799, Arthur St. Clair papers; *The Philadelphia Gazette*, 22 and 30 August, 1799.

14. *The Western Spy*, 20 and 27 August 1799; *The Philadelphia Gazette*, 6 September 1799; St. Clair to McHenry, 19 August 1799, Arthur St. Clair papers; Galloway to Drake, 12-23 January 1839, George Rogers Clark papers, 8J245.

15. *The New York Spectator*, 17 November 1826; Harrison to Eustis, 6 August 1811, Esarey 1: 542; M. Dawson, *Historical Narrative*, 41–42.

16. Slover's "Narrative," *Pennsylvania Archives*, 2nd series, 14: 717; commissary notes, 17, 19, 21, and 24 December 1795, U.S. Army papers, box 1/folder 7; Shane interview.

17. Mission diary, 18 May 1802, L. H. Gipson, *Moravian Indian Mission*, 164. This volume contains most of the documents relating to life on the White River at this period.

18. Joseph A. Parsons, Francis P. Prucha (1962), Reginald Horsman (1967), Paul Woehrmann, and Bernard W. Sheehan have provided broad accounts of United States Indian policy at the turn of the century. A recent discussion of the condition of the Indians is in Richard White, ch. 11.

19. For land negotiations see Dwight L. Smith (1949) and the Indian Claims Commission, *Indians of Ohio, Indiana*. The most satisfactory biography of Harrison is by Freeman Cleaves.

20. Quotation from John Gibson and Francis Vigo to Harrison, 6 July 1805, Esarey 1: 141. See also letters in ibid., 1: 147, 161, 164, 180; and documents in Gipson, 379, 385, 545.

21. Lasselle to Thomas Jefferson, 12 June 1806, *TPUS* 10: 57; Harrison to William Hargrove, 12 November 1807, Esarey, *Harrison*, 1: 273.

22. Speech of Blackbeard, 1807, Shawnee File.

23. Mission diary, 4 August 1803, Gipson, 256.

24. The sickness is referred to in Gipson, 220–21, 359–62, 381–83, 529.

9. A Revolution on the White River

1. The comment on Lalawéthika's appearance was made by Benjamin Youngs of the Shakers in 1807: E. D. Andrews, "Shaker Mission," 120. Other descriptions of him are in the letters of James Witherell, 20 and 27 April 1816, B. F. H. Witherell papers; George Winter ms., "On The Prophet"; and J. J. Lutz, "Methodist Missions," 165. Quotations about his character come from Shane (see ch. 2 n. 1); Thomas Forsyth to William Clark, 15 January 1827, Thomas Forsyth papers (1), 9T37; and Andrews, 122. On this see also Charles Blue-Jacket interviewed by Lyman Draper, 1868, Draper notes, 23S167.

2. The Prophet was reported to have had two wives, four sons, and three daughters. One son, John Prophet, married Pene-e-pe-es-ce, a daughter of Spybuck (Charles Tucker to Draper, 26 June and 16 August, 1887, Tecumseh papers, 3YY112,1YY95; Pene-e-pe-es-ce interviewed by Draper, 1868, Draper notes, 23S172). John Prophet's family is mentioned in the records of the Shawnee mission school in Kansas and in the 1857 census of the Kansas Shawnees.

3. Mission diary, 14 March 1805, L. H. Gipson, *Moravian Indian Mission*, 339–40, supplies the quotation. This volume collects most of the documents, but the "revolution" is also treated by J. Heckewelder, *Narrative*, 409–17. Heckewelder was not on the

White, but received reports: David Zeisberger to Heckewelder, 10 May 1806, North-west Territory Collection (2); John to Polly Heckewelder, 14 May 1806, John Heck-ewelder papers. For Beata: J. Miller, *Delaware Integrity*, 70–71.

4. Andrews, 123.

5. Shane states that Lalawéthika was preceded as a prophet by Pengahshega. As Lalawéthika began preaching at Wapakoneta in the fall of 1805 (Shane; *The Virginia Argus* [Richmond], 6 September 1806; Andrews, 122–23), I surmise the Shawnee witch-finding on the White in May and June referred to his predecessor (diary, 19 June 1805, Gipson, 361–62; Hendrick Aupaumut to Henry Dearborn, 21 May 1805, Shawnee File).

6. Andrews, 122–23. The common description of Lalawéthika's first vision, taken from S. G. Drake, *Aboriginal Races*, 624, is erroneous. The "foreign" journal that supplied Drake with his information was, in fact, *The New Monthly Magazine and Literary Jour-nal*, series 2, 2 (1821): 60–70, but it referred to Handsome Lake, a Seneca prophet, not Lalawéthika.

7. Primary accounts of the Prophet's message are: diary, 3 December 1805, Gipson, 392; Andrews, passim, from which the quotations are taken; Thomas Worthington and Duncan McArthur to Thomas Kirker, 22 September 1807, Simon Kenton papers, 7BB49; speech of the Trout, 4 May 1807, *MPHC* 40: 127; B. Drake, *Life of Tecumseh*, 219; Nelson journal, 1807–1808, 61–64, George Nelson papers; the Prophet, August 1808, L. Esarey, *Harrison*, 1: 299; Shane; W. V. Kinietz and E. W. Voegelin, *Shawnese Traditions*, 3, 41–42; Forsyth to Clark, 15 January 1827, Thomas Forsyth papers (1), 9T37; and J. Tanner, *Narrative*, 155–58.

8. The Prophet was reluctant to accept the finality in the Christian concept of damna-tion, which he acquired indirectly through Delaware traditions. In the early days he emphasized opportunities for repentance, claiming that penitents could be pardoned up to four times for a particular offense; in 1824 he was mellower still, and taught that ultimately all souls passed to Heaven, some after punishment.

9. Forsyth's reference to the Prophet's introduction of a dance raises the possibility that it may have been a prototype of the Shawnee fall bread dance, first recorded in 1859. Injunctions associated with that dance, such as the condemnation of adultery and drunkenness, are redolent of the Prophet's teachings, while traditions from the nine-teenth century attributed it to one who had visited Waashaa Monetoo (M. R. Harring-ton, ms., "Shawnee Indian Notes," 102, 121–25; J. Gregg, *Commerce of the Prairies*, 387–89).

10. This and the following three quotations are from the speech of the Trout.

11. The Delaware prophetic tradition is examined by Howard H. Peckham (1947), A. F. C. Wallace (1956), Charles Hunter, Melburn D. Thurman (1973), and Gregory E. Dowd (1986, 1992). A Shawnee belief that the tribe had lost the Creator's affections, and de-clined accordingly, made it particularly susceptible to prophets advocating reform as a way of regaining sacred favor. Nonetheless, the sources do not suggest that the type of messianic nativism associated with Neolin played a major role in their resistance to white expansion between 1770 and 1805. Indeed, some currents ran against it, in-cluding the desire for Euro-American manufactures acquired by trade or warfare. A sign of its revival occurred in a Shawnee speech made at Fort Wayne in 1803 (Drake, *Life of Tecumseh*, 21), but even when it recaptured attention more fully in 1805 most of the tribe rejected the prophets.

There is a possibility that Lalawéthika's doctrines were influenced by the prophecy that began among the Iroquois in 1798. An Indian in a Seneca town on the Allegheny (New York) had a dream in February 1799 that closely resembled the Prophet's first vision. The Seneca spoke of the torture of sinful souls in a house where a drunkard was offered "melted pewter" to drink (M. H. Deardorff, "Religion of Handsome Lake," 89). The greatest of these Iroquois prophets, Handsome Lake, began his ministry in the same town a few months afterward. News of the Iroquois visions may have reached Lalawéthika prior to his ministry. A New York Indian agent reported in 1807 that "for two years past" the "western Indians" had been sending messages to Handsome Lake (Deardorff, 96). However, I believe that both drew independently upon traditions that already existed. Handsome Lake can be studied by reference to A. F. C. Wallace (1952, 1973).

12. Shane says Tecumseh brought his band back to Ohio in 1805, invited by the Wapakoneta chiefs, who wanted to unify the Shawnee nation. Yet some Shawnees were still on the White River in 1806. There are no references to the Indian village above the mouth of Stony Creek before 1806. It stood on a ridge above the west bank, and may have been formed by Tecumseh and the Prophet after their split from the Wapakoneta Shawnees. I am assuming that Lewis also lived there, because he was associated with Tecumseh's band in 1806 and later headed a Shawnee-Mingo town in Logan County. The location of the Stony Creek village is indicated by Andrews, 117–18; J. Antrim, *Champaign and Logan Counties*, 135; *History of Logan County and Ohio*, 364; Daniel Spellman to Draper, 28 September 1862, Tecumseh papers, 3YY61; and E. W. Voegelin, *Indians of Northwest Ohio*, 319–20. Abraham Luckenbach's diary of 1808 (Shawnee File) evidently confuses this town with a Mingo village to the north.

13. Gipson, 621. Shane has an interesting account of the Delaware witch trials, but was not himself an eyewitness.

14. Gipson, 621. E. P. Olmsted, *Blackcoats*, 181–84, has material on Joshua's origins.

15. Gipson, 621.

16. Mission diary, 13 March 1806, ibid., 412.

17. Ibid., 17 March 1806, 415.

18. William Henry Harrison to Delawares, April 1806, M. Dawson, *Historical Narrative*, 83.

19. Badger diary, 13 May 1806, Badger, *Memoir*, 145. The Wyandot deputation to Beata is mentioned in Gipson, 381–82.

20. Badger, 14 June 1806, 160, but see also pp. 147–48; the diary of Quintus F. Atkins, 12 and 13 July, 1806; Wallace, *Death and Rebirth of the Seneca*, 297.

10. Surely God Is in This Place!

1. John Johnston interviewed by Lyman Draper, 1843, Tecumseh papers, 11YY9; Isaac Brock to Lord Liverpool, 29 August 1812, Britain/CO 42/352: 105.

2. *The Virginia Argus* (Richmond), 6 September 1806.

3. My entry on Black Hoof in *ANB* revises the old sketch in T. L. McKenney and J. Hall, *Indian Tribes of North America*, 1: 234–47.

4. Speech of Blackbeard, 1807, Shawnee File. This discussion of Black Hoof's land policy is based upon the speech of Black Hoof and Henry Dearborn's reply, February 1802, Dearborn to William Henry Harrison, 23 February 1802, and Thomas Jefferson's speech, 19 February 1807, all in ibid.; Shawnees to Dearborn, 1807, U.S. SoW/LR/U 2: 0949; Indian petitions, 16, 21 January 1809, Daniel Parker papers; Johnston to Draper, 13 September 1847, Tecumseh papers, 11YY31; H. Harvey, *History of the Shawnee Indians*, 129–31, 134–37.

5. Johnston to William Eustis, 15 April 1809, G. Thornbrough, *Letter Book*, 33.

6. Shane (for the prophetess and the eclipse); J. Badger, *Memoir*, 147.

7. The only sketch of Lewis (died 1826) is in McKenney and Hall, 1: 168–71; but see Johnston to Eustis, 7 January 1812, U.S. SoW/LR/R 46: 1021, and Indian agreement with William Hull, 8 June 1812, ibid., 45: 0243.

8. Speech of Mekoches, William Claus papers, 7: 124; Alexander McKee to Matthew Elliott, May 1795, ibid., 7: 46. Foundation sketches of Blue Jacket can be found in *DCB* and *ANB*.

9. My account of Roundhead in *ANB* needs revising in the light of material in Frontier Wars papers, volume 11U.

10. E. D. Andrews, "Shaker Mission," 123.

11. Amherstburg council, 8 June 1805, *MPHC* 23: 39. References to the western confederacy between 1804 and 1807 include M. Wherry to Amos Stoddard, 12 September 1804, U.S. SoW/LR/R 2: 0466; James Bruff to James Wilkinson, 29 September 1804, 19 March 1805, ibid., 2: 0461, 0506; Charles Reaume to Josiah Dunham, 4 June 1807, ibid., 6: 1805; Pierre Chouteau, 1 September and 20 November, 1807, ibid., 5: 1419, 1550; Nicholas Boilvin to Dearborn, 14 September 1807, ibid., 4: 1121; Charles Jouett to Eustis, 30 June 1810, ibid., 38: 4616; Robert Forsyth to Thomas McKee, 19 May 1805, Canada/IA 10: 9598; William Claus to J. Green, 24 July 1805, ibid., 10: 9615; Jacques Lasselle to Thomas Jefferson, 12 June 1806, *TPUS* 10: 57; Harrison to Jefferson, 5 July 1806, L. Esarey, *Harrison*, 1: 194; William Wells to Harrison, 20 August 1807, ibid., 1: 239; Harrison to Dearborn, 11 July 1807, ibid., 1: 222; *The Western Spy*, 22 July 1806; Indian speech, 28 June 1806, William Claus papers, 9: 139; Hull to Dearborn, 28 October 1805, 9 September 1807, *MPHC* 40: 77, 197; Frederick Bates to Thomas Hunt, 22 July 1807, Indians collection; and *The Western Sun*, 14 July 1810. The only historian to appreciate this significant movement is R. White, *Middle Ground*, 511–13.

12. Moore to Edward Tiffin, 18 February 1806, Simon Kenton papers, 7BB26. The documents for this incident are filed in volume 7 of the Kenton papers, except for Tiffin to Thomas Worthington, 20 February and 1 March, 1806, Thomas Worthington papers, and the statement of Big Snake, Captain Snake, and Lewis, 19 February 1806, *The Scioto Gazette*, 10 March 1806.

13. Shawnee speech, 20 March 1806, Simon Kenton papers, 7BB31. According to Joseph Vance to Benjamin Drake, Tecumseh papers, 2YY108, he was one of a party of whites who visited Stony Creek at this time. Tecumseh spoke of the Indians' goodwill. Mayor Joseph Vance, the informant's father, believed him, but William Ward and Simon Kenton remained doubtful. I have no contemporary references to this visit.

14. M. Dawson, *Historical Narrative*, 85.

15. Hull to Dearborn, 28 July 1806, *TPUS* 10: 65; *The Western Spy*, 1, 22 July 1806.

16. *The Virginia Argus* (Richmond), 6 September 1806.

17. Jefferson to Shawnees, 19 February 1807, Shawnee File.

18. Wells to Dearborn, 20–23 April, 1808, U.S. SoW/LR/R 33: 0923.

19. Wells to Dearborn, 19 April 1807, U.S. SoW/LR/R 14: 4566; William Kirk to Dearborn, 28 May 1807, ibid., 9: 2854.

20. Wells to Hull, 5 September 1806, J. F. Clarke, *Campaign of 1812*, 310.

21. The material in this section is drawn from the Shaker journal published by Andrews.

22. R. McNemar, *Kentucky Revival*, 130–32; J. P. MacLean, "Shaker Mission to the Shawnee Indians," 228–29.

11. Prophets and Pilgrims

1. William Wells to Henry Dearborn, 19 and 25 April, 1807, U.S. SoW/LR/R 14: 4566, 4568.

2. Traditional accounts were preserved by Henry R. Schoolcraft (1834) and William W. Warren, but see William Hull to Dearborn, 4 August 1807, and the report of A. B. Woodward, 14 August 1807, *MPHC* 40: 169, 174.

3. Speech of the Trout, 4 May 1807, *MPHC* 40: 127; *The Missouri Gazette*, 19 July 1809; Shawnees to James Hamilton, 8 February 1752, S. Hazard, *Minutes*, 5: 569; Mekoche speech, 1795, William Claus papers, 7: 124; B. Drake, *Life of Tecumseh*, 21.

4. Statement of Letourneau, 21 May 1807, Jasper Grant papers, folder 6.

5. Dunham to Hull, 20 May 1807, *MPHC* 40: 123; Dunham to Ojibwas and Ottawas, 26 May 1807, U.S. SoW/LR/R 6: 1804.

6. John Askin to his father, 1 and 8 September, 1807, M. M. Quaife, *Askin Papers*, 2: 568, 572.

7. Schoolcraft, "Discourse," 103–105.

8. J. Tanner, *Narrative*, 155–58.

9. See ch. 2, n. 10, and M. R. Harrington, ms., "Shawnee Indian Notes," 169–72.

10. Nelson journal, 1807–1808, pp. 61–64, George Nelson papers.

11. Thomas Forsyth to William Clark, 15 January 1827, Thomas Forsyth papers (1), 9T37; G. Catlin, *Letters and Notes*, 2: 115–19. Melburn D. Thurman, "Shawnee Prophet's Movement," argues that Lalawéthika's religion may have passed to the Pacific Northwest and formed the basis of the "prophet" and ghost dance cults of 1870 and 1890. This is entirely plausible, but there is no conclusive evidence that the Prophet's influence extended that far.

12. Harrison to William Eustis, 3 December 1809, L. Esarey, *Harrison*, 1: 393; Dearborn to Harrison, 1808, ibid., 1: 284; Francis Vigo and John Gibson to Harrison, 6 July 1805, ibid., 1: 141; Johnston to Eustis, 1 July 1809, U.S. SoW/LR/R 24: 8062; and works by Paul Woehrmann and Paul A. Hutton.

13. Wells to Dearborn, 31 March 1807, U.S. SoW/LR/R 14: 4516.

14. Compare Shane's account with Wells to Dearborn, 19 April 1807, U.S. SoW/LR/R 14:4566, Wells to Shawnees, 22 April 1807, ibid., 14: 4569; and Dearborn to Wells, 15 May 1807, Shawnee File.

15. *The Scioto Gazette*, 4 June 1807; *The Western Spy*, 8 June 1807; Hull to Dearborn, 15 June 1807, *MPHC* 40: 137.

16. William Kirk to Dearborn, 20 July 1807, U.S. SoW/LR/R 9: 2874; Roundhead to Whiteman and Moore, 6 June 1807, Tecumseh papers, 3YY72; Blacksnake and Black Hoof to James McPherson, 9 June 1807, Frontier Wars papers, 5U181; Black Hoof to Whiteman, 15 June 1807, ibid., 5U182; speech of Sandusky Wyandots, 9 June 1807, Edward Tiffin papers.

17. Whiteman's accounts of 1839 and 1846 treat the episode with a different emphasis: narrative, 18 October 1839, and interview by Lyman Draper, 1846, both in Simon Kenton papers, 9BB7, 9BB1. The council is also mentioned by James Ward, interviewed by Draper, 1845, ibid., 9BB54.

18. The contemporary documents are the council minutes, 24–25 June 1807, from which quotations are taken, Frontier Wars papers, 5U183, and Kirk to Dearborn, 20 July 1807, U.S. SoW/LR/R 9: 2874. Later reminiscences vary enormously in value, but all need careful evaluation and cross-checking. The best are those by Whiteman; Simon Kenton, interviewed by John H. James, 1832, Simon Kenton papers, 5BB106; and J. C. Vance (undated, Tecumseh papers, 2YY108, and in *The Cincinnati Gazette*, 4 November 1841); and the account of Richard Hunt, and others, 24 August 1840, Tecumseh papers, 3YY134. Less reliable are the interviews given by James Ward and Christopher Wood (Wood, interviewed by Draper, 1852, Simon Kenton papers, 8BB52). Ward's is shot through with errors, and contains a ridiculous story of Tecumseh squaring up to Black Hoof. Among slighter references see Henry Brown's testimonial for Kirk, 27 March 1809, U.S. SoW/LR/R 25: 8188; *Sketches of Springfield*, 14; *History of Clark County*, 221; interviews by Draper, 1863, Draper notes, 17S87, 18S83; J. R. McBeth to J. L. A. Ward, 7 February 1866, Simon Kenton papers, 5BB71; and William Renick to Draper, 16 March 1867, ibid., 5BB19.

19. This Captain Johnny was apparently unrelated to the famous Kekewepelethy, who also used that name and who died about 1808, for whom see my article in *ANB*. The younger man is described in Draper's interviews with Whiteman (see n. 17 above), Henry McPherson and Joseph Markle, 1863, Draper notes, 17S272, 19S44, and John H. Renick, 1866, ibid., 21S95; and in J. B. Finley, *Life Among the Indians*, 508–12.

20. Black Hoof and Blacksnake to Tiffin, 28 June 1807, Edward Tiffin papers; Black Hoof, Blacksnake, Big Snake, and Butler to Whiteman, 29 June 1807, Frontier Wars papers, 5U184.

12. An Engine Set to Work by the British

1. Staunton petition, 8 July 1807, U.S. SoW/LR/R 15: 4729.

2. Wells to Henry Dearborn, 14 July, 4, 14, and 30 August, and 30 September 1807, U.S. SoW/LR/R 15: 4710, 4732, 4727, 4746, 4791; Wells to William Henry Harrison, 20 August 1807, L. Esarey, *Harrison*, 1: 239; Wells to John Gerard, 22 August 1807, Simon Kenton papers, 7BB44; James McPherson to William Ward, 16 August 1807, ibid., 7BB40; report of Simon Kenton and others, September 1807, ibid., 7BB46.

3. Kirk to Daniel Drake, 16 September 1807, Tecumseh papers, 3YY74; Wells to Dearborn 30 August 1807, U.S. SoW/LR/R 15:4746.

4. Joseph Browne to Dearborn, 23 March 1807, *TPUS* 14: 110; Harrison to Dearborn, 13 August 1807, Esarey 1: 229; Wells to Harrison, 20 August 1807, ibid., 1: 239; Charles Reaume to Josiah Dunham, 4 June 1807, U.S. SoW/LR/R 6: 1805; statements of Francis Ducharme, 6 July 1807, and Joseph Watson, 8 July 1807, ibid., 9: 2806.

5. William Claus to Prideaux Selby, 16 February 1808, William Claus papers, 9: 175. Well-considered accounts of the crisis are given by Ernest A. Cruikshank (1927) and J. C. A. Stagg.

6. McKee to William Halton, 11 June 1807, Canada/IA 2: 627.

7. Wells to Harrison, 20 August 1807, Esarey 1: 239.

8. Wells to Dearborn, 14 August 1807, U.S. SoW/LR/R 15: 4727.

9. Harrison to Dearborn, 11 July and 29 August 1807, Esarey 1: 222, 243.

10. Relevant papers of Hull were published as "Documents Relating to Detroit and Vicinity," 112–240. See also *TPUS* 10: 63, 130, 131; Dunham to Dearborn, 12 June 1807, U.S. SoW/LR/R 6: 1808; and Indian petition, 26 July 1807, Daniel Parker papers.

11. Jefferson to Dearborn, 12 and 28 August, 1807, Daniel Parker papers.

12. Erastus Granger to Dearborn, 18 and 25 August and 25 December 1807, U.S. SoW/LR/R 7: 2277, 2279, 2328; Jasper Parrish to Dearborn, 3 September 1807, ibid., 11: 3479.

13. Dearborn to Hull, 24 March 1807, *TPUS* 10: 93; Black Hoof, Chaukalowaik (Tail's End), Dameenaytha (Butler), and Big Snake to Dearborn, 12 December 1807, U.S. SoW/LR/R 4: 1189; report of Kenton and others, September 1807, Simon Kenton papers, 7BB46.

14. Hull to Dearborn, 9 September 1807, *MPHC* 40: 197.

15. Hull to Dearborn, 9 September 1807, *MPHC* 40: 197; Thomas Worthington and Duncan McArthur to Thomas Kirker, 22 September 1807, Simon Kenton papers, 7BB49.

16. Harrison to Shawnees, August 1807, Esarey 1: 249; Harrison to Dearborn, 5 September 1807, ibid., 1: 247; the Prophet to Harrison, August 1807, ibid., 1: 251.

17. Worthington and McArthur to Kirker, 22 September 1807, Simon Kenton papers, 7BB49.

18. Kirker's papers relating to this affair are filed in volume 7 of the Simon Kenton papers. See Kirker to Shawnees, 19 August 1807, ibid., 7BB43; Worthington and McArthur to

Kirker, 22 September 1807, ibid., 7BB49; McArthur to Robert Means, 24 October 1807, Duncan McArthur papers (1).

19. Jefferson to Adams, B. Drake, *Life of Tecumseh*, 219. See also Wells to Dearborn, 20 October, 5 and 21 December 1807, U.S. SoW/LR/R 15: 4816, 4856, 4858; Johnston to Dearborn, 31 December 1807, ibid., 9: 2833; Jefferson to Dearborn, 2 August 1808, Daniel Parker papers.

20. Jouett to Dearborn, 1 December 1807, *TPUS* 7: 496; Hendrick Aupaumut to Wells, 26 February 1808, U.S. SoW/LR/R 3: 0950.

21. Wells to Dearborn, 7 January 1808, U.S. SoW/LR/R 15: 4881.

22. Wells to Dearborn, 16 January 1809, U.S. SoW/LR/R 33: 1317; Thomas Forsyth, "The Main Poque," Tecumseh papers, 8YY57; Forsyth to William Clark, 15 January 1827, Thomas Forsyth papers (1), 9T37; and article by R. D. Edmunds (1985).

23. Selby to McKee, 15 November 1807, Ironside letterbook, George Ironside papers; Francis Gore to James Craig, 5 January 1808, Britain/CO 42/136: 167.

24. Claus to McKee, 7 October 1807, Canada/IA 11: 9740; Claus to Johnson, 2 November 1807, William Claus papers, 9: 161.

25. Craig to Gore, 6 and 28 December 1807, Britain/CO 42/136: 153, 158.

26. Claus to McKee, 20 December 1807, Ironside letterbook, George Ironside papers; Gore to Claus, with instructions, 29 January 1808, Canada/IA 11: 9770.

13. The Open Door

1. William Wells to Henry Dearborn, 20–23 April 1808, U.S. SoW/LR/R 33: 0923.

2. William Henry Harrison to Dearborn, 19 May 1808, L. Esarey, *Harrison*, 1: 290.

3. James to Ruth Miller, 10 November 1811, James Miller papers; Harrison to William Eustis, 18 November 1811, Esarey, 1: 618; G. Thornbrough, *John Badollet*, 159, 167, 182; A. Walker, *Journal of Two Campaigns*, 33–34; George Winter ms. "On The Prophet"; A. McCollough, *Battle of Tippecanoe*, 24–25, 27.

4. The first reference to Lalawéthika's new name is William Claus to Francis Gore, 27 February 1808, Esarey, 1: 285; Wells to Dearborn, 6 March 1808, U.S. SoW/LR/R 15: 4934.

5. Wells to Dearborn, 20–23 April, 1808, U.S. SoW/LR/R 33: 0923.

6. Diary of Abraham Luckenbach, 1808, Shawnee File; Kirk to Dearborn, 12 April and 10 December 1808, and 12 February 1809, U.S. SoW/LR/R 25: 8114, 8143, 8157; Wells to Dearborn, 20–23 April 1808 ibid., 33: 0923; G. Thornbrough, *Letter Book*, 33, 37, 46; C. F. Klinck and J. T. Talman, *John Norton*, 173–75; J. A. Green, "Schillinger," 82.

7. Quotation from Hull to Dearborn, 9 September 1807, *MPHC* 40: 197.

8. Black Hawk, *Life*, 10: Wells to Dearborn, 20–23 April, 1808, U.S. SoW/LR/R 33: 0923.

9. Statement of John Conner, 18 June 1808, U.S. SoW/LR/R 33: 1016; Wells to Dearborn, 5 and 30 June 1808, ibid., 33: 0988, 1014.

10. *The Western Sun*, 2 July 1808; Harrison to Dearborn, 12 July 1808, Esarey, 1: 295.

11. Speech of Tenskwatawa, Esarey 1: 299; Harrison to Dearborn, 1 September and 9 November 1808, and 14 February 1809, Esarey, 1: 302, 321, and U.S. SoW/LR/R 23: 7538.

12. Wells to Dearborn, 5 June 1808, U.S. SoW/LR/R 33: 0988; Claus to Prideaux Selby, 3 May 1808, William Claus papers, 16: 196; Claus to Gore, 16 May 1808, ibid., 16: 208; diary of Claus, 16 May 1808, ibid., 9: 194.

13. Claus to Shawnees, 25 March 1808, Britain/CO 42/136: 180; Gore to Claus, 29 January 1808, Canada/IA 11: 9770. Reginald Horsman's *Matthew Elliott* is a consistently sound account of the British Indian Department.

14. Gore to Sir James Craig, 8 April 1808, Canada/IA 2: 843; Canada/IA 27: 15761, 15786, 15801.

15. Claus to Selby, 25 March 1808, Esarey, 1: 287; Claus to Sir John Johnson, 5 May 1808, William Claus papers, 16: 207.

16. The account of Tecumseh's visit depends upon Gore to Craig, 27 July 1808, Canada/IA 11: 9901; Speech of Gore, 11 July 1808 and Indian reply, 13 July 1808, ibid; 11: 9884, 9891; Claus diary, William Claus papers, 9: 194.

17 Elliott to William Halton, 19 May 1809, Canada/IA 3: 990, for the return of the belt to Brownstown.

18. Harrison to Eustis, 18 and 26 April and 3 May, 1809, Esarey, 1: 340, 342, 344; Wells to Harrison, 8 April 1809, ibid., 1: 337; Wells to Dearborn, 31 December 1807, 23 January 1808, 5 and 30 June, 1808 U.S. SoW/LR/R 15: 4863, 4885, and 33: 0988, 1014; Hull to Eustis, 16 June and 2 August 1809, Shawnee File; Elliott to Halton, 19 May 1809, Canada/IA 3: 990; and Thornbrough, *Letter Book*, 49, 51.

19. Wells to Dearborn, 7 and 23 January, 2 April and 20–23 April 1808, U.S. SoW/LR/R 15: 4881, 4885, and 33: 0927, 0923.

20. Certificate by Billy Caldwell, 1 August 1816, Billy Caldwell papers; N. Matson, *Memories of Shaubena*, 19; and biography by James Dowd.

21. Boilvin to William Clark, 21 April 1808, U.S. SoW/LR/R 20: 6205; John Johnson to John Mason, 19 September 1808, U.S. SoW/LR/U 3: 1242. American difficulties with these Indians figure in the letters of Lewis, Clark, and the commanders of Fort Madison, Alpha Kingsley and Horatio Stark, filed in the U.S. SoW/LR/R for 1808 and 1809.

22. Thornbrough, *Letter Book*, 18 May 1809, p. 51; Harrison to Eustis, 5 July 1809, Esarey, 1: 349.

23. Attempts to put the Prophet behind the disaffection were made in Lewis to the Sacs and Foxes, May 1808, U.S. SoW/LR/R 25: 8312; Clark to Dearborn, 5 and 29 April 1809, ibid., 20: 6175, 6209; and *The Missouri Gazette*, 5 April 1809. A comparison should be made with Boilvin's reports of 21 April, 28 May, 2 August, and 17 October, 1809 (U.S. SoW/LR/R 20: 6205, and 18: 5616, 5598, 5651), and the enclosures in Stark to Eustis, 10 November 1809, ibid., 31: 0481.

24. Harrison to Eustis, 18 and 26 April, 3 and 16 May 1809, Esarey, 1: 340, 342, 344, 346; Wells to Harrison, 8 April 1809, ibid., 1: 337; Wells to Dearborn, 31 March 1809, U.S. SoW/LR/R 33: 1405; Harrison to Johnston, 4–12 May, 1809, John Johnston papers (1).

25. Thornbrough, *Letter Book*, 49, 52; Johnston to Eustis, 1 July 1809, U.S. SoW/LR/R 24: 8062.

26. Kingsley to Dearborn, 19 April 1809, U.S. SoW/LR/R 25: 8177; James House to Eustis, 9 May 1809, ibid., 23: 7602; Jouett to Eustis, 1 September 1809, ibid., 24: 8067; Clark to Eustis, 25 June 1809, ibid., 20: 6275.

27. I take Harrison's reference to a Sac mission to the Prophet (Harrison to Dearborn, 18 February 1808, Esarey, 1: 283) to be a garbled reference to the 1807 delegation reported in Hendrick Aupaumut to Wells, 26 February 1808, SoW/LR/R3:0950. See also Claus diary, 16 July 1808, William Claus papers, 9: 194; *The Missouri Gazette*, 4 October 1809; and Black Hawk, 11.

14. A Treaty Too Far

1. Speech of Shawnees, 14 April 1809, U.S. SoW/LR/R 25: 8189; William Eustis to John Johnston, 23 May 1809, 16 January 1810, John Johnston papers (1); minutes of meetings, 10 February 1810, 17 October 1811, Society of Friends minutes; G. Thornbrough, *Letter Book*, 46, 61.

2. Johnston to Harrison, 24 June 1810, L. Esarey, *Harrison*, 1: 430; Johnston to Eustis, 3 July 1810, U.S. SoW/LR/R 38: 4614; C. F. Klinck and J. T. Talman, *John Norton*, 174–75.

3. Wyandots to Samuel Huntington, 8 May 1810, John Johnston papers (1); Johnston to Eustis, 6 November 1810, U.S. SoW/LR/R 38: 4649.

4. Shane interview; Harrison to Eustis, 14 June, 18 July, and 24 December 1810, Esarey 1:422, 446, 496; and Wyandots to Hull 27 June 1810, U.S. SoW/LR/R 37: 3872. The chronology of Tecumseh's 1809 tour is uncertain. Shane has him visiting the Sandusky in the summer, but the presence of Lewis in his party suggests that Tecumseh had already come through the Shawnee communities in Ohio. Johnston's account of Tecumseh at Wapakoneta implies that that event occurred in the fall. I have assumed, therefore, that Shane's dating was slightly in error.

5. Hull to Eustis, 6 July 1810, U.S. SoW/LR/R 37: 3867.

6. C. Atwater, *History*, 140, 236–37; Atwater, *Remarks Made on a Tour*, 119.

7. Eustis to Harrison, 5 and 15 July 1809, Esarey 1: 347, 356. Primary sources for the treaties of 1809 are in Esarey; Thornbrough, *Letter Book*; and C. J. Kappler, *Indian Affairs*, vol. 2. Among other sources I have drawn upon are the statement of William Wells, U.S. SoW/LR/R 33: 1579; Johnston's notes, 26 May 1808, U.S. SoW/LR/U 3: 1199 (for Winamek); Indian Claims Commission, *Indians of Ohio, Indiana*, 1: 79, 132–34; E. W. Voegelin, E. J. Blasingham, and D. R. Libby, *Miami, Wea, and Eel River Indians*, 387–413; and accounts by Dwight L. Smith (1949) and James A. Clifton (1977).

8. Quotations from treaty proceedings may be found in the "Journal," Esarey, 1: 362.

9. After the treaty of Fort Wayne the Potawatomi annuities stood at $2,400. At Greenville (1795) the United States awarded annuities to a large number of tribes, partly in response to the Indian argument that the land was held in common and distinctions were inappropriate. The Potawatomis thus received as much as the Shawnees in that treaty, although they had no villages within the ceded area and the Shawnees had lost their homelands, as well as hunting grounds south of the Ohio, for which they received no compensation. Thereafter, the Americans identified individual tribes as the owners of territories being purchased, and the Shawnees were accordingly shut out of the 1809 treaty. So, too, should have been the Potawatomis, but Harrison admitted them, presumably to facilitate the treaty. While the Potawatomis had done well from treaty annuities, the Shawnees fared badly. Apart from the $1,000 awarded at Greenville, they had a salt annuity (1803), and the Michigan band was supposed to have a one-fifth share in $1,000 under the Swan Creek treaty of 1805. Shawnee annuities were regularly delivered short, to pay for alleged horse thefts. In 1807–1810 a total of $985 was deducted. After 1809 the Miamis, Delawares, Ojibwas, Ottawas, Potawatomis, Wyandots, Weas, Eel Rivers, and Kaskaskias all received more annuities than the Shawnees.

10. Johnston to Eustis, 25 July 1810, U.S. SoW/LR/R 38: 4620.

11. McIntosh to Madison, 3 September 1810, U.S. SoW/LR/R 38: 5285; Badollet to Gallatin, 24 June and 25 September 1810, G. Thornbrough, *John Badollet*, 151, 167; and correspondence in *TPUS* 8: 25, 29.

12. Wyandots to Hull, 30 September 1809, *MPHC* 40: 304.

13. Speech of Tecumseh, 21 August 1810, Esarey, 1: 468.

14. Harrison to Eustis, 28 August 1810, Esarey, 1: 470.

15. Harrison to Eustis, 14–19 June and 6 August 1810, Esarey, 1: 422, 456. The quotation is from the latter document.

16. Speech of Tecumseh, 20 August 1810, Esarey, 1: 463; Harrison to Eustis, 6 June and 28 August 1810, ibid., 1: 433, 470.

17. Speech of Tecumseh, 15 November 1810, enclosed in Matthew Elliott to William Claus, 16–18 November 1810, Britain/CO 42/351: 40, 42; Harrison to Eustis, 28 August 1810, Esarey, 1: 470.

18. Harrison to Eustis, 14–19 and 26 June and 28 August 1810, Esarey, 1: 422, 433 470;

Harrison to Johnston, 16 June 1810, U.S. SoW/LR/R 37: 3868; Thomas Forsyth to John Gibson, 26 July 1812, Thomas Forsyth letter.

19. Harrison to Eustis, 25 April, 2 and 15 May, 14–19 and 26 June 1810, 6 June 1811 (quotation), Esarey, 1: 417, 419, 420, 422, 433, 512; report of Michel Brouillet, 30 June 1810, Albert Gallatin Porter papers; statement of John Shaw, 24 June 1810, *The Western Sun*, 14 July 1810.

15. The Moses of the Family

1. Matthew Elliott to William Claus, 10 June 1810, Canada/IA 27: 16099; William Henry Harrison to William Eustis, 26 June 1810, L. Esarey, *Harrison*, 1: 433.
2. Harrison to Eustis, 25 April, 2 and 15 May, 14–19 June, and 4 and 18 July 1810, Esarey, 1: 417, 419, 420, 422, 438, 446; William Clark to Eustis, 20 July 1810, U.S. SoW/LR/R 35: 2577; John Badollet to Albert Gallatin, 24 June 1810, G. Thornbrough, *John Badollet*, 151.
3. The Prophet said that Tecumseh was "daily" expected to return to Prophetstown from the Detroit early in June (Harrison to Eustis, 15 June 1810, Esarey, 1: 426), which indicates that he had then been absent some time. Tecumseh made no visit to the British, across the Detroit River, on this trip, or to the Americans in Detroit itself, and I think it safe to presume that he was visiting the Wyandots, Shawnees and Three Fires of that region, probably in connection with an intertribal meeting he and his brother were then organizing. See Harrison to Eustis, 15 May, 14–19 June, 18 July, and 24 December 1810, ibid., 1: 420, 422, 446, 496; William Hull to Eustis, 12 July 1810, U.S. SoW/LR/R 37: 3877.
4. Harrison to Eustis, 14–19 June 1810, Esarey, 1: 422; Badollet to Gallatin, 25 September 1810, Thornbrough, *John Badollet*, 167.
5. Harrison to Eustis, 26 June, 4 July, and 28 August 1810, Esarey, 1: 433, 438, 470; *The Western Sun*, 23 and 30 June, 1810; Harrison to John Johnston, 16 June 1810, U.S. SoW/LR/R 37: 3868; deposition of Michel Brouillet, 30 June 1810, Albert Gallatin Porter papers.
6. In addition to materials in Esarey see Benjamin Parke and others to Eustis, 25 April 1810, U.S. SoW/LR/R 39: 5790, and Randolph petition, 6 August 1810, William Henry Harrison papers (1).
7. Johnston to Eustis, 3 and 25 July and 7 August 1810, U.S. SoW/LR/R 38: 4614, 4620, 4623; Harrison to Eustis, 4 July 1810, Esarey, 1: 438; Brouillet, deposition, 30 June 1810, Albert Gallatin Porter papers.
8. Harrison to Eustis, 22 and 28 August, 1810, Esarey, 1: 459, 470; speech of Tecumseh, 21 August 1810, ibid., 1: 468.
9. Harrison to Eustis, 11 and 18 July, and 1 and 6 August, 1810, Esarey, 1: 444, 446, 453, 456.
10. Harrison to Eustis, 25 July 1810, Esarey, 1: 449; J. B. Dillon, *Indiana*, vi, 441–42 (quotation).
11. Harrison to the Prophet, 19 July 1810, Esarey, 1: 447; Harrison to Eustis, 6 August 1810, ibid., 1: 456.
12. Floyd to his wife, 14 August 1810, Tecumseh papers, 2YY118.
13. J. Law, *Vincennes*, 82–92. The first publication of the story I know is in *The National Recorder*, 12 May 1821, but Tecumseh's words are here quoted from the more authoritative M. Dawson, *Historical Narrative*, 155–59. Other versions were published in 1825, 1834, and 1844. For late eyewitness testimony recalling the incident see James S. Whitaker interviewed by Lyman Draper, 1863, Draper notes, 18S128; Joseph Mc-

Cormick interviewed by Draper, Tecumseh papers, 3YY109; and Augustus Jones to Draper, 4 February 1885, ibid., 3YY106.

　　With the exception of the words of John Gibson (taken from Dawson) other quotations in this section come from Harrison to Eustis, 22 August 1810, enclosing Tecumseh's speeches of 20–21 August, 1810, Esarey, 1: 459. This is the principal authority for the council, but reference has also been made to Harrison to Eustis, 28 August 1810, ibid., 1: 470; *The Western Sun*, 18 and 25 August 1810; Badollet to Gallatin, 25 September 1810, Thornbrough, *John Badollet*, 167; R. B. McAfee, *Late War*, 13–14; and the *Chicago Tribune*, 6 March 1886.

14. Dawson, 158–59. According to a resident of Vincennes and critic of Harrison, William McIntosh, Tecumseh did not rule out visiting the President himself: McIntosh to James Madison, 3 September 1810, U.S. SoW/LR/R 38: 5285.

16. Tecumseh's Diplomacy

1. William Clark to William Eustis, 20 July and 28 September 1810, U.S. SoW/LR/R 35: 2577, 2633; journal of Edward Hebert, August 1811, ibid., 36: 3304; L. Esarey, *Harrison*, 1: 474.

2. James Witherell to Theophilus Harrington, 19 November 1810, Tecumseh File; William Henry Harrison to Eustis, 6 June 1811, Esarey, 1: 512.

3. Speech of Tecumseh, 15 November 1810, enclosed in Matthew Elliott to William Claus, 16–18 November, 1810, Britain/CO 42/351: 40, 42.

4. Harrison to Eustis, 26 June 1810, 7 August 1811, Esarey, 1: 433, 548.

5. Clark to Eustis, 20 July 1810, U.S. SoW/LR/R 35: 2577. Among the papers relating to the Cole affair in the Ninian Edwards papers the statements of Stephen Cole, James Murdough, Maurice Blondeau, Gomo, Wanatee, and William Clark are most useful. In addition, consult Benjamin Howard to Ninian Edwards, 15 November 1810, E. B. Washburne, *Edwards Papers*, 56.

6. Matson's "Sketch of Shaubena," 415–16, *Memories of Shaubena*, 11, 19–20, and *Pioneers of Illinois*, 231–32, contain the traditions. The latter added the Racine snippet, and said that Tecumseh and his party wore eagle feathers in their hair, and clothes of white buckskin. Indian villages of 1810 are mapped in H. H. Tanner, *Atlas*, map 20.

7. J. W. Biddle, "Recollections," 53–54; A. Grignon, "Seventy-two Years' Recollections," 267–68.

8. Howard to Edwards, 29 July 1811, Washburne, 66; Clark to Eustis, 23 November 1811, U.S. SoW/LR/R 43: 8364.

9. Black Hawk, *Life*, 11; *The Missouri Gazette*, 4 October 1809.

10. W. H. Keating, *Narrative*, 1: 236.

11. A. Stoddard, *Sketches*, 214–15. Sources for the Missouri Shawnees are Shawnees to James Madison, 29 March 1811, U.S. SoW/LR/IA: 0550; Clark to Madison, 10 April 1811, ibid., 0548; *The Missouri Gazette*, 14 March 1811; and U.S. SoW/LR/R 18: 5622, 19: 5940.

12. Thomas Forsyth to Clark, 25 December 1812, E. H. Blair, *Indian Tribes*, 2: 278; Harrison to Eustis, 6 August 1810, Esarey, 1: 456; speech of Tecumseh, 20 August 1810, ibid., 1: 463.

13. Wyandots to Madison, 24 October 1811, U.S. SoW/LR/R 49: 3663. Other source materials are Wyandots to Hull, 27 June 1810, ibid., 37: 3872; Hull to Eustis, 6 July 1810, ibid., 37: 3867; E. P. Olmstead, *Blackcoats*, 158; G. Thornbrough, *Letter Book*, 83; J. Badger, *Memoir*, 125; J. Heckewelder, *History*, 295–99, and the article by Otway Curry.

　　The prevalent view that the witch-hunts of 1809 and 1810 were prompted by the Prophet to destroy political enemies is contradicted by the evidence. It arose from the eagerness of some officials to see the Prophet behind any untoward event. Thus, Harrison blamed the execution of Leatherlips upon the Prophet, and asserted the assassination squad was led by Roundhead (B. Drake, *Life of Tecumseh*, 118), but the reverse was true. Leatherlips was the victim of Tarhe's party, the opponents of Roundhead and the Prophet, and the executioners were from the Sandusky. The witch-hunts of 1809–1810 should rather be set within the context of the widespread sickness. They occurred principally among groups hostile to the Prophet, such as the Delawares, the Missouri Shawnees, and the pro-American faction of the Sandusky Wyandots.

14. *The Missouri Gazette*, 16 August 1809; Benjamin Mortimer diary, 4 June 1810, Olmstead, 158; account of Nicholas Biddle, 1810, N. W. Schutz, *Shawnee Myth*, 207; account of Godfrey Lesieur, March 1872, Tecumseh papers, 8YY48. Lesieur was under twelve at the time of Tecumseh's visit, and probably got his information from his father. He erroneously dated the chief's arrival in 1809, but his statement that it occurred a year after the Missouri witch-hunt began clearly puts it in 1810.

15. Harrison to Eustis, 6 August 1811, Esarey, 1: 542. The dispute can be followed in Clark to Eustis, 20 July and 12 September, 1810, 22 January 1811, U.S. SoW/LR/R 35: 2577, 2623, 2868; Pierre Chouteau to Eustis, 19 July and 13 October 1810, ibid., 35: 2574, 2656; *The Missouri Gazette*, 21 June and 31 October 1810; Eustis to John Johnston, 18 February 1811, Shawnee File.

16. L. Houck, *Spanish Regime in Missouri*, 2: 393–97. By the account of Edward Meatt, 24 March 1886 (Tecumseh papers, 1YY126), who married Mrs. Maisonville's granddaughter, François Maisonville died in New Madrid County, aged about fifty. The couple's children were all dead in 1886, but a grandson, Joseph, survived. Meatt remembered seeing Mrs. Maisonville when he was seven or eight years old. See also Robert Wilson to Lyman Draper, 28 June 1887, Tecumseh papers, 1YY129.

17. Brownstown council to Tecumseh and the Prophet, 26 September 1810, Thornbrough, *Letter Book*, 86; ibid., 83, 87; Esarey, 1: 480, 496; U.S. SoW/LR/R 37: 3927, 3958, 3964, 3966; Canada/IA 27: 16156, 16159, 16163; C. F. Klinck and J. T. Talman, *John Norton*, 285–86.

18. Johnston to Harrison, 14 October 1810, Esarey, 1: 476 (quotation); Johnston to Eustis, 20 October 1810, U.S. SoW/LR/R 38: 4646; Thornbrough, *Letter Book*, 76, 78, 90–91.

19. Speech of Tecumseh, enclosed in Elliott to Claus, 16–18 November, 1810, Britain/CO 42/351: 40, 42; Harrison to Eustis, 7 November 1810, Esarey, 1: 483.

17. An Uncommon Genius

1. William Henry Harrison to William Eustis, 7 August 1811, L. Esarey, *Harrison*, 1: 548.
2. Harrison's address to the Indiana Territorial Legislature, 12 November 1810, and Harrison to Eustis, 24 December 1810, ibid., 1: 487, 496.
3. Johnston to Eustis, 8 February 1811, U.S. SoW/LR/R 38: 4682; Harrison to Eustis, 24 December 1810, Esarey, 1: 496; James Rhea to Jacob Kingsbury, 21 March 1811, Kingsbury letterbooks; Eustis to Harrison, 7 March 1811, William Henry Harrison papers (2).
4. Benjamin Hawkins to Eustis, 8 April and 21 July 1810, 22 May 1811, U.S. SoW/LR/R 37: 3782, 3886, 4165; report, 11 June 1810, ibid., 37: 3854; Christian Limbaugh to Eustis, 27 May 1811, ibid., 37: 4167; Lower Creeks to Hawkins, 18 July 1810, ibid., 37: 3892; T. S. Woodward, *Reminiscences*, 88.
5. Harrison to Eustis, 6 June 1811, Esarey, 1: 512; William Clark to Eustis, 24 May (enclosing Iowa speeches) and 3 July 1811, U.S. SoW/LR/R 35: 2889, 2923; John Lalime to Clark, 3 June 1811, ibid., 35: 2898; Samuel Levering to Ninian Edwards, 12 August

1811, ibid., 36: 3311; Matthew Elliott to William Claus, 6 July 1811, Canada/IA 27: 16294 (quotation).

6. Harrison to Eustis, 6 June 1811, Esarey, 1: 512; Harrison to Clark, 19 June 1811, ibid., 1: 519.

7. John Shaw to Johnston, 18 August 1811, U.S. SoW/LR/R 38: 4625; Samuel Tupper to Eustis, 16 July 1811, 22 February 1812, ibid., 40: 6929, and U.S. SoW/LR/U 6: 2543.

8. Harrison to Eustis, 6 and 19 June, 1811, Esarey, 1: 512, 518; Harrison to Clark, 19 June 1811, ibid., 1: 519.

9. Harrison to Eustis, 2 July 1811, Esarey, 1: 526; Erastus Granger to Eustis, 11 August 1811, 6 May 1812, U.S. SoW/LR/R 36: 3590, 44: 9690; Robert Forsyth to Rhea, 10 March 1812, ibid., 48: 2771; Clark to Eustis, 22 March 1812 (which incorrectly identifies the Iroquois concerned as Canadian), ibid., 43: 8516; C. F. Klinck and J. T. Talman, *John Norton*, 286; W. L. Stone, *Red Jacket*, 291; and C. M. Snyder, *Red and White*, 43.

10. Iowa speech, May 1811, U.S. SoW/LR/R 35: 2892; affidavit of Rebecca Cox, 13 June 1811, ibid., 36: 3283; Thomas Forsyth to Benjamin Howard, 11 February 1812, ibid., 45: 0101; the letters of Lalime and Levering (n. 5, above); and the reports of Ninian Edwards, 7 June to 11 August 1811, filed in ibid., 36: 3271, 3275, 3278, 3280, 3287, 3301.

11. Indian speeches, 17 August 1811, U.S. SoW/LR/R 36: 3317; Levering to Edwards, 12 August 1811, ibid., 36: 3311; journal of Edward Hebert, August 1811, ibid., 36: 3304; speech of Edwards, July 1811, Ninian Edwards papers.

12. Harrison to Eustis, 25 June 1811, Esarey, 1: 524; Harrison to Tecumseh, 24 June 1811, ibid., 1: 522.

13. Account of Thomas Wilson, Tecumseh papers, 5YY9; J. Law, *Vincennes*, 98–105; Harrison to Eustis, 10 July 1811, Esarey, 1: 532; Tecumseh to Harrison, 4 July 1811, ibid., 1: 529.

14. Eustis to Harrison, 17 and 20 July, 1811, Esarey, 1: 535, 536.

15. The basic account of the Vincennes council, from which quotations other than Badollet's are drawn, is Harrison to Eustis, 6 August 1811, Esarey, 1: 542. Other sources are Harrison to Eustis, 24 July and 13 August, 1811, ibid., 1: 537, 554; John Badollet to Albert Gallatin, 6 August 1811, G. Thornbrough, *John Badollet*, 182; *The Western Sun*, 27 July 1811; and R. B. McAfee, *Late War*, 16.

16. The story of the Deaf Chief comes from M. Dawson, *Historical Narrative*, 184–85, appendix, n. 6. In turn, this depends substantially upon Harrison to Eustis, 7 August 1811, Esarey, 1: 548, and Barron's narrative in *The Western Sun* for 18 and 25 April, 1812. Barron may have expanded his story for Dawson, but his suggestion that the Deaf Chief was assassinated because he was never again seen in Vincennes is disproved by Harrison to Eustis, 25 September 1811, Esarey, 1: 589.

17. Quotations from Harrison to Eustis, 6, 7 August 1811, Esarey, 1: 542, 548.

18. Storm on the Wabash

1. Harrison to Miamis, Weas, and Eel Rivers, September 1811, L. Esarey, *Harrison*, 1: 576.

2. Speeches at Fort Wayne, 4 September 1811, Esarey, 1: 577. For other Indian responses, H. W. Beckwith, "Fort Wayne Manuscript," 73, 76.

3. Harrison to William Eustis, 25 September 1811, Esarey, 1: 589. The old headman may have been Joe Renard.

The following December a Kickapoo named Little Deer, who often acted for Pamawatam, announced that "the chief of . . . the Kickapoos which had joined the

Prophet" intended visiting Vincennes (Harrison to Eustis, 4 December 1811, Esarey, 1: 656). Shortly afterward a party of Indians en route to Vincennes arrived at Fort Harrison, where their Kickapoo spokesman admitted he had attended the September council, that he had supported the Prophet, and that his brother had been killed in the battle of Tippecanoe (*The Western Sun*, 28 December 1811). This may have been Pamawatam, who subsequently also reported losing a brother in the battle (Pamawatam to Ninian Edwards, 8 June 1812, U.S. SoW/LR/R 45: 0322).

It was reported that early in September the British furnished guns, ammunition and presents to the Prophet's party (Reuben Atwater to Eustis, 21 January 1812, ibid., 42: 7436), but the remark may have been prompted by the visit some Weas made to Fort Malden about that time. The Weas were not in the battle of Tippecanoe.

4. John Badollet told Albert Gallatin (G. Thornbrough, *John Badollet*, 199) that the atrocities were committed by Winamek's band. He accused Winamek, who was "frequently in town, genteely dressed," of bad faith. However, this assumes that Winamek had control of his men, who seem to have been turning to Tecumseh and the Prophet.

5. Quotation from Adam Walker's account (Esarey, 1: 697). Harrison's force, initially over 1,000 men, was reduced by sickness, and the need to leave garrisons at Vincennes and Forts Harrison and Boyd. His field return of 12 October 1811 (ibid., 1: 597) lists just under 1,000, including 350 regulars. Harrison said that he quit Fort Harrison for the last leg of his march with about 880 men (Harrison to Charles Scott, 13 December 1811, ibid., 1: 666), but reinforcements brought his final battle force to around 950 soldiers. See also A. Pirtle, *Battle of Tippecanoe*, 71, 111–14.

Primary sources for the campaign are collected in Esarey; *The Western Sun*, 28 December 1811, and 8 February, 18 April, and 23 June, 1812; and A. McCollough, *Battle of Tippecanoe*. However, readers are warned that the account attributed to Shabeni in the last is a pure invention. Additional details can be gleaned from John Parker Boyd to Richard Cutts, 16 December 1811, Arthur Mitten Collection; Boyd to James Taylor, 27 December 1811, William Henry Harrison papers (1); the John Parker Boyd papers; John to Catherine McCoy, 26 October 1811, McCoy letter; U.S. Infantry, 4th Regiment, orderly and letterbook; C. to Adam Larrabee, 5 February 1812, Frontier Wars papers, 9U1; R. G. Carlson, "George P. Peters"; battlefield plan, 1840, William Henry Harrison papers (4); Thomas Brown, "Meanderings on the Field of Battle," 1828–1829, Tippecanoe County Folder; William Bruce, reminiscences, 1851; John Tipton to William Polke, 12 September to 1833, William Polke papers; and L. Cass, "Policy and Practise," 434.

6. H. R. Schoolcraft, *Travels*, 129.

7. For the numbers of Indians present see Esarey, 1: 599, 616, 2: 12; Thomas Forsyth to Benjamin Howard, 11 February 1812, U.S. SoW/LR/R 45: 0101; John Johnston to Eustis, 28 November 1811, ibid., 46: 0989; G. Thornbrough, *Letter Book*, 110; *The Western Sun*, 4 January 1812.

8. Early statements about the role of the Prophet were made by Harrison to Eustis, 29 October 1811, Esarey, 1: 604; Josiah Snelling to Harrison, 20 November 1811, ibid., 1: 643; James to Ruth Miller, 10 November 1811, James Miller papers; William Clark to Eustis, 23 November 1811, U.S. SoW/LR/R 43: 8364; and Johnston to *Liberty Hall*, 30 November 1811, *The Western Sun*, 11 January 1812.

9. For Indian leaders see Esarey, 1: 705; R. B. McAfee, *Late War*, 35; M. Dawson, *Historical Narrative*, 232; and L. Cass, "Indians of North America," 97.

10. Indian casualties are discussed in Elliott to Isaac Brock, 12 January 1812, Esarey, 1: 616; Johnston to Eustis, 28 November 1811, U.S. SoW/LR/R 46: 0989; John Lalime to Howard, 4 February 1812, ibid., 45: 0099; Forsyth to Howard, 11 February 1812, ibid., 45: 0101; and Cass, "Indians of North America," 97.

19. Red Sticks and Earthquakes

1. A detailed recital of the sources for Tecumseh's southern journey is given in my paper "Early Pan-Indianism," which the present chapter revises but does not replace. Jim Blue-Jacket junior belonged to the Ohio Shawnees. After emigrating to Kansas, he served the United States against the Seminoles in 1837 and 1838, and died in Kansas in 1848.

2. Enclosures in Willie Blount to William Eustis, 16 September 1811, SoW/LR/R 34: 2232; *The Missouri Gazette,* 12 October 1811; Henry S. Halbert to Lyman Draper, 14 February 1884, Tecumseh papers, 4YY59. In "Early Pan-Indianism" (p. 279) I incorrectly identified Tecumseh as the sender of a message to the Chickasaws in July 1811, but in fact this was an invitation from the Missouri Indians to join a campaign against the Osages: Alexander Smyth to Eustis, 19 March 1811, SoW/LR/R 40: 6629.

3. Halbert's material may be found in Tecumseh papers, vols. 4YY and 10YY, and is summarized in Halbert and T. H. Ball, *Creek War,* and in my article.

4. Pushmataha's opposition to Tecumseh is mentioned in his obituary in *The National Journal* (Washington, D.C.), 28 December 1824.

5. *The Missouri Gazette,* 12 October 1811, contains the report of Tecumseh "finally" recruiting three hundred Choctaws.

6. This paragraph depends upon A. J. Pickett, *History,* 511–15, who names several eyewitnesses as his informants. Contemporary sources for Tecumseh's visit to the Creeks are Hawkins to Wade Hampton, 21 September 1811, SoW/LR/R 37: 4252; Hawkins to Eustis, 30 September and 3 October 1811, and 13 January 1812, ibid., 37: 4256, 4260, and 44: 0015; Return Jonathan Meigs to Eustis, 4 December 1811, ibid., 47: 1650; letter of 8 December 1811 in Blount to Eustis, 12 December 1811, ibid., 42: 7716; Hawkins to Creeks, 16 June 1814, *ASPIA* 1: 845; deposition of Samuel Manac, 2 August 1813, Halbert and Ball, 91; *The Republican and Savannah Ledger,* 17 October and 5 November 1811; and Eustis to Hawkins, 5 October 1811, U.S. SoW/LS/IA, vol. C: 101.

   The most important of the subsequent sources are T. L. McKenney, *Memoirs,* 1: 164; the George Stiggins narrative in T. A. Nunez, "Creek Nativism"; T. S. Woodward, *Reminiscences*; and the statement of Tustenuckochee, 22 August 1883, Tecumseh papers, 4YY2. Students are again warned against using the influential but bogus accounts of J. F. H. Claiborne. See my "Early Pan-Indianism," 288, and the paper by Henry S. Halbert (1898).

   A reliable and comprehensive account of the Creek troubles of this period is still needed, but useful insights are given in works by Halbert and Ball, Frank H. Akers, Frank L. Owsley (1981), Douglas Barber, J. Leitch Wright (1986), Florette Henri, Benjamin W. Griffith, H. D. Southerland and J. E. Brown, and Joel Martin.

7. Nunez, 147; E. Denny, *Military Journal,* 71–72.

8. The northern delegation was believed to be carrying British muskets, and although Hawkins left Tuckabatchee without knowing Tecumseh's plans, he assumed the chief was hostile and would encourage the acceptance of the war pipe.

9. Quotations from Hawkins to Eustis, 3 October 1811, and the account in *The Republican and Savannah Ledger,* 17 October 1811. See also Hopoithle Mico to James Madison, 15 May 1811, U.S. SoW/LR/IA: 0554.

10. The term "red stick" or "red club" related to the red-painted war clubs used to raise war parties (Wright [1986], 157; Talosee Fixico to Hawkins, 5 June 1813, *ASPIA* 1: 847).

11. Stiggins and Pickett both mention Tecumseh's reference to the comet, but the first to link the two was *The Halcyon Luminary* (New York) for June 1812: S. G. Drake, *Aboriginal Races,* 624.

12. Big Warrior quotation: Woodward, 103. For Creek rivalry see Hopoithle Mico to the British, 1 September 1811, Britain/CO 23/58: 88; Hawkins to Big Warrior, 26 July 1813, U.S. SoW/LR/U 8: 3098; Hawkins to Thomas Pinckney, 26 April 1814, U.S. SoW/LR/R 56: 0608; and my articles on McQueen and Big Warrior in *ANB*.

13. Frank L. Owsley (1985) treats Josiah Francis.

14. John Shaw to James Rhea, 3 March 1812, U.S. SoW/LR/R 48: 2772; Reuben Atwater to Eustis, 21 January 1812, ibid., 42: 7436; William Wells to Eustis, 10 February and 1 March 1812, ibid., 49: 3709, 3773; letter of 8 December 1811 (see n. 6 above); and M. Hardin to Henry Clay, 2 December 1812, Frontier Wars papers, 7U6.

15. The quotation is from W. W. Stringfield, *North Carolina Booklet*, 13–15. Stringfield may have obtained the tradition from Cherokees he commanded in the Civil War, or from his father, who reputedly served with Junaluska in the Creek War of 1813–1814. For the Chickasaws: James Neelly to Eustis, 29 November 1811, U.S. SoW/LR/R 47: 2217; Chickasaws to Eustis, 26 November 1811, U.S. SoW/LR/U 4: 1948.

16. W. G. McLoughlin, "New Angles." J. L. Penick, *New Madrid Earthquakes*, and E. P. Olmstead, *Blackcoats*, 150–51, are also relevant.

17. Meigs to Eustis, 14 March 1812, U.S. SoW/LR/R 47: 1719.

18. The earliest reference to Tecumseh's prediction of the earthquake that I have found is in *The Halycon Luminary*, mentioned in n. 11.

19. *The Western Sun*, 16 June 1812.

20. Rebuilding the Union

1. William Henry Harrison to William Eustis, 6 August 1811, L. Esarey, *Harrison*, 1: 542, and William Clark to Eustis, 22 March 1812, U.S. SoW/LR/R 43: 8516, supply the quotations. In addition see R. B. McAfee, *Late War*, 17, and the letter to Lyman Draper, 8 November 1884, Tecumseh papers, 8YY46.

2. *The New York Herald*, 21 December 1811; *The Missouri Gazette*, 21 March 1812.

3. J. D. Hunter, *Memoirs*, 39.

4. Clark to Eustis, 20 February 1810, U.S. SoW/LR/R 35: 2307; Pierre Chouteau to Eustis, 16 April 1810, ibid., 35: 2449; E. B. Clemson to Eustis, 28 March 1810, ibid., 35: 2464; *The Missouri Gazette*, 12 September 1811.

5. The Osage-Shawnee peace is noticed in *The Missouri Gazette*, 9 May 1812.

6. L. Cass, "Indians of North America," 101. Cass led the attack on Hunter. For discussion see R. Drinnon, *White Savage*, and J. Sugden, "Early Pan-Indianism," 292–93.

7. *The New York Spectator*, 13 November 1826. Further comment, along the same lines, was published in *The National Gazette and Literary Register* (Philadelphia), 10 January 1827.

8. Hunter, 43–48. This account is confused. It says that Tecumseh visited the band on the Great Osage River, which was led by Clermont. In fact, this chief headed the Arkansas, not the Missouri, Osages.

9. Clark to Eustis, 23 November 1811, 13 February and 12 and 22 March 1812, U.S. SoW/LR/R 43: 8364, 8483, 8508, 8516; Ninian Edwards to Eustis, 3 March 1812, ibid., 44: 9332; Horatio Stark to Daniel Bissell, 22 January and 7 February 1812, ibid., 42: 7771, 7784; Nicholas Boilvin to Benjamin Howard, 5 January 1812, ibid., 44: 9320; John Lalime to Howard, 4 February 1812, ibid., 45: 0099; Maurice Blondeau, 7 January 1812, ibid., 44: 9321; Thomas Forsyth to Clark, 1 November 1811, Thomas Forsyth papers (2); *The Western Sun*, 5 May and 7 July 1812.

10. Edwards to Eustis, 3 March 1812, U.S. SoW/LR/R 44: 9332; Clark to Eustis, 22 March 1812, ibid., 43: 8516.

11. Stark to Bissell, 26 January 1812, U.S. SoW/LR/R 42: 7772.

12. Edwards to Eustis, 23 March 1812, U.S. SoW/LR/R 44: 9344.
13. Edwards to Eustis, 3 March 1812, U.S. SoW/LR/R 44: 9332, and the doubtful report in Matthew Elliott to Isaac Brock, 12 January 1812, Esarey, 1: 616.
14. Little Turtle said on 25 January that Tecumseh had just reached the Wabash with eight men (Esarey, 2: 18), but a month later some of the Shawnee's followers were claiming that he had not yet come home: John Shaw to James Rhea, 3 March 1812, U.S. SoW/LR/R 48: 2772. The quotation is from Canada/IA 28: 16512.
15. Harrison to Eustis, 4 March 1812, William Henry Harrison papers (2); B. Drake, *Life of Tecumseh*, 156.
16. James to Ruth Miller, 10 November 1811, James Miller papers; Josiah Snelling to Harrison, 20 November 1811, Esarey, 1: 643; Harrison to Eustis, 7 January 1812, ibid., 2: 3.
17. In addition to documents in Esarey see John Johnston to Eustis, 28 November 1811, U.S. SoW/LR/R 46; 0989; Thomas Fish and Enos Terry to Return Jonathan Meigs, 14 January 1812, ibid., 46: 1681; Lalime to Howard, 4 February 1812, ibid., 45: 0099; William Wells to Eustis, 10 February 1812, ibid., 49: 3709; Robert Forsyth to Rhea, 10 March 1812, ibid., 48: 2771; Harrison to Eustis, 10 December 1811, Daniel Parker papers; and *The Western Sun*, 7 December 1811, and 4 and 11 January 1812.
18. Esarey prints many documents, but details also come from Johnston to Eustis, 4 December 1811, U.S. SoW/LR/R 46:0994; Reuben Atwater to Eustis, 21 January 1812, ibid., 42: 7436; G. Thornbrough, *Letter Book*, 116; *The Western Sun*, 7, 21 and 28 December 1811, and 11 January 1812; Harrison to Eustis, 10 December 1811, Daniel Parker papers; and James to Amy Witherell, 21 January 1812, B. F. H. Witherell papers.
19. Brock to Major Taylor, 4 March 1811, F. B. Tupper, *Sir Isaac Brock*, 96; Brock to Sir George Prevost, 3 December 1811, ibid., 130; William Claus to James Brock, 9 December 1811, Canada/IA 3: 1222.
20. Edwards to Eustis, 10 February 1812, U.S. SoW/LR/R 44: 9316. The raids are detailed in various accounts in Esarey, vol. 2; Thornbrough, *Letter Book*; the files of *The Western Sun* and *The Missouri Gazette*; the Ninian Edwards papers; and the Return Jonathan Meigs papers (1), box 1/ folders 4–5. I have also used more than fifty reports in U.S. SoW/LR/R 42–48. They cannot be itemized here, but the dispatches written and forwarded by Bissell, Clark, Edwards, Howard, and Johnston are particularly valuable.
21. Speech of Gomo, April 1812, Ninian Edwards papers.
22. Johnston to Eustis, 21 May 1812, U.S. SoW/LR/R 46: 1064.
23. Harrison to Eustis, 22 April 1812, Esarey, 2: 41.
24. Statement of Samuel Manac, 2 August 1813, H. S. Halbert and T. H. Ball, *Creek War*, 91; Benjamin Hawkins to John Armstrong, 28 July 1813, *ASPIA* 1: 845.
25. Jackson to Willie Blount, 4 June 1812, J. S. Bassett, *Andrew Jackson*, 1: 225. For the Creek raids see J. Caller to Eustis, 6 April 1812, U.S. SoW/LR/R 43: 8574; depositions of John Gill and others (ibid., 43: 8575) and of Nathan and William Lott and William Wormack (ibid., 45: 0297); Blount to Eustis, 25 and 26 July 1812, ibid., 42: 7954, 8024; James Neelly to Eustis, 5 June 1812, ibid., 47: 2242; William to J. J. Henry, 25 June 1812, ibid., 42: 8028; letters of Hawkins to Eustis between 5 April and 7 September 1812, ibid., 45: 0106, 0230, 0273, 0325, 0339, 0347, 0350, 0397, 0425; letters of Big Warrior, June and July 1812, ibid., 45: 0276, 48: 2865; Nimrod Doyle to Hawkins, 3 May 1813, *ASPIA* 1: 843; Bassett, 1: 225; *TPUS* 6: 283; Hawkins to Edmund P. Gaines, 8 July 1812, War of 1812 mss.; and Halbert and Ball, 101.

21. Last Days of Peace

1. Elliott to William Claus, April 1812, and Tecumseh's speech, Canada/IA 28: 16512; L. Esarey, *Harrison*, 1: 616, 2: 15, 53; G. Thornbrough, *Letter Book*, 102, 116, 149; Wells to William Eustis, 1 March 1812, U.S. SoW/LR/R 49: 3773; John Shaw to James Rhea, 3 March 1812, ibid., 48: 2772; Claus to Isaac Brock, 16 June 1812, E. A. Cruikshank, *Invasion of Canada*, 32.

2. For the delegation to Harrison and its aftermath see Esarey, 1: 707, 2: 25, 26, 32; Thornbrough, 102, 108; Wells to Eustis, 10 February 1812, U.S. SoW/LR/R 49: 3709; Harrison to Shaw, 6 March 1812, ibid., 48: 3084; Harrison to Eustis, 4 March 1812, William Henry Harrison papers (2); and M. M. Crawford, "Lydia B. Bacon's Journal," 385–86.

3. Speech of Gomo, April 1812, Ninian Edwards papers; E. P. Olmstead, *Blackcoats*, 151; speech of Pamawatam, 8 June 1812, U.S. SoW/LR/R 45: 0322.

4. Wells to Eustis, 1 March 1812, U.S. SoW/LR/R 49: 3773; Robert Forsyth to Rhea, 10 March 1812, ibid., 48: 2771; Shaw to Rhea, 3 March 1812, ibid., 48: 2772; Shaw to Eustis, 3 March 1812, ibid., 48: 3042; *The Western Sun*, 7 July 1812; Esarey, 2: 41; Thornbrough, 110, 149.

5. Wells to Eustis, 1 March 1812, U.S. SoW/LR/R 49: 3773; Robert Cooper to Thomas Johnson, 5 April 1812, ibid., 46: 1043; Willie Blount to Eustis, 1 May 1812, with enclosures, ibid., 42: 7854; statement of Solomon Thorn, 7 April 1812, ibid., 46: 1046; and James Neelly to Eustis, 13 May 1812, ibid., 47: 2238.

6. The principal material on the council comes from the report in Esarey, 2: 50; Benjamin Stickney to William Hull, 25 May 1812, ibid., 2: 53; Stickney to Return Jonathan Meigs, 8 June 1812, Thornbrough, 139; and Claus to Brock, 16 June 1812, Cruikshank, *Invasion of Canada*, 32.

7. Tecumseh to the Wyandots and British, May 1812, Cruikshank, 33.

8. Thornbrough, 120; E. W. Voegelin and D. B. Stout, *Indians of Illinois and Northwestern Indiana*, 228–29; Forsyth to Rhea, 10 March 1812, U.S. SoW/LR/R 48: 2771; Thomas Forsyth to Ninian Edwards, 8 June 1812, ibid., 44: 9410.

9. Thornbrough, 140, 149, 154, 158; Edwards to Eustis, 23 June and 21 July 1812, U.S. SoW/LR/R 44: 9415, 9431; John Johnston to Benjamin Howard, 9 July 1812, with enclosure, *TPUS* 14: 578; J. Bradbury, *Travels*, 227.

10. Thomas Forsyth to Gibson, 26 July 1812, Thomas Forsyth letter; report of Antoine Leclair, 14 July 1812, U.S. SoW/LR/R 44: 9423.

11. Reports on the growth of Prophetstown are published in Esarey, 2: 48, 58, 66, particularly Samuel Hopkins to Isaac Shelby, 27 November 1812, ibid., 2: 231. See also Edwards to Eustis, 12 May 1812, U.S. SoW/LR/R 44: 9362, and materials in n. 8 above.

12. Sources for the Illinois concentration include Thomas Forsyth to Edwards, 8 June 1812, U.S. SoW/LR/R 44: 9410; Edwards to Eustis, 12 May and 23 June 1812, ibid., 44: 9362, 9415; Voegelin and Stout, 228–32, 334–39; J. Jablow, *Indians of Illinois and Indiana*, 360–61, 368–73, 384; and D. J. Berthrong, *Indians of Northern Indiana and Southwestern Michigan*, 142–46.

    The Winnebago movements appear from the report of Leclair, 14 July 1812, U.S. SoW/LR/R 44: 9423, and J. A. Jones, A. E. Smith, and V. Carstensen, *Winnebago Indians*, 120–30, 140. For Main Poc see also William Clark to Eustis, 22 March 1812 (quotation), ibid., 43: 8516; Robert Forsyth to Rhea, 10 March 1812, ibid., 48: 2771; and Thomas Forsyth to Edwards, 13 July 1812, ibid., 44: 9428. What I assume was an embassy from Main Poc to the Prophet in January is mentioned in Wells to Eustis, 10 February 1812, ibid., 49: 3709.

13. In addition to the sources given above in n. 10 see Dickson to Claus, 18 June 1812, and Dickson's statement in W. Wood, *British Documents*, 1: 424, 426.

14. Harrison to Eustis, 7 July 1812, Esarey, 2: 66.
15. Stickney's letters of 20–30 June, 1812 (Thornbrough, 140, 144, 149) and Wells to Harrison, 22 July 1812 (Esarey, 2: 76) are the main sources for Tecumseh's visit to Fort Wayne. J. G. Talbott to Lyman Draper, 23 September and October 1881, Tecumseh papers, 5YY50–52; Stephen Johnston to Draper, 23 August 1880, ibid., 11YY3; and John Johnston interviewed by Draper, 1843, ibid., 11YY9 are also relevant.

Tecumseh's knowledge of Hull's movements is uncertain. There is evidence that his fellow Shawnee and friend James Logan brought Hull's proclamation to Fort Wayne, in which case Tecumseh's gleanings may have been considerable: bill receipted by Logan, 10 July 1812, War of 1812 mss.

22. War Across the Detroit

1. Tecumseh's arrival at Fort Malden is noticed in James Taylor to James Eubank, 11 July 1812, James Taylor papers; William Wells to William Henry Harrison, 22 July 1812, L. Esarey, *Harrison*, 2: 76; Isaac Brock to George Prevost, 17 August 1812, E. A. Cruikshank, *Invasion of Canada*, 156; and R. Lucas, "Journal," 366.
2. Jasper Grant to Thomas Grant, 20 February 1807, Jasper Grant papers, folder 6. Most dispatches for this and the following chapter are conveniently available in Cruikshank; "Copies of Papers," *MPHC*, vol. 15; and Wood, *British Documents*, vol. 1. Useful British reminiscences are John Richardson (1902) and Thomas Vercheres de Boucherville, reprinted with an American narrative of James Foster by Milo M. Quaife (1940). Robert Lucas provided the best American journal of the campaign, but the accounts of James Dalliba, Adam Walker, and Josiah Snelling have important details, while the diaries of Lydia Bacon (edited by M. M. Crawford) and William K. Beall and the *Journal of an American Prisoner* (edited by G. M. Fairchild) offer the perspective of American prisoners held at Amherstburg. The minutes of William Hull's court-martial (J. G. Forbes, 1814) are essential, but subsequent vindications by Hull (*Memoirs*) and his grandson, J. F. Clarke (*Campaign of 1812*) are worth consulting.

R. B. McAfee (1816) and Alec R. Gilpin have full accounts of the war from the American point of view, but for a broader picture the histories by Harry L. Coles, Reginald Horsman, and John K. Mahon are recommended. George C. Chalou surveys relations between Britain, the United States, and the northern Indians during the conflict.
3. Fort Malden: report of 8 September 1812, U.S. SoW/LR/U 6: 2568.
4. The number of Indian warriors at Amherstburg was variously estimated between two hundred and four hundred, but Elliott to William Claus, 15 July 1812 (Cruikshank, 62) and the testimony of Aaron Forbush (Forbes, 146) are particularly authoritative. See also Forbes, 101; Lucas, 366, 373–74; Beall, 790, 793; Thomas Forsyth to Benjamin Howard, 7 September 1812, U.S. SoW/LR/R 45: 0458; and Abraham Luckenbach to Return Jonathan Meigs, 5 April 1813, Return Jonathan Meigs papers (1), box 2/folder 8.
5. For Elliott's opinion see his letter to Claus, 8–11 August, 1812, Canada/IA 28: 16397.
6. Tecumseh's desire for action is reported in John B. Glegg to Edward Baynes, 11 November 1812, and St. George to Brock, 15 July 1812, Cruikshank, 227, 61.
7. Brock to Baynes, 29 July 1812, Cruikshank, 106.
8. Letters to John Lovett, 26 and 28 August, 1812, M. Edgar, *Brock*, 264; *Tales of Chivalry and Romance* (George Procter), 78–79; J. Richardson, *Canadian Brothers*, 1: 55; and Beall, 793.

9. St. George to Brock, 8 July 1812, Cruikshank, 44. It was possibly on this occasion that the Indian chiefs undertook to discourage their warriors from scalping (William H. Merritt narrative, Wood, 3: 549).

10. Martin Hardin to Henry Clay, 2 December 1812, Frontier Wars papers, 7U6; Shane interview (see ch. 2, n. 1).

11. Wells to William Henry Harrison, 22 July 1812, Cruikshank, 78 (quotation); letters of 20 and 27 July, 1812 in ibid., 77; Wells to Harrison, 30 July 1812, William Wells papers; Zachary Taylor to Harrison, 9 August 1812, Esarey, 2: 82; and Benjamin Stickney to Harrison, 21 July 1812, G. Thornbrough, *Letter Book*, 167.

12. Hull's proclamation, Cruikshank, 58.

13. For the poor state of British morale and American expectations of an easy victory see Cruikshank, 61, 62, and *The Western Sun*, 11 and 18 August and 8 September 1812.

14. Elliott to Claus, 15 July 1812, Cruikshank, 62. In addition see Elliott to Claus, 26 July 1812, Canada/IA 28: 16396.

15. St. George to Brock, 15 July 1812, Cruikshank, 61.

16. Cass to Hull, 17 July 1812, Cruikshank, 71; ms. diary of John Robison; Lucas, 378–82; Forbes, 20, 105–106; Fairchild, 11; Beall, 798–99; A. Walker, *Journal of Two Campaigns*, 69; W. F. Coffin, *1812*, 200.

17. James to Isabella Denny, 17 July 1812, James Denny papers, box 1/folder 1.

18. Hull to William Eustis, 9 July 1812, Cruikshank, 50.

19. Robison diary; Lucas, 384–87. Foster's account (Quaife [1940], 246–54) mentions Tecumseh, but Lucas, a major source for Foster, has no reference to the chief at this point.

20. Sources for the skirmish are Quaife, 81–84 (Boucherville), 256–61 (Foster); Elliott to Claus, 26 July 1812, Canada/IA 28: 16396; Henry Procter to Brock, 26 July 1812, Cruikshank, 89; James to Isabella Denny, 27 July 1812, James Denny papers, box 1/folder 1; Wells to Harrison, 3 August 1812, William Wells papers; Robison diary; Lucas, 391–92; Charles Askin narrative, 1812, Charles Askin papers; Wood, 3: 550–51; Walker, 70; Beall, 803; and Coffin, 199.

21. Quotations from Wood, 3: 549, and Procter to Roger Sheaffe, 20 November 1812, Henry Procter papers. See also Procter to Brock, 11 August 1812, Cruikshank, 135; Hull to Eustis, 4 August 1812, ibid., 115; McArthur to Thomas Worthington, 4 August 1812, Thomas Worthington papers; Samuel to Eliza Williams, 5 August 1812, Williams, "Memoirs," ms., vol. 2, Samuel Williams papers (1); C. F. Klinck and J. T. Talman, *John Norton*, 300; Cass, "Policy and Practise," 422–29.

22. Elliott to Claus, 8 August 1812, Canada/IA 28: 16397. James Denny had earlier reported that two men had been killed trying to reach Detroit (James to Isabella Denny, 27 July 1812, James Denny papers, box 1/folder 1).

23. John Anderson to Meigs, 10 August 1812, J. N. Crouch, 11 August 1812, and Calvin Austin to Meigs, 11 August 1812, all in Return Jonathan Meigs papers (1), box 1/folder 6. Gilpin, 97–98, refers to this incident but his source has not yet been traced.

24. The description of the battle is based upon Elliott to Claus, 8 August 1812, Canada/IA 28: 16397; Richardson, *War of 1812*, 26–33; James Taylor to James Eubank, 12 August 1812, James Taylor papers; Hull to Eustis, 7 August 1812, Cruikshank, 125; Procter to Brock, 11 August 1812, ibid., 135; Robison diary; Lucas, 395–99; Taylor Berry to Eubank, 8 August 1812, William Hull papers; Charles Askin narrative, 1812, Charles Askin papers; Forbes, 67–73; and J. Dalliba, *Battle of Brownstown*, 8–9.

25. Hull to Eustis, 4 August 1812, Cruikshank, 115.

26. Brush's march: Williams, "Memoirs," vol. 2, Samuel Williams papers (1); letters of Brush in U.S. SoW/LR/R 42: 8081, and Meigs papers, box 1/folder 6.

27. Berry to Eubank, 8 August 1812, William Hull papers; Hull to Eustis, 8 August 1812, Cruikshank, 126.

23. The Moon of Plums

1. J. Richardson, *War of 1812*, 34.
2. J. Richardson, *War of 1812*, 212, and *Canadian Brothers*, 1: 174. The latter is a novel, based on Richardson's wartime experiences, but contains some valid observations about the personalities at Amherstburg.
3. Hull to William Eustis, 8 August 1812, E. A. Cruikshank, *Invasion of Canada*, 126. Informed estimates of the number of Indians in the skirmish vary, from the two hundred given by Boucherville, who was present (Quaife, *War on the Detroit*, 84–106), through two hundred to three hundred (C. F. Klinck and J. T. Talman, *John Norton*, 300) to about four hundred (Matthew Elliott to William Claus, 8 August 1812, Canada/IA 28: 16397). The official British report of the action is Henry Procter to Isaac Brock, 11 August 1812, Cruickshank, 135. American accounts are James to Ruth Miller, 27 August 1812, James Miller papers; J. G. Forbes, *Report of the Trial*, 107–108; James Taylor to James Eubank, 12 August 1812, James Taylor papers; Hull to Eustis, 13 August 1812, Cruikshank, 139; Lewis to Thomas Peckham, 8 September 1812, ms.; R. Lucas, "Journal," 400–403; A. Walker, *Journal of Two Campaigns*, 59–63; and, particularly useful for Tecumseh, J. Dalliba, *Battle of Brownstown*, passim.
4. Cass to Return Jonathan Meigs, 12 August 1812, Cruikshank, 137; officers to Charles Scott, 12 August 1812, Daniel Parker papers, box 14; James to Isabella Denny, 15 August 1812, James Denny papers, box 1/folder 1; Hull to Eustis, 26 August 1812, Cruikshank, 184; and, for allied reinforcements from Michilimackinac, documents in ibid., 150, 248.
5. Elliott to Claus, 8–11 August 1812, and George Ironside, 31 July 1812, Canada/IA 28: 16397, 16396.
6. The role of Main Poc is given in Thomas Forsyth to Benjamin Howard, 7 September 1812, U.S. SoW/LR/R 45: 0458. Main Poc's emissaries claimed that Detroit had fallen, and invited Indians to Fort Malden. One band of Potawatomis, under Shequenebea, a prophet-warrior; Esh-kee-bee; and Black Partridge, was inspired to make an abortive raid down the Illinois River.
7. Brock to Procter, October 1812, G. Auchinleck, *History*, 103.
8. John Bachevoyle Glegg gave the account to F. B. Tupper (*Sir Isaac Brock*, 242–45).
9. William Hamilton Merritt's account in W. Wood, *British Documents*, 3: 554; Brock to one of his brothers, 3 September 1812, Britain/CO 42/353: 226; James FitzGibbon to Tupper, 27 September 1845, Ferdinand Brock Tupper papers.
10. FitzGibbon to Tupper, 27 September 1845, Ferdinand Brock Tupper papers.
11. Brock to Hull, 15 August 1812, Cruikshank, 144.
12. The Indian force is generally put at six hundred (for example by Aaron Forbush, in Forbes, 147), but I have assumed this included John Norton's detachment, for which see Klinck and Talman's *John Norton* and Norton to Glegg, 11 August 1812, Canada/IA 487: 4451. On the American side, I have taken the adjutant-general's report of 1,060 men fit for duty, exclusive of both the Michigan militia and McArthur and Cass's detachment, which was sent south to open communications, to be more consistent with the British return of prisoners than Hull's attempt to minimize his forces: Lucas, 413–14; Cass to Eustis, 10 September 1812, Cruikshank, 218; Hull, *Memoirs*, 123; J. Snelling, *Remarks*, 12–13.
13. Merritt, in Wood, 3: 554. Lucas, 412, says that some Indians had appeared behind the fort when the surrender was made.
14. Robert Wallace interviewed by John D. Shane, Tecumseh papers, 7YY96, and Wallace to R. C. Langdon, 1842, J. F. Clarke, *Campaign of 1812*, 443. John Anderson claimed his house in Detroit and its outlying buildings were confiscated by the British, who assumed from their use by American soldiers that they were public property. Tecumseh,

he claimed, made the house his headquarters. It contained one and a half stories, was large, was painted white, and had three rooms papered (Anderson to William Woodbridge, 8 November 1819, William Woodbridge papers).

15. W. S. Hatch, *A Chapter*, 113–15.
16. Chambers to Procter, 24 August 1812, Cruikshank, 175; Askin journal, ibid., 243–47; Chambers, 17 January 1815, *MPHC* 16: 45; B. Drake, *Life of Tecumseh*, 226–27.
17. Hull, *Memoirs*, 119, gives the number of American soldiers at the River Raisin.
18. The sash story was published by W. James, *Full and Correct Account*, 1:291–92. A prejudiced historian, but not a man to fabricate material, James probably had an eyewitness for the incident, possibly Robert Nichol, who was both present and one of the author's subscribers. James is also the source of the popular story that before crossing the river to attack Detroit, Brock asked Tecumseh for his opinion "in case of his proceeding further." The chief weighed a roll of elm bark down with four stones, and used a scalping knife to sketch the topography of the country, including the roads and rivers. The story of the sash, but without the elm bark, was supported by an informant of James FitzGibbon (n. 10, above). See also British general orders, 16 August 1812, Cruikshank, 148.
19. Samuel Huntington to Eustis, 27 September 1812, U.S. SoW/LR/R 45: 0468.

24. Attack and Counterattack

1. Brock to George Prevost, 18 September 1812, W. Wood, *British Documents*, 1: 592.
2. Brock to Liverpool, 29 August 1812, Britain/CO 42/352: 105. Technically, the British Prime Minister was then the First Lord of the Treasury.
3. Brock to Prevost, 28 September 1812, Wood, 1: 596.
4. N. Atcheson, "Compressed View," 137–38; M. Edgar, *Brock*, 279; Procter to Roger Sheaffe, 28 November 1812, Henry Procter papers.
5. Prevost to Bathurst, 5 October 1812, Britain/CO 42/147: 207; Liverpool to Prevost, 9 December 1812, ibid., 147: 237; *The Kingston Gazette*, 16 October 1813; Prevost to John Borlase Warren, 5 and 20 October 1812, Canada/IA 487: 4461, 4465; Bathurst to Prevost, 3 June 1814, Britain/CO 43/23: 150.
6. Benjamin Stickney to William Henry Harrison, 29 September 1812, G. Thornbrough, *Letter Book*, 172.
7. Some Miamis were already with the hostiles, but there is doubt about the inclinations of the others, who abandoned their villages to concentrate on the Mississinewa. They took little part in the attack on Fort Wayne, and sued for peace when threatened by the Americans; but they did not attend the Piqua conference with the U.S. commissioners, and the Delawares and Ohio Shawnees were convinced that they had gone over to Tecumseh. See L. Esarey, *Harrison*, 2: 164, 173, 186; Thornbrough, 172; and Matthew Elliott to William Claus, 3 February 1813, Canada/IA 28: 16435.
8. Commissioners' report, 10 September 1812, U.S. SoW/LR/R 49: 4162; Edward Tupper to Return Jonathan Meigs, 26 January 1813, Return Jonathan Meigs papers (1), box 2/folder 4.
9. On powder see Ninian Edwards to William Eustis, 21 September 1812, U.S. SoW/LR/R 44: 9431.
10. Brock to Prevost, 18 September 1812, Wood, 1: 592; Procter to Roger Sheaffe, 12 September 1812, Ferdinand Brock Tupper papers; Procter to Brock, 3 October 1812, Canada/C 677: 111; Charles Askin journal, 23 August 1812, E. A. Cruikshank, *Invasion of Canada*, 248; Claus to John Johnson, 8 October 1812, William Claus papers, 17: 70; report from Cleveland, 8 September 1812, U.S. SoW/LR/U 6: 2568; William Foster to Eustis, 22 September 1812, U.S. SoW/LR/R 44: 9603.

11. Quotation from Daniel Curtis to Jacob Kingsbury, 21 September 1812, H. H. Peckham, "Recent Documentary Acquisitions."

12. Edwards to Eustis, 8 August 1812, and Thomas Forsyth to Benjamin Howard, 7 September 1812, U.S. SoW/LR/R 44: 9438, 45: 0458.

13. Fort Harrison: Zachary Taylor to Harrison, 10 and 13 September, 1812, Esarey, 2: 124, 134; John Gibson to John Armstrong, 31 March 1813, ibid., 2: 406; return of provisions burned, Thomas Richardson to Gibson, 12 August 1812, Gibson to Harrison, 12 September 1812, and William Russell to Gibson, 16 September 1812, all in William Henry Harrison papers (1); Gibson to Eustis, 9 and 16 September, 1812, U.S. SoW/LR/R 44: 9764, 9769; Russell to Eustis, 23 September 1812, ibid., 48: 2890; Samuel Hopkins to Eustis, 13 September 1812, ibid., 45: 0449; and J. B. Dillon, *Indiana*, 491.

14. Gibson to Colonel Hargrove, 18 September 1812, Esarey, 2: 138; *The Western Sun*, 8 September 1812; R. B. McAfee, *Late War*, 376; Dillon, 492–93.

15. Muir to Procter, 26 and 30 September, 1812, Canada/C 677: 97, 102.

16. John Bickley to Thomas Barr, 23 November 1811, Frontier Wars papers, 7U7; Harrison to Eustis, 13 October and 24 December, 1812, Esarey, 2: 173, 252; John Johnston to Harrison, 23 October 1812, ibid., 2: 186; Edward Munger to Meigs, 30 December 1812, Return Jonathan Meigs papers (1), box 2/folder 3.

17. Nathan Newsom diary, ms., 13–21 October, 1812, for the pillage of Roundhead's village.

18. Sources for the skirmish are: Hopkins to Isaac Shelby, 27 November 1812, Esarey, 2: 231; Joseph Bartholomew to Jonathan Jennings, 11 December 1812, U.S. SoW/LR/R 54: 8153; Shane interview; and the William M. Crockett ms., which quotes Lieutenant Little's account of 30 November 1812 and identifies the location of the fight as Boyd's farm, Perry Township, Tippecanoe County.

19. Johnston to Harrison, 4 February 1813, William Henry Harrison papers (2); Johnston to Meigs, 16 February 1813, Return Jonathan Meigs papers (1), box 2/folder 5; Procter to Roger Sheaffe, 13 January 1813, Wood, 2: 3. The evidence for Tecumseh's wife is given in J. Sugden, *Tecumseh's Last Stand*, 251, and William Walker, interviewed by Lyman Draper, 1868, Frontier Wars papers, 11U26, who believed the British later gave her a pension.

20. Harrison to Armstrong, 11 February 1813, Esarey, 2: 356; Munger to Meigs, 30 December 1812, Return Jonathan Meigs papers (1), box 2/folder 3; Elliott to Claus, 3 February 1813, Canada/IA 28: 16435 (quotations); Shane (including the Prophet story); C. F. Klinck and J. T. Talman, *John Norton*, 315.

21. Andrew Jackson to George Campbell, 15 October 1812, J. S. Bassett, *Andrew Jackson*, 1: 236; James Robertson to William Anderson, 4 March 1813, Arthur Mitten collection; Elliott to Claus, 3 February 1813, Canada/IA 28: 16435. A few Creeks were already with the northern Indians, and both groups probably participated in the battle of the River Raisin in January: Edward Dewar to G. McDonnell, 19 October 1812, Canada/C 677: 136; Nimrod Doyle to Benjamin Hawkins, 3 May 1813, *ASPIA* 1: 843.

22. A good account of this affair by Rembert W. Patrick misses the role of Seekaboo, for which see Creeks to Hawkins, 5 December 1812, U.S. SoW/LR/R 45: 0604, and Hawkins to David Mitchell, 13 September 1812, M. B. Pound, *Benjamin Hawkins*, 217. The Creeks said Seekaboo came from Nauchee, on the Coosa River, and "had been to the Shawnees and heard the deception of the white people there." See also Hawkins to Eustis, 24 August, 7 and 20 September, and 29 October, 1812, U.S. SoW/LR/R 45: 0397, 0425, 0473, 0557. Seekaboo went back to the Upper Creeks, participated in their war against the United States, and fled with its survivors to the Seminoles in 1814. He fought the Americans in the Seminole war of 1818, and died a year

or so afterward (statements of Himonubbee, 24 June and 9 November 1887, Tecumseh papers, 10YY2, 10YY4).

23. Robert Dickson to Prevost, 15 February 1813, Canada/C 257: 52 (quotation). McAfee, A. R. Gilpin, and G. Glenn Clift (1961) describe the battle.

25. Fighting Groundhogs

1. Procter to Roger Sheaffe, 17 April 1813, Canada/C 678: 230; embarkation return, 23 April 1813, W. Wood, *British Documents*, 2: 38.
2. Differences between Prevost and Procter are illustrated in Prevost to Earl Bathurst, 27 February 1813, Britain/CO 42/150: 90.
3. Procter to Sheaffe, 28 November 1812, Henry Procter papers.
4. Procter to Sheaffe, 30 October 1812, Canada/C 677: 163.
5. Robert Dickson to Noah Freer, 16 March 1813, Canada/C 257: 64; Dickson to Sheaffe, 22 March 1813, ibid., 257: 67; report of Auguste LaRoche and Louis Chevalier, 4 April 1813, U.S. SoW/LR 53: 7328; Thomas Forsyth to Benjamin Howard, 7 May 1813, ibid., 50: 4943; Robert Gilmore to Allan McLean, 27 March 1813, William Woodbridge papers; H. Lindley, *Captain Cushing*, 100; Charles Marvin to Joseph Larwill, 27 April 1813, Larwill Family papers, box 1/folder 4; Procter to Robert McDouall, 16 April 1813, Henry Procter papers; Harrison, 25 April 1813, William Henry Harrison papers (1); E. Darnell, *Journal* (Timothy Mallary narrative), 77.
6. Procter to McDouall, 16 April 1813, Henry Procter papers.
7. Eleazor Wood in G. W. Cullum, *Campaigns*, 389–90. British accounts of the siege are Procter, 11 May 1813, Henry Procter papers; Procter to Prevost, 14 May 1813, Wood, 2: 33; Peter Chambers to Freer, 13 May 1813, Canada/C 678: 244; S. Byfield, "Narrative," 67–71; and J. Richardson, *War of 1812*. Among abundant American documents see Esarey, 2: 431, 435, 438, 440, 442, 450; Lindley, *Captain Cushing*; Eleazor Wood, cited above; A. Bourne, "Siege of Fort Meigs"; *The Weekly Register*, 12 June 1813; and "Siege of Fort Meigs," *Register of the Kentucky Historical Society*. A useful secondary account has been written by Larry Nelson.
8. Daniel Cushing to his family, 8 June 1813, Lindley, 127.
9. Clay's force is usually given as 1,200 men, but the return of 7 May 1813 (Green Clay papers) implies otherwise. The force consisted of two regiments. One investigation (report, 1813, War of 1812 mss.) concluded that William Dudley's regiment consisted of 866 men, not 800 as commonly believed.
10. John Norton (C. F. Klinck and J. T. Talman, *John Norton*, 321) refers to Tecumseh's role in opposing Miller's sortie. He was not at Fort Meigs, but was well acquainted with some who were, both British and Indians, and his account is generally well informed. The casualties are taken from Wood (Cullum, 399–400) but may have been higher. This seems to have been the severest of the actions on the south bank, which were said to have cost the Americans a total of 64 killed and 124 wounded (*The Western Intelligencer*, published in Worthington, Ohio, 9 June 1813; Jesup Couch to Thomas Worthington, 25 May 1813, Thomas Worthington papers).
11. W. Hibbert, "Pictorial Map" (map annotated by William Sebree).
12. Ms. narrative of George Carter Dale, written about 1837; Shawnee chiefs to Harrison, 19 May 1813, William Henry Harrison papers (2).
13. Byfield, 70.
14. G. Ewing to J. H. James, 2 May 1818, Tecumseh papers, 2YY180.
15. Combs to Clay, 6 May 1815, Tecumseh papers, 6YY20; Combs to *Historical Record*, October 1871, H. S. Knapp, *Maumee Valley*, 205; T. Christian, "Campaign of 1813," 5.

16. Byfield, 69–70.
17. John Plummer and Joseph Markle interviewed by Lyman Draper, 1863, Draper notes, 19S244, 249.
18. Richardson, 154.
19. The fullest narratives by survivors of the massacre were given by Combs in 1815 (quotation), cited above in n. 15; Combs to G. M. McLaughlin, 18 February 1863, Tecumseh papers, 6YY22; the narratives by Dale and Christian; and that by Joseph Underwood, April 1871, Tecumseh papers, 6YY23.
20. The perpetrator(s) of the massacre are mentioned in Klinck and Talman, 321; Richardson 153–54; the annotation to Richardson's 1842 edition by James Cochran, 88; and Draper's 1863 interviews with William Caldwell, Robert Reynolds, and John Tofflemyer, Draper notes, 17S212, 17S243, and 20S218.
21. Combs mentioned Tecumseh in all his accounts, but see especially his letter of 1863 (n. 19) and Combs to Draper, Tecumseh papers, 6YY21. For Elliott's conduct: Samuel Finley to Thomas Worthington, 1 June 1813, Thomas Worthington papers, and more doubtfully in Draper's interviews with John McCormick and William Caldwell in 1863 (Draper notes, 17S201, 17S212).
22. An account dated 19 May 1813 claimed that American prisoners reported that "Tecumseh, in particular, was much enraged at the conduct of the Indians" (*The War*, 1: 209). Other papers carrying the story included *Liberty Hall*, 25 May 1813 and *The Kingston Gazette*, 27 July 1813. Ewing and Richardson refer to the use of a tomahawk.
23. S. R. Brown, *Authentick History*, 1: 100; Samuel Stivers interviewed by Draper, 1863, Draper notes, 19S120.
24. A. Edwards to John Armstrong, 28 September 1813, U.S. SoW/LR/R 52: 6533, and Ewing's letter.
25. Lindley, 107; Harrison to Armstrong, 18 May 1813, Esarey, 2: 450.
26. On the Shawnees, Shawnee chiefs to Harrison, 19 May 1813, enclosed by John Wingate to Harrison, 15 June 1813, William Henry Harrison papers (2); Esarey, 2: 463; Shane; Adam Brown interviewed by Draper, 1868, Frontier Wars papers, 11U74; and Combs to the *Historical Record*, October 1871. The Wyandot exchange proposal is treated in William Claus to Christopher Myers, 6 February 1813, Henry Procter papers; Procter to Harrison, 7 May 1813, Britain/CO 42/151: 10; and *The Weekly Register*, 15 January 1814.
27. Lindley, 105. The British return of casualties is in Canada/C 678: 254. Harrison reported his losses in the fort and on the south bank at 81 killed and 188 wounded. Those sustained by Dudley's command on the north bank are not precisely known. American searches of the area throughout May yielded over 50 bodies, although it was supposed others had been buried (Lindley, 105–108). The British counted 547 prisoners, but Procter asserted that more than 80 others were later surrendered by the Indians (Wood, 2: 39). Some of these were wounded, and a few subsequently died (William Irvine to Clay, 7 June 1813, Green Clay papers). The return of Clay's brigade, 7 May 1813, and James Degarnett to Clay, 6 June 1813 (both in the Clay papers), indicate that some of Boswell's regiment may also have landed and suffered with Dudley.
28. Sheaffe to Prevost, 8 May 1813, Canada/C 678: 221; Francis de Rottenburg to Prevost, 13 May 1813, ibid., 243.

26. An Adequate Sacrifice to Indian Opinion

1. J. Sugden, *Tecumseh's Last Stand*, 17.
2. *Tales of Chivalry and Romance*, 80–81. George Procter, who was evidently the author of the sketch on Tecumseh in this volume, did not come to Canada until 1814, but his

sources were excellent, for in 1819 he married General Procter's eldest daughter. Not only the general, but also his wife, son, and daughters knew Tecumseh at Amherstburg in 1813: Henry Procter to Thomas Talbot, 23 September 1813, J. H. Coyne, *Talbot Papers*, 193; Robert McDouall to Procter, 4 June 1813, Henry Procter papers; C. F. Klinck, "Anonymous Literature"; and G. F. G. Stanley, *War of 1812*, 406, 458.

3. William Walker to Lyman Draper, 22 November 1870, Frontier Wars papers, 11U97.

4. M. M. Quaife, *War on the Detroit*, 140–41. Boucherville confused the occasion on which the banquet occurred, but almost certainly had an historical incident in mind.

5. Letter to Hyacinth Lasselle, 26 May 1813, Lasselle papers; Woodbridge to Clay, December 1823, William Woodbridge papers; Procter to Ebenezer Reynolds, 14 January 1813, Henry Procter papers; Sugden, 257.

6. Procter to McDouall, 14 May 1813, Canada/C 678: 240; Richard Mentor Johnson to John Armstrong, 14 June 1813, U.S. SoW/LR/R 54: 8295. An American report (Green Clay to William Henry Harrison, 20 June 1813, L. Esarey, *Harrison*, 2: 474) has Tecumseh near the mouth of the River Rouge, but this may have been a temporary encampment.

7. Procter to McDouall, 4 July 1813, W. Wood, *British Documents*, 2: 40; Procter to Prevost, 5 July 1813, Canada/C 679: 185; C. F. Klinck and J. T. Talman, *John Norton*, 340. Richard Mentor Johnson's regiment of mounted Kentucky volunteers actually struck at the River Raisin: Johnson to Armstrong, 3 July 1813, U.S. SoW/LR/R 54: 8305.

8. Procter to Prevost, 4 July 1813, Wood, 2: 42.

9. W. F. Coffin, *1812*, 207–13. Reynolds said the incident occurred at the end of the siege of Fort Meigs in May, but as the Indians had then dispersed the remarks attributed to Tecumseh would have been inapplicable at that time. If it happened at all, and some of the details strike me as convincing, the most likely occasion was the June council.

10. Clay to Harrison, 20 June 1813, Esarey, 2: 474; H. Lindley, *Captain Cushing*, 112; Procter to McDouall, 19 June 1813, Canada/C 679: 110.

11. Lindley, 116–17.

12. Dickson to Freer, 23 June 1813, Canada/C 257: 86; ms. account of Lewis Bond, 53; Procter to Roger Sheaffe, 13 January 1813, Wood, 2: 3; Maurice Blondeau to Ninian Edwards, February 1813, U.S. SoW/LR/R 52: 6460; report of Auguste LaRoche and Louis Chevalier, 4 April 1813, ibid., 53: 7328; Thomas Forsyth to Benjamin Howard, 7 May 1813, ibid., 50: 4943; D. Robinson, *History of the Dakota*, 85–88.

13. Elliott to William Claus, 29 August 1813, Canada/IA 28: 16527; Procter to Prevost, 9 August 1813, Wood, 2: 44; Procter to McDouall, 19 June 1813, Canada/C 679: 155.

14. Returns, 29–30 July, 1813, Green Clay papers; Harrison to Armstrong, 23 July 1813, Esarey, 2: 494. For the second siege of Fort Meigs I have relied upon Procter to Prevost, 9 August 1813, Wood, 2: 44; J. Richardson, *War of 1812*, 177–78; S. Byfield, "Narrative," 75; reports in Esarey, 2: 474, 493, 494, 495, 499, 500, 501, 506; Lindley, 118–24; letter to Frankfort, Kentucky, *Argus*, 4 August 1813, Tecumseh papers, 6YY84; J. C. Bartlett to Lewis Cass, 22 July 1813, Return Jonathan Meigs papers (1), box 3/folder 11; Harrison to Return Jonathan Meigs, 2 August 1813, William Henry Harrison papers (1); diary of Joseph Larwill, Larwill Family papers; John O'Fallon to William Croghan, 1 August 1813, Tecumseh papers 6YY86; and William Gaines to Lyman Draper, 25 November and 4 December, 1881, ibid., 5YY46–47.

15. The report of J. Battersby to Edward Baynes, 31 July 1813, Canada/C 679: 517, that Tecumseh destroyed an American advance of twelve men, was erroneous.

16. For Tecumseh see Klinck and Talman, 340–41; Harrison to Armstrong, 4 August 1813, Esarey, 2: 510; and Gaines to Draper, 15 May 1882, Tecumseh papers, 7YY73.

17. Procter to Prevost, 9 August 1813, Wood, 2: 44.

18. Extracts from journal of the Creek agency, 12 August 1813, SoW/LR/U 8: 3266; James Robertson to William Anderson, 4 March 1813, Arthur Mitten collection; reports by

Hawkins (*ASPIA* 1: 839, 840, 842, 851), Big Warrior (ibid., 1: 843), Alex Cornells (ibid., 1: 845) and Talosee Fixico (ibid., 1: 847).

19. In addition to the above, see letters to Willie Blount by James Robertson (5 March 1813) and Harry Toulmin (28 July 1813), U.S. SoW/LR/R 50: 4811, 5167.

20. Letters of Hawkins (*ASPIA* 1: 839, 840), Big Warrior (ibid., 1: 841, 843), and Talosee Fixico (ibid., 1: 847). In addition to the four Indians killed at the Hickory Ground and Little Warrior, three men, including two brothers, were slain at the town of Hoithlewaulee. The woman was held responsible for the Duck River murders of 1812 because it was a false report of her death that had prompted that raid. Two Okfuskee Creeks were also executed for the murder of a white man on the post road. One was disemboweled with a knife.

21. Moshulatubbee to George Gaines, 15 July 1813, U.S. SoW/LR/R 50: 5111; reports by Cornells, Talosee Fixico, Cussita King, and Hawkins in *ASPIA* 1: 845, 847, 849.

22. Big Warrior and Coweta chief to Hawkins, 4 August 1813, *ASPIA* 1: 851; Hawkins to David Mitchell, 27 July 1813, with enclosures, U.S. SoW/LR/U 8: 3096; Hawkins to James Wilkinson, 27 July 1813, U.S. SoW/LR/R 51: 5790; James Lyon to Blount, 17 July 1813, ibid., 50: 5079.

23. Pierre Chouteau to Armstrong, 5 March 1813, U.S. SoW/LR/R 51: 5623; Gaines to John Mason, 22 July 1813, with enclosures, ibid., 50: 5110; Moshulatubbee to Gaines, 8 August 1813, ibid., 50: 5163; Return Jonathan Meigs to Armstrong, 23 August 1813, ibid., 55: 9216; John Sibley to Armstrong, 3 and 6 October, 1813, ibid., 57: 1224, 1293; John Pitchlynn to Blount, 18 September 1813, U.S. SoW/LR/U 9: 3418; Cussita King to Hawkins, 10 July 1813, *ASPIA* 1: 849; J. G. Forbes, *Sketches*, 200–205.

24. Cornells to Hawkins, 22–23 June, 1813, *ASPIA* 1: 845.

25. E. H. West, "Prelude"; Mateo González Manrique to Juan Ruiz Apodaca, 6 September 1813, with enclosures, Spain/Papeles Procedentes de Cuba, 1794; Ferdinand Claiborne to Armstrong, 12 August 1813, with enclosures, U.S. SoW/LR/R 51: 5785; affidavits of W. Pierce, David Tate, and John M'Coombs, ibid., 50: 5153, 5203; Big Warrior to Hawkins, 4 August 1813, *ASPIA* 1: 851.

26. Reports of Hawkins between 23 August and 23 October, 1813, *ASPIA* 1: 851, 852, 857.

27. B. W. Griffith, *McIntosh and Weatherford*, 111.

28. F. H. Akers, *Unexpected Challenge*, 155; Creeks and Seminoles to Charles Cameron, 11 September 1813, Britain/CO 23/60: 110, 111. When Peter McQueen visited Pensacola again, in January 1814, after the Creek war had begun, he was refused arms and ammunition by the Spaniards, and had to be content with food supplies only: report of Manrique, 8 January 1814, Spain/Papeles Procedentes de Cuba, 1795.

29. West, 249; reports of Hawkins, 6 and 28 June, 1813, *ASPIA* 1: 840, 847.

27. Father, We See You Are Drawing Back!

1. Matthew Elliott to William Claus, 29 August 1813, Canada/IA 28: 16527; Richard Mentor Johnson to William Henry Harrison, 20 September 1813, William Henry Harrison papers (2). The sources for this and the following chapter are fully detailed in J. Sugden, *Tecumseh's Last Stand*. Since its publication some fresh material on these events has been uncovered, some of it used here, but it supports the conclusions of my earlier volume.

2. Council minutes, 23 August 1813, Canada/C 257: 139; Peter Chambers to Noah Freer, 26 August 1813, ibid., C 679: 445. Tecumseh did not speak at the council, which he apparently regarded as a Wyandot affair, but William Walker, who was fourteen years old at the time, believes that the Shawnee chief was present: Walker interviewed by Lyman Draper, 1868, Frontiers Wars papers, 11U26.

3. This Indian council is mentioned by J. Van Horne, *Narrative*, 15.
4. Procter to Francis de Rottenburg, 23 October 1813, W. Wood, *British Documents*, 2: 323.
5. J. Richardson, *War of 1812*, 207.
6. Speech of Tecumseh, 18 September 1813, Britain/WO 71/243: 381.
7. Procter in Britain/WO 71/243: 411. These are the minutes of Procter's court-martial.
8. Hall, ibid., 411.
9. Procter, ibid., 351.
10. Warburton, ibid., 11.
11. Tecumseh K. Holmes to Lyman Draper, 20 April and 4 May, 1882, Tecumseh papers, 7YY67, 129. This is the only one of several stories told by local Canadians to stand upon respectable eyewitness testimony.

28. Our Lives Are in the Hands of the Great Spirit!

1. Bullock to Richard Friend, 6 December 1813, J. Richardson, *War of 1812*, 230.
2. William Caldwell interviewed by Lyman Draper, 1863, Draper notes, 17S212.
3. *Tales of Chivalry and Romance*, 80.
4. Richardson, 212.
5. Allan McLean in W. F. Coffin, *1812*, 228. The Procters remembered it as "Father, tell your young men to be firm and all will be well" (*Tales of Chivalry and Romance*, 83).
6. Elliott to Claus, 24 October 1813, William Claus papers, 10: 111. The only accounts crediting the British with killing any of their enemies are the letter of James Johnson, 12 October 1813 (*The Missouri Gazette*, 6 November 1813) and the statement of one of Johnson's volunteers in *The Western Spy*, 30 October 1813.
7. J. C. Fredriksen, "Kentucky," 103. Allied survivors of the battle support the version of Tecumseh's death given here. A map of the field, prepared in 1814 with the apparent assistance of the Indian Department, indicates the spot where Tecumseh died, in advance of his position in the line, and notes, "Great chief Tecumseh in advance was killed by the enemy" (map of George Williams, 9 August 1814, Canada/National Map Collection). John Norton, who knew followers of Tecumseh, wrote that "the intrepid Tecumthai" was last "seen rushing boldly forward upon the hostile ranks, when victory seemed to incline to their side" (C. F. Klinck and J. T. Talman, *John Norton*, 343). That Tecumseh's body was not recovered, which is the burden of the testimony, further argues that it was too far ahead to be retrieved safely. For Desha's comments see Desha to A. Mitchell, 4 October 1840, J. A. Padgett, "Joseph Desha," 301.
8. Trisler to his father, 8 October 1813, Durrett miscellaneous mss.; S. R. Brown, *Views of the Campaigns*, 71–72, 105; Rowland, 9 October 1813, *The War*, 2: 91.
9. Stuart S. Sprague discussed Johnson's political campaign. Samuel Baker offers one example of bogus reporting. As late as 1886 he was claiming to have witnessed Tecumseh's death, but he had forgotten his earlier admission that it was his brother, and not he, who had been in the battle: J. Sugden, *Tecumseh's Last Stand*, 144; Baker to Lyman Draper, 9 and 19 June, 1861, Simon Kenton papers, 11BB31.
10. The New York *Plebeian*, 13 April 1843, reporting a speech Johnson made in Oswego. For other accounts by Johnson see Sugden, 139–40, and Jonathan Roberts to Luther Bradish, 20 August 1851, James Hamilton papers.
11. Dispatches of the Johnson brothers are in *The Missouri Gazette*, 6 November 1813, and Richard Mentor Johnson to John Armstrong, 21 November 1813, U.S. SoW/LR/R 54: 8326. Contemporary accounts linking Johnson to Tecumseh's death were given by Robert B. McAfee, Trisler, and Brown, all reviewed in Sugden, 134, 137–38, and in contributions to *The Missouri Gazette*, 20 November 1813, and *The Western Spy*, 30

October 1813. In the last, one of Johnson's regiment maintained that Tecumseh had "certainly" been killed by Johnson.

12. Reprinted from *The Chicago Democrat* by *The Kentucky Gazette*, 30 January 1840.

13. Hubbard to Draper, 4 September 1875, Tecumseh papers, 9YY104.

14. Ap-ta-ke-sic (Half Day)'s account is given in Henry W. Blodgett to Augustus H. Burley, 23 January 1893, Ottawa File. Fictionalized versions of it appear in D. B. Cook, *Six Months*, 85–87, but Cook refers to him as a Christian Ottawa named Noon Day. Other Indian witnesses incriminating Johnson (*The Western Citizen* [Paris, Kentucky], 7 February 1824; T. L. McKenney, *Memoirs*, 1: 181) are unidentified.

15. Henry Rowe Schoolcraft to L. Bradish, 5 May 1851, Henry Rowe Schoolcraft papers; *Louisville Weekly Journal*, 9 December 1859.

16. Account of the Davidsons, 1831, Tecumseh papers, 7YY141.

17. Forsyth to Ninian Edwards, 31 March 1816, R. G. Thwaites, "Letter Book," 345.

18. In addition to sources given in Sugden, see Thomas Bodley's statement in *The Ohio Republican* (Dayton), 25 October 1813, and J. P. Hedges, "Early Recollections."

19. D. Duffy, "Fate of Tecumseh," 22; Harrison to John Tipton, 2 May 1834, typescript from original supplied by Doug Clanin; Robert Reid to Robert Patterson, 25 October 1813, Robert Patterson papers.

20. *The Columbus Sentinel*, 3 January 1832; ms. journal of Daniel R. Dunihue; "Lines Written," Dunihue mss.

29. Since Our Great Chief Tecumtha Has Been Killed

1. James to Amy Witherell, 27 April 1816, B. F. H. Witherell papers. Paukeesaa was eighteen when he received the civil chieftainship, and cannot possibly have commanded the band's confidence. However, an Indian who held that office, and was thereby termed "the Shawnee King," made at least two speeches in 1814. One, at Dundas on 21 November (Canada/IA 29: 17384) warned that the British, like the French before them, were not fulfilling their promises to the Indians, and the other complained about William Caldwell, who had succeeded the late Matthew Elliott as Indian superintendent of Amherstburg (ibid., 29: 17518). This Indian appears to have been Yealabaheah, who had succeeded Paukeesaa by 1816 (Indian speeches to Lewis Cass, 1816, Cass papers [2]). Yealabaheah, who had been with Paukeesaa on the visit to Quebec, evidently left Canada in 1817, taking his family back to the Wabash (George Ironside to William Claus, 24 October 1817, George Ironside papers).

   Tecumseh's younger brother Kumskaukau also slipped back toward the Wabash, but died on his way, at the River Raisin. This occurred "a few years" before 1825 (T. L. McKenney and J. Hall, *Indian Tribes of North America*, 1: 78; Shane). However, Paukeesaa and the Prophet remained in Canada until 1825.

2. Speeches of the Prophet, 20 November 1814 and 8 February 1816, Canada/IA 29: 17381, 18828. This period is treated in J. Sugden, *Tecumseh's Last Stand*, ch. 7, and by R. D. Edmunds (1983).

3. Speech of Naiwash, 6 October 1814, Canada/IA 29: 17250.

4. Edward Nicolls to Alexander Cochrane, 12 August 1814, Alexander Cochrane papers, 2328: 59; "Return of Muscogee or Creek Indians," Britain/WO 1/143: 174.

5. J. Sugden, "Southern Indians in the War of 1812."

6. The other Shawnee recipients were Cuthenwaga, Big Nancy, George Blue-Jacket, Joe Parks, Betsey, and Sally Wilson (return of claims, George Ironside papers). See also speeches of the Prophet and Yealabaheah to Cass, 1816, Lewis Cass papers (2).

7. James to Amy Witherell, 27 April 1816, B. F. H. Witherell papers.

8. Ironside to Claus, 24 May 1820, Ironside letterbook, George Ironside papers.

    James A. Clifton (1984) and Richard White, *Middle Ground*, 520–23, represent the Prophet to have narrated the eleven Shawnee folktales collected by Charles Trowbridge in Detroit (Trowbridge, "Indian Tales") and contend that the stories reflect Tenskwatawa's opinion of Shawnee society and his own role within it. Thus, some of them treat antisocial behavior and the decay of old traditions, and the efforts of individuals, aided by supernatural helpers, to confront them. For example, "Pukeelauwau, Thrown Away," tells how a boy, abandoned by his father and village, develops the skills of hunting with the help of a guardian spirit. Ultimately, he rediscovers his people, survives initial mockery, and achieves chieftainship. This, White speculates, is an allegory of the experiences of Tecumseh and the Prophet. Separated from most of their nation, as they were on the White River, they also returned, aspiring to lead and restore their people through divine assistance.

    Although ingenious, this theory is seriously flawed. First, the identification of Tenskwatawa as the narrator of the tales can be questioned. Certainly, Trowbridge, to whom they were dictated, made no such claim when forwarding them to Lyman Draper in 1874, even though he knew Draper had a special interest in Tecumseh and the Prophet. Rather, he stated the tales came from "one of these old 'story tellers'" he had occasionally met among the Indians (Trowbridge to Draper, 14 March 1874, covering "Indian Tales"). In fact, the very day Trowbridge sent the stories he wrote a separate letter to Draper on the subject of Tecumseh, again without making any connection with the tales (Tecumseh papers, 5YY6). The Prophet could have supplied the material, but Trowbridge had alternative Shawnee informants.

    Second, even supposing the Prophet was the narrator, to sustain the interpretation here being put on them, the stories would have to be original creations of Tenskwatawa, in their basic elements rather than minor matters of detail. However, they might equally have been versions of well-established and popular Shawnee folktales, and not substantially the invention of this particular narrator. Without a body of Shawnee folklore to provide a comparison, the question cannot be settled either way, but Shawnee folktales, reworked to varying extents, seem to have had a considerable longevity. What is evidently a variation of one of Trowbridge's tales, "Motshee Linnee," appears in J. Gregg, *Commerce of the Prairies*, 386–88.

    The suspicion that these tales were not primarily original creations of their narrator, whether he was Tenskwatawa or not, is strengthened by reference to the folklore of other Algonquian tribes. The themes in the Shawnee stories seem to be part of the common stock. As Margaret Fisher, "Mythology," observes, the hero of Algonquian stories is frequently "an anonymous poor boy—orphaned, or otherwise neglected or mistreated—whom the supernatural powers befriend" (p. 233). The Shawnee story of "Pukeelauwau, Thrown Away," then, seems not to have been constructed as an allegory of the Prophet's career, but to have been merely a traditional folktale. The relevance of Trowbridge's "Indian Tales" to the Prophet is certainly plausible in principle, but without further evidence the claim must be approached with caution and an open mind.

9. G. Catlin, *Letters and Notes*, 2: 117–18.

10. Charles Tucker interviewed by Draper, 1868, Draper notes, 23S173; W. P. Ross to Draper, 23 December 1882, Tecumseh papers, 4YY62. From the late nineteenth century it was strongly claimed that Paukeesaa was the father of a well-known Shawnee chief named Big Jim, who died in 1901. Big Jim's descendants have supported the claim but after examining the materials, I am not satisfied that Big Jim was Paukeesaa's son. Some Shawnee genealogist may one day clarify the point.

11. Letter of J. A. Chute, 1837, J. J. Lutz, "Methodist Missions," 164.

12. Shawnees to John Johnston, 27 April 1815, L. U. Hill, *John Johnston*, 85; J. J. Lutz, "Methodist Missions," 165.

13. Shawnee traditions can be sampled in Erminie W. Voegelin papers, especially box 11; W. A. Galloway, *Old Chillicothe*, 162–63; N. W. Schutz, *Shawnee Myth*, 247–49; J. Howard, *Shawnee!*, 214, 216. A fictional recounting, supposedly based on Indian traditions, is Marion Campbell's *The Boyhood of Tecumseh* (1940).

14. Howard, 220–21; Richard C. Adams, *The Adoption of Mew-Seu-Qua, Tecumseh's Father.* . . . (1917); *The Toronto Star*, 21 July 1933.

15. An "Indian" biography of Tecumseh was written by a mixed-blood Cherokee, John M. Oskison. More recent Indian tributes include the pageant, *Tecumseh*, hosted by the Six Nations at the Forest Theatre, near Brantford, Ontario, in 1988; and the establishment of a Great Lakes Native American Center at Prophetstown in 1996.

16. J. Sugden, *Tecumseh's Last Stand*, 5–6, 219–20; letter to J. C. Patterson, 29 September 1893, Canniff papers; A. Falls to Lyman Draper, 7 February 1885, Tecumseh papers, 6YY110. An American vessel, the *Tecumseh*, was sunk in the battle of Mobile Bay in 1864.

17. *The Canadian Review, and Literary and Historical Journal* I (1824): 432. G. Longmore, *Tecumthe, A Poetical Tale, in Three Cantos*, edited by Mary Lu MacDonald (1993) is a definitive edition of the poem.

18. For other Tecumseh items by Richardson see A. H. U. Colquhoun, *Tecumseh and Richardson*, and the New York *Literary World* for 3 May 1851. His work inspired an early British novelette, "Tecumseh, Chief Warrior of the Shawanoes," *Fraser's Magazine for Town and Country* 13 (1836): 499–511. A biography of Richardson has been published by David R. Beasley.

19. Norman Shrive, *Charles Mair, Literary Nationalist* (1965).

20. Lloyd Roberts, *Tecumseh* (Toronto, 1930), 28. More recent Canadian educational biographies include Greg Price, *Tecumseh: Maker of Nations* (1980) and Betty Jane Wylie, *Tecumseh* (1982).

21. Bliss Carman's poem is reprinted in William Rose Benet and Norman Cousins, *Poetry of Freedom* (New York, 1945). It was written in 1918.

22. The other Steuben titles are *Der Rote Sturm* (1931), *Tecumseh der Berglöwe* (1932), *Der Strahlende Stern* (1934), and *Schneller Fuss und Pfeilmädchen* (1935). Michael Friedrichs surveys the whole subject in his forthcoming paper, "Tecumseh's Fabulous Career in German Fiction."

23. *The Hesperian* 1 (1838): 386.

24. John D. Shane scrapbooks, Kentucky papers, 26CC.

25. H. W. Smith, *Virgin Land* (1950), 172.

26. Tecumseh papers, 1YY87.

27. J. C. A. Stagg, *Mr. Madison's War*, 330. R. G. Gunderson, *The Log Cabin Campaign* (1957) deals with Harrison's campaign.

28. G. H. Orions, "Cannons Through the Forest," 218.

29. B. Gilbert, *God Gave Us This Country*, 334–35. For some Tecumseh relics see Canada/IA 1993: file 6828; Tecumseh papers, 7YY47, 131–35, 13YY12; and the Tecumseh file.

30. Modern plays include Claude Dunster, *Tecumseh, A Play* (1965); Allan W. Eckert, *Tecumseh, A Play* (1974); and Mark Dunster, *Tecumseh* (1979). Thom's novel inspired a TV movie, *Tecumseh, the Last Warrior* (1995), produced by Francis Ford Coppola for TNT and starring Jesse Borrego as Tecumseh.

31. L. Cass, "Indians of North America," 98.

Appendix: Family Portraits

1. Johnson to Samuel G. Drake, 25 April 1838, R. M. Johnson letter.
2. B. J. Lossing, *Pictorial Field-Book*, 189, 283. For his final sentence Lossing relied upon B. F. H. Witherell's "Reminiscences," 301–302. Witherell remarked that Captain John Grant once saw Tecumseh and Procter at the head of their troops, the chief attired in the uniform of a brigadier-general with a scarlet coat and cocked hat, but keeping his blue breechcloth, red leggings, and moccasins. A resident of Grosse Point, George Moran, recalled Tecumseh in his common buckskin suit, with fringe at the seams and shoulders. About his head he had tied a red and blue handkerchief "in the neat and peculiar manner of the Hurons or Wyandotts." Both descriptions influenced Lossing when he bowdlerized the Le Dru drawing.
3. G. I. Quimby, "Discovered." Among the accession records of the Field Museum of Natural History see especially Emily O'Fallon to Mrs. Grant, 4 December 1893, and O'Fallon to Harlow N. Higinbotham, 26 January 1894. I examined the portrait in 1989.
4. T. L. McKenney and J. Hall, *Indian Tribes of North America*, 1: xlvi–liii, lvi–lvii. Henry Inman made copies of 108 of the 147 War Department portraits, but these do not include the likeness of "Pah-gue-sah-ah, Son of Tecumseh."
5. The original has disappeared, but a Lehman and Duval lithograph was published in 1836, and a copy of the painting was made by Charles Bird King (J. O. Lewis, *Aboriginal Port Folio*, no. 9; H. J. Viola, *Indian Legacy*, 55, 58; A. J. Cosentino, *Charles Bird King*, 57, 59–60, 73, 183).
6. A copy by Inman survives in the Peabody Museum, Harvard University, and a lithograph was published by McKenney and Hall, facing page 1: 88. See ibid., 1: xlvi–liii, lv–lvi, 98.
7. R. David Edmunds, *Shawnee Prophet*, 230, n. 5.
8. National Archives of Canada, *A Place in History*, 40–43.

BIBLIOGRAPHY

A: Manuscript Sources

Accession records. Field Museum, Chicago.

Additional manuscripts. Mss. 38259, 38346, 38362–63, 38365, 38577. The British Library, London.

Alder, Jonathan. Narrative. OHS.

Allen County folder. Indiana State Library, Indianapolis.

Armstrong, John. Papers. IHS.

Askin, Charles. Papers. BHC.

Askin, John. Papers. BHC.

Atkins, Quintus F. Diary. Western Reserve Historical Society, Cleveland, Ohio.

Ayer, Edward E. Manuscripts. The Newberry Library, Chicago.

Bishop, Levi. Papers. BHC.

Bond, Lewis. Narrative. Library of Congress, Washington, D.C.

Boone, Daniel. Papers (C). SHSW/D.

Boyd, John Parker, Papers. Eli Lilly Library, Bloomington, Indiana.

Britain/Admiralty papers. North American Station, Adm. 1/vols. 503–508. Public Record Office, Kew.

Britain/Colonial Office Papers [Britain/CO], cited by class, volume, and page. CO 23/vols. 58–61 (Bahamas); CO 42/45–83 (Quebec); CO 42/89–162 (Lower Canada); CO 42/316–56 (Upper Canada); CO 42/16–22 (Canada Miscellaneous); CO 5 (Indian Trade); CO 43/23 (Earl Bathurst). Public Record Office, Kew.

Britain/Foreign Office Papers [Britain/FO], cited by class, volume, and page. FO 5/vols. 127, 139. Public Record Office, Kew.

Britain/War Office Papers [Britain/WO], cited by class, volume, and page. WO 1/vol. 96 (In-letters); WO 1/143–44 (South); WO 17/151[3] (monthly returns); WO 27/112[1] (inspections); WO 71/243 (Procter court-martial). Public Record Office, Kew.

Brown, Henry. Papers. Cincinnati Historical Society, Ohio.

Bruce, William. Reminiscences. Indiana State Library, Indianapolis.

Buell, Joseph. Diary. Marietta College Collection. OHS.

Burton, Clarence Monroe. Papers. BHC.

Butler, Richard. Journal. Durrett Miscellaneous Manuscripts. University of Chicago.

Caldwell, Billy. Papers. Chicago Historical Society.

Canada Papers. Chicago Historical Society.

Canada/C Military Papers, Record Group 8 [Canada/C], cited by volume and page. Vols. 246–58, 673–87, 911–14 (microfilms C/2848–53, 3171–74, 3231, 3278). National Archives of Canada, Ottawa.

Canada/Indian Affairs Papers, Record Group 10 [Canada/IA], cited by volume and page. Vols. 1–12, 26–30, 1993 (microfilms C/10996–11000, 11007–11008, 11130), and vols. 486–87. National Archives of Canada, Ottawa.

Canada/National Map Collection. National Archives of Canada, Ottawa.

Canniff Papers. Archives of Ontario, Toronto.

Cass, Lewis. Letter, 1821. State Historical Society of Wisconsin, Madison.

Cass, Lewis. Papers (1). BHC.

Cass, Lewis. Papers (2). William L. Clements Library, Ann Arbor, Michigan.

Catlin, George B. Papers. BHC.

Clark, George Rogers. Papers (J). SHSW/D.

Claus, William. Papers (MG19/f1), cited by volume and page. Vols. 1–17 (microfilms C/1478–1482). National Archives of Canada, Ottawa.

Clay, Green. Papers. BHC.

Cochran, James. The War in Canada, 1812–15. Welch Regiment Museum, Cardiff, Wales.

Cochran, James. Annotations to his copy of J. Richardson, *War of 1812* (1842), cited by book page number. Welch Regiment Museum, Cardiff, Wales.

Cochrane, Alexander. Papers, cited by volume and page. National Library of Scotland, Edinburgh.

Crockett, William M. Account. Indiana State Library, Indianapolis.

Dale, George Carter. Narrative. State Historical Society of Wisconsin, Madison.

Dearborn, Henry. Papers. Chicago Historical Society.

Denny, James. Papers. OHS.

Draper, Lyman C. Notes (S) SHSW/D.

Drake, Benjamin. Letter to, 1821. State Historical Society of Wisconsin, Madison.

Drake, Daniel. Papers (0). SHSW/D.

Dunihue Manuscripts. Eli Lilly Library, Bloomington, Indiana.

Dunihue, Daniel R. Journal. Indiana State Library, Indianapolis.

Dunn, Jacob P. Papers. Indiana State Library, Indianapolis.

Durrett Miscellaneous Manuscripts, University of Chicago.

Edwards, Ninian. Papers. Chicago Historical Society.

English, William H. Papers. IHS.

Farney, A. B. Papers. Fort Malden National Historic Site, Amherstburg, Ontario.

Forsyth, Thomas. Letter, 1812. Chicago Historical Society.

Forsyth, Thomas. Papers (1) [T]. SHSW/D.

Forsyth, Thomas. Papers (2). Missouri Historical Society, St. Louis.

Frontier Wars Papers (U). SHSW/D.

Godfroy, Gabriel. Papers. BHC.

Gowman, Thomas. Pioneer Life in Upper Canada. Archives of Ontario, Toronto.

Grant, Jasper. Papers. Ms. 10178 of Ussher Papers. National Library of Ireland, Dublin.

Haldimand, Frederick. Papers. Add. Mss. 21760–63, 21765–72, 21775, 21782–83, 21842, 21845, 21876. British Library, London.

Hamilton, James. Papers. Historical Society of Pennsylvania, Philadelphia.

Hardin, Martin D. Papers. Chicago Historical Society.

Harmar, Josiah. Papers (1). William L. Clements Library, Ann Arbor, Michigan.

Harmar, Josiah. Papers (2) [W]. SHSW/D.

Harrington, M. R. Shawnee Indian Notes. The Newberry Library, Chicago.

Harrison, William Henry. Papers (1). IHS.

Harrison, William Henry. Papers (2). Library of Congress, Washington, D.C.

Harrison, William Henry. Papers (3). Chicago Historical Society.

Harrison, William Henry. Papers (4) [X]. SHSW/D.

Harrison, William Henry. Papers (5). BHC.

Harrison, William Henry. Papers (6). Cincinnati Historical Society, Ohio.

Hatch, William S. Papers. Cincinnati Historical Society, Ohio.

Heckewelder, John. Papers. American Philosophical Society, Philadelphia.

Heth, Harvey, to J. H. Larwell, 1812. IHS.

Hinde, Thomas Spottswood. Papers (Y). SHSW/D.

Horsfield, Timothy. Letters. American Philosophical Society, Philadelphia.

Hull, William. Papers. BHC.

Indian Languages. Related papers. American Philosophical Society, Philadelphia.

Indiana Territory Collection. IHS.

Indians Collection. Missouri Historical Society, St. Louis.

Invoices for Indian Goods, 1810. IHS.

Ironside, George. Papers. BHC.

Johnson, Richard Mentor. Letter, 1838. IHS.

Johnston, John. Papers (1). OHS.

Johnston, John. Papers (2). Cincinnati Historical Society, Ohio.

Jones, Frank J. Papers. Cincinnati Historical Society, Ohio.

Jones, Nehemiah. Papers. BHC.

Jordan, Walter K. Letters. Indiana State Library, Indianapolis.

Keen, Greenbury. Diary. OHS.

Kenton, Simon. Papers (BB). SHSW/D.

Kentucky Papers (CC). SHSW/D.

Kickapoo File. Great Lakes–Ohio Valley Ethnohistory Archive, Glenn A. Black Laboratory, University of Indiana, Bloomington.

Kingsbury, Jacob. Letterbooks. BHC.

Kirker, Thomas. Papers. OHS.

Lacey, Mary Ruth. Papers. BHC.

Larwill Family papers. OHS.

Lasselle papers. Indiana State Library, Indianapolis.

Logan, James. Letterbooks. American Philosophical Society, Philadelphia.

Lorimier, Louis. Miscellaneous papers. Missouri Historical Society, St. Louis.

Lossing, Benson J. Papers. BHC.

Love, James Young. Papers. Filson Club. Louisville, Kentucky.

Lyon, Lucius. Papers. William L. Clements Library, Ann Arbor, Michigan.

McAfee, Robert B. Papers. Filson Club, Louisville, Kentucky.

McArthur, Duncan. Papers (1). Library of Congress, Washington, D.C.

McArthur, Duncan. Papers (2). OHS.

McArthur, Duncan. Papers (3). BHC.

McClung Historical Collection. Lawson McGhee Library, Knoxville, Tennessee.

McCoy, John. Letter, 1811. Indiana State Library, Indianapolis.

McDonell, John. Papers. BHC.

McKee, Alexander. Papers. National Archives of the United States, Washington, D.C.

McPherson, James. Petition, 1834. U.S. History manuscripts, Eli Lilly Library, Bloomington, Indiana.

McWhorter, Lucullus V. Papers. Washington State University, Pullman, Washington.

Marietta College Collection. OHS.

Meigs, Return Jonathan. Papers (1). OHS.

Meigs, Return Jonathan. Papers (2). Eli Lilly Library, Bloomington, Indiana.

Miller, James. Papers. OHS.

Mitten, Arthur. Collection. IHS.

Morgan, George. Papers. Carnegie Library of Pittsburgh, Pennsylvania.

Morgan, George. Letterbook. Pennsylvania State Archives, Harrisburg.

Naylor, Isaac. Reminiscences. Indiana State Library, Indianapolis.

Nelson, George. Papers. Metropolitan Public Library of Toronto, Ontario.

Newsom, Nathan. Diary. OHS.

Northwest Territory Collection (1). OHS.

Northwest Territory Collection (2). IHS.

Ottawa File. Great Lakes–Ohio Valley Ethnohistory Archive, Glenn A. Black Laboratory, University of Indiana, Bloomington.

Parker, Daniel. Papers. Historical Society of Pennsylvania, Philadelphia.

Patterson, Robert. Papers. American Philosophical Society, Philadelphia.

Peckham, Lewis. Letter, 1812. IHS.

Photographs. Royal Anthropological Institute, London.

Pickett, Albert J. Papers. State of Alabama Department of Archives and History, Montgomery.

Polke, William. Papers. Eli Lilly Library, Bloomington, Indiana.

Porter, Albert Gallatin. Papers. IHS.

Porter, Augustus Seymour. Papers. BHC.

Prince, William. Folder. IHS.

Procter, Henry. Papers. National Archives of the United States, Washington, D.C.

Robison, John. Diary. OHS.

St. Clair, Arthur. Papers. OHS.

Sargent, Winthrop. Papers. OHS.

Shabbona papers. Chicago Historical Society.

Shawnee File. Great Lakes–Ohio Valley Ethnohistory Archive, Glenn A. Black Laboratory, University of Indiana, Bloomington.

Shelby, Isaac. Papers. Library of Congress, Washington, D.C.

Schoolcraft, Henry Rowe. Papers. BHC.

Society of Friends. Minutes of meetings. OHS.

Spain/Papeles Procedentes de Cuba, legajo 25A, 25B, 39, 177, 1794, 1795, 1856. Archivo General de Indias, Seville, Spain.

Stickney, Benjamin F. Letter, 1816. IHS.

Swearingen, Henry. Letter, 1811. IHS.

Tardiveau, Barthelemi. Papers. Chicago Historical Society.

Taylor, James. Papers. BHC.

Taylor, Zachary. Letter, 1812. IHS.

Tecumseh File. Fort Malden National Historic Site, Amherstburg, Ontario.

Tecumseh papers (YY). SHSW/D.

Tennessee papers (XX). SHSW/D.

Thames, Battle of. File. Fort Malden National Historic Site, Amherstburg, Ontario.

Tiffin, Edward. Papers. OHS.

Tippecanoe County folder. Indiana State Library, Indianapolis.

Todd, Robert. Papers. Eli Lilly Library, Bloomington, Indiana.

Trowbridge, Charles C. Indian Tales. State Historical Society of Wisconsin, Madison.

Tupper, Ferdinand Brock. Papers. Archives of Ontario, Toronto.

United States. Record Group 107. Secretary of War/Letters Received/Registered series [U.S. SoW/LR/R], microfilm M 221, cited by reel and frame. National Archives, Washington, D.C.

United States. Record Group 107. Secretary of War/Letters Received/Unregistered series [U.S. SoW/LR/U], microfilm M 222, cited by reel and frame. National Archives, Washington, D.C.

United States. Record Group 75. Secretary of War/Letters Received/Indian Affairs [U.S. SoW/LR/IA], microfilm M 271, cited by frame. National Archives, Washington, D.C.

United States. Record Group 75. Secretary of War/Letters Sent/Indian Affairs [U.S. SoW/LS/IA], microfilm M 15. National Archives, Washington, D.C.

United States. Muster rolls and payrolls of militia and regular organizations in the battle of Tippecanoe, November 1811. Microfilm T 1085. National Archives, Washington, D.C.

United States Army papers. OHS.

Unites States Infantry. Fourth Regiment. Orderly and letterbook, 1811. IHS.

Voegelin, Erminie Wheeler. Papers. The Newberry Library, Chicago.

War of 1812 manuscripts. Eli Lilly Library, Bloomington, Indiana.

Wayne, Anthony. Papers (1). Historical Society of Pennsylvania, Philadelphia.

Wayne, Anthony. Papers (2). Chicago Historical Society.

Wells, William. Papers. Chicago Historical Society.

Wilkinson, James. Papers. Chicago Historical Society.

Williams, John R. Papers. BHC.

Williams, Samuel. Papers (1). OHS.

Williams, Samuel. Papers (2). Eli Lilly Library, Bloomington, Indiana.

Winchester, James. Papers. BHC.

Winchester, James. Dispatch book. Eli Lilly Library, Bloomington, Indiana.

Winter, George. On The Prophet. Tippecanoe County Historical Society, Lafayette, Indiana.

Witherell, B. F. H. Papers. BHC.

Woodbridge, William. Papers. BHC.

Woodward, Augustus B. Papers. BHC.

Worthington, Thomas. Papers. OHS.

Yeates, Jasper. Papers. Historical Society of Pennsylvania, Philadelphia.

B: Principal Newspapers

The Carlisle Gazette
The Fredonian (Chillicothe)
The General Advertiser (Philadelphia)
The Kentucky Gazette (Lexington)
The Kentucky Reporter(Lexington)
The Kingston Gazette
The Knoxville Gazette
Liberty Hall (Cincinnati)
The Missouri Gazette (St. Louis)
The National Intelligencer (Washington, D.C.)
The Quebec Gazette
The Republican and Savannah Ledger
The Scioto Gazette (Chillicothe)
The Upper Canada Gazette (York)
The Weekly Register (Baltimore)
The Western Spy (Cincinnati)
The Western Sun (Vincennes)

C: Select Published Sources

Abernethy, Thomas Perkins. *Western Lands and the American Revolution*. 1937; reprinted New York, 1959.

Adams, Henry. *History of the United States of America*. 9 vols. New York, 1891–1896.

Akers, Frank Herman. *The Unexpected Challenge: The Creek War of 1813–1814*. Ph.D. diss., Duke University, 1975.

Alford, Thomas Wildcat. *Civilization*. Norman, Oklahoma, 1936.

Allen, Robert S. *His Majesty's Indian Allies*. Toronto, 1992.

American National Biography. Cary, North Carolina, forthcoming.

The American Pioneer. 2 vols. Cincinnati, 1842–1843.

American State Papers, Indian Affairs. 2 vols. Washington, D.C., 1832–1834.

Andrews, Edward Deming, ed. "The Shaker Mission to the Shawnee Indians." *Winterthur Portfolio* 7 (1972): 113–28.

Anson, Bert. *The Miami Indians*. Norman, Oklahoma, 1970.

Antrim, Joshua. *The History of Champaign and Logan Counties*. Bellefontaine, Ohio, 1872.

Atcheson, Nathaniel. "A Compressed View of the Points to be Discussed in Treaty with the United States of America. . . ." *The Pamphleteer* 5 (1815): 105–39.

Atwater, Caleb. *Remarks Made on a Tour to Prairie du Chien. . . .* Columbus, Ohio, 1831.

Atwater, Caleb. *A History of the State of Ohio*. Cincinnati, 1838.

Auchinleck, Gilbert. *A History of the War Between Great Britain and the United States. . . .* Toronto, 1855.

Badger, Joseph. *A Memoir of Rev. Joseph Badger*. Hudson, Ohio, 1851.

Bakeless, John. *Daniel Boone, Master of the Wilderness*. New York, 1939.

Bakeless, John. *Background to Glory*. Philadelphia, 1957.

Barber, Douglas. "Council Government and the Genesis of the Creek War." *The Alabama Review* 38 (1985): 163–74.

Barce, Elmore. *The Land of the Miamis*. Fowler, Indiana, 1922.

Bassett, John S., ed. *Correspondence of Andrew Jackson*. 7 vols. Washington, D.C., 1926–1935.

Beall, William K. "Journal of William K. Beall, July–August 1812." *American Historical Review* 17 (1911–12): 783–808.

Beard, Reed. *The Battle of Tippecanoe*. Chicago, 1889.

Beasley, David R. *The Canadian Quixote*. Erin, Ontario, 1977.

Beckwith, Hiram W., ed. "The Fort Wayne Manuscript." *Fergus Historical Series* 26 (1883): 63–95.

Berthrong, Donald J. *Indians of Northern Indiana and Southwestern Michigan*. New York, 1974.

Bickley, Francis, ed. *Report on the Manuscripts of Earl Bathurst*. London, 1923.

Biddle, James W. "Recollections of Green Bay in 1816–17." *Collections of the State Historical Society of Wisconsin . . . 1854* 1 (1855): 49–63.

"Biographical Notices and Correspondence—War of 1812." *Western Reserve and Northern Ohio Historical Society Tracts* 19 (1873): 1–4.

Black Hawk: *Life of Black Hawk*. 1834; reprinted New York, 1994.

Blair, Emma Helen, ed. *The Indian Tribes of the Upper Mississippi Valley and Region of the Great Lakes*. 2 vols. Cleveland, Ohio, 1911.

Blair, Samuel. "Narrative." *The South-Western Monthly* 2 (1852): 140.

Bond, Beverley W. *The Civilization of the Old Northwest*. New York, 1934.

Bourne, Alexander. "The Siege of Fort Meigs, Year 1813." *Northwest Ohio Quarterly* 17 (1945): 139–54, and 18 (1946): 39–48.

Bradbury, John. *Travels in the Interior of America. . . .* 1819; reprinted Cleveland, Ohio, 1904.

Brannan, John, ed. *Official Letters of the Military and Naval Officers of the United States During the War with Great Britain. . . .* Washington D.C., 1823.

Brice, Wallace A. *History of Fort Wayne*. Fort Wayne, Indiana, 1868.

Brown, John P. *Old Frontiers*. 1938; reprinted New York, 1971.

Brown, Joseph. "Sketch of the Captivity of Colonel Joseph Brown. . . ." *The South-Western Monthly* 1 (1852) 10–16, 72–78.

Brown, Samuel R. *Views of the Campaigns of the North-Western Army* Philadelphia, 1814.

Brown, Samuel R. *An Authentick History of the Second War for Independence*. 2 vols. Auburn, New York, 1815.

Brymner, Douglas, ed. *Public Archives of Canada Report for 1896*. Ottawa, 1917.

Buell, John Hutchinson. "A Fragment from the Diary of Major John Hutchinson Buell. U.S.A." *The Journal of the Military Service Institution of the United States* 40 (1907): 102–13, 260–68.

Burnet, Jacob. *Notes on the Early Settlement of the North-Western Territory*. Cincinnati, 1847.

Burt, A. L. *The United States, Great Britain, and British North America*. 1940; reprinted New York, 1961.

Butterfield, Consul W. *History of the Girtys*. Cincinnati, 1890.

Byfield, Shadrach. "A Narrative of a Light Company Soldier's Service in the 41st Regiment of Foot. . . ." *The Magazine of History with Notes and Queries* 11 (1910): 57–96.

Calloway, Colin G. *Crown and Calumet*. Norman, Oklahoma, 1987.

Calloway, Colin G. *The American Revolution in Indian Country*. New York, 1995.

"Campaigns in the Canadas." *Quarterly Review* 27 (1822): 405–49.

Carlson, Richard G., ed. "George P. Peters' Version of the Battle of Tippecanoe (November 7, 1811)." *Vermont History* 45 (1977): 38–43.

Carr, John. "Early History of the Southwest—Narrative of John Carr." *The South-Western Monthly* 2 (1852): 73–80, 197–200.

Carter, Clarence E., and John Porter Bloom, eds. *The Territorial Papers of the United States*. 28 vols. Washington, D.C., 1934–1975.

Cass, Lewis. "Indians of North America." *North American Review* 22 (1826): 53–119.

Cass, Lewis. "Policy and Practise of the United States and Great Britain in Their Treatment of Indians." *North American Review* 24 (1827): 365–442.

Catlin, George. *Letters and Notes on the Manners, Customs, and Condition of the North American Indians*. 2 vols. London, 1841.

Caughey, John W., ed. *McGillivray of the Creeks*. Norman, Oklahoma, 1938.

Chalou, George Clifford. *The Red Pawns Go to War*. Ph.D. diss., Indiana University, 1971.

Christian, Thomas. "Campaign of 1813 on the Ohio Frontier," *Western Reserve and Northern Ohio Historical Society* 23 (1874): 4–7.

Cist, Charles, ed. *The Cincinnati Miscellany*. 2 vols. Cincinnati, 1845–1846.

Claiborne, J. F. H. *Mississippi*. 1880; reprinted Baton Rouge, 1964.

Clanin, Douglas E., ed. *The Papers of William Henry Harrison, 1800–1815*. Indianapolis, 1994 in progress.

Clark, Jerry Eugene. *Shawnee Indian Migration*. Ph.D. diss., University of Kentucky, 1977.

Clarke, James Freeman. *History of the Campaign of 1812 and Surrender of the Post of Detroit*. New York, 1848.

Clarke, Peter Dooyentate. *Origin and Traditional History of the Wyandotts*. Toronto, 1870.

Cleaves, Freeman. *Old Tippecanoe*. New York, 1939.

Clift, G. Glenn, ed. "War of 1812 Diary of William B. Northcutt." *Register of the Kentucky Historical Society* 56 (1958): 165–80, 253–69, 325–43.

Clift, G. Glenn. *Remember the Raisin!* Frankfort, Kentucky, 1961.

Clifton, James A. *The Prairie People*. Lawrence, Kansas, 1977.

Clifton, James A. *Star Woman and Other Shawnee Tales*. New York, 1984.

Coates, B. H., ed. "A Narrative of an Embassy to the Western Tribes. . . ." *Memoirs of the Historical Society of Pennsylvania* 2 (1827): 61–131.

Coffin, William F. *1812; The War, and the Moral.* Montreal, 1864.

Coles, Harry L. *The War of 1812.* Chicago, 1965.

Colquhoun, A. H. U., ed. *Tecumseh and Richardson.* Toronto, 1924.

Cook, Darius B. *Six Months Among Indians, Wolves, and Other Wild Animals.* Niles, Michigan, 1889.

"Copies of Papers on File in the Dominion Archives at Ottawa . . . Pertaining to . . . the Period of the War of 1812." *MPHC*, vols. 15 (1890) and 16 (1892).

Corbitt, D. C. and Roberta Corbitt, eds. "Papers from the Spanish Archives Relating to Tennessee and the Old Southwest." *East Tennessee Historical Society Publications*, vols. 22 (1950), 23 (1951), 27 (1955), and 28 (1956).

Corkran, David H. *The Creek Frontier, 1540–1783.* Norman, Oklahoma, 1967.

Cotterill, Robert S. *The Southern Indians.* Norman, Oklahoma, 1954.

Coyne, James H. ed. *The Talbot Papers.* Ottawa, 1908.

Cranbrook Institute of Science Newsletter 13 (1943): 6–7.

Crawford, Mary M., ed. "Mrs. Lydia B. Bacon's Journal, 1811–1812." *Indiana Magazine of History* 40 (1944): 367–86, and 41 (1945): 59–79.

Cresswell, Nicholas. *The Journal of Nicholas Cresswell.* London, 1925.

Cruikshank, Ernest A. "The *Chesapeake* Crisis as It Affected Upper Canada," *Ontario Historical Society Papers and Records* 24 (1927): 281–322.

Cruikshank, Ernest A., ed. "Contemporary Narratives by Captain W. H. Merritt. . . ." *Niagara Historical Society* 9 (1902).

Cruikshank, Ernest A., ed. *Documents Relating to the Invasion of Canada and the Surrender of Detroit, 1812.* 1912; reprinted New York, 1971.

Cruikshank, Ernest A., ed. *The Correspondence of Lieutenant-Governor John Graves Simcoe.* 5 vols. Toronto, 1923–1931.

Cruikshank, Ernest A. and A. F. Hunter, eds. *The Correspondence of the Honourable Peter Russell.* 3 vols. Toronto, 1932–1936.

Cullum, George W., ed. *Campaigns of the War of 1812–15 Against Great Britain.* New York, 1879.

Curry, Otway. "The Doomed Wyandott." *The Hesperian* 1 (1878): 43–46.

Dalliba, James. *A Narrative of the Battle of Brownstown.* New York, 1816.

Darnell, Elias. *A Journal . . . of the Hardships . . . of those Heroic Kentucky Volunteers and Regulars, Commanded by General Winchester. . . .* Paris, Kentucky, 1813.

Davies, Kenneth G. ed. *Documents of the American Revolution.* 19 vols. Shannon, Ireland, 1972–1978.

Davis, John. "Narrative of John Davis." *The South-Western Monthly* 1 (1852): 211–14.

Dawson, Moses. *Historical Narrative of the Civil and Military Services of Major-General William Henry Harrison.* Cincinnati, 1824.

Deardorff, Merle H. "The Religion of Handsome Lake," In *Symposium on Local Diversity in Iroquois Culture*, edited by W. N. Fenton, 77–107. Washington, D.C., 1951.

Denny, Ebenezer. *Military Journal of Major Ebenezer Denny.* Philadelphia, 1859.

Dictionary of Canadian Biography. Toronto, Vol. 3, 1974 to Vol. 7, 1988.

Dillon, John B. *History of Indiana.* Indianapolis, 1859.

"Documents Relating to Detroit and Vicinity, 1805–1813." *MPHC* 40 (1929): passim.

Dowd, Gregory Evans. *Paths of Resistance.* Ph.D. diss., Princeton University, 1986.

Dowd, Gregory Evans. *A Spirited Resistance: The North American Indian Struggle for Unity, 1745–1815.* Baltimore, 1992.

Dowd, James. *Built Like a Bear.* Fairfield, Washington, 1979.

Downes, Randolph C. *Council Fires on the Upper Ohio.* Pittsburgh, 1940.

Drake, Benjamin. *Life of Tecumseh, and of His Brother The Prophet*. 1841; reprinted New York, 1969.

Drake, Samuel G. *The Aboriginal Races of North America*. 1832; reprinted New York, 1880.

Drinnon, Richard. *White Savage: The Case of John Dunn Hunter*. New York, 1972.

Duffy, Dennis. "The Fate of Tecumseh." *The Beaver* 73 (1993): 20–23.

Edgar, Matilda. *General Brock*. Toronto, 1905.

Edgar, Matilda, ed. *Ten Years of Upper Canada in Peace and War*. Toronto, 1890.

Edmunds, R. David. *The Potawatomis*. Norman, Oklahoma, 1978.

Edmunds, R. David. *The Shawnee Prophet*. Lincoln, Nebraska, 1983.

Edmunds, R. David. *Tecumseh and the Quest for Indian Leadership*. Boston, 1984.

Edmunds, R. David. "Main Poc: Potawatomi Wabeno." *American Indian Quarterly* 9 (1985): 259–72.

Egglestone, Edward, and Lillie Egglestone Seelye. *The Shawnee Prophet; or, the Story of Tecumseh*. 1879; reprinted London, n.d.

Ellet, Elizabeth F. *The Women of the American Revolution*. 3 vols. New York, 1850.

Ellet, Elizabeth F. *Pioneer Women of the West*. New York, 1852.

Engelman, Fred L. *The Peace of Christmas Eve*. London, 1962.

Esarey, Logan, ed. *Messages and Letters of William Henry Harrison*. 2 vols. Indianapolis, 1922.

Evans, E. Raymond. "Dragging Canoe." *Journal of Cherokee Studies* 2 (1977): 176–89.

"Extract from Reminiscences of a Western Traveller." *Southern Literary Messenger*, March 1835, 336–40.

Fairchild, G. M., ed. *Journal of an American Prisoner at Fort Malden and Quebec in the War of 1812*. Quebec, 1909.

Faragher, John Mark. *Daniel Boone*. New York, 1992.

Ferguson, Roger James. *The White River Indiana Delawares*. Ph.D. diss., Ball State University, 1972.

Filson, John. *The Discovery, Settlement, and Present State of Kentucke*. 1784; reprinted New York, 1962.

Finley, James B. *Life Among the Indians*. Cincinnati, 1868.

Fisher, Margaret W. "The Mythology of the Northern and Northeastern Algonkians in Reference to Algonkian Mythology as a Whole." In *Man in Northeastern North America*, edited by F. Johnson, 226–62. 1946; reprinted New York, 1980.

Flick, A. C., et al., eds. *The Papers of Sir William Johnson*. 13 vols. Albany, New York, 1921–1962.

Fliegel, Carl J., ed. *Index to the Records of the Moravian Missions Among the Indians of North America*. New Haven, 1970.

Flint, Timothy. *The First White Man of the West*. 1847; reprinted Cincinnati, 1851.

Forbes, James G. *Report of the Trial of Brig. General William Hull*. New York, 1814.

Forbes, James G. *Sketches, Historical and Topographical, of the Floridas*. New York, 1821.

Foreman, Grant. *The Last Trek of the Indians*. Chicago, 1946.

Fredriksen, John C. *Free Trade and Sailors' Rights*. Westport, Connecticut, 1985.

Fredriksen, John C. ed. "Kentucky at the Thames, 1813." *Register of the Kentucky State Historical Society* 83 (1985): 93–107.

Friedrichs, Michael. "Tecumseh's Fabulous Career in German Fiction" (forthcoming).

Galbreath, C. B. "Tecumseh and His Descendants." *Ohio Archaeological and Historical Society Publications* 34 (1925): 143–53.

Galloway, William A. *Old Chillicothe*. Xenia, Ohio, 1934.

Gatschet, A. S. "Tecumseh's Name." *The American Anthropologist* 8 (1895): 91–92.

Gibson, Arrell M. *The Kickapoos*. Norman, Oklahoma, 1963.

Gifford, Jack Jule. *The Northwest Indian War, 1784–1795*. Ph.D. diss., University of California, 1964.

Gilbert, Bil. *God Gave Us This Country: Tekamthi and the First American Civil War*. New York, 1989.

Gilpin, Alec R. *The War of 1812 in the Old Northwest*. East Lansing, Michigan, 1958.

Gipson, Lawrence Henry, ed. *The Moravian Indian Mission on White River*. Indianapolis, 1938.

Goebel, Dorothy Burne. *William Henry Harrison*. Indianapolis, 1926.

Goltz, Herbert C. W. *Tecumseh: The Man and the Myth*. M.A. diss., University of Wisconsin–Milwaukee, 1966.

Goltz, Herbert C. W. *Tecumseh, The Prophet, and the Rise of the Northwestern Indian Confederacy*. Ph.D. diss., University of Western Ontario, 1973.

Goodpasture, Albert V. "Indian Wars and Warriors of the Old Southwest, 1730–1807." *Tennessee Historical Magazine* 4 (1918): 3–49, 106–45, 155–56, 161–210, 252–89.

Grant, C. L., ed. *Letters, Journals, and Writings of Benjamin Hawkins*. 2 vols. Savannah, Georgia, 1980.

Green, James A. *William Henry Harrison*. Richmond, Virginia, 1941.

Green, James A., ed. "Journal of Ensign William Schillinger, a Soldier of the War of 1812." *Ohio Archaeological and Historical Publications* 41 (1932): 51–85.

Gregg, Josiah: *Commerce of the Prairies*. 1844; reprinted Norman, Oklahoma, 1954.

Griffith, Benjamin W. *McIntosh and Weatherford, Creek Indian Leaders*. Tuscaloosa, Alabama, 1988.

Grignon, Augustin. "Seventy-two Years' Recollections of Wisconsin." *Collections of the State Historical Society of Wisconsin 1856* 3 (1857): 195–295.

Gurd, Norman St. Clair. *The Story of Tecumseh*. Toronto, 1912.

Hagan, William T. *The Sac and Fox Indians*. Norman, Oklahoma, 1958.

Halbert, Henry S. "Some Inaccuracies in Claiborne's History in Regard to Tecumseh." *Publications of the Mississippi Historical Society* 1 (1898): 101–103.

Halbert, Henry S., and Timothy H. Ball. *The Creek War of 1813 and 1814*. 1895; reprinted University, Alabama, 1969.

Hall, General. "Indian Battles and Murders." *The South-Western Monthly* 1 (1852): 331–36, and 2 (1852): 11–16.

Hamer, Philip M., ed. "The British in Canada and the Southern Indians." *East Tennessee Historical Society Publications* 2 (1930): 107–34.

Handley, Samuel. "Narrative." *American Historical Magazine* 2 (1897): 86–90.

Hanna, Charles A. *The Wilderness Trail*. 2 vols. New York, 1911.

Harvey, Henry. *History of the Shawnee Indians*. Cincinnati, 1855.

Hassig, Ross. "Internal Conflict in the Creek War of 1813–1814." *Ethnohistory* 21 (1974): 251–71.

Hatch, William S. *A Chapter in the History of the War of 1812 in the Northwest*. Cincinnati, 1872.

Hatheway, G. G. *The Neutral Indian Barrier State*. Ph.D. diss., University of Minnesota, 1957.

Haywood, John. *The Civil and Political History of the State of Tennessee*. Knoxville, 1823.

Hazard, Samuel, ed. *Minutes of the Provincial Council of Pennsylvania*. 10 vols. Harrisburg, 1851–1852.

Hazard, Samuel, et al., eds. *Pennsylvania Archives*. 138 vols. Philadelphia and Harrisburg, 1852–1949.

Heath, Herschel. *The Indians as a Factor in the War of 1812*. Ph.D. diss., Clark University, 1926.

Heckewelder, John. *History, Manners, and Customs of the Indian Nations. . . .* 1819; reprinted New York, 1971.

Heckewelder, John. *A Narrative of the Mission of the United Brethren. . . .* 1820; reprinted Cleveland, Ohio, 1907.

Hedges, John P. "Early Recollections." *Indiana Magazine of History* 8 (1912): 171–73.

Henri, Florette. *The Southern Indians and Benjamin Hawkins, 1796–1816*. Norman, Oklahoma, 1986.

Hibbert, Wilfrid. "The Recently Discovered Pictorial Map of Fort Meigs and Environs." *Bulletin of the Historical Society of Northwestern Ohio*, bulletin 4, vol. 6 (1934).

Hill, Leonard U. *John Johnston and the Indians in the Land of the Three Miamis*. Piqua, Ohio, 1957.

History of Clark County, Ohio. Chicago, 1881.

History of Logan County and Ohio. Chicago, 1880.

History of Madison County, Ohio. Chicago, 1883.

Hopkins, T. M. *Reminiscences of Colonel John Ketcham*. Bloomington, Indiana, 1860.

Horsman, Reginald. *Matthew Elliott, British Indian Agent*. Detroit, 1964.

Horsman, Reginald. *Expansion and American Indian Policy, 1783–1812*. East Lansing, Michigan, 1967.

Horsman, Reginald. *The War of 1812*. London, 1969.

Horsman, Reginald. *The Frontier in the Formative Years, 1783–1815*. New York, 1971.

Hosmer, H. L. *Early History of the Maumee Valley*. Toledo, Ohio, 1858.

Houck, Louis, ed. *The Spanish Regime in Missouri*. 2 vols. Chicago, 1909.

Howard, James. *Shawnee! The Ceremonialism of a Native Indian Tribe and Its Cultural Background*. Athens, Ohio, 1981.

Howe, Henry, ed. *Historical Collections of Ohio*. 2 vols. 1847; reprinted Cincinnati, 1902.

Hull, William. *Memoirs of the Campaign of the North Western Army of the United States, A.D. 1812*. Boston, 1824.

Hunter, Charles. "The Delaware Nativist Revival of the Mid-Eighteenth Century." *Ethnohistory* 18 (1971): 39–49.

Hunter, John Dunn. *Memoirs of a Captivity Among the Indians of North America*. London, 1823.

Hutton, Paul A. "William Wells: Frontier Scout and Indian Agent." *Indiana Magazine of History* 74 (1978): 183–222.

Indian Claims Commission. *Indians of Ohio, Indiana, Illinois, Southern Michigan, and Southern Wisconsin*. New York, 1974.

Jablow, Joseph. *Indians of Illinois and Indiana*. New York, 1974.

Jacobs, James R. *The Beginnings of the U.S. Army, 1783–1812*. 1947; reprinted Port Washington, New York, 1972.

James, James A. *Life of George Rogers Clark*. Chicago, 1928.

James, James A., ed. *George Rogers Clark Papers*. 2 vols. Springfield, Illinois, 1912–1926.

James, William. *A Full and Correct Account of the Military Occurrences of the Late War Between Great Britain and the United States of America*. 2 vols. London, 1818.

Jennings, Francis. *The Ambiguous Iroquois Empire*. New York, 1984.

Johnston, John. "Account of the Present State of Indian Tribes Inhabiting Ohio." *Archaeologia Americana* 1 (1820): 269–99.

Johnston, John. "Recollections of the Last Sixty Years." In *The Cincinnati Miscellany*, edited by C. Cist, 2: 233–34, 241–42, 249–50, 260–61, 268–69, 297–99, 305–306, 313–14, 324–26, 329–30, Cincinnati, 1845–1846.

Jones, David. *A Journal of Two Visits Made to Some Nations of Indians on the West Side of the Ohio. . . .* Burlington, New Jersey, 1774.

Jones, J. A., Alice E. Smith, and Vernon Carstensen. *Winnebago Indians*. New York, 1974.

Juday, Richard Roland. *The Battle of Piqua*. Dayton, Ohio, 1976.

Kappler, Charles J., ed. *Indian Affairs, Laws, and Treaties*. Vol. 2. Washington, D.C., 1904.

Keating, William H. *Narrative of an Expedition to the Source of St. Peter's River. . . .* 2 vols. Philadelphia, 1826.

Keith, Alice B., ed. *The John Gray Blount Papers*. 3 vols. Raleigh, North Carolina, 1952–1965.

Kellogg, Louise P., ed. *Frontier Advance on the Upper Ohio, 1778–1779*. Madison, Wisconsin, 1916.

Kellogg, Louise P., ed. *Frontier Retreat on the Upper Ohio, 1779–1781*. Madison, Wisconsin, 1917.

Kelsay, Isabel Thompson. *Joseph Brant, 1743–1807: Man of Two Worlds*. Syracuse, New York, 1984.

Kinietz, W. Vernon, and Erminie Wheeler Voegelin, eds. *Shawnese Traditions: C. C. Trowbridge's Account*. Ann Arbor, Michigan, 1939.

Kinnaird, Lawrence, ed. *Spain in the Mississippi Valley, 1765–1794*. 3 vols. Washington, D.C., 1946–1949.

Klinck, Carl F. "Some Anonymous Literature of the War of 1812." *Ontario History* 49 (1957): 49–60.

Klinck, Carl F., ed. *Tecumseh: Fact and Fiction in Early Records*. Englewood Cliffs, New Jersey, 1961.

Klinck, Carl F., and James T. Talman, eds. *The Journal of Major John Norton, 1816*. Toronto, 1970.

Klopfenstein, Carl G. *The Removal of the Indians from Ohio, 1820–1843*. Ph.D. diss., Case Western Reserve University, 1955.

Knapp, H. S. *History of the Maumee Valley*. Toledo, Ohio, 1872.

Knapp, Samuel Lorenzo. *Lectures on American Literature*. . . . New York, 1829.

Knopf, Richard C., ed. "Two Journals of the Kentucky Volunteers, 1793 and 1794." *Filson Club History Quarterly* 27 (1953): 247–81.

Knopf, Richard C., ed. "A Precise Journal of General Wayne's Last Campaign." *American Antiquarian Society* 64 (1954): 273–302.

Knopf, Richard C., ed. "A Surgeon's Mate at Fort Defiance." *Ohio Historical Quarterly* 66 (1957): 57–86, 159–86, 238–68.

Knopf, Richard C., ed. *Anthony Wayne, a Name in Arms*. 1960; reprinted Westport, Connecticut, 1975.

Kohn, Richard H. *Eagle and Sword*. New York, 1975.

Lankford, George E. "Losing the Past: Draper and the Ruddell Indian Captivity." *The Arkansas Historical Quarterly* 49 (1990): 214–39.

Law, John. *The Colonial History of Vincennes*. Vincennes, Indiana, 1858.

Lewis, James Otto. *The Aboriginal Port Folio*. Philadelphia, 1835–1836.

Lindley, Harlow, ed. *Captain Cushing in the War of 1812*. Columbus, Ohio, 1944.

Long, John. "1813 Letter." *The Register of the Kentucky Historical Society* 47 (1949): 253–54.

Longmore, George. *Tecumthe, a Poetical Tale, in Three Cantos*, edited by Mary Lu MacDonald. London, Ontario, 1993.

Lorrain, Alfred M. *The Helm, the Sword, and the Cross*. Cincinnati, 1862.

Lossing, Benson J. *Pictorial Field-Book of the War of 1812*. 2 vols. New York, 1868.

Lucas, Robert. "The Robert Lucas Journal." *The Iowa Journal of History and Politics* 4 (1906): 343–437.

Lutz, J. J. "The Methodist Missions." *Kansas Historical Collections* 9 (1905–1906): 160–235.

McAfee, Robert B. *The Late War in the Western Country*. 1816; reprinted Ann Arbor, Michigan, 1966.

McAfee, Robert B. "The McAfee Papers." *Register of the Kentucky Historical Society* 26 (1928): 4–23, 108–36, 236–48.

McClung, John A. *Sketches of Western Adventure*. 1832; reprinted Cincinnati, 1838.

McCollough, Almeda, ed. *The Battle of Tippecanoe*. Lafayette, Indiana, 1973.

McConnell, Michael N. *The Search for Security*. Ph.D. diss., William and Mary College, 1983.

McConnell, Michael N. *A Country Between: The Upper Ohio Valley and Its Peoples, 1724–1774*. Lincoln, Nebraska, 1992.

McCrane, R. C., ed. "William Clark's Journal of General Wayne's Campaign." *Mississippi Valley Historical Review* 1 (1914): 418–44.

McDonald, John: "The Tragical Death of Wawillowa." *The Western Christian Advocate*, 22 April 1836.

McDonald, John: *Biographical Sketches of General Nathaniel Massie, General Duncan McArthur. . . .* Cincinnati, 1838.

M'Ferrin, John B. *History of Methodism in Tennessee*. 3 vols. Nashville, 1869–1873.

McKenney, T. L. *Memoirs*. 2 vols. New York, 1846.

McKenney, Thomas L., and James Hall. *The Indian Tribes of North America*. 3 vols. 1836–1844; reprinted Edinburgh, 1933.

MacLean, J. P. "Shaker Mission to the Shawnee Indians." *Ohio Archaeological & Historical Publications* 11 (1903): 215–29.

MacLean, J. P. "The Kentucky Revival and Its Influence on the Miami Valley." *Ohio Archaeological and Historical Society Proceedings* 12 (1903): 242–86.

McLoughlin, William G. "New Angles of Vision on the Cherokee Ghost Dance Movement of 1811–1812." *American Indian Quarterly* 5 (1979): 317–46.

McNemar, Richard. *The Kentucky Revival*. 1808; reprinted New York, 1846.

McWhorter, Lucullus V. *The Border Settlers of Northwestern Virginia*. Dayton, Virginia, 1915.

Mahon, John K. *The War of 1812*. Gainesville, Florida, 1972.

Martin, Joel W. *Sacred Revolt: The Muskogees' Struggle for a New World*. Boston, 1991.

Matson, Nehemiah. "Sketch of Shaubena, Pottowattamie Chief." *Collections of the State Historical Society of Wisconsin* 7 (1876): 415–21.

Matson, Nehemiah. *Memories of Shaubena*. Chicago, 1878.

Matson, Nehemiah. *Pioneers of Illinois*. Chicago, 1882.

May, John. *Journal and Letters of John May. . . .* Cincinnati, 1873.

Michigan Pioneer and Historical Society Historical Collections. 40 vols. Lansing, 1877–1929.

Miller, Jay. *Delaware Integrity* (forthcoming).

Minutes of Debates in Council on the Banks of the Ottawa River . . . November 1791. Philadelphia, 1792.

Moore, John H., ed. "A Captive of the Shawnees, 1779–1784," *West Virginia History* 23 (1962): 287–96.

National Archives of Canada. *A Place in History*. Ottawa, 1991.

Nelson, Larry L. *Men of Patriotism, Courage, and Enterprise! Fort Meigs in the War of 1812*. Canton, Ohio, 1985.

Niebaum, John H. "The Pittsburgh Blues." *Western Pennsylvania Historical Magazine* 4 (1921): 110–22, 175–85, 259–70.

Nunez, Theron A., ed. "Creek Nativism and the Creek War of 1813–14." *Ethnohistory* 5 (1958): 1–47, 131–75, 292–301.

Nuttall, Thomas: "Thomas Nuttall's Travels in the Old Northwest." *Chronica Botanica* 14 (1951): 1–88.

Olmstead, Earl P. *Blackcoats Among the Delaware*. Kent, Ohio, 1991.

Orions, G. H. "Cannons Through the Forest." *Ohio History* 72 (1963): 195–219.

Oskison, John Milton. *Tecumseh and His Times*. New York, 1938.

Owsley, Frank L. *Struggle for the Gulf Borderlands*. Gainesville, 1981.

Owsley, Frank L. "Prophet of War: Josiah Francis and the Creek War." *American Indian Quarterly* 11 (1985): 273–93.

Padgett, James A., ed. "Joseph Desha, Letters and Papers." *Register of the Kentucky Historical Society* 51 (1953): 286–304.

Palmer, William P., et al., eds. *Calendar of Virginia State Papers and Other Manuscripts*. 11 vols. Richmond, Virginia, 1875–1893.

Parkman, Francis. *The Conspiracy of Pontiac*. 1851; reprinted New York, 1962.

Parsons, Joseph A. "Civilizing the Indians of the Old Northwest, 1800–1810." *Indiana Magazine of History* 56 (1960): 195–216.

Pate, James Paul. *The Chickamauga*. Ph.D. diss., Michigan State University, 1969.

Patrick, Rembert W. *Florida Fiasco*. Athens, Georgia, 1954.

Pearce, Roy Harvey. *The Savages of America*. Baltimore, 1967.

Peckham, Howard H. *Pontiac and the Indian Uprising*. 1947; reprinted Chicago, 1961.

Peckham, Howard H., ed. "Recent Documentary Acquisitions to the Indiana Historical Society Library Relating to Fort Wayne." *Indiana Magazine of History* 44 (1948): 409–18.

Penick, James Lal. *The New Madrid Earthquakes*. Rev. ed. Columbia, Missouri, 1981.

Perkins, Bradford. *Castlereagh and Adams*. Berkeley, California, 1964.

Perrin du Lac, F. M. *Travels Through the Two Louisianas*. London, 1807.

Pickett, Albert James. *History of Alabama*. 2 vols. Charleston, 1851.

Pirtle, Alfred. *The Battle of Tippecanoe*. Louisville, Kentucky, 1900.

Pound, Merritt B. *Benjamin Hawkins: Indian Agent*. Athens, Georgia, 1951.

Pratt, Julius W. *Expansionists of 1812*. 1925; reprinted Gloucester, Massachusetts, 1957.

Prucha, Francis Paul. *American Indian Policy in the Formative Years*. Cambridge, Massachusetts, 1962.

Prucha, Francis Paul. *The Sword of the Republic*. Bloomington, Indiana, 1977.

Quaife, Milo M., ed. "Henry Hay's Journal from Detroit to the Mississippi River." In *Proceedings of the State Historical Society of Wisconsin* 62 (1915): 208–61.

Quaife, Milo M., ed. *The John Askin Papers*. 2 vols. Detroit, 1928–1931.

Quaife, Milo M., ed. "General James Wilkinson's Narrative of the Fallen Timbers Campaign." *Mississippi Valley Historical Review* 16 (1929): 81–90.

Quaife, Milo M., ed. *War on the Detroit*. Chicago, 1940.

Quimby, George I. "Discovered: A Possible Tecumseh Portrait." *Chicago Natural History Museum Bulletin* 25, no. 9 (1954): 3.

Rains, John. "Narrative of John Rains." *The South-Western Monthly* 2 (1852): 263–67.

Ramsey, J. G. M. *The Annals of Tennessee. . . .* Charleston, 1853.

Randall, E. O. "Tecumseh, the Shawnee Chief." *Ohio Archaeological and Historical Society Publications* 15 (1906): 418–97.

Raymond, Ethel T. *Tecumseh: A Chronicle of the Last Great Leader of His People*. Toronto, 1915.

Remini, Robert V. *Andrew Jackson and the Course of American Empire, 1767–1821*. New York, 1977.

Rice, Otis K. *Frontier Kentucky*. Lexington, 1975.

Richardson, John. *Tecumseh; or, The Warrior of the West*. London, 1828.

Richardson, John. *Richardson's War of 1812*. 1826–1827; reprinted Toronto, 1902.

Richardson, John. *The Canadian Brothers*. 2 vols. 1840; reprinted Toronto, 1976.

Robertson, James. "Correspondence." *The American Historical Magazine* 1–5 (1896–1900).

Robinson, Doane. *A History of the Dakota or Sioux Indians*. 1904; reprinted Minneapolis, 1967.

Saliers, Earl A. "The Siege of Fort Meigs." *Ohio Archaeological and Historical Society Publications* 18 (1909): 520–41.

"Scalping of Thomas Everett. . . ." *The South-Western Monthly* 1 (1852): 265–67.

Schaaf, Gregory. *Wampum Belts and Peace Trees*. Golden, Colorado, 1990.

Schoolcraft, Henry Rowe. *Travels in the Central Portions of the Mississippi Valley*. New York, 1825.

Schoolcraft, Henry Rowe. "Discourse Delivered Before the Historical Society of Michigan." In *Historical and Scientific Sketches of Michigan* 103–105. Detroit, 1834.

Schoolcraft, Henry Rowe, ed. *Information Respecting the History, Condition, and Prospects of the Indian Tribes of the United States*. 6 vols. Philadelphia, 1853–1860.

Schutz, Noel William. *The Study of Shawnee Myth in an Ethnographic and Ethnohistorical Perspective*. Ph.D. diss., Indiana University, 1975.

Sheehan, Bernard W. *Seeds of Extinction: Jeffersonian Philanthropy and the American Indian*. Chapel Hill, North Carolina, 1973.

Shelby, John. "Letter." *The South-Western Monthly* 2 (1852): 141.

"The Siege of Fort Meigs." *Ohio Archaeological and Historical Quarterly* 28 (1919): 280–85.

"The Siege of Fort Meigs." *Register of the Kentucky Historical Society* 19 (1921): 54–62.

Sipe, Chester Hale. *The Indian Chiefs of Pennsylvania*. Butler, Pennsylvania, 1927.

Sipe, Chester Hale. *The Indian Wars of Pennsylvania*. Harrisburg, Pennsylvania, 1929.

Sketches of Springfield. Springfield, Ohio, 1852.

Smith, Dwight L. *Indian Land Cessions in the Old Northwest, 1795–1809*. Ph.D. diss., Indiana University, 1949.

Smith, Dwight L., ed. "From Greene Ville to Fallen Timbers." *Indiana Historical Society Publications* 16 (1952): 237–326.

Smith, William H., ed. *The St. Clair Papers*. 2 vols. 1881; reprinted Freeport, New York, 1970.

Snelling, Josiah. *Remarks on General William Hull's 'Memoirs. . . .'* Detroit, 1825.

Snyder, Charles McCool, ed. *Red and White on the New York Frontier: A Struggle for Survival; Insights from the Papers of Erastus Granger, Indian Agent, 1807–1819*. Harrison, New York, 1978.

Sosin, Jack M. *Whitehall and the Wilderness*. Lincoln, Nebraska, 1961.

Sosin, Jack M. "The British Indian Department and Dunmore's War." *The Virginia Magazine of History and Biography* 74 (1966): 34–50.

Sosin, Jack M. *The Revolutionary Frontier, 1763–1783*. New York, 1971.

Southerland, Henry DeLean, and Jerry Elijah Brown. *The Federal Road Through Georgia, the Creek Nation, and Alabama, 1806–1836*. Tuscaloosa, Alabama, 1989.

Sparks, Rex M. *Tecumseh's Deer Creek Village (1795–1796)*. London, Ohio, 1974.

Spencer, Oliver M. *The Indian Captivity of O. M. Spencer*. 1834; reprinted Chicago, 1917.

Spencer, Rex Leroy. *The Gibraltar of the Maumee: Fort Meigs in the War of 1812*. Ph.D. diss., Ball State University, 1988.

Sprague, Stuart S. "The Death of Tecumseh and the Rise of Rumpsey Dumpsey." *The Filson Club History Quarterly* 59 (1985): 455–61.

Stagg, J. C. A. *Mr. Madison's War*. Princeton, New Jersey, 1983.

Stanley, George F. G. *The War of 1812*. Toronto, 1983.

Stevens, Frank E. *The Black Hawk War*. Chicago, 1903.

Stevens, Paul Lawrence. *His Majesty's "Savage" Allies*. Ph.D., diss., State University of New York, 1984.

Stocker, Harry E. "A History of the Moravian Mission Among the Indians on the White River in Indiana." *Transactions of the Moravian Historical Society* 10 (1917): 230–408.

Stoddard, Amos. *Sketches, Historical and Descriptive, of Louisiana*. Philadelphia, 1812.

Stone, William Leete. *Life of Joseph Brant-Thayendanegea*. 2 vols. 1838; reprinted St. Clair Shores, Michigan, 1970.

Stone, William Leete. *The Life and Times of Red Jacket, or Sa-go-ye-wat-ha*. 1841; reprinted St. Clair Shores, Michigan, 1970.

Stringfield, William W. *The North Carolina Booklet*. Raleigh, 1903.

Sugden, John. "The Southern Indians in the War of 1812: The Closing Phase." *The Florida Historical Quarterly* 61 (1982): 273–312.

Sugden, John. *Tecumseh's Last Stand*. 1985; reprinted Norman, Oklahoma, 1989.

Sugden, John. "Early Pan-Indianism: Tecumseh's Tour of the Indian Country, 1811–1812." *American Indian Quarterly* 10 (1986): 273–304.

Sugden, John. *The Shawnees in Tecumseh's Time*. Nortorf, West Germany, 1990.

Swanton, John R. *The Indians of the Southeastern United States*. Washington, D.C., 1946.

Sword, Wiley. *President Washington's Indian War*. Norman, Oklahoma, 1985.

Talbert, Charles G. *Benjamin Logan, Kentucky Frontiersman*. Lexington, 1962.

Tales of Chivalry and Romance. Edinburgh, 1826.

Tanner, Helen Hornbeck. "Cherokees in the Ohio Country." *Journal of Cherokee Studies* 3 (1978): 94–102.

Tanner, Helen Hornbeck. "The Glaize in 1792." *Ethnohistory* 25 (1978): 15–39.

Tanner, Helen Hornbeck, ed. *Atlas of Great Lakes Indian History*. Norman, Oklahoma, 1986.

Tanner, Helen Hornbeck, ed. *The Settling of North America: The Atlas of the Great Migrations into North America from the Ice Age to the Present*. New York, 1995.

Tanner, John. *A Narrative of the Captivity and Adventures of John Tanner*. New York, 1830.

Thornbrough, Gayle, ed. *Outpost on the Wabash, 1787–1791*. Indianapolis, 1957.

Thornbrough, Gayle, ed. *Letter Book of the Indian Agency at Fort Wayne, 1809–1815*. Indianapolis, 1961.

Thornbrough, Gayle, ed. *The Correspondence of John Badollet and Albert Gallatin, 1804–1836*. Indianapolis, 1963.

Thurman, Melburn D. *The Delaware Indians*. Ph.D. diss., University of California, 1973.

Thurman, Melburn D. "The Shawnee Prophet's Movement and the Origins of the Prophet Dance." *Current Anthropology* 25 (1984): 530–31.

Thwaites, Reuben G., ed. "Letter Book of Thomas Forsyth, 1814–1818." *Collections of the State Historical Society of Wisconsin* 11 (1888): 316–55.

Thwaites, Reuben G., and Louise P. Kellogg, eds. *Documentary History of Dunmore's War, 1774*. Madison, Wisconsin, 1905.

Thwaites, Ruben G., and Louise P. Kellogg, eds. *The Revolution on the Upper Ohio, 1775–1777*. Madison, Wisconsin, 1908.

Thwaites, Reuben G., and Louise P. Kellogg, eds. *Frontier Defense on the Upper Ohio, 1777–1778*. Madison, Wisconsin, 1912.

Trigger, Bruce, ed. *Handbook of North American Indians*. Vol. 15, *Northeast*. Washington, D.C., 1978.

Tucker, Glenn. *Poltroons and Patriots*. 2 vols. Indianapolis, 1954.

Tucker, Glenn. *Tecumseh: Vision of Glory*. Indianapolis, 1956.

Tupper, Ferdinand Brock. *The Life and Correspondence of Major General Sir Isaac Brock, K.B.* London, 1845.

Van Hoose, William H. *Tecumseh, an Indian Moses*. Canton, Ohio, 1984.

Van Horne, James. *A Narrative of the Captivity and Sufferings of James Van Horne*. Middleburg, Vermont, 1817.

Viola, Herman J. *The Indian Legacy of Charles Bird King*. Washington, D.C., 1976.

Voegelin, Charles F. (Carl), and Erminie W. Voegelin. "Shawnee Name Groups." *American Anthropologist* 37 (1935): 617–35.

Voegelin, Erminie W. *Indians of Northwest Ohio*. New York, 1974.

Voegelin, Erminie W., Emily J. Blasingham, and Dorothy R. Libby. *Miami, Wea, and Eel River Indians of Southern Indiana*. New York, 1974.

Voegelin, Erminie W., and David B. Stout. *Indians of Illinois and Northwestern Indiana*. New York, 1974.

Voegelin, Erminie W., and Helen Hornbeck Tanner. *Indians of Northern Ohio and Southeastern Michigan*. New York, 1974.

Voegelin, Erminie W., and Helen Hornbeck Tanner. *Indians of Ohio and Indiana Prior to 1795*. 2 vols. New York, 1974.

Wainwright, Nicholas B., ed. "George Croghan's Journal. . . ." *Pennsylvania Magazine of History and Biography* 71 (1947): 313–444.

Walker, Adam. *A Journal of Two Campaigns of the Fourth Regiment of U.S. Infantry in the Michigan and Indiana Territories*. Keene, New Hampshire, 1816.

Wallace, A. F. C. "New Religions among the Delaware Indians, 1600–1900," *Southwestern Journal of Anthropology* 12 (1956): 1–21.

Wallace, A. F. C. "Political Organization and Land Tenure Among the Northeastern Indians, 1600–1830." *Southwestern Journal of Anthropology* 13 (1957): 301–21.

Wallace, A. F. C. *The Death and Rebirth of the Seneca*. New York, 1973.

Wallace, A. F. C., ed. "Halliday Jackson's Journal to the Seneca Indians, 1798–1800." *Pennsylvania History* 19 (1952): 117–47, 325–49.

The War. 3 vols. New York, 1813–1815.

Warren, William W. *History of the Ojibwa Nation*. 1885; reprinted Minneapolis, 1957.

Washburne, E. B., ed. *The Edwards Papers*. Chicago, 1884.

Washington, Thomas. "The Attack on Buchanan's Station." *The Annals of the Army of Tennessee and Early American History* 1 (1878): 370–81, 426–28.

Welsh, William J. and D. C. Skaggs, eds. *War on the Great Lakes*. Kent, Ohio, 1991.

Weslager, C. A. *The Delaware Indians*. New Brunswick, New Jersey, 1972.

West, Elizabeth H., ed. "A Prelude to the Creek War of 1813–1814." *Florida Historical Quarterly* 18 (1940): 247–66.

Whitaker, Arthur P. *The Spanish American Frontier, 1783–1795*. 1927; reprinted Lincoln, Nebraska, 1969.

White, Leslie A., ed. *Lewis Henry Morgan*. Ann Arbor, Michigan, 1959.

White, Richard. *The Middle Ground: Indians, Empires, and Republics in the Great Lakes Region, 1650–1815*. New York, 1991.

Wickliffe, Charles A. "Tecumseh and the Battle of the Thames." *Register of the Kentucky Historical Society* 60 (1962): 45–49.

Wilcox, Frank. *Ohio Indian Trails*. 1933; reprinted Pittsburgh, 1970.

Wilkinson, James. *Memoirs of My Own Times*. 3 vols. Philadelphia, 1816.

Williams, Edward G., ed. "The Journal of Richard Butler, 1775." *The Western Pennsylvania Historical Magazine* 46 (1963): 381–95, and 47 (1964): 31–46, 141–56.

Withers, Alexander S. *Chronicles of Border Warfare*. 1831; reprinted Cincinnati, 1891.

Witthoft, John, and William A. Hunter. "The Seventeenth-Century Origins of the Shawnees." *Ethnohistory* 2 (1955): 42–57.

Woehrmann, Paul. *At the Headwaters of the Maumee*. Indianapolis, 1971.

Wood, William, ed. *Select British Documents of the Canadian War of 1812*. 4 vols. Toronto, 1920–1928.

Woodward, Thomas S. *Reminiscences of the Creek or Muscogee Indians*. 1859; reprinted Tuscaloosa, Alabama, 1939.

Wright, J. Leitch. *Anglo-Spanish Rivalry in North America*. Athens, Georgia, 1971.

Wright, J. Leitch. *Britain and the American Frontier, 1783–1815*. Athens, Georgia, 1975.

Wright, J. Leitch. *The Only Land They Knew*. New York, 1981.

Wright, J. Leitch. *Creeks and Seminoles: The Destruction and Regeneration of the Muskogulge People*. Lincoln, Nebraska, 1986.

Young, Bennett H. *The Battle of the Thames*. Louisville, Kentucky, 1903.

Zaslow, Morris, and Wesley B. Turner, eds. *The Defended Border*. Toronto, 1964.

INDEX